The
COMPLETE
COOK

The
COMPLETE
COOK

EDITED BY SOPHIE HALE
& JOSEPHINE BACON

INTERNATIONAL
CULINARY
SOCIETY

A QUINTET BOOK

This 1987 edition published by
International Culinary Society
Distributed by Crown Publishers Inc.
225 Park Avenue South
New York, New York 10003

ISBN 0-517-63530-5

This book was designed and produced by
Quintet Publishing Limited
6 Blundell Street
London N7 9BH

Designer: Phil Mitton
Editors: Susie Ward, Fanny Campbell, Shaun Barrington

Printed and manufactured in Hong Kong
h g f e d c b a

Contents

Introduction

HOW TO USE THIS BOOK

THE COMPLETE COOK is a practical guide to success in the kitchen and at the table — whether you are preparing a simple meal for two or a grand feast for ten. Over a thousand recipes — from scrumptious soups to mouth-watering desserts, from summer salads to winter casseroles, and from Austrian Bagels to Yorkshire Curd Tart — offer a wide variety of culinary choices, both to the traditional and to the more adventurous home cook.

The book is divided into 18 sections that cover appetizers or starters, such as Soups and Hors d'Oeuvres and Snacks; main dishes, including Fish and Seafood, Mutton and Lamb, and Pork and Ham; accompaniments like Salads, Pickles and Preserves, and Drinks; and sweets, among them Hot Desserts, Confectionery, and Cakes, Cookies, Pastries and Breads. The section on Eggs, Milk and Cheese presents a selection of recipes concentrating on these staple foods, using them as starters, main dishes or puddings. The section is a good starting point for one way of using this book: working from the refrigerator or freezer towards the recipe. For the last-minute cook, a quick inventory of the fridge contents and a check on the relevant contents page may produce a Cheese Roll or a Welsh Rarebit, according to the time and ingredients available.

The color photographs spread throughout THE COMPLETE COOK — over half of the recipes are illustrated — are useful both as guides toward achieving the desired result and suggestions as to how to garnish and serve dishes. Step-by-step instructions following the sections are also helpful, not only for their concisely worded advice on how to tackle such tasks as making a soufflé, jointing a chicken, preparing julienne vegetables or beating strudel paste, but also for their telling series of color photographs. Many basic cookbooks give such hints to their readers in words, but viewing each stage of the real process is the next best thing to an actual cooking lesson.

THE COMPLETE COOK will guide you when it comes to basic preparation: if a recipe calls for, say, shortcrust pastry, then a full explanation of how to make it is given. Where basic recipes form a part of a dish, they are capitalized in the ingredients list to indicate their inclusion in the book as recipes in their own right. A quick glance at the index at the back of the book, or the table of contents at the start of each section, will tell you, for instance, how to go about making Vinaigrette for your Summer Avocado Salad, or Tomato Sauce for your Red Mullet Provençal, or Thick Chocolate Frosting for your Habsburger Torte.

The popularity of ethnic restaurants and travel abroad have introduced Western palates to many foreign dishes in recent years, and THE COMPLETE COOK provides recipes for many of the more familiar dishes, from starters such as Hummus and Samosas, to more exotic entrées that include Lamb Dhansak, Malaysian Chicken and Thai Beef with Spinach. THE COMPLETE COOK has a truly international flavor, traveling from Western and Eastern Europe, through North and South America, to the Orient and the Middle East; and you can bring the tastes of all these nations into your own kitchen — at a much cheaper price than going out to eat.

THE COMPLETE COOK also caters for the vegetarian, starting with just simple vegetable side dishes or soups, and leading to imaginative and filling meals that appeal to vegetarians and non-vegetarians alike. Just a few such dishes are Stuffed Eggplant, Cheesy Onion Quiche, Curry Noodles and Vegetable Lasagne.

Those with a discerning sweet tooth are well provided for in THE COMPLETE COOK, with myriad delicious recipes, ranging from the quick and easy to the sophisticated — although the latter are not in the least

For the preparation of vegetables for crudités, see page 29.

daunting to create, whatever you may have assumed from sampling the fare at a fancy patisserie. Whether you want to make the likes of Sailors' Delght or Nun's Pretzels, or Queen of Puddings and Gâteau des Rois — and whether you are celebrating a child's birthday or entertaining your friends — you can do it with THE COMPLETE COOK as your guide.

Where appropriate, interesting general information accompanies some of the recipes. These tidbits include historical background on dishes that have been adapted from centuries-old recipes, as well as simple suggestions on what kinds of vegetables to serve with main dishes.

So, indulge yourself — and your family and guests — with the culinary treats you will find on the following pages. You won't believe how easy it is to make so many delicious dishes — and to earn so many glowing compliments!

Hors d'Oeuvres and Snacks

Artichokes with Tomato Sauce
Serves 4

Ingredients

4 large artichokes	1tbsp. tomato paste
1-2tbsp. oil	2tsp. fresh oregano,
1 large onion, chopped	chopped
2 cloves garlic, chopped	lemon juice
15oz. can tomatoes,	salt and freshly ground
mashed	black pepper

Rinse the artichokes thoroughly under the cold tap and leave them upside down to drain. Bring a very large pan of salted water to a boil, put the artichokes in and boil fast for 30-50 minutes, depending on the size. When an outer leaf comes away at a gentle tug, the artichokes are ready.

Meanwhile, make the sauce. Heat the oil in a pan and fry the onion and garlic until transparent. Add the tomatoes, tomato paste and oregano and reduce until the sauce is of pouring consistency but not sloppy. Season with salt and pepper and a dash of lemon juice to taste.

Drain the artichokes. When cool, pull out the tiny inner leaves together with the hairy inedible "choke." Spoon in some tomato sauce.

Stand each artichoke in a pool of sauce on an individual dish and serve.

Stuffed Eggplant
Serves 4 or 8

Ingredients

4 eggplant	2tbsp. fresh herbs, chopped
olive oil	salt and freshly ground
1 large onion, chopped	black pepper
2-3 cloves garlic, crushed	¼lb. Mozzarella cheese
4 large tomatoes, skinned	4tbsp. brown breadcrumbs
and chopped	a little butter

Preheat the oven to 400°F.

Wash the eggplants. Cut in half lengthwise and score the cut surface deeply with a knife. Sprinkle with salt and leave, cut surface down, for 30 minutes.

Meanwhile, heat 1-2tbsp. oil in a pan and fry the onion and garlic until translucent. Transfer to a bowl and mix in the tomatoes and chopped herbs.

Add more oil to the pan. Rinse the eggplants and pat dry. Put them, cut surface down, in the pan and cook gently for about 15 minutes. They absorb a lot of oil, so you will need to keep adding more.

Scoop some of the flesh out of the eggplants, mash and mix it with the rest of the filling. Season well.

Pile the filling onto the eggplants and top with thinly sliced Mozzarella. Sprinkle with breadcrumbs and dot with butter. Arrange eggplants in a greased ovenproof dish and bake for 20 minutes until the cheese has melted and the breadcrumbs are crispy.

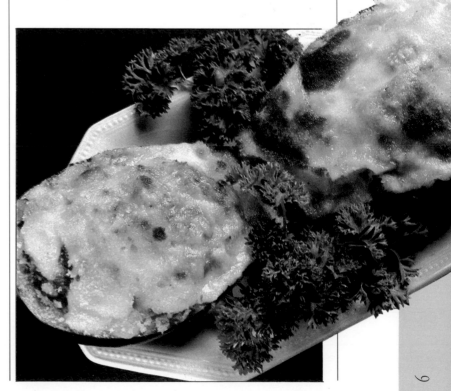

Avocado with Blue Cheese
Serves 4

This makes a delicious start to a summer meal, but can also be served as a light lunch for two. Stilton can be substituted with another mild blue cheese.

Ingredients

²/₃ cup crumbled Stilton or blue cheese	freshly ground black pepper
4tbsp. Mayonnaise	3 ripe avocado pears, peeled
4tbsp. plain yogurt	
2tbsp. parsley sprigs	1tbsp. walnut pieces
lemon juice to taste	4 lettuce leaves

Mash together the cheese, mayonnaise, yogurt and parsley. Season to taste with lemon juice and black pepper.

Halve the avocados. Remove the pits, scoop out the flesh and retain the skins. Dice flesh and put into a mixing bowl with the walnut pieces. Add the cheese dressing and mix well.

Arrange each lettuce leaf on a small plate, and spoon the avocado mixture back into four of the skins.

Summer Avocado Salad
Serves 4

Ingredients

2 ripe avocados	1 cup cooked long-grain rice
1tbsp. lemon juice	
2 grapefruit	1 sweet yellow pepper, seeded
1 small lettuce	
¼ cucumber	salt and freshly ground pepper
²/₃ cup Vinaigrette	
¾ cup cooked shrimp	

Peel the avocados. Cut them in half and remove the pits. Cut the flesh in slices and sprinkle with the lemon juice to prevent discoloration.

Using a small sharp knife, cut a slice from the grapefruit exposing the flesh. Cut round in strips, removing all the white pith. Cut into each section between the membranes of each slice. At the end you will have segments of grapefruit without skin. Squeeze the juice of the membranes by hand over the fruit.

Line the serving dish or dishes with washed, drained lettuce leaves and cucumber slices.

Pour some of the Vinaigrette over the grapefruit.

Mix the cooked shrimp with the rice and remaining dressing.

Cut the yellow pepper in thin strips. Retaining some for the garnish, chop the remainder and mix with the rice and shrimp. Season well.

Arrange the prawn and rice mixture in the dishes on the cucumber and lettuce.

Top with sliced avocado and grapefruit and serve garnished with reserved pepper rings.

Avocado Dip
Serves 3-4

Ingredients

1 large avocado	dash Tabasco
½ cup cream cheese	2tbsp. lemon juice
½ small onion, finely chopped	salt and pepper

Mash the flesh of the avocado. Add the remaining ingredients, mixing them in very well. Spoon the mixture into a serving dish and cover it well. Refrigerate until required.

Serve with raw vegetables or crackers as a dip or spread.

Note Do not make this too long before you intend to serve it as avocado discolors easily.

Avocado with Honey Sauce
Serves 6-8

The sweetness of the honey, the naturally nutty flavor of the avocado and the citrus tang of the grapefruit make this an interesting combination.

Ingredients
1 onion, finely chopped	½ cup olive oil
1tsp. dry mustard	4 large avocados
⅔ cup honey	1 large grapefruit, peeled,
½ cup lemon juice	seeded and sectioned

First make the honey sauce. In a large mixing bowl, combine the onion, mustard, honey, lemon juice and olive oil. Mix thoroughly. Chill for 30 minutes.

Halve the avocados and remove the pits. Cut each avocado half into wedges approximately the same size as the grapefruit sections. Remove the outer skin.

Arrange the avocado wedges alternately with grapefruit sections in small dishes. Spoon some of the honey sauce over each portion and serve.

Avocado Fish
Serves 4

Ingredients
2 avocados	1 clove garlic, crushed
juice of 1 lemon	1 cup cooked long-grain
½ cup canned tuna fish,	rice
drained	rind of lemon
⅔ cup natural yogurt	good pinch paprika
1tsp. cumin powder	

Slice the avocados lengthwise. Remove the pits. Remove some of the flesh and sprinkle lemon juice into the shells and onto the flesh.

Mix the tuna with the diced avocado flesh.

In a small bowl mix the yogurt, cumin and crushed garlic. Stir well. Add the cooked rice and the avocado and tuna mixture.

Pile the filling into the avocado shells and serve garnished with lemon rind and paprika.

Variation Substitute ¾ cup cooked shrimp for the tuna.

Chopped Calf's Liver
Serves 8

A variation of the more familiar chopped chicken liver, this recipe is a specialty of Eastern Europe.

Ingredients
½ cup beef stock	1 large stalk celery, finely
1lb. fresh calf's liver, cubed	chopped
1 clove garlic, finely	½ cup diced onions
chopped	2tbsp. sherry
1lb. fresh chicken livers,	1tsp. brandy
halved	2tbsp. unflavored dry
2 hard-boiled eggs, finely	breadcrumbs
chopped	½tsp. salt
½ cup Mayonnaise	1tsp. white pepper
½ cup diced green pepper	

Heat the beef stock in a medium-sized saucepan. Add the calf's liver cubes and garlic and cook, stirring frequently, for 10 to 12 minutes, or until the liver is thoroughly cooked. Remove the liver cubes and set them aside. Discard the cooking liquid.

Put the chicken livers in a saucepan and add enough cold water to cover. Bring the liquid to a boil and simmer for 15 minutes, or until the livers are thoroughly cooked. Drain well.

Put the calf's liver, chicken livers, eggs, Mayonnaise, green pepper, celery, onions, sherry, brandy, breadcrumbs, salt and white pepper into a large mixing bowl. Mash the ingredients together with a fork until the mixture has a fine and even consistency. Cover the bowl and refrigerate for at least 2 hours before serving.

Quick Blue Cheese Pâté
Serves 4

If Stilton is not available use any other mild blue cheese such as Roquefort or Danish Blue.

Ingredients
2 cups crumbled Stilton or	3tbsp. Mayonnaise
blue cheese	freshly ground black
4tbsp. unsalted butter,	pepper
softened	4 pecan halves
2tbsp. port	

Mash together or process the cheese, butter and port until smooth. Quickly mix in the mayonnaise and a little pepper.

Taste for seasoning, then spoon into four small individual dishes. Press a pecan half on top of each, then cover and chill.

Serve with hot toast and a watercress salad.

Lima Bean Pâté
Serves 4

Ingredients

³/₄lb. lima beans	salt and freshly ground
approx. 1 cup cream	black pepper
cheese	sprigs of mint

Boil the lima beans lightly in salted water until tender.

Mash or put through a vegetable mill with enough cream cheese to make a thick paste. Season with salt and pepper. Press into individual dishes and garnish each with a sprig of mint.

Serve with triangles of wholewheat toast.

Stuffed Date Patties
Serves 6-8

This dish of stuffed dates on veal patties is traditionally served with Pickled Lemons.

Ingredients

5tbsp. butter or margarine	32 unsalted roasted
1lb. ground veal	almonds
good pinch thyme	32 dried dates, pitted

Melt 2tbsp. of the butter or margarine in a small skillet. Add the veal and thyme and cook over a low heat for 15 minutes, or until the veal is thoroughly browned. Drain off any fat that has accumulated in the skillet. Set the veal aside.

Preheat the oven to 375°F. When the veal is cool enough to handle, form it into 32 small patties each with a diameter of about 1in.

Arrange the patties on a greased cookie sheet.

Insert an almond into each date. Top each veal patty with a stuffed date.

Melt the remaining butter or margarine, pour over the patties and bake in the preheated oven for 10 minutes. Serve hot.

Sautéed Chicken Livers
Serves 8

Featuring two different kinds of wine, this recipe has a decidedly Continental flavor.

Ingredients

¹/₄ cup chicken fat	1 clove garlic, finely
1¹/₂lb. fresh chicken livers	chopped
1 cup white wine	1 small shallot, finely
¹/₄ cup dry sherry	chopped
1tbsp. chopped parsley	good pinch salt
1tbsp. finely chopped	good pinch ground white
onion	pepper

Melt the chicken fat in a large skillet over a low heat. Add the chicken livers and sauté until browned, about 5 minutes. Add the remaining ingredients, raise the heat to medium, cover and cook for 5 minutes.

Remove the cover and cook until the liquid is almost gone, stirring occasionally.

Serve with crackers or crusty bread.

Chicken Livers with Avocado
Serves 6

Ingredients

2tbsp. butter	²/₃ cup yogurt
1 medium onion, sliced	salt and pepper
1¹/₂lb. chicken livers	1 avocado, sliced
juice of half a lemon	chopped parsley
¹/₄ cup dry vermouth	

Heat the oil, add the onion and cook until it has softened but not browned. Add the chicken livers and cook them, stirring from time to time, for about 5 minutes. Add the lemon juice and vermouth. Cover and cook for a further 8 minutes.

Stir in the yogurt, season to taste, and cook just long enough to warm the yogurt through. Spoon onto a shallow serving dish, lay the avocado slices along the livers and scatter with parsley.

Variation For a richer dish use sour cream instead of the yogurt.

Chopped Chicken Livers
Serves 6-10

Ingredients

1lb. fresh chicken livers	¹/₂ cup chopped onion
¹/₄ cup Mayonnaise	¹/₂tsp. salt
2 hard-boiled eggs	¹/₂tsp. freshly ground black
2 stalks celery, chopped	pepper

Put the chicken livers into a saucepan and cover completely with cold water. Bring to a boil and cook for 10 to 12 minutes. Drain the livers well.

In a large mixing bowl, combine the livers with the Mayonnaise and eggs. Mash the mixture with a fork. Add the celery, onion, salt and pepper. Mash until the mixture has as even, fine consistency.

Put the mixture into a serving bowl, cover, and chill for at least 1 hour before serving. Serve with crusty bread, melba toast or crackers.

Ceviche
Serves 6

This dish can be traced back to the Peruvian Incas. The fish "cooks" in the lime juice.

Ingredients

1 cup fresh lime juice	1tsp. salt
1 cup fresh lemon juice	good pinch black pepper
4 dried red chili peppers, finely ground	2½lb. sole or flounder fillets, cut into 1-in. square pieces
2 large Spanish or red onions, thinly sliced	1 large head lettuce
2 cloves garlic, finely chopped	

In a large glass or ceramic dish, combine the lime juice, lemon juice, ground chili peppers, onions, garlic, salt and pepper. Stir well. Add the fish pieces and submerge them in the marinade.

Cover and chill for 4 hours. Serve cold on a bed of lettuce.

Corn on the Cob with Olive Butter
Serves 4

Ingredients

4 corn on the cob	1tbsp. parsley, chopped
¼tsp. sugar	2tsp. capers
4tbsp. butter	salt and freshly ground pepper
1 green onion, washed and sliced	1tbsp. lemon juice
12 green or stuffed olives	½tsp. grated lemon rind

Remove the hairy husk and trim the stalk end of the corn. Cook in unsalted water with the sugar for 15 minutes. The cooking time will depend on the freshness of the corn — corn freshly picked and cooked immediately may need only 5 minutes cooking time.

Melt the butter on a very low heat, add the sliced green onion and olives, allow to cook for 1 minute. Add the parsley, capers, seasoning, lemon juice and rind.

Drain the corn and serve hot with the olive butter spooned on each.

Note If using frozen corn, follow cooking instructions on the packet.

Crudités with Hot Anchovy Dip
Serves 6-8

Ingredients

1½-2lb. crisp mixed raw vegetables, cut into manageable pieces, such as:	cauliflower flowerets radishes mushrooms
carrots	**Dip**
celery	½ cup butter
green, red and yellow peppers	2 cloves garlic, crushed
cucumber	8 anchovies
	1¼ cup heavy cream

Prepare the vegetables and arrange them on a serving platter. Keep cold.

Prepare the dip. Heat the butter in a pan and add the garlic. Drain the anchovies and pat dry with paper towels. When the garlic has softened, pound the anchovies into the pan until you have a smooth paste.

Beat in the cream and bring back to a boil. Cook, stirring until the dip has thickened slightly. Serve hot. If you use a small copper pan or a fondue pan, you can serve the dip in the pan you cooked it in.

Stuffed Vine Leaves
Makes approx. 60

These are usually served with a bowl of chilled yogurt.

Ingredients

1 packet preserved vine leaves (vacuum packed)	1 tsp. mint
2 tbsp. vegetable oil	2 tbsp. currants
2 large onions, finely chopped	salt and freshly ground pepper
½ cup brown rice, cooked	1¼ cups boiling water
¼ cup pine nuts, chopped	⅔ cup olive oil
4 tbsp. parsley, freshly chopped	juice of 2 lemons

Preheat the oven to 325°F.

Rinse the vine leaves and blanch in boiling water for 2 minutes or treat according to the instructions on the packet.

Heat the vegetable oil on a low heat and cook the chopped onions for about 3 minutes, until they are translucent.

Add the cooked rice and stir gently. Add the chopped pine nuts, parsley, chopped mint, currants and seasoning.

Gradually stir in the boiling water, cover and cook for about 10 minutes, until the water is absorbed but the rice still has a bite.

Smooth the leaves on a board and arrange 1 tsp. stuffing on each. Fold the stem end and the sides in and roll up firmly.

Line an ovenproof dish with any leaves which are left over. Put a layer of stuffed leaves in the dish, ensuring the seam side is downwards. When one layer is complete, sprinkle with oil and lemon juice.

Continue packing layers until finished, sprinkling each with oil and lemon juice. Depending on the size of dish, you may need more oil and lemon juice. Cover with foil and weight with empty baking pans to keep rolls in shape.

Cook in the preheated oven for 1 hour and remove from the heat. Allow to cool; excess liquid will be absorbed. Chill before serving.

Transfer to a serving dish and garnish with lemon wedges.

Extra rolls may be kept in the freezer for future treats.

Egg Salad
Serves 6

Ingredients

6 hard-boiled eggs	1 large pimento, chopped
4 tbsp. Mayonnaise	2 tbsp. sweet pickle relish
1 carrot, diced	1 tbsp. Dijon-style mustard
1 large stalk celery, diced	½ tsp. celery salt
1 small onion, finely chopped	1 tsp. Worcestershire sauce
2 tbsp. chopped green pepper	1 tsp. cayenne pepper
	1 tsp. paprika
	lettuce

In a large mixing bowl, combine all the ingredients except the paprika. Mix roughly with fork until the consistency, texture and color of the mixture is even throughout.

Arrange the egg salad on a bed of lettuce. Sprinkle with paprika. Chill for 10 minutes before serving.

Garlic Mushrooms
Serves 4

Ingredients

16 open mushrooms, about 1½ in. across	5 tbsp. fresh mixed herbs, chopped
2 slices wholewheat bread, crumbled	a little oil
⅔ cup warm milk	salt and freshly ground black pepper
4 cloves garlic	few sprigs of watercress

Preheat the oven to 350°F.

Wipe the mushroom caps clean. Remove, chop and reserve the stalks.

Soak the breadcrumbs in milk until soft, then squeeze out excess milk.

In a mortar, pound the garlic with herbs and enough oil to make a paste. Pound in the stalks. Mix together with the breadcrumbs and season well with salt and pepper.

Spoon the filling into the mushroom caps and arrange them in a lightly oiled ovenproof dish. Bake for about 15 minutes in the preheated oven until mushrooms are soft and juicy and filling has crisped a little on the top.

Serve hot, garnished with sprigs of watercress.

Herring and Apple Salad
Serves 4

Ingredients

1 jar (approx. 12oz.) pickled herring	1 large crisp apple, sliced ²/₃ cup sour cream

Drain the liquid from the jar of herrings and cut them into slices. Add the onions from the jar together with the apple and sour cream. Mix all together well.

Refrigerate until required and serve with black bread if possible.

Chopped Herring Marseilles
Serves 6-8

Ingredients

8 large salt herring fillets	4tbsp. vinegar
¹/₃ cup finely chopped onion	3 slices white bread, trimmed and shredded
2 apples, peeled, cored and finely chopped	2tbsp. sugar
3 hard-boiled eggs, finely chopped	2¹/₂tbsp. olive oil

Soak the herring overnight in cold water in a large mixing bowl. Drain well and chop finely.

In a mixing bowl combine the herring with the remaining ingredients. Mix thoroughly until the consistency is even throughout. Cover and chill for at least 4 hours before serving.

Finnish Herring
Serves 4

Ingredients

²/₃ cup farmer's cheese, preferably home-made	fresh dill to taste
4tbsp. cream	1 hard-boiled egg, chopped
1tbsp. French mustard	1 jar (approx. 12oz.) pickled herring
1tbsp. sugar	

Mix everything except the herrings together very well. Add a little of the liquid from the herrings if the mixture is very stiff.

Drain the rest of the liquid from the herrings and cut the herrings into slices, together with their onions. Add the herrings and onions to the yogurt mixture and stir to coat the herring well. Refrigerate until required.

German Herring Salad
Serves 4

You can use a jar of pickled herring or any other herring you can obtain at a delicatessen. Use more herring if you like and add some small pieces of cold meat, such as roast beef. This sounds an odd combination but is surprisingly good.

Ingredients

3 salt herrings, filleted and very finely chopped	1 large tart apple, peeled and very finely chopped
2 large cooked potatoes, very finely chopped	1 large pickled cucumber, very finely chopped
1 large cooked beet, very finely chopped	²/₃ cup sour cream watercress to garnish

Combine all the ingredients and mix well. Pack the mixture into a small ring mold if you like and refrigerate it until required. Unmold it and put some watercress in the center of the ring.

Herring and Beet Salad
Serves 6

This piquant herring salad is a delicious way to start a meal. Serve it on a bed of lettuce with thin rounds of crusty bread.

Ingredients

1lb. herring fillets	¹/₂tsp. dried dill
²/₃ cup cooked beets, diced	2tbsp. olive oil
3 green onions (including tops), diced	¹/₄ cup lemon juice
2tbsp. white wine vinegar	¹/₂tsp. black pepper
¹/₂tsp. dried tarragon	¹/₄ cup orange juice
	1tbsp. Dijon-style mustard

Combine all the ingredients in a blender or food processor and chop finely.

Spoon the salad into a serving bowl, cover tightly and refrigerate for at least 1 hour before serving.

Mushroom and Herring Salad
Serves 6-8

Ingredients

1¼lb. beets, cooked and diced
1lb. baby potatoes, cooked and diced
1lb. canned pear sections, drained and cut into small pieces
2lb. bottled herring pieces, drained

2 medium onions, finely sliced
1 cup red wine vinegar
½tsp. black pepper
good pinch salt
1 cup quartered mushrooms
2 cups sour cream
½ cup white wine

Toss all the ingredients together in a large mixing bowl. Cover and chill for at least 3 hours before serving.

Special Pickled Herring
Serves 6

Ingredients

1½lb. pickled herring (rollmops)
½ cup raspberry vinegar
¼lb. small onions, diced
1tsp. freshly ground black pepper

½tsp. tarragon
½ cup white wine
1 cup cooked peas

Preparation Drain the herring well and set aside. Discard any onions or other ingredients packed with the herring.

Put the raspberry vinegar, onions, pepper, tarragon and white wine in a large glass or ceramic, but not metal, bowl.

Add the herring, which should be completely covered by the liquid; if not, add equal amounts of white wine and vinegar until the herring is covered. Cover the bowl and chill for at least 12 hours.

Just before serving, add the peas to the herring and marinade and mix gently.

Kipper Pâté
Serves 6-8

Ingredients

1lb. kipper fillets
1⅓ cup farmer's cheese
1tsp. paprika

juice of 1 lemon
pepper

Poach the kipper fillets, drain them and remove the skin.

Liquidize them with the farmer's cheese, paprika and lemon juice until smooth and season to taste. Spoon into individual pots or one serving dish.

Refrigerate until required, and serve with toast and lemon wedges.

Variation To make a softer mixture, add a little cream.

Lesco
Serves 6-8

Ingredients

5tbsp. chicken fat
1 medium onion, finely chopped
2 cloves garlic, chopped
2lb. tomatoes, skinned, seeded and coarsely chopped
1½lb. green peppers, seeded and cut into strips

½tsp. salt
1tsp. black pepper
3tbsp. paprika
2oz. black olives, pitted and diced
1 cup tomato paste
1½lb. beef sausage, thinly sliced
6-8 eggs

Melt the chicken fat in a large saucepan. Add the onion and garlic and cook for 10-12 minutes over a low heat.

Add the tomatoes, green peppers, salt, pepper, paprika and olives. Turn the heat up to medium, cover and cook for 15 minutes.

Add the tomato paste and sausage. Reduce the heat to low and simmer, covered, for 30 minutes.

After the Lesco has cooked for 25 minutes, fry the eggs on both sides until the whites are firm.

Serve the Lesco in soup bowls, topping each portion with a fried egg.

Stuffed Melon
Serves 6

This delicious first course takes an ordinary melon and turns it into something special.

Ingredients

3 oranges, peeled, seeded and sectioned
1 large pink grapefruit, peeled, seeded and sectioned
6tbsp. Triple Sec or other orange-flavored liqueur
3tbsp. grenadine syrup
½ cup fresh pomegranate seeds
1tbsp. finely chopped fresh mint
3 small cantaloupe melons, halved and seeded

In a small mixing bowl, combine the orange and grapefruit sections, Triple Sec, grenadine syrup, pomegranate seeds and mint. Refrigerate for 1 hour.
 Spoon the fruit mixture evenly into the cantaloupe halves.

Mixed Herb Platter
Serves 6

This delightful dish of fresh herbs and feta cheese is the traditional Iranian way to begin a meal. Serve with pitta bread.

Ingredients

medium-sized bunch flat-leaved parsley
small bunch mint sprigs
small bunch green onions
3oz. fresh chives
small bunch fresh tarragon
small bunch coriander leaves
small bunch watercress
2 small heads Belgian endive
½lb. feta cheese, broken into small pieces

Arrange the ingredients in piles on a large platter, preferably silver or pewter.

Hummus
Serves 6-8

This garlicky chick-pea or garbanzo bean dip is a favorite appetizer in the Middle East. Serve it with warmed pitta breaad or crudités.

Ingredients

1lb. cooked chick-peas (garbanzo beans), drained
½ cup tahini (sesame seed paste)
1 medium-sized onion, quartered
½ cup fresh lemon juice
2 cloves garlic, chopped
½tsp. dried coriander
½tsp. ground cumin
½tsp. salt
½tsp. freshly ground black pepper
1½tbsp. water
3tbsp. fresh parsley, coarsely chopped

Put the chick-peas, tahini, onion, lemon juice, garlic, paprika, coriander, cumin, salt, pepper and water into a food processor or electric blender. Blend until smooth and creamy.
 Pile the hummus into a serving dish and garnish with the parsley.

Mozzarella and Avocado Bees
Serves 2

Ingredients

1 ripe avocado
¼lb. Mozzarella cheese
1tbsp. olive oil
1tbsp. tarragon vinegar
salt and freshly ground black pepper

Cut the avocado in half and remove the pit. With a spatula carefully remove the flesh from each half of the avocado in one piece.
 Lay the avocado halves flat-side downwards and cut horizontally into ¼-in. slices.
 Cut semi-circular slices of the same width from the Mozzarella, with 4 extra semi-circles for wings.
 Arrange the cheese slices between the avocado slices to form the striped body of the bee, and arrange the wings at the sides.
 Mix the oil and vinegar together and season well. Pour over the bees and serve.

Baby Potatoes with Caviar
Serves 6

Ingredients

6 medium-sized baby potatoes
1oz. black caviar or lumpfish roe
1oz. red caviar or lumpfish roe
8 hard-boiled egg yolks, crumbled
3 lemons, quartered

Cook the potatoes in a large pot of boiling water until they are tender, about 20 to 30 minutes. Drain well.

When the potatoes are cool enough to handle, cut them in half lengthwise. Scoop a small pocket out of each half with a teaspoon.

Fill six of the potato halves with the black caviar; fill the remaining halves with the red caviar. Sprinkle the crumbled egg yolks over each potato.

Put both a red and black potato half on each plate and garnish with lemon wedges.

Pâté Rothschild
Serves 6-8

Ingredients

1lb. fresh chicken livers, finely chopped
1lb. fresh calf's liver, finely chopped
2 eggs, beaten
3oz. cooked haricot beans, mashed
2tbsp. lemon juice
4tbsp. cream
1 clove garlic, finely chopped
bay leaf, crumbled
good pinch salt
good pinch black pepper
$\frac{1}{4}$ cup chicken fat
$\frac{1}{4}$ cup brandy
$\frac{1}{4}$ cup dark sherry

Preheat the oven to 375°F. Put all the ingredients in a large wooden mixing bowl and combine thoroughly.

Pack the pâté mixture into a small loaf pan. Smooth the top. Bake for 1½ hours.

Remove the pâté from the oven and leave it to cool. Invert the loaf pan and turn out the pâté.

Cover and chill for at least 3 hours before serving.

Stuffed Peppers
Serves 4

Ingredients

2 large green peppers (or 1 red and 1 green)
1 cup ricotta cheese
1 small pickled cucumber, finely chopped
1tbsp. chopped parsley
1tbsp. chopped dill
salt and pepper
crisp lettuce to serve

Remove the stalk end of the peppers and discard the cores and seeds. Mix the ricotta with the pickled cucumber, parsley, dill and salt and pepper.

Stuff the mixture into the peppers and refrigerate for several hours. With a very sharp knife, cut the peppers into slices about ½in. thick.

Serve the pepper slices on a bed of crisp lettuce.

Variation Use farmer's or cottage cheese instead of ricotta, or a mixture of low-fat soft cheeses.

Pilchard Pâté
Serves 4-6

This pâté can also be used as a dip or as a stuffing for tomatoes or celery.

Ingredients

12oz. can pilchards or herrings in tomato sauce
1 cup cottage cheese
2tbsp. lemon juice
1 clove garlic, crushed
salt and pepper

Blend everything together well until smooth. Chill.

Either serve in individual pots, garnished with a slice of tomato or some parsley, or turn the mixture into a serving dish.

Smoked Mackerel Pâté
Serves 3-4

This makes a very firm pâté — you can make a softer mixture by adding more yogurt. It would then make a dip, for carrot sticks etc. This freezes very well.

Ingredients

approx. ½lb. smoked mackerel fillets
⅔ cup yogurt
2tsp. grated horseradish
1tbsp. lemon juice
salt and pepper

Skin the fish and remove any bones. Liquidize all the ingredients together. Spoon into individual dishes or one serving dish. Refrigerate until required.

Serve with toast and lemon wedges.

Smoked Mackerel Cream
Serves 4

Ingredients

10oz. smoked mackerel
  fillet
juice of 1 lemon
1 clove garlic, crushed
2tbsp. vegetable or olive oil

¼ cup cream cheese
2tbsp. parsley, finely
  chopped
salt and freshly ground
  pepper

Remove the skin from the mackerel and check for any bones which may be left. Mash in a bowl with a fork. Sprinkle with the lemon juice.

Mix the crushed garlic, oil and cream cheese in a bowl. Gradually add the fish and the parsley. (Alternatively feed the ingredients into a food processor and mix for a few seconds.) Season well.

Serve in small ramekins with triangles of brown toast and lemon wedges.

Shrimp-Stuffed Vine Leaves
Serves 8

Ingredients

olive oil
1 large onion, chopped
1 clove garlic, chopped
½ cup chopped green
  pepper
½ cup chopped carrot
¾ cup brown rice

2½ cups water or stock
salt and freshly ground
  black pepper
1½ cups peeled shrimps
2tbsp. parsley, chopped
soy sauce to taste
1 packet vine leaves

Preheat the oven to 350°C.

Heat a little oil in a pan and fry the onion and garlic until soft. Stir in the green pepper, carrot and rice. Pour on the water or stock. Bring to a boil and season with salt and pepper. Cover and turn the heat down low. Simmer without stirring for about 40 minutes.

Stir in the shrimps and cook for a further 10 minutes until liquid has been absorbed and rice is tender. Stir in the parsley and season with soy sauce to taste.

Divide the mixture between the vine leaves and roll into tight parcels.

Pack the vine leaves in an ovenproof dish. Pour enough olive oil over to coat, cover the dish and bake for 30 minutes until heated through.

Shrimp Bush
Serves 4

Ingredients

24 large shrimp, cooked, in
  shells

bunch of parsley or
  watercress

Preparation Arrange the shrimp with the tails over the rim of a large glass goblet.

Stand on a glass plate and make a garland with the remaining shrimp and parsley or watercress round the plate.

Serve with Mayonnaise or Aïoli.

Smoked Salmon Pâté
Serves 3-4

Ingredients

¼lb. smoked salmon pieces
2tbsp. fresh parsley,
  chopped
freshly ground black
  pepper

juice of 2 lemons
¼ cup cream cheese
2tbsp. heavy cream

Select a few small pieces of smoked salmon and retain for garnish. Pound, press through a strainer or blend the remainder, then add a good shake of black pepper and lemon juice and mix well.

Add the smoked salmon and chopped parsley to the cream cheese and heavy cream. Mix well.

Serve in small ramekins with triangles of toast.

This mixture can also be piped on crackers or toast to serve as canapés decorated with small curls of smoked salmon.

Spinach and Carrot Terrine
Serves 4-6

Ingredients

2lb. spinach, washed, stalks
   removed
2 egg whites
1tsp. salt
freshly ground white
   pepper
nutmeg
ground ginger
$\frac{1}{2}$ cup heavy cream

Filling

14oz. carrots, peeled and
   trimmed
2 egg whites
1tsp. salt
freshly ground white
   pepper
$\frac{1}{2}$ cup heavy cream
butter to grease the terrine
   dish
1 cup Chaudfroid Sauce
carrot cutouts to decorate
aspic to finish

Squeeze the spinach into a heavy-bottomed pan, cover and cook with only the water adhering to the leaves over a low heat for 5-8 minutes, stirring occasionally. When soft, allow to cool. Squeeze out the excess liquid and then purée in a blender.

Gradually beat the egg whites into the spinach. Add the salt, pepper, nutmeg and ginger to taste. Stand the bowl over ice and beat in the cream a little at a time.

Cut up the carrots and cook in salted water until tender. Make up the carrot filling just as you made up the spinach mixture.

Grease the terrine dish and carefully fill it with alternate layers of spinach and carrot mixture. Cover the dish with foil and stand it in a roasting pan of simmering water in the oven. Cook for 45 minutes. Allow to cool.

When the terrine is cool, cover the top of it with a layer of chaudfroid sauce. When this has set, decorate with carrot cutouts and glaze with aspic.

Summer Lunch Bowl
Serves 1

This is lovely and refreshing for a warm summer's day — add an ice cube if necessary to cool it down.

Ingredients

1 cup yogurt or
   a mixture of yogurt
   and sour cream
slices of cucumber
chopped green onion

chopped chives
1tbsp. cream cheese
1 radish
salt and pepper

Add the vegetables and chives to the yogurt in a pretty bowl. Crumble in the cream cheese. Season to taste. Serve well chilled.

Variation Add the raw vegetables of your choice to the yogurt.

Sweet and Sour Salmon
Serves 8

Ingredients

3 medium onions, sliced
3 lemons, sliced
scant cup honey
$\frac{1}{3}$ cup seedless raisins
bay leaf
8 thin salmon steaks

1tsp. salt
3 cups water
8 crushed ginger snaps
$\frac{1}{2}$ cup cider vinegar
$\frac{1}{2}$ cup sliced blanched
   almonds

Combine the onions, lemon slices, honey, raisins, bay leaf, salmon steaks, salt and water in a large saucepan. Cover and cook over a low heat for 30 minutes. Remove the fish.

Add the ginger snaps, vinegar and almonds to the fish stock. Cook over a low heat. Stir until smooth. Pour over the fish, and serve either warm or cold.

Stuffed Tomatoes I
Serves 4

Ingredients

4 large tomatoes, peeled	lemon juice
⅔ cup cream cheese	1tbsp. grated onion
milk	pepper
2tbsp. lumpfish roe	

Cut the tops off the tomatoes, scoop out the seeds (reserve the tops and seeds for use in a soup).

Mix the cream cheese with a little milk, just to soften it. Add the lumpfish roe and lemon juice to taste. Stir in the grated onion. Season with pepper (you shouldn't need salt as the roe will be fairly salty).

Mix everything together well and stuff the tomatoes with the mixture. Refrigerate until required.

Serve on crispy lettuce with some hot French bread.

Stuffed Tomatoes II
Serves 4

Ingredients

4 large tomatoes	1 fresh green chili pepper, seeded and sliced
¼ cup long-grain rice, cooked	½tsp. curry powder (optional)
salt and freshly ground pepper	¼ cup almonds, chopped
2tbsp. oil	1tsp. chopped fresh coriander or parsley
1 large onion, sliced	⅓ cup cooked ground beef, lamb or chicken
1 green pepper, seeded and sliced	

Remove the top of the tomatoes. Scoop out the centers into a bowl.

Add the cooked long-grain rice. Season well.

Heat the oil and fry the onion over a low heat for 3 minutes. Add the sliced pepper and chili pepper. Sprinkle with the curry powder and continue cooking for 2 minutes. Add the chopped almonds.

Finally sprinkle in the chopped coriander or parsley. Add the meat and mix well.

Fill each tomato with the rice mixture. Brush the tomatoes with oil. Then cook in the oven for about 15 minutes at 350°F.

Tuna Pâté
Serves 2-3

Ingredients

7oz. tin tuna fish	1 drop Tabasco sauce
1 clove garlic, crushed	freshly chopped parsley to taste
½tsp. cayenne	
2tbsp. fresh lemon juice	salt and pepper to taste
¼ cup heavy cream	

Drain the tuna fish.

Mash with all the other ingredients and season to taste.

Turn into a dish and refrigerate for 3 hours.

Tarama Salad
Serves 6-8

Ingredients

3 large potatoes
3tbsp. milk
1/2 cup red caviar or smoked cod's roe
6tbsp. water
1/4 cup lemon juice
1 small onion, finely chopped
3/4 cup olive oil

Peel and dice the potatoes. Cook them in boiling water until very soft, about 20 minutes.

Drain the potatoes and put them into a mixing bowl. By hand or with an electric beater, mash the potatoes, slowly adding the milk, until smooth.

Add the caviar or cod's roe and water to the potatoes. Mix well.

Add the lemon juice and onion to the mixture and mix briefly. Slowly beat in the olive oil.

Continue to beat until a smooth paste is formed.

Serve with cucumber and tomato slices and warmed pitta bread.

Vegetable Caviar
Serves 6-8

Serve this delectable vegetarian dish in exactly the same way as real caviar — by itself, accompanied by thin slices of dark bread and perhaps a squeeze of lemon.

Ingredients

1 small eggplant, peeled
1 small squash, halved and seeded
3 large green peppers, seeded
1/2tsp. salt
1/2tsp. black pepper
1/2tsp. finely chopped garlic
3tbsp lemon juice
6tbsp. vegetable oil
3tbsp. fresh parsley, finely chopped

Preheat the oven to 475°F. Put the eggplant, squash and green peppers in a baking dish. Bake for 30 minutes and remove the peppers. Bake the eggplant and sqash for 15 minutes longer.

Cut the peppers into strips. Cut the eggplant into cubes. Scoop the pulp from the squash and discard the skin.

Combine the eggplant, peppers and squash in a medium-sized mixing bowl. Chop and mix thoroughly until the mixture is well combined. Add the salt, black pepper, garlic, lemon juice, vegetable oil and parsley. Blend thoroughly.

Chill for at least 2 hours before serving.

Vegetarian "Chopped Liver"
Serves 6

Ingredients

1/2lb. chick peas (garbanzo beans), cooked and drained
1/2lb. red kidney beans, cooked and drained
1 hard-boiled egg, finely chopped
1/4lb. canned mackerel fillets in tomato sauce
1/2 cup finely chopped onion
4tbsp. slivered carrot
2tbsp. lemon juice
1tbsp. red wine

Combine all the ingredients in a large wooden chopping bowl. Mash them into a paste with a fine and even consistency.

Spoon the mixture into a serving bowl. Cover and chill for at least 2 hours. Serve with crackers, dark bread or on a bed of lettuce.

Vegetable Cream Cheese
Makes approx. 3/4lb.

Ingredients

1 1/3 cups cream cheese
2 green onions, chopped
2 carrots, grated
2 radishes, chopped
2 sticks celery, chopped
small piece fennel, chopped
1/2 green pepper, chopped
1tbsp. chopped chives
1/2tsp. paprika
salt and pepper

Combine all the ingredients and mix well.

Use the mixture as an hors d'oeuvre, served in small bowls, or as a spread for open sandwiches (try pumpernickel or rye bread).

Bean Pancake
Makes 16

Ingredients

1⅓ cups split or whole mung
  beans, washed
¼ cup glutinous rice
1tbsp. soy sauce
1tbsp. roasted sesame
  seeds, crushed
½tsp. baking soda
1 cup bean sprouts,
  blanched and dried
1 clove garlic, peeled and
  crushed
4 green onions, trimmed
  and chopped

¾ cup shredded cooked
  lean pork
salt and pepper to taste
sesame oil for frying
Sauce
¼ cup soy sauce
1 clove garlic, peeled and
  crushed
2tbsp. rice vinegar
2 green onions, finely
  sliced lengthwise
pinch of sugar

Pick over then soak the mung beans and glutinous rice in water for at least 8 hours.

Rinse well, removing as many green skins as possible, drain, then put into a food processor and grind to a batter the consistency of heavy cream. Add soy sauce, sesame seeds and bicarbonate of soda.

When ready to cook, add the bean sprouts, garlic, green onion and pork. Season to taste. Heat the sesame oil in a pan. Spoon or ladle in just over ⅔ cup of the mixture and, using the back of a spoon, spread it into a thick pancake. Drizzle a little of the sesame oil over the surface, cover and cook over a medium heat until the underside is cooked.

Now invert a lightly oiled plate over the pancake. Remove from the heat and turn the skillet over so that the pancake is on the plate. Slip the pancake, uncooked-side down, back into the pan, and continue cooking for a further 3-4 minutes.

Keep warm while cooking the remaining batter and serve in quarters with the dipping sauce, made by blending together its ingredients.

Pork Spring Rolls
Makes 20

Ingredients

2tbsp. finely chopped
  onions
3 cloves garlic, crushed
½in. ginger, scraped and
  shredded
2 red chili peppers,
  shredded
oil for frying
½lb. pork, finely ground
1tsp. turmeric

10 spring roll wrappers, cut
  in half
flour and water paste to
  seal
Sauce
⅓ cup vinegar
1½ cloves garlic
salt and black pepper
6 pieces chili pepper, sliced

Fry the onions, garlic and ginger with the chili peppers and oil. Add the pork, cook for 5 minutes, stirring until the meat changes color. Add seasoning and turmeric. Cook for 2 minutes, and cool.

Fill rolls, sealing with flour and water paste. Then deep fry in hot oil until they turn crispy and brown.

Mix together all the sauce ingredients and serve in a small bowl as a dip for the rolls.

Cheese and Garlic Straws
Makes 20

Ingredients

1lb. Puff Pastry
juice of 2-3 garlic cloves
¼ cup milk
1tsp. paprika

1tbsp. Parmesan cheese,
  grated
salt and cayenne pepper

Roll out the puff pastry on a floured board into a rectangle, as thinly as possible.

Stir the garlic juice into most of the milk and brush the pastry with half of it.

Mix the paprika and Parmesan, and season with a little salt and cayenne. Sprinkle half of it over one half of the pastry.

Fold the pastry and roll out as thinly as possible.

Repeat with the remaining garlic milk and Parmesan mixture and roll out to a rectangle not more than ¼in. thick. Brush with milk and cut into strips about ½in. wide and 6in. long.

Arrange the straws at least 1in. apart, on greased cookie sheets and bake for 7 to 10 minutes in a preheated 425°F oven until well-risen and golden brown.

Serve warm, piled onto each other, log-cabin style.

Cheese Cutlets
Makes 6

Ingredients

1 tbsp. Ghee or butter
1 cup milk
1 cup cottage cheese
¾ cup farina
1 medium onion, finely chopped
2 green chili peppers, seeded and finely chopped

1 tbsp. chopped coriander leaves
½ tsp. salt
2 tbsp. flour
½ cup milk
breadcrumbs
oil for deep frying

Melt the ghee or butter over medium heat, add the milk, cottage cheese, farina, onions, chili peppers, coriander leaves and salt and mix thoroughly. Stirring constantly, cook until the mixture leaves the sides and a ball forms, about 3-4 minutes.

Spread the mixture ¾ in. thick on a greased cookie sheet. Cut into 1-in. squares and chill for about 2 hours.

Make a smooth batter with the flour and milk. Dip each square into the batter and then roll it in bread-crumbs.

Heat the oil and deep fry the cutlets for 2-3 minutes over a high heat till crisp and golden. Serve with chutney.

Chop
Spicy ground lamb wrapped in potato
Makes about. 20

Ingredients

2 tbsp. oil
1 large onion, finely sliced
2 cloves garlic, crushed
½ in. ginger, grated
¾ tsp. ground turmeric
½ tsp. chili powder
1 tsp. salt
good pinch of salt
1 tbsp. raisins (optional)
2 tsp. vinegar
1 lb. ground lamb

1 tsp. Garam Masala
1 egg (lightly beaten)
breadcrumbs
oil for shallow frying
1¼ lb. potatoes, peeled and boiled
1 tsp. ground, roasted cumin
½ tsp. ground, roasted, dried red chili peppers (optional)

Heat the oil in a large skillet over a medium high heat. Add the onion, garlic and ginger and fry for 4-5 minutes, stirring constantly, until the onion becomes pale gold.

Add the turmeric, chili powder, salt, sugar, raisins (if used) and vinegar, mix thoroughly with the onion and fry for 1 minute. Add the lamb and mix with the spices.

Cover, lower heat, and, stirring occasionally, cook for about 20 minutes. Remove the cover, turn the heat up and, stirring constantly, cook until all the liquid has evaporated and the lamb is dry.

Mix in the Garam Masala, remove from the heat, and set aside to cool.

Mash the potatoes with the cumin, ground chili peppers, if used and salt. Divide into about 20 balls.

Take a ball and make a depression in the middle with your thumb, to form a cup shape. Fill the center with the meat mixture and re-form the potato ball, making sure no cracks appear. Make all the Chop in this manner.

Dip in the egg, one at a time, and roll in the breadcrumbs.

Heat the oil over a very high heat in a large skillet and fry until golden brown, turning once after about a minute.

Deviled Eggs
Makes 8

Ingredients

4 hard-boiled eggs, halved lengthwise
1½ tbsp. finely chopped onions
2 green chili peppers, seeded and finely chopped

1 tbsp. coriander leaves, chopped
½ tsp. salt
2 tbsp. mashed potato
oil for deep frying
1 tbsp. plain flour
¼ cup water

Remove the yolks and mix with the onions, chili peppers, coriander leaves, salt and mashed potatoes. Put the mixture back into the egg whites. Chill for 30 minutes.

Heat the oil in a pan over high heat. While the oil is heating, make a batter with the flour and water. Be careful not to allow the oil to catch fire.

Dip eggs into the batter and gently put into the hot oil. Fry until golden, turning once. Drain and serve warm.

Falafel
Chick-Pea Balls
Serves 4

Ingredients

1 cup chick-peas	2 eggs, beaten
3 cloves garlic, finely chopped	lemon juice
1 onion, finely chopped	wholewheat flour mixed with wheatgerm for coating
1 tsp. ground cumin	
1 tsp. ground coriander	oil
1 tbsp. fresh parsley, finely chopped	cayenne pepper
	olives, gherkins, pickled peppers (optional)
1 tbsp. tahini paste	

Soak the chick-peas overnight, then cook in boiling water until they can be mashed with a fork.

In a large bowl, mash the chick peas with the garlic, onion, cumin, coriander, parsley and tahini. Add enough egg and lemon juice to make a dough.

Form the dough into 1½in. balls, roll in flour and wheatgerm to coat and fry in hot oil until crispy. Drain on paper towels.

Serve hot or cold with a dip of tahini paste mixed with olive oil and lemon juice, and sprinkled with cayenne pepper. Serve with olives, gherkins and pickled peppers if you like. Alternatively, stuff the falafel into envelopes of pitta bread with a salad of shredded leaves, peppers and a few chopped chili peppers.

Devils on Horseback
Makes 12

Ingredients

12 prunes, soaked	12 toothpicks
6 slices fatty bacon	

Put the soaked prunes in a small saucepan, cover with water, bring to a boil and simmer for 5 minutes. Drain and allow to cool slightly.

Remove the pits from the prunes and reshape.

Cut the rind from the bacon, cut each slice in half and smooth out with a spatula. Put a piece of foil on the broiler pan and arrange the slices of bacon on the foil. Cook for 2 minutes under a hot broiler. Do not allow to crisp.

When slightly cooled, wrap the bacon pieces around the prunes and finish cooking under the broiler or in the oven if more convenient.

Secure with toothpicks, and serve hot with pre-dinner drinks.

Deep Fried Pastries
makes 12

Kalonji is also known as nigella. It is a small black seed.

Ingredients

1 scant cup flour	1½ tbsp. oil
½ tsp. salt	¼ cup hot water
pinch kalonji	oil for deep frying
pinch ground roasted nutmeg	

Sift the flour and salt together. Mix in the cumin. Blend in the oil.

Add enough water to make a stiff dough. Knead for 10 minutes until soft and smooth.

Divide the dough into 12 balls. Roll each ball into thin rounds 4in. across. Make 5 or 6 small cuts in the rounds.

Heat the oil in a skillet over medium heat. Add a pastry round and fry until crisp and golden. Drain on paper towels. Serve warm with chutney.

Garlic Buttered Nuts
Makes 2 cups

Ingredients
2 cups shelled almonds, cashews or peanuts, or a mixture	1tbsp. oil
2tbsp. butter	2-3 cloves of garlic, finely crushed
	rock salt

Loosen and remove the almond skins by pouring boiling water over them and refreshing in cold water. Toast the peanuts briefly and rub off the brown skins.

Melt the butter and oil with the garlic in a heavy skillet and toss the nuts in it over a moderate heat for 3 to 5 minutes or until they are crisp and golden.

Drain on paper towels and sprinkle with rock salt. Serve warm.

Variation For Deviled Garlic Nuts, add a little cayenne to the rock salt.

Curried Vegetable Fritters
Makes 20

Ingredients
4tbsp. gram (chick-pea) flour	potatoes, cut into very thin rounds
2tsp. oil	cauliflower, cut into ¾in. flowerets
1tsp. baking powder	
½tsp. salt	fresh chili pepper, left whole
5tbsp. water	pumpkin, cut into thin slices
Any of the following vegetables can be used:	green pepper, cut into thin strips
eggplant, cut into very thin rounds	oil for deep frying
onions, cut into ⅛in. rings	

Mix all the batter ingredients together and beat until smooth.

Wash the slices of vegetables and pat dry.

Heat the oil in a wide skillet till very hot.

Dip each vegetable slice into the batter and lower into the hot oil. Put as many slices as you can in the oil. Fry till crisp and golden.

Drain and serve with Coriander Chutney.

Mexican Pastries
Makes 20

Ingredients
¾lb. Puff or Shortcrust Pastry	½ spicy sausage finely chopped
milk or beaten egg to seal	½tbsp. tomato paste
deep fat for frying	1 hard-boiled egg, chopped
1tbsp. oil	3tbsp. raisins
½ small onion, peeled and chopped	4 stuffed olives, cut into rings
1 clove garlic	1 small gherkin, chopped
½ cup ground pork	seasoning

Make the pastry or thaw if you are using frozen. Cover and leave to rest in the refrigerator while preparing the filling.

Heat the oil and fry the onion and garlic without browning. Add the ground pork and stir until the meat browns. Add the sausage and tomato paste. Cover and cook very gently for 10-15 minutes. Draw from the heat and leave to cool, then stir in the hard-boiled eggs, raisins, olives, gherkin and seasoning to taste. Leave to cool completely.

Roll out the pastry on a floured board and cut into 4in. rounds. Divide the filling between them. Damp the edges half-way round, then fold into a half circle. Seal the edges by knocking up with the back of a knife, then flute them or mark with the prongs of a fork, to seal.

When all the pastries are made, fry in hot oil for 10 minutes until golden and cooked through. Drain thoroughly on paper towels and serve hot or warm.

Variation Instead of deep frying the pastries, you can bake them at 425°F in a preheated oven for 12 minutes.

Fish Savories with Spicy Tomato Sauce
Serves 4

Leftover poached salmon, trout or canned fish such as tuna or salmon can be used.

Ingredients
½lb. fish, cooked	salt and freshly ground pepper
2tbsp. butter	1tbsp. chopped parsley
1 small onion, peeled and sliced	1 egg, beaten
½lb. potatoes, cooked and strained	dried breadcrumbs
	oil for frying
2 drops Tabasco sauce	⅔ cup Spicy Tomato Sauce
1tsp. tomato ketchup	

Make sure that all the bones are removed from the cooked fish.

Melt the butter and sweat the onion until tender. Add the potatoes, seasoning and parsley to the onion in a bowl, and finally add the fish and mix well.

Mix with a little of the beaten egg. Add a few drops of water to the remaining egg. Flour the hands and form the mixture into small balls and chill in the refrigerator.

Roll the fish balls in the egg and water mixture, and then in the dried crumbs. Fry the balls in deep fat or in a skillet one-third filled with oil which has been heated.

Arrange on a plate. Spear the balls with cocktail sticks and serve around a dish of hot Spicy Tomato Sauce.

Hi-Speed Pizzas
Makes 4 small pizzas

Ingredients

½lb. flour	good pinch fresh marjoram
½tsp. salt	or ½tsp. dried oregano
1tsp. baking powder	¼ cup stoned black olives
4tbsp. olive oil	⅓lb. Cheddar cheese, thinly
water to mix	sliced
1 cup Concentrated	1 clove garlic, finely
Tomato Sauce	chopped

Sift together the flour, salt and baking powder, and add the oil and enough water to make a very sticky dough.

Divide into 4 and press each piece into a well-oiled 6in. round pizza or pie pan.

Top each with the tomato sauce, marjoram or oregano, olives and cheese, and sprinkle with the garlic.

Bake for 15-20 minutes in a preheated oven at 450 °F until the dough is cooked and the cheese is browned and bubbling.

Variation You can add chopped ham, crisp bacon, strips of salami, sliced button mushrooms or sliced red pepper.

Green Banana Balls
Makes 8

Ingredients

1 green banana, halved	½tsp. salt
1 fresh green chili pepper,	1tbsp. chopped onion
seeded and chopped	1tsp. plain flour
½tbsp. chopped coriander	oil for deep frying
leaves	

Boil the banana till soft. Peel and cool.

Mash the banana with the chili pepper, coriander leaves, salt, onion and flour. Divide the mixture into 8 small balls and flatten.

Heat the oil and fry the balls, turning once, till crisp and golden.

Galloping Horses
Fried Pork and Fruit Snacks
Makes 16

Make up the filling just before using — it binds together better when still warm.

Ingredients

1½tbsp. peanut or	1tbsp. Worcestershire sauce
vegetable oil	1tbsp. brown sugar or to
1 clove garlic, peeled and	taste
crushed	freshly ground black
1 red chili pepper, seeded	pepper
and chopped	pieces of fresh pineapple
few stems fresh coriander,	mandarin segments, cut
stems chopped and	almost through vertically
leaves reserved	and opened out like a
⅓lb. pork with a	book, skin-side down.
reasonable proportion of	canned lychees, well-
fat to lean, finely ground	drained
¼ cup salted peanuts,	
crushed coarsely with	
pestle and mortar	

Heat the oil in a wok, fry the garlic and chili pepper without browning, then add the coriander stems. Now add the meat and cook until the color changes. Add the peanuts, Worcestershire sauce if used, sugar and pepper. Continue cooking, stirring occasionally, for 10 minutes or until the mixture is cooked but not too dry.

Arrange the pieces of prepared fruit on a serving dish and top each with a spoonful of the pork mixture. Lightly press with fingers to stick.

Garnish with the reserved coriander leaves. Serve.

Tapenade
Serves 6

Ingredients

½ cup black olives	1tbsp. capers
2-3 cloves of garlic,	½ cup olive oil
coarsely chopped	medium French loaf, thinly
5tbsp. chopped canned	sliced.
anchovies	

Pit and coarsely chop the olives and blend them with the garlic, anchovies and capers, adding the oil gradually.

Toast the bread on one side. Spread the untoasted side thickly with the mixture and cook under a hot broiler until the edges are well browned. Serve warm.

This can also be served on fingers of crisp, buttered toast.

Samosas
Makes 20

Ingredients

3tbsp. oil
pinch whole cumin seeds
1lb. potatoes, diced into
 ½in. cubes
1 fresh green chili pepper,
 seeded and finely
 chopped
pinch turmeric
½tsp. salt

¾ cup peas
1tsp. ground roasted
 cumin
Dough
½lb. plain flour
1tsp. salt
3tbsp. oil
approx. 4 cups hot water
oil for deep frying

To make the filling, heat the oil in a heavy skillet over medium high heat and add the cumin seeds. Let them sizzle for a few seconds.

Add the potatoes and green chili pepper and fry for 2-3 minutes. Add the turmeric and salt and, stirring occasionally, cook for 5 minutes.

Add the peas and the ground roasted cumin. Stir to mix. Cover, lower heat and cook a further 10 minutes until the potatoes are tender. Cool.

For the dough, sift together the flour and salt. Rub in the oil. Add enough water to form a stiff dough. Knead for 10 minutes until smooth.

Divide into 12 balls. Roll each ball into a round of about 6in across. Cut in half.

Pick up one half, flatten it slightly and form a cone, sealing the overlapping edge with a little water. Fill the cone with 1½tsp. of the filling and seal the top with a little water.

Continue making the samosas until all the ingredients are used up.

Heat oil in a skillet over medium heat. Put in as many samosas as you can into the hot oil and fry until crisp and golden.

Drain and serve with a chutney.

Wholewheat Samosas
Makes 16

Ingredients

½lb. wholewheat flour
½tsp. salt
4tbsp. oil
4tbsp. water
Filling
1tbsp. oil
½ cup ground lamb
1 potato, peeled, cooked
 and diced

1tsp. fresh mint, chopped
pinch coriander
pinch curry powder
salt and freshly ground
 pepper
3tbsp. water
2tbsp. cooked peas
1tbsp. yogurt
oil for deep frying

Sprinkle the flour and salt into a bowl and pour the oil over the flour. Rub in with finger tips, as if making Shortcrust Pastry, until the mixture is in fine crumbs. Gradually add the water and mix to a stiff dough.

Turn onto a floured work surface and knead for a few minutes, until smooth. Put the dough in an oiled plastic bag and allow to stand for at least 30 minutes.

To make the filling, heat the oil in a skillet and brown the lamb, separating the ground meat with a spoon or fork.

Add the diced potato, mix with meat, sprinkle with mint, coriander, curry powder and season well. Fry for 2 minutes. Add the water and cook for 5 minutes on a low heat.

Add peas and yogurt. Allow to cool. Taste for seasoning.

Knead the dough on a floured surface for 2 minutes. Roll into a sausage shape and divide into 8. Put the other pieces of pastry back into the oiled bag while making the samosas.

Flatten into a 7in. square, using a rolling pin. Cut two triangles. Wet the open ends with cold water and seal one side.

Fill the open end with the mixture, seal the edge well. Flute the wide edge with the finger tips and press the other two edges with floured fingers to form an even strip. Shape and fill remaining dough as described.

Heat the oil to 360°F in a deep pan. Fry two or three at a time, turning from time to time. Drain on paper towels.

Serve hot as an appetizer or as a light meal with salad.

These can be made even smaller and used as cocktail snacks.

Julienne Vegetables

I Slicing vegetables such as carrots and celery for crudités like this makes the hors d'oeuvres more attractive. (Steamed Julienne vegetables look highly professional as part of the main dish). Square off the sides of root vegetables so that they are block-shaped.

2 Slice finely, using a good, sharp knife.

3 Stack the slices and slice again into 'matchsticks'. Soaking Julienne vegetables in iced water makes them curly.

Soups

Avocado Soup
Serves 4

Ingredients

2 large ripe avocados | juice of 1 lemon
2½ cups yogurt | salt and pepper
1 clove garlic, crushed

Halve the avocados, remove the pits and peel them. Blend all the ingredients together. Serve very well chilled, garnished with chives if desired.

The thickness of the soup will depend as much on the size of the avocados as the thickness of the yogurt used. You can thin it down with a little milk or cream if you need to.

Eggplant Soup
Serves 6-8

This unusual soup shows a touch of Turkish influence.

Ingredients

½ cup olive oil | 4¼ cups beef stock
1 cup mushrooms, | ½tsp. dried parsley
  quartered | pinch salt
1 large onion, coarsely | pinch white pepper
  chopped | pinch dried thyme
1 large tomato, cut into | pinch dried marjoram
  eighths | pinch grated nutmeg
1 large eggplant, peeled
  and diced

Heat the olive oil in a large pot over a low heat. Add the mushrooms, onion and tomato and sauté for 10 minutes.

Add the remaining ingredients to the pot. Cover and simmer for 35 to 40 minutes. Serve hot.

Cold Apple Soup
Serves 4-6

Fruit soup is popular throughout Central Europe. This version could be also made with plums, pears, peaches or cherries.

Ingredients

3 medium tart cooking | 2 whole cloves
  apples, peeled and cored | pinch salt
⅔ cup water | 1tbsp. white wine
⅓ cup sugar | 2 cups yogurt
juice of ½ lemon | ⅔ cup sour cream
1tbsp. cinnamon | (optional)

Cube the apples and cook them with the water, sugar, lemon juice, cinnamon, cloves and salt until they are soft. Remove the cloves.

Mash the apples and leave them to cool. Add the wine and yogurt to the apples and mix together well.

Serve, well chilled, with the sour cream if desired.

A thinly sliced red-skinned apple can be used as a garnish.

Bean Soup
Serves 4-6

Ingredients

1¼ cups dry white beans | 1 slice lemon
1-2tbsp. oil | soy sauce
1 onion, chopped | salt and freshly ground
1 clove garlic, chopped | black pepper
2 carrots, chopped | parsley
2 stalks celery, sliced
3 tomatoes, peeled (or a
  small can)

Soak the beans overnight. Bring to a boil in a large pan of water (about 4 cups) and simmer until tender.

Meanwhile, heat oil in a skillet and cook the onion and garlic until soft. Add carrots, celery and tomatoes, in that order, stirring all the while.

Tip vegetables into the pan with the cooked beans. Add the slice of lemon and soy sauce. Taste and adjust seasoning.

Heat through and serve sprinkled with chopped parsley. The soup may be partly puréed if you like.

Beet and Cabbage Borscht
Serves 6-8

The perhaps unlikely combination of beets and red cabbage makes a deliciously rich and hearty soup. The addition of the sausages makes it into more of a meal. Although the sour cream is not cooked with the soup, it is an essential part of it.

Ingredients

butter or margarine	bay leaf
2 slices bacon, chopped	1 clove garlic, crushed
1lb. cooked beets, peeled and diced	1tbsp. sugar
2tbsp. flour	3½pt. beef stock
2tbsp. vinegar	salt and pepper
1½lb. red cabbage, finely shredded	1lb. spicy sausages, chopped (optional)
	⅔ cup sour cream

Heat the butter and fry the bacon. Add the beets and toss them for 1 minute. Add the flour and stir well off the heat. Return to the heat and add the vinegar, mixing it in well.

Add the cabbage, bay leaf, garlic, sugar, stock, salt and pepper. Bring to a boil and then simmer, covered, for 1 hour, adding a little more stock if necessary. If you are using the sausages, add them 5 minutes before serving.

Serve hot with a generous spoonful of sour cream in each bowl.

Hearty Beef Soup
Serves 8

Ingredients

1lb. beef brisket or chuck, thinly sliced	3tbsp. chopped green pepper
1lb. beef bones, split into pieces	pinch salt
1 large turnip, diced	pinch black pepper
1 onion, quartered	4tbsp. chopped chives
2 stalks celery, finely chopped	¼ cup red wine
1 carrot, halved	4pts. water
	½lb. egg noodles

Put all the ingredients except the noodles into a large soup pot. Bring to a boil, reduce the heat and simmer, tightly covered, for 5-6 hours. Add the noodles.

Raise the heat to medium and cook for a further 12-15 minutes. Serve hot.

Chilled Borscht
Serves 6

Ingredients

1lb. cooked beets, peeled	⅔ cup sour cream
4 cups chicken stock	dill
juice of 1 lemon	salt and pepper

Liquidize the beets, with the stock, lemon juice, half of the sour cream, dill, salt and pepper. You can make the mixture as smooth as you like, but you may prefer to leave it a little chunky with small pieces of beet floating in it.

Refrigerate as long as possible (overnight is best) and serve well chilled with the remaining sour cream and perhaps a couple of ice cubes in each bowl.

Broccoli and Orange Soup
Serves 6

Ingredients

1lb. broccoli, chopped	1¼ cups yogurt
1 medium onion, chopped	1tbsp. cornstarch
1tbsp. oil	2tbsp. water
juice of 2 oranges	salt and pepper
2½ cups chicken stock	grated orange rind

Reserve some small pieces of broccoli for garnish.

Heat the oil and cook the onion until it has just softened but not browned. Add the broccoli and stir. Cook, covered, for a few minutes and then add the orange juice and stock. Bring to a boil, cover and simmer for about 20 minutes, until the broccoli is soft. Purée the soup in a blender.

Mix the cornstarch and water to a smooth paste and stir into the soup, adding the yogurt, with salt and pepper to taste. Return the soup to the heat and cook for a further 5 minutes.

Serve, garnished with the reserved broccoli and orange rind.

Use frozen broccoli if fresh is not available. If you prefer, this soup can be served cold.

Carrot and Coriander Soup
Serves 6

Ingredients

2tbsp. butter
1 medium onion, sliced
1½lb. carrots, sliced
1tsp. ground coriander

4 cups vegetable stock
⅔ cup sour cream
salt and pepper
fresh coriander or parsley

Heat the butter, add the onion and cook until it has just softened but not browned. Add the carrots and ground coriander and stir well. Leave the carrots to cook gently for 3 minutes. Add the stock and bring the mixture to a boil, then simmer, covered, for 25 minutes.

Liquidize the soup, adding the sour cream. Adjust the seasoning. Serve very cold, garnished with fresh coriander or parsley

Use a chicken stock if preferred. Herb bouillon cubes are very good for this soup.

Chard Soup with Lentils
Serves 6-8

Kale or fresh spinach may be substituted for the chard.

Ingredients

2 cups brown lentils
8 cups water
¼ cup olive oil
2 large onions, finely
  chopped
6 cloves garlic, coarsely
  chopped
1½ cups Swiss chard leaves,
  torn, tough stems removed

2tbsp. chopped fresh
  coriander
½tsp. salt
pinch black pepper
4tbsp. lemon juice

Pick over the lentils and wash them. Put the lentils into a large saucepan and add the water. Cover and cook over a medium heat for 1 hour.

When the lentils have cooked for 50 minutes, heat the olive oil in a skillet over a low heat. Add the onions, garlic and chard and sauté for 8 minutes, stirring constantly.

Add the chard mixture to the lentils. Add the coriander, salt, pepper and lemon juice and stir well. Cover the saucepan and simmer over a low heat for 20 minutes. Serve hot.

Celeriac Soup
Serves 6-8

Ingredients

6¼ cups chicken stock
2 large celeriac, peeled
  and sliced
3 stalks coarsely chopped
  celery

¼ cup chopped leeks
1 small endive, chopped
2 large carrots, diced
½tsp. salt
½tsp. white pepper

In a large soup pot, bring the chicken stock to a boil. Add the remaining ingredients, reduce the heat to low and simmer for 40 minutes. Serve hot.

German Carrot Soup
Serves 4-6

Carrots, apples and onions may seem an odd combination, but this delicious soup is a traditional dish along the Rhine.

Ingredients

1lb. carrots, peeled and
  sliced
bay leaf
3 cups chicken stock
1tsp. brown sugar
5tbsp. butter
3 medium onions, peeled
  and halved

1 large tart apple, peeled,
  cored and sliced
salt and freshly ground
  pepper
a little lemon juice
a little chopped chervil

Put the carrots into a large skillet with the bay leaf, chicken stock, and brown sugar. Bring to a boil, then simmer until nearly tender.

Meanwhile, heat the butter in another skillet, add the sliced onions and apple with a little salt and pepper. Fry until soft and golden brown. Add the contents of the skillet to the carrots, and continue cooking until all the vegetables are very soft. Strain and reserve the liquid. Remove the bay leaf.

Press through a strainer or liquidize the vegetable mixture until very smooth. Return to the liquid. Reheat and adjust the seasoning, adding a little lemon juice if necessary.

Serve sprinkled with chopped chervil.

German Carrot Soup

Oriental Chicken Soup
Serves 6

Serve prawn or shrimp crackers with this slightly spicy, unusual soup.

Ingredients

2 chicken joints, skinned	1 large green pepper, seeded and coarsely chopped
1 medium onion, peeled and quartered	¼ cup Chinese egg noodles
1in. root ginger, peeled and sliced	soy sauce
4¼ cups good chicken or vegetable stock	freshly ground pepper
	2 green onions, sliced, to garnish

Wipe the chicken joints and place in a large pan. Add the onion and ginger to the pan with the stock. Bring to a boil, then cover and simmer gently for 20 minutes, or until the chicken is very tender. Remove from the heat and allow to cool slightly.

Remove the onion from the pan, then lift out and bone the chicken joints. Reserve the meat. Skim any fat from the liquid left in the pan.

Add the pepper to the liquid in the pan. Finely chop the reserved chicken, and add to the pan with the noodles and a little soy sauce and ground pepper. Bring back to a boil, then simmer gently for 5 minutes. Taste for seasoning, and add a little more soy sauce if necessary.

Spoon into individual bowls and garnish with the sliced green onions.

Cheese and Onion Soup
Serves 4-6

Ingredients

1-2 tbsp. oil	1½ cups grated Cheddar cheese
2 medium onions, sliced	salt
5 cups stock	soy sauce
½lb. potatoes	

Heat the oil in a large saucepan and stir-fry onions until lightly browned. Add stock and bring to a boil.

Meanwhile, peel the potatoes and grate them into the saucepan. Turn down the heat and simmer until potatoes have cooked and soup has thickened.

Add the grated cheese, stirring to melt. Season to taste with salt and soy sauce.

Serve with wholewheat bread and a crisp green salad.

Cold Cherry Soup
Serves 8

This unusual soup is made using both red and black cherries and is served cold.

Ingredients

4 cups cold water	2tbsp. lemon juice
2½ cups sugar	1 cup red wine
pinch cinnamon	pinch dried dill
3 cups fresh or canned red cherries, stoned	½tsp. ground white pepper
	2tbsp. tepid water
3 cups fresh or canned black cherries, stoned	1tbsp. arrowroot

In a medium-sized saucepan, combine all the ingredients except the tepid water and arrowroot. Bring to a boil over a medium heat. Partially cover the saucepan and reduce the heat to low. Simmer for 1 hour.

In a small bowl, combine the arrowroot and tepid water. Stir well. Stir the mixture into the soup and turn the heat up to medium. Continue stirring until the soup begins to bubble. Reduce the heat to low. Simmer the soup, uncovered, for 2 minutes.

Pour the soup into a glass bowl and chill for 1 hour. Serve cold.

Jellied Lemon Chicken Soup
Serves 4

Ingredients

4 cups chicken stock	1 tsp. sugar
5tsp. gelatin	⅔ cup sour cream
¼ cup lemon juice	

Bring the stock to a boil, remove from the heat, sprinkle over the gelatin and stir to dissolve. Add the lemon juice and sugar and stir well.

Leave this to cool and when it is beginning to set, beat in the sour cream. Pour into individual dishes or glasses and leave to set firm. The mixture may separate into two layers, but this will simply add to its charm.

Chicken in the Pot with Soup
Serves 6-8

This dish, the queen of all chicken soups, is traditionally served with Kreplach and Matzo Balls.

Ingredients

2 large parsley sprigs
1 large parsnip
1 small leek
dill sprig
5pts. water
2 stalks celery, halved
2 large onions, halved

5 carrots, halved
2-lb. chicken, cut into pieces
1tsp. salt
½tsp. black pepper
pinch ground white pepper
6tbsp. fine egg noodles

Tie the parsley, parsnip, leek and dill together with kitchen string.

Fill a large soup pot with the water. Add the bunch of vegetables and herbs and the celery, onions, carrots and chicken pieces. Bring the liquid to a boil. Add the salt, black pepper and white pepper. Reduce the heat to low. Simmer for 1 hour 45 minutes.

Remove and discard the bunch of vegetables and herbs. Add the egg noodles to the pot. Simmer for 10 minutes, stirring occasionally.

Serve the soup with the vegetables and chicken pieces in large deep bowls.

Clam Chowder
Serves 4

Ingredients

1-2 dozen clams or 1 can clams
⅔ cup white wine
1¼ cups water
bay leaf
bouquet garni
¼lb. fatty bacon
2tbsp. butter
1 medium onion, diced
2 leeks, washed and chopped
1 green pepper, seeded, blanched and diced

1 stalk celery, diced
1 cup diced potato
salt and freshly ground pepper
few sprigs fresh thyme or ½tsp. dried thyme
4-6 fresh tomatoes, skinned, or 15-oz. can tomatoes
1tbsp. chopped parsley
8 cream crackers, crushed

Poach fresh clams for about 10 minutes in the white wine and water with a bay leaf and bouquet garni added. If using canned, poach for 5 minutes.

Cut the fatty bacon into small pieces. Melt the butter in a saucepan and add bacon. After about 2 minutes add the onion, leeks, diced pepper, diced celery and diced potato. Sweat the vegetables for about 6 minutes then add the clam liquor with seasoning, thyme and chopped tomatoes.

Make the liquid up to approximately 4 cups with water. Bring the soup to a boil, reduce heat and simmer until the vegetables are tender. Add the clams a few minutes before serving.

Serve the chowder sprinkled with crushed crackers and parsley.

Corn Chowder
Serves 4

Ingredients

4 slices fatty bacon
1 medium onion, peeled and diced
1 potato, peeled and cubed
12oz. can corn kernels or frozen corn

2½ cups chicken stock
salt and freshly ground pepper
1¼ cups milk
drop Tabasco
1tbsp. chopped parsley

Remove any rind from the bacon slices and cut into small pieces.

On a low heat cook the bacon in a saucepan in its own fat. When there is a little fat in the pan, turn up the heat and allow to crisp. Add the onion and fry for 1 minute.

Add the potato cubes, stir round, then add half the corn with the chicken stock and seasoning. Bring to a boil and simmer for 30 minutes. Allow to cool slightly and liquidize the soup in a blender or food processor.

Return to the saucepan and stir in the milk and the remaining corn. Heat through over a low heat. Add Tabasco and taste for seasoning.

Serve sprinkled with chopped parsley.

Corn Chowder

Midwest Corn Chowder
Serves 4-6

Ingredients

¾ cup finely chopped
    bacon
1 onion, chopped
¼ cup sliced celery
1¼ cups diced potatoes
2 cups water
1 bay leaf

1 tsp. salt
pinch black pepper
2 cups milk
⅔ cup whipping cream
1 cup corn, cut from the
    cob

In a saucepan, sauté the bacon until well browned. Stir in the onion and cook for a further 2 minutes. Add the celery, potatoes, water, bay leaf and salt. Simmer gently until potatoes are tender, about 20-30 minutes.

In a smooth bowl mix the flour with 1 tbsp. milk. Stir until smooth and add to potato mixture. Add the remaining milk and stir. Heat the soup until it thickens.

Slowly stir in the cream and corn. Heat mixture gently but thoroughly. Add the black pepper, stir, and serve.

Fish Chowder
Serves 4

Ingredients

1 lb. white fish, boned
2 tbsp. butter
1 large onion, peeled and
    finely chopped
1-2 cloves garlic, peeled
    and crushed
4 potatoes, peeled and
    diced
14 oz. can tomatoes
few sprigs of thyme
few sprigs of parsley

1-2 bay leaves or 1
    bouquet garni
salt and freshly ground
    black pepper
pinch cayenne pepper
1¼ cups hot water
⅔ cup milk
8 plain crackers, crushed
1 tbsp. chopped parsley

Make sure the fish is boned as far as possible, as most people object to fish bones. Cut into even-sized pieces.

Melt the butter and sweat the onion, crushed garlic and diced potato for about 5 minutes. Add the can of tomatoes with the herbs and seasoning. Pour in the hot water.

Bring to a boil and simmer for about 20 minutes, or until potatoes are cooked. Add the fish for about the last 10 minutes of cooking. Taste for seasoning and

make sure all the fish is cooked. Add the milk and stir over a low heat for a few minutes.

Put the crackers in the bottom of the soup bowls and pour over the soup. Sprinkle with chopped parsley. Serve with warm French bread or crispy rolls.

Zucchini and Fennel Soup
Serves 4-6

This Italian soup is delicious served with garlic bread.

Ingredients

1 bulb fennel, approx. ½ lb.
1 tsp. lemon juice
4 tbsp. butter or margarine
1 lb. zucchini, sliced
1 medium onion, sliced
salt and freshly ground
    pepper

4 tbsp. flour
2½ cups good chicken or
    vegetable stock
⅔ cup light cream
chopped chives or parsley

Trim the fennel and quarter. Cook in boiling salted water with the lemon juice until tender — about 20 minutes. Drain thoroughly.

Heat the butter or margarine in a large pan and add the sliced vegetables with a little salt and pepper. Cover, and cook slowly for 15 minutes. Slice the drained fennel and add to zucchini mixture. Raise the heat and cook, stirring constantly for 1 minute, then stir in the flour, followed by the stock. Bring to a boil, then cover and simmer for 20 minutes.

Strain the soup, reserving the liquid. Press through a strainer or liquidize the vegetables until smooth. Return to the pan with the liquid and the cream. Reheat, adding more stock or water if the soup is too thick, and taste for seasoning.

Sprinkle with the chopped chives or parsley just before serving.

Melt the butter or margarine in a saucepan. Add the onions and sauté for 3 minutes. Stir in the flour and milk. Slowly bring the mixture to a boil and add the corn, salt and pepper.

Cook over a low heat for 15 minutes, and serve hot.

Cucumber Soup
Serves 4

Ingredients

1 large cucumber, peeled	salt and pepper
2¼ cups yogurt	walnuts, chopped
dill or mint	(optional)

Remove a thumb-length piece of cucumber and reserve it. Cut the rest of the cucumber into chunks. Liquidize it with the yogurt, herbs, salt and pepper.

Refrigerate the soup and serve very cold, with the reserved cucumber diced finely. Scatter some chopped walnuts over the soup if desired.

Variation Use half milk, half yogurt and include a pickled cucumber, chopped, ¾ cup diced cooked chicken, plenty of chopped fresh herbs and 2 chopped hard-boiled eggs.

Persian Cucumber Soup
Serves 4

Ingredients

1 large cucumber, finely grated	2 hard-boiled eggs, finely chopped
2½ cups yogurt	1 large clove garlic, crushed
2tbsp. tarragon vinegar	1tsp. sugar
dill	⅔ cup cream
2tbsp. raisins soaked in 2tbsp. tea for 1 hour	salt and pepper

Combine all the ingredients and stir thoroughly. Refrigerate for a minimum of 3 hours and serve very cold.

Variation You may prefer to substitute mint or tarragon for the dill, and add chopped apples, celery, fennel or radishes.

Cock-A-Leekie Soup
Serves 4

Ingredients

1 large chicken joint or 1 chicken carcass	3 cups water
1 onion, peeled	2tbsp. brown rice
bay leaf	6 prunes, soaked in water
bouquet garni	1lb. leeks, washed
salt and freshly ground pepper	1tbsp. chopped parsley

Put the chicken joint or cooked carcass with the quartered onion in a saucepan. Add the bay leaf and bouquet garni with a sprinkling of seasoning. Pour on the water and bring to a boil. Simmer for 1 hour.

Strain into a bowl, remove the chicken joint, skin it and chop the meat into small pieces. If using a carcass, remove any meat left and leave aside.

Skim any fat from the stock and return to the saucepan. Make up to 5 cups with water or more chicken stock.

Sprinkle in the brown rice, bring to a boil and simmer until the rice is almost cooked, approximately 20 minutes. Add the prunes and continue cooking for 5 minutes.

Make a cross through the center of each leek, having first removed any discolored outside leaves. Wash thoroughly under a running tap. Chop into slices about ½in. thick. Add to the soup. Cook on a simmering heat for a further 10-15 minutes. Stir in the cooked chicken and heat through.

Serve hot, garnished with parsley.

With wholewheat bread, this makes an excellent snack meal.

Cream of Corn Soup
Serves 8

Ingredients

4tbsp. butter or margarine	4 cups milk
3tbsp. onion, finely chopped	2 cans corn kernels
2tbsp. flour	1tsp. salt
	black pepper to taste

Garlic Chicken Soup
Serves 8

The simple yet pungent flavor of this traditional country soup was thought to arouse the taste buds for the courses to follow. This recipe can be traced back to the 17th century.

Ingredients

6½ cups chicken stock	½ cup onion, chopped
¼ cup white wine	1tbsp. green onion,
1lb. chicken, boned,	chopped
skinned and shredded	
1 good cup garlic cloves,	
peeled and quartered	

Combine the chicken stock, white wine and shredded chicken meat in a medium-sized saucepan. Simmer over a low heat for 15 minutes.

Add the garlic cloves, chopped onions and green onions to the soup. Simmer for 10-12 minutes longer and serve.

This soup is especially good with chunks of crusty French bread.

Garlic Soup
Serves 6-8

Variations on this rich and tasty soup are found throughout the Spanish-speaking world.

Ingredients

½ cup olive oil	7½ cups boiling water
8 cloves garlic	2tsp. salt
1tsp. paprika	1tsp. fresh ground black
pinch cayenne pepper	pepper
6 slices stale white bread,	6 eggs, beaten
cubed	

Heat the olive oil in a large heavy saucepan. Add the garlic and sauté until golden brown. Stir in the paprika and cayenne pepper. Add the bread cubes and sauté until they are firm and golden. Carefully add the boiling water to the pan, making sure the fried bread cubes are not broken. Add the salt and pepper. Cover the pan and simmer for 1 hour.

Slowly pour the beaten eggs into the pan, stirring constantly. Simmer until the eggs are firm. Serve at once.

Fruit Soup
Serves 6

This fruit soup can be made with nearly any fruit in season.

Ingredients

2 ripe peaches, halved and	1¼ cups strawberries
pitted	¼ cup ripe cherries, pitted
4 ripe plums, halved and	4tbsp. lemon juice
pitted	4 cups water
3 ripe apricots, halved and	½ cup sugar
pitted	1 cup white wine
2 apples, peeled, cored and	1½ cups sour cream
halved	

Put the fruit, lemon juice, water and sugar in a large pot. Simmer, covered, over a medium heat for 25 minutes.

Turn the heat off. Mash the fruit with a fork into a thick paste. Add the wine. Simmer over a low heat for 5 minutes.

Chill and add a dollop of sour cream to each bowl of soup just before serving.

Fish Soup
Serves 8-10

Deliciously light and savory, this Russian fish soup is traditionally made during the summer and autumn months.

Ingredients

6¼ cups water	½ cup heavy cream
1 good cup onions, finely	1 cup white wine
chopped	pinch white pepper
2tsp. fresh parsley, finely	1 clove garlic, crushed
chopped	2 large cucumbers, peeled
pinch lemon rind, finely	and sliced
grated	4 tomatoes, peeled, seeded
bay leaf	and diced
pinch black pepper	¼ cup black olives, pitted
1lb. halibut steaks, diced	and halved

In a very large soup pot, combine the water, onions, parsley, lemon rind, bay leaf and black pepper. Bring the liquid to a boil, reduce the heat and simmer for 2 minutes.

Add the fish to the pot and simmer for 5 minutes. Reduce the heat to low and simmer for a further 5 minutes.

Add the cream, white wine, white pepper, garlic, cucumbers and tomatoes. Simmer over a low heat for 5 minutes. Do not let the soup boil.

Remove the pot from the heat. Stir in the olives. Leave the pot to stand for 30 seconds. Stir again and serve.

Gazpacho
Serves 4-6

The basic soup is smooth and icy, and the guests add garnishes of their choice until the soup is very thick, and full of crunchy vegetables.

Ingredients

1½ lb. ripe tomatoes, peeled
  and seeded
2-3 cloves garlic, peeled
6 slices crustless
  wholewheat bread, diced
1 green pepper, cored,
  seeded and quartered
1 red pepper, cored, seeded
  and quartered
4 tbsp. good olive oil
4 tbsp. red wine vinegar
1 large cucumber, peeled
1 large Spanish onion,
  peeled and quartered
2½ cups tomato juice
12 ice cubes

salt and freshly ground
  pepper
few drops Tabasco

Garnishes

1 small cucumber, peeled
  and chopped
1 red pepper, cored, seeded
  and chopped
1 green pepper, cored,
  seeded and chopped
6 green onions, trimmed
  and sliced
2 tomatoes, peeled and
  chopped
garlic flavored croûtons
  (optional)

Either process or liquidize the tomatoes until smooth. With the machine still running, drop in the garlic, diced bread, peppers and gradually add the oil and vinegar. Cut the cucumber into 1-in. chunks and add with the onion to the mixture. Process until the soup is very smooth.

Tip into a bowl, stir in the tomato juice and ice cubes and season to taste with salt, pepper and Tabasco. Chill until ready to serve. If the soup seems too thick, add more ice cubes.

Spoon the soup into individual bowls. Arrange bowls of vegetables and croûtons, if used, on a tray, so everyone can help themselves.

Green Soup
Serves 4-6

This is a useful way of using up odd amounts of vegetables which tend to lurk in the refrigerator. Use any green vegetables you have in whatever quantity you like — this is only a rough guide.

Ingredients

1 tbsp. oil
1 medium onion, sliced
½ lb. zucchini, sliced
½ lb. spinach, washed and
  picked over
handful of sorrel, washed
  and picked over

½ bunch watercress
4 cups chicken stock
⅔ cup sour cream
1 egg yolk
salt and pepper

Heat the oil, add the onion and cook until it has just softened but not browned. Add the vegetables and stock. Stir and bring to a boil and then simmer, covered, for 20 minutes.

Mix the sour cream with the egg yolk. Liquidize the soup, adding the sour cream mixture slowly. Adjust the seasoning. Serve hot or cold.

Harvest Soup
Serves 4-6

Ingredients

1-2 tsp. oil
1 onion, chopped
2½ cups pumpkin, peeled
  and diced
½ lb. carrots, sliced
2 potatoes
juice of ½ lemon
5 cups stock

salt and freshly ground
  black pepper
1 zucchini, sliced
  (optional)
handful snap beans, sliced
  (optional)
basil leaves

Heat the oil in a large saucepan and fry the onion until translucent. Add pumpkins, carrots and potatoes and pour the lemon juice over. Sweat, covered, for 5 minutes.

Add stock and seasoning and simmer until potatoes are cooked. Blend or part-blend the soup. If liked, add zucchini and beans and simmer for a further 4 minutes. Check seasoning.

Serve garnished with basil leaves. This soup can also be served sprinkled with Parmesan cheese.

Harvest Soup

Kohlrabi and Chicken Soup
Serves 8

Fresh kohlrabi, a root vegetable, can be purchased at most well-stocked grocery stores.

Ingredients

3lb. chicken, cut into
  pieces
3 medium onions, halved
7½ cups chicken stock
1 leek
½tsp. salt
pinch black pepper

3 fresh kohlrabi, peeled
  and cut into small pieces
2tbsp. fresh parsley,
  coarsely chopped
3tbsp. margarine
¼ cup white wine

Put the chicken, onions, chicken stock, leek, salt and pepper in a large soup pot. Simmer, covered, over a medium heat for 50 minutes. Add the kohlrabi, parsley, margarine and wine. Simmer, covered, for an additional 35 minutes. Remove the chicken and use it in another dish. Serve the soup hot.

Curried Lentil Soup
Serves 4-6

Serve with wholemeal bread and cheese to make a filling, nutritious meal.

Ingredients

1 cup lentils
2 medium onions, finely
  chopped
2 cloves garlic, finely
  chopped
1in. root ginger, peeled
  and finely chopped
1 fresh green chili pepper,
  seeded and finely
  chopped
2tbsp. oil
½tsp. ground coriander
½tsp. ground cumin
pinch cayenne pepper, to
  taste

2 stalks celery, coarsely
  chopped
1 red pepper, cored, seeded
  and coarsely chopped
4 medium tomatoes, peeled
  and coarsely chopped
2 slices rindless, fatty
  bacon (optional),
  coarsely chopped
5 cups chicken or vegetable
  stock
salt and freshly ground
  black pepper
fresh coriander leaves,
  chopped

Pick over the lentils, wash thoroughly and leave to drain. Mash or blend the onions, garlic, ginger and chili pepper to form a thick paste.

Heat the oil in a heavy pan and quickly fry the ground coriander, cumin and cayenne pepper. After 5 seconds, add the onion paste and fry for a further 5 seconds. Add the celery, red pepper, tomatoes and bacon, if used and stir-fry for 1 minute.

Stir in the lentils, stock and salt and pepper to taste. Bring to a boil, then cover and simmer for about 40 minutes. Taste for seasoning, then stir in the fresh, chopped coriander.

Serve very hot with warm, crusty bread and cheese.

Family Lentil Soup
Serves 4

Ingredients

2tbsp. oil
1 large onion, peeled
1 carrot, scraped
2 sticks celery, washed
1¼ cups red lentils, washed
1 sprig parsley
1 bay leaf

1 bouquet garni
salt and freshly ground
  pepper
5 cups stock
1tbsp. chopped parsley
wholewheat bread croûtons

Heat the oil over a low heat in a large saucepan.

Dice the vegetables finely, add to the oil and allow to cook for 4 minutes.

Add the lentils, parsley, bay leaf, bouquet garni, seasoning and stock. Bring to a boil and simmer gently for about 35 minutes, until the lentils are cooked. If necessary, skim the surface from time to time.
time.

Taste for seasoning and adjust. Serve with chopped parsley sprinkled on top and a dish of croûtons.

Variation Cream of Lentil Soup can be made by liquidizing the soup and reheating slowly with 4tbsp. milk and 2tbsp. cream.

Lentil and Tomato Soup
Serves 4

Ingredients

¾ cup red lentils
1 large onion, peeled
1 small turnip, peeled
1 parsnip, peeled
2 stalks celery, washed
15-oz. can tomatoes
4¼ cups stock or water

bay leaf
bouquet garni
salt and freshly ground
　pepper
wholewheat croûtons
1tbsp. chopped parsley

Wash and rinse the lentils, removing any discolored or black pieces.

Chop the vegetables roughly into even-sized pieces.

Put the lentils, vegetables, tomatoes and stock or water into a large saucepan with the bay leaf and bouquet garni. Season well.

Bring the soup to a boil and remove and skim. Lower the heat to allow liquid to simmer for about 35 minutes, until vegetables and lentils are tender. Allow to cool slightly.

Liquidize the soup in a blender or food processor or rub through a strainer with a wooden spoon. If the mixture is too thick, add a little more stock, milk or water. Reheat and taste for seasoning.

Serve with wholemeal bread croûtons and a sprinkling of chopped parsley.

Curried Squash or Zucchini Soup
Serves 6

Ingredients

1tbsp. oil
1 large onion, chopped
2tbsp. curry powder
1 large zucchini, peeled
　and chopped

4¼ cups chicken stock
⅔ cup yogurt
2tbsp. mango chutney

Heat the oil, add the onion and cook until it has just softened but not browned. Stir in the curry powder and cook it for 1 minute. Add the zucchini and stir well. Add the stock.

Bring to a boil and then simmer until the zucchini is soft.

Blend the soup and return it to the pan. Keep warm while you mix the yogurt and chutney together. Stir into the soup and serve immediately.

If you prefer to make this in advance, don't add the yogurt mixture until you reheat it. You could serve a little shredded coconut with this and additional chutney if desired.

Cream of Mushroom Soup
Serves 4-6

Ingredients

4 cups mushrooms
4tbsp. butter
1 small onion, peeled and
　finely chopped
5 cups chicken stock
bouquet garni
bay leaf

2tbsp. white wine
1tbsp. wholemeal flour
salt and freshly ground
　pepper
4tbsp. heavy cream
pinch paprika

Wash the mushrooms and retain two for garnish. Chop the remainder roughly.

Heat half the butter in a large saucepan on a low heat. Add the onion and cook for 3 minutes. Add mushrooms and stir for a further 2 minutes.

Add the stock, bouquet garni, bay leaf and white wine. Bring to a boil and simmer for 15 minutes. Allow to cool slightly.

Liquidize the soup in a blender or food processor. If this is not possible, press with a wooden spoon through a strainer.

Heat the remaining butter in a cleaned saucepan, add the flour until a roux (a paste of flour and butter) is made. Cook for 1 minute, then gradually add the mushroom soup, stirring briskly. Season well. Add half the cream just before serving.

Mix the remaining cream with the paprika. Pour the soup into bowls and swirl the cream mixture on top. Decorate with the reserved mushrooms, sliced. Serve with fresh wholewheat bread.

Mushroom Soup
Serves 4

Ingredients

2tbsp. butter
1 large onion, sliced
4 cups sliced mushrooms
grated nutmeg

1tbsp. flour
$\frac{2}{3}$ cup chicken stock
$1\frac{1}{4}$ cups yogurt
2tbsp. sherry (optional)

Preparation Heat the butter and cook the onion until it has just softened but not browned. Add the mushrooms, stir and leave them to cook for 2 minutes. Add more butter if necessary.

Add nutmeg to taste, and the flour and stir well. Slowly add the stock, stirring until the mixture is smooth. Bring to a boil and then simmer for 5 minutes. Stir in the yogurt and just warm it through.

Add the sherry and serve hot.

Pork Soup with Ginger
Serves 6

The ginger greatly enhances the flavor of this soup. The fish sauce and vinegar are also evident, but do not overpower. It is quite a meal in itself, with all the meaty pieces.

Ingredients

6 cups pork or chicken
  stock
2tbsp. light soy sauce
1 clove garlic, peeled and
  crushed
1in. ginger, scraped and
  sliced
1 medium-sized onion,
  peeled and sliced
1tbsp. sugar
1tbsp. fish sauce (optional)

1tbsp. lime juice or vinegar
$\frac{1}{4}$ cup finely shredded pork
  fillet
$\frac{1}{4}$ cup diced pig's liver
  (optional)
1-2tbsp. seasoned
  cornstarch
2-3tbsp. oil
seasoning
green onions or coriander
  leaves

Green Pea Soup

Simmer the stock and soy sauce together while preparing the other ingredients.

Pound the garlic, ginger and onion together with a pestle and mortar or blender and add them to the stock. Cook for 5 minutes, then add the sugar, fish sauce, if used, and lime juice or vinegar.

Dip the pork and liver pieces in seasoned cornstarch. Fry in hot oil until the meats change color, keeping the pieces of meat as separate as possible. Pour off any excess oil and add the meats to the soup. Simmer for 20-30 minutes or until the meat is tender.

Taste for seasoning and serve garnished with chopped green onions or coriander leaves.

Green Pea Soup
Serves 4

Ingredients

2 cups dried green peas
2tbsp. butter
1 large onion, diced
4 cups stock or water
$\frac{1}{4}$tsp. sugar
salt and freshly ground
  pepper

1tsp. chervil
bay leaf
bouquet garni
$\frac{2}{3}$ cup milk
4tbsp. light cream

Soak the dried peas in cold water overnight.

Melt the butter in a large saucepan. Add the onion and cook over a low heat for 4 minutes.

Add the peas with $\frac{2}{3}$ of the stock or water, bring to a boil and simmer until cooked. (This will take about 35 minutes.) Allow to cool slightly.

Liquidize the peas in a blender or food processor or press with a wooden spoon through a strainer. Return to the saucepan, add the sugar, seasoning and herbs.

Over a low heat, add the remaining stock or water and simmer for 10 minutes. Gradually add the milk and continue cooking on a low heat for a further 5 minutes. Remove the bouquet garni and bay leaf, taste for seasoning. Stir in the cream just before serving.

Serve with slices of wholewheat bread, brown rolls or croûtons.

Variation Use frozen peas for this recipe if preferred. Reduce initial cooking time to 15 minutes.

Green Pea and Lettuce Soup
Serves 4

Ingredients

4 cups chicken stock or
  water
1 large potato, peeled and
  sliced
8oz package frozen peas
3 green onions or 1 small
  onion, peeled
1 bay leaf

1 bouquet garni
sprig parsley
salt and freshly ground
  pepper
1 lettuce, washed
2tbsp. light cream
1tbsp. green onion,
  chopped.

Put the stock or water in a large saucepan. Add the potato, bring to a boil and simmer for 15 minutes.

Add the frozen peas and simmer for a further 5 minutes.

Chop the green onions or finely chop the small onion if green onions are not available.

Add the onions, bay leaf and bouquet garni and sprig of parsley with some seasoning.

Gradually add the lettuce, torn into strips, and simmer for a further 10 minutes.

Allow to cool slightly and liquidize in a blender or food processor or rub through a strainer.

Taste for seasoning and reheat if serving hot. Garnish each bowl with a swirl of cream and a little chopped green onion.

French Onion Soup
Serves 8

Served in individual bowls topped with melted cheese, this soup is a French classic.

Ingredients

2tbsp. vegetable oil
2tbsp. butter
2lb. onions, coarsely
  chopped
2tbsp. flour
7½ cups vegetable stock
½tsp. salt

12 slices Swiss cheese
16 thin slices cut from a
  French loaf
2tsp. olive oil
2 cloves garlic, finely
  chopped

Heat the vegetable oil and butter in a large deep saucepan. Add the onions and sauté over a medium heat for 5 minutes. Reduce the heat to low and simmer for a further 20 minutes, stirring frequently.

Sprinkle the onions with the flour and continue cooking, stirring constantly, for 3 minutes.

Add the vegetable stock and salt. Simmer, covered, for 35 minutes over a low heat. While the soup simmers, coarsely chop 4 of the cheese slices. Preheat oven to 325°F.

Brush the bread slices with the olive oil and arrange them in a single layer on a baking sheet. Sprinkle the bread with the garlic and the chopped cheese. Bake for 15 minutes and set aside.

When the soup is done, place 2 bread slices in each of 8 individual deep soup bowls. Fill each bowl with soup and top with a slice of cheese. Place the bowls on the center rack of the oven and raise the heat to 350°F. Bake for 5 to 7 minutes or until the cheese begins to soften and turn brown.

Remove the bowls from the oven, allow to cool for 1 minute and serve.

Potato Soup
Serves 6

Ingredients

5tbsp. butter
1 onion, finely chopped
1lb. potatoes, cubed
1 carrot, grated
salt to taste
½tsp. white pepper

1tsp. caraway seeds
3 cups water
2tbsp. cream of wheat
3 cups milk
3tbsp. chopped parsley
½ cup sour cream

Melt the butter in a saucepan and brown the onions.

Add the potatoes, carrot, salt, pepper and caraway seeds. Stir until all the ingredients are slightly soft. Add the water and bring to a boil. Stir in the cream of wheat and cook over a low heat for 20 minutes, stirring frequently.

Add the milk and parsley, bring to boiling point, and serve with the sour cream.

Cheesy Potato Soup
Serves 4-6

Ingredients

5tbsp. butter or margarine
2 large potatoes, peeled and sliced
2 large onions, sliced
2 cloves garlic, chopped
salt and freshly ground pepper

4¼ cups beef stock
1 cup grated Cheddar cheese
thin slices toasted French bread with a little extra grated cheese

Heat the butter or margarine in a large, heavy pan and add the sliced vegetables with a little salt and pepper. Stir well, cover and simmer for about 10 minutes, or until the vegetables are softened and slightly golden in color. Add the stock and simmer gently for 15 to 20 minutes, or until the soup has thickened and the vegetables are very tender.

Strain the soup, reserving the liquid.

Press through a strainer or liquidize the vegetables until smooth, then return to the liquid with the grated cheese. Reheat, stirring constantly, until the soup is thick and creamy. Taste for seasoning.

To serve, toast bread and cover with extra grated cheese, then broil until brown and bubbling. Spoon the soup into warmed bowls, and float cheese-topped toast slices on top.

Russian Egg Drop Soup
Serves 8-10

Ingredients

8 cups chicken stock
2½ cups chicken, cooked and shredded
¼ cup white wine
2½ cups fine egg noodles
½tsp. salt

pinch dill
½ cup finely chopped celery
2 large carrots, quartered
sprig parsley
4 eggs, well beaten

Pour the chicken stock into a large saucepan. Add the chicken meat, wine, egg noodles, salt, dill, celery, carrots and parsley. Bring the soup to a boil. Reduce the heat and simmer for 18-20 minutes over a low heat.

Bring the soup back to a furious boil. Beat the eggs in with a fork. Remove the pan from the heat when the eggs become cloud-like, and serve immediately.

Scotch Broth
Serves 4-6

Ingredients

1lb. scrag end of lamb
4¼ cups water
salt and freshly ground pepper
bay leaf
2-3tbsp. pearl barley

2tbsp. dried peas, soaked
2 carrots, scraped
1 large onion
1 small turnip, peeled
3 leeks, washed
1tbsp. chopped parsley

Put the trimmed meat in a large saucepan with the water, 1tsp. salt, pepper and bay leaf. Add the pearl barley and peas. Bring to a boil and simmer for 1 hour. Remove the meat and cut into small pieces.

Cut the carrots into dice, the onions into small dice and the turnip into slices and then small dice. Cut a cross down the leeks and wash thoroughly, then slice.

Skim away any fat that has risen to the surface of the broth. Add the carrots, onions and turnips and bring back to a boil and skim. Simmer for a further 15-20 minutes. Then add the leeks and cook for a further 10 minutes with the meat.

Skim any fat from the surface with paper towels. Toss in the chopped parsley, and serve with slices of wholemeal bread.

Scotch Barley Soup
Serves 8

Ingredients

5tbsp. butter or margarine
6 carrots, grated
3 onions, coarsely chopped
2 turnips, cubed

8 cups water
1½ cups pearl barley
1tsp. salt
black pepper to taste
chopped parsley

Melt the butter or margarine in a large saucepan. Add the carrots, onions and turnips and sauté for 5 minutes. Add the water and bring to a boil.

Add the barley, salt and pepper. Cook over a low heat for 2 hours. Stir in the parsley and serve.

Scoth Broth

Sour Soup
Serves 8

This unusual soup gets its savory flavor from the veal.

Ingredients

1 tbsp. olive oil	2 beaten eggs
1 large carrot, finely chopped	2 slices bread, soaked in water and squeezed out
¼ cup chopped celery	½ tsp. salt
2 onions, diced	pinch black pepper
1½ cups water	1 cup cooked rice
½ oz. chopped parsley	½ tsp. fresh dill, chopped
4 cups sauerkraut or pickled cucumber juice	1½ lb. ground veal

Heat the olive oil in a large saucepan over a medium heat. Add the carrots, celery and onions and sauté for 8 minutes, stirring frequently. Add the water and parsley to the saucepan and bring to a boil. Cook for 1 minute. Add the sauerkraut or cucumber juice and reduce the heat slightly. Cook for 15 minutes.

In a large mixing bowl, combine the eggs, bread, salt, pepper, rice, dill and veal. Mix with a fork until the consistency is even. Form the veal mixture into balls approximately 1 in. in diameter.

Drop the meatballs into the simmering soup and reduce the heat to low. Simmer for 40 minutes and serve.

Shellfish Bisque
Serves 4

Ingredients

24 large shrimp	3 stalks parsley
2 tbsp. butter	2 tbsp. brandy
1 medium onion, peeled and diced	4 tbsp. white wine
1 carrot, peeled and diced	4¼ cups water or fish stock
sprig of thyme or pinch dried thyme	2 tbsp. butter
bay leaf	1 tbsp. flour
bouquet garni	salt and freshly ground pepper
	4 tbsp. cream

Wash the shrimp thoroughly. Remove the shells and crush them in a plastic bag with a rolling pin.

Melt the butter in a saucepan and sweat the onions and carrots over a low heat for about 5 minutes, then add 8 of the shrimp.

Add thyme, bay leaf, bouquet garni and parsley at the side of the pan.

Pour the brandy into a ladle and heat, set alight and pour over the shellfish and vegetables. Add the white wine and simmer for 2 minutes.

Pour the stock into a saucepan and add the crushed shrimp shells. Bring to a boil and simmer for 35 minutes.

Mix the butter and flour together with the fingertips into a paste and form into small balls.

Pass the soup through a fine strainer. Return the soup to the saucepan, and stirring over a low heat add the balls of flour and butter until the mixture has thickened. Taste for seasoning and add the rest of the shrimp for the last 5 minutes cooking time.

Stir in the cream just before serving.

Variation Lobster or crayfish shells may be crushed, brought to a boil and simmered with the vegetables. Continue to make soup as in method given above. If the lobster meat has already been eaten, canned lobster may be used as a garnish or the soup may be served without the meat.

Spinach Soup
Serves 6

Ingredients

1 tbsp. oil	1 clove garlic, crushed
1 large onion, sliced	4¼ cups chicken stock
1½ lb. spinach, washed and picked over	1¼ cups yogurt
	salt and pepper

Heat the oil, add the onion and cook until it has just softened but not browned. Add the spinach and garlic and stir. Add the stock, bring to a boil and then simmer, covered, for 15 minutes. Liquidize the soup, adding the yogurt slowly. Adjust the seasoning. Serve hot or cold.

Use well-thawed frozen spinach if you prefer. About 1 lb. would do.

Cold Tomato Soup
Serves 6

Cold Tomato Soup

Ingredients

2½ cups tomato juice
2½ cups yogurt
3 green onions, chopped
1 green pepper, chopped

*1 large tomato, skinned
    and chopped*
salt and pepper

Blend the juice and yogurt and pour the mixture into a large bowl. Add the onions, pepper and tomato and season to taste.

Serve well chilled, with some ice cubes floating in the soup.

Variations You can add or subtract ingredients to this according to what you have handy. Try sliced avocados; shrimp; fresh basil; chopped olives; cucumber cut into fine dice; raw sliced mushrooms; chopped fennel; fried croûtons.

Fresh Tomato and Vodka Soup
Serves 6

An unusual start for a dinner party, this soup is equally good served hot or cold. If you don't like vodka, you can omit it, but the soup won't be quite the same.

Ingredients

1 cup sliced green onions
1 medium onion, sliced
*1 small fresh green chili
    pepper, seeded and
    sliced*
1 clove garlic, sliced
2½ cups tomato juice
*salt and freshly ground
    pepper*

*2lb. ripe tomatoes, peeled,
    seeded and chopped*
a little brown sugar
⅔ cup vodka
*a few chopped chives to
    garnish*

Put the green onions, onion, chili pepper and garlic into a large pan with half the tomato juice, and a little salt and pepper. Cover and cook over low heat until the onions are very soft — about 40 minutes.

Add the tomatoes to the pan with a little brown sugar and the remaining tomato juice. Cook uncovered, over medium heat for 20 minutes. Strain the soup and reserve the liquid.

Press through a strainer or liquidize the vegetables until very smooth. Return to the liquid, and if the soup seems too thin, reduce over high heat. Taste, and adjust the seasoning.

The soup can be served hot or chilled — either way add the vodka and chives just before serving.

Fresh Tomato and Vodka Soup

Vegetable Cream Soup
Serves 6

This delicious soup has a creamy texture yet uses no milk products.

Ingredients

½ cup olive oil	½ cup leeks, finely chopped
4 cloves garlic, finely chopped	⅓ cup spinach, finely chopped
1 onion, coarsely chopped	1 cup baby peas, cooked
½ lb. green beans, trimmed and quartered	1 cup lima beans cooked
1 cup zucchini, peeled and coarsely chopped	¾ cup jellied cranberry sauce
1 cup yellow squash, peeled and coarsely chopped	1 tbsp. parsley, finely chopped
⅓ cup carrots, sliced	2 tbsp. fresh basil, coarsely chopped
⅓ cup turnips, peeled and cubed	1 tsp. salt
1 cup celery, coarsely chopped	pinch ground white pepper
2 cups potatoes, peeled and cubed	6¼ cups water

In a large saucepan, combine all the ingredients. Mash with a fork.

Cover and simmer for 40 minutes over a low heat. Mash again. Replace the lid and simmer for an additional 20 minutes over a low heat. Serve hot.

Quick Chilled Summer Soup
Serves 4-6

Perfect for a meal on the patio, this soup can also be taken in a thermos bottle for summer picnics.

Ingredients

1 large cucumber, peeled	1¼ cups good chicken or vegetable stock, chilled
2 ripe avocados, peeled	salt and pepper to taste
juice of ½ lime	3 drops Tabasco
1 tbsp. fresh coriander leaves, chopped	lime slices and a few crushed ice cubes
1¼ cups plain yogurt, chilled	

Cut the cucumber into 2-in. chunks, and quarter the avocados, discarding the pits. Either liquidize or process the cucumber and avocados with the lime juice, coriander and yogurt, until very smooth. Tip into a bowl and stir in the stock.

Season to taste with salt, pepper and a little Tabasco. If necessary, add a little more lime juice and, if the soup is too thick, add a little milk, stock or water.

Chill well. Just before serving, stir in a few crushed ice cubes. Spoon into chilled bowls, and float lime slices on the top.

Vegetable Garlic Basil Soup
Serves 8

This hearty traditional French soup can be a meal in itself. Serve with crusty bread.

Ingredients

5 tbsp. olive oil	1 tbsp. green onions, finely chopped
1 cup finely chopped onions	2 celery stalks, coarsely chopped
5 cloves garlic, finely chopped	1¼ cups fresh green beans, trimmed and quartered
5 pts. water	1¼ cups zucchini, thinly sliced
¼ cup white beans cooked	4 tbsp. dried basil
1 lb. fresh tomatoes, peeled, seeded and coarsely chopped	2 tbsp. tomato paste
1½ cups carrots, coarsely chopped	½ tsp. salt
1½ cups baby potatoes, diced	½ tsp. black pepper

Heat 2 tbsp. of the oil in a large saucepan. Add the onions and garlic and sauté over a low heat for 5 minutes.

Add the remaining ingredients, including the rest of the oil, and simmer over a medium heat for 30 minutes, stirring occasionally. Serve hot.

Consommé
Serves 4

Ingredients

1 pt. brown stock	¼ cup lean ground beef
salt and freshly ground pepper	1 small leek
2 egg whites with shells	2 tbsp. parsley, chopped
	2 tbsp. dry sherry

Make sure the brown stock is as free of fat as possible. Season well. Beat the egg whites until slightly frothy and mix with the ground beef. Mix with ½ pt. cold stock.

Bring the remaining stock to the boil with the chopped leek and parsley. Turn the heat off. Gradually add the beaten egg and beef mixture, stirring the stock to distribute the egg mixture evenly. Add the egg shells after crushing them in a plastic bag.

Bring the mixture back to simmering point, stirring while it is heating. Stop stirring when bubbles appear on the surface and allow the egg white to come to the surface. Allow pan to simmer very slowly almost off the heat for about 10 minutes.

Arrange a strainer lined with cheesecloth over another saucepan or bowl. Carefully pour the stock through.

Allow the consommé to stand for a few minutes, then add the sherry. Use as required.

Country Vegetable Soup
Serves 6

A hearty soup, full of natural goodness and flavor.

Ingredients

2lb. mixed root vegetables — carrots, celery, Jerusalem artichokes, leeks, onions, parsnips, potatoes, swedes, turnips, etc.

5tbsp. butter or margarine

2 cloves garlic, sliced

bay leaf

salt and pepper to taste

1¼ cups good chicken or vegetable stock

a little grated cheese to garnish (optional)

Wash and prepare the vegetables, trimming and peeling where necessary, and slice them.

Heat the butter or margarine in a large pan and add the vegetables, garlic, bay leaf, and a little salt and pepper. Stir well, then cover and cook slowly for 15 minutes, stirring occasionally. Add the stock, bring to a boil, then cover and simmer gently for 30 minutes or until the vegetables are tender. Remove the bay leaf.

Strain the soup, reserving the liquid. Coarsely mash or blend half the vegetables. Add to the liquid. Press through a strainer or liquidize the remaining vegetables until they form a thick purée. Add to the soup, reheat and taste for seasoning.

Spoon into individual bowls and serve sprinkled with grated cheese, if wished.

Scholar's Vegetable Soup
Serves 6-8

Ingredients

1lb. ripe tomatoes, seeded and finely chopped

4 large carrots, peeled and quartered

2 cups chopped celery

3 leeks, cut into sections

2 cups fresh green peas

¾ cup lentils

1tsp. salt

1 small head cauliflower, cut into flowerets

bay leaf

½tsp. black pepper

1tbsp. diced green pepper

7½pts. water

1 large Spanish onion, halved

2 vegetable stock cubes

Combine all the ingredients in a large soup pot. Bring to a boil, reduce the heat to medium and simmer for 3 hours, stirring occasionally.

Serve hot in large soup bowls.

Watercress Soup
Serves 4

Ingredients

2tbsp. butter

1 large onion, chopped

½lb. potatoes, peeled

5 cups stock

salt and freshly ground black pepper

3 bunches watercress

cream

Melt the butter in a large saucepan, add the onion and cook, stirring, until transparent.

Add the potatoes, stock and seasoning. Bring to a boil, then simmer until potatoes can be mashed with a fork.

Wash watercress and discard tough stalks and yellow leaves. Reserve a few sprigs for garnish, roughly chop the rest and add to the soup. Continue cooking for 2 minutes.

Allow the soup to cool slightly, then blend in a liquidizer. Allow to cool completely. Taste and adjust seasoning.

Chill and serve with reserved sprigs of watercress and a swirl of cream.

Chicken Broth
Serves 4

Ingredients

1½ tbsp. butter	2 stalks parsley
1 onion, peeled and diced	1pt. Chicken Stock
3 leeks, washed	¼ cup cooked chicken
1 bouquet garni	⅓ cup vermicelli
1 bay leaf	2tbsp. chopped parsley

Melt the butter in a saucepan and cook the onion over a low heat until transparent.

Prepare the leeks by removing the coarse outer leaves, trim off the coarse tops and then cut a cross down the center of the leek, i.e., two lengthwise cuts to the white part. This enables the mud to be washed off easily under a cold running faucet.

Add the leeks to the onion and stir well. Drop the bouquet garni, bay leaf and parsley stalks into the saucepan.

Pour the stock in and simmer for 10 minutes after bringing to a boil.

Taste for seasoning, add the cooked chicken and vermicelli. Simmer for a further 7 minutes then add the chopped parsley. Taste for seasoning before serving. Remove bouquet garni, bay leaf and parsley stalks.

Watercress and Potato Soup
Serves 6

Ingredients

3tbsp. butter or margarine	2½ cups chicken stock
1 medium onion, chopped	2 cups yogurt
1lb. potatoes, peeled and sliced	1 egg
2 bunches watercress	salt and pepper

Heat the butter, add the onion and cook until it has just softened but not browned. Add the potatoes and watercress. Stir and leave on a low heat for 3 minutes. Add the stock and simmer for 20 minutes. Mix the yogurt with the egg.

When the potatoes are soft, liquidize the soup, adding the yogurt mixture slowly. Serve hot or cold.

Chicken Stock
Makes 3½pts

Ingredients

2 onions, peeled and sliced
2 carrots, scraped and
   sliced
3 stalks celery
2 bay leaves
2 stalks parsley

1 bouquet garni
6 peppercorns, slightly
   crushed
3-lb. boiling fowl
6-8pt. water

Place all the ingredients in a large saucepan and bring to the boil. Add giblets if available, reduce heat and simmer for 1½ hours. Check that the chicken is tender, allow to cook in the stock.

Remove the chicken and strain stock for use in soup and sauces.

To make 1-1½pts. stock with remnants of a cooked bird use all the scraps and carcass of cooked chicken. Begin with only 3½pts. water.

Brown Stock
Makes 3pts

Ingredients

1-lb. shin of beef
2lb. beef and veal bones
2 onions, peeled and sliced
2 carrots, peeled and sliced

1 bouquet garni
1 bay leaf
6 peppercorns, crushed
4pt. water

Slice the meat thinly and arrange in a roasting pan with the roughly chopped bones and vegetables. Place in a hot oven (400°F) to brown. After 30 minutes, when the bones and meat are brown, drain off the fat and transfer the meat and bones into a large saucepan. Add the herbs and peppercorns, with the water, to the bones and vegetables.

Bring to a boil, remove any scum with a slotted spoon and allow to simmer for 1½-2 hours. Strain when cool and allow any fat to solidify on top. Use as required — any excess can be stored in the freezer for special dishes, such as consommé.

Brown stock can also be made in smaller quantities in the oven in a casserole when it is being used for long-term cooking. To make in a pressure cooker follow manufacturer's instructions.

Waste-Nothing Vegetable Stock

Ingredients

1-2tbsp. oil
2 large onions, chopped
1 clove garlic, chopped
2 carrots, sliced
2 stalks celery, sliced
juice ½ lemon
1 large potato, peeled and
   diced
½ cup lentils, presoaked
cabbage or cauliflower
   stalks
outer leaves of cabbage,
   lettuce etc.

any vegetables past their
   prime, such as soft
   tomatoes or mushrooms
fresh herbs, chopped
3½pts. water, including
   any leftover from
   cooking vegetables,
   tomato juice drained
   from cans, etc.
salt and freshly ground
   black pepper.
2-3tbsp. soy sauce

Heat the oil in a large saucepan and stir-fry the onion and garlic until transparent.

Add the carrots, celery and lemon juice. Turn the heat to low, cover the pan and sweat the vegetables stirring occasionally, for 5-10 minutes.

Add the remaining vegetables and herbs and pour over the water. Season well and simmer, covered, for about 40 minutes, until vegetables are mushy.

Blend the stock and add soy sauce to taste. Keep in the fridge to use within a couple of days or freeze in ice cube trays.

Court-Bouillon
To cook 6lb. fish

Used for cooking salmon, trout, crayfish and lobster.

Ingredients

4pt. water
2tsp. salt
1 cup carrots, peeled and
   sliced
1 cup onions, peeled and
   sliced
2tbsp. parsley stalks

4tbsp. white wine or white
   wine vinegar
2 bouquets garnis or 2 bay
   leaves
sprigs of thyme
6 slightly crushed
   peppercorns

Place the ingredients except the peppercorns in a fish kettle or large saucepan. Bring the liquid to a boil and skim.

Simmer for approximately 3-5 minutes then add the crushed peppercorns, continue simmering for a further 10-20 minutes. Allow to cool and strain through a fine colander or strainer.

Use as required. After cooking fish in the court-bouillon the stock can be used several times if strained each time.

To store, pour into a plastic bag set in a bowl or plastic container and freeze until cooking fish again.

The bag may be taken out when frozen and sealed. This quantity is for large fish (weighing about 6lb.) and may be halved for smaller quantities.

Fish Stock

To make a good fish stock, add the fish trimmings to the Court-Bouillon, leaving out the vinegar. The vegetables should not be simmered for longer than 30 minutes, or the stock will become bitter.

Note After fish has been cooked in the Court-Bouillon the liquid becomes a fish stock.

Making a Stock

The secret of stocks is slow gentle simmering. If the liquid is the slightest bit greasy, vigorous boiling will produce a murky, fatty-tasting stock. Skimming, especially for meat stocks, is vital too — as fat and scum rise to the surface they should be lifted off with a perforated spoon, perhaps every 10 or 15 minutes. Vegetables and bones should be evenly well browned — but not burned — to make good brown stock.

Eggs, Milk and Cheese

Asparagus and Egg Napoleon
Serves 6

This is a kind of millefeuille made with a quick rough-puff pastry, and filled with asparagus and scrambled egg. The pastry can be made several days in advance and crisped up before use.

Ingredients

	Filling
2¼ cups plain flour	24 spears cooked
good pinch salt	asparagus (fresh or
½ cup cold butter or block	canned)
margarine, diced	⅓ cup butter
½ cup cold lard or	9 eggs
vegetable fat, diced	1¼ cups light or heavy
approx. 7tbsp. icy water	cream
3tsp. lemon juice	salt and freshly ground
beaten egg to glaze	pepper

First make the pastry. Lightly cut the fats into the flour and salt until the fats become thumb-nail sized flakes. Stir in the water and lemon juice using a round-bladed knife, adding more water if needed. You should have a soft but not sticky, lumpy-looking dough. Wrap well and chill for about 30 minutes.

Sprinkle a work surface and rolling pin with flour, and carefully roll out the dough to a rectangle 15×5in. Fold the top third of the pastry down and the bottom third of the pastry up to make a three-layered square of pastry. Turn the pastry so the fold is on your left, and roll and fold the pastry as before. Wrap and chill for 15 minutes. Repeat the rolling, folding and chill procedure twice more, so the pastry has been folded a total of 6 times.

Grease 2 large cookie sheets. Roll out the pastry to a rectangle 14×9in. (or the length of your cookie sheets), and ⅛in. thick. Cut the rectangle in half to make 2 thin rectangles 14in long. Put on the cookie sheets and prick well. Brush with beaten egg, then bake in the heated oven at 400°F until golden and crispy — about 10 minutes. Cool on a wire rack, then trim off the edges, and cut each sheet into 6 strips.

When ready to eat, gently warm the pastry and asparagus tips. Melt the butter in a heavy pan. Beat the eggs till frothy with half the cream and a little salt and plenty of pepper. Tip into the pan and stir over low heat until the eggs are lightly scrambled. Remove from the heat and taste for seasoning. Stir in the rest of the cream.

Put a strip of pastry on each of 6 plates. Divide the scrambled eggs between the pastry bases, then arrange 4 spears of asparagus on top of each. Cover with the remaining pastry strips. Serve straight away.

Variation Replace the asparagus with strips of smoked salmon, cooked smoked haddock, or kipper fillets.

Baked Eggs with Green Peas and Cream
Serves 4

Ingredients

1lb. green peas, fresh	4tbsp. butter
(shelled weight)	salt and pepper
1tsp. sugar	8 eggs
sprigs of fresh mint	⅔ cup single cream

Boil the peas with the sugar and mint for 10 to 15 minutes or until just tender.

Drain, discarding the mint, and mash to a rough purée.

Stir in the butter, and season with salt and pepper to taste.

Divide the pea purée between 4 greased ramekin dishes and break 2 eggs over the top of each.

Pour the cream over the eggs and bake for 7 to 10 minutes at 400°F, until the eggs are just set. Serve immediately.

Variation "Mushy peas" are a woefully neglected vegetable, and this is a delicious and unusual way of serving them. Warm the contents of a 15 oz. can, beat in a little butter, season with plenty of salt and pepper and proceed as for the green pea purée.

Eggs with Curly Kale
Serves 2-4

Ingredients

1lb. curly kale	½ cup grated Cheddar
4 eggs	cheese
2tbsp. butter	salt and freshly ground
4tbsp. all-purpose flour	black pepper
1¼ cups milk	

Wash the kale and discard the stalks. Pack into a saucepan with a very little water, cover and cook slowly for about 20 minutes until tender. Drain and cut up roughly with a knife and fork. Put the kale in the bottom of a heatproof serving dish and keep warm. Soft-boil the eggs.

Meanwhile, make the cheese sauce. Melt the butter in a pan and stir in the flour. Cook, stirring for a few minutes. Gradually add the milk. Continue to stir until the sauce has thickened. Add the cheese. When it melts, season.

Plunge the eggs in cold water and remove the shells. Lay them on the bed of kale and cover with the sauce. Heat the dish through in the oven or under the broiler.

Bulgarian Eggs
Serves 2 or 4

Ingredients

4 eggs	salt and pepper
1¼ cups yogurt	2tbsp. butter, melted
1 small clove garlic,	½tsp. paprika
crushed	

Softly poach the eggs. Mix the yogurt with the garlic, salt and pepper and warm it through gently but don't let it boil. Spoon it into four shallow dishes. Put one egg, well drained, into each dish.

Add the paprika to the melted butter and drizzle it onto the eggs. Serve immediately, with hot French or pitta bread.

Tea Eggs
Makes 12

Ingredients

12 eggs	1tsp. five-spice powder
2tsp. salt	1tbsp. red Chinese tea
3tbsp. light soy sauce	leaves
2tbsp. dark soy sauce	

Boil the eggs in water for 5-10 minutes. Remove and gently tap the shell of each egg with a spoon until it is cracked finely all over.

Put the eggs back in the pan and cover with fresh water. Add the salt, soy sauces, five-spice powder and tea leaves (the better the quality of the tea, the better the result). Bring to the boil and simmer for 30-40 minutes. Leave the eggs to cool in the liquid.

To serve, peel off the shells — the eggs will have a beautiful marbled pattern. They can be served either on their own or as part of a mixed hors d'oeuvre, whole or cut into halves or quarters.

Curried Eggs
Serves 4

Ingredients

2tbsp. oil	½tsp. salt
1 large onion, finely sliced	big pinch sugar
½tsp. ground turmeric	8 hard-boiled eggs
½tsp. chili powder	½ cup water

Heat the oil in a skillet over medium high heat and fry the sliced onion for 3-4 minutes until lightly browned.

Add turmeric, chili, salt and sugar and, stirring constantly, fry for another 2-3 minutes. Add the eggs and mix until well covered with the spices.

Add the water, bring to the boil, lower heat, cover and cook for about 10 minutes until the gravy thickens.

Country Herb Eggs

Country Herb Eggs
Serves 2

This is the perfect dish for a light lunch. Accompany with plenty of crusty bread and a green salad.

Ingredients

3tbsp. butter	½tsp. fresh thyme
1 clove garlic, crushed	salt and pepper
½tbsp. parsley, chopped	4 fresh eggs
½tsp. fresh sage, chopped	
2-3 blades fresh rosemary, bruised	

Melt the butter over a low heat and add the garlic, herbs and seasoning. Cook gently for about 5 minutes until the garlic is transparent.

Boil the eggs for 3½-4 minutes and shell them.

Add the eggs to the herb and garlic butter and turn them for a minute. Remove the rosemary blades and serve immediately.

Piperade
Serves 3-4

Ingredients

2tbsp. butter	4 eggs
1 medium onion, thinly sliced	salt and pepper
1-2 cloves of garlic, crushed	a slice of hot buttered toast per person
1 red pepper, seeded and thinly sliced	1tbsp. parsley, chopped
2 large tomatoes, skinned, seeded and coarsely chopped	

Melt the butter in a heavy saucepan and cook the onions, garlic and pepper over a moderate heat for 15 minutes. Add the tomato and cook for a further 5 minutes.

Beat the eggs with a little salt and pepper and pour into the vegetables.

Turn down the heat and stir until the eggs are thick and creamy. Be careful not to overcook them.

Serve immediately piled on the toast and sprinkled with parsley.

Variation For a more substantial version, add 1 cup cubed cooked ham with the tomatoes.

Lox and Onion Omelet
Makes 4

Lox is the Yiddish name for smoked salmon, and this dish is perfect for a light lunch. It is traditionally served with toasted bagels.

Ingredients

8 eggs
1/2 lb. lox (smoked salmon), cubed
1 onion, finely chopped
black pepper to taste
4tsp. butter

Beat the eggs in a bowl. Stir in the salmon, onion and pepper.

Melt 1tsp. of the butter in a small skillet. Add a quarter of the egg mixture and cook over a low heat until the omelet has set. Keep warm while you make 3 more omelets in the same way.

Scrambled Eggs with Smoked Salmon
Serves 2

For the most delicious breakfast there is, serve this with chilled Champagne or Buck's fizz. The secret of perfect scrambled eggs is to remove them from the heat just before they begin to set, as they will continue cooking on the plate. Have thin triangles of wholemeal toast buttered and kept hot on warmed plates so that all that remains to be done once the eggs are cooked is to pop the cork.

Ingredients

6 medium-sized eggs beaten with 1tbsp. milk
freshly ground black pepper
2tbsp. butter
1/4lb. smoked salmon, cut into 1/2in. squares
pinch cayenne
hot buttered toast

Beat the eggs with some pepper.

Melt the butter in a large heavy-bottomed skillet over a low heat. Stir in the eggs and smoked salmon. Keep stirring, moving the spoon all over the bottom of the pan to prevent the eggs from sticking.

As soon as the eggs are thick and creamy, pile them onto the hot toast, sprinkle over a little cayenne and serve.

Avocado Soufflé Omelets
Makes 2

Ingredients

1 green pepper
3tbsp. butter
1 ripe avocado
few drops of lemon juice
4 eggs, separated
salt and freshly ground black pepper

Seed and slice the green pepper. Heat a little of the butter in a pan and fry it until soft. Set aside.

Cut the avocado in half. Remove the pit and remove the flesh from the shell in one careful movement with a palette knife. Slice the avocado and sprinkle with lemon juice.

Beat the egg yolks and season with salt and pepper. Whisk the whites and fold the two together.

Heat half the remaining butter in a pan and pour in half the omelet mixture. Arrange half the avocado and green pepper on one side of it. When lightly set, fold the omelet in two, slide out of the pan and keep hot until you have made the second omelet in the same way. Serve immediately.

Omelet with Cheese and Horseradish
Serves 2

Ingredients

4 eggs
1tbsp. water
salt and pepper to taste
a little butter

½ cup grated Cheddar
   cheese
1tsp. fresh horseradish,
   finely chopped or grated

Mix the eggs, water, salt and pepper.

Heat the skillet and add a touch of butter. When fairly hot pour in the eggs.

Sprinkle with the cheese and horseradish when the omelet is nearly cooked.

Serve immediately with a tomato salad.

Mushroom Omelet Surprise
Serves 2

Ingredients

¼lb. mushrooms
⅔ cup milk
1tbsp. butter
1tbsp. flour
1tbsp. grated Parmesan
   cheese

salt and freshly ground
   black pepper
4 eggs, separated

Peel or wipe the mushrooms and slice. Put them in a small, heavy-bottomed pan with a little of the milk and poach gently until very black and juicy. Remove the mushrooms with a slotted spoon and arrange them in the bottom of a shallow greased heatproof dish about 7in. in diameter.

Heat the butter in a pan and when it has melted, add the flour. Stir well and remove from the heat. Add the milk that the mushrooms have been cooked in and stir in enough extra milk to make a thick sauce. Stir in the

cheese and season well.

Beat the yolks into the cheese sauce. Beat the whites until they form soft peaks and fold into the sauce.

Pour the mixture over the mushrooms and cook under a preheated broiler until the omelet is nearly set and golden on top.

Spiced Omelet
Makes 1

Ingredients

2 eggs
4 cardamoms (skinned
   and ground)
1tsp. coriander seed, finely
   crushed
4tbsp. chick pea (gram)
   flour

2tbsp. yogurt
1tbsp. Ghee (Clarified
   Butter)
parsley, chopped
   (optional)

Beat the eggs well. Add the cardamom, coriander and flour and stir gently. Add the yogurt and beat thoroughly. Leave to stand for 30 minutes.

Heat the ghee in a large pan and pour in the egg mixture. Tip the pan so that the egg covers the whole of the bottom of the pan. Leave for a moment or two to set the eggs.

Slide the omelet from the pan, sprinkle with chopped parsley and serve immediately.

Grapefruit Cheese Jelly
Serves 4

This can be served as an accompaniment to cold poultry or fish. It can also be served as a dessert. Use another citrus-flavored jello if you prefer.

Ingredients

1 large grapefruit, peeled
½lb. lime jello

½ cup cream cheese

Cut the grapefruit into small chunks. Make up the jello according to the instructions, using ¼ cup less water than the package says. Pour half the jello into a bowl and leave to cool before mixing with the cream cheese until smooth. Add the grapefruit. Pour the mixture into a moistened small ring mold and refrigerate until set.

Spoon on the remaining jello (which should not set if you have left it out of the refrigerator; if it does, melt it gently and spoon over the set jello when cooled). Refrigerate until set. Unmold before serving.

Kukuye
Serves 6

Ingredients

12 eggs
1 large onion, finely
   chopped
8 zucchini, thinly sliced
1½tsp. ground turmeric

½tsp. salt
½tsp. black pepper
1tsp. sugar
¼ cup Ghee (Clarified
   Butter)

Beat the eggs in a mixing bowl. Add the onion, zucchini, turmeric, salt, pepper and sugar. Mix well.

In a large skillet, heat the clarified butter over a low heat until it is very hot. Add the egg mixture, cover, and cook for 5 to 7 minutes. If the omelet is entirely solid, remove it from the pan and serve, cut into wedges. If the omelet is still semi-solid, replace the lid and cook for a further 2 minutes.

Pancakes
Makes 8-10

Ingredients

2½ cups milk
2¼ cups flour
pinch of salt

2 eggs
butter or oil for frying

Mix the milk and flour together until smooth. Add the salt and eggs and beat in well. Leave the mixture to rest for at least 15 minutes and up to 2 hours.

Heat a little butter or oil in a heavy skillet (preferably one used only for pancakes). Tip out excess butter. Pour in just enough batter to coat the bottom of the skillet.

Fry on one side only if the pancakes are to be filled.

Stuffed Pancakes with Cheese and Herbs
Makes 9-10

Ingredients

5tbsp. plain flour
5tbsp. wholewheat flour
pinch salt
1 egg
⅔ cup milk
1tbsp. melted butter

Filling

1lb. farmer's cheese
2tsp. cream
1 fat clove garlic, crushed
2tbsp. fresh herbs, finely
   chopped
1tbsp. green onion,
   chopped

To make the pancake batter, sift the flour and salt into a bowl. Make a well in the middle of it and add the egg.

Gradually beat in the milk. When half of the milk has been added, beat in the melted butter. Continue beating in the milk until you have a thin batter. Allow the batter to stand for half an hour.

Meanwhile, prepare the filling. Combine the farmer's cheese with the rest of the ingredients and mix well.

To fry the pancakes, oil a heavy-bottomed skillet 7in. in diameter. Put it on the heat and when it is very hot, add 2tbsp. of the batter. Tilt the pan so that the batter covers the base. Cook until the pancake is beginning to brown on the underside and then turn over and cook the top. You may have to throw the first pancake away, as it will absorb the excess oil in the pan.

Continue making pancakes, keeping them warm, until all the batter is used up. Divide the filling between them, rolling the pancakes around it into a cigar shape.

Arrange the stuffed pancakes in an ovenproof dish and heat through in a moderate oven or microwave.

Cheese and Celery Pancakes
Makes 8-10

Ingredients

1 recipe Pancakes
2 cups farmer's cheese
1 egg
½tsp. paprika
salt and pepper

4 stalks canned or cooked
   celery, drained and
   sliced
melted butter

Make the pancakes as directed in the recipe.

Mix the farmer's cheese, egg, paprika, salt and pepper together well. Put a spoonful of the cheese mixture onto each pancake on the cooked side and spread it a little. Divide the celery among the pancakes. Fold each pancake into a packet or roll it, tucking in the edges.

Put the filled pancakes in a buttered oven dish and drizzle a little melted butter over the top. Warm through in the oven at 350°F for 25 minutes.

Serve with a spoonful of yogurt or sour cream on top of each pancake if liked.

Variation Substitute cooked asparagus for the celery.

Mandarin Pancakes
Makes 10-12

Ingredients

2¼ cups all-purpose flour
pinch of salt

1 scant cup boiling water
3tbsp. peanut or sesame oil

Sift the flour and salt into a bowl or food processor. Gradually add sufficient boiling water and a third of the oil to form a soft but not sticky dough. Knead for 2-3 minutes or 30 seconds in the food processor. Allow to rest for 30 minutes.

Divide the dough into 20-24 pieces. Roll out each evenly into 15-in. or 7-in. rounds. Brush the surface of half the rounds with oil and sandwich pairs together, matching the size as nearly as possible

When all the pancakes are ready, brush the surface of a heavy skillet sparingly with oil. Even better, have two skillets to speed up the process. Put the pancakes in one at a time and cook over a gentle heat until the pancake is puffy but not colored. Turn over and cook a further 2-3 minutes.

Mushroom Pancakes
Makes 8-10

Ingredients

1 recipe Pancakes	2 tbsp. canned red
butter	pimentos, finely chopped
1 large onion, finely	²/₃ cup sour cream
chopped	salt and pepper
1 lb. mushrooms, chopped	melted butter

Make the pancakes as directed.

Melt the butter, add the onion and cook until it has softened but not browned. Add the mushrooms and cook until soft. Drain off excess liquid. Mix in the pimentos, sour cream, salt and pepper.

Put a spoonful of the mixture onto each pancake on the cooked side. Roll up the pancakes, tucking in the edges. Put the rolled pancakes in a buttered oven dish and drizzle a little melted butter over the top. Warm through in the oven at 350°F for 25 minutes.

Serve with extra sour cream if desired.

Buttermilk Pancakes
Makes 8-10

These pancakes are not the paper-thin crêpe type but fairly thick and spongy. Serve them warm with extra butter and, if you like, some maple syrup.

Ingredients

2¼ cups flour	2 eggs
1 tsp. baking powder	2 cups buttermilk
1 tsp. bicarbonate of soda	4 tbsp. melted butter
1 tsp. salt	butter or oil for frying

Sift the dry ingredients into a large bowl. Beat the eggs until they are light and fluffy. Stir the buttermilk into the eggs. Fold this into the dry ingredients and mix until smooth. Add the melted butter and stir well.

Heat your pancake pan until it is very hot. Add a little fat and when it has melted, pour off any excess. Cook the pancakes (about ½ cup batter per pancake, depending on the size of the pan) until golden on each side. Keep pancakes warm in a low oven while you cook the rest of the batter.

Spinach Pancakes
Makes 8-10

Ingredients

1 recipe Pancakes	1 egg
1 lb. spinach, washed and	grated nutmeg
picked over	salt and pepper
1 cup cottage cheese	melted butter

Make the pancakes as directed.

Cook the spinach without any excess water. Drain it very well (between two plates is the most effective way). Mix the cooked spinach with the cottage cheese, egg, and nutmeg, salt and pepper to taste.

Spread a spoonful of the mixture onto each pancake on the cooked side. Roll or fold the pancakes, tucking in the edges well. Put the filled pancakes into a buttered oven dish and drizzle a little melted butter over the top. Warm through in the oven at 350°F for 25 minutes.

Serve with a spoonful of yogurt or sour cream on top of each pancake if you like.

Smoked Salmon Pancakes
Makes 4-6

Although this seems an extravagant recipe, the use of smoked salmon pieces instead of the more expensive whole slices should help you economize.

Ingredients

½ recipe Pancakes	1 egg
¾ cup chopped smoked	pepper
salmon pieces	butter
1 cup cream cheese	

Make the pancakes as directed.

Mix the chopped smoked salmon with the cream cheese, egg and pepper. Put a spoonful of the mixture onto each pancake on the cooked side. Roll up the pancakes, tucking in the edges. Fry the pancakes gently in butter to warm them through.

These are rather rich but would be even more delicious served with sour cream.

Tuna Crêpes
Serves 6-8

Ingredients

2 7-oz. cans tuna, drained	6 eggs, beaten
2-oz. can anchovies, drained	1 cup+2tbsp. flour
2tbsp. chopped parsley	1 cup. cold water
½tsp. salt	2tsp. finely chopped onion
½tsp. pepper	2tbsp. vegetable oil

In a medium-sized mixing bowl, combine the tuna, anchovies, parsley, salt and pepper. Flake the tuna with a fork and mix until evenly blended. Set the filling aside.

In another mixing bowl, combine the eggs, flour, water and onions. Mix the batter thoroughly.

Lightly grease a large heavy skillet with the vegetable oil. Place over a medium heat. Ladle 3tbsp. of the batter at a time into the pan, spreading it evenly, and cook for 3 to 5 minutes, or until the crêpe is solid but still slightly moist. Place 1tbsp. of the tuna filling on the crêpe and fold it over. Remove from pan and set aside on a large cookie sheet. Repeat the process until all the batter and filling are used up.

Preheat the oven to 450°F. Put the cookie sheet in the oven and bake for 8 minutes. Serve hot.

Herb Roulade
Serves 6

Ingredients

½ cup Cheddar cheese, grated	**Filling**
⅓ cup Parmesan cheese, grated	3tbsp. Mayonnaise
1 cup crumbled crustless brown bread	4 large lettuce leaves
⅔ cup sour cream	2tbsp. olive oil
3tbsp. full-cream milk	1tsp. wine vinegar
1tbsp. parsley	salt and freshly ground pepper
1tbsp. snipped chives	French mustard to taste
1tbsp. chervil	1tbsp. basil leaves, chopped
4 eggs, separated	4 tomatoes, peeled, quartered and seeded
salt and freshly ground pepper	

Grease a jelly roll pan 13×9in. and line with waxed paper.

Mix the Cheddar and Parmesan, breadcrumbs, cream, milk, herbs and egg yolks. Beat the egg whites until stiff and mix in quickly. Add salt and pepper to taste.

Spoon into the prepared pan and bake in a preheated oven at 400°F for 10 minutes, or until firm and golden. Remove from the oven and cover with a damp, clean dishcloth and leave to cool.

Turn out the roulade on to a sheet of non-stick wax paper and trim the edges. Spread the roulade with the mayonnaise and cover with lettuce leaves. In a liquidizer or food processor, quickly reduce the oil with the vinegar, salt, pepper, mustard and basil to a smooth dressing.

Arrange the tomatoes on the lettuce leaves. Spoon over the basil dressing, and roll up the roulade like a jelly roll. Serve immediately.

Spinach Roulade
Serves 4

Ingredients

1½lb. fresh spinach, washed and picked over	salt and pepper
1tbsp. butter	⅔ cup farmer's cheese
4 eggs, separated	⅔ cup sour cream
grated nutmeg	4 green onions, finely chopped

Cook the spinach without any extra water. Drain it very well (press it between two plates) and either chop the spinach very finely by hand or run it in a food processor just enough to chop it.

Add the butter, egg yolks, grated nutmeg and salt and pepper to taste. Mix together very well. Beat the egg whites until they are stiff. Fold a spoonful of the beaten whites into the spinach mixture to lighten it and then fold in the remaining whites. Mix through carefully. Turn the mixture into a jelly roll pan 15×10in. which has been lined with waxed paper or foil. Bake at 400°F for 10 minutes only.

While the spinach is cooking, mix the farmer's cheese with the sour cream and green onions. Season to taste. Have a clean dish towel spread on a board and when the spinach mixture is cooked, turn it upside down onto the dish towel. Carefully peel off the waxed paper or foil.

Spread the cheese and sour cream mixture over the spinach, taking care not to tear the surface. Using the dish towel to help you, roll the spinach up into a roll and onto serving plate. Serve immediately.

Although this is usually served hot, it is, in fact, very good cold.

Cheese Soufflé
Serves 4

Ingredients
4tbsp. unsalted butter	freshly ground white
½ cup plain flour	pepper, a generous
1 cup millk	amount
5 eggs, separated	cayenne pepper, according
1¼ cups grated Cheddar	to taste (¼tsp. makes it
cheese	quite hot)
salt	pinch mustard powder

Melt the butter and mix in the flour. Add the milk and stir until smooth. Remove from the heat when mixture has thickened. Add the egg yolks, one at a time. Add the cheese, salt, spices, freshly ground white pepper, cayenne pepper and mustard.

Whisk the egg whites until they stand in peaks. Stir a little egg white into the cheese mixture to loosen it, then fold in the rest.

Turn the mixture into a buttered soufflé dish and bake in a preheated oven at 400°F for 25 minutes, or until the soufflé is brown and risen.

Cheese and Spinach Soufflé
Serves 4

Ingredients
4 cups spinach, washed	6 eggs
and picked over	1 cup cottage cheese
¼ cup butter or margarine	grated nutmeg
½ cup flour	salt and pepper
2 cups milk	

Cook the spinach without any extra water. Drain it very well (between two plates).

While the spinach is cooking, melt the butter and stir in the flour off the heat. Slowly add the milk and return the pan to the heat. Separate the eggs and add the yolks, one at a tme, mixing after each one. Add the cooked and drained spinach, cottage cheese, nutmeg, salt and pepper to taste. Mix everything together well.

Beat the whites until they are stiff. Take a scoop of the whites and fold it gently into the spinach mixture to lighten it a little and then incorporate the rest of the whites into it, mixing it in lightly. Turn the soufflé mixture into it, mixing it in lightly. Turn the soufflé mixture into a greased soufflé dish measuring about 8½×3½in. Bake at 375°F for 30 minutes.

Zucchini Soufflé
Serves 6

French flair combines with a Middle Eastern influence to create this unusual and delicious soufflé.

Ingredients
4tbsp. butter	1 cup crumbled feta cheese
5tbsp. finely chopped	1lb. zucchini, finely
onion	chopped
4tbsp. flour	pinch salt
1 cup milk	pinch black pepper
1tbsp. grated Parmesan	4 egg yolks
cheese	5 egg whites

Preheat the oven to 350°F. Melt the butter in a large saucepan over a medium heat. Add the onion and sauté for 2 minutes. Add the flour and cook for an additional 2 minutes.

Add the milk and cook, stirring constantly, until the sauce begins to bubble and thicken. Add the Parmesan and feta cheeses and stir until well mixed.

Add the zucchini, salt and pepper. Reduce the heat to low and cook for 1 minute.

Stir in the yolks one at a time. When all the egg yolks are blended, remove the saucepan from the heat.

Beat the egg whites until they are stiff. Fold the egg whites into the zucchini mixture. Pour the mixture into a buttered soufflé dish and bake for 45 minutes, or until the soufflé is puffed and browned. Serve at once.

Belgian Endive Soufflé
Serves 4

Ingredients
3 heads of Belgian endive	1¼ cups milk
salt	½ cup grated cheese
1tbsp. lemon juice	4 eggs, separated
1tbsp. butter	1tbsp. dry brown
2tbsp. flour	breadcrumbs

Trim the endive and cook in salted water to which you have added the lemon juice. This will stop it discoloring.

When the endive is tender, drain and set aside. When it is cool, press the water out from between the leaves with your fingers. Chop the endive very finely.

Meanwhile, melt the butter in a heavy-bottomed pan. Stir in the flour. Remove from the heat and stir in the milk. Return to the heat and stir until the sauce has thickened. Add the cheese and cook for a further minute. Allow to cool.

When the sauce has cooled, mix in the endive, then the egg yolks.

Beat the egg whites until they form soft peaks and fold into the endive mixture. Spoon into a greased soufflé dish and sprinkle the top with breadcrumbs.

Bake in a preheated oven at 400°F for 20-25 minutes until lightly set, well risen and golden on top. Serve this soufflé with a strongly flavored salad, such as watercress garnished with slivers of orange.

Leek and Stilton Bake
Serves 4

Ingredients

1lb. small leeks
6 eggs
1 slice wholemeal bread,
  crumbled

2tbsp. cider vinegar
¼lb. Stilton cheese

Preheat the oven to 400°F.

Trim and wash the leeks. Steam for 10-15 minutes. Lay them in a greased ovenproof dish.

Beat the eggs with the vinegar and breadcrumbs and crumble in the Stilton. Pour over the leeks and bake for 30 minutes until risen and golden.

Crab and Asparagus Tart
Serves 4

Ingredients

6oz. Shortcrust Pastry
2 eggs plus 1 yolk
⅔ cup heavy cream
1tbsp. brandy
½lb. crabmeat
2tbsp. butter

4tbsp. flour
⅔ cup milk
2tbsp. grated Cheddar
  cheese
salt and cayenne pepper
8 asparagus spears, cooked

Roll out the pastry and line a 8-in. quiche or flan dish standing on a greased cookie sheet.

Beat the eggs, cream and brandy together. Flake the crabmeat with a fork and stir into the egg mixture.

Melt the butter in a heavy-bottomed pan and add the flour. Stir and cook for a few minutes. Remove from the heat and gradually stir in the milk. Return to the heat and continue stirring until the sauce thickens. Add the cheese and seasoning.

Stir the crab mixture into the cheese sauce and pour into the flan. Decorate the top with asparagus spears, pressing them into the filling. Bake in a preheated oven at 375°F for 35-40 minutes till lightly set.

Summer Posy Mousse
Serves 4

If you cannot get the herbs and edible flowers in this posy, other seasonal herbs can be substituted.

Ingredients

1tbsp. (2 envelopes)
  powdered gelatin
2tbsp. warm water
2 eggs, separated, plus 1
  egg white
⅔ cup heavy cream
¼lb. blue cheese, crumbled
3tbsp. sour cream
salt and freshly ground
  white pepper
few drops Tabasco or hot
  sauce

The posy
nasturtium flowers and
  leaves
borage flowers and leaves
summer savory
sprigs of mint, fennel and
  dill

Put the gelatin and water into a small bowl and stand it in a pan of simmering water. Stir well until the gelatin has dissolved.

Beat the egg yolks with half the heavy cream, the sour cream and the gelatin. Mash in the cheese. Whip the remaining heavy cream, fold into the mixture, season and add Tabasco to taste. Chill.

Whisk the egg whites until soft peaks form. Fold them into the mixture. Oil a ring mold, pour in the mousse and chill until set.

Dip the mold into hot water, invert a plate over it and turn the mousse out. Fill the center with a posy of edible flowers and delicate leafy herbs. Serve with brown bread.

Salmon and Chive Cocottes

Salmon and Chive Cocottes
Serves 4

Ingredients

butter
6oz. cooked salmon, boned
½ cup grated Cheddar
  cheese
3 eggs

2 egg yolks
1½ cups light cream
1tbsp. snipped chives
salt and freshly ground
  pepper

Butter 4 small individual dishes.

Skin and flake the salmon and divide among the dishes.

Mix together the cheese, eggs, egg yolks, cream and chives. Season, then pour over the salmon in the dishes. Place in a roasting pan half-filled with hot water. Bring to the boil on top of the stove, then bake in the heated oven at 375°F for 15 minutes or until firm to the touch. Either serve at once, or leave to cool.

Ham and Cheese Mousse
Serves 4

Ingredients

1 cucumber
1 cup chopped ham
1 cup cream cheese
2tsp. mustard

2 eggs
4tsp. gelatin
3tbsp. boiling water

Slice the cucumber and line a moistened small ring mold or dish with half the slices. Mix the ham into the cheese with the mustard and eggs.

Mix the gelatin with the water until it has dissolved. Add this to the ham mixture. Fold in the remaining cucumber slices and spoon the mixture into the prepared mold. Leave to set for a minimum of 6 hours, or overnight.

Unmold and serve with salad.

Crunchy Pepper and Tuna Mousse
Serves 6

Set in a Tupperware or plastic container instead of a glass bowl, this tangy, textured mousse makes a picnic treat.

Ingredients

8oz. can tuna, drained
  and flaked
2 hard-boiled eggs, coarsely
  chopped
1 red pepper, cored, seeded
  and coarsely chopped
1 green pepper, cored,
  seeded and coarsely
  chopped
1tbsp. butter or margarine
2tbsp. flour
⅔ cup milk

3tbsp. water
½tbsp. gelatin
⅔ cup Mayonnaise
⅔ cup heavy cream,
  whipped
2tbsp. lemon juice
salt and freshly ground
  pepper
tomato ketchup, to taste
  (optional)
lemon slices or pepper
  rings

Mix together the tuna, eggs and peppers until well blended.

Melt the butter in a small pan, and stir in the flour followed by the milk. Bring to a boil, stirring constantly. Simmer for two minutes. Tip on to a large plate and allow the sauce to cool completely.

Meanwhile, put the water into a small pan and sprinkle in the gelatin. Leave to soak for 5 minutes, then gently melt over low heat.

Mix the cooled sauce into the tuna mixture with the melted gelatin, mayonnaise, and whipped cream. Season to taste with lemon juice, salt and pepper and tomato ketchup, if used.

Spoon into a glass bowl, cover and chill until firm. Garnish with thin lemon slices or pepper rings, and serve with a green salad and crusty bread.

Onion Tart
Serves 4

Ingredients

6oz. Shortcrust Pastry
1tbsp. butter
1tbsp. oil
good 2 cups onions, finely
  chopped
2 eggs plus 1 yolk
2 cups light cream

1-2tbsp. grated Cheddar
  cheese
1-2tbsp. chopped parsley
salt and freshly ground
  black pepper
pinch cayenne

Heat the oven to 375°F.

Line an 8-in. quiche pan with the pastry.

Heat the butter and oil in a pan. Stir in the onions. Cover the pan, turn down the heat and sweat for about 5 minutes, stirring occasionally until the onions are soft and transparent.

Beat the eggs, cream and cheese togther and add the onions and parsley. Season with salt and pepper and cayenne to taste, pour into the pastry-lined pan and bake in the middle of the oven for 30-40 minutes until golden and set.

Variation For Onion and Blue Cheese Tart combine 1-2tbsp. crumbled blue cheese with the cream before beating it with the eggs. Omit the Cheddar, parsley and cayenne pepper.

Cheesy Onion Quiche
Serves 6-8

This is a favorite country recipe from Alsace.

Ingredients

1 cup Cheddar cheese,
  grated
1¹⁄₃ cup all-purpose flour
5tbsp. cold butter, diced
pinch each salt and
  cayenne pepper
1 egg, beaten

Filling
1¹⁄₂lb. medium-sized onions
5tbsp. butter or margarine
salt and freshly ground
  pepper
bay leaf
²⁄₃ cup white wine
1 egg
3tbsp. milk
¹⁄₄lb. Cheddar cheese, sliced

First make the pastry. Mix the grated cheese with the flour, butter and seasonings, until the mixture resembles fine breadcrumbs. Pour in the beaten egg, and mix until the mixture forms a soft but not sticky dough. Turn out onto a floured surface and roll out fairly thickly, then use to line a 8-in. quiche dish. Bake blind in a preheated oven at 375°F for 10 to 15 minutes or until the pastry is looking golden and crisp.

While the pastry is cooking, prepare the filling. Slice the onions. Heat the butter or margarine in a large skillet, then add the onions, a little salt and pepper, and the bay leaf. Fry over a high heat, stirring constantly, until the onions are golden. Add the wine, and cook over medium heat, stirring frequently until all the liquid has evaporated. Remove the bay leaf. Mix the egg with the milk.

Spoon the onion mixture into the cooked pastry case, pressing the filling down well. Arrange the cheese slices on top of the onions, then carefully pour on the egg mixture. Bake in a preheated oven for 15 minutes or until the quiche is golden brown.

Serve hot or warm.

Tomato and Sage Cheese Quiche
Serves 4

If sage cheese is not available use another hard, herb-flavored cheese. A firm goat's cheese is also a very good substitute.

Ingredients

4 large tomatoes
6oz. Shortcrust Pastry
¹⁄₄lb. sage cheese
3 eggs

²⁄₃ cup milk
salt and freshly ground
  black pepper

Pour boiling water over the tomatoes. After a minute the skins will begin to split. Refresh with cold water. Peel the tomatoes and slice them thickly.

Line an 8-in. quiche pan with the pastry and crumble the cheese into it. Arrange the tomato slices to cover the cheese.

Break the eggs into a bowl and lightly beat with the milk and seasoning. Pour egg mixture over the tomatoes, gently pressing them down with a fork.

Bake in the center of a preheated oven at 400°F for 15-20 minutes, until set and golden.

Spinach Quiche
Serves 4

Ingredients
6oz. Shortcrust Pastry
2lb. spinach
2tbsp. butter
salt and freshly ground
    black pepper
nutmeg

1¼ cups light cream
2 eggs plus 1 yolk
⅓ cup grated Parmesan
    cheese
½ cup mushrooms, sliced

Roll out the pastry and use to line a 8-in. quiche pan.

Wash the spinach and discard the tough stalks. Squeeze it into a large saucepan with the water still clinging to it and add three quarters of the butter. Cook, tightly covered, over a low heat, stirring occasionally, until soft (about 5-8 minutes).

Purée the spinach in a blender and season to taste with salt, pepper and nutmeg.

Beat the cream, eggs and cheese together and stir in the spinach. Pour spinach mixture into a prepared pie crust and arrange the mushroom slices on top. Dot with the remaining butter and bake for 30-40 minutes in a preheated oven at 375°F until set and slightly browned on top.

Kipper Mousse Quiche
Serves 6-8

Ingredients
1½ cups cornflakes,
    crushed
¾ cup all-purpose flour
pinch each salt and pepper
5tbsp. cold butter, diced
1 small egg, beaten

Filling
1lb. kipper fillets, cooked
1⅓ cups cottage cheese
    with chives
a little lemon juice
freshly ground black
    pepper
⅔ cup heavy cream,
    whipped
lemon slices

First make the pastry. Blend together the cornflakes, flour, salt and pepper and butter, until the mixture resembles breadcrumbs. Add the beaten egg, and mix to a soft but not sticky dough.

Turn out onto a well floured board and roll out fairly thickly. Use to line a 8-in. ovenproof china quiche dish. Bake blind in a preheated oven at 375°F for 10 to 15 minutes or until the pastry is crisp and golden brown. Allow to cool completely.

Meanwhile make the filling. Skin and flake the cooked, cooled kipper fillets. Liquidize or press the cottage cheese through a strainer until smooth. Add the flaked fish with the lemon juice and black pepper. Liquidize or process until very smooth and light.

Fold this mixture into the whipped cream. Taste for seasoning, adding more lemon juice and pepper if necessary. Spoon mixture into the pastry case and chill well.

Garnish the quiche with lemon slices, and serve well chilled with lemon wedges and a cucumber salad.

Pumpkin Tart
Serves 4-6

Ingredients
6oz. wholewheat or white
    self-rising flour
pinch salt
2tbsp. oil
water to mix

Filling
1lb. pumpkin flesh
4 eggs
⅔ cup heavy cream
⅔ cup milk
2 large tomatoes, peeled
    and chopped
1tbsp. chopped fresh basil
    leaves
freshly ground black
    pepper

To make the pastry sift the flour with the salt. Rub in the oil with your fingertips and add enough water to make a dough. Chill. Roll out. Line a greased 8-in. quiche pan.

Remove the rind and seeds from the pumpkin and cut into slivers. Pack into a pan with very little water and cook over a low heat, covered. Check the pan occasionally to make sure the pumpkin hasn't dried out. After about 20 minutes you should be able to mash it into a purée.

Beat the eggs with the cream and milk. Mix in the pumpkin, tomato and basil and pour into the pastry-lined pan. Bake in a preheated oven at 375°F for 45 minutes until set and golden.

Leek Quiche
Serves 4

Ingredients

pie plate 8in. lined with Shortcrust Pastry	1 large onion, chopped
2tbsp. butter	1⅓ cup cottage cheese
1lb. leeks, trimmed and chopped	3 eggs
	salt and pepper
	pinch ground allspice

Prick the pastry case with a fork, line it with uncooked rice or beans and bake it for 10 minutes at 350°F. Discard the rice or beans.

Heat the butter and soften the leeks and onion in it for 5 minutes. Mix the cottage cheese with the remaining ingredients.

Cover the bottom of the lined pie plate with the cooked leeks and onions. Spoon over the cottage cheese mixture. Bake for 35 minutes.

This is equally good hot, cold, or warm.

Blue Cheese Pâté
Makes approx. 10oz.

This mixture is useful as a filling for fruit (especially good with pears) or choux pastry, for stuffed tomatoes or celery, or as a salad dressing, in which case add more cream or creamy milk.

Ingredients

1 cup farmer's cheese
¼lb. blue cheese
2-4tbsp. cream

Liquidize the cheeses with just enough cream to reach the required consistency. Refrigerate the mixture until required. It will firm up considerably.

Cheese and Herb Pâté
Makes approx. 1¼lb.

If you don't eat all this divine pâté, created by John Tovey of the Miller Howe Hotel in the English Lake District, just by constant "tasting", you will find it amazingly versatile — as a vegetable stuffing, a spread, slipped under the skin of a chicken before roasting, with fruit, as a dressing for hot vegetables, stuffing for veal or pork, on broiled meats. Use any available fresh herbs.

Ingredients

⅔ cup melted butter	1tbsp. chopped chervil
3 cloves garlic, crushed	1tbsp. finely chopped chives
1tbsp. finely chopped parsley	1lb. cream cheese
	salt and pepper

Melt the butter slowly and leave it to cool a little. Combine all the other ingredients and gently fold in the cooled butter. Pot it and refrigerate it until needed. It keeps for several weeks if well wrapped. Use as required.

Date and Cream Cheese Spread
Makes approx. 10oz.

Fresh dates are so different from the more widely known semi-dried variety. They are not as sweet as the boxed ones and lend themselves to interesting combinations. This spread can be used on bread (try wholewheat) or as a cocktail appetizer on crackers.

Ingredients

⅓ cup cream cheese
2tbsp. milk
½lb. fresh dates, finely chopped
1tbsp. finely grated lemon rind

Mix the cheese with the milk to a smooth cream. Add the dates and lemon rind and mix together well.

Welsh Rarebit
Serves 2 or 4

Ingredients

4 slices bread	¼ cup strong ale or beer
4tbsp. butter	2tsp. hot mustard
2 cups grated Cheddar cheese	salt and pepper to taste

Toast the bread on both sides.

Melt the butter in a heavy saucepan over a low heat. Add the cheese and ale, stirring all the time. Add the mustard, salt and pepper.

Spread on the toast and broil until browned and bubbling.

Vegetable Cheese Custard
Serves 10

Ingredients

1tbsp. oil	3 eggs
1 medium onion, chopped	⅔ cup cream cheese or cottage cheese
14oz. can tomatoes	
fresh basil, chopped, to taste	1 cup yogurt
salt and pepper	1 cup grated Cheddar cheese

Heat the oil, add the onion and cook until just softened but not browned. Drain the tomatoes (reserve the juice for use in a sauce or soup) and add them to the onion together with the basil, salt and pepper. Cook for 5 minutes, breaking the tomatoes up as they cook. Turn the contents of the pan into a lightly greased ovenproof dish.

Mix the remaining ingredients, except the grated cheese, together well, in a blender or food processor. Pour the mixture over the tomatoes and scatter the grated cheese on top. Bake at 350°F for 30 minutes.

Variation The recipe can be adapted to use any vegetable or combination of vegetables you like: fresh tomatoes instead of canned, 1lb. zucchini, lightly fried with an onion and fresh marjoram and thyme added; ¾lb. button mushrooms, lightly fried with an onion and a little grated nutmeg added; a ratatouille of onions, zucchini, eggplant and tomatoes with oregano; sautéed leeks with grated nutmeg. Try ricotta, farmer's cheese, or drained yogurt instead of the cream cheese.

You may care to make a quiche with this mixture, in which case line a pie shell 9in. in diameter, which has been baked for 10 minutes, with the prepared vegetables and spread the cheese mixture over the vegetables. Top with the grated cheese and bake as above.

Light Cheese Tart
Serves 4-6

Ingredients
1tbsp. butter
1 large onion, sliced
4 eggs
1⅓ cups farmer's cheese
1⅓ cups cream cheese
2tbsp. chopped chives
salt and pepper
part-baked Shortcrust
  Pastry case approx. 8in.
  in diameter

Heat the butter, add the onion and cook until it has just softened but not browned. Beat the eggs until they are very light and fluffy. Mix the cheeses with the cooked onion, chives, salt and pepper. Carefully fold the cheese mixture into the beaten eggs and spoon this into the pastry case. Bake at 350°F for 30 minutes, or until set.

Serve cold (preferably the next day) with a crisp salad. This freezes very well.

Broccoli and Tomato Cheesecake
Serves 4-6

Ingredients
2 cups wholewheat cracker
  crumbs
4tbsp. butter, softened
Filling
½lb. broccoli flowerets
1 large tomato
2 cups farmer's cheese
salt and freshly ground
  white pepper
pinch nutmeg
2 eggs,separated
a little gelatin melted in
  warm water (optional)

Combine the crumbs and the butter and press down well into a greased 8-in. quiche pan with a loose bottom.

Steam the broccoli flowerets over boiling salted water until tender. Carefully slice some of the flowerets for decoration. Immerse the tomato in boiling water for a minute, refresh in cold water, peel and seed.

Mash the farmer's cheese with most of the broccoli and the tomato and season well with salt, pepper and a good pinch of nutmeg. Beat in the egg yolks.

Beat the whites until they form soft peaks and fold into the mixture. Pour the filling over the crumb base and bake in a preheated oven at 350°F for about 20-25 minutes until slightly risen and just set.

Allow to cool. When cold, remove from the tin and decorate the top with the remaining sliced broccoli flowerets. Brush with the melted gelatin if you like and chill before serving.

Cheese Roll
Serves 4

Ingredients
12oz. Puff Pastry
1½ cups grated Cheddar
  cheese
⅔ cup cream cheese
⅔ cup farmer's cheese
1 egg
chopped parsley or mint, to
  taste
salt and pepper
egg white to glaze

Roll the pastry out as thinly as possible. Mix the remaining ingredients, except the egg white, until smooth. Spread the mixture over the pastry. Fold over to make a flattish roll, sealing the edges well. Brush with the egg white. Transfer to a moistened cookie sheet and bake at 400°F for 20 minutes.

Serve hot, with sour cream if liked.

Whisking Eggs

Frothy Whisked, usually with a fork, just enough to mix them and prevent them pouring out of the jug or bowl separately. This makes them easier to add gradually to mixtures.

Soft Peak Whisked until the egg white will just hold its shape when the whisk is lifted, the points that are dragged up by the rising whisk flopping over softly. Used to add to fairly liquid mixtures such as cake batters or whipped cream.

Medium Peak Whisked until the egg whites will stand in peaks when the whisk is lifted, but with the tips of the peaks just flopping over like wilted leaves. For incorporating into soft mixtures such as soufflés, ice creams, sorbets and sherbets. The idea is to have the two mixtures the cook is combining as close to each other in consistency as possible. It is very difficult to add over-whisked (too stiff and too dry) egg whites to, say, a soft chocolate mousse mixture — the egg whites break up into islands and by the time you have stirred and struggled to get the mixture smooth, most of that carefully incorporated air has been knocked out.

Stiff Peak Whisked until the egg white will stand up in rigid pointed (not floppy) peaks when the whisk is lifted. Used mainly for meringue, at which point the sugar is added.

To Make a Soufflé

1 Fold not-too-stiffly whisked whites into the base. Continue until there are no large patches of egg white, then stop. Do not overmix.

2 Brush out the soufflé dish with melted butter, then — for a crusty edge — dust with breadcrumbs. Fill dish only two-thirds full.

3 A paper collar — also buttered and breadcrumbed — pinned in place will allow the soufflé to rise to the top of the dish.

4 Draw a knife through the mixture first one way then at angles to break up any air pockets.

5 Running a finger around the edge of the soufflé mixture ensures a top-hat shape when baked.

6 Carefully peel away the collar, if used, before serving.

Fish and Seafood

Fisherman's Stew
Serves 8-10

Ingredients

2lb. fresh halibut steaks	1tsp. grated orange peel
2lb. white fish (preferably mixed), cleaned	1tsp. dried thyme
2lb. haddock steaks	1tbsp. roughly chopped parsley
2lb. cod-fish steaks	bay leaf
9tbsp. olive oil	pinch of saffron threads
2 medium onions, coarsely chopped	1/2tsp. salt
6oz. thinly sliced leeks	1/2tsp. black pepper
6 cloves garlic, finely chopped	5 cups cooked rice

Rouille

7 cups water	2 green chilies, seeded and coarsely chopped
2 cups white wine	1/2tsp. hot pepper sauce
3lb. tomatoes, peeled, seeded and coarsely chopped	1/2 cup chopped pimento
	3tbsp. unflavored breadcrumbs

Trim the skin and bones from the fish steaks. Fillet the whole fish. Cut the fish steaks and fillets into 1-in. cubes. Reserve the trimmings, heads and bones.

Heat 3tbsp. of the olive oil in a large saucepan. Add the onions, leeks and a third of the chopped garlic. Cook over a low heat, stirring occasionally, for 5 minutes.

Add 6 cups of the water, the white wine and reserved fish trimmings to the pan. Cover and simmer over a low heat for 5 minutes.

Add the tomatoes, orange peel, thyme, parsley, bay leaf, saffron, salt and pepper. Raise the heat slightly and simmer, covered, for 15 minutes. Remove the cover and simmer for a further 10 minutes.

Prepare the Rouille. Combine the remaining garlic with the green chili peppers, hot pepper sauce, pimento, remaining olive oil and breadcrumbs. Mix well.

Put the mixture into a saucepan and add the remaining water. Simmer over a moderate heat for 10 minutes. Put the sauce into a serving bowl and set aside.

When the fish broth is ready, strain it through a cheesecloth into another saucepan.

Bring the strained stock to a boil over a medium heat. Add the fish pieces and cook for 10 minutes. Reduce the heat to low and cook for a further 5 minutes.

Heat the rice through and divide it among the soup bowls. Ladle the soup on top. Serve with the Rouille.

Fish in Bean Paste Sauce
Serves 2-3

Ingredients

1 1/2lb. red snapper or bream	3 green chili peppers, seeded and roughly chopped
1/2 medium onion, peeled and chopped	1/4 cup water
2 cloves garlic, crushed	seasoning to taste
2tbsp. bean paste	green onion or coriander leaves
1/2oz. fresh ginger	
oil for frying	
1tsp. sugar	

Wipe the fish, then make three slashes on each side with a sharp knife.

Pound half the onion, one garlic clove and the bean paste together until creamy. Slice and shred the ginger.

Half fry the fish in oil on both sides, then lift out. Fry the reserved onion and garlic in the fat in the skillet until just browning. Stir in the bean paste mixture and fry for 1-2 minutes to bring out the flavor. Add the sugar and green chili peppers.

Pour in the water. Bring to the boil then lower the fish into the sauce. Cover and cook for a further 5-10 minutes or until the fish is cooked through.

Garnish with chopped green onion or fresh coriander leaves.

Family Fish Pie
Serves 4

Ingredients

1lb. haddock or cod, filleted	4tbsp. butter
approx. 1 1/4 cups milk or milk and water	4tbsp. flour
	salt and freshly ground pepper
2 tomatoes, skinned and sliced	2lb. potatoes, peeled and sliced
1/4 cup mushrooms, washed and sliced	1 egg
	2 tbsp. milk

Poach the fish in the milk or milk and water. Allow to cool in the liquid. Strain the liquid into a measuring cup and add enough to make up to 1 1/4 cups if necessary for the Béchamel Sauce. Remove the skin from the fish, and flake.

Arrange the tomatoes and mushrooms on the bottom of a pie plate. Make up the Sauce using half the butter, season well, mix with the fish and pour into the pie plate.

Cook, mash or press the potatoes through a strainer, mix with a little beaten egg and milk, season well. Pipe or pile on top of the fish mixture and dot with the remaining butter.

Bake at 350°F for about 25 minutes, and serve garnished with parsley sprigs.

Paella Marrano
Serves 10

Ingredients

¼ cup olive oil	1 green pepper, seeded and
1lb. beef sausage, sliced	finely chopped
¾lb. cooked shelled	1 large tomato, peeled,
shrimps	seeded and finely
¾lb. cooked shelled mussels	chopped
2lb. chicken, cut into small	4 cloves garlic, finely
pieces	chopped
1lb. salmon steak, cut into	2½ cups rice
small pieces	pinch of saffron threads
1lb. haddock fillets, cut	1½ quarts boiling water
into small pieces	a few cooked shrimps and
1tsp. salt	mussels in their shells to
½tsp. black pepper	garnish
⅓ cup finely chopped	1 cup peas
onions	lemon wedges

In a medium-sized heavy skillet, heat 3tbsp. of the olive oil. Add the sausage slices and brown well over a low heat. Remove the sausage slices and set aside.

In the same pan, brown the chicken pieces over a moderate heat for 10 to 20 minutes, or until thoroughly cooked. Remove the pieces and set aside.

Drain the fat from the skillet. Add the rest of the oil and heat over a low heat. Add the shellfish, fish pieces, salt, pepper, onions, green pepper, tomatoes and garlic. Sauté for 15 to 20 minutes or until the fish are cooked but still firm. Set aside.

Preheat the oven to 400°F. In a large paella pan or flameproof casserole combine the sautéed fish and vegetables with the rice, saffron and boiling water. Stir well and bring to a boil over a high heat. Remove the pan from the heat.

Arrange the pieces of sausage, shrimps and mussels in their shells and the peas over the rice mixture. Bake, uncovered, for 30 minutes, or until all the liquid is absorbed.

Remove the pan from the oven and cover with a clean dish towel. Leave it to stand for 5 minutes. Serve with lemon wedges for garnish.

Gefilte Fish
Serves 8-10

Ingredients

2lb. fresh white fish fillets	1tbsp salt
(reserve the heads, skin	1½tsp. black pepper
and bones)	4 large onions, finely
2lb. fresh carp fillets	chopped
(reserve the heads, skin	4 eggs, beaten
and bones)	4tbsp. matzo meal
2lb. fresh pike or trout	2 tbsp. sugar
fillets (reserve the heads,	2 carrots, cut into fine
skin and bones)	julienne strips
2 quarts cold water	3 carrots, peeled and cut
	into 1in. rounds

Put the reserved fish heads, skin and bones into a large stock pot. Add the water, 1tsp. of the salt, and the pepper. Bring the liquid to a boil and cook, uncovered, over a high heat for 40 minutes. Strain the fish stock into another pot and discard the heads, skin and bones.

Finely chop the fish fillets. Put the chopped fish into a large bowl and add the onions, eggs, matzo meal, sugar, remaining salt, julienne carrots and another cup cold water. Mix well until the consistency is even. Shape the fish mixture into balls about 2in. in diameter.

Bring the strained fish stock to a boil over a low heat. Add the carrot slices. Drop the fish balls into the stock and cover the pot. Simmer over a low heat for 1 hour. Remove the cover and simmer for another 45 minutes. Remove the pot from the heat and let the gefilte fish cool in the liquid to room temperature.

Remove the gefilte fish and put them into a glass or ceramic serving bowl. Strain the stock again and pour it over the fish. Add the sliced carrots from the stock. Cover the bowl and chill for 2 hours before serving. Serve with horseradish sauce.

Salt-Broiled Fish
Serves 2

This method of cooking a whole fish is very simple and quite delicious. After marinating with salt, the fish is cooked over a high heat causing the oils and the salt to give a succulent, moist result.

Ingredients

2 small mackerel or red	finely grated daikon (white
snapper (or any	radish or mooli) or
medium-sized fish),	lemon slices
gutted, head and tail	4tbsp. soy sauce
left on	
salt	

Wash and dry the fish on paper towels. Thread two skewers through the body of the fish as handles for broiling. Wrap the tail and fins, if liked, in small pieces of foil to prevent them burning when cooking. Sprinkle the surfaces of the fish, inside and out, with salt and leave for 30 minutes.

Broil or barbecue for at least 5-10 minutes on each side, depending on the size of the fish. The flesh should look milky and flake easily. Do not overcook.

Serve garnished with the daikon or slices of lemon and a bowl of soy sauce so that the fish can be dipped into it before eating.

Stuffed Fish
Serves 6-8

This mixture of fish stuffed with dates may seem odd, but it is very tasty.

Ingredients

¾ cup cooked rice	black pepper to taste
4tbsp. chopped almonds	1 cup dates, pitted
4tbsp. sugar	6lb. firm, white-fleshed fish,
½ cup butter	cleaned
½tsp. ground ginger	1 onion, sliced
salt to taste	1tbsp. cinnamon

Preheat the oven to 350°F. Combine the rice, almonds, sugar, 2tbsp. of the butter, ginger, salt and pepper in a mixing bowl. Mix well. Stuff the dates with the mixture and close the openings with toothpicks. Pack the cavity of the fish with the stuffed dates.

Grease a large baking dish with the remaining butter. Put the fish in the dish and top with the onion slices. Bake until the fish flakes easily with a fork, about 25 to 30 minutes.

Remove the dates from the fish and arrange the fish on a serving platter. Arrange the dates around the fish and dust with the cinnamon.

Fish Kebabs
Serves 4

Ingredients

2 thick cod steaks	1tbsp. roughly chopped
8 medium mushrooms	parsley
8 bay leaves	1 bay leaf
8 cooked shrimps	1 small onion, thinly sliced
1 green pepper, seeded and	in rings
blanched	½tsp. paprika
1 red or yellow pepper,	1 cup long grain rice,
seeded	uncooked
2 zucchini, thickly sliced	3½ cups water
Marinade	½tsp. turmeric
4tbsp. oil	a little oil
6tbsp. lemon juice	lemon wedges
salt and freshly ground	parsley sprigs
pepper	

Cut the cod steaks into 12 even-sized pieces and thread onto the skewers one piece at a time. Alternate with mushrooms, bay leaves, shrimps, squares of peppers and slices of zucchini.

Combine the oil, lemon juice, seasoning, parsley, bay leaf, onion and paprika and pour over the fish. Leave to marinate for at least 3 hours, turning the kebabs from time to time.

Add the water with turmeric added to the rice and cook as directed on the package.

Paint the broiling rack with oil to prevent sticking and broil the skewered food for about 4 minutes each side until the cod is cooked.

Serve on a warm bed of rice with Spicy Tomato Sauce and a crisp green salad.

Smoked Fish Croquettes
Makes 16

Ingredients

1lb. finnan haddie, or	1 hard-boiled egg
smoked cod or mackerel	few drops Worcestershire
⅔ cup milk	sauce
1 small onion, finely	1tbsp. parsley, chopped
chopped, or 6 green	1 egg, beaten
onions	1½ cups dried
1½lb. potatoes, peeled and	breadcrumbs
boiled	oil for frying

Poach the smoked fish in a little milk and a knob of butter. Allow the fish to cool in the liquid then remove and flake the fish into a bowl

Chop up the green onions and add to the fish mixture. If using an onion in place of green onions sweat in butter until boiled but do not allow to brown.

Press the potatoes through a strainer or ricer to prevent lumps, and add 4tbsp. of fish liquid. Add the chopped hard-boiled egg, Worcestershire sauce, chopped parsley, and a shake of pepper. Taste before salting, as the fish may be salty. Mix the ingredients well.

With floured hands form into sausage-shaped cylinders about 2in. long. Chill in the refrigerator and then coat in egg and crumbs.

Fry in hot oil and serve with crisp vegetables or a salad.

Note It is handy to make up a double amount and store the extra in the freezer until needed.

Smoked Fish Salad
Serves 6

Ingredients

½ cup heavy cream	3 stalks celery, chopped
1¼ cups farmer's cheese	¼ cup canned sweet
1½lb. smoked mackerel or	pimentos, chopped
trout, boned and	1tbsp. lemon juice
skinned	salt and pepper

Whip the cream and fold it into the drained farmer's cheese. Add the fish, flaked, and the remaining ingredients, combining them all gently so as not to break the fish up too much. Refrigerate until required.

You can put the salad into a ring mold and turn it out onto a bed of shredded lettuce. Decorate it with the rest of the can of pimentos, cut into thin strips.

Jellied Fish
Serves 6

This cold fish dish is of Eastern European ancestry. Any firm white fish fillets may be used.

Ingredients

2lb. fish heads and trimmings
2 cups water
1 cup white wine
1 stalk celery, diced
bay leaf
2tbsp. coarsely chopped parsley

2 onions, quartered
½tsp. black pepper
2tbsp. lemon juice
pinch of salt
2tbsp. olive oil
2lb. fish fillets

Put all the ingredients except the fish fillets in a medium-sized saucepan. Bring the liquid to a boil over high heat. Reduce the heat to medium, cover, and cook for 1 hour.

Strain the fish stock through a fine strainer into another saucepan. Add the fish fillets to the fish stock, cover, and simmer over low heat for 20 minutes.

Carefully remove the fish fillets and put them into a deep dish. Pour the stock over the fish and chill until the stock jells. Serve cold.

Spiced Fish
Serves 6

Ingredients

¼ cup lemon juice
½tsp. ground ginger
½tsp. finely chopped garlic
pinch of ground cumin
½tsp. paprika

pinch of cayenne pepper
pinch of ground turmeric
½tsp. salt
1 cup white wine
3lb. flounder fillets

Preheat the oven to 375°F. In a small mixing bowl, combine all the ingredients except the flounder fillets. Mix well.

Arrange the fillets in a large baking dish and pour the sauce over them. Bake for 15 minutes. Serve hot.

Finnan Haddie Soufflé
Serves 4

Ingredients

1lb. finnan haddie (smoked haddock)
1¼ cups milk
2tbsp. butter
4tbsp. flour
salt and freshly ground pepper

pinch cayenne
pinch of grated nutmeg
4 egg yolks
2tbsp. half and half
6 egg whites

Poach the finnan haddie in the milk with a quarter of the butter for about 10 minutes over a low heat until just cooked.

Drain the liquid and make up to 1¼ cups with a little water if necessary. Skin and flake the fish.

Melt the remaining butter in a saucepan and make a roux with the flour. Season the fish liquid and add the cayenne and nutmeg. Be careful with the salt as smoked fish can be salty. Add the fish liquor to the roux and make a thick smooth sauce. Add a little of the warm sauce to the egg yolks mixed with the half and half and then return to the sauce. Lastly add the flaked fish.

Prepare a 7-in. soufflé dish by oiling well. Put the

other half of the fish in the bottom of the dish. Beat the egg whites until fluffy but not too stiff and fold carefully into the mixture. Turn into the soufflé dish and bake for about 30-35 minutes at 400°F.

Serve immediately with a crisp salad for lunch or supper, or as the fish course or appetizer for a dinner party.

Baked Striped Bass
Serves 4

Ingredients

2lb. striped bass, gutted and cleaned
4tbsp. Green Butter
½ lemon, sliced

1 small onion, peeled and quartered
fresh thyme sprigs
sprigs of parsley

Smear the fish inside and out with the Green Butter. Arrange the lemon slices, quartered onion, sprig of thyme and parsley in the stomach slit.

Make an S-shaped cut in the fish back and stuff the thyme sprigs into it. Bake for 25 minutes at 350°F.

Serve with Gribiche Sauce and extra Green Butter.

The fish may be cooked wrapped in foil, if preferred.

Red Mullet Provençal
Serves 2

Red mullet has a very delicate taste and is best prepared simply either by broiling or baking in foil. It has no gall and does not need to be gutted; indeed the liver is considered a delicacy.

Ingredients

4 red mullet
2tbsp. butter
1¼ cups Tomato Sauce
1 green or red pepper, seeded and diced
1tbsp. port or sherry

salt and freshly ground pepper
pitted black olives
lemon wedges
4 anchovy fillets

Rub the fish with melted butter and cook under a hot broiler for 2 minutes each side. Arrange in an ovenproof dish.

Mix the Tomato Sauce with the diced pepper and the port or sherry. Season the fish well and pour the sauce over it, then arrange the olives. Bake for 20 minutes at 350°F.

Serve either hot, garnished with lemon wedges and anchovy fillets, or chilled as an hors d'oeuvre.

Deviled Herring
Serves 4

Ingredients

4 herrings, filleted	1tsp. capers, chopped
4tsp. French mustard	½tsp. tarragon, dried
4tsp. breadcrumbs	1 green onion, finely
Sauce	chopped
⅔ cup vegetable oil	salt and freshly ground
3tbsp. white wine vinegar	pepper

Preheat the broiler. Make 3 slits in the backs of each of the boned herrings. Arrange on the broiler pan.

Spread the mustard over the fish and sprinkle with breadcrumbs. Brush with a little vegetable oil and broil under a high heat for 5 minutes. Lower heat to medium and continue cooking for a further 5 minutes.

Put all the sauce ingredients in a screw-top jar and shake well. Serve separately in a sauceboat, either hot or cold.

Herrings in Oatmeal with Mustard Sauce
Serves 4

Ingredients

4 herrings, filleted	¼ cup coarse oatmeal
4tbsp. milk	oil for frying
1tbsp. seasoned flour	lemon wedges
1 egg, beaten	Mustard Sauce

Fillet the herrings or ask the fish shop to do this for you. Wash thoroughly under cold running water, and flatten out.

Steep the herring in the milk for about half an hour, drain and dip in seasoned flour.

Dip the fish in beaten egg and then coat generously in coarse oatmeal.

Shallow fry in hot oil, stomach side down first, until crisp and golden on both sides.

Serve with wedges of lemon and Mustard Sauce. Baby potatoes are usually served with this dish.

Baked Salt Herring
Serves 4-6

Herring Yemen-style was originally prepared over an open fire. This recipe has been adapted for use in modern kitchens.

Ingredients

4 salt herrings, cut into	pinch of black pepper
small pieces	1 large pimento, finely
4tbsp. chopped coriander	chopped
leaves	1tbsp. chopped parsley
1tbsp. fresh or 1tsp. dried	¾ cup finely chopped
marjoram	onion
pinch of salt	

Put the herring pieces in a large glass or ceramic, not metal, baking dish. Cover the herring with the coriander, marjoram, salt, pepper, pimento, parsley and onion. Cover the dish and marinate in the refrigerator for 6 hours.

Preheat the broiler. Remove the herring pieces from the marinade and put them in an ovenproof dish. Broil them until they are lightly browned, about 15 minutes, and serve immediately.

"Solomon Gundy"
Soused Herrings
Serves 4

Ingredients

8 herrings, filleted	bay leaf
1 tsp. salt	1¼ cups vinegar
freshly ground pepper	1¼ cups water
1tsp. whole allspice	
8 peppercorns, slightly	
crushed	

Fillet the herrings or ask the fish shop to do this for you. Season the inside of the washed herrings.

Roll each fish from head to tail and secure with a wooden cocktail stick or toothpick. Arrange fish in a baking dish or casserole.

Put the remaining ingredients in a saucepan, bring to a boil and simmer for 5 minutes, then allow to cool slightly.

Pour over the fish and bake in the oven at 325°F, covered either with foil or a lid, for about 1 hour.

Allow to cool in the liquid and serve with a green salad.

Stuffed Baked Mackerel
Serves 4

Ingredients

4 mackerel	3tbsp. breadcrumbs
salt and freshly ground	1tbsp. chopped parsley
pepper	1tsp. chopped mint
2tbsp. lemon juice	salt and freshly ground
4tbsp. oil	pepper
1 medium onion, finely	2tbsp. butter
chopped	lemon wedges
½ cup white currants, fresh	
or canned and drained	

Clean the fish, remove head, slit down the stomach and remove backbone. Sprinkle with salt, pepper and a little of the lemon juice.

Heat half the oil and sauté the onion, then add the white currants and mix well.

Combine breadcrumbs, parsley, mint, lemon juice, and seasoning together, add onion and white currants and mix well.

Stuff into mackerel and secure edges together with a cocktail stick or toothpick.

Put the fish in remaining oil in a casserole, dot with butter and bake at 400°F for 15 minutes then reduce heat to 350°F for a further 15-20 minutes until fish is tender.

Serve garnished with lemon wedges.

Baked Perch
Serves 4-6

This recipe is traditionally made with mushat, a fish native to the Sea of Galilee. Perch is a good substitute.

Ingredients

8 large perch fillets
pinch of salt
pinch of black pepper
¼ cup coarsely chopped
  onion

3tbsp. coarsely chopped
  parsley
½ cup white wine
¼ cup lemon juice
¼ cup olive oil

Preheat the oven to 375°F. In a large baking pan, arrange the perch fillets skin side down. Sprinkle with the salt and pepper and top with the onion.

Combine the parsley, wine, lemon juice and olive oil in a small mixing bowl. Mix thoroughly.

Pour half the olive oil mixture over the fish and bake for 10 minutes. Baste the fish with the remaining olive oil mixture and bake for 10 minutes longer. Serve immediately.

Pike Quenelles
Serves 4

Quenelles are traditionally made with pike but other fish can be used. It is a rather difficult dish to make by hand and is easier if a food processor is used.

Ingredients

4 eggs
1 cup+2tbsp. sifted flour
1¼ cups milk
4tbsp. butter
1½lb. pike or grey mullet
4tbsp. suet
salt and freshly ground
  pepper

3tbsp. heavy cream, lightly
  beaten
1 cup Béchamel Sauce
1tbsp. tomato paste
½ cup cooked, peeled
  shrimps

Remove the skin and bones from the fish, put the flesh in the food processor and pulverize.

Make a thick mixture by stirring 2 of the eggs, sifted flour and milk together. Beat briskly over a low heat, add butter and stir until a thick mixture is made, almost like a choux pastry. Allow to cool.

Add the suet, then the flour mixture. Season, then add the yolks of the remaining 2 eggs and mix well in the processor. Add the lightly beaten cream.

Wet a board and form the mixture into small sausage-sized portions. If the mixture is not holding together add a beaten egg white.

Bring a saucepan of salted water to a boil and reduce to simmering. Drop a quenelle into the water. Cook for a few minutes (never boil) and test for flavor. Correct if necessary, then simmer the rest.

For the sauce, add the tomato paste and shrimps to the Béchamel and serve hot with the warm quenelles.

Baked Red Snapper
Serves 8

Any large fish can be cooked in this way.

Ingredients

1 large red snapper
¼ cup red wine vinegar
½ cup olive oil
1 cup white wine
2½ cups water

2tsp. sugar
1tsp. salt
2 cloves garlic, finely
  chopped

Clean and fillet the fish. Reserve the head and bones. In a saucepan, combine the reserved fish trimmings with the vinegar, olive oil, wine, water, sugar, salt and garlic. Cover and simmer over a low heat for 30 minutes. Strain the fish stock mixture through a fine strainer or cheesecloth.

Preheat the oven to 425°F. Put the red snapper fillets in a large baking pan. Pour the fish stock mixture over the fillets. Bake for 30 minutes. Keep warm. Pour off the cooking liquid and serve in a gravy boat on the side.

Red Snapper à la Creole
Serves 4

Ingredients

2-3lb. red snapper or red
  mullet
salt and freshly ground
  pepper
juice of 1 lemon
few sprigs of thyme
1 bay leaf
sprig parsley
4 allspice berries, crushed
4 cloves
Stuffing
½ onion
2tbsp. butter
mushroom stalks from ½
  cup mushrooms,
  chopped

2tbsp. fresh breadcrumbs
4tbsp. chopped parsley
salt and freshly ground
  pepper
Sauce
1¼ cups white wine
2tbsp. butter
1 large onion, peeled and
  finely chopped
2 large tomatoes, peeled
½ cup mushrooms, sliced
15oz. can tomatoes

Clean and wash the snapper thoroughly. Sprinkle inside and out with seasoning and lemon juice. Make an S-shaped cut in the back and stuff with thyme, bay leaf, parsley, allspice and cloves.

Make the stuffing by sweating the onion in the butter until it is transparent, about 4 minutes on a low heat. Add chopped mushroom stalks and continue cooking for a further 2 minutes. Add the breadcrumbs and 1tbsp. of the parsley and seasoning. Put the stuffing into the fish stomach.

Lay the fish in a flat dish and pour the wine over it. Bake for about 20 minutes at 350°F, covered with a lid or piece of foil.

Meanwhile melt the butter in a frying pan, add the chopped onion and cook until it is transparent. Add the chopped fresh tomatoes and sliced mushrooms and cook for a few minutes on a low heat. Then add the canned tomatoes, season and simmer for about 10 minutes.

After the fish has cooked for 20 mintues pour the sauce over. Continue cooking for a further 10-15 minutes.

Serve sprinkled with extra parsley.

Variation For a truly traditional touch add oysters and shrimps with the tomatoes.

Baked Stuffed Salmon
Serves 6

This recipe was originally for pike, which may be hard to obtain. It works well with any large freshwater fish.

Ingredients

1 medium onion, finely chopped	2tbsp. finely chopped parsley
5tbsp. butter	¼ cup grated Parmesan cheese
3 cloves garlic, diced	
5tbsp. finely chopped mushrooms	4lb. salmon, cleaned and scaled, without backbone, but with the head and tail left intact
1 cup seasoned fresh breadcrumbs	
½ cup milk	½ cup sour cream, chilled
6 anchovies, ground to a paste	1tsp. salt
	1tsp. black pepper
1tbsp. capers	3tbsp. lemon juice

Prepare the stuffing first. In a medium-sized skillet, brown the onions and garlic in the butter. Cook for 2 or 3 minutes. Stir in the mushrooms and cook for a further 5 minutes.

In a large mixing bowl, combine the breadcrumbs, milk, anchovies, capers, parsley and Parmesan cheese. Mix thoroughly. Set the stuffing aside.

Preheat the oven to 425°F. Rinse the fish inside and out, and pat completely dry. Fill the cavity of the fish with the stuffing. Pour the butter, mushrooms and onions over the fish. Bake the fish for 45 to 50 minutes,

basting with the pan juices every 5 to 7 minutes.

While the fish is cooking, combine the sour cream, salt, pepper and lemon juice in a small bowl. Chill.

Remove the fish from the oven. Remove the stuffing from the cavity of the fish and put it in a large mixing bowl. Add half the fish drippings and half the onions and mushrooms from the baking pan. Mix well. Put the stuffing back into the fish. Reduce the oven temperature to 250°F. Return the fish to the oven for 5 minutes.

Pour the remaining fish drippings, along with the remaining mushrooms and onions from the baking pan, into a small saucepan. Add the sour cream, mix and cook over a low heat, stirring frequently until heated through. Do not allow the sauce to boil.

Arrange the fish on a serving plate. Pour some of the sauce over the fish. Serve the remainder of the fish sauce separately.

Poached Salmon
Serves 8-10

This method can also used for striped bass or large trout.

Ingredients

7-8lb. salmon	bay leaf
½ lemon	1 sprig parsley
½ onion, halved	cold Court Bouillon

Prepare the salmon by slitting the stomach and removing the insides from head to tail. Wash the cavity under cold running water. (The fish can also be gutted by removing the head and drawing the entrails out with the curved handle of a soup ladle. This means the stomach remains whole and is better to dress for a buffet table. However, many fish are bought already gutted.)

Put the lemon, onion, bay leaf and parsley sprig in the cavity.

Half fill a fish kettle with the Court Bouillon and lower the fish into the liquid, bring to a boil gently and then simmer over a low heat for about 45 minutes. Remove from the heat and allow to cook for some hours in the fish liquid.

Do not cook over a high heat or the fish will split.

Remove the fish from the liquid and allow it to drain for about 1 hour if using cold, as a Dressed Salmon. Alternatively serve the salmon hot with Hollandaise or Mousseline Sauce.

Alternative Method As fish kettles are fairly large, the smallest being around 18in. long, many people do not want the expense of buying one or the storage problem for an occasional large fish. It is possible to cook a fairly large fish in a modern oven if you have a large roasting pan. Pour the Court Bouillon to about a quarter of the way up the pan and place the fish diagonally across. The head may be cut off and the tail wrapped in foil to make the fish fit. Cook the head beside the fish. Pour over as much liquid as the pan will take and cover with a double sheet of foil or another large roasting pan.

Allow 10 minutes for each 1lb. using this method at 325°F. Cool as instructed above.

Dressed Salmon
Serves 8-10

The salmon will look very elegant if you use an extra cucumber, sliced wafer thin, and arrange the slices to cover all the fish flesh, overlapping like scales.

Ingredients

1 poached salmon with head and tail
1¼ cups aspic jelly
1 cucumber, peeled

12 stuffed olives
2 lemons
watercress

Remove the top skin of the salmon and any grey bits on the pink flesh with the back of a knife. Arrange on a serving platter.

Make the aspic jelly as directed on the package with boiling water and allow to cool.

Paint the salmon with the aspic and allow to set slightly. After about 30 minutes pour a little more aspic all over the fish. Allow to set.

Slice the cucumber very thinly and cut each slice in half. Cut the olives into thin slices. The lemon can be scored with a sharp knife before halving, then slicing it thinly.

Arrange the cucumber slices in a wavy pattern along one edge of the fish. Use the olives to mark the backbone. Paint each slice with aspic before arranging.

Use the halved lemon slices for the other side of the fish, then pour over another coating of almost-setting aspic. Any excess aspic may be chopped and arranged round the fish when it has set.

Serve the salmon with Mayonnaise or Green Sauce.

Salmon en Croûte
Serves 4

Ingredients

3lb. tail end of salmon
1¼ cups Court Bouillon
1 medium onion, peeled and finely chopped
6 green onions, washed and chopped
½ cup mushrooms, washed and finely chopped
2tbsp. butter

2tbsp. tomato paste
1tbsp. fresh parsley, chopped
salt and freshly ground pepper
1lb. Puff Pastry, thawed if frozen
beaten egg to glaze

Poach the salmon in the Court Bouillon for about 15-20 minutes. Allow to cool in the liquid.

Remove the fish and then reduce the liquid by boiling to about one-third. Skin each side and carefully remove the two top fillets of fish, then lift out the bones and two further fillets will appear underneath. The vegetables for the stuffing may be chopped in the blender or food processor.

Melt the butter in a skillet and cook the onions and green onions over a low heat for about 5 minutes. Add the finely chopped mushrooms and continue cooking for a further 3 minutes. Add the tomato paste and 2tbsp. of the reduced fish liquid. Season well and add the parsley. Allow to cool.

Divide the pastry in two, with one piece bigger than the other, and roll out the smaller piece. Cut it into a simple fish shape, with a slightly pointed nose coming out to a flat head, a rounded body and a fan tail. Make a paper pattern about 12in. long as a guideline, if necessary.

Arrange two pieces of fish on the pastry with the broad ends meeting in the middle and the narrower parts at either end. Cover with the stuffing and then put the other two pieces of fish neatly on top.

Dressed Salmon

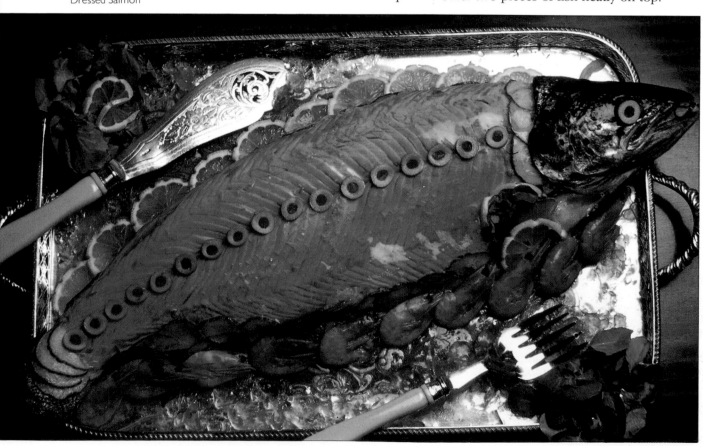

Roll out the larger half of the pastry about 2in. bigger than the previous one. Dampen the edges with cold water and lay over the fish, tucking the extra pastry underneath and molding it to secure and improve the fish shape.

Cut the remaining strips of pastry into crescents for decoration and thin strips to decorate the tail with fins. Make several slits down the back to allow the steam to escape.

Arrange the decorations, paint with beaten egg and bake at 425°F for 20 minutes. If the pastry is browning too quickly, turn down the heat after 15 minutes.

Serve hot or warm with Hollandaise Sauce.

Salmon Fish Cakes
Makes 12

Ingredients

2lb. peeled and sliced potatoes	1tbsp. finely chopped parsley
1 cup cooked salmon, flaked and boned	1 egg
1/2 cup coley or haddock, cooked, flaked and boned	lemon wedges
	fat for deep frying
1tbsp. tomato ketchup	**Coating**
1tsp. Worcestershire sauce	1 egg
salt and freshly ground pepper	2tbsp. water
	1 cup dried breadcrumbs

Boil the potatoes until soft, drain and mash through a ricer or press through a strainer. It is important that the potato is free from lumps.

Mix the flaked fish into the potatoes, gradually add seasonings and parsley, and bind with beaten egg.

Flour a board and, using a 2-in. biscuit or cookie cutter, shape the cakes. Put them onto a tray or cookie sheet and chill in the freezer or top of the fridge for at least 30 minutes.

Flour your hands and dip each cake into the beaten egg mixed with the water, and then coat with the breadcrumbs. Press the crumbs well into the cakes. Chill for a further 30 minutes.

Fry in deep fat for about 4-5 minutes until crisp. Serve with wedges of lemon.

The fried cakes can be refrigerated or frozen and reheated as required.

Rich Salmon Fish Cakes
Serves 8

Ingredients

3lb. canned salmon, drained	1/2 cup butter or margarine, softened
1tsp. salt	4tbsp. flour
black pepper to taste	1/2 cup heavy cream
3/4 cup chopped onion	3/4 cup vegetable oil

Chop the salmon very finely in a mixing bowl. Add salt and pepper. Add the onions, butter, flour and cream and mix until smooth. Shape the mixture into cakes.

Heat the vegetable oil in a large heavy skillet. Cook the salmon cakes in batches until golden brown on both sides.

Salmon with Lime and Walnut Oil
Serves 4

Ingredients

4 salmon steaks	7tbsp. chilled, sweet butter
salt to taste	2tbsp. lime juice
black pepper to taste	3tbsp. walnut oil
rind of 1 lime	

Season the salmon steaks with salt and pepper. Preheat the oven to 250°F.

Cut the lime rind into julienne strips. Blanch strips in boling water for 1 minute. Drain well.

Heat 2 tbsp. of butter in a large skillet. Add the salmon and sauté over a medium-high heat until lightly browned, about 4 minutes per side. Transfer the salmon to a plate, cover, and keep warm in oven.

Add the lime juice, lime rind and walnut oil to pan. Stir well and cook over a low heat until the mixture is just heated through. Beat in the remaining butter 1 tbsp. at a time. Be careful not to let the sauce get too hot. Remove the pan from the heat and let it cool slightly if necessary. The saucc should be slightly thick, the same consistency as hollandaise sauce. Season with salt and pepper and remove from heat.

Remove the salmon from oven. Spoon sauce over steaks and serve.

Salmon Cutlets with Anchovy Butter
Serves 4

Ingredients

4 anchovies	a little oil
1½tbsp. milk	4 salmon cutlets
4tbsp. butter	parsley sprigs
pepper and hot pepper sauce to taste	4 lemon wedges

First make the anchovy butter. Soak the anchovies in the milk for ½ hour, then mash with a wooden spoon until creamy. Cream in the butter and season. Chill until needed.

Preheat the broiler to high. Oil the broiling rack.

Put a small knob of anchovy butter (divide a quarter of the mixture in four) on each cutlet and arrange so each gets an even heat. Broil for 4 minutes.

Turn the cutlets with a spatula and place another quarter of the butter among the steaks. Broil on the second side for 4 minutes. Reduce the heat and allow to cook for a further 3 minutes, less if the cutlets are thin.

Serve with a quarter of the remaining anchovy butter in a neat pat on top of each cutlet. Garnish with parsley sprigs and lemon wedges.

Salmon Loaf
Serves 8

Ingredients

5½ cups flour	1tsp. black pepper
1 cup unsalted butter, softened	1½ cup white wine
½ cup vegetable shortening	1lb. mushrooms, quartered
2tsp. salt	2 egg yolks
1 cup iced water	1 cup chicken broth
2lb. fresh salmon, skinned and boned	4tbsp. lemon juice
1½lb. cabbage, shredded	4tbsp. chopped fresh dill
1 cup roughly chopped onion	4 hard-boiled eggs, chopped
	2tbsp. sugar

In a large mixing bowl, combine the flour, a quarter of the butter, the vegetable shortening and half the salt. Mix together with a wooden spoon until the dough has a flaky texture. Add the iced water and mix until smooth. Divide the dough into 2 equal portions. Wrap each half in plastic wrap and refrigerate for 3½ hours.

Put the salmon, remaining butter, cabbage, onion, pepper, wine, mushrooms, remaining salt, egg yolks,

chicken broth, lemon juice, dill and sugar into a large saucepan. Simmer for 1 hour, or until most of the liquid has evaporated.

Flake the salmon with a fork. Stir gently and add the chopped hard-boiled eggs. Stir gently again. Set the mixture aside.

Roll out half the chilled dough on a lightly floured surface into a rectangle about 1in. thick. Dust with flour, and then roll the dough out into a sheet ⅛in. thick. Trim the sheet into a rectangle 8×16in. Repeat with the remaining dough, but trim the sheet to 10×16in.

Put the smaller dough rectangle on a large, greased cookie sheet. Arrange the salmon filling evenly on the dough, leaving a 1-in. border around the edges. Put the larger dough sheet over the filling. Press the edges of the top and bottom dough sheets together with a fork. Chill for 15 minutes.

Preheat the oven to 400°F. Bake the loaf for 1 hour. Serve immediately.

Salmon and Spinach Pie
Serves 4

Ingredients

1lb. frozen chopped spinach	1tbsp. chopped parsley
¾lb. salmon, poached	salt and freshly ground black pepper
1pt. Béchamel Sauce	½lb. Puff Pastry, thawed if frozen
2 hard-boiled eggs, chopped	½ beaten egg to glaze
1tsp. dill	

Cook the frozen spinach in a little salted water as directed on the package. (If using fresh spinach you will need to cook approximately 2lb.) Drain well and line the bottom of a buttered pie plate with it.

Mix the boiled, boned and skinned salmon with the Béchamel Sauce (which can be made with the liquid in which the fish was poached) and hard-boiled eggs. Mix in the dill and parsley and pour the mixture on top of the spinach.

Roll out the Puff Pastry 2in. larger than the pie plate. Cut a 1-in. wide strip from the outer edge of the pastry. Brush the rim of the plate with water and fit the pastry strip round it. Lift the remaining piece of pastry over the rolling pin and transfer to the pie plate. Press the edges together, and trim with a sharp knife held at an angle away from the dish. To seal the edges firmly together hold the knife horizontally towards the pie plate and make a series of shallow cuts around the edge. Flute the edges with your thumb and forefinger and pull in the flutes with the back of a knife.

To make decorative leaves, cut remaining pastry into 1½-in. strips using the rolling pin or ruler as a guide. Every 2½in. cut the strips at an angle to make diamond shapes. Score lines on the diamonds to make the veins of the leaves.

Make a hole in the middle of the pie by making a cross with a knife and fold back each quarter. Arrange the leaves in a decorative pattern around the middle and brush with beaten egg.

Bake in a preheated oven at 425°F until pastry is well risen and golden brown — approximately 30 minutes. Cover with foil or waxed paper if pastry shows any sign of browning too much.

Salmon Mousse
Serves 4

Ingredients

½lb. salmon, cooked and flaked (or use canned salmon)
1tbsp. grated Parmesan cheese
salt and freshly ground white pepper
lemon juice

1¼ cups aspic or equivalent and heavy cream, mixed in a proportion of 3 to 1
2 egg whites
thin slices of unpeeled cucumber

Mix the salmon with the cheese in a blender and season with salt, pepper and lemon juice to taste.

Reserving a little of the aspic mixture to glaze the mousse, stir the rest into the fish. When the mixture is cold, beat the egg whites until they form soft peaks and fold into the fish. Turn into a greased mold or soufflé dish and chill until set.

Unmold if liked, decorate with cucumber slices and glaze with remaining aspic. Chill again before serving.

Coulibiac
Serves 4

This is an elegant Russian fish pie which has become a classic of French cuisine.

Ingredients

1lb. salmon
4tbsp. butter
salt and freshly ground pepper
8 green onions, washed and chopped or 1 onion, finely chopped
1 cup boiled rice
½ cup mushrooms, washed and sliced

2 hard-boiled eggs
grated rind and juice of ½ lemon
1tbsp. fresh dill or 1tsp. dried
1tbsp. chopped parsley
2tbsp. sour cream
1lb. Puff Pastry, thawed if frozen
1 egg, beaten

Cut half the butter into small pieces and dab over salmon, season and wrap loosely in foil. Bake in a preheated oven at 300°F for 25-30 minutes. Unwrap and allow to cool.

Melt the remaining butter and add the green onions or very finely chopped onion. Gradually stir in the boiled rice and mushrooms. Allow to cool.

Remove the skin and bones carefully from salmon and leave in large flakes. Mix with the boiled rice and mushrooms, chopped hard-boiled egg, lemon rind and juice, dill, parsley and seasoning. Lastly add the sour cream.

Roll out the pastry to 14×14in., then divide into four 7-in squares. Put a quarter of the salmon in the middle of each square and turn dampened corners over and crimp the edges. Brush with beaten egg and bake in a hot oven 350°F for about 20 minutes.

Serve garnished with watercress and baked mushrooms, and accompanied by Hollandaise Sauce or a bowl of sour cream mixed with fresh chives.

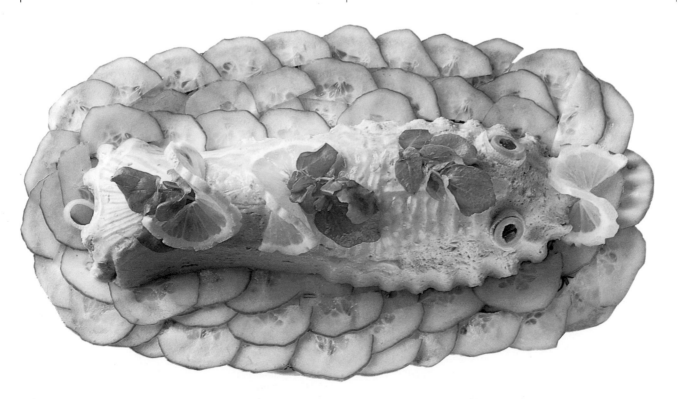

Salmon Mousse

Skate in Caper Sauce
Serves 4

Ingredients

4 wings of skate	salt and freshly ground
1¼ cups water	pepper
1tbsp. vinegar	1tbsp. butter
1 small onion, peeled and	2tbsp. flour
sliced	5tbsp. capers, chopped
bay leaf	2tbsp. fresh parsley

Put the skate wings in a baking dish and pour over the water, vinegar, sliced onon and bay leaf. Season with salt and pepper. Bake, covered at 350°F for about 15 to 20 minutes.

In a saucepan make a roux with the butter and flour and make into a sauce with 1¼ cups of the fish liquor, strained from the skate. Add the chopped capers and parsley.

Pour the sauce over the fish and serve with sautéed potatoes and a crisp green vegetable.

Variation If skate is unavailable use halibut or turbot.

Sardines Provençal
Serves 4

Ingredients

2lb. fresh or frozen	2 eggs, beaten
sardines	2lb. spinach
salt and freshly ground	2tsp. vegetable oil
pepper	2tbsp. half and half
4tbsp. fresh breadcrumbs	2tbsp. grated Parmesan
1tsp. anchovy essence	cheese
1tsp. mixed fresh herbs or	2tsp. vegetable oil
½tsp. dried	
1tsp. freshly chopped	
parsley	

Allow sardines to thaw if frozen. Slit down the stomach and remove the backbone. Season each and leave open.

Mix half the breadcrumbs, seasoning, anchovy essence and herbs in a bowl and add a little of the beaten egg.

Put some of this mixture in each fish and fold over.

Blanch the spinach in boiling water for 2 minutes if using fresh, and for 4 if using frozen. Drain carefully.

Season well with salt and pepper. Mix with half and half and remaining egg. Arrange spinach in the bottom of an ovenproof dish with the sardines on top. Sprinkle the fish with a mixture of the remaining breadcrumbs and the Parmesan cheese. Brush with oil and bake at 350°F until the fish are golden brown.

Poached Sole
Serves 6-8

Ingredients

⅔ cup dry vermouth	3¾ cups water
2 large onions, sliced	½tsp. dried thyme
4 parsley sprigs	4lb. sole fillets
bay leaf	6 tomatoes
2tbsp. fresh basil or ½tsp.	4 egg yolks, beaten
dried	1 cup heavy cream
1tbsp. black pepper	lemon slices
⅔ cup chopped celery	

To make the poaching liquid, combine the vermouth, onions, parsley, bay leaf, basil, black pepper, celery, water, thyme and salt in a large pot. Simmer over a low heat for 30 minutes.

Arrange the fillets on a large square of cheesecloth. Top with the tomatoes and wrap with the cheesecloth.

Strain the stock into a fish poacher or large saucepan. Add the wrapped fish and tomatoes. Cover and simmer gently over a low heat for 10 minutes.

Remove the fish and tomatoes from the poacher. Remove the cheesecloth and arrange the fillets on a warm serving platter. Keep warm while you make the sauce.

Beat the egg yolks and cream into the remaining stock in the poacher. Cook over a medium heat, stirring constantly, for 5 minutes, or until the sauce thickens. Do not let it boil.

Pour the sauce over the fish and serve with lemon slices.

Goujons of Sole
Serves 4

Ingredients

4 soles, filleted and	dry breadcrumbs
skinned	oil for frying
flour or matzo meal to coat	
1 egg, beaten with 1tbsp.	
water	

Cut each fish fillet into two pieces and then cut each half in strips diagonally.

Flour the strips and shake off excess. Dip in egg mixture then roll in breadcrumbs. Deep fry until golden brown.

Serve with lemon wedges.

Fillets of Sole in White Wine with Mushrooms
Serves 4

Ingredients

4 large sole, filleted	sprig of parsley
²/₃ cup white wine	4 peppercorns
²/₃ cup water	1tbsp. butter
1 small onion, peeled and sliced	2tbsp. flour
6 small mushrooms	2tbsp. half and half
bay leaf	sprigs of watercress

Roll the fillets of sole head to tail and arrange in an ovenproof dish.

Pour the wine, water, onion, mushroom stalks, herbs and seasoning over them. Bake at 350°F, covered with a buttered paper or foil or lid, for 15-20 minutes.

Strain the liquid from the fish and make into to ²/₃ cup with extra water or wine if necessary. Poach the mushroom caps in this liquid for a few minutes — remove and keep warm.

Make a roux with the butter and flour and make up a sauce with the fish liquid.

Add the half and half to the sauce just before serving, pour it over the warmed fish, and serve with the mushroom caps, sprigs of watercress and, perhaps, Duchesse potatoes.

Sole Dugléré
Serves 4

Ingredients

4tbsp. butter	salt and freshly ground pepper
1 onion, peeled and chopped	²/₃ cup white wine
3 tomatoes, peeled and chopped	2tbsp. flour
8 sole fillets	1 tomato, peeled and sliced
	few sprigs of parsley

Melt half the butter in a skillet and add the chopped onions. Sweat over a low heat for a few minutes. Add the tomatoes and simmer for a further 2 minutes.

Fold each fillet in three and lay on top of the tomato and onion mixture, add seasoning and white wine and simmer for a further 12 minutes. Remove the fish to a serving dish and keep warm.

Reduce the sauce by about half over a medium heat. Make a roux with the remaining butter and flour. Add the strained liquid to make a sauce.

Mask the fish with the sauce and serve garnished with tomato slices and sprigs of parsley.

Sole Véronique
Serves 4

Ingredients

4oz. green grapes	6 peppercorns
4tbsp. butter	salt
¹/₂ small onion, diced	²/₃ cup white wine or white wine and water
2tbsp. breadcrumbs	4tbsp. flour
salt and freshly ground pepper	2tbsp. half and half
2lb. whole sole	watercress
bay leaf	
1 small onion, peeled and sliced	

Dip the grapes in boiling water for about 5 seconds. Cut in half, remove skin and discard the seeds.

To make the stuffing, melt the butter and sweat the onion over a low heat for about 4 minutes. Mix with breadcrumbs and about half the grapes, chopped, and seasoning.

Fillet the fish and wrap them, skinned side inwards, around stuffing. Lay in an ovenproof dish and add bay leaf, onion and seasonings; finally, pour on the wine. Add enough fish stock to come halfway up the dish, and bake at 350°F.

When the fish is cooked, remove the fillets and keep warm. Place the liquid in a saucepan and reduce to about ²/₃ cup. Make Velouté Sauce from the remaining butter, the flour, reduced fish liquor and enough milk for 1¹/₄ cups sauce.

Finally add the half and half to the slightly cooled sauce, pour over the fish and decorate with the remaining grapes and sprigs of watercress.

Variation If sole is unavailable use small flounders.

Sole Meunière
Serves 4

Ingredients

2 Dover soles, filleted	1tbsp. fresh parsley, chopped
1 cup+2tbsp. flour	
4tbsp. butter	1 lemon

Flour the fillets of sole and shake off excess.

Melt the butter and shallow fry the fillets for about 3 minutes either side.

Arrange the fillets on a warmed serving dish and keep warm.

Add the parsley to the juices in the pan. Add a little extra butter if necessary. Pour over the fish and serve with wedges of lemon.

Savory Baby Herrings

Savory Baby Herrings
Serves 4

Ingredients

1lb. baby herrings or
 pilchards
salt and freshly ground
 black pepper
½ cup cream cheese
1tsp. fresh parsley, chopped

1 clove of garlic
1 egg, beaten with 1tbsp.
 water
dried breadcrumbs
oil for frying

Remove the heads from the little herrings and open down the belly slit and remove the backbone. Wash the fish under cold running water and drain on kitchen towels. Season with salt and pepper.

Mix the cream cheese with a little seasoning, chopped parsley and a crushed clove of garlic. Cream the ingredients together well.

Stuff each herring with a little of the cream cheese mixture and shape the fish by folding over. Dip the fish in beaten egg and then in the crumbs, coating well.

Deep fry for about 3-4 minutes until golden brown. Drain on paper towels, and serve hot.

Barbecued Squid with Lime
Serves 3-4

Ingredients

2-3 large fresh squid, 1½-
 2lb. uncleaned weight
salt and pepper to taste

oil
6-10 wedges lime

Clean the squid (or ask the fish shop to do it for you). Season, then brush them with oil, before barbecuing for 8-12 minutes. (They can also be cooked under a broiler or in a skillet with oil.)

Slice into rings after cooking and serve hot with the lime wedges.

Trout "Au Bleu"

Trout "Au Bleu"
Serves 4

Ingredients

4 really fresh trout
3 cups well seasoned Court
 Bouillon, luke warm

⅔ cup white wine vinegar

Gut the trout just before cooking but do not scale. Put in a wide saucepan.

Pour the white wine vinegar and Court Bouillon over it and allow to simmer for about 10 minutes. Do not allow to boil or the fish will split.

Serve with hot or warm lemon wedges and Hollandaise Sauce.

Trout Chaudfroid

Trout Chaudfroid
Serves 4

An excellent summer meal or buffet dish.

Ingredients

4 trout	*canned pimento*
⅔ cup Chaudfroid Sauce	*stuffed olives, sliced*
cucumber peel	*watercress*

Cook the trout "au bleu" and allow to cool.

Remove the heads and top skin. Lift top fillet from fish carefully and remove the bone. Lay fillet back on the fish.

Coat with sauce. Garnish with cucumber peel cut into thin strips, diamond-shaped pieces of pimento, and sliced stuffed olives to make flowers and leaves. Surround head end with sprigs of watercress.

Trout with Almonds
Serves 4

Ingredients

4 trout, cleaned	*¾ cup flaked almonds*
⅔ cup milk	*4 sprigs of parsley or*
2tbsp. seasoned flour	*watercress*
2-4tbsp. butter	

Dip the trout in half the milk and then into the seasoned flour.

Melt half the butter in a skillet and lightly fry the almonds — alternatively this can be done without butter in a non-stick skillet. Shake and turn the almonds to brown evenly. Remove them and keep warm.

Melt the remaining butter and shallow fry the trout on both sides for about 4 minutes each side. Arrange the almonds on top of the trout during the last 2 minutes of cooking.

Replace each fish eye with a sprig of parsley or watercress, and serve hot.

Variation Remove the top skin, showing the pink flesh, after cooking and arrange the almonds on top and re-heat for a few minutes under the broiler.

Trout with Avocado and Ham
Serves 4

These days trout are so easily available that traditional ways of cooking them can seem a little plain. This unusual filling will transform them.

Ingredients

4×8oz. trout, cleaned	*8 thin slices bacon*
4tbsp. lemon juice	*2tbsp. flour*
1 large ripe avocado pear	*5tbsp. butter*
3oz. sliced lean ham	*lemon wedges*
salt and freshly ground	
* pepper*	

Preparation Sprinkle the trout inside and out with half the lemon juice and a little salt.

Peel the avocado and remove the pit. Liquidize or process the flesh with the remaining lemon juice until smooth. Add the ham, and blend until the ham is finely chopped but not puréed. Season to taste. Spoon this stuffing into the fish cavities.

Stretch the bacon slices with the back of a knife, and wrap two slices securely around each fish. Dust the fish with the flour.

Heat the butter in a large skillet, and fry the fish for 4 to 5 minutes on each side, till the flesh is opaque and the skin is browned.

Serve at once with lemon wedges.

Two Trout Mousse
Serves 4-6

An unusual combination of fresh and smoked trout.

Ingredients

1tbsp. butter	*²/₃ cup heavy cream*
1tbsp. flour	*½ cup smoked trout*
1¼ cups milk	*½ cup cold, poached trout,*
2 egg yolks	*boned*
1tsp. grated horseradish or	*2 sticks celery, finely*
2tsp. bottled horseradish	*chopped*
sauce	*lemon juice to taste*
salt and freshly ground	*½ large cucumber, peeled*
pepper	*and thinly sliced*
²/₃ cup sunflower or	
safflower oil	

Melt the butter in a small pan, stir in the flour, followed by the milk. Bring to a boil, stirring constantly until sauce is smooth and creamy. Simmer for 1 minute, then leave to cool completely.

In a liquidizer or food processor mix the egg yolks with the horseradish and a little salt and pepper. With the machine running, slowly pour in the oil to make a thick mayonnaise. Add the cooled sauce and mix well. Turn into a mixing bowl. Stiffly whip the cream and add to the mayonnaise mixture.

Flake both types of trout, discarding the skin. Carefully fold into the mayonnaise mixture. Add lemon juice and season to taste.

Use half the cucumber slices to line the base and sides of a 7-8in. glass soufflé dish. Spoon in half the fish mixture. Cover with a layer of cucumber slices, then the remaining fish mixture. Decorate with the remaining cucumber slices. Cover and chill for at least 2 hours.

Serve with slices of toast or buttered pumpernickel bread, and a green salad.

Steamed Trout with Hazelnuts and Zucchini
Serves 2

Ingredients

2×1-lb. trout	*bunch fresh chives*
2 zucchini	*½ cup hazelnut oil*
juice of ½ lemon	*2tbsp. hazelnuts*

Fillet the trout or ask your supermarket assistant to do this. Skin the fish and put them on a plate or dish which will fit over a saucepan, for steaming, skinned side down.

Cut the zucchini into matchstick pieces and sprinkle with a little of the lemon juice. Put the zucchini on top of the fish. Steam the fish for about 8 minutes or until cooked.

Meanwhile, snip the chives into small pieces, mix with the remaining lemon juice, hazelnut oil and the hazelnuts which have been put into a blender. Alternatively, place the nuts in the blender or food processor and blend, then add the other ingredients and mix well.

Remove trout onto warmed plates and pour the hazelnut dressing over them.

Serve with boiled baby potatoes and a crisp green salad.

Tuna Wholewheat Rolls
Serves 4

Ingredients

4 wholewheat rolls, crusty	4tbsp. canned or cooked
2tbsp. butter or margarine	corn kernels
2 green onions, washed	2tsp. lemon juice
and sliced	1/2tsp. paprika
4 mushrooms, washed and	salt and freshly ground
sliced	pepper
1 small can tuna fish,	
drained	

Cut a slice from the top of each roll about 1½in. in diameter and scoop out some of the inside.

Melt the butter or margarine in a small skillet, add the sliced green onions and mushrooms. Allow to cook over a low heat for 2 minutes.

Remove from the heat and stir in the remaining ingredients, including the breadcrumbs from the rolls. Season to taste.

Stuff the rolls with the filling and replace the lids. Wrap each in a square of foil and bake at 400°F for 10 minutes to heat through. Remove from the oven and unwrap the foil.

Serve with a crispy green salad for a light lunch.

Tuna Mousse
Serves 4

Ingredients

7oz. can tuna, drained	1tbsp. chopped parsley
1tbsp. lemon juice	2tsp. gelatin
1/4 cup Mayonnaise	1/2 cup boiling water
1/4 cup sour cream	2 egg whites
1tbsp. chopped onion	salt and pepper

Put the tuna, lemon juice, Mayonnaise, sour cream, chopped onion and parsley in a food processor or blender and mix together until smooth.

Dissolve the gelatin in the boiling water. Add to the tuna mixture and mix in well. Beat the egg whites until stiff and fold them into the mixture. Adjust the seasoning and turn the mixture into a moistened mold (a small ring mold looks nice). Refrigerate until set and then unmold.

Decorate with watercress and/or thin slices of orange.

Tuna-Stuffed Potatoes
Serves 4

Ingredients

4 large potatoes, scrubbed	4tbsp. sour cream
4 tomatoes, skinned and	salt and freshly ground
chopped	pepper
4 green onions, washed	7oz. can tuna fish, in oil
and chopped	

Make a cross on the potato skins and bake for 1 hour at 350°F or until cooked.

Halve the potatoes and scoop out the cooked potato, retaining the skins.

Mix all ingredients together, season well and pile back into the potato skins.

Reheat before serving.

Deep-Fried Baby Herrings
Serves 4

Ingredients

1½lb baby herrings or	oil for frying
pilchards	lemon wedges
3/4 cup seasoned flour	parsley sprigs

Pat the small herrings dry with paper towels.

Toss the fish in seasoned flour and deep fry in hot oil for a few minutes until golden brown and crisp.

Serve with lemon wedges, parsley sprigs and Tartare Sauce. Offer thinly sliced wholewheat bread and butter.

Whiting Bercy
Serves 4

Ingredients

4×10oz. whiting	juice of 1/2 lemon
4tbsp. butter	salt and freshly ground
2 small onions	pepper
3/4 cup white wine	1tbsp. butter creamed
1tbsp. fresh parsley,	together with 2tbsp. flour
chopped	1/2 cup fresh breadcrumbs

Fillet the fish and make fish stock with the trimmings and heads.

Fold fillets over with a small knob of butter in each and poach in the fish stock for about 8 minutes. Remove fillets and keep warm.

Melt the remaining butter and toss finely chopped onion in it for a few minutes; cook on a low heat without browning. Add the wine and allow to reduce slightly. Finally add the strained fish stock, chopped parsley, lemon juice, salt and pepper.

Bring to a boil and remove from the heat. Beat the flour and butter mixture into the liquid.

Beat over the heat for a few minutes until sauce thickens. Pour over fillets which have been kept warm. Sprinkle with breadcrumbs and top with little knobs of butter.

Heat through in a hot oven or brown under the broiler for a few minutes.

Variation This is also a good way to cook sole or cod.

Tuna-Stuffed Potatoes

Dressed Crab
Serves 2

Ingredients

1 crab, cooked
a little olive oil
2tbsp. white breadcrumbs
1-2tbsp. Mayonnaise
½tsp. French mustard
salt and freshly ground
  pepper

juice of ½ lemon
fresh parsley, finely
  chopped
paprika
1 egg, hard-boiled
lettuce

Put the boiled crab on a board and twist the claws until they separate from the body. Crack the claws open with a hammer. Take a skewer and remove the white meat from the claws and put in a bowl.

Take hold of the crab firmly with both hands and with the thumbs push the body section away from the shell.

Take out and discard the following: the small sac or stomach bag which is attached to the large shell, any green-tinged material in the large shell and, lastly, the grey spongy parts known as "dead man's fingers."

Scrape the brownish meat from the shell into a second bowl.

Cut the body into two and scrape any white meat left into the first bowl.

Tap the shell to remove the ragged sharp edge. Wash and scrub the inside and outside of the shell thoroughly and rinse well (do not use soap). Dry off the shell and brush with some olive oil.

Mix the white breadcrumbs with the brown meat and cream well with the Mayonnaise, French mustard and seasonings.

Arrange the white meat mixed with lemon juice and salt and pepper on each side of the shell and the brown meat down the middle.

Garnish with rows of chopped parsley, paprika and separate lines of the finely chopped white and yolk of the hard-boiled egg.

Serve on a bed of lettuce surrounded by the small claws, with thinly sliced wholewheat bread and butter. Serve extra Mayonnaise separately, if you like.

Chili Crab
Serves 4

Ingredients

2 cooked crabs (1½lb.
  each)
1in. piece fresh ginger,
  scraped
2 fresh red chilies or 2 tsp.
  chili sauce
2 cloves garlic, crushed
4-6 tbsp. vegetable oil

1 cup tomato ketchup
1tsp. brown sugar
⅔ cup hot water
1 beaten egg (optional)
salt
fresh coriander to garnish
chunks of cucumber and
  pieces of toast to serve

Remove the large claws and turn each crab onto its back, with the head facing away from you. Use your thumbs to push the body up from the main shell. Discard the stomach sac and "dead man's fingers" (the lungs and any green matter); leave the creamy brown meat in the shell and cut in half. Cut the body section in half with a strong knife and crack the claws with a sharp tap from a hammer or cleaver. Crack, don't splinter them.

Pound the ginger, seeded chilies and garlic together. Fry in hot oil for 1-2 minutes without browning. Add tomato ketchup, chili sauce, sugar and water, and mix well. When almost boiling add all the crab over a high heat.

Just before serving stir in the beaten egg, which will scramble in the sauce if desired; taste for seasoning and serve at once garnished with fresh coriander leaves, together with the cucumber and toast.

Chili Crab

Dressed Crab (see page 94)

Papaya Crab
Serves 4

Ingredients

2 ripe papayas, 10-12oz.
  each
2tbsp. whipped cream
½ cup Mayonnaise

lime or lemon juice
a little white pepper
½ cup crabmeat

Split the papayas and remove the seeds and "strings."

Mix the whipped cream with the Mayonnaise. As homemade Mayonnaise is so much richer than a commercial brand, you may need to add a little more whipped cream to lighten it.

Flavor to taste with lime or lemon juice and a little white pepper.

Combine the dressing with the crabmeat and pile into the pawpaw halves.

Serve chilled.

Variation For Melon Crab use two small melons, halved and deseeded, instead of the papayas. The fragrant, orange or peach-fleshed varieties of melon, such as Charentais and Cantaloupe, are particularly good for this.

Baked Avocado with Crab

Crab with Eggs
Serves 4

Ingredients

4-6oz. cooked crabmeat
1tsp. sugar
1 small piece ginger,
  scraped and crushed in
  garlic press
2tsp. light soy sauce

seasoning
4 eggs, beaten
a little butter or oil for
  frying
4-6 green onions, finely
  chopped

Pick over the crabmeat and remove any shell or cartilage. Stir the sugar, ginger and soy sauce into it and season to taste.

Add this to the beaten eggs and scramble in fat in a pan for 1 minute.

Add green onions and serve at once.

Baked Avocado with Crab
Serves 4

Ingredients

2 ripe avocados
7oz. can of crabmeat or
  the meat from 1 cooked
  crab
1tbsp. lemon juice
2tbsp. white wine
few drops of hot pepper
  sauce

2tsp. tomato paste
salt and freshly ground
  pepper
1¼ cups Béchamel Sauce
1tbsp. parsley, finely
  chopped

Cut the avocados in half carefully and remove the pits and some of the flesh.

Sprinkle the crab meat and chopped avocado flesh with lemon juice and white wine.

Add the rest of the ingredients to the béchamel sauce and fill the halved avocados, piling the mixture up as high as it will go without spilling.

Bake at 350°F until golden brown. Serve sprinkled with chopped parsley.

Variation This dish can be made with tuna fish in place of crab.

Dressed Lobster

1 medium-sized boiled lobster	lemon juice and salt and pepper or Mayonnaise

Crack the pincer claws with a small hammer and take out the meat with a skewer.

Cut the lobster lengthways from head to tail, using a sharp knife. Remove the stomach bag on the right side of the head and also the grey spongy parts known as "dead man's fingers."

Remove the coral, wash and retain for decoration. Now remove all the meat from the shell. Keep the green liver meat which is edible.

Flavor the meat with lemon juice and seasoning or mayonnaise and return to the shell. Serve on a bed of lettuce.

Note Lobsters are best at about 1¾-2½lb. as this will give two good servings. Look for a healthy lobster with the tail curled under the body.

To prepare and cook a live lobster, first take a skewer or sharp knife and drive through the cross which is on the head. Grip the lobster firmly behind the head and plunge into a large saucepan of boiling salted water. A bay leaf, sprig or parsley or bouquet garni may be added. Cook for 15 minutes for each 1lb of lobster. Allow to cool in the liquid. Leave the antennae on, as they form part of the decoration if serving in the shell. When cool, twist off the claws, retaining small claws for garnish.

Oysters à l'Américaine
Serves 4

Ingredients

24 oysters	1 cup grated Gruyère cheese
2 cups fresh breadcrumbs	
4tbsp. butter	
freshly ground black pepper	

Remove the oysters from the shell and wash the deep shells thoroughly. Drain and wipe the oysters on paper towels.

Fry half the breadcrumbs in melted butter until golden brown. Sprinkle a few fried breadcrumbs in the bottom of the 24 deep shells. Season with pepper.

Return oysters to prepared shells, sprinkle with a mixture of breadcrumbs and Gruyère cheese and brown in the oven at 425°F. Serve immediately.

Lobster Newburg
Serves 4

Most hot lobster dishes are best made with freshly cooked lobster, which means killing the lobster just before cooking it. For those who find this difficult, the delicious Lobster Newburg is a welcome recipe as it can be made with a cooked lobster.

Ingredients

2lb. lobster, cooked	3 egg yolks
2tbsp. butter	⅔ cup heavy cream
salt and freshly ground pepper	2 cups cooked rice, hot
	1tbsp. chopped parsley
2tbsp. brandy	lemon twists

Cut down the soft shell under the tail with scissors. Peel away the hard shell to leave the tail whole. Crack the claws with a small hammer and carefully remove the meat with a skewer.

Melt half the butter in a skillet over a very low heat. Add the claw meat and the tail meat cut into sections, season well and and heat through for about 3 minutes.

Heat the brandy in a ladle and set it alight to flambé the lobster by pouring the lighted brandy over the lobster meat. When the flames die down, remove the skillet from the heat.

In a bowl, mix egg yolks, cream and the remaining butter cut into little pieces with more seasoning.

Return the lobster meat to the lower heat and gradually pour over it the egg mixture, stirring with a wooden spoon until the sauce becomes thick and creamy.

Serve on hot boiled rice garnished with chopped parsley and lemon twists.

Lobster Newburg

Moules Marinière
Serves 4

Ingredients

2lb. mussels	bay leaf
4tbsp. butter	sprigs fresh parsley
1 medium onion, finely chopped	2tbsp. chopped parsley (optional)
1-2 cloves garlic, finely crushed	2tbsp. heavy cream (optional)
1¼ cup white wine	

Make sure the mussels are properly prepared before cooking. They should be alive — tap with a wooden spoon and if any remain open discard at once. Wash and scrub the shells thoroughly under cold running water and remove the "beard." Put in a bowl of cold water and change the water several times to remove the sand.

Heat butter in a very large saucepan or skillet. Add the chopped onion and garlic. Allow to sweat gently in the butter without browning.

Add the wine, bay leaf and sprigs of parsley. Turn up the heat and add the cleaned mussels. Shake over the heat for about 6-10 minutes until all the mussels are open.

Discard any mussels which do not open. Divide the mussels among serving bowls and, if liked, add the cream and chopped parsley to the juice. Heat for a further minute and pour over the mussels.

Serve with warm French bread and extra plates for empty shells.

Oysters en Brochette
Serves 4

Ingredients

24 oysters	4 slices of toast, cut in long strips
⅔ cup dry white wine and water	1 cup fresh white breadcrumbs
1tbsp. oil	
freshly ground black pepper	2tbsp. butter
12 slices of bacon, rind removed	¾tsp. cayenne pepper

Drain the opened oysters over a strainer lined with cheesecloth to catch the oyster juice. Heat the wine and water and oyster liquid in a saucepan and add a shake of pepper.

Allow the oysters to remain in the liquid for a few minutes without boiling. Remove when plumped up.

Cut the bacon slices in half, stretch with the back of a knife, and cook in a little oil over a low heat until the fat starts to run. Do not crisp.

Wrap the bacon around the oysters and thread onto skewers.

Put the skewers under a hot broiler for a few minutes, turning from time to time, then put them on the strips of toast, and keep warm.

Fry the breadcrumbs in the butter until golden and mix with cayenne. Sprinkle on the brochettes and serve immediately.

Variation This recipe can also be made with mussels.

Shrimp Curry
Serves 4

Ingredients

2 small potatoes, peeled and thinly sliced	bay leaf
	bouquet garni
1 onion, peeled and finely chopped	½ cauliflower, washed and broken into flowerets
2 cloves garlic, crushed	¾lb. shrimps, cooked and shelled
1-2tbsp. oil	
2tbsp. curry powder	1tbsp. lemon juice
15oz. can tomatoes	salt and freshly ground pepper
1tbsp. tomato paste	
¼ cup fish stock or water	1 cup long grain rice, cooked
2 cups small mushrooms	

Parboil potatoes for 3 minutes. Drain and set aside.

Sauté the onion and garlic in the oil for several minutes until the onion is transparent, then add the curry powder and fry, mixing with the onions for a few minutes.

Add the tomatoes, paste and fish stock or water and chopped mushroom stalks. Add herbs. Bring to a boil, then lower heat.

Add the parboiled potatoes, the cauliflower and the mushrooms to the mixture and simmer for 25 minutes.

Add the shrimps and lemon juice and simmer for a further 10 minutes on a low heat. Season to taste.

Serve on a bed of cooked rice with poppadums and chutneys.

Shrimp Curry

Scallops au Gratin
Serves 4

Ingredients

8-16 bay scallops, depending on size	bay leaf
1-2oz. butter	bouquet garni
1 small onion, peeled and finely chopped or 6 green onions, cleaned and chopped	salt and freshly ground pepper
	mashed potatoes
	1½tbsp. butter
1 clove garlic, crushed (optional)	1½tbsp. flour
⅔ cup white wine	1-2tbsp. half and half
⅔ cup fish stock or water	2tbsp. fresh breadcrumbs, dried
	1tbsp. Parmesan cheese

Cut the scallops into slices. Melt the butter in a saucepan. Sweat the onion or green onion and garlic over a low heat for about 3 minutes.

Add the sliced scallops, cook for a further 1 minute and then add the wine and water or fish stock with the bay leaf and bouquet garni. Season well.

Bring to a boil and turn the heat down low and simmer for about 6 minutes. Allow to cool.

Strain the liquor from the scallops, retaining the vegetables. Discard the bay leaf and bouquet garni.

Pipe a border of mashed potatoes around 8 deep, cleaned scallop shells.

Make a roux with the butter and flour, make a sauce with the fish liquor. Taste for seasoning, add half and half.

Add the onion mixture, then the scallops to the sauce and divide the mixture between the shells.

Sprinkle with a mixture of breadcrumbs and Parmesan cheese. Brown in a hot oven or under the broiler and serve hot.

Note If using 8 scallops, you will only need 4 shells and 1tbsp. half and half. One shell is sufficient for a fish course but 2 will be needed for a main course.

Shrimp-Stuffed Zucchini
Serves 2-4

Ingredients

4 zucchini	1¼ cups Béchamel Sauce
½ cup shrimps	1tbsp. Parmesan cheese, grated
1 hard-boiled egg	

Cut a small slice lengthwise along the zucchini and scoop out a little of the flesh and chop it finely.

Blanch the zucchini for 2 minutes in boiling water.

Add the shrimps, chopped egg and chopped zucchini to the Béchamel Sauce.

Fill the zucchini with the mixture and sprinkle with Parmesan cheese. Bake at 350°F for 15-20 minutes.

Shellfish Paella
Serves 4

Ingredients

1lb. cod or halibut	1 red pepper, seeded
2½ cups Court Bouillon	1 green pepper, seeded
4tbsp. oil	⅔ cup white wine and water
2 cloves garlic, crushed	
3 medium onions, peeled	4 cups mussels
1½ cups long grain rice	1 cup peeled shrimps
pinch of saffron threads or ¼tsp. turmeric	1tbsp. parsley, chopped
	lemon wedges
2½ cups fish or chicken stock	4-8 large cooked shrimps (optional)

Poach the cod in Court Bouillon for 5 minutes.

Put the oil in a large pan and sweat the garlic and 2 of the onions, one thinly sliced and the other finely chopped, for about 4 minutes without browning.

Add the rice to the pan and stir over the heat for a few minutes until rice just begins to color.

Strain the cod and retain the stock. Add saffron or turmeric to the stock and pour it over the rice, stirring from time to time over a low heat. Cook covered with a lid or foil for the first 10 minutes.

Blanch the peppers for 2 minutes, then dice firmly, add to the rice and stir well.

In another saucepan, put the other onion, finely chopped, with the water and wine mixture and a good shake of pepper. Bring to a boil and add the cleaned mussels. Cook for 10 minutes until steamed open.

Add the strained mussel liquor to the rice and stir well. Cook for a further 5 minutes or until the rice is tender.

Add the chunks of white fish, shrimps and mussels.

Serve hot, sprinkled with parsley and garnished with lemon wedges. Decorate with extra shrimps if you like.

Bay Scallops with Mushrooms
Serves 4

Ingredients

⅔ cup dry white wine	2 tomatoes, skinned and chopped
⅔ cup water	
1 small onion, peeled and sliced	8 bay scallops, cleaned
4 peppercorns	2½tbsp. flour
1 bay leaf	1 egg yolk
1 stalk parsley	1tbsp. half and half
¼lb. mushrooms, washed	few drops of lemon juice
4tbsp. butter	2tbsp. fresh breadcrumbs, dried
1 medium onion, peeled and finely chopped or 8 green onions, washed and chopped	lemon wedges
	parsley

Put the first six ingredients in a saucepan, bring to the boil and simmer for about 10 minutes.

Remove the mushroom stalks and chop finely. Slice the caps, retaining 16 slices for garnish.

Melt half the butter in a frying pan and sweat the chopped onion or spring onions and chopped mushrooms stalks over a low heat for about 4 minutes. Add the tomatoes and cook for 3 minutes.

Add the sliced scallops to the strained wine mixture and poach over a low heat for about 8 minutes. Remove the scallops with a slotted spoon and then poach the mushroom slices for about 2 minutes. Strain the liquid into a measuring jub and make up to 1¼ cups, if necessary, with wine or water.

Make a roux wih the remaining butter and the flour and make into a sauce with the fish liquor. Allow to cool slightly then add a little sauce to the egg yolk, mix well and return the mixture to the sauce. Stir over a low heat for about 1 minute. Allow to cool slightly, add the cream and, lastly, the sliced mushrooms.

Divide the onion, mushroom and tomato mixture between the shells or spread on the bottom of the serving dish, if using one big dish.

Add the scallops to the mushroom sauce, taste for seasoning and add a few drops of lemon juice to taste. Pour into the shells or serving dish and sprinkle with crumbs and garnish with mushrooms. Heat through in the oven at 350°F for 10-15 minutes.

Serve garnished with parsley and lemon wedges.

Variations Milk may be substituted for the wine.

For **Curried Scallops** add 1tsp. curry powder to the onion and tomato mixture and fry for about 1 minute over a high heat. Add the mixture to the sauce. Water or fish stock may be used in place of wine for the curry. Serve with lemon wedges.

Selection

When buying fish and shellfish, absolute freshness is essential. Bright eyes and stiff flesh are the signs of fresh fish. Dull eyes and limp flesh with a slight ammonia smell indicate stale fish.

It is best to buy the fish the day it is to be cooked. Store it in the refrigerator loosely covered and try not to keep it longer than 24 hours before cooking.

Preparation of Fish

Ideally, fish should be prepared just before cooking but time does not always permit this. If it is to be cooked in a stock it is often advantageous to allow it to cool in the fish liquid.

Most people are not keen on cleaning or gutting fish and it is fortunate that fish shops are so helpful with preparation. However, for those who are prepared to do the work themselves, this is how it should be done.

To scale fish: lay fish on paper towels and hold by the tail. Scrape the scales away from the tail towards the head using the blunt side of a knife. Rinse under cold water.

To Clean and Fillet Flat Fish

Slit behind the head on the dark skin side, remove the entrails from the cavity and rinse in cold water. Pat dry with a clean cloth or paper towels. Remove the fins with a sharp knife or scissors.

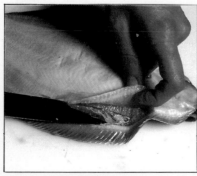

1 Begin filleting the fish by cutting into head end against the bone.

2 Cut the fillet away carefully with the skin attached to it, leaving the bone as clean as possible.

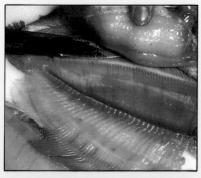

3 Turn the fish over, insert the knife at the head and carefully remove the second fillet in the same way. The flat fish is now filleted. One fillet has thick black skin, the other white. The bone can now be used for stock.

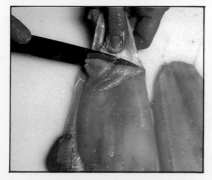

4 To skin the fish, hold the tail firmly and work fillet away from the skin from tail to head, with a sharp knife. The skin can also be used for fish stock.

To Clean and Bone Round Fish

1 To clean, retaining the head, slit from under the head down to the tail.

2 Remove entrails by hooking the finger under the throat and pulling down towards the tail. Wash well. A rubber glove may be used for this step.

3 If the head is not required — as with, for example, mackerel and herring — cut it off with a sharp knife before boning.

4 Slip the sharp knife under the bone on each side of the fish in turn, open and remove the bones.

5 An alternative method, which may be easier for the inexperienced, is to turn the fish open-side downwards. Press down on the back with the heel of the hand and loosen the bone.

6 Turn the fish over and, starting at the tail end, place the blade of the knife under the bone and push along the spine to release. Feel the surface of the fish with the fingers to ensure there are no stray bones. The round fish is now ready to be cooked.

Dressing Crab

1 Lay the crab on its back and twist off the claws. Then twist off the legs — do not pull them.

2 Prise the apron up by pulling at the pointed end near the mouth to remove the body from the shell.

3 Remove the dead men's fingers. These are soft and spongy and are found at the sides of the body and stomach sac which lies behind the head.

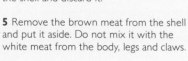

4 Strip out the cartilaginous membrane from the shell and discard it.

5 Remove the brown meat from the shell and put it aside. Do not mix it with the white meat from the body, legs and claws.

6 With the thumbs, break the shell along the visible lines to enlarge the opening. Use a hammer if it is tough. Wash out the shell and scrub it if necessary.

7 Remove the white meat from the body, claws and legs. Crack the claws and legs with a hammer or lobster cracker. Use a lobster pick or skewer to help you extract all the flesh.

8 Mix brown meat with a little Mayonnaise (and brown breadcrumbs if you like). Spoon it down the center of the shell. Put white meat at each end. Cover the dark meat with lines of parsley, chopped egg white and yolk.

Poultry and Game

Spanish Chicken and Rice
Serves 8

Rice with chicken is a classic Spanish meal, hearty and easy to prepare. Serve it with a simple salad, a glass of wine and a simple dessert.

Ingredients

2tbsp. chicken fat
2 3-lb. chickens, cut into serving pieces
pinch of salt
pinch of black pepper
1¾ cups finely chopped onion
4 cloves garlic, finely chopped
1½tbsp. sweet paprika
4 ripe tomatoes, skinned, seeded and finely chopped
2 cups shelled peas
½tsp. crumbled saffron threads
3tbsp. finely chopped parsley
1½lb. rice
5 cups boiling water

Melt the chicken fat in a large paella pan or saucepan. Add the chicken pieces, salt and pepper and cook over a moderate heat for 40 minutes. Turn the chicken pieces frequently.

Remove the chicken pieces from the pan and set them aside.

Add the onions, garlic, paprika, tomatoes, peas, saffron and parsley to the pan. Cook over a low heat for 10 minutes, stirring frequently.

Return the chicken to the pan. Add the rice and boiling water. Stir well and bring to a boil over a high heat. Reduce the heat to low. Cover the pan and simmer for 40 minutes.

Remove the pan from the heat. Remove the lid and leave it to stand for 5 minutes before serving.

Cantonese Chicken
Serves 3

Hoisin sauce is a plum sauce widely available in supermarkets.

Ingredients

2½-lb. chicken
salt
1tbsp. cornstarch
2tbsp. sherry
2tbsp. liquid honey
oil for deep frying
green onion curls
cucumber slices
hoisin sauce

Rinse the chicken inside and out thoroughly. Plunge it into a large pan of boiling water for 1 minute. Lift out carefully, drain and dry thoroughly. Tie up by the feet and dry out for 3-4 hours. Rub the skin with salt and suspend overnight in a cool, dry place.

Blend the cornstarch and sherry, then stir in the honey. Rub the skin of the chicken with this mixture and leave for several hours or overnight.

Lift the chicken into a frying basket and lower into a larger pan of deep fat, lifting out several times to allow the fat to regain heat. The chicken will be cooked in 50-60 minutes and the skin will be crisp and golden.

Drain thoroughly and cut into even-sized, smallish pieces. Serve garnished with green onions and pieces of cucumber and hoisin sauce for dipping.

Barbecued Spiced Chicken
Serves 4

Hoisin sauce is a Chinese plum sauce which is widely available in supermarkets.

Ingredients

3-lb. chicken, cut into 4 pieces
8 shallots
2 cloves garlic, peeled and crushed
½in. ginger, peeled and sliced
1 stem lemon grass
1tsp. chili powder
4tbsp. soy sauce
2tbsp. hoisin sauce
3tbsp. oil
salt
oil for frying
½ cup chicken stock

Slash the flesh of the chicken quarters several times. Finely chop the shallots and set aside. Pound the garlic, ginger, lemon grass and chili powder together. Mix with soy sauce, hoisin sauce and oil and pour over the chicken pieces. Leave to marinate for 30 minutes.

Heat oil in a wok, fry the onions without browning, lift the chicken pieces out of the marinade and fry on both sides to seal. Reduce the heat, cook for 10 minutes. Transfer to the barbecue to complete cooking.

Add the marinade to the remaining ingredients in the pan. Fry, then add stock. Cook for 5 minutes and serve this sauce with the chicken.

Season well and add a few drops of lemon juice. Place the sliced avocado in the remaining lemon juice.

Arrange the salad in a bowl which has been lined with sliced tomatoes.

Decorate with slices of blanched pepper and the sliced avocados. Arrange parsley or watercress around the dish.

Note If preparing in advance sprinkle the avocados with lemon juice.

Any wholewheat pasta shapes can be used, such as shells, spirals or short-cut macaroni.

Chicken in Coconut Milk
Serves 4

Ingredients

3-lb. chicken, cut into 8 pieces	1-in. piece fresh ginger
1tbsp. sugar	2 stems lemon grass
3½ cups shredded coconut	5tbsp. coconut or vegetable oil
2½ cups boiling water	2tbsp. chili powder or to taste
4 small onions	salt to taste
2 cloves garlic	

Rinse the pieces of chicken and dry them on paper towels. Put in a bowl, sprinkle with sugar and toss in the bowl to release their juices.

Dry fry 1 cup of coconut in a large skillet or wok turning all the time until it becomes dry, crisp and golden. Pound with a pestle and mortar until the oil begins to show.

Turn the remaining coconut into a deep bowl and make coconut milk by pouring the boiling water over it, leaving to soak for 15 minutes, then squeezing out the liquid. Leave liquid to stand for another 15 minutes, then spoon off 4tbsp.

Peel and chop the onions and garlic and scrape and chop the ginger. Pound them with the lemon grass.

Heat the oil in the wok. Fry the pounded ingredients for several minutes to bring out the flavor. Lower the heat, add the chili powder and cook for 3-4 minutes, stirring all the time. Add the spooned off coconut milk and salt. Stir as the mixture comes to the boil to prevent curdling. Add the chicken pieces turning frequently so that the mixture coats each piece. Reduce the heat and stir in the remaining coconut milk. Cook over a gentle heat for 45-50 minutes or until the chicken is tender.

Just before serving, spoon some of the sauce into the pounded coconut. Mix well, then return this to the wok. Stir without breaking up the chicken and cook for a further 5 minutes.

Boned Highland Chicken
Serves 6-8

Ingredients

4-lb. chicken, boned	rind of 1 lemon
6tbsp. butter	juice of ½ lemon
1 large onion, peeled	4tbsp. stock
2 sticks celery, washed	freshly ground pepper
½ cup medium oatmeal	butter or vegetable oil
1tbsp. chopped parsley	

Preheat the oven to 350°F.

To bone the chicken, place the chicken, breast side downwards, on the board and split the bird down the back with a very sharp knife.

Chicken in Baked Potatoes
Serves 4

Ingredients

4 even-sized large potatoes	4tbsp. sweetcorn kernels, cooked
1½ cups chicken, chopped	2tbsp. Mayonnaise
1 green pepper, seeded and chopped	2 tomatoes, skinned
1 green onion, washed and chopped	salt and freshly ground pepper

Wash and scrub the potato skins. Prick with a fork. Arrange on the oven shelves and bake at 400°F for 45-60 minutes.

Alternatively, boil the potatoes for 15 minutes, drain and then bake in the oven for 25-35 minutes, depending on size. Potatoes can also be baked in a microwave oven — one potato will take 5 minutes but four will need 20 minutes. Crisp in the oven if liked.

Cut the potato lengthwise and scoop out some of the flesh from each potato half. Reserve and mix with remaining ingredients. Season to taste.

Fill the potatoes and reheat for a few minutes in the oven.

Potatoes can be prepared and stuffed then kept in the refrigerator until needed. Heat through before serving.

Chicken Avocado Pasta Salad
Serves 4

Ingredients

3 cups cooked pasta	2 tomatoes, skinned and sliced
6 green onions, washed	1 red pepper, seeded
1 cup Mayonnaise	parsley or watercress (optional)
2 ripe avocados	
1½ cups cooked chicken, chopped	
salt and freshly ground pepper	

Put the cooked pasta in a bowl. Chop the green onions finely and add to the pasta with the mayonnaise.

Remove the skins from the avocados, cut them in half and remove the stones. Cut 8 thin slices for garnish and chop the remainder. Add to the pasta and mayonnaise mixture with the cooked chicken.

Ease the skin and flesh from the carcase with the knife and fingers. Insert the knife between the ball and socket of the thigh joint and remove the sinews. Take out the thigh bones, which should come away cleanly.

Hold the joint between the finger and thumb and gradually work the meat from the drumstick. Remove the wing joint from the body and carefully work the flesh from the breastbone without cutting the skin. Remove the breastbone completely. Flatten out the bird on a board ready for stuffing.

To make the stuffing, melt the butter in a saucepan, dice the onion and cook over a low heat for 5 minutes. Remove strings from celery with a potato peeler and dice finely. Add the celery to the onion, cook for a further 3 minutes. Sprinkle in the oatmeal and stir for a few minutes with the buttery vegetables. Add parsley, lemon rind and juice. Add a little stock until the stuffing holds together.

Lay the stuffing in the cavity of the chicken, reform its shape and sew up with a trussing needle and thin string.

Rub over the skin of the chicken with the squeezed lemon half, season with pepper, spread with a little butter or paint with vegetable oil and roast in foil for 1 hour 40 minutes. Remove foil for the last 20 minutes.

Chicken Curry with Noodles
Serves 6-8

Ingredients

4 cups boiling water	4 fresh red chili peppers,
1lb. shredded coconut	seeded or 2tsp. chili
4lb. egg noodles or rice	powder
noodles	1-2tsp. powdered turmeric
3-lb. chicken, cut into	peanut oil for frying
quarters	4-5tbsp. chick-pea flour
salt to taste	1-2tbsp. Worcestershire
1lb. onions, peeled	sauce
3 cloves garlic, peeled and	coriander leaves
crushed	

First make coconut milk by pouring the boiling water over the coconut, leaving it to stand for 15 minutes, then squeezing out the liquid.

Break some of the rice noodles into 1-in. lengths and deep fry until crisp. Drain on paper towels.

Put the chicken joints in a pan. Add 9 cups of water and some salt. Bring to a boil, then cover and simmer for 45-60 minutes or until the chicken is tender. Lift the chicken joints from the pan, cool and remove the meat and cut into small pieces. Discard the skin and bones. Strain the stock and reserve.

Meanwhile pound the onions, garlic and chili peppers, or chili powder, to a paste in a food processor. Add turmeric. Fry in hot oil until it gives off a rich aroma. Stir in the coconut milk and 4½ cups of the reserved chicken stock. Simmer for 15 minutes.

Blend the chick-pea flour with a little of the cold stock or water to make a cream. Slowly stir one ladleful of liquid from the pan into the cream, then pour this back into the pan. Simmer over a low heat, stirring until the soup thickens a little. Add the chicken pieces, salt and Worcestershire sauce. Turn into a serving tureen and scatter with fresh coriander leaves.

Cook the noodles in plenty of boiling water and spoon noodles into the bowls first, then top with the curried chicken. Serve fried noodles separately.

Chicken Biriani
Serves 4

Ingredients

1 cup long-grain rice,	1tbsp. flour
preferably basmati	¼tsp. chili powder
1tbsp. salt	5tbsp. yogurt
2 large onions, peeled	1tbsp. lemon juice
2 cloves garlic, crushed	4tbsp. water
1-in. piece root ginger,	1tsp. ground coriander
grated	¼tsp. ground cinnamon
4tbsp. slivered almonds	⅓tsp. turmeric
6tbsp. vegetable oil	1 hard-boiled egg
2-3 boned chicken portions	1 tomato, skinned

Wash the rice several times. Allow to soak in a large bowl of water and salt for at least 1 hour.

Slice half an onion finely into rings and reserve. Put the remaining onion, garlic, ginger, 1tbsp. oil and some water in an electric grinder or food processor with a few slivered almonds. Grind to a paste.

Heat the remaining oil on a fairly high heat and fry the onion rings until golden brown. Remove with a slotted spoon and drain on paper towels.

Fry the remaining slivered almonds until golden on each side and drain with the onion rings.

Cut the chicken into small pieces and toss in seasoned flour mixed with the chili powder. Fry until golden and drain on kitchen paper.

Fry the paste in the oil in the pan. Add the yogurt, 1tbsp. at a time, with the lemon juice. Add 4tbsp. water and return the chicken to cook over a low heat for 15 minutes.

Add the coriander, cumin and cinnamon to the chicken after 5 minutes and stir well.

Meanwhile cook the rice in 4¼ cups boiling salted water with the turmeric for 10 minutes and drain.

Spread the drained rice on top of the chicken casserole. Add the almonds.

Cover the mixture with foil and then the casserole lid, and bake in the oven at 300°F for 35 minutes.

To serve, mix the chicken and rice well with a fork and turn into a heated serving dish. Garnish with sliced hard-boiled eggs, tomato and browned onion rings.

Chicken Creole
Serves 6-8

Ingredients

8 chicken pieces
¾ cup peeled shrimp
2 tbsp. olive oil
½ tsp. dried tarragon
2 cloves of garlic, crushed
a few drops hot pepper
   sauce or cayenne

1 large onion, thinly sliced
1 red pepper, cored and
   thinly sliced
Concentrated Tomato
   Sauce

Score the chicken pieces and put them in a dish, with the shrimp at one end. Pour over them a mixture of the oil, tarragon, garlic and hot pepper sauce or cayenne. Leave to marinate for at least an hour before cooking.

Drain the marinade into a skillet. Remove the shrimp and reserve until needed.

Fry the chicken in the heated marinade for 7 to 10 minutes, turning occasionally, until well browned. Arrange in a roasting pan.

Fry the onion and sweet pepper in the oil left in the pan until the onion begins to brown, then arrange over the chicken.

Pour the Tomato Sauce over the vegetables and chicken, cover the pan with foil, and cook at 350°F for 30 minutes.

Remove the foil, turn up the heat to 425°F and bake for another 20 minutes, adding the shrimp 5 minutes before serving, to heat them through.

Chicken Casserole with Ginger
Serves 4-6

Ingredients

3-lb. chicken
1-in. piece fresh ginger,
   scraped and chopped
1 large onion, peeled and
   sliced
2 cloves garlic, crushed
4-6 tbsp. oil

2½ cups water or chicken
   stock
1 unripe papaya
2 tbsp. Worcestershire sauce
a good handful of washed
   spinach leaves
salt and pepper

Cut the chicken into eight or more pieces, dry on kitchen towels and set aside. Fry the ginger, onion and garlic in hot oil until soft and tender, but not colored. Lift out and reserve.

Reheat the fat in the pan and fry the chicken pieces on all sides until golden, turning frequently. Add water or stock and seasoning. Stir in the onion, garlic and ginger. Cover and cook over a gentle heat until the chicken pieces are almost cooked — about 35-45 minutes depending on the size.

Wash and cut the papaya in half, remove the seeds and outer skin. Slice evenly and add to the chicken. Cover and cook until the papaya is tender — about 5 minutes.

Bring up to a rapid boil, add the Worcestershire sauce and spinach. Cover and cook for 1 minute. Taste for seasoning and serve.

Chicken Casserole with Coconut Milk
Serves 4

Ingredients

3lb. chicken or 4 chicken quarters
4 cloves garlic, crushed
¾ cup cider vinegar
½-1 tsp. black peppercorns, crushed
2½ cups shredded coconut

1¾ cups boiling water
1½ cups chicken stock or water
oil for frying
1tbsp. soy sauce
cucumber matchsticks and tomato slices to garnish

Wipe the chicken and cut into eight pieces, then the thigh and drumstick into two pieces and the breast and wing into a further two portions. Similarly cut each of the chicken quarters, if using, into two. Place in a glass or glazed bowl, add the garlic, vinegar and peppercorns. Mix well then leave to marinate for 1 hour.

Prepare coconut milk by putting the coconut in a bowl, pouring the boiling water over it, leaving to stand for 15 minutes, then squeezing out the liquid.

Turn the marinaded chicken pieces into a pan with the stock or water. Bring to a boil, but do not cover, then simmer for 25-30 minutes, adding a little extra water if necessary to keep the chicken moist. When the chicken is tender lift out and reduce the cooking liquid to ⅔ cup and set aside.

Clean the pan, add oil and fry the chicken pieces until they are brown all over. Keep warm on a serving dish. Add the coconut milk to the reduced sauce in another pan. Add soy sauce and cook for 4-5 minutes.

Pour over the chicken pieces and garnish with cucumber matchsticks and tomato slices. Serve with freshly boiled rice.

Chicken Buried in Salt
Serves 4

The Chinese claim that this method of cooking ensures that the bird is full of vitamins and is especially good eaten on its own just before going to sleep!

Ingredients

2-lb. fresh chicken
2-in. piece fresh ginger
salt and pepper

7lb. coarse salt (depending on size of casserole)

Preheat the oven to 400°F.

Remove the giblets from the chicken; dry inside and out with paper towels. Tie at the neck with a piece of string and tie up over a bowl so that the chicken will drain and dry.

Peel and bruise the ginger; place it inside the body cavity of the bird and wrap the chicken in a sheet of oiled greaseproof paper. Tie with a piece of string.

Cover the base of an ovenproof casserole with some of the salt. Place the chicken on the salt and spoon the remaining salt over it to complete cover. Cover with a tight fitting lid or foil.

Set in the preheated oven and cook for 1½ hours. Cool a little, then lift the chicken parcel out of the casserole carefully spooning out some of the salt first; it will be hot.

Unwrap the parcel and serve the chicken on a platter, cut up into small portions.

Chicken Curry
Serves 4

Ingredients

1 medium size chicken, cut into pieces and skinned
2 cloves garlic, chopped
1tsp. turmeric
1 onion, finely chopped
1tbsp. curry powder
2 cups water

2 bay leaves
cornstarch
4 bananas, green if possible
2 slices ginger, finely chopped
fresh lemon juice, to taste

Prick the chicken pieces with a fork and rub with a mixture of garlic and turmeric.

Fry half the onion until soft, add the chicken pieces and cook until tender and browned. Keep hot.

To make the curry sauce, fry the rest of the onion. When soft, add the curry powder and cook for 5 minutes, stirring. Add the water and one of the bay leaves. Cook until the sauce thickens, if necessary adding a little cornstarch. Serve the curry sauce separately.

Split each banana into two. Sprinkle the bananas with chopped ginger and fry them in a non-stick skillet with the other bay leaf.

Add the lemon juice to taste and serve with the cooked chicken.

Chicken Breasts with Sesame Seeds
Serves 6

Ingredients

2 eggs
fresh rosemary, chopped
black pepper, freshly ground
2tbsp. fine matzo meal

3tbsp. sesame seeds
2¼lb. chicken breasts (boneless), cut into small pieces
vegetable oil for frying

Mix together the eggs, rosemary and black pepper.

Mix together the matzo meal and sesame seeds.

Dip pieces of the chicken into the egg then the sesame mixture.

When the oil is sizzling drop in the chicken pieces.

When the chicken is golden-brown on one side, sprinkle generously with pepper and turn, sprinkling the other side when it has browned as well.

Drain on kitchen paper and serve.

Chicken Paprika
Serves 6-8

This delectable chicken dish is the perfect centerpiece for a holiday dinner. Although most cookbooks suggest serving it with egg noodles, for true authenticity it should be served on a bed of rice.

Ingredients

4-lb. chicken, cut into	*4tbsp. flour*
pieces	*4tsp. paprika*
1 cup margarine	*¼tsp. salt*
½ cup grated carrots	*pinch of black pepper*
1 cup chopped onions	*½ cup red wine*
3 cloves garlic, quartered	*3½ cups chicken stock*

Place all the ingredients except for half the chicken stock in a large soup pot. Simmer, covered, over a low heat for 1 hour.

Add the remaining stock, reduce the heat to very low and simmer, covered, for 1 hour longer.

Serve on a bed of rice.

Chicken Peanut Casserole
Serves 4

Ingredients

3tbsp. vegetable oil	*4 chicken drumsticks*
2tbsp. butter	*1¼ cups chicken stock*
2 onions, peeled and diced	*2tbsp. peanut butter*
1 clove garlic, crushed	*bouquet garni*
2tbsp. flour	*4tbsp. yogurt*
salt and freshly ground	*¼ cup roasted peanuts,*
pepper	*chopped*
pinch of paprika	*parsley or watercress*
4 chicken thighs	

Heat the oil and butter in a skillet, turn to low heat and cook the onions and garlic for 4 minutes.

Mix the flour with seasoning and paprika and toss the chicken pieces in flour.

Remove the onion to the casserole and, on a higher heat, brown the chicken pieces evenly. Remove, when golden brown, to the casserole dish.

Add any remaining flour to the juices in the pan, mix well and gradually add the stock and peanut butter. Mix and pour over the chicken in the casserole. Add bouquet garni. Cook on top of the stove at a slow simmer for 40 minutes or in the oven at a temperature of 350°F for 50 minutes.

Arrange the chicken on a heated serving dish. Stir the yogurt into the sauce and coat the chicken with the sauce.

Sprinkle with chopped peanuts and garnish with parsley or watercress.

Chicken with Kumquats
Serves 6

Kumquats look like miniature oranges. They are the only citrus fruit which are eaten whole, with the peel.

Ingredients

2 3-lb. chickens, cut into	*5tbsp. honey*
pieces	*1tsp. cayenne pepper*
¼ cup orange juice	*4tbsp. lemon juice*
5tbsp. apricot jam	*¾lb. kumquats, boiled for*
5tbsp. peach jam	*10 minutes, drained*

Preheat the oven to 400°F. Arrange the chicken pieces in a large, lightly greased baking dish and bake for 30 minutes.

Combine the orange juice, apricot jam, peach jam, honey, cayenne pepper and lemon juice in a mixing bowl. Mix well.

After the chicken has baked for 30 minutes, brush the pieces with half the orange juice mixture. Reduce the oven temperature to 350°F and bake for 15 minutes.

Turn the chicken pieces over and brush them with the remaining orange juice mixture. Arrange the kumquats in the pan with the chicken. Bake for 15 minutes longer.

Pour the pan juices over the chicken and kumquats before serving.

Chicken and Mushroom Lasagne
Serves 4-6

Ingredients

1 onion, peeled and diced	*salt and freshly ground*
2tbsp. butter	*white pepper*
½ cup mushrooms, washed	*9 sheets "non cook"*
and sliced	*lasagne*
2 cups cooked chicken,	*2tbsp. fresh breadcrumbs*
diced	*2tbsp. grated Parmesan*
1tbsp. chopped parsley	*cheese*
2 cups Béchamel Sauce	

Cook the onion in the butter over a low heat for about 3 minutes. Add the mushrooms and cook for a further 2 minutes. Add the chicken to the mushroom and onions, season well and mix with chopped parsley. Make up the Béchamel Sauce, season well. Place about 4tbsp. sauce in the bottom of an ovenproof dish. Cover with one third of the chicken mixture. Put sheets of lasagne on top to cover. (If using fresh it can be cooked in boiling water for 3 minutes.)

Place a further 4tbsp. sauce on top of the lasagne and a further third of the chicken mixture. Continue with third layer of lasagne, top with remaining Béchamel Sauce.

Mix the fresh crumbs with the cheese and sprinkle on top. Bake in the oven at a temperature of 350°F for 25 minutes until golden brown.

Chicken Satay
Serves 4

Ingredients

Marinade
2¼ cups boiling water
1 cup shredded coconut
1 green onion, washed and
    chopped
1in. fresh ginger, grated
grated rind of 1 lemon
pinch ground cinnamon
6 cardamom pods
1tsp. cumin
1tsp. ground coriander
1tbsp. chopped parsley
1½lb. boneless chicken

Satay Sauce
¾ cup peanuts
4 shallots, peeled and
    chopped
2 cloves garlic, peeled
6 macadamia, almond or
    cashew nuts
2 stems lemon grass
    (optional)
3tbsp. coconut or peanut
    oil
2-3tsp. chili powder
1¼ cup coconut milk
tamarind water made from
    1tbsp. tamarind pulp or
    dried, soaked in 4tbsp.
    hot water and squeezed
    out
1tbsp. brown sugar
salt to taste
chopped green onion

Pour the boiling water over the coconut. Leave for 15 minutes, then squeeze out. Measure out 1¼ cups of the liquid and reserve it. Mix the rest with the marinade ingredients. Cut chicken breasts and thighs into small pieces or use a whole chicken if liked. Cut meat from breasts and legs as needed. Marinate the chicken overnight in the refrigerator or at least for several hours. Remove from marinade and thread on to wooden or metal skewers.

To make the sauce, first toast the peanuts in a hot oven for about 20 minutes. Rub off the skins in a dish towel and grind for just a few seconds in the liquidizer. Do not reduce the nuts to a powder — this would spoil the consistency of the sauce.

Grind or pound the onions and garlic and grind or pound the macadamia nuts and lemon grass.

Fry the onion mixture in hot oil, then add the nut and lemon grass paste. Reduce the heat, add the chili powder and cook for 2 minutes.

Stir all the time while adding the reserved coconut milk. Allow to come to the boil, then reduce the heat and add tamarind water, sugar, salt to taste and peanuts. Cook for 2-3 minutes and stir frequently until the sauce thickens.

Broil the chicken skewers for 4 minutes each side under a high heat, then allow to cook for a further 4 minutes each side under a medium heat.

Serve with satay sauce dip and a green salad, the sauce garnished with green onion.

Chicken Escalopes
Serves 4

Ingredients

4 chicken breasts, boned
salt and freshly ground
    pepper
4tbsp. bran
pinch paprika

1 egg, beaten
2tbsp. butter
3tbsp. vegetable oil
lemon wedges to garnish

Cut the chicken breasts in half and place each half between a sheet of foil or plastic wrap and beat to an escalope shape with a rolling pin. Season each side well. Mix the bran with the paprika. Dip chicken in beaten egg, and coat evenly with bran. Heat the butter and oil in a skillet and, over a medium to high heat, fry the chicken breasts on both sides until golden. They will need about 5 minutes on each side. Turn the heat down after the first 5 minutes. Keep warm in a low oven. Garnish with lemon wedges.

Oriental Chicken and Mushroom Stew
Serves 4

Ingredients

*1½ cups boned chicken,
    with skin*
4 large mushrooms, wiped
2 medium carrots
*1 cup fresh or canned
    bean sprouts*
4 small potatoes, scrubbed
2in. square tofu (optional)

1-2tbsp. vegetable oil
*1 cup well-flavored chicken
    stock*
2tbsp. sugar
2tbsp. dry sherry
3tbsp. soy sauce
8 snow peas
cress to garnish

Cut the chicken into ¾-in. cubes. Wash and trim the vegetables and cut into small chunks.

For the best flavor, the vegetables should then be parboiled separately in lightly salted water, rinsed and drained.

Heat the oil in a large saucepan over high heat.

Drop the chicken pieces into the oil and stir-fry to coat in oil. Add the carrots and tofu, if using, and then the mushrooms, bean sprouts and potatoes.

Stir-fry for 3 minutes, until the chicken and vegetables are lightly cooked and evenly coated with oil. Ladle the stock over them, add the sugar, dry sherry and soy sauce, and bring to a boil.

Cover and simmer for 15 minutes, until the simmering stock is glossy and reduced by one-third.

Trim the snow peas and slice diagonally into 1-in. slices. Parboil them in lightly salted water, and add to the chicken and vegetables just before serving.

Serve hot or at room temperature in individual bowls, arranging the vegetables attractively. Garnish with cress.

Chinese Chicken with Pineapple and Cashew Nuts
Serves 4-6

Serve with plain boiled rice and jasmine tea for a quick and tasty Chinese meal.

Ingredients

*1lb. chicken breasts,
    skinned and boned*
3tsp. cornstarch
*12oz. can pineapple
    chunks in natural juice*
2tbsp. dry sherry
2tbsp. oil
*1-in. piece fresh root ginger,
    peeled and sliced*

*2 cloves garlic, peeled and
    sliced*
½ cup cashew nuts
*6 green onions, trimmed
    and sliced*
salt

Quarter the chicken breasts and chop roughly. Coat with 1tsp. of the cornstarch, and set aside.

Drain the juice from the pineapple, and measure a scant cup. Mix with the remaining cornstarch and the sherry.

Heat the oil in a wok or large skillet, and add the sliced ginger and garlic. Stir-fry for a few seconds, then add the chicken. Stir-fry over high heat, making sure the chicken pieces remain separate. When the chicken has become golden brown (after about 2 minutes), add the cashew nuts, and stir-fry for 1 minute. Add the pineapple and the juice mixture.

Bring to a boil, stirring constantly, and cook for another minute. Stir in the green onions, and add salt to taste. Serve immediately.

Cold Chicken Millefoglie
Serves 4-6

Ingredients

¾lb. Puff Pastry dough	2 pinches cayenne pepper
½ cup Basic Garlic	1tbsp. lemon juice
Dressing	½ cup stiffly whipped
8-10 canned artichoke	cream
hearts, quartered	1⅓ cups cold cooked
½tbsp. oil	chicken, cut or torn into
1 clove of garlic, crushed	bite-sized pieces
1tsp. ground coriander	salt and pepper
½tsp. ground cumin	2tbsp. finely chopped
½tsp. turmeric	parsley
½tsp. paprika	1tbsp. Mayonnaise or Aïoli

Roll the pastry dough out thinly and cut into 3 strips approximately 4in. wide. Prick all over with a fork and bake for 7 to 10 minutes at 450°F until well-risen and browned. Cool on a wire rack until needed.

Warm the Basic Garlic Dressing and pour over the artichoke hearts. Set aside for at least 1 hour.

To make the sauce for the chicken, heat the oil and add to it the garlic, coriander, cumin, turmeric, paprika, and cayenne. Stir over a moderate heat for several minutes. Remove from the heat and add the lemon juice, and either pour or strain the mixture into the cream. Fold the chicken into the sauce and season with salt and pepper to taste.

To assemble the Millefoglie, put one slice of cooked pastry on a serving dish and spread over it half the chicken mixture. Drain the dressing from the artichoke hearts, mix into them the parsley and put half of this on top of the chicken. Top with the second piece of pastry, the remaining chicken, and the rest of the artichoke mixture.

Spread the underside of the final pastry slice with the mayonnaise or Aïoli and press it gently, sticky side down, onto the artichoke and parsley mixture.

Chicken Stuffed with Fruit and Nuts
Serves 6

Ingredients

3½-lb. oven-ready chicken	½ cup prunes, pitted and
salt and freshly ground	coarsely chopped
pepper	4tbsp. roasted almonds,
2 medium onions, peeled	roughly chopped
2 slices crustless wholewheat	4tbsp. roasted hazelnuts,
bread, finely crumbled	roughly chopped
½ cup butter	¼ cup pine nuts
1 large cooking apple,	1tbsp. raisins
peeled and cored	1¼ cups good chicken stock
½ cup apricots, coarsely	1tbsp. fresh thyme
chopped	

Wipe the chicken inside and out and season inside. Quarter one of the onions and put in a roasting pan.

Grate or grind the bread to form fine crumbs. Set aside. Finely chop the other onion. Heat half the butter in a skillet and slowly cook the onion until soft and golden.

Add the apple, apricots and prunes to the onion and fry for 1 minute. Then add the chopped almonds, hazelnuts, pine nuts and raisins to the pan. Take the pan off the heat and mix in the breadcrumbs. Add 1tbsp. of the stock and season with salt and pepper. Cool, then use to stuff the chicken. Stand the chicken

on the onion in the roasting pan. Rub with the remaining butter, sprinkle with salt and pepper and the thyme. Roast at a temperature of 400°F in a preheated oven for about 1¼ hours, basting frequently.

Remove the cooked chicken to a warmed serving dish, and keep warm. Add the stock to the pan, and bring to a boil on top of the stove, stirring to dislodge all the meat juices. Skim off any fat. Boil the gravy till reduced by a third. Season to taste, then strain and serve.

Variation This is a delicious way of cooking the Christmas turkey.

Chicken Garam Masala
Serves 4

Ingredients

1 cup chopped onions	1tsp. salt
1tbsp. grated fresh ginger	½ cup tomatoes, skinned
2 cloves garlic	and chopped
3tbsp. Ghee (Clarified	1 medium chicken, jointed
Butter) or butter	and skinned
1tsp. cumin seeds	2tbsp. coriander seeds,
1tsp. ground coriander	chopped
1tsp. turmeric	1tsp. Garam Masala
1tsp. chili powder	2¼ cups water

Liquidize the onion, ginger and garlic to a smooth paste.

Heat the ghee or butter in a heavy-based saucepan. Add the onion mixture. Cook, stirring frequently, until golden brown. Add 1tbsp. water to prevent the mixture from sticking to the pan, more if required.

Add the cumin seeds, ground coriander, turmeric, chili powder and salt. Stir in well.

Add the tomatoes. Cook until the tomatoes are reduced to a pulp. Again, add a little water if the mixture is sticking to the pan.

Gently add the chicken pieces. Cook, still stirring, until the chicken turns golden brown and has absorbed the flavor of the spices.

Add the water to make the sauce.

Cover and cook on a low heat for 35 minutes, or until the chicken is tender. Do not let it fall off the bone.

Sprinkle with the chopped coriander and garam masala. Cover again and cook for a further 10 minutes.

Holiday Fried Chicken
Serves 8

This Italian version of fried chicken makes an excellent buffet dish.

Ingredients

1tsp. salt	*3tbsp. lemon juice*
½tsp. black pepper	*1 cup olive oil*
pinch ground nutmeg	*1 cup+2tbsp. flour*
pinch ground cinnamon	*2 eggs, beaten*
½tsp. finely chopped garlic	*lemon wedges*
2 small chickens, cut into small pieces	

In a small mixing bowl, combine the salt, pepper, nutmeg, cinnamon and garlic. Mix well. Rub the chicken pieces with the mixture and then sprinkle them with the lemon juice.

Heat the oil in a large heavy skillet over a moderate heat until it is very hot.

Dip half the spiced chicken pieces in the flour and then in the egg. Sauté, turning frequently, for 20 minutes. Keep the pieces from the first batch in a warm oven while cooking the remainder.

Serve hot with lemon wedges.

Deep-fried Soy Chicken
Serves 4

Morsels of chicken marinated in soy sauce become a rich reddish brown. Fresh ginger gives a tang to the marinade and is frequently used to accompany chicken in Japanese cooking.

Ingredients

1½lb. boned chicken, skin attached	**Marinade**
6tbsp. cornstarch	*4tbsp. soy sauce*
vegetable oil for deep frying	*2tbsp. dry sherry*
1 lemon, washed, dried and quartered	*1tsp. sugar*
	pinch of ginger
4 sprigs parsley, washed and patted dry	*lemon quarters*
	parsley sprigs

Cut the chicken into large bite-size chunks. Mix the marinade ingredients and pour over the chicken. Mix well so that the chicken is evenly covered. Set aside to marinate for 30 minutes.

Drain the chicken and coat with cornstarch. Wait for a few minutes so that the coating can set.

In a small saucepan, heat oil for deep frying to 350°F. Carefully put the chicken in the oil, a few pieces at a time, and deep-fry for about 3 minutes, until crisp and brown.

Remove piece by piece and drain.

Serve garnished with lemon quarters and sprigs of parsley.

Glazed Chicken Wings
Serves 8

Ingredients

3lb. chicken wings	*pinch cayenne*
4tbsp. Tomato Sauce	*½ cup white wine*
½tsp. garlic powder	*4tbsp. honey*
½tsp. onion powder	*4tbsp. apricot preserve*
pinch ground ginger	*2tbsp. peach preserve*

Preheat the oven to 375°F. Cut the tips from the wings (discard or save them for stock). Spread the chicken wings in one layer in a large greased pan. Bake for 30 minutes.

Meanwhile, mix together the tomato sauce, garlic powder, onion powder, ginger, cayenne pepper and wine in a small bowl.

Spoon the mixture over the chicken wings and bake for a further 30 minutes. While the wings are cooking, mix together the honey, apricot and peach preserves in a small bowl. Brush the glaze over the chicken wings. Raise the heat to 400°F and bake for a further 10 to 15 minutes, or until the wings are golden and glazed.

Fried Chicken Wings
Serves 3-4

Ingredients

2 cloves garlic, crushed	*1tsp. sugar*
3tbsp. oil	*2tbsp. white wine*
3 pinches cayenne	*salt and pepper*
½tsp. oregano	*10 chicken wings*
1tsp. paprika	*seasoned flour*
2tsp. vinegar	

Combine the garlic, half the oil, the cayenne, oregano, paprika, vinegar, sugar, white wine and plenty of salt and pepper. Cut a few slits in each chicken wing and put them in a large plastic bag. Pour over the marinade and knot the top of the bag. Put the bag in a bowl to prevent leaking, and leave in a cool place for 2 to 4 hours. Drain the chicken wings of the marinade and toss them in the seasoned flour. Fry in the remaining oil for approximately 10 minutes, turning occasionally, until well browned. Drain on paper towels and serve hot with brown rice and salad.

Double Garlic Chicken
Serves 4

Ingredients

3 heads garlic (about 35 cloves)
3½-4lb. roasting chicken
¾ cup cream cheese or low fat soft cheese
1tbsp. chives, chopped

1tbsp. parsley, chopped
salt and pepper
½lb. seedless green grapes
1 sprig of rosemary
2tbsp. butter

Plunge the unpeeled garlic, except for 2 cloves, into a pan of boiling water for 30 seconds, drain and peel. Boil for a further 2 minutes, drain and set to one side.

Peel one of the remaining garlic cloves and cut it in half. Rub the cut side of the garlic over the breast and legs of the chicken, then slice it and its other half.

Peel and crush the last garlic clove and blend it with the cream or low fat cheese, chives and parsley. Season well with salt and pepper.

Work your fingers under the skin of the chicken breast, carefully freeing it from the meat without tearing it.

Pack the cheese mixture between the loosened skin and the meat, covering the breast completely.

Stuff the body of the chicken with the blanched garlic and the grapes, together with most of the rosemary.

Put the chicken in an oiled roasting pan and tuck slices of garlic and the remaining blades of rosemary between the legs and wings and the body of the chicken.

Sprinkle the breast with salt and dot it with the butter. Cover the breast and feet with foil.

Bake for approximately an hour and a half at 350°F, until the juice no longer runs pink, removing the foil for the last 20 minutes of cooking to crisp the skin.

Drunken Chicken
Serves 4-6

Ingredients

3-lb. fresh chicken
½in. fresh ginger, scraped and sliced
2 green onions
7½ cups water or to cover

1tsp. salt
1¼ cups dry sherry
brandy (optional)
green onion curls to garnish

Wipe the chicken inside and out. Place the ginger and green onion in the body cavity. Set the chicken in a large pan or flameproof casserole and cover with water. Bring to a boil, skim and cook for 15 minutes. Turn off the heat and allow the chicken to stay in the cooking liquid for 3-4 hours, by which time it will be cooked. Lift out and drain well. Reserve 1¼ cups of the stock. Cool and skim.

First of all remove the leg joints — divide each into a drumstick and thigh. Now cut away the wings to include some of the breast. Cut away the breast still on the bone and divide it into two pieces. Arrange these chicken portions in a shallow glass or glazed dish (only use enamel if it is unchipped). Rub salt into the skin of the chicken, leave for several hours or overnight.

Next day mix the sherry and a few tablespoons of brandy, if you like, with an equal amount of chicken stock and pour over the chicken pieces. Cover with plastic wrap or a lid and leave in a refrigerator or cool place for at least 2 or 3 days; turn over occasionally.

When ready to serve, cut into chunky pieces through the bone and arrange on a serving platter garnished with green onion curls.

pineapple. Cover and cook in a preheated oven at a temperature of 350°F for 1 hour.

Garnish with strips of blanched pepper and pineapple rings.

Poulet au Roquefort
Serves 4

Ingredients

4 chicken pieces	¼lb. Roquefort or other
1tbsp. butter	blue cheese
salt and pepper	2tsp. cornstarch
1¼ cups yogurt	1tbsp. water

Brown the chicken in butter and remove it to a casserole. Season well. Blend the yogurt and blue cheese together until the mixture is smooth.

Mix the cornstarch and water and add to the yogurt mixture. Pour over the chicken. Cover and bake at 350°F for 50 minutes. Uncover and return to the oven for a further 10 minutes.

Jellied Chicken Salad
Serves 4

Ingredients

5oz. package of lemon jelly	½ cup farmer's cheese
1¼ cups boiling water	1 stick celery, chopped
juice of 1 lemon	4 thin slices of lemon
2 cups diced cooked chicken	

Dissolve the jelly in the boiling water and add the lemon juice. Stir well and set aside ⅓ cup. Leave the jelly to cool.

Mix in the chicken, cheese and chopped celery and put the mixture into a serving dish. Refrigerate until set. If the reserved jelly in the cup has set, melt it by standing the cup in a pan of boiling water.

Put the lemon slices on top of the chicken mixture and carefully spoon over the reserved jelly. Leave to set before serving.

Lemon Chicken with Wholewheat Spaghetti
Serves 2

Ingredients

4 thick slices cooked chicken	6oz. wholewheat spaghetti
	oil
1¼ cups Béchamel Sauce	parsley sprigs
2tsp. lime juice	lemon wedges
juice of ½ lemon	

Heat the chicken in the Béchamel Sauce which has had the lime and lemon juice added.

Cook the pasta 2-3 minutes if fresh (12 minutes if dried) in boiling salted water with a few drops of oil added. Drain and toss in a little butter.

Serve with the chicken in sauce, garnished with parsley sprigs and lemon wedges.

Malaysian Chicken
Serves 4

Ingredients

2 green onions, washed	½tsp. paprika
2 stalks celery, washed	½tsp. cumin
1 onion, peeled	4tbsp. oil
1 clove garlic	1⅓ cups toasted shredded
1 red pepper, seeded	coconut
1 chili pepper, seeded	2½ cups chicken stock
4 portions chicken	¼lb. pineapple, chopped
1tbsp. flour	8 strips of blanched red
salt and freshly ground pepper	pepper
	4 pineapple rings

Prepare the vegetables and purée in a blender or food processor.

Toss the chicken portions in seasoned flour with paprika and cumin added.

Heat the oil in a casserole or skillet and fry the chicken until golden. Turn the heat to low and add the puréed vegetables. Mix well with the chicken.

Add the coconut, chicken stock, seasoning and

Traditional Roast Chicken
Serves 6

Ingredients

3½-4lb. roasting chicken, with liver
1tsp. salt
2 cloves garlic, finely chopped
1tbsp. ground ginger
1tsp. cayenne
1¾ cups fresh breadcrumbs
2 stalks chopped celery
½ cup chopped mushrooms
¼ cup shredded carrots
2tbsp. vegetable oil
1tbsp. chopped fresh parsley or 1tsp. dried
½tsp. dried thyme
½tsp. dried marjoram
4tbsp. butter or margarine, melted
1 cup boiling water
3lb. potatoes, cut into sixths
3 large onions, cut into sixths

Preheat the oven to 350°F. Place the cleaned chicken on a greased roasting pan. Reserve the chicken liver. Sprinkle the skin with ½tsp. each of the salt, garlic, ginger and cayenne pepper. Roast the chicken for 30 minutes.

While the chicken roasts, prepare the stuffing. In a mixing bowl, combine the breacrumbs with the celery, mushrooms, carrots, oil, and the remaining salt, garlic, ginger and cayenne pepper. Add the parsley, thyme and marjoram. Mix well.

Put the chicken liver in a small saucepan and add enough cold water to cover. Bring to a boil and cook until the liver is done, about 10 minutes. Drain well. Chop the liver coarsely. Add the chopped liver to the stuffing mixture. Add the melted butter or margarine and a boiling water. Mix well.

Remove the chicken from the oven and fill the cavity with the stuffing. Arrange the potato and onion pieces around the chicken in the roasting pan. Return the chicken to the oven and roast for 1½ to 2 hours basting with the pan drippings every 30 minutes.

Sprinkle the chicken, potatoes and onions with paprika after the final basting.

Lemon Chicken with Wholewheat Spaghetti

Penang Chicken Curry
Serves 4

Penang Chicken Curry doesn't look special under its mound of fried onions, but the smell really is special and the taste is out of this world.

Ingredients

3-lb. fresh chicken, divided into 8 pieces
2½ cups shredded coconut just over 1 cup boiling water
1tbsp. tamarind, pulp or dried
⅔ cup water
1tsp. yeast extract
2-4 fresh chili peppers or 1-2 tsp. chili powder
2 macadamia nuts or almonds
2 stems lemongrass
1-in. piece fresh ginger
2 cloves garlic
1-2tsp. ground turmeric
4tbsp. coconut or cooking oil
salt
piece cinnamon
6 green or white cardamom pods, bruised but left whole
2 large onions, finely sliced and deep fried or a handful of chopped coriander to garnish

Wipe the chicken and set aside. Make coconut milk by pouring the boiling water over the shredded coconut, leaving it to stand for 15 minutes, then squeezing out the liquid. Soak the tamarind in the water for 10 minutes, squeeze out, and reserve the juice. Pound the prepared and chopped chili peppers, nuts, lemongrass, ginger and garlic into a paste with the yeast extract; if using dried chili, add it to the paste. Stir in the turmeric.

Heat the oil and fry the spice mixture for a few minutes without browning. Stir in the chicken pieces until they are all coated with the spices. Add salt. Pour in the coconut milk and tamarind juice. Add the cinnamon and cardomom pods. Cook uncovered over a gentle heat for 35-45 minutes until almost all the sauce has cooked away. Taste for salt. Test the chicken pieces with a skewer. When tender, serve in a hot bowl. This is traditionally served with a topping of crispy fried onions, but you may prefer to use chopped coriander instead.

Ingredients

3-lb. chicken	¹/₂tsp. Szechuan
3tbsp. soy sauce	peppercorns, crushed
3tbsp. dry sherry	1 piece dried tangerine
salt	peel, crushed
3 green onions	2tbsp. wine vinegar
2tbsp. seasoned cornstarch	approx ²/₃ cup chicken
deep fat for frying	stock
1-2 dried red peppers (or	salt to taste
more if you like this dish	
hot), dry fried then	
crushed	

Cut the chicken into eight pieces first and then each of these into a further two or three pieces. Marinate for 3-4 hours in soy sauce together with sherry, salt and one chopped green onion. Chop the remaining green onions and set aside for garnish.

Drain the chicken pieces and reserve the marinade. Dust the chicken with cornstarch and deep fry in two or three lots for about 7 minutes or until golden and crisp. Lift out and keep warm.

In another pan, heat a little oil and fry the pepper, peppercorns and crushed tangerine rind for a minute. Add the cooked chicken pieces and toss all together. Pour in the vinegar and cook over a higher heat until the vinegar evaporates. Keep moving the chicken around in the pan. Add sufficient stock to the marinade to make up to a scant cup Pour into the pan. Do not cover.

Cook for 15 minutes or until the liquid evaporates, stirring occasionally. Serve at once sprinkled with green onions.

Paper-Wrapped Chicken
Serves 3-4

Ingredients

2 chicken breasts, skinned	1 small bunch green
and boned	onions, washed and
3tbsp. soy sauce	dried
1tbsp. dry sherry	¹/₄lb. cooked ham
1tbsp. granulated sugar	oil for deep frying
pinch of freshly ground	stir-fried snow peas or
black pepper	broccoli to garnish
1¹/₂in. fresh ginger, scraped	
and sliced, then crushed	
in garlic press	

Cut the chicken into pieces the size of your little finger. Marinate in a mixture of soy sauce, wine or sherry, sugar, black pepper and ginger.

Meanwhile cut the green onions into 2¹/₂-in. lengths and the ham into small pieces. Prepare 7-in. squares of waxed paper to make the parcels. Brush the paper with oil, then lay a piece of marinated chicken in the middle, top with a little green onion, ham and another piece of chicken. Fold the paper up almost corner to corner to make a triangle. Fold sides to middle to make an envelope shape, then tuck the flap in to form a neat parcel. (Seal with a staple if your prefer, but do warn your guests when they open their parcels.) Repeat with the remaining ingredients.

Fry several parcels at a time in hot oil for 2-3 minutes. Do not overcook or let the paper turn brown. Serve hot, garnished with snow peas or broccoli and any remaining green onions.

Salt-Broiled Chicken
Serves 4

Salt-broiling accentuates the succulent taste of chicken.

Ingredients

8 small boned chicken	salt
thighs, skin intact	lemon wedges
2tbsp. sherry	

Sprinkle the chicken thighs with sherry and leave to stand for 5 to 10 minutes to tenderize. Thread onto skewers.

Sprinkle both sides liberally with salt.

Broil over (or under) a hot flame for 10 minutes, turning occasionally, until the skin is golden and the flesh is cooked but still moist.

Serve hot or at room temperature, garnished with lemon wedges.

Chicken with Tangerine Peel
Serves 4-6

Szechuan peppercorns and dried tangerine peel are available at oriental grocers. If you cannot get them, use crushed whole allspice and dry your own tangerine peel in the oven.

cavity to prevent damage to the skin or breast.

Allow to cool slightly, then lift out and chop into bite-sized pieces to serve. Serve scattered with green onions.

The sauce can be reserved and used again, several times in fact, with the flavor improving on each occasion as it gets stronger and matures.

Chicken in Mole Sauce
Serves 6

This Mexican dish is an ideal way of using up leftover chicken or turkey. Totally unsweetened chocolate is best for this dish; it can sometimes be found at Caribbean grocers.

Ingredients

1 large chicken, jointed	1/2tsp. coriander seeds
1 medium onion, coarsely chopped	2tbsp. whole almonds or pecans
6 tomatoes, peeled, or 15oz. can tomatoes	2tbsp. peanuts
3 red chili peppers, seeded and chopped	1/2-in cinnamon stick, broken up
2 cloves garlic	2tbsp. olive oil
2tbsp. sesame seeds	2oz. plain chocolate

Put the chicken pieces and onion in a pan. Season and add water to cover. Simmer, covered, for 20 minutes. Remove the chicken and drain on a paper towel. Reserve the stock.

To make the sauce, blend together the cooked onion, tomatoes, chili peppers and garlic. Grind the seeds, nuts and cinnamon. Heat the olive oil in a large, heavy-based saucepan and brown the chicken. Add the tomato mixture and the ground nut mixture. Cook for 5 minutes. Add half the chicken stock and the chocolate, broken into pieces. Stir over a low heat until the chocolate is dissolved.

Bring to a boil and simmer until the chicken is cooked, adding more stock if necessary.

Spicy Roast Chicken
Serves 4

Ingredients
3 1/2-lb. chicken, cleaned

Stuffing
1tbsp. oil
1/4 cup finely chopped onion
1 large potato, boiled and diced
2 eggs, boiled and chopped
1/2 cup peas, boiled
1/2tsp. salt
pinch of pepper
1—2 green chili peppers, chopped
1tbsp. coriander leaves, chopped
1 1/2tbsp. ground almonds

Marinade
1/4lb. onions, cut up
2-3 cloves garlic
1-in. ginger root
1/2tsp. ground turmeric
1/2tsp. chili powder
1/2tsp. Garam Masala
2tbsp. blanched almonds
1/2 cup yogurt
1tsp. salt
4tbsp. oil

Heat the oil in a pan over a medium high heat. Fry the onion until lightly golden. Add all the remaining stuffing ingredients and fry for another 2-3 minutes. Pack into the body cavity of the chicken.

Blend together all the marinade ingredients except the oil. Stir the oil into the blended mixture. Rub the chicken all over with the marinade and set aside for 5-6 hours.

Roast the chicken in a preheated oven at 425°F for 20 minutes. Cover with foil, lower heat to 375°F and bake for a further 1 1/2 hours. Remove the cover for the last 30 minutes of the cooking time.

To serve, place the chicken on a platter and offer the sauce separately in a bowl.

Red-Cooked Chicken
Serves 4-6

Ingredients
3-lb. fresh chicken
1 clove garlic, peeled and crushed
1/2in. fresh ginger, scraped and chopped
scant cup chicken stock

scant cup each light and dark soy sauce
1 star anise
1tbsp. sugar
2tbsp. sherry
green onions

Plunge the chicken into a pan of boiling water to completely cover it. Cook for 3-4 minutes. Carefully lift out and drain.

Put breast-side down in another large pan or flameproof casserole and add the garlic, ginger, chicken stock, soy sauces, star anise, sugar and sherry. Allow to come to a boil, cover and simmer for 45-60 minutes or until the chicken is tender, turning it over two or three times so that it is evenly cooked in the rich sauce. Turn by inserting a roasting fork into the body

Tandoori Chicken
Serves 4

This utterly delicious and extremely easy-to-make dish is good with *Nan* (Indian bread). Several points are worth noting. You need small pieces of chicken, otherwise it is difficult to cook them thoroughly by broiling. Baby chickens, cut up, would be excellent, or ask your butcher to cut a larger bird into small pieces. You can use more marinade if you like. If using fresh chickens you can freeze the marinaded chicken uncooked. It freezes well but, as always with poultry, make sure it is thoroughly defrosted before cooking.

Ingredients
1¼ cup yogurt	1 tbsp. oil
1 in. piece root ginger, crushed	1 tsp. ground coriander
2 cloves garlic, crushed	a few drops red coloring (optional)
salt and pepper	3½-4 lb. roasting chicken, cut into 8 pieces
¼ tsp. garam masala	lemon wedges
½ tsp. red chili pepper	

Mix everything except the chicken and lemon together in a large bowl.

Remove the skin from the chicken and put the pieces into the yogurt mixture to marinate for 24 hours. Turn the pieces from time to time.

Broil the marinated chicken for at least 10 minutes on each side, basting with the juices. Serve with the lemon wedges.

Sesame Chicken
Serves 4

Ingredients
1 tbsp. cornstarch	1 large clove garlic, crushed
3 tbsp. water	salt and pepper
1¼ cups yogurt	4 pieces of chicken
3 tbsp. tahini	2 tbsp. sesame seeds

Mix the cornstarch and water to make a smooth paste and add the yogurt, tahini, garlic, salt and pepper.

Put the chicken pieces in a shallow ovenproof dish; prick the skin with a fork. Spread the yogurt mixture over the chicken. Bake, uncovered at 350°F for 50 minutes, basting from time to time.

Scatter the sesame seeds over the chicken and put under the broiler for 5 minutes to brown.

Stuffed Baby Chickens
Serves 4

Ingredients
2 cups yogurt	4 baby chickens, skin removed
1 tbsp. cornstarch	½ cup rice, cooked
4 tbsp. water	6 tbsp. raisins
1½ tsp. ground cumin	4 tbsp. flaked almonds
1½ tsp. ground cinnamon	
salt and pepper	

First prepare the yogurt sauce. Put the yogurt into a saucepan. Mix together the cornstarch and water. Stir into the yogurt. Put on a medium heat, bring to a boil and then reduce the heat and simmer gently for 10 minutes, stirring from time to time. Remove from the heat and add the cumin, cinnamon, salt and pepper. Leave to cool while you stuff the baby chickens.

Mix the rice, raisins, almonds and salt and pepper together and stuff the mixture inside the baby chickens. Tie the legs together with string or thread. Place the baby chickens in a shallow oven dish. Spoon over the prepared yogurt mixture. Bake at 350°F for 1 hour. Baste with the sauce after 30 minutes. Remove from the oven dish and put them onto a serving dish. Spoon over the sauce.

Serve with a brightly colored vegetable, such as carrots or peas.

Yakitori
Serves 4

Ingredients
6 tbsp. soy sauce	4 chicken thighs, boned
¼ cup sake	4 green onions, or ½ green pepper, seeded and cut into 8 pieces
½ cup mirin or sweet sherry	
8 chicken livers (optional)	

Heat the soy sauce, sake and mirin together, stirring all the time until it comes to a boil. Cook without a cover for 2-3 minutes until it has reduced to two-thirds, then cool.

Meanwhile clean the chicken livers, cutting away any threads with scissors. Cut the chicken thighs into even-sized pieces for broiling, about 1 in. Cut the green onions into the same size lengths. Thread the halved chicken livers, if you are using them, onto skewers with the chicken pieces and green onion or green pepper.

Pour the marinade into a jam jar and dip each skewer of food into this. Set under a hot broiler or over a barbecue. Dip in the marinade three or four times during the 10 minute cooking period.

Serve at once to enjoy this succulent dish at its best.

Curry-fried Turkey
Serves 4

Ingredients

1½lb. turkey breasts, boned and skinned	½tsp. ground turmeric
2 cloves garlic, peeled	½tsp. salt
1-in. piece fresh root ginger, peeled	1tsp. ground cumin
3 medium tomatoes, peeled	½tsp. ground fennel
1tsp. tomato paste	pinch ground nutmeg
½tbsp. fresh coriander leaves	pinch ground cinnamon
	2 drops Tabasco
	2tbsp. oil

Freeze the turkey until very firm. Slice very thinly, using a sharp knife or the slicing disc of a food processor, then turn into a shallow glass or china bowl. Using the metal blade, liquidize or process the garlic with the ginger.

Add all the remaining ingredients, except for the oil and blend for 20 seconds. Tip into the bowl and stir into the sliced turkey until well mixed. Cover and leave to marinate overnight in the fridge.

When ready to serve, heat the oil in a heavy skillet or heavy deep-frying pan. Add the meat and the marinade and fry over medium high heat for about 10 minutes, stirring frequently, until the turkey is golden brown and slightly crispy.

Serve hot with Nutty Rice Pilau or Spicy Potatoes or cold with a tossed green salad, and a rice salad.

Variation Replace the turkey with lean steak, chicken breasts, fillet of lamb or pork, or pheasant breasts.

Deviled Turkey Legs
Serves 4

Ingredients

4 cooked turkey legs or thighs	pinch ground ginger
melted butter or margarine	salt
breadcrumbs, browned	black pepper
1tsp. mustard powder	1tsp. cayenne pepper

Chop unsightly bits of bone off legs and thighs. Score the flesh deeply with a sharp knife and brush with melted butter.

Put breadcrumbs in a bowl and mix the rest of the ingredients with them.

Spread the breadcrumb mixture over the turkey pieces, pressing it well into the scored cuts, and leave them to stand for an hour.

Broil on a greased broiling pan until crisp and brown.

Serve at once with pats of butter.

Lemon Turkey
Serves 4

Ingredients

1¼lb. turkey fillet	salt and pepper
juice and rind of 2 lemons	1tbsp. cornstarch
⅔ cup chicken stock	1tbsp. water
½tsp. sugar	⅔ cup yogurt

Cut the turkey fillets lengthwise into thin strips. Put them in a shallow pan and add the lemon juice and a little grated rind, the stock, sugar, salt and pepper. Poach the turkey on a gentle heat for 20 minutes.

Mix the cornstarch and water to a smooth paste. Add this to the pan and stir around to thicken the poaching liquid. Add the yogurt and cook for a further 5 minutes on a gentle heat. Adjust the seasoning.

Serve with a colorful vegetable — carrots or mangetout would go well.

Roast Turkey
Serves 6-8

Ingredients

9-lb. turkey	2tbsp. vinegar
1 green pepper, finely chopped	2tsp. turmeric
2tsp. ginger	2tsp. black pepper
2 onions, finely chopped	2tsp. Garam Masala
4½ cups half-cooked brown rice	

Wash the turkey and remove its skin.

For the stuffing, mix together the green pepper, ginger, onions, rice and ½tsp. vinegar and pack it into the bird.

Prepare a paste of turmeric, black pepper, garam masala, and the rest of the vinegar. Rub it onto the bird.

Cover with foil and bake in the oven at 325°F for 20 minutes for each 1lb.

Baste frequently with butter and the turkey's own fat.

Remove the foil to brown the turkey 20 minutes before taking it out of the oven.

Turkey Mole
Serves 8

This authentic Mexican dish uses unsweetened chocolate and has a rich, cinnamon taste that is quite unusual.

Ingredients

8-10lb. turkey, cut into 8 serving pieces	$\frac{1}{2}$tsp. ground cinnamon
1$\frac{1}{2}$ cups finely chopped onions	$\frac{1}{2}$tsp. ground cloves
3 tomatoes, skinned, seeded and coarsely chopped	1 cup finely chopped almonds
$\frac{2}{3}$ cup chopped seedless white raisins	$\frac{1}{2}$tsp. salt
$\frac{1}{2}$tsp. ground coriander	pinch black pepper
1tsp. cayenne pepper	2 cups boiling chicken stock
2 cloves garlic, finely chopped	$\frac{1}{4}$ cup chicken fat
	2 cups cold chicken stock
	1$\frac{1}{2}$oz. unsweetened chocolate

Put the turkey pieces in a large saucepan and cover with water. Cover the pan and cook over a high heat for 15 minutes. Reduce the heat to medium and cook for a further 45 minutes.

Meanwhile, combine the onions, tomatoes, white raisins, coriander, cayenne pepper, garlic, cinnamon, cloves, almonds, salt, pepper and boiling chicken stock in a large wooden mixing bowl. Mix to a paste.

In a large skillet, melt the chicken fat over a low heat. Add the chopped vegetables and spice mixture. Fry for 5 minutes, stirring constantly.

Add the cold chicken stock and chocolate to the pan. Cook for 10 to 12 minutes over a moderate heat, or until the chocolate has completely melted. Stir constantly until the chocolate is evenly distributed throughout the sauce.

Preheat the oven to 450°F. Remove the turkey pieces from the skillet and drain well. Pat the pieces dry with paper towels. Arrange the turkey pieces in a large baking dish in a single layer. Bake, uncovered, for 30 minutes.

Pour the sauce over the turkey pieces and lower the heat to 350°F. Cook for a further 30 minutes. You can sprinkle the dish with sesame seeds before serving.

Turkey Fillets in Wine Sauce
Serves 4

Ingredients

1$\frac{1}{4}$lb. turkey fillet	$\frac{2}{3}$ cup farmer's cheese
1tbsp. seasoned flour	1$\frac{1}{4}$ cups button mushrooms, sliced
2tbsp. butter	grated nutmeg
$\frac{2}{3}$ cup chicken stock	salt and pepper
$\frac{2}{3}$ cup dry white wine	

Pass the turkey through the seasoned flour. Brown it lightly in the butter. Add the stock and wine and simmer it, covered, for 30 minutes.

Add the farmer's cheese, together with the mushrooms and nutmeg. Check the seasoning. Stir gently and cook for a further 10 minutes.

You could use turkey steaks for this but they would need longer cooking time — another 10 minutes before adding the farmer's cheese.

Peking Duck
Serves 8

Ingredients

4-lb. duckling	16 Mandarin Pancakes
3tbsp. honey	4tbsp. hoisin sauce
2tbsp. water	a little dark soy sauce to taste
salt	
bunch green onions	
$\frac{1}{2}$ cucumber, peeled and cut into thin, finger-like strips	

Bring a large pan of water to a boil and plunge in the duckling to scald the skin. Carefully lift out and drain thoroughly. Secure the legs with string and leave to drip over a bowl overnight in a cool dry place.

Blend the honey, water and salt together and use to brush over the duck skin. Hang up again and leave for 2-3 hours. Repeat and leave to dry completely for a further 3-4 hours.

Set the duck on a rack over a roasting pan and place in the centre of a hot oven (450°F). Immediately reduce the oven temperature to moderate (350°F) and cook for 1$\frac{1}{4}$ hours. Check that the skin is crisp (do not

baste the duckling) and, if you think it necessary, increase the oven temperature for the last 15 minutes.

Meanwhile remove the root from the green onions. Cut in half lengthwise and cut in half again. Pop in ice cold water. Prepare cucumber, drain and dry on paper towels. Prepare the mandarin pancakes and the sauce.

Carve the duckling at the table; traditionally only the skin was eaten, but these days most people carve the skin and meat togther into 1½-in. pieces. This is then dipped into the prepared sauce and deftly rolled up in a pancake with some of the green onions before eating.

Crispy Duck
Serves 4

Ingredients

First Marinade	**Second Marinade**
3-lb. duck	4 slices fresh ginger
6 green onions	16 cloves
6tbsp. wine	4 cloves star anise
2tbsp. soy sauce	2 fennel bulbs
	hoisin sauce

Wash and dry the duck. Crush the green onions and add the remaining ingredients of the first marinade.

Put the green onions only inside the duck, rub the marinade all over the outside of the duck and leave it for 2 hours.

Remove the green onions and put in their place 2 slices of ginger.

Spread the green onions, the other 2 slices of ginger and the other ingredients of the second marinade on and around the duck. Steam the duck for an hour, cool it and drain it.

Heat enough oil to almost cover the duck in a deep skillet.

Once the oil is hot, remove the pan from the heat and place the duck gently in it, taking care not to burn yourself. Spoon the oil over the duck and fry until the duck is browned all over, returning it to the heat only if the oil cools down too much.

Serve with hoisin sauce.

Chinese Duck
Serves 4

Ingredients

4-lb. fresh duckling	1tbsp. dark soy sauce
4tbsp. cooking oil	1tbsp. sugar
2 cloves garlic, chopped	1/2tsp. five spice powder
1-in. piece fresh ginger, thinly sliced	3 points star anise
	2 cups duck stock or water
3tbsp. bean paste	salt to taste
2tbsp. light soy sauce	green onion to garnish

Use the duck giblets to make a duck stock; strain and reserve 2 cups. Heat the oil, fry the garlic without browning, then add the duck. Fry, turning frequently, until the outside is slightly brown. Lift out the duck.

Add the ginger, then the bean paste to the pan. Cook to bring out the flavors. Add light and dark soy sauces, sugar and five spice powder.

Return the duck to the pan and fry it in this mixture to coat the outside of the duck. Add the star anise, duck stock and seasoning to taste. Cover and cook over a gentle heat until the duck is tender, stirring occasionally. Allow 2-2½ hours. Skim off any fat or oil, then leave in the sauce to cool.

Cut into serving portions. Skim the sauce and pour it over each helping, which will set like a jelly. Garnish with green onion. Serve with rice.

Duck Breasts with Hazelnuts and Orange Potato Balls
Serves 4-6

This potato mixture can be made in advance, then fried just before serving. Duck breasts are now available from many supermarkets.

Ingredients

2lb. potatoes, peeled	2tbsp. flour
rind and juice of 3 large oranges	oil for deep-frying
	2 large duck breasts, boned
4tbsp. butter	2tbsp. oil
3 egg yolks	1/2 small onion
3 small eggs	2/3 cup duck or chicken stock
salt and freshly ground pepper	
	1 large onion
1 cup hazelnuts or filberts	1tsp. chunky marmalade

First make the potato balls. Halve the potatoes and cook in boiling salted water until tender. Drain well, then return to the pan and dry over low heat for 1 minute. Blend or process the potatoes, the juice of 2 oranges, egg yolks, and 2 of the eggs until smooth. Add salt and pepper to taste. Spoon on to a plate, cover and chill until firm.

Roll tablespoonfuls of the potato mixture into balls. Finely chop two thirds of the nuts. Roll the potato balls in seasoned flour, then in the remaining egg, beaten, and finally roll in the nuts. Chill for 15 minutes or until ready to cook.

Heat the oil to 350°F and fry the balls a few at a time till golden brown. Drain on paper towels and keep warm.

Trim the duck breasts if necessary. Heat the 2tbsp. oil in a skillet and fry the duck for about 3 minutes on each side for rare meat, longer for medium and well done meat. Drain and keep warm. Fry the remaining hazelnuts or filberts in the fat in the pan for a couple of minutes or until browned. Drain and remove. Finely chop the onion and add to the pan. Fry for a couple of minutes to soften then add the reserved flour. Fry for 1 minute stirring constantly, then stir in the stock. Bring to a boil, stirring, then simmer for 2 minutes.

Stir the remaining orange rind and juice into the sauce with the marmalade. Bring to a boil and season to taste. Thinly slice the duck, adding any juices to the sauce. Arrange the duck slices on a warmed serving dish with the potatoes. Stir the fried nuts into the sauce and spoon over the meat. Serve immediately with the fried potato balls.

Roast Duck with Spaetzle
Serves 6

Spaetzle or spätzen are an extremely popular form of egg noodle. They go well with any sort of roast meat, but particularly with roast duck.

Ingredients

2-3lb. duck, split and cleaned, with the fat retained	2 cups cold water
	4tbsp. lemon juice
	1/2 cup orange juice
1lb. flour	3tbsp. blackcurrant or blackberry jam
2tsp. salt	
5 eggs	1/2tsp. black pepper

Preheat the oven to 325°F. Put the duck halves, skin-side up, in a roasting pan. Roast the duck for 1 hour.

While the duck cooks, make the spaetzle. Place the flour in a large mixing bowl. Make a well in the centre of the mound. Sprinkle 1tsp. of salt in the well. Break the eggs into the well and mix them into the flour. Gradually add the water (more or less as needed) and mix to form a stiff dough.

Turn the dough out onto a lightly floured work surface and knead it vigorously until it is smooth and elastic. Roll or shape the dough into narrow strips. With a sharp knife, cut the strips into tiny pieces.

Bring 6½pt. water to a furious boil in a very large pot. Drop the spaetzle into the water. (Since each spaetzle must be able to float to the top of the water as it cooks, you may prefer to cook them in batches in less boiling water.) After the spaetzle rise to the top, boil for a further 15 minutes. Drain the spaetzle well and set them aside.

After the duck has roasted for 1 hour, drain off the drippings, reserving ¼ cup.

In a small bowl, combine the lemon juice, orange juice, jam and pepper. Brush the skin of the duck with the mixture. Return the duck halves to the oven, skin-side up, and roast for 1 hour longer, draining off the drippings from the pan twice during the cooking time.

With a sharp knife, remove all the skin and meat from the duck halves and shred them coarsely. Discard the bones. Put the shredded meat and skin into a large serving bowl.

Bring 6½pt. water to a furious boil in a large pot. Return the cooked spaetzle to the water for 1 minute. Drain the spaetzle well and add them to the shredded duck. Add the reserved duck drippings and salt to taste. Toss well and serve hot.

Duck with Pineapple
Serves 4

Ingredients

4 pieces of duck (or 5-lb.
   duck cut into 4)
salt and pepper
2tsp. cornstarch
4 slices canned pineapple
   and juice from can

2tsp. cornstarch
⅔ cup sour cream
½tsp. paprika

Prick the duck and season well. Put the pieces on a wire rack in a roasting pan so that the fat runs off the duck. Roast at 425°F for 10 minutes then reduce the heat to 350°F for a further hour. Mix the cornstarch with a little pineapple juice.

When the duck is cooked, remove the pieces from the pan and place each one on a piece of pineapple on a clean dish. Keep them warm while you make the sauce.

Remove as much fat as possible from the pan, leaving the juices. Mix the cornstarch mixture into the juices over a gentle heat, cooking this for 2 minutes. Add the rest of the pineapple juice and warm the sauce through. Add the sour cream and stir it thoroughly.

Spoon the sauce over the duck. Sprinkle the paprika over the top and either serve it immediately or keep it warm in a low oven for up to 15 minutes.

Braised Coriander Duck
Serves 6

Ingredients

5-6-lb. duck, cut into 6
   servings and trimmed of
   fat
4tbsp. lemon juice
½tsp. ground cumin
½tsp. salt
½tsp. black pepper

4tbsp. olive oil
3 cups lager beer
1lb. rice
1½ cups cooked peas
5tbsp. finely chopped fresh
   coriander leaves

Brush the duck with a mixture of the lemon juice, cumin, salt and pepper. Put on a plate, cover and refrigerate for 4 to 5 hours.

In a large flameproof casserole, heat the olive oil over a medium heat. Add the duck pieces and brown them on all sides. Pour off all but 1tbsp. of the fat.

Add the lager beer to the casserole and bring to a boil. Cover and reduce the heat to low. Simmer for 50 minutes.

Remove the duck pieces from the casserole. Set them aside and keep warm.

Remove 3 cups of the liquid from the casserole and bring it to a boil in a medium-sized saucepan over a high heat. Add the rice, stir, bring to a boil again and cover tightly. Reduce the heat to low and simmer for 18 minutes.

Stir the peas and coriander leaves into the rice. Cover, remove from the heat and allow to stand for 1 minute.

Arrange the duck pieces on a bed of rice and serve.

Hot Game Pie with Fried Apples and Onions
Serves 4-6

Wild duck is particularly good cooked this way, although any sort of game can be used. Try to mix at least two types of game for the best flavor.

Ingredients

2¼ cups plain wholewheat
  flour
large pinch salt
2tbsp. white vegetable fat,
  diced
⅓ cup butter or cooking
  margarine, diced
1 egg
1-2tbsp. milk

Filling

1lb. cooked game, boned
3 bacon slices
6 tart apples, quartered
  and cored
2 large onions, peeled
4tbsp. butter
1tsp. sugar
salt and freshly ground
  pepper
mild paprika, to taste
⅔-1 cup leftover game
  gravy
1 beaten egg to glaze

Make the pastry first. Put the flour and salt in a bowl and rub in the fats until the mixture resembles fine crumbs. Mix the egg with 1tbsp. of the milk and add to the mixture to form a soft but not sticky dough. If too dry add a little more milk. Wrap and chill while preparing the filling.

Cut or shred the game into bite-size chunks. Coarsely chop the bacon, and slice the unpeeled apples. Slice the onions.

Heat half the butter in a skillet, and fry the bacon till golden brown and crispy. Drain and remove. Fry the onions till soft and golden. Drain and remove. Heat the remaining butter and quickly fry the apple slices with the sugar till caramelized. Drain and remove.

Layer up the filling in a greased soufflé dish in this order: onion, bacon, apple, game, onion, apple, game, apple, onions and finally bacon. Add seasoning with each layer. Pour over enough of the gravy to come ⅔ the way up the dish.

Roll out the pastry on a floured board to an oval 2in. larger than the dish. Cut a strip the width of the rim of the dish. Brush the rim with a little of the beaten egg. Stick the pastry strip on to the rim then brush with egg. Cover the soufflé dish with the pastry. Seal well and flute the edges. Cut a small steam-hole in the top. Decorate the soufflé with any trimmings of pastry if wished. Glaze with beaten egg.

Bake in the preheated oven at 400°F for 10 minutes, then reduce the heat to 375°F and bake for a further 20 minutes or until the pastry is crisp and golden brown. Serve hot.

Pheasant Pojarski Cutlets
Serves 6

Ingredients

½lb. pheasant breasts,
  boned and skinned
1¼ cups fresh white bread
  crumbs
⅔ cup sour cream
1tbsp. port
pinch of salt
2 drops Tabasco

freshly ground black
  pepper
6 slices wholewheat bread,
  toasted
6 mushrooms
2tbsp. butter
6 sprigs parsley

Dice the pheasant and liquidize or process for 10 to 15 seconds, until finely chopped. Add the crumbs, cream, port and seasonings and blend for 30 seconds or until very smooth. Fry a teaspoonful of the mixture and taste for seasoning — it should not be too bland. Turn into a bowl and allow to chill until firm — about an hour.

Cut the toast into circles 3in. in diameter and put on a cookie sheet.

Put the chilled pheasant mixture into a piping bag fitted with a star nozzle, and pipe the mixture neatly on the toast circles. Bake in the preheated oven (400°F) for 10 to 15 minutes until golden and firm to touch.

While they are cooking, fry the mushrooms using the butter and drain on paper towels.

Serve each cutlet capped with a mushroom and garnished with a sprig of parsley. Accompany with Mushroom Sauce and a green salad.

Variation The pheasant can be replaced with chicken, veal, scallops, or fillet of sole.

Pheasant Pojarski Cutlets

Jointing a Chicken

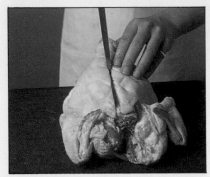

1 Turn the chicken over so that the backbone is uppermost. Cut through to the bone along the line of the spine.

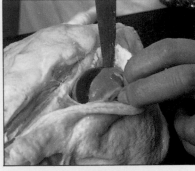

2 Where the thigh joins the backbone there is a fleshy 'oyster' on each side. Cut round them to loosen them from the carcass so that they come away when the legs are severed.

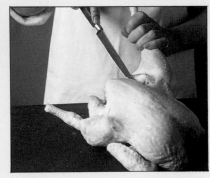

3 Turn the bird over and pull a leg away from the body. Cut through the skin only, as far round the leg as possible, close to the body.

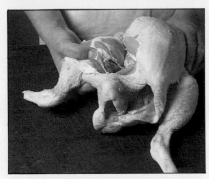

4 Pull the leg away from the body and twist it down so that the thigh bone pops out of its socket on the carcass and is exposed.

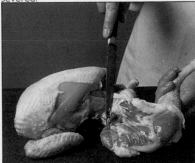

5 Cut the leg off, taking care to go between thigh, bone and carcass and to bring the 'oyster' away with the leg. (Turn over briefly to check.) Repeat the process for the other leg.

6 Now for the breast. Carefully cut down each side of the breast bone to free the breast flesh a little.

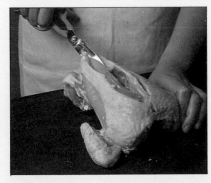

7 Use scissors to cut through the small bones close to the breast. Cut away the breast bone.

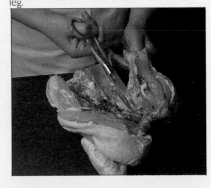

8 Open up the bird. Cut each wing and breast off the carcass with scissors, starting at the tail end and cutting up to and through the wing bone near the neck.

9 Cut the wing join in two, leaving about one third of the breast attached to the wing.

10 Cut off the almost meatless pinions (which can be used for stock, along with the carcass) from each wing.

11 Lay the legs skin-side down on the board and cut through where the thigh and lower leg bones meet.

12 With the heal end of a heavy knife (or a cleaver) chop the feet bones off the drumsticks.

Boning a Chicken

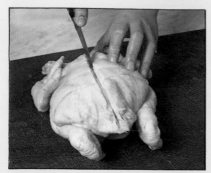

1 Put the chicken breast-side down on a board. Cut through to the backbone.

2 Feel for the fleshy 'oyster' at the top of each thigh and cut round it. Cut and scrape the flesh from the carcass with a sharp knife held as close as possible to the bone.

3 Continue along both sides of the backbone until the rib-cage is exposed. At the joint of the thigh and pelvis, cut between the bones at the socket so that the legs stay attached to the flesh and skin, and not to the body carcass.

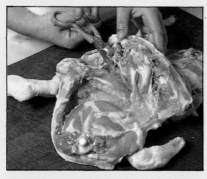

4 Keep working right round the bird then use scissors to cut away most of the rib cage, leaving only the cartilaginous breast-bone in the centre.

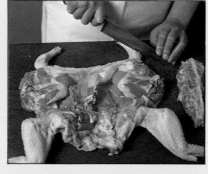

5 Using a heavy knife cut through the foot joints to remove the knuckle end of the drumsticks.

6 Working from the inside thigh end scrape one leg bone clean, pushing the flesh down towards the drumstick until you can feel the thigh bone. Repeat on the other leg.

7 Working from the drumstick ends, scrape the lower leg bones clean in the same way and remove them. Remove as many tendons as possible from the legs as you work.

8 Now for the wings. Cut off the pinions with a heavy knife.

9 Scrape the wing bones clean as you did the leg bones.

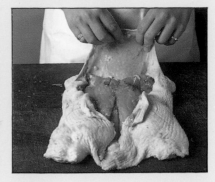

10 Carefully free the breastbone with the knife, working from the middle of the bird towards the tail.

11 Take great care not to puncture the skin, which has not flesh under it at this point so is easily torn.

12 You should now have a beautifully boned bird. Keep the neck flap of skin intact to fold over once the chicken is stuffed.

Mutton and Lamb

Baby Lamb
Serves 8

This dish is traditionally made with chops from a young goat, but the recipe is often adapted to lamb, which is more readily available.

Ingredients

4lb. lamb rib chops	2 cloves garlic, finely
3tbsp. olive oil	chopped
½tsp. salt	1½ cups cold water
pinch black pepper	2 egg yolks
4tbsp. coarsely chopped	2tbsp. lemon juice
parsley	

Put the lamb chops in a large heavy skillet. Add the oil, salt, pepper, parsley and garlic. Pour the water over the meat and spices, cover, and simmer over a low heat for 1 hour.

In a small mixing bowl, combine the egg yolks and lemon juice. Pour over the lamb and cover. Simmer for another 3 minutes and serve.

Capered Cutlets
Serves 4

Ingredients

1-2tbsp. oil	1tbsp. water
1 medium onion, sliced	1¼cups yogurt
8 lamb cutlets	2 egg yolks
salt and pepper	2tbsp. capers
1¼cups beef stock	chopped parsley
2tsp. cornstarch	

Heat the oil, add the onion and cook until softened but not browned. Add the cutlets and brown them. Drain off excess fat and season well. Add the stock, bring to the boil and simmer for 30 minutes, or bake at 350°F.

Mix the cornflour with the water and add it to the pan. Stir over a gentle heat to thicken the sauce. Mix the yogurt and egg yolks with the capers and add them to the pan. Warm through on a gentle heat. Sprinkle with the chopped parsley and serve immediately.

Fragrant Lamb Stew
Serves 6

Ingredients

2 cups canned moist	6 cloves
coconut	2 cardamom pods
2 cups hot water	6-7 curry leaves
2lb. lamb, cut into 1-in.	1½tsp. salt
cubes	2tbsp. Ghee (Clarified
2-3 green chili peppers	Butter)
1in. ginger, cut into thin	1 small onion, finely
strips	chopped
2 large onions, diced	½tsp. freshly milled pepper
2-in. piece of stick	1tbsp. flour
cinnamon	

Blend together the coconut and water until smooth.

In a large saucepan, put the lamb, chili peppers, ginger, onions, cinnamon, cloves, cardamom, curry leaves, salt and about 2 cups of the coconut milk and bring to boil.

Cover, lower heat and simmer for 45 minutes. Add the remaining coconut milk and cook for a further 10 minutes. Remove from the heat.

In a small pan, heat the ghee and fry the onion until lightly browned. Add the pepper and the flour and, stirring constantly, mix the flour with the fried onion and ghee. Add a little of the meat gravy and mix until smooth.

Add this to the stew and, stirring constantly, bring to the boil. Serve hot with rice.

Fragrant Lamb Stew

Crown Roast of Lamb with Apricot Rice Stuffing
Serves 6

This is an excellent party dish as it can be prepared in advance.

Ingredients

2 rib sections of lamb loins	2 stalks celery
1tbsp. oil	2½ cups dried apricots,
freshly ground pepper	soaked or 1 large can
Stuffing	apricots
½ cup long-grain or risotto	1tbsp. white raisins
rice	1tbsp. mixed nuts, chopped
1tbsp. butter	1 egg, beaten
1 onion, peeled and finely	1tbsp. parsley, chopped
chopped	salt and freshly ground
	pepper

Ask the butcher to prepare the crown roast or, if this is not possible, have the rib sections chined. Remove the skin from the fatty side of the joints. Cut along the fat about 1½ in. from the top of the bone and remove fat and meat from the tops of the bones. Scrape the little end bones clean with a knife. Turn the meat over the cut between the cutlets to enable the joint to bend.

Stand the two pieces of meat up with the bones at the top. Turn fatty sides in and sew together at the top and bottom of the joints to make the crown roast. Brush over with oil and sprinkle with pepper.

For the stuffing, partially cook the rice for 10 minutes, rinse and allow to drain and cool. Heat the butter and oil and cook the onion for 4 minutes over a low heat. Add the chopped celery, chopped apricots (if using canned apricots retain 8 drained halves for garnish), white raisins and nuts. Lastly stir in the rice. Turn into a bowl and allow to cool. Mix with the egg yolk and parsley.

Fill the center of the roast with the stuffing. Cover with a piece of foil.

Cover the individual tips of the bones with foil to prevent charring. Then completely cover with foil. Roast in the oven for 1½-2 hours at 350°F, depending on the size of the cutlets.

Remove the crown roast to a heated platter and make gravy to accompany roast in the usual way. If using canned apricots, a little juice may be added to the gravy. Remove the string before carving between the cutlets.

Note Any excess stuffing may be used to stuff apricot halves which can be brushed with oil and cooked in the oven for the last 30 minutes of cooking time.

Kashmiri Lamb with Fennel Seeds
Serves 6

Ingredients

1¾tsp. whole fennel seeds	2lb. lamb, cut into 1-in.
6tbsp. oil	cubes
good pinch of asafetida	2tsp. paprika
(optional)	2tsp. chili powder
2-in. piece of stick	1½tsp. ground ginger
cinnamon	1tsp salt
4 cardamom pods	2 cups yogurt, lightly
4 cloves	beaten

Put the fennel seeds in a grinder and grind until fine.

Heat oil in a large saucepan over a high heat. Add the asafetida (if used) and after 2 seconds add the cinnamon, cardamom and cloves and let them sizzle for 4-5 seconds.

Add the lamb and fry, stirring constantly, for about 5-7 minutes. Add the paprika, chili, ginger and salt and fry for another 2-3 minutes.

Add the yogurt, mix with the lamb, and cook for 10 minutes. Add the fennel, stir well to mix, cover, lower heat to very low and cook for about 1 hour, stirring occasionally, until the meat is tender and the gravy thickened. Serve with rice.

Lamb Chops with Apricot Marsala Sauce
Serves 4

Ingredients

1½ cups dried apricots	1 onion, peeled and finely
⅔ cup orange juice	chopped
4tbsp. Marsala	1tbsp. flour
2tbsp. butter	2½ cups chicken stock
1tbsp. oil	parsley sprigs
4 double lamb chops	

Cut the apricots in half and soak in the orange juice and Marsala for at least 4 hours.

Melt the butter and oil on a medium-high heat and brown the chops on each side. Transfer to an ovenproof dish.

Lower the heat and cook the finely chopped onion for 3 minutes. Sprinkle the flour on the onion and stir well with the juices in the pan.

Add the stock gradually and the strained liquid from the apricots. Stir continuously and bring to the boil. Season well. Stir in the apricots.

Pour the sauce over the chops and cook in the oven, covered with a lid or foil, for 45 minutes.

Serve garnished with parsley sprigs and boiled baby potatoes in their skins with peas or green beans.

Lamb Biryani
Serves 8

Ingredients

2lb. lamb, cut into large pieces
2lb. basmati rice
1in. ginger
4 cloves garlic
4tbsp. coriander leaves
1tbsp. mint leaves
4 green chili peppers
8 cloves
2×1-in. pieces of stick cinnamon
1tsp. black cumin seeds
¼ nutmeg

6 cardamom pods, skinned
6-8tbsp. milk
1tsp. saffron threads
¾ cup Ghee (Clarified Butter)
3 large onions, halved and finely sliced
2tsp chili powder
juice of 2 lemons
2 cups yogurt
3tsp. salt
6½ pints water

Wash the meat and leave in a strainer or colander to allow all the water to drain off.

Wash the rice in several changes of water. Soak for 15 minutes in water and then leave in a strainer to drain.

Blend the ginger, garlic, coriander, mint and green chili peppers to a fine paste.

Grind together 4 cloves, 1 piece of stick cinnamon, ½tsp. black cumin seeds, nutmeg and 3 cardamom pods to a fine powder.

Warm 2tbsp. milk and soak the saffron in it. Put aside.

Heat the ghee and fry the onions until golden brown. Drain and put aside, reserving the ghee.

Put the meat in a large bowl, add the coriander paste and, with the back of a wooden spoon, beat the meat for 15-20 minutes, turning the meat frequently.

To the meat add the chili powder, lemon juice, yogurt, 2tsp. salt, the powdered spices and half the fried onions, mix and put aside for 3-4 hours.

In a saucepan, melt the ghee again over a medium high heat and add the meat and the marinade. When it starts to boil, lower the heat, cover and, stirring occasionally, cook for about 1 hour until the meat is tender and the gravy thickened.

While the meat is being cooked, bring the water to a boil in a large saucepan. Add the remaining spices and salt.

When the water is boiling rapidly, add the drained rice, bring it back to the boil and boil the rice for 3-4 minutes until the rice is nearly cooked. Remove and drain the rice.

Lightly grease a large casserole dish big enough to hold all the rice and meat, and put half the cooked rice evenly over the bottom. Put the meat and gravy on the rice and the remaining rice on top.

Sprinkle the saffron milk, the remaining milk and the rest of the fried onions on top. Cover tightly with aluminum foil and then the lid and put in a preheated oven at 375°F for about 45 minutes until the rice is cooked.

Lamb Chop Kebabs
Serves 6

Ingredients

1½lb. lamb chops
2 cups yogurt
1½tsp. salt
1in. ginger, grated
8 cloves garlic, crushed

¾tsp. Garam Masala
1tbsp. poppy seeds, ground
2-3 green chili peppers, ground
2tbsp. oil

Remove excess fat from the chops. Wash and pat dry.

Lightly beat the yogurt and mix in all the ingredients.

Add the lamb chops and marinate for at least 6 hours. You can marinate them for 24 hours, but the meat should be covered and refrigerated, then returned to room temperature before broiling.

Take the chops out of the marinade and place on a cookie sheet. Cook under a preheated broiler for 8-10 minutes on each side.

Lamb Chop Kebabs

Lamb Dhansak
Serves 4-6

Doddy is a vegetable widely available in Indian supermarkets and grocers' stores.

Ingredients

$2^1/_3$ cups red lentils, washed
pumpkin, peeled and cut
   into 1-in. pieces
$^3/_4$ lb. doddy, peeled and
   cut into 1-in. pieces
1 medium potato, peeled
   and diced
1 medium onion, chopped
1 tsp. ground turmeric
2 tsp. salt
3 medium tomatoes,
   chopped
$1^1/_2$lb. lamb, cut into 1-in.
   cubes

4 tbsp. oil
1-in. ginger, grated
3 cloves garlic, crushed
3 dried red chili peppers,
   ground
$1^1/_2$tsp. ground coriander
$1^1/_2$tsp. ground cumin
$^1/_2$tsp. ground mustard
$^1/_2$tsp. fenugreek seeds,
   ground
$1^1/_2$tsp. samba powder
   (optional)

Put the lentils, pumpkin, doddy, potato, onion, turmeric and salt in a large saucepan, and add enough water to cover it by $1^1/_2$in. Bring to the boil and simmer until tender. Add the tomatoes and cook for a further 10 minutes. Pass the lentils and vegetables through a strainer and put aside.

Boil the meat in a little water for about 45 minutes until tender. Put aside.

Heat the oil in a large saucepan over a medium heat. Add all the spices and fry for 1-2 minutes, stirring constantly, so that they do not stick. If necessary, sprinkle on a few drops of water to prevent the spices from burning. Add the lentils and lamb and simmer on a low heat for about 30 minutes. (The lentils should be quite thick.)

Lamb Extravaganza
Serves 4-6

Ingredients

1 lb. lamb fillet
3 tbsp. paprika
2 tbsp. chili powder
2 tbsp. fresh coriander,
   chopped
2 tbsp. fresh parsley,
   chopped
6 tbsp. crème fraîche or
   thick yogurt
3 tbsp. oil
2 cloves garlic
1 onion, finely chopped

$1^1/_2$ cups mushrooms, sliced
1 red pepper, seeded and
   sliced
2×8oz. cans pineapple
   slices in own juice,
   quartered
$1^1/_4$ cups strong black coffee
4 tsp. cornstarch and water
   to mix
lime and coriander to
   garnish

Cut the meat into 1-in. cubes. Mix together the paprika, chili, coriander, parsley and crème fraîche in a bowl. Coat the meat with this mixture.

Heat the oil in a deep skillet and lightly fry the garlic and vegetables for 2-3 minutes. Drain. Cook the meat for 10 minutes stirring occasionally, and mix in the vegetables.

Add the pineapple and coffee and simmer for 10 to 15 minutes. Blend the cornstarch with a little cold water and add to the pan. Stir until the sauce thickens. Adjust the seasoning.

Garnish with slices of lime and sprigs of coriander. Serve with brown rice.

Lamb in Dill Sauce with Tagliolini
Serves 4

Ingredients

4tbsp. oil	1lb. fresh tagliolini verdi or
1 medium onion, peeled	fettucini
and diced	1tbsp. butter melted
1lb. ground lamb	nutmeg
2tbsp. fresh white	2 egg yolks
breadcrumbs	1¼ cups sour cream
salt and freshly ground	2tsp. dried dill
pepper	juice of 1 lemon
1tbsp. parsley, chopped	dill or parsley, freshly
1 egg, beaten	chopped
½tsp. Worcestershire sauce	

Heat half the oil in a skillet and cook the onion over a low heat until soft and transparent. Drain from the pan with a slotted spoon and reserve the remaining oil. Put the onion in a mixing bowl and allow to cool.

Add the ground lamb to the onion with the breadcrumbs, seasoning, beaten egg and Worcestershire sauce.

Mix well and with floured hands shape the mixture into balls 1in. in diameter. Roll them lightly in seasoned flour.

Add the remaining oil to the skillet and brown the meatballs over a high heat for about 1 minute each side. Reduce heat and continue cooking for about 8 minutes.

Cook the fresh green tagliolini or fettucini for 2-3 minutes in boiling salted water with a few drops of oil. Drain the pasta and toss in a little melted butter with a shake of nutmeg. Arrange meatballs on the pasta and keep warm for a few minutes until the sauce is made.

To make the sauce, mix the egg yolks with a little cream and then add the dill. Add the remaining cream to the juices in the pan in which the meat was fried. Stir well, add some of the warm cream to the egg and return to the pan. Add lemon juice and warm through.

Pour the warmed sauce over the meatballs, sprinkle with fresh dill or parsley and serve immediately. Do not boil the sauce if you are reheating it.

Lamb with Fennel and Lemon Sauce
Serves 6

This dish comes from Greece. If you wish, you can replace the lamb with pork, chicken, veal or turkey.

Ingredients

2 bulbs fennel, trimmed	⅔ cup red wine
and sliced	2½ cups good lamb, veal or
2tbsp. oil	chicken stock
2lb. lean, boneless lamb,	bouquet garni
cubed	salt and freshly ground
2 medium onions, finely	pepper
chopped	2 eggs
2tbsp. parsley, chopped	4tbsp. lemon juice
1tbsp. flour	

Blanch the fennel in boiling, salted water for 5 minutes. Drain, reserving the stock for soup and refresh the fennel with cold water. Drain thoroughly, and set aside.

Heat the oil in a heavy, flameproof casserole or pan and quickly brown the meat on all sides — this may have to be done in several batches. Drain well, remove and set aside on a plate.

Add the blanched fennel and the chopped onion and parsley to the casserole and cook over low heat for 10 minutes until soft and golden, stirring occasionally. Stir in the flour, cook for 1 minute, then stir in the wine, half the stock, and the bouquet garni, and bring to the boil, stirring constantly. Replace the meat, add a little salt and pepper, then cover and simmer gently for 1½ hours or until tender, stirring from time to time.

Make the sauce just before serving — beat the eggs with the lemon juice.

Bring the remaining stock to a boil, remove from the heat and leave to cook for 1 minute. Then pour the hot stock onto the egg mixture, beating all the while. Remove the casserole from the heat, and stir in the sauce. Taste and adjust seasoning. Cover and leave to stand in a warm place, or on top of a hot plate for 10 minutes, for the flavors to blend. Serve with baby potatoes or plain boiled rice.

Lamb Kidneys in Red Wine
Serves 4

Ingredients

12 lamb kidneys, skinned	1½ cups mushrooms,
1 tbsp. flour	washed and sliced
salt and freshly ground	2 tomatoes, skinned and
pepper	chopped
4 tbsp. butter	⅔ cup red wine
1 onion, peeled and sliced	1 tbsp. chopped parsley

Remove the core from each kidney and cut in half. Dredge with seasoned flour.

Heat the butter and gently cook the onion on a low heat. Remove from the pan into an ovenproof dish.

Sauté the kidneys for a few minutes on either side until golden brown. Add mushrooms and continue cooking for about 2 minutes.

Add the tomatoes and red wine. Spoon into the ovenproof dish, cover with foil and bake for 25 minutes at 350°F.

Serve individual portions in a ring of rice on the plate and garnish with parsley.

Lamb Kebabs
Serves 3

Ingredients

1 lb. lean, boneless lamb,	⅛ nutmeg
cut into 1-in. cubes	1 clove
1 medium onion	2 peppercorns
3 cloves garlic	1 tsp. salt
1-in. ginger	1 tsp. chili powder
1-in. piece of stick	⅔ cup yogurt
cinnamon	Ghee (Clarified Butter) for
2 cardamom pods, skinned	basting
1 tsp. poppy seeds	lemon wedges

In a blender or food processor, blend together the onion, garlic and ginger, adding a little water if necessary.

Grind the cinnamon, cardamom, poppy seeds, nutmeg, clove and peppercorns to a fine powder.

Place the lamb in a large bowl, add the onion paste, powdered spices, salt, chili powder and yogurt, and mix thoroughly. Cover the bowl with plastic wrap and place in the refrigerator overnight to marinate.

Divide the meat among 6 skewers. Put under a hot broiler and baste occasionally with the ghee. Turn once or twice and cook until tender — about 10 minutes.

Serve hot with wedges of lemon.

Lamb Korma
Serves 6

A korma is a mild curry, and because it is popular with everyone it is frequently served by Indian Muslims at the Festival of Id, which celebrates the end of Ramadan, the period of fasting. Chicken is often cooked in this manner and indeed this recipe can be adapted using chicken.

Ingredients

2 large onions, sliced	1 tomato, peeled and
4 cloves garlic	chopped
1-in. piece root ginger,	pinch grated nutmeg
finely chopped	pinch ground cinnamon
oil	pinch ground cloves
2 lb. boned shoulder of	salt and pepper
lamb, trimmed and	⅔ cup water
cubed	2 tsp. cornstarch
1 tbsp. ground coriander	1 tbsp. water
2 tsp. ground cumin	⅔ cup yogurt
1 tsp. ground turmeric	

Put half the onions into a blender with the garlic and ginger and blend until smooth. Fry the remaining onion in oil until soft. Remove from the pan and reserve it.

Brown the cubed meat, adding more oil if necessary. Remove the meat and keep it with the reserved onion. Add the blended mixture to the pan, stir well and fry for 5 minutes. Lower the heat and add the coriander, cumin and turmeric. Cook these for a further 3 minutes. Add the tomato and cook for 2 minutes. Add the remaining spices and cook them on a gentle heat for 5 minutes, stirring occasionally.

Return the meat and onions to the pan with the ⅔ cup of water, bring to a boil, then cover and simmer for 30 minutes. Mix the cornstarch with the tablespoon of water and add it to the yogurt. Stir the yogurt into the lamb and warm the sauce through.

Serve with rice, chapatis, poppadums and chutney.

Lamb Kebabs

In a saucepan, put the ground lamb, lentils cardamom, peppercorns, onions, garlic, ginger, chili powder, salt and water. Bring to a boil over a medium high heat. Cover, lower the heat and simmer until the lentils are tender and all the water absorbed.

Place the mixture in a food processor or liquidizer and blend until smooth. Mix in the beaten egg, and divide into 16-18 small balls.

Combine the ingredients for the filling and put aside.

Take a minced lamb and lentil ball, and with your thumb, make a depression in the middle to form a cup shape. Fill the center with a little filling and re-form into a smooth ball. Flatten slightly.

Heat the oil in a large skillet and fry the meatballs, turning once until nicely browned. Drain.

Serve hot with wedges of lemon and a salad.

Lamb and Okra Stew
Serves 6

The okra in this stew gives it a natural thickness and savory taste. Be careful not to overcook the okra, or it will become stringy.

Ingredients

3 tbsp. butter or margarine	1½ cups Chicken Broth
2½ lb. boneless stewing lamb, cubed	½ tsp. salt
½ cup chopped onion	½ tsp. black pepper
1 tsp. ground cumin	½ tsp. sugar
8 oz. can tomatoes	1 lb. fresh okra
4 tbsp. tomato purée	½ cup water
	½ cup white vinegar

Melt 1 oz. of the butter or margarine in a large skillet. Add the lamb cubes and sauté until they are browned on all sides. Add the onion, cumin, tomatoes, tomato purée, chicken broth, salt, pepper and sugar to the skillet. Cook over a low heat, stirring frequently, for 5 minutes.

Preheat the oven to 325°F. Transfer the lamb mixture from the skillet to a medium-sized casserole. Cover the dish and bake for 90 minutes.

Trim the okra and cut it into thin slices. Soak the slices in the water and vinegar for 20 minutes. Drain and pat the okra dry with paper towels.

Melt the remaining butter or margarine in a small skillet. Add the okra slices and sauté for 6 minutes, stirring frequently.

After the casserole has baked for 90 minutes, add the okra slices to it. Stir well, cover the dish, and bake for a further 40 minutes. Serve hot.

Lamb and Lentil Meatballs
Serves 4

Ingredients

1 lb. lean ground lamb	½ cup water
½ cup lentils, washed and drained	1 egg, lightly beaten
2 large black cardamom pods, skinned	**Filling**
	1 medium onion, finely chopped
6 black peppercorns	3 green chili peppers, chopped
1 medium onion, chopped	
3 cloves garlic, crushed	3 tbsp. coriander leaves, chopped
1-in. ginger, grated	
½ tsp. chili powder	oil for frying
1 tsp. salt	lemon wedges

Lamb with Spinach
Serves 4-6

Ingredients

6 tbsp. oil	¾ in. ginger, grated
4 cardamom pods	½ tsp. ground turmeric
2-in. piece of stick cinnamon	1 tsp. chili powder
3 bay leaves	1½ lb. lamb, cut into 2-in. cubes
2 medium onions, finely sliced	1 tsp. salt
	1½ lb. frozen spinach, chopped
2 cloves garlic, crushed	

Heat the oil in a large saucepan, add the cardamom, cinnamon and bay leaves and let them sizzle for 4-5 seconds.

Add the onions, garlic and ginger and fry until the onions are golden brown. Add the turmeric and chili and fry for another minute. Add the lamb and salt and mix well with the spices.

Cover, lower heat to very low and cook for about 30 minutes, stirring occasionally.

Add the spinach and continue to cook until all the liquid has evaporated.

Lamb Tikka
Serves 4

Ingredients

1¼lb. leg of lamb (in a single thick slice)
1¼ cups natural yogurt
1tsp. chili powder
1tsp. crushed coriander
1tsp. Garam Masala
½tsp. salt

juice of 1 fresh lime or lemon
8 lettuce leaves
2 tomatoes, sliced
12 slices of cucumber
1 small onion, peeled and finely sliced
1 lemon or lime, quartered

Leg of lamb sliced about ½in. thick is best for this dish. Remove any bone or gristle. Cut into ½-in. cubes.

Mix yogurt with the spices, salt and lime or lemon juice in a plastic bag or a flat dish. Add the meat to the marinade and allow to soak for several hours. Turn from time to time.

Divide the meat onto 4 skewers and cook under a hot broiler, turning every two minutes.

Serve each portion off the skewer with Pilau Rice and a green salad. Garnish with the remaining ingredients and accompany with the sauce of your choice.

Lamb-Stuffed Artichokes
Serves 8

Ingredients

1tbsp. olive oil
1 onion, finely chopped
¼ cup pine nuts
1lb. ground lamb
2tbsp. chopped parsley
½tsp. black pepper
pinch salt

8 large artichokes, stems trimmed and outermost leaves removed
4 cups water
2tbsp. butter
½ cup lemon juice

Heat the oil in a small saucepan. Add the onion and pine nuts and cook for 3-5 minutes over a low heat.

Combine the lamb with the onions and pine nuts in a small mixing bowl. Add the parsley, pepper and salt. Mix thoroughly.

Stuff the artichokes with the meat mixture, inserting small quantities between the leaves with a teaspoon.

Place the artichokes upright in 2 large saucepans, 4 in each pot. Fill each pot with half the water. Reduce the heat to low and cover the pots. Steam the artichokes for 45 minutes and then drain well.

In a small saucepan, melt the butter and add the lemon juice. Pour the mixture over the artichokes and simmer for 15 minutes. Serve warm.

Lamb with Onions
Serves 6

Ingredients

2lb. lamb, cut into 1-in. cubes
½tsp. ground turmeric
½tsp. chili powder
1tsp. ground cumin seeds
1tsp. ground coriander seeds
1-in. ginger, grated

2 cloves garlic, crushed
1½ cups yogurt
1tsp. salt
4 large onions
10tbsp. oil
4 cardamom pods
2-in. piece stick cinnamon
3 cloves

Marinate the lamb with the turmeric, chili, cumin, coriander, ginger, garlic, yogurt and salt and set aside for 3-4 hours.

Cut three of the onions in half and finely slice them. Chop the remaining onion.

Heat the oil in a large saucepan over a medium high heat and fry the sliced onions, stirring occasionally, until golden brown. Drain on paper towels and put aside.

In the remaining oil add the cardamom, cinnamon and cloves and let them sizzle for 4-5 seconds. Add the chopped onion and fry until lightly browned. Add the meat and spices and fry, stirring constantly, for about 5-7 minutes.

Cover, turn down heat to very low and simmer for about 1 hour until tender. Add two thirds of the fried onions and mix with the meat and cook for another minute.

Serve garnished with the remaining onions.

Hard-Boiled Eggs Wrapped in Spiced Meat
Serves 4

Ingredients

1½ cups lamb, finely ground	3 cloves garlic, crushed
2tbsp. coriander leaves, finely chopped	3tbsp. onion, finely chopped
1tsp. salt	3tbsp. lemon juice
2-3 green chili peppers, finely chopped	1 egg, beaten
	4 hard-boiled eggs
	oil for deep frying

Mix the ground lamb well with the coriander, salt, chili peppers, garlic, onion, lemon juice and the beaten egg, and divide into 4 portions.

Wrap each portion round a hard-boiled egg, making sure the egg does not show through at any point.

Deep fry over a medium high heat for about 4-5 minutes until nicely browned.

Cut in half lengthwise to serve.

Marinated Lamb Chops
Serves 4

Ingredients

8 rib lamb chops	**Sauce**
2tbsp. oil	2tbsp. oil
2tbsp. soy sauce	1 onion, finely chopped
1tsp. brown sugar	2tbsp. sherry
salt and freshly ground pepper	2tbsp. water
1tsp. lemon juice	2tbsp. red currant jelly
	1tsp. ground coriander
	1 small can pineapple pieces
	1tbsp. parsley

Put the chops in a plastic bag with the oil, soy sauce, brown sugar, seasoning and lemon juice. Leave to marinate for several hours. Turn the bag around on a dish to help the meat to contact the marinade.

Arrange the chops on a rack in a roasting pan and roast in a preheated oven at 400°F for 15-20 minutes.

Make the sauce by cooking the onion in the oil for 3 minutes. Add the remainder of the marinade from the chops and simmer for a few minutes. Add the sherry, water, red currant jelly, coriander, seasoning and pineapple pieces. Simmer for 15 minutes. The sauce may be liquidized before serving. Alternatively mix 1tsp. cornstarch with 1tbsp. water, add a little warmed sauce and return to the saucepan. Stir until sauce is slightly thickened.

Serve the chops on a bed of rice, sprinkled with chopped parsley. Pour or pass the sauce, as you like.

Light Lamb Curry
Serves 6

Ingredients

6tbsp. oil	1in. ginger, grated
3 medium potatoes, peeled and halved	1tsp. ground turmeric
4 cardamom pods	½tsp. chili powder
2-in. piece of stick cinnamon	1tsp. salt
2 bay leaves	good pinch sugar
1 large onion, finely sliced	1tbsp. vinegar
2 cloves garlic, crushed	2lb. lamb, cut into 1-in. cubes
	4 cups water

Heat the oil in a large saucepan over a medium high heat, and fry the pieces of potato until evenly browned. Put aside.

Put the cardamom, cinnamon and bay leaves in the hot oil and let them sizzle for 4-5 seconds. Add the onions, garlic and ginger and fry until the onions are golden brown.

Add the turmeric, chili, salt, sugar and vinegar and fry for another minute.

Add the lamb, mix with the spices and fry, stirring constantly, for 10-15 minutes, until all the meat juices have evaporated.

Add the water and bring to a boil. Cover, lower heat and cook for 40 minutes, stirring occasionally.

Add the potatoes, cover again and cook for a further 20 minutes until the meat and potatoes are tender. Serve with rice.

Marinated Lamb Chops

Rack of Lamb in a Garlic Crust
Serves 4-6

Ingredients

2 racks of lamb of 6-8 chops each, chined
3 cloves of garlic, peeled
sprig rosemary
1tbsp. oil
3tbsp. fresh white breadcrumbs

2tbsp. redcurrant or guava jelly, warmed
1tbsp. parsley, chopped
½tsp. French mustard
salt and pepper

Turn the lamb racks bone side up and cut a narrow slit between each chop at the meaty end.

Slice a clove of garlic and stuff each slit with a sliver of garlic and a blade of rosemary.

Put the lamb racks, fat side up, into an oiled roasting pan and cut several shallow diagonal slashes in the fat.

Crush the remaining garlic cloves and mix with the breadcrumbs, warmed jelly, parsley and mustard, and season well with salt and pepper.

Smear this mixture over the lamb racks and leave for 1-2 hours. Roast for 25-35 minutes at 450°F, until well browned but still pink in the center.

Persian Lamb Stew
Serves 6-8

Lots of fresh parsley is crucial to this dish. Use the flat-leaved kind for maximum flavor

Ingredients

½ cup butter
12 green onions, finely chopped
3 cups finely chopped parsley
3½lb. lean lamb, cubed
3pts. water
⅓ cup fresh lemon juice

1 lemon, cut into small wedges
1½lb. cooked (or canned) red kidney beans, drained weight
scant 1tbsp. salt
2tsp. freshly ground black pepper

Preparation Melt half the butter in a medium stockpot. Add the onions and parsley and sauté until the parsley turns a dark green.

Melt the remaining butter in a large skillet. Add the cubed lamb and sauté until the cubes are lightly browned.

Add the lamb to the stockpot. Add the water, lemon juice and lemon wedges. Stir well, cover and simmer for 1 hour 15 minutes. Stir in the kidney beans, salt and pepper. Cover and simmer for another 20 minutes, or until the lamb is tender. Serve with rice.

Sauté of Lamb with Cranberries
Serves 4

Ingredients

2tbsp. oil
4 loin lamb chops, trimmed
1lb. onions, thinly sliced
2 medium carrots, peeled and thinly sliced or grated

½ cup fresh cranberries
2tbsp. port
2tbsp. redcurrant jelly
2tbsp. stock
salt and freshly ground pepper
1tbsp. parsley, chopped

Heat the oil in a sauté pan or heavy deep skillet, and brown the chops on each side. Drain and remove. Add the onions and cook slowly over low heat for 10 minutes. Stir in the carrots and cook for a further 5 minutes. Add the cranberries, port, red currant jelly and stock. Bring to a boil, then add the chops. Shake the pan well, then cover and simmer for 20 minutes, turning the chops after 10 minutes.

When the chops are tender, taste for seasoning. The sauce should not be too thin, however. If the cranberries are particularly juicy, remove the chops and keep warm, then boil the liquid rapidly to reduce to a thick glaze. Spoon over the chops and serve garnished with the parsley.

Lamb with Almonds and Yogurt
Serves 6-8

Ingredients

2lb. onions	*2tsp. poppy seeds, ground*
2lb. lamb, cut into 1-in.	*7 cloves garlic, crushed*
cubes	*1in. ginger, grated*
1tsp. ground coriander	*6 cardamom pods, slightly*
1tsp. ground cumin	*crushed*
1tsp. chili powder	*½ cup almonds, blanched*
1½tsp. salt	*and slivered*
1 cup oil	*1 cup light cream*
2 cups yogurt	
½tsp. Garam Masala	

Peel all the onions and finely chop half of them. Finely slice the other half.

Put the lamb in a large bowl, add the chopped onions, coriander, cumin, chili and salt, mix with the meat and marinate for 4-5 hours.

Heat the oil in a large skillet and fry the sliced onions until brown. Drain them on paper towels and blend to a fine paste in a liquidizer or food processor without adding any water. (Keep the oil for making the curry.)

Put the yogurt, Garam Masala and poppy seeds in a bowl, add the onion paste, mix thoroughly and put aside.

Heat 6tbsp. of the reserved oil in a large saucepan over a medium high heat. Add the garlic and ginger and fry until very lightly golden.

Add the lamb and the spices and mix with the oil. Lower the heat and cook, stirring occasionally, until all the liquid that comes out of the lamb has been absorbed.

Add the yogurt paste, cardamom and almonds and mix with the meat. Cover and cook for about 30 minutes until the lamb is tender and the gravy very thick.

Add the cream and stir gently to mix. Cook for a further 10 minutes.

After the gravy has thickened and the lamb is tender, it can be transferred to an ovenproof dish, the cream gently mixed in and then put in a preheated oven at 350°F for 10 minutes.

Simple Cassoulet
Serves 6-8

Ingredients

1lb. navy beans	*4 cloves garlic, crushed*
½lb. piece, smoked bacon	*2tbsp. tomato paste*
bay leaf	*1tsp. sugar*
½lb. Toulouse or Polish	*seasoned flour*
sausage, cut into 1-in.	*3tbsp. olive oil*
chunks	*2 medium onions, sliced*
½tsp. dried thyme	*½tsp. dried oregano*
2lb. boned shoulder or	*1¼ cups red wine*
breast of lamb cut into	*salt and pepper*
1½in. chunks	*⅔ cup stock or water*

Wash the navy beans and soak them in cold water overnight.

Change the water, add the bacon and the bayleaf and simmer, covered, for an hour. Drain, discard the bay leaf and cut the bacon into 1-in. chunks. Put the bacon, beans and Toulouse or Polish sausage into a large casserole.

Roll the meat in seasoned flour and brown in oil.

Transfer to the casserole.

Fry the onions and garlic in the remains of the oil until they begin to brown. Add the tomato paste, sugar, herbs, wine and plenty of salt and pepper. Simmer for a couple of minutes, then pour into the casserole together with the stock or water.

Put the casserole, uncovered, into a hot oven (400°F) for 20 minutes, stirring gently from time to time. Cover the casserole, turn down the heat to 325°F for a further 2½ hours, stirring occasionally, until the lamb and beans are tender. (You may need to add a little more water if it looks like getting dry.)

Souvlakia
Serves 4

This dish is particularly delicious when cooked on a barbecue.

Ingredients

1lb. leg of lamb	*salt and freshly ground*
12 bay leaves	*pepper*
juice of ½ lemon	*1tsp. oregano*
2tbsp. olive oil	*lemon quarters*

Allow one skewer for each person. Cut the lamb into 1-in. cubes and thread onto the skewers with pieces of bay leaf in between. Leave space at either end of the skewers to enable them to rest on the broiler rack.

Beat the lemon juice into the olive oil, season with salt, pepper and oregano and leave the lamb to marinate in the mixture in a plastic bag for at least 1 hour.

Cook under the hot broiler for about 10 minutes turning occasionally, so that the lamb becomes well seared on the outside and tender and juicy inside.

Serve immediately with quarters of lemon to squeeze over the meat, a tomato and cucumber salad and a dish of rice.

Souvlakia

Wheat Grain Lamb
Serves 6

Ingredients

1lb. wholewheat grains
5 cardamom pods
1-in. piece of stick
   cinnamon
6 cloves
1in. ginger
4 cloves garlic
³⁄₄ cup Ghee (Clarified
   Butter)
4 medium onions, finely
   sliced
1¹⁄₂lb. boneless lamb, cut
   into 1-in. cubes

1tsp. ground turmeric
2tsp. chili powder
1tbsp. ground poppy seeds
3tbsp. shredded coconut
2tbsp. coriander leaves,
   chopped
1tbsp. mint leaves, chopped
2tbsp. salt
³⁄₄ cup yogurt
juice of 2 limes

Soak the wheat in plenty of water overnight. Drain. Put the wheat and some water in a large saucepan and bring to a boil. Cook until tender and mushy.

Grind the cardamom, cinnamon and cloves to a fine powder and the ginger and garlic to a fine paste.

In a large saucepan, heat the ghee and fry the onions until golden. Remove one-third of the fried onions and put aside.

Add the ginger and garlic paste, the lamb, turmeric, chili powder, poppy seeds, coconut, coriander and mint leaves, the salt and half the ground spices and stir-fry for 5-6 minutes.

Add the yogurt and mix thoroughly. Lower the heat. Cover and cook for about 30 minutes.

Add the remaining ground spices and continue to cook for about another 30 minutes until the meat is tender. Remove from the heat.

Add the boiled wheat and beat with the back of a wooden spoon until the meat disintegrates.

Add the lime juice and stir well. Bring to a boil again and boil for 5 minutes.

Serve garnished with the remaining fried onions.

Spicy Lamb Rissoles
Serves 4

This is an excellent dish for using up leftover lamb from a joint. These rissoles are also well suited to being made in advance and frozen until needed.

Ingredients

1 cup ground cooked lamb
2tbsp. vegetable oil
1 large onion, peeled and
   finely chopped
¹⁄₂tsp. oregano
1 clove garlic, crushed
1tbsp. lemon juice
1 cup cooked long-grain
   rice
salt and freshly ground
   pepper

pinch ground cumin
¹⁄₂tsp. paprika
1tbsp. chopped parsley
3 eggs
2tbsp. water
1tbsp. flour
1¹⁄₂ cups dried
   breadcrumbs
oil for frying
1¹⁄₂ cups Spicy Tomato
   Sauce

Heat the oil in a large skillet and cook the onion for 4 minutes. Push to one side of the pan and fry the lamb, separating the meat with a fork or spoon.

Mix the oregano, garlic, lemon juice and cooked rice and allow to cool in a mixing bowl.

Add the seasoning, cumin, paprika and parsley to the lamb mixture and mix well. Add a little beaten egg to bind the mixture together.

Mix the remaining eggs with 2tbsp. water.

With floured hands form rice and lamb mixture into 2-in. rissole shapes. Dip into the egg and water, and then into the breadcrumbs. Arrange on a tray and chill for at least 15 minutes before frying.

Heat the oil in a deep fryer and fry for 4-5 minutes. Serve hot with the sauce and crisp green salad.

Spicy Lamb Rissoles

Spiced Lamb and Cheese Meatloaf
Serves 4-6

Serve this meatloaf with Ratatouille (minus the cheese), or cold with relish and Rainbow Salad.

Ingredients

½lb. large spinach leaves, washed
4oz. finely crumbled Crustless wholewheat bread
1lb. lean lamb, trimmed and coarsely ground
2 eggs, lightly beaten
2tbsp oil
1 medium onion, finely chopped

2 cloves garlic, crushed
1 green chili, seeded and finely chopped
1tsp. ground coriander
½tsp. ground cumin
salt and freshly ground pepper
¼lb. Gruyère cheese, sliced

Grease a 2-lb. bread pan, and line the base with waxed paper.

Remove the stalks from the spinach and blanch in boiling salted water for 1 minute. Drain and rinse with cold water. Drain well, pat dry with paper towels, then line the prepared tin with the spinach leaves so they completely cover the sides and base. Save any spinach leaves which are left over.

In a mixing bowl combine the breadcrumbs, lamb and eggs until thoroughly blended.

Heat the oil in a pan, add the onion, garlic and chili and fry for 2 minutes. Stir in the spices and fry for 1 minute. Allow to cool, then add to the bowl with a little salt and pepper. Chop any remaining spinach and add to the lamb mixture. Mix all these ingredients together until smooth and well blended.

Pack half the meat mixture into the bread pan. Cover with the sliced cheese, then with the remaining meat mixture. Press down firmly with the back of a spoon. Cover the pan with foil, then stand it in a roasting pan half-filled with hot water. Bake in the preheated oven at 375°F for 1¾ to 2 hours. Turn out and serve sliced.

Stuffed Vine Leaves
Serves 4-6

This is a Bulgarian version of a dish which appears throughout the Middle East. Vine leaves can be bought at delicatessens, either canned or salted in brine. If you have your own vines, it is gratifying to be able to make use of the leaves.

Ingredients

1tbsp. oil
1 onion, chopped
¼ cup rice
2tsp. paprika
1 medium tomato, peeled and chopped
2 cups beef stock
1lb. ground lamb
salt and pepper

parsley, finely chopped
1tsp. dried marjoram
½lb. vine leaves (if using preserved leaves, otherwise about 35 fresh leaves)
2 eggs
1⅓ cups yogurt

Heat the oil, add the onion and cook until it has just softened but not browned. Add the rice and paprika and stir around well. Add the tomato and cook for 3 minutes. Add half the stock to the pan and bring the mixture to the boil. Add this sauce to the ground meat and season with salt and pepper, parsley and marjoram. Mix together very well

Rinse the leaves if using preserved leaves or blanch them if using fresh leaves. Remove the stems. Put a teaspoonful of the meat mixture into each leaf on the rough side and roll it up, tucking in the edges. Squeeze each roll to pack it firmly. Fit the rolls closely into a flameproof oven dish and pour over the remaining beef stock. Put a plate on the vine leaves (to keep them from rising up), cover and simmer for 45 minutes.

Mix the eggs and yogurt and when the vine leaves are cooked, carefully drain off the liquid and mix it with the egg and yogurt. Pour the mixture back into the vine leaves and either warm through on a very gentle heat or bake at 350°F for 10 minutes.

Casseroled Leg of Lamb
Serves 6-8

Ingredients

7-8lb. leg of lamb, boned and tied
1tsp. salt
3 bay leaves
1 cup red wine vinegar
2 cups water
1¼ cups diced onions
4tbsp. coarsely chopped fresh parsley

½tsp. dried thyme
½tsp. black pepper
4 large tomatoes, coarsely chopped
2tbsp. chicken fat or olive oil

Rub the leg of lamb with the salt. Put the lamb in a large casserole.

In a small saucepan combine the bay leaves, vinegar, water, onions, parsley, thyme, pepper and tomatoes. Bring the liquid to a boil over a high heat. Cook for 1 minute and remove the saucepan from the heat. Cool the mixture to room temperature and pour it over the lamb. Leave the lamb to marinate in the refrigerator for 6 hours, uncovered. Turn the lamb every 1½ hours.

Preheat the oven to 375°F. Melt the chicken fat in a small saucepan over a medium heat. Remove the lamb from the refrigerator. Pour the chicken fat or olive oil over the lamb. Roast the lamb for 2 hours, basting every 30 minutes. (If the liquid in the casserole starts to boil too fast, reduce the heat to 350°F).

Simple Lamb Curry
Serves 4

Ingredients

1lb. boneless lamb	1½tsp. ground cumin
3 onions	1tsp. chili powder
4 cloves garlic	½tsp. Garam Masala
1in. ginger	1tsp. salt
3 tomatoes	¼ cup yogurt, slightly
3tbsp. Ghee (Clarified	beaten
Butter)	1 cup water
2tsp. ground coriander	

Wash and dry the meat. Cut into 1-in. cubes.

In a blender or food procesor, blend together the onion, garlic and ginger to a fine paste.

Plunge the tomatoes into boiling water for 10 seconds. Peel and chop them and put aside.

Heat the ghee in a large saucepan and fry the onion paste, stirring constantly, until golden brown.

Add the coriander, cumin, chili, Garam Masala and salt and stir-fry for 1-2 minutes.

Add the meat and fry for a few minutes with the spices.

Add the yogurt, mix well and fry for a further minute.

Add the water and, when it starts to boil, lower the heat. Cover and cook for about 40 minutes, stirring occasionally.

Add the tomatoes, stir well to mix, cover again and cook for a further 25-30 minutes until the meat is tender and the gravy slightly thickened.

Orange Lamb Chops
Serves 4

Ingredients

2tbsp. oil	salt and pepper
8 lamb chops	⅔ cup yogurt
1tsp. ground cinnamon	1 egg yolk
juice of 2 oranges	

Heat the oil, add the chops and brown them. Remove them to a flameproof oven dish. Add the cinnamon to the pan and stir it around. Add the orange juice and bring it to a boil, scraping the sediment from the bottom of the pan. Pour the juice over the lamb, season well, cover and bake at 350°F for 1 hour.

Mix the yogurt with the egg yolk. Take the chops from the dish and keep them warm. Add the yogurt mixture to the pan and warm it through on a gentle heat.

Return the chops to the sauce and serve immediately.

Sweet and Sour Lamb
Serves 6

Ingredients

½ cup oil	3 medium tomatoes,
1½lb. onions, halved and	chopped
sliced	2 cups water
½tsp. chili powder	3tbsp. vinegar
pinch ground turmeric	2tsp. sugar
1in. ginger, grated	1tsp. salt
1½lb. lamb, cut into 1-in.	
cubes	

Heat the oil in a saucepan over a medium high heat and fry the onions until golden brown. Add the chili, turmeric and ginger and fry, stirring constantly, for 1-2 minutes. Add the lamb and tomatoes and continue to fry for another 8-10 minutes, until the meat is browned.

Add the water, stir well and bring to a boil. Lower heat, cover and cook for about 45 minutes. Add the vinegar, sugar and salt and cook for another 15 minutes.

Tarragon Lamb
Serves 6

Ingredients

2lb. boned shoulder of	1 medium onion, chopped
lamb, trimmed and	3tbsp. butter or margarine
cubed	2tbsp. flour
1tsp. salt	1tbsp. tarragon vinegar
1tbsp. dried tarragon or	1 egg yolk
2tbsp. fresh, chopped	⅔ cup sour cream
2½ cups water	pepper

Put the lamb into a large pan with the salt, tarragon, water and onion. Bring to the boil and then cover and simmer for about 1 hour, or until the meat is tender. At this stage you might care to cool the lamb overnight and skim off the fat before continuing.

In a clean pan melt the butter and stir in the flour off the heat. Add a little stock from the meat and stir it in well to make a smooth sauce. Return this mixture to the meat and add the vinegar. Cook for 5 minutes. Mix the egg yolk into the sour cream. Add several spoonsful of the hot liquid, a little at a time, and then return the mixture to the pan on a very gentle heat. Stir through well.

Variation Substitute dill for the tarragon if you prefer.

Preparing Lambs' Kidneys

I Nick the membrane with a knife and pull it off.

2 Cut the kidneys lengthways through the core to give even halves.

3 Use scissors to remove all the white gristle and fat from the center (the 'core'). Tuck the scissor points right in to snip out as much of the core as possible.

Beef and Veal

Hamburgers with Spicy Tomato Sauce
Serves 4

Ingredients

1lb. lean ground beef
1 onion, peeled and finely
  chopped
1 green pepper, seeded
2tbsp. fresh breadcrumbs
1 egg
1tsp. Worcestershire sauce
salt and freshly ground
  pepper

Sauce
1tsp. oil
1 clove garlic, crushed
1 carrot, scraped and
  grated
1 onion, peeled and finely
  chopped
1 chili pepper seeded and
  chopped (optional)
7oz. can peeled tomatoes
²⁄₃ cup stock or water
bay leaf
¹⁄₂tsp. oregano

Put the meat in a bowl with the very finely chopped onion.

Chop the pepper into very small dice. If you prefer, both onion and pepper can be chopped in a blender.

Add the breadcrumbs. Mix with a beaten egg and add the Worcestershire sauce and seasoning.

Divide the mixture into 8 parts and shape into rounds. A manual hamburger shaper can be used for this purpose. Place on a tray in the refrigerator to chill while making the sauce.

To make the sauce, heat the oil in a saucepan and cook the garlic and grated carrot over a low heat for 4 minutes. Stir well and then add remaining ingredients. Season well. Simmer for at least 20 minutes on a low heat.

Brush the hamburgers over with oil and broil over a high heat for 4 minutes each side. If you like beef well cooked give the burgers an additional 3 minutes.

Cottabulla
Jamaican Meatloaf
Serves 8

Ingredients

¹⁄₂lb. stale white bread,
  crusts removed
2lb. ground beef
2 medium onions, finely
  chopped
2 eggs
1tsp. ground coriander

1tsp. dried oregano
1tsp. paprika
3 cloves of garlic, crushed
pinch cayenne
1tsp. sugar
salt and freshly ground
  black pepper

Soak the bread in the water, squeeze out and crumble. Mix all the ingredients together thoroughly, seasoning with plenty of salt and pepper.

Pack into a large soufflé dish leaving a slight hollow in the middle. Cover with foil and bake for 40 to 50 minutes at 375°F until cooked through, but still slightly pink in the middle.

While it is still hot, put a plate slightly smaller than the baking dish on top of the foil and weight it with some heavy cans. Leave until cold and firm, remove the weights and refrigerate until needed.

Slice into wedges and serve in its cooking dish.

Variation This can also be served hot. There is no need to weight it.

Shaped into patties, rolled in seasoned flour and fried, broiled or barbecued, this mixture makes sensational hamburgers!

Beef with Carrots
Serves 4-6

Ingredients

2tbsp. oil
1 large onion, chopped
1¹/₂lb. stewing beef, cubed
1lb. carrots, sliced
1tsp. ground cumin

1tsp. sugar
¹/₄ cup beef stock
salt and pepper
1 cup yogurt

Heat the oil, add the onion and cook until it has just softened but not browned. Add the beef and brown in the oil. Add the carrots, cumin and sugar, and stir well. Add the stock and seasoning. Bring to the boil, cover and bake at 275°F for 3 hours.

Remove from the oven, stir in the yogurt carefully and heat through gently before serving.

Indian Kebab
Serves 4

Ingredients

1 egg
1lb finely ground beef
1tsp. coriander seeds, ground
¹/₂tsp. chili powder
¹/₂tsp. cumin
¹/₂tsp. Garam Masala
2 cloves garlic, crushed
salt to taste

1 onion, grated or liquidized
breadcrumbs (optional)
2tbsp. oil
1 lemon, sliced, pits removed
1 onion, sliced into rings
1 tomato, peeled and sliced

Mix the lightly beaten egg and beef in a bowl. Add the spices, garlic, salt and grated onion to the beef and use breadcrumbs to stiffen and bind the mixture if necessary.

Oil your fingers and the skewers. Wrap the meat around the skewers in cigar shapes. Brush the meat with oil and cook under a moderate broiler until evenly browned.

Serve garnished with lemon, onion and tomato slices.

Mediterranean Beef Casserole
Serves 4

This is an excellent dish to prepare in advance as the flavor improves when the dish is reheated

Ingredients

1¹/₂lb. lean chuck steak
2 slices bacon
2tbsp. seasoned flour
4tbsp. oil
2 onions, peeled and diced
2 cloves garlic, crushed
2 stalks celery, washed
1 carrot, washed and sliced
2 red peppers, seeded and diced
15oz. can tomatoes
1¹/₄ cups stock or water
4tbsp. red wine

salt and freshly ground black pepper
1-2 bay leaves
1 bouquet garni
sprig of fresh or 1tsp. dried thyme
¹/₄lb. mushrooms
3¹/₂ cups pasta
1tbsp. butter
pinch of nutmeg
1tbsp. parsley, freshly chopped (optional)

Mediterranean Beef Casserole

Trim the meat to remove excess fat or gristle, cut into small ¹/₂-in. cubes. Toss the cubes in seasoned flour.

Heat half the oil in a skillet on a high heat, turn down a little and fry the meat on all sides to seal. Drain on to a plate and leave the meat juices in the skillet.

Put the remaining oil in an ovenproof casserole and cook the onion over a low heat for about 3 minutes. Add crushed garlic.

Remove the strings from the celery with a sharp knife and then cut into neat slices. Add to the onions. Add the carrot and diced peppers, toss all vegetables in the oil over a low heat for 2 minutes. Add the meat and tomatoes to the casserole.

Pour the stock into the skillet and mix with the meat juices and the red wine over a low heat. Pour over the meat and vegetables. Add the herbs.

Bring to the boil and cook in the oven at 350°F for 1 hour or until meat is tender. Add mushrooms, either sliced or whole, halfway through the cooking time The casserole may be cooked on top of the stove but must only simmer gently for about 45 minutes.

Cook the pasta in boiling salted water with a few drops of oil added for approximately 12 minutes. Drain and toss in a little melted butter with a shake of pepper and nutmeg.

Serve the pasta with the casserole which may be garnished with chopped parsley.

Little Meatballs
Serves 8

Ingredients

2lb. beef chuck steak, ground
3½tsp. tomato paste
2 cups chicken stock
4tbsp. grape jelly
½tsp. salt
pinch ground white pepper
1 clove garlic, finely chopped
pinch dried oregano
pinch dried rosemary
2tbsp. chicken fat
½tsp. dried dill
½tsp. dried basil

In a large mixing bowl combine the ground beef, tomato paste, ½ cup of the chicken stock, grape jelly, salt, white pepper, garlic, oregano and rosemary. Mix well. Shape the mixture into meatballs approximately 1in. in diameter.

In a large saucepan, melt the chicken fat over a low heat. Add the meatballs and brown for 5 minutes. Add the remaining chicken broth and the dill and basil. Simmer for 15 minutes over a very low heat. Serve warm.

Beef Cobbler
Serves 6-8

Ingredients

2lb. stewing beef
½ cup seasoned flour
4tbsp. oil
1lb. onions, cut into 1-in. chunks
4-5 cloves garlic, crushed
¾lb. large carrots, cut into ½-in. rounds
2tsp. dried mixed herbs
1tsp. sugar
1tbsp. paprika
1tbsp. tomato paste
1¼ cups red wine
1¼ cups stock or water
salt and pepper
2¼ cups plain flour
2½tsp. baking powder
4tbsp. butter or shortening
⅔ cup cold milk and water

Trim the meat of fat and membrane and cut into 1½in. chunks. Roll in the seasoned flour and fry rapidly in the oil in batches until browned all over. Transfer the meat to a large casserole and sprinkle with any remaining seasoned flour.

Fry the onions and garlic until they begin to brown and add to the casserole together with the carrots, herbs, sugar, paprika, tomato paste, wine, stock or water, and plenty of salt and pepper.

Stir gently and put the uncovered casserole into a hot oven for 20 minutes. Stir after 10 minutes.

Cover the casserole with foil, put its lid on and cook at 325°F for a further 2 hours, stirring from time to time. Add more stock or water if it looks dry.

To make the baking powder biscuit topping, sift the flour and baking powder together and rub in the butter or shortening until the mixture resembles fine breadcrumbs.

Add plenty of salt and pepper and enough milk and water to make a soft dough.

Roll out to ½in. thick on a well-floured surface and stamp out circles 1½-2in. across.

Taste the stew and adjust the seasoning, adding a little more stock or water if necessary.

Arrange the biscuit circles on top of the stew and cook, uncovered, at 400°F for 20 to 30 minutes, until the biscuits are puffy and well browned.

Cholent
Serves 8-10

Ingredients

1 cup dried lima beans
1½ cups dried red kidney beans
1¼ cups dried yellow split peas
1¼ cups dried lentils
4tbsp. butter or margarine
4 large onions, quartered
2 cloves garlic, crushed
1tsp. black pepper
1tsp. salt
2tsp. paprika
4lb. beef brisket
3 cups white wine
1½lb. potatoes, peeled and quartered

Preheat the oven to 450°F. Put the dried peas and beans in separate bowls. Add 3 cups of cold water to each bowl and leave the pulses to soak overnight. Drain well.

Melt the butter or margarine in a large heavy pot. Add the onions and brown them. Add the garlic, pepper, salt and paprika. Add the brisket and brown it.

Add the wine, 4¼ cups cold water, all the pulses and the potatoes. Bring the liquid to a boil. Cover the pot tightly and place it in the oven. Bake for 1 hour, then reduce the heat to 300°F and bake for a further 90 minutes.

Remove the brisket from the pot and let it rest for 10 minutes before slicing. Arrange the peas, beans and potatoes around the brisket and spoon over the broth.

Stuffed Peppers
Serves 4

Ingredients

4 large green peppers
1lb. ground beef
½ cup cooked rice
1 small onion, finely chopped
pinch salt
½tsp. black pepper
1 egg yolk
¼ cup red wine

⅔ cup chopped mushrooms
1½tsp. raspberry or cider vinegar
1 medium tomato, seeded and chopped
¼ cup fresh lemon juice
2tbsp. sugar
pinch paprika
2tbsp. brandy

Preheat the oven to 375°F. Cut the tops off the green peppers and carefully discard the seeds. Blanch the peppers in a large pot of boiling water for 3 minutes. Drain well and set aside.

In a large mixing bowl combine the ground beef, rice, onion, salt, pepper, egg yolk, wine and half the mushrooms. Mix well. Stuff the blanched peppers with the mixture.

Place the peppers on their sides in a large baking dish. Add the vinegar and enough water to fill the dish to a depth of 2 inches. Cover the dish and bake for 35 minutes.

When the peppers have been in the oven for 30 minutes, combine the remaining mushrooms with the tomatoes, lemon juice, sugar, paprika and brandy in a small saucepan. Cover the saucepan and simmer over a very low heat for 5 minutes. Pour the mixture over the stuffed peppers.

Reduce the oven temperature to 300°F and bake the stuffed peppers, uncovered, for a further 15 minutes. Serve warm.

Beef Patties
Serves 4

Ingredients

1lb. ground beef
2 eggs
1 medium onion, chopped
1 large clove garlic, finely chopped
pinch ground rosemary

1 blade mace, broken between your fingers
dash soy sauce
pepper
fine matzo meal
vegetable oil for frying

Mix together all ingredients except for matzo meal and vegetable oil and shape into a dozen patties.

Coat both sides in matzo meal.

Heat vegetable oil until quite hot and fry the patties until brown on both sides.

Beef Patties

Corned Beef Stuffed Potatoes
Serves 4

Children of all ages will love this meal in a potato.

Ingredients

4 large potatoes, scrubbed
1tsp. oil
1tsp. salt
4tbsp. butter
1 medium onion, peeled and finely chopped
2 cloves garlic, peeled and crushed
1 stick celery, finely chopped
½ green pepper, cored, seeded and finely chopped

1 cup wiped and finely chopped button mushrooms
12-oz. can corned beef, diced
salt and freshly ground pepper
¾ cup grated Cheddar cheese

Rub the potatoes with the oil and salt and bake in a preheated oven at 180°C for about 1½ hours, or until tender.

Meanwhile, heat the butter in a skillet, add the vegetables and stir-fry over medium heat for about 5 minutes or until slightly softened.

When the potatoes are ready, slice in half and scoop out the insides. Mash well and mix with the corned beef. Stir into the vegetables in the skillet and reheat. Season to taste.

Heat the broiler. Pile the mixture back into the potato skins. Sprinkle the cheese over the potatoes and broil until golden and bubbling. Serve immediately.

Beef Goulash
Serves 8

There is perhaps no dish so readily identifiable with Hungary than goulash. There are at least 80 standard variations calling for a variety of different ingredients. Below is a traditional beef goulash recipe.

Ingredients

5tbsp. butter or margarine
1 large onion, coarsely chopped
1 large tomato, peeled, seeded and coarsely chopped
1 medium-sized green pepper, seeded and finely diced
4lb. lean beef sirloin, cut into small pieces

3 cups beef stock
2tbsp. flour
3tbsp. poppy seeds
2tbsp. Hungarian sweet paprika
¼ cup dry red wine
1 cup water
1lb. egg noodles
4tbsp. sour cream

Melt the butter or margarine in a large saucepan over a low heat. Add the onion, tomato and green pepper and sauté for 5 minutes.

Add the beef, beef stock, flour, poppy seeds, paprika and red wine. Simmer for 30 minutes. Add the water, cover, and simmer for 90 minutes.

While the goulash simmers, cook the egg noodles in a large pan of boiling water. Drain well. Serve the goulash on a bed of noodles, and drizzle the cream over the dish.

Boeuf Dijonnaise
Serves 4-6

You may be able to buy fillet ends, which are much cheaper than the better end of the fillet and will do perfectly well for this type of dish.

Ingredients

2tbsp. oil
1 large onion, sliced
1½lb. fillet of beef, cut into strips

1tbsp. seasoned flour
1¼ cups beef stock
2tbsp. Dijon mustard
⅔ cup yogurt

Heat the oil, add the onion and cook until it has softened but not browned. Pass the beef strips through the seasoned flour and then brown them lightly. Add the stock and mustard to the pan, stirring well. Cover and simmer for 15 minutes. Stir the yogurt in and gently warm it through.

Serve with rice and salad.

Beef Satay
Serves 4

Ingredients
2 green onions, washed
1in. fresh root ginger,
 grated
2 cloves garlic, crushed
8 cardamom pods
1tsp. cumin seeds
1tsp. coriander seeds
juice of 1 lemon
1tsp. grated or ground
 nutmeg
2 bay leaves
2tbsp. oil
1½lb. chuck steak

Sauce
6tbsp. peanut butter
1tbsp. brown sugar
2 chili peppers, seeded
1tsp. sugar
⅔ cup beef stock
juice and rind of 1 lemon

Place all the ingredients except the meat in a blender to make a paste.

Trim the meat and cut into small squares. Mix with the paste and allow to marinate for several hours, then thread the meat onto skewers.

Make the sauce by mixing all the ingredients except the lemon juice together in a saucepan. Bring to the boil and simmer for about 20 minutes. Add the lemon juice.

While the sauce is cooking turn the broier on to high heat and allow the skewered meat to cook. Turn every 2 minutes for the first 6 minutes, then lower the heat and continue cooking. The time will depend on whether you like your meat slightly rare or well cooked.

Accompany with boiled rice.

Korean Beef with Vegetable Noodles
Serves 4

Ingredients

½lb. rump or sirloin steak, thinly sliced
1tbsp. sugar
3tbsp. soy sauce
4 green onions
1 clove garlic, crushed
2tbsp. sesame seeds, roasted
¼lb. transparent noodles, soaked in water for 20 minutes
40 Chinese mushrooms, soaked in water for 30 minutes
1 onion, peeled and sliced
1 carrot, peeled and cut into fine matchstick-like pieces
2 zucchini or ½ cucumber, trimmed and cut into sticks
½ red pepper, seeded and cut into strips
4 button mushrooms, sliced
3 cups bean sprouts, washed and drained
sesame oil for cooking
1-2 eggs, separated
salt and pepper

Chill the steak so that it is easier to slice finely and cut it into 2in. strips. Mix with the sugar, two-thirds of the soy sauce, one of the green onions, finely chopped, the garlic and a few crushed sesame seeds. Leave to marinate for an hour or two.

Cook the soaked and drained noodles in boiling water for 5 minutes. Drain well and separate by pulling apart. Drain the mushrooms and slice. Prepare the onion, carrot, zucchini or cucumber, red pepper, button mushrooms, bean sprouts and green onions.

Heat a little oil in a skillet or wok. Break the egg yolks and pour them into the pan. When they are set, remove them onto paper towels. Heat the pan again and pour in the egg whites. When these are set, drain, then cut up the yolk and white into strips or diamond shapes for the garnish.

Drain the marinade from the beef. Heat a little more sesame oil and stir-fry the beef until it changes color. Add the carrot and onion next. Cook for 2 minutes then add all the other vegetables, tossing all the time until they are just cooked. Add noodles and soy sauce and taste for seasoning. Cook for 1 more minute.

Turn out onto a serving dish and garnish attractively with egg strips, the remaing green onion, chopped, and the rest of the sesame seeds.

Ground Beef Curry
Serves 4-6

Ingredients

1-2tsp. oil
1 large onion, sliced
1 clove garlic, crushed
1½lb. lean ground beef
2tsp. ground coriander
2tsp. ground cumin
1tsp. turmeric
½tsp. ground ginger
salt
1tbsp. cornstarch
½ cup water
1¼ cups yogurt

Heat the oil, add the onion and garlic, and cook until they have just softened but not browned. Add the beef, a little at a time, and brown it well. Drain off any excess fat which may accumulate. Add the spices and salt and stir them in well. Cook for 5 minutes, stirring constantly.

Mix the cornstarch with the water to a smooth paste. Add to the meat, together with the yogurt. Stir well, cover and cook for 25 minutes on a gentle heat.

Serve with rice and usual curry accompaniments.

Parsee Beef Curry
Serves 6

Ingredients

1lb. lentils
1lb. lean beef
2 large onions, finely chopped
2 eggplants, coarsely chopped
1 green pepper, finely chopped
2 potatoes, peeled and coarsely chopped
1lb. spinach, washed and chopped
5tsp. Ghee (clarified butter) or butter
5 cloves garlic, crushed
1tbsp. fenugreek seeds
1tbsp. cumin
1tsp. chili powder
1tsp. coriander seeds
1tsp. mint
salt

Wash the lentils and put them into a pan with the beef. Add the chopped vegetables and cover with water. Bring to the boil and simmer until the vegetables and meat are cooked.

Remove the meat and blend the vegetables and the lentils.

Heat the ghee or butter and fry the garlic, fenugreek, cumin, chili, coriander and mint. Add the lentils and meat, mix well and bring slowly to the boil, add salt to taste. Serve with rice.

Ground Beef with Dill
Serves 4-6

Ingredients

1-2tbsp. oil
1 large onion, chopped
1½lb. ground beef
1tbsp. dried dill
salt and pepper
⅔ cup yogurt

Heat the oil, add the onion and cook until it has just softened but not browned. Add the beef and brown it. Drain off any excess fat. Add the dill, salt and pepper, cover and simmer for 30 minutes. Stir in the yogurt and warm it through gently.

Serve with rice or pasta and a crisp salad.

Ground Beef Curry

Beef Stroganoff
Serves 4

Ingredients

³/₄lb. fillet or rump steak
2tbsp. butter
2tbsp. vegetable oil
1 small onion, peeled and
  finely chopped
3 green onions, washed
1tbsp. flour
pinch paprika
salt and freshly ground
  pepper

¹/₂lb. mushrooms, washed
  and sliced
1tbsp. brandy
2tbsp. madeira or sherry
²/₃ cup beef stock
4tbsp. sour cream
1tbsp. chopped parsley
onion rings

Trim the steak and cut into thin strips about 2in. long.

Heat the butter and oil in a skillet and cook the onion for about 4 minutes over a low heat until translucent. Add the chopped green onions, retaining a few rings of green for final garnish.

Meanwhile mix the flour with the paprika and seasoning and coat the meat strips evenly.

Add the sliced mushrooms to the onions and sauté gently for another 2 minutes. Remove the onions and mushrooms with a slotted spoon, leaving as much fat behind as possible.

Over a fairly high heat fry the meat for a few minutes — less for fillet steak than for rump. Heat the brandy in a ladle and ignite it with a match. Pour over the steak and allow to flame. Remove the meat and mix with the onion and mushrooms.

Add the madeira or sherry and any leftover flour and paprika to the pan and stir well. Gradually add the stock, scraping all meat juices from the bottom of the pan. Add the meat, mushrooms and onions to the sauce and reheat for about 2-3 minutes. Turn the heat low. Add 2-3 tablespoons sour cream and mix well.

Serve in a ring of rice garnished with parsley, sour cream, onion rings, and a sprinkling of paprika. A crisp green salad or crisply cooked green vegetables, such as snow peas or string bean, makes an excellent accompaniment to this luxurious but quickly prepared dish.

Barbecued Ribs of Beef
Serves 6-8

Ingredients

1 tbsp. vegetable oil
3 lb. beef ribs, cut into 2-in.
  pieces
1 tsp. salt
pinch pepper
1 tsp. paprika
1 tsp. dry mustard
1 tbsp. sugar

1 tbsp. Worcestershire sauce
½ cup tomato ketchup
½ cup water
½ cup cider vinegar
¼ cup finely chopped
  onion
1 clove garlic, finely
  chopped

Preheat the oven to 350°F. Heat the vegetable oil in a flameproof casserole. Add the rib pieces and brown on all sides. Pour off the fat. Add the remaining ingredients to the casserole. Cover and bake for 2 hours. Remove the cover for the last 30 minutes. Arrange on a dish with parsley and serve.

Steak au Poivre Vert
Serves 4

Ingredients

4 tbsp. unsalted butter
1 full tbsp. green
  peppercorns
1 tbsp. brandy

sea salt, freshly ground, to
  taste
4 steaks, 8 oz. each

Liquidize the butter, peppercorns, brandy and salt until smooth.

Spread the flavored butter on the steaks and broil under high heat until cooked the way you like them.

Beef Strudel
Serves 4-6

Ingredients

1 tbsp. oil
1 large onion, finely
  chopped
1 lb. lean ground beef
1 cup cooked rice
2 hard-boiled eggs,
  chopped

⅔ cup cottage cheese
salt and pepper
¾ lb. Shortcrust Pastry
egg for glazing
⅔ cup sour cream

Heat the oil, add the onion and cook until it has just softened but not browned. Add the meat, a little at a time, and brown it. Drain off excess fat. Add the cooked rice, chopped eggs, cottage cheese, salt and pepper. Mix thoroughly and leave it to cool.

Roll out the pastry until it is very thin. Spread the meat mixture over the pastry and carefully roll it up. Tuck the ends in well, sealing them with water. Glaze with the beaten egg (or just the white if preferred). Slide the roll carefully onto a greased cookie sheet.

Bake at 350°F for 30 minutes. Serve with the sour cream.

Stir-Fried Beef with Baby Corn and Green Peppers

Stir-Fried Beef with
Baby Corn and Green Peppers
Serves 4-6

Ingredients

1 lb. piece of lean chuck
  steak
1 tbsp. cornstarch
4 tbsp. oil
3 green peppers, cored,
  seeded, halved and
  thinly sliced
1 green chili pepper, seeded
  and thinly sliced

1 small onion, peeled,
  halved and thinly sliced
2 cloves garlic, sliced
1 in. piece root ginger,
  peeled and thinly sliced
½ tsp. superfine sugar
10 oz. can baby corn,
  drained
1-2 tbsp. soy sauce, to taste
2 tbsp. sherry

Cut the meat into wafer-thin slices, either by hand, or by processor (it is best to semi-freeze the meat first if using this method). Coat with the cornstarch, and set aside.

Heat 1 tbsp. of the oil in a wok or large skillet. Add the sliced peppers, chili pepper and onion. Stir-fry over high heat for 2 minutes. Drain thoroughly and set aside.

Heat the remaining oil in the wok or pan, add the garlic and ginger and fry for a few seconds. Add the meat and sugar and stir-fry over high heat for 1 minute, add the corn and stir-fry for another minute. Season with the soy sauce and sherry, and stir-fry the whole mixture for 30 seconds.

Finally, add the pepper mixture and stir-fry for 1 or 2 minutes to heat through and blend the flavors. Serve immediately.

Beef Napoleon
Serves 6

Ingredients

2 heads garlic
3tbsp. olive oil
4tbsp. robust red wine
2tbsp. green onions, finely chopped
3tsp. French mustard
2½tsp. fresh thyme or ½tsp. dried thyme

salt and pepper
1 beef fillet, weighing about 2lb.
2tbsp. chopped parsley
1lb. Puff Pastry

To prepare the marinade, peel and crush 3 of the garlic cloves and mix with 2tbsp. of the oil, the wine, green onions, 1tsp. of the mustard, the thyme, and plenty of salt and pepper.

Lay the fillet at the bottom of a large plastic bag and pour the marinade over it. Seal the top of the bag, put it on a plate in case of leaks, and leave to marinate in a cool place for 6-8 hours.

Heat the remaining oil in a large skillet until very hot.

Lift the meat out of its marinade and fry it quickly on all sides to seal in the juices; this should take no more than 2 minutes.

Cool the beef and return to its marinade. Freeze for an hour — more if you like your fillet really rare.

Simmer the remaining unpeeled garlic cloves for 20 to 25 minutes, until soft. Drain, peel and mash with a fork to a sticky paste.

Stir in the remaining mustard and the parsley, and season with salt and pepper to taste.

Take the beef out of the freezer and leave to thaw the marinade. Roll out the pastry to a thickness of ¼in. — large enough to wrap the beef generously.

Drain the meat and add 1tbsp. of its marinade to the garlic and parsley mixture.

Lay the beef in the middle of the pastry and spread the garlic and parsley mixture over it.

Wet the edges of the pastry with a little water, bring them up over the sides of the meat, and press them together. Seal the ends.

Put the pastry-wrapped beef, seam side down, on a well greased cookie sheet, brush the top with a little milk or egg yolk, and bake for 15 to 20 minutes at 450°F, until the pastry is cooked. If, after this time, the pastry is cooked but the fillet is too rare, turn down the heat to 375°F and cook for a further 7 to 10 minutes, and test again. Serve immediately.

Variation For Beef Garibaldi, spread the beef with half a cup of Pesto instead of the garlic and parsley paste.

Boiled Beef
Serves 8

This substantial dish is remarkably simple to prepare. The method is ideal for making less expensive beef cuts tender.

Ingredients

3lb. beef flank
2 cups beef broth
2 cups chicken broth
2 cups white wine
3 large onions, quartered
1 sprig parsley
2 bay leaves
6 potatoes, peeled and quartered
4 large carrots, peeled and halved

1lb. green beans, trimmed and halved
5 small beets, peeled and quartered
1 large turnip, peeled and cubed
1 clove garlic, crushed
½tsp. salt
½tsp. black pepper

Put all the ingredients into a large, heavy pan. Simmer, covered, over a medium heat for 1 hour. Reduce the heat to low and simmer for 1 hour longer.

Remove the beef from the pan and leave to stand for 10 minutes before slicing.

Serve the beef slices in bowls with the vegetables and broth ladled over them.

Pickled Beef Tongue
Serves 8

Ingredients

4-5-lb. smoked beef tongue
2 cups white wine vinegar
3 large onions, quartered
¾ cup sugar
bay leaf
1 whole clove

pinch white pepper
2tbsp. honey
pinch cinnamon
2tbsp. pickling spice, tied up in cheesecloth

In a large pot, cover the smoked beef tongue with water. Bring the water to a boil. Skim off the fat that rises to the surface. Reduce the heat to low and cover the pan. Simmer for 3 to 4 hours, or until tender, depending on the size of the tongue. Remove the pot from the heat and leave the tongue to cook in the liquid. Skim off the fat.

Put 2¾ cups of the cooking liquid into a saucepan. Discard the remaining cooking liquid or save it for stock. Add the vinegar, onions, sugar, bay leaf, clove, white pepper, honey and cinnamon. Bring the mixture to a boil and simmer for 5 minutes. Add the pickling spice. Remove the clove and simmer for a further 5 minutes. Remove the bay leaf and spice bag. Pour the liquid over the tongue. Chill for at least 90 minutes and serve.

Sauerbraten
Serves 8-10

There are as many different versions of Sauerbraten as there are localities in Germany and Austria. You need to begin this dish 5 days before you want to serve it.

Ingredients

4lb. beef brisket
2 cups red wine vinegar
2 cups white wine
2tsp. whole cloves
1tsp. whole black
  peppercorns
2 bay leaves
2 small onions, coarsely
  chopped
3 cloves garlic, quartered

1 large seedless orange
  with peel, sliced
¼ cup lemon juice
1 cup water
1tbsp. salt
2tbsp. butter
1 cup whole cooked (or
  canned) tomatoes,
  drained
1 cup tomato paste

Put the beef brisket in a large bowl or deep dish. Cover it with the vinegar, wine, cloves, peppercorns, bay leaves, onion, garlic, orange slices, lemon juice and water. Cover the bowl or dish tightly. Refrigerate for 4 days, turning the meat over daily.

On the fifth day, remove the meat from the marinade and pat dry with paper towels. Reserve the marinade. Melt the butter in a large casserole or heavy pot. Add the meat and brown well on all sides. Add the tomatoes, tomato paste and reserved marinade. Cover tightly and simmer for 2½ hours, or until the meat is tender.

Remove the meat from the casserole or pot and leave to stand for 10 minutes before slicing.

Strain 2¾ cups of the cooking liquid through a strainer into a saucepan. Bring the liquid to a boil and simmer for 5 minutes. Serve this as gravy with the sliced Sauerbraten.

Steak and Ale
Serves 6

Ingredients

2lb. rump steak (6 pieces)
Dijon mustard
freshly ground black
  pepper
vegetable oil for frying
12 black peppercorns

12 green peppercorns
8 whole allspice berries
1¼ cups sliced mushrooms
1 cup Guinness or brown
  ale
1tsp. Worcestershire Sauce

Coat the steaks with a thin layer of Dijon mustard and lots of freshly ground pepper. Fry in oil as for rare steaks. Carefully lift out the meat and set aside.

Add to the pan juices the peppercorns, allspice and mushrooms. Cook for 2 minutes. Add the Guinness and cook on a high heat for a minute, then add the Worcestershire sauce.

Lay the steaks in an ovenproof dish and pour over them the Guinness mixture. Cover dish with foil and bake at 350°F for an hour.

Steak and Ale

Spiced Brisket I
Serves 4

Ingredients
Marinade

salt to taste
freshly ground black
  pepper
2 tbsp. red and green
  peppercorns
3 garlic cloves, mashed
1 tsp. soy sauce
1 tsp. paprika
2 tsp. prepared mustard

2lb. brisket of beef
1 onion, chopped
1 green pepper, chopped

Combine the ingredients for the marinade and spread generously over the brisket. Leave to stand for an hour at room temperature, turning every 15 minutes.

Sauté the diced onion and green pepper until soft and place at the bottom of a roasting pan. Place the brisket fat side up and baste well with the marinade. Cover and roast for 2 hours at 350°F.

Remove the roast and cool slightly until it can be sliced, then return to the oven and roast for another 20 minutes, until cooked.

Spiced Brisket II
Serves 6

Ingredients

3lb. brisket of beef
8 slices bacon, rind
  removed
2 onions, coarsely chopped
2 cloves

1 blade mace
1 tbsp. allspice berries
6 black peppercorns
water

Clean and dry the meat, trimming off excess fat if necessary.

Cover the bottom of a casserole dish with 4 slices of bacon and the onion.

Put the meat on the bacon and onion and lay the remaining slices of bacon on top. Add the spices and water so that the meat is nearly covered.

Cover the casserole and cook in a slow oven at 325°F for 3 hours or until tender.

Thai Beef with Spinach
Serves 4

Ingredients

1/2lb. chuck steak
1 1/4 cups unsweetened
  canned coconut milk
1 tsp. brown sugar
1 tbsp. mixed chopped nuts
1 tbsp. soy sauce
2 cloves garlic, crushed
1 onion, peeled
1 in. fresh root ginger

2 fresh chili peppers, seeded
salt and freshly ground
  pepper
juice of 1/2 lemon
1 tbsp. cornstarch
1lb. frozen spinach or 2lb.
  fresh spinach
4 tbsp. yogurt

Trim off excess fat from the meat, and cut into thin strips.

Put the coconut milk, sugar, nuts and soy sauce into a saucepan. Mix the beef with these ingredients and bring to the boil. As soon as the mixture bubbles, turn the heat down and allow to simmer for about 10 minutes.

In a blender or food processor make a paste with the garlic, onion, fresh ginger, chili peppers, a little salt and lemon juice. Mix this paste with the cornstarch and a little cold water. Add some of the hot liquid from the beef to the mixture before stirring into the beef. Cover and simmer gently for about 30-40 minutes until meat is cooked.

Cook the spinach as directed on the packet if using frozen. For fresh spinach wash and remove large stems and cook in a small amount of boiling salted water for about 5 minutes. Drain cooking water into a bowl and use to add to sauce if it has reduced too much. Arrange drained spinach in a hot serving dish. Put beef on top of the spinach and trickle yogurt on top.

Serve with plain boiled rice.

Veal Paprika
Serves 4-6

In Hungary, "paprika" in the title of the recipe usually means the dish will contain not only paprika but also sour cream. You could adapt this recipe using chicken or pork.

Ingredients

1 tbsp. oil	2 green peppers, seeded
2 tbsp. butter	and sliced
1 lb. onions, sliced	3 tomatoes, peeled and
1½ lb. braising veal, cubed	chopped
2 tbsp. paprika	1¼ cups veal or beef stock
1 large clove garlic,	salt and pepper
crushed	⅔ cup sour cream

Heat the oil and butter, add the onions and cook until they have just softened but not browned. Add the veal and let it color slightly. Stir in the paprika and cook it for 2 minutes. Add the garlic, peppers and tomatoes and stir everything together well. Add the stock, salt and pepper, bring to the boil and simmer, covered, for 45 minutes. Stir in the sour cream and warm it through gently.

Serve this with green noodles — the contrasting colors make it a very pretty dish.

Veal and Eggplant Casserole
Serves 4

Ingredients

1½ lb. veal, cubed	½ lb. tomatoes, peeled and
1 tbsp seasoned flour	chopped
2-3 tbsp. oil	⅔ cup dry white wine
2 tsp. paprika	salt and pepper
2 large eggplants	2 eggs
1 large onion, chopped	1¼ cups yogurt

Lightly coat the veal in the seasoned flour. Heat the oil and brown the meat lightly. Add the paprika and stir. Remove the meat.

Cut the eggplants in half lengthwise and scoop out the flesh carefully, leaving the shells intact. Brown the shells in the hot oil (add more if necessary) and remove them from the pan. Add the onions and chopped eggplant flesh to the pan and brown everything lightly. Add the tomatoes and cook just to soften everything. Add the wine, browned meat, salt and pepper, cover and cook on a gentle heat for 30 minutes.

Put the browned eggplant shells in a shallow oven dish and fill them with the meat mixture. Spoon any extra meat around the shells. Cover and bake at 350°F for 20 minutes.

Mix the eggs and yogurt with a little salt and pepper and pour over the eggplant. Return to the oven uncovered, for a further 10 minutes, until the topping is set and lightly colored.

Braised Veal Chops with Parsley Dressing
Serves 6-8

Ingredients

1 cup+1 tbsp. butter or	1 cup chicken stock
margarine	4 tbsp. vegetable oil
½ cup finely chopped	1 cup unflavored
onions	breadcrumbs
½ cup finely chopped	½ cup ground ham
carrots	1 tsp. lemon juice
1 tsp. dried basil	3 tbsp. finely chopped
½ tsp. salt	parsley
½ tsp. black pepper	8 loin veal chops, 1 in. thick
1½ cups white wine	

In a medium-sized saucepan combine 1 cup butter or margarine with the onions, carrots, basil, salt, pepper, wine and chicken stock. Cover and simmer for 10 minutes over a medium heat.

Heat the vegetable oil in a small skillet. Add the breadcrumbs and brown for 3 to 5 minutes over a low heat. Stir in the ham, lemon juice, parsley and the remaining butter or margarine. Cook over a low heat, stirring frequently, for 2 to 3 minutes.

In a large flameproof casserole, arrange the veal chops in a single layer. Pour the broth mixture over the chops, and then the seasoned breadcrumb mixture.

Cover and cook over a medium heat for 40 minutes, or until the veal is tender.

Veal Clou de Giroffe
Serves 4

Ingredients

1¾ lb. leftover veal roast	2 tsp. French mustard
freshly ground black	pinch ground cloves
pepper	½ cup heavy cream
2 cups grated Jarlsberg	
cheese	

Cut the meat into slices ¼ in. thick and arrange them in a well-greased roasting pan. Sprinkle with ground pepper to taste.

Mix cheese, mustard, cloves and heavy cream. Spread the mixture evenly over the meat. Bake for 6 minutes in the oven at 400°F, then broil until golden brown, taking care not to let the meat burn. Serve immediately.

Shoulder of Veal with Mushrooms and Spinach Fettucini
Serves 4

Ingredients

3-3½lb. boned rolled shoulder of veal
1tbsp. oil
1 small onion, peeled and sliced
salt and freshly ground pepper
4tbsp. dry white wine
2½ cups Béchamel Sauce

2½ cups mushrooms, washed and sliced
1tbsp. freshly chopped parsley
1½lb. fresh spinach fettucini
½tsp. oil
2tbsp. butter
nutmeg, freshly grated

Put the boned rolled shoulder in a roasting pan. Pour the oil over it, scatter the sliced onions on top and season well. Pour on the wine. Cook in the oven at 400F for 1½ hours, turning the temperature down to 350°F for the last hour.

Make the Béchamel Sauce, season well and add mushrooms; cook for 5 minutes.

Cook the fettucini in boiling salted water with a few drops of oil added. Fresh fettucini will take 2 minutes. Drain and toss in butter; arrange in a warm serving dish.

Slice the meat after allowing it to stand for 10 minutes. Arrange sliced meat on the pasta and keep warm.

Drain the fat from the roasting pan, add 4tbsp. water, boil, then add meat juices to the mushroom sauce and stir well. Coat the sliced veal, and serve hot.

Sautéed Sherry Veal
Serves 6

Ingredients

1 cup olive oil
1 cup green olives, pitted and halved
1½ cups mushrooms, coarsely chopped
1 cup finely chopped onions
2 green peppers, seeded and finely chopped
4 cloves garlic, finely chopped

4 ripe tomatoes, peeled, seeded and finely chopped
3lb. thin veal scallops
1 cup+2tbsp. flour
pinch salt
pinch black pepper
½ cup dry sherry
½ cup water

Heat half the olive oil in a large heavy skillet. Add the olives, mushrooms, onions, green pepper, garlic and tomatoes. Cook, stirring frequently, for 15 minutes over a low heat. Set aside.

Dredge the veal scallops in a mixture of flour, salt and pepper.

In another pan, heat the remaining olive oil over a low heat. Add the veal scallops, in batches if necessary, and cook for 3 to 4 minutes per side. As they are cooked, set them aside in a warm place.

Drain the oil and fat from the pan. Add the sherry, water and cooked vegetables. Cover and simmer for 8 minutes over a medium heat. Pour the sauce over the veal and serve hot.

Osso Buco
Serves 4

Ingredients

2tbsp. vegetable oil
4tbsp. butter
1 onion, peeled and sliced
1 clove garlic, crushed
2lb. shank of veal
⅔ cup white wine

1¼ cups chicken or veal
  stock
1lb. tomatoes or 15oz. can
  peeled tomatoes
1 lemon, rind and juice
1-2tbsp. parsley

Heat the oil and butter in a heavy saucepan. Add the onion and garlic and cook for 3-4 minutes on a fairly low heat without browning. Remove onto a plate.

Brown the veal on all sides on a medium heat. Add white wine and stock. Allow to cook for a few minutes. Either add the onion to the saucepan, standing the veal upright to prevent the marrow coming out of the bone, or transfer all ingredients into an ovenproof casserole in the same way.

Add chopped tomatoes and simmer on top of the stove or in the oven at 350°F for about 1 hour or until the meat is tender. Add a few drops of lemon juice to the veal.

Mix the grated rind of a lemon with the chopped parsley and sprinkle over the Osso Buco. Serve with Risotto Milanese.

Veal Scallops with Red Wine
Serves 8

Ingredients

½ cup flour
½tsp. salt
½tsp. ground white pepper
3lb. thinly sliced veal
  scallops
8tbsp. olive oil
2 large onions, coarsely
  chopped

3 cloves garlic, finely
  chopped
2tbsp. coarsely chopped
  parsley
½ cup red wine
½ cup sweet sherry
2 cups water
5tbsp. tomato paste

Saltimbocca

On a large ceramic plate mix the flour, salt and pepper together. Lightly dredge the veal slices in the mixture.

Heat the olive oil in a large heavy skillet. Add the veal, onions and garlic and cook over a medium heat for 3 to 5 minutes, or until both sides of the veal slices are browned. Remove the veal slices and keep warm.

Add the parsley, wine, sherry, water and tomato paste to the pan. Stir well and bring to a boil over a high heat. Cook for 3 minutes. Cover and simmer for 10 minutes longer. Serve the sauce spooned over the veal scallops.

Saltimbocca
Serves 4

Ingredients

8 thin slices veal, about
  3×4in.
8 thin slices cooked ham or
  prosciutto, about 3×4in.
8 thin slices mozzarella
  cheese
fresh or dried sage
2tbsp. olive oil
2 cloves of garlic, crushed

juice of 1 large lemon
salt and pepper
4tbsp. butter
½ cup white wine
1tbsp. finely chopped green
  onions (green part only)
1tbsp. parsley, chopped
sprigs of parsley
lemon wedges

On each slice of veal lay a slice of ham, a slice of cheese and either a quarter of a well-bruised leaf of fresh sage or a tiny pinch of dried sage. Roll up and secure with a cocktail stick.

Mix the olive oil, garlic, and half the lemon juice, and season with salt, pepper and a little fresh or dried sage.

Pour over the veal rolls and leave in a cool place to marinate for 2 to 4 hours.

To cook, heat the butter in a large skillet and gently sauté the veal rolls for about 10 minutes, turning occasionally.

Turn up the heat and add the wine, chopped green onions, and the remaining lemon juice.

Allow the sauce to bubble and reduce for 5 minutes. Check the seasoning.

Sprinkle with the chopped parsley and serve immediately, garnished with parsley sprigs and lemon wedges.

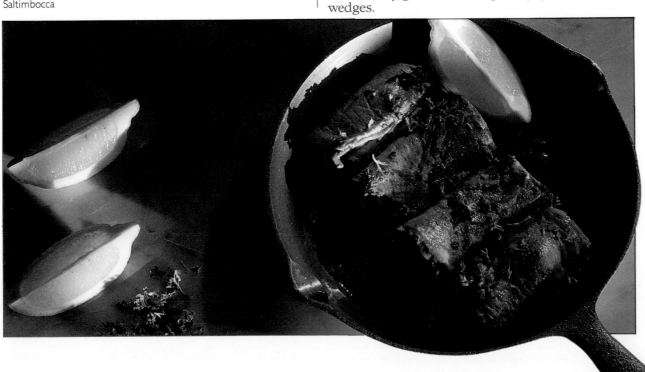

Stuffed Veal Shoulder
Serves 6-8

Ingredients

1lb. ground veal	2 cups cold water
1lb. ground beef	2 eggs
$\frac{1}{2}$lb. ground chicken	1tsp. salt
$\frac{1}{4}$ cup finely chopped onion	$\frac{1}{2}$tsp. white pepper
	4-5lb. veal shoulder, boned
2tbsp. finely chopped green onions	1 clove garlic, crushed
	4 hard-boiled eggs
1 cup soft breadcrumbs	5tbsp. butter or margarine

In a large mixing bowl, combine the ground veal, beef, chicken, onion, green onions, breadcrumbs, water, eggs, salt and pepper. Mix thoroughly until the stuffing has an even consistency.

With a sharp knife, cut the veal shoulder almost in half horizontally, where it is thickest. The veal shoulder should lie flat on a large cutting board. Rub the cut surface of the veal with the garlic and then cover it with a large piece of waxed paper. Pound the veal with a meat pounder until the meat is flattened.

Remove the paper and spread half the flattened veal shoulder with half the stuffing mixture. Arrange the hard-boiled eggs on top of the stuffing. Spread the remaining stuffing mixture over the eggs.

Fold the veal over and tie with strong kitchen string at 2in. intervals and put the veal in a shallow roasting pan filled with 2in. water. Roast for 2 hours at 375°F. Remove the veal from the oven. Remove the roast from the pan and put it on a carving board. Cut and remove the string. Let the roast stand for 10 minutes before slicing.

Melt the butter or margarine in a small saucepan. Add the drippings from the roasting pan. Stir well and simmer for 10 minutes, uncovered, until the gravy is slightly reduced and thickened. Serve separately.

Vitello Tonnato
Serves 6

This summery Italian dish of cold roast veal in a tuna fish sauce should be made a day or so in advance. Ask the butcher to bone the veal for you — you will need some bones for the sauce.

Ingredients

2-lb. piece boned leg or fillet of veal	**Sauce**
	3 egg yolks
2 carrots, peeled and halved	scant cup olive oil
	1-2tbsp. lemon juice
2 onions, peeled and halved	6$\frac{1}{2}$oz. can tuna fish
	salt and freshly ground pepper
2tbsp. butter	1tbsp. capers
1lb. veal bones	lemon wedges

Trim the veal and tie into a neat cylinder if necessary. Coarsely chop the carrots and onions. Put half the vegetables in a roasting pan and set the meat on top. Rub with the butter and roast in the heated oven at 400°F for 1$\frac{1}{2}$ to 1$\frac{3}{4}$ hours, basting frequently. Remove from the pan and allow to cool completely.

Put the remaining vegetables and the veal bones into a large saucepan, and add the vegetables and meat juices from the roasting pan. Barely cover with water and bring to the boil, skimming frequently. Simmer for 1$\frac{1}{2}$ to 2 hours. Strain, discarding the bones and vegetables. Boil the stock rapidly to reduce to 1$\frac{1}{4}$ cups. Cool.

In the meantime, prepare the sauce. With the egg yolks and oil, make a thick mayonnaise. Add 1tbsp. of the lemon juice. Drain and flake the tuna fish, and gradually process or liquidize with the sauce. Add enough stock to make a sauce of coating consistency. Season to taste, adding more lemon juice if necessary.

Remove the string from the meat and slice it thinly. Put the sliced veal into a terrine and spoon over the sauce. Cover and chill overnight for the flavors to blend.

Garnish with the capers and lemon wedges. Serve with crusty bread and a crisp salad.

Stuffed Cabbage Rolls
Serves 8

This is the Hungarian version of stuffed cabbage. It is unique in that the sauce is neither red nor sweet.

Ingredients

10 large white cabbage leaves	pinch salt
	pinch white pepper
4tbsp. chicken fat	1tsp. Hungarian sweet paprika
2lb. ground veal	
2$\frac{1}{2}$ cups cooked rice	1 cup cold water
3 cloves garlic, quartered	
$\frac{1}{2}$ cup finely chopped onion	

Cook the cabbage leaves in a large pot of boiling water for 5 to 8 minutes or until they are soft. Drain well and set aside.

In a large saucepan, melt the chicken fat. Add the veal, rice, garlic, onions, salt and pepper. Cook over a low heat, stirring often, until the veal loses its raw look. Cover and simmer for 20 minutes, stirring frequently.

Add the paprika to the veal mixture and cook, stirring frequently, for 2 minutes.

Spoon 3tbsp. of the veal mixture on to the center of each cabbage leaf. Roll up the cabbage leaves, tucking in the edges of the leaves as you roll.

Place the cabbage rolls in a large saucepan. Add the water and cover. Simmer over a low heat for 50 minutes. Serve warm.

Preparing Veal or Beef Kidney

1 Remove as much of the white 'core' as possible with scissors.

2 Slice the kidney thinly. Veal kidney (which is smaller and pale) is usually cooked at this stage. Beef kidney is chopped smaller for mixing with other meats.

Preparing Veal Liver

1 With a small sharp knife remove the fine membrane that covers the liver. Hold the knife aginst the liver and gently pull away the skin.

2 Cut into very fine slices with a long, thin knife. Remove any 'tubes' carefully — they are unpleasantly tough when cooked.

Pork and Ham

Sausage and Bacon Kebabs
Serves 4

Ingredients

16 cocktail sausages	4 tomatoes
8 slices bacon	2 tbsp. vegetable oil
8 mushrooms	salt and freshly ground
1 green pepper, seeded	pepper
1 red pepper, seeded	1¼ cups Spicy Tomato
4 bay leaves	Sauce

You will need 4 large or 8 small skewers to prepare the kebabs. If cocktail sausages are not easily available, simply twist the link sausages, into two.

Roll the bacon after flattening each slice with a knife. Each slice will make 2 small rolls.

Remove the mushroom stalks and cut the peppers into squares.

Thread sausages, bacon rolls, mushrooms, peppers and bay leaves alternately onto the skewers. Lay in a flat dish and pour the oil over. Season well. Turn in the oil for 5 minutes until well coated.

Prepare the Spicy Tomato Sauce.

Put the kebabs under a heated broiler and turn the skewers round every 2 minutes until the food is evenly browned on all sides. When it is golden brown turn the heat to medium and cook for 3-4 minutes each side. Lay the tomatoes on the broiling rack for the last few minutes of cooking. (Tomatoes are best cooked separately as they tend to fall off skewers when cooked.)

Lay the kebabs on a bed of rice and serve with the Spicy Tomato Sauce. If you wish to remove the skewers use a fork to slide the food off.

Bacon and Potato Supper
Serves 4-6

Ingredients

4 slices lean bacon	6 green onions, trimmed
2 lb. potatoes, peeled	and finely chopped
2 cloves garlic, peeled and	1 tbsp. parsley, chopped
crushed	¼ lb. Cheddar cheese
1¼ cups sour cream	salt and freshly ground
3 eggs	pepper

Heat the broiler, then broil the bacon until crisp. Drain on paper towels.

Coarsely grate the potatoes. This is much quicker if you have a food processor. Remove the excess water from the potatoes by squeezing well, then draining on paper towels.

Mix the garlic, cream, eggs, green onions and parsley. Crumble the bacon and add. Mix the grated potatoes with the grated cheese in a bowl, then stir in the egg and cream mixture. Season to taste, then pour into a greased shallow ovenproof baking dish.

Place in the heated oven and bake at 400°F for 30 to 40 minutes until golden brown and crispy.

Serve with a crisp green salad.

Sausage and Bacon Kebabs

Sausage and Bacon Rolls with Tomato Rice
Serves 4

Ingredients

1 cup long-grain rice	½ tsp. salt
2¼ cups beef stock	8 sausages
2 tsp. tomato paste	8 slices bacon
1 small onion, peeled and chopped	⅔ cup Spicy Tomato Sauce

Wash the rice several times and drain.

Mix the beef stock, tomato paste and onion with the salt and bring to the boil. Pour over the rice and fork through to stop grains sticking together. Cover and simmer until all liquid is absorbed, about 15 minutes.

Turn the broiler on high and brown the sausages on each side for 3 minutes. Allow to cool slightly and then wrap bacon slices around the sausages.

Broil for a further 5 minutes under a medium heat. Alternatively bake in the oven at 350°F in the tomato sauce for 15 minutes after browning under the broiler.

Arrange the sausage and bacon rolls on the tomato rice and pour the sauce on top.

Pork Dijonnaise
Serves 4

Serve noodles tossed in butter and black pepper or creamy mashed potatoes to complement the rich piquant sauce.

Ingredients

4 pork chops	2 egg yolks
2 tbsp. oil	2 tbsp. Dijon mustard
2 shallots, peeled and finely chopped	1 tbsp. parsley, finely chopped
1¼ cups dry white wine	4 tbsp. sour cream
bouquet garni	
salt and freshly ground pepper	

Trim the chops and pat dry.

Heat the oil in a heavy sauté pan or skillet, and brown the chops on both sides. Stir in the shallots and cook for 1 minute. Add the wine, bouquet garni and a little salt and pepper. Stir well, bring to a boil, then cover and cook very gently for 20 minutes, or until the chops are tender.

Combine the yolks with the mustard and parsley. Drain the juices from the meat and skim off the fat. Then, beating all the while, pour the hot juices on to the egg yolk mixture. Beat well, then add the sour cream.

Taste the sauce for seasoning then pour over the chops. Reheat without boiling and serve immediately.

Variation Replace the chops with boneless chicken breasts or veal chops.

Stuffed Pork Chops with Pasta Bows
Serves 4

Ingredients

1 tbsp. oil	1 tbsp. fresh white breadcrumbs
1 small onion, peeled and finely diced	4 thick pork chops
½ cup mushrooms, washed and finely chopped	2 cups Concentrated Tomato Sauce
½ tsp. dried or 1 tsp. chopped fresh sage	½ lb. pasta bows
1 tsp. freshly chopped parsley	2 tbsp. butter
½ tsp. grated lemon rind	freshly grated nutmeg
salt and freshly ground pepper	bunch watercress

Heat the oil and cook the finely diced onion over a low heat for 4 minutes, add finely chopped mushrooms and cook for a further 2 minutes.

Add sage, parsley, lemon rind, salt and pepper to the breadcrumbs in a small mixing bowl. Tip the onion and mushrooms into the bowl and mix well.

Cut a slit in each chop at the fat end. Fill the slit with the onion and mushroom stuffing. Put the chops under the broiler for 4 minutes each side. Dry on paper towels to remove excess fat.

Arrange the chops in an ovenproof dish, pour over the tomato sauce, cover with foil and bake for 25 minutes at 350°F.

Cook the pasta bows for about 10 minutes, drain and toss in melted butter. Add a shake of pepper and nutmeg.

Serve the bows and chops garnished with watercress.

Stuffed Pork Chops with Pasta Bows

Fried Pork with Mushrooms and Water Chestnuts
Serves 4-6

The pork can be replaced with lean steak, or boneless, skinned chicken breasts for a change of flavor.

Ingredients
1lb. pork fillet, roughly chopped
1tsp. cornstarch
4tbsp. oil
1 small onion, peeled and finely chopped
1in. ginger, peeled and finely chopped
2½ cups sliced button mushrooms

1 cup water chestnuts, drained and sliced
1tbsp. soy sauce, or to taste
2tbsp. sherry
1tbsp. hoisin sauce, or to taste
1tbsp. sesame seeds

Coat the pork with cornstarch and set aside.

Heat half the oil in a wok or large skillet, and add the onion and ginger. Stir-fry for 1 minute, then add the mushrooms and water chestnuts and stir-fry for another minute. Add half of the soy sauce, fry for 30 seconds, then remove the vegetables to a plate.

Wipe out the wok or pan, add the remaining oil and heat. Add the meat, and stir-fry over high heat to separate the pieces and brown evenly. After 2 minutes, add the remaining soy sauce, the sherry, hoisin sauce (a plum sauce, widely available) and all the vegetables.

Stir-fry for 2 minutes, then transfer to a serving dish and serve immediately, sprinkled with sesame seeds.

Stir Fry Pork
Serves 4-6

Ingredients
1lb. pork fillet
a piece of pork fat or oil
1 onion, peeled and chopped
1 clove garlic, peeled and crushed
2 green chili peppers, seeded and pounded

½lb. green beans, cut into 1-in. lengths
1½tsp. Worcestershire sauce
salt and sugar to taste
coriander leaves to garnish
plain boiled rice to serve

Trim the pork and cut into small pieces. Render the fat from the pork. When all the fat is in the pan, discard it and heat the oil, if preferred.

Fry the onion, garlic and chili pepper until it gives off a rich aroma; do not allow to brown. Push to the side of the pan and stir in the pork fillet pieces. Turn all the time until the meat changes color. Cook for 2-3 minutes.

Now add the beans and toss all the ingredients well. Add the Worcestershire sauce, if used, sugar and salt to taste.

Garnish with fresh coriander leaves and serve with plain rice.

Pork Fillet en Croûte
Serves 4-6

Ingredients

3 medium-sized or 2 large pork fillets	rind and juice of 1 lemon
Stuffing	1 egg, beaten
2 tbsp. oil	½lb. Puff Pastry
1 small onion, peeled	**Gravy**
½ cup rice	1 tbsp. flour
1¼ cups stock or water	1 tsp. dried sage or 1 tbsp. chopped fresh sage
1 small apple, peeled and diced	salt and freshly ground pepper
1 tbsp. white raisins	2-3 tbsp. white wine
1 tbsp. mixed nuts	⅔ cup stock

Trim the fat and gristle from the fillets. Cut into 6-in. lengths.

For the stuffing, heat the oil in a skillet and cook the onion for 2 minutes. Add the rice and stir well for a further 2 minutes. Pour in the stock or water with a pinch of salt. Cover and cook for 5 minutes. Remove the lid and fork through the rice, then add the diced apple, white raisins, nuts, lemon rind and juice. Mix through with a fork, cover and continue cooking for 5 minutes. When all the stock has been absorbed the rice should be slightly undercooked. Put the mixture into a bowl and allow to cool. Mix in most of the egg, leaving a little for glazing the pastry.

Put 2-3 lengths of fillets, slightly flattened, on a board. Cover with rice stuffing. Top with the remaining lengths of fillets and tie neatly into a cylinder with string.

Brush over with oil and wrap loosely in foil. Roast at 400°F for 35 minutes. Allow to cool and retain any meat juices for use in the gravy.

Roll the thawed pastry into an even shape, about 10in. square. Put the cooled meat, with string removed, in the center. Fold the pastry over the meat and dampen the edges with cold water. Turn the pastry package over so that the fold is underneath. Fold the ends neatly, cutting a square out and placing flaps over like a package. Put on a cookie sheet.

Roll out any scraps of pastry and cut out leaves. Alternatively, cut out decorative shapes with a cookie cutter. Wet the shapes and arrange them on the croûte. Make sure there are several slits in the pastry to allow steam to escape.

Brush over with the remaining egg. Cook in the oven at 425°F for a further 10 minutes.

For a gravy, scrape the meat juices into a saucepan. Add the flour, seasoning, white wine and stock. Beat well and serve in a heated sauceboat when thickened.

Pork Satay
Serves 2-3

Ingredients

5½ cups shredded coconut	2 tsp. coriander seeds
2 cups water	6 blanched almonds
1lb. pork fillet	1-2 stems lemon grass, peeled and sliced
1 tbsp. brown sugar	½tsp. ground turmeric (optional)
½-in. cube blanchan (optional)	2 tbsp. coconut or peanut oil
2 medium-sized onions, peeled	cucumber cubes
3-6 red chili peppers, seeded	

Soak 8-12 bamboo skewers in water for at least an hour to prevent them from burning under the broiler.

Make the coconut milk by putting the shredded coconut in a bowl, pouring the boiling water over it and leaving to stand for 15 minutes. Squeeze out the liquid and refrigerate it until needed.

Cut the pork into even-sized pieces, about the size of your thumb nail, and sprinkle with sugar to help release the juices. If using blanchan, fry it in a foil parcel in a dry skillet or on a skewer over the gas flame. Make the onions and chili peppers into a paste in the food processor.

Pound the coriander seeds, then add the nuts and the bulb part of the lemon grass and grind using a pestle and mortar. Add turmeric and salt and then stir this into the onion mixture in the food processor.

Pour in the coconut milk and oil. Switch the machine on and then off. Pour the contents into a shallow bowl containing the pork. Marinate for an hour or two.

Thread five or six pieces of pork onto each skewer. Broil or cook over charcoal for an even more authentic flavor. Baste with the marinade.

When tender, serve hot with cubes of cucumber.

Peppery Pork
Serves 4

Ingredients

1tbsp. oil	10oz. can tomatoes
4 pork steaks (or	2tsp. cornstarch
equivalent amount of	1tbsp. water
fillet)	⅔ cup yogurt
pinch chili powder	salt

Heat the oil, add the pork and lightly brown it. Drain off excess fat. Sprinkle the chili powder over it and stir it around. Add the tomatoes and bring the liquid to a boil, breaking up the tomatoes a little.

Mix the cornstarch with the water to a smooth paste and add to the pan. Stir until the sauce has thickened. Add the yogurt and mix it in well. Season with salt. Bake at 350°F for 1 hour.

Serve with rice or noodles. You may prefer more or less chili powder.

Pork Fillets in Brandy Cream Sauce
Serves 4

Ingredients

1½lb. pork fillet	3 cups Herbed Rice
1tbsp. flour	2tbsp. brandy
salt and freshly ground	pinch nutmeg
pepper	⅔ cup half-and-half
2tbsp. butter	4 lemon wedges
2tbsp. oil	bunch watercress
1 onion, peeled and finely	
chopped	

Trim the pork fillets. Remove any gristle and excess fat. Cut into diagonal slices. Beat out to about ½in. thick.

Mix the flour with the seasoning and coat each slice evenly.

Heat the butter and oil in a skillet and cook the onions for 4 minutes. Remove onto a plate with a slotted spoon.

Prepare and cook the Herbed Rice.

On a medium heat sauté the pork fillet slices for about 4 minutes each side until golden brown. Heat the brandy in a ladle and set alight. Pour onto the pork and allow to flambé.

Serve the Herbed Rice on a warmed serving dish. Arrange the pork slices on top and keep warm in a low oven.

Add nutmeg and half-and-half to the skillet and stir over a low heat to combine the meat juices and cream. Pour the sauce over the meat.

Garnish with the lemon wedges and watercress and accompany with a crisp green salad.

Baked Ham and Broccoli
Serves 4

Ingredients

8 slices cooked ham	½ cup grated cheese
8 flowerets fresh or frozen	3 cups cooked pasta shapes
broccoli	salt and freshly ground
2½ cups Mornay Sauce	pepper
1tsp. dried mustard	1tsp. ground nutmeg

Lay out slices of ham on a board.

Wash and drain fresh broccoli. If using frozen, blanch in boiling water for 3 minutes, drain well.

Roll the broccoli flowerets neatly in the ham.

When making up the Mornay Sauce, grated Cheddar may be used or a mixture of Parmesan cheese. Add the dried mustard and mix well.

Butter an ovenproof dish, spread the pasta over the bottom, season with a shake of pepper and nutmeg. Arrange the filled ham on top.

Pour over the sauce and finish with sprinkled grated cheese. Cook for 20 minutes at 350°F or until cheese is golden on top.

Baked Ham and Broccoli

Ham in Sour Cream I
Serves 4

Ingredients

1tbsp. oil or butter	⅔ cup dry white wine
1 onion, sliced	1lb. cooked ham, sliced
2tsp. flour	⅔ cup sour cream
1 cup canned tomatoes	freshly ground pepper

Heat the oil, add the onion and cook until it has softened but not browned. Add the flour and stir it off the heat until smooth. Add the tomatoes and wine. Break the tomatoes up a little and cook gently for a minute. Add the ham and let it warm through. Stir in the sour cream and season with pepper to taste.

Variation Serve on a bed of noodles, with 3tbsp. grated Parmesan sprinkled over the top and flash it under a hot broiler just to brown the top.

Ham in Sour Cream II
Serves 6-8

Ingredients

3lb. ham	¼lb. button mushrooms
1¼ cups chicken stock	2tbsp. cornstarch
grated lemon rind	2tbsp. water
bay leaf	1¼ cups sour cream
2 cups sliced carrots	pepper
2 large onions, sliced	

Put the ham into a large pan with water to cover. Bring to a boil and then reduce the heat, cover and simmer for 45 minutes. Pour off the cooking liquid (reserve it to use as stock for a lentil soup).

Remove the skin from the ham and return it to the pan with the stock, lemon rind, bay leaf, carrots, and onions. Bring to a boil and then cover and simmer for a further 45 minutes. Add the mushrooms, whole.

Mix the cornstarch with the water and stir in the sour cream. Add to the pan and stir in well. Add some pepper (it shouldn't need any salt), cover and simmer for 20 minutes.

Slice the ham and serve it with the sauce spooned over.

Burmese Pork Curry
Serves 6

Ingredients

2lb. lean pork, cut into 1-in. pieces	4 stems lemon grass, peeled
1lb. onions, peeled	1in. ngapi or blanchan (optional)
8 cloves garlic, peeled and crushed	1tsp. turmeric
2in. piece fresh ginger, scraped and chopped	4tbsp. peanut oil for frying
2½tsp. chili powder	1¼ cups stock or water
	coriander leaves to garnish

Put the pork pieces on a dish. Slice half the onions and put the remainder into a food processor with the garlic, ginger, chili powder, the lower 2½in. of the lemon grass (bruise and reserve the top of the stem), ngapi if used and turmeric. Make these ingredients into a coarse paste.

Fry the pork pieces in the hot oil until they change color, then increase the heat and add the paste. Fry for 2 minutes, then add the remaining onion slices. When the pork is well coated with the spice mixture, pour on the stock or water. Add salt and the lemon grass tops. Cover and cook for 1½ hours or until the pork is tender.

Cook uncovered for a further 15 minutes, if liked, to reduce the liquid. Remove the lemon grass. Add more chili powder if a hotter curry is preferred.

Sprinkle with fresh coriander and eat with rice.

Lion's Head Meatballs
Serves 2-3

Ingredients

1lb. lean pork, finely ground with a little fat	2tbsp. cornstarch
4-6 canned water chestnuts, finely chopped	peanut oil for frying
1tsp. finely chopped ginger	1¼ cups chicken stock
1tbsp. finely chopped onion	a little sugar
2tbsp. soy sauce	seasoning
seasoning to taste	¼lb. each Chinese leaves and spinach leaves, washed, dried and shredded
beaten egg to bind	

Mix the pork, water chestnuts, ginger, onion, 1tbsp. of the soy sauce and the seasoning together. Bind with sufficient beaten egg to form into balls. Toss the balls in a little seasoned cornstarch and make a paste with the remaining cornstarch and water.

Fry the balls in the hot oil to brown all over, then transfer them to another pan or flameproof casserole. Add stock, sugar, seasoning and the remaining soy sauce. Cover and simmer for 20-25 minutes, then increase the heat and add the Chinese leaves and spinach. Cook for 3-4 minutes.

Lift out the vegetables with a draining spoon onto a serving platter. Arrange the meatballs on top and keep warm.

Thicken the gravy with the cornstarch paste and pour over just before serving.

Deep-Fried Wonton with Apricot Sauce
Makes 40-50

Ingredients

1 package wonton wrappers (40-50 approx.), thawed	salt and freshly ground black pepper
1 cup chopped pork meat with a little fat	flour and water paste
	oil for deep frying
¾ cup raw shrimp	**Apricot sauce**
2 green onions, finely chopped	1lb. apricot jam
	3-4tbsp. light vinegar
1-2tsp. oyster sauce (optional)	2-3 tbsp. hot water

If the wrappers are frozen leave them out to thaw. When thawed remove them from the package. Gently ease up the top one at a corner and slowly lift, pushing your finger between this and the next one to prevent tearing. Place each one on top of the other in a pile on the counter, covered with a sheet of waxed paper and a slightly damp cloth to prevent drying out. Any torn wrappers can be used for patches, should you accidently damage any while filling them.

Prepare the filling by blending meat and shrimp in a food processor. Add green onions, oyster sauce, if used, and seasoning to taste. Now you are ready to fill the wrappers.

Lay the wrappers out on the counter, say 10 at a time (leave the rest covered). Place a tiny spoonful of the filling in the center of each wrapper. Dampen two edges with flour and water paste and fold over to form a triangle which is slightly off center. Now put two tiny pieces of filling on each side of the center mound. Draw the mid points of the triangle over the filling and press down. The wings will then fall back.

Deep fry for 1-2 minutes. Drain well.

To prepare the sauce, warm the jam, vinegar and water together, strain and pour into a bowl.

To serve, put the sauce in a bowl surrounded by the wonton puffs.

Pork Baked Beans
Serves 6

Ingredients

2tbsp. butter	4 small leeks, sliced
1lb. salt pork, cubed	1 cup chopped carrots
2 onions, finely chopped	4 raw potatoes, washed and cubed
2 cloves garlic, crushed	⅔ cup tomato juice
1lb. dried navy beans, soaked in cold water overnight	⅔ cup red wine
	1¼ cups strong black coffee

Melt the butter and add the pork, onions and garlic. Cook gently until the onion is soft and transparent. Season to taste.

Put the beans in a large casserole, add the pork and onion mixture, and stir in the leeks, carrots, potatoes, tomato juice, red wine and coffee. Mix well. Put the covered casserole into the oven and bake for 2½ to 3 hours at 350°F until the beans are tender and most of the liquid absorbed. If the beans are still firm and all the liquid has been absorbed, add extra coffee and continue to cook until tender.

Check the seasoning and serve hot with fresh crusty bread.

Pork Baked Beans

Pork and Bean Casserole
Serves 4

Ingredients

¾ cup red kidney beans, soaked	15-oz. can tomatoes
¼lb. bacon	1tsp. chili powder
½lb. loin or leg of pork	½tsp. cumin
¼lb. bacon hock	bay leaf
1tbsp. flour	bouquet garni
salt and freshly ground pepper	⅔ cup beer
1 large onion, sliced	1¼ cups stock
	1tbsp. parsley, chopped

Cook the red kidney beans for 15 minutes in cold water that has been brought to a boil.

Remove the rind from the bacon. Cut it into small pieces and cook in a skillet.

Trim fat and gristle from pork and bacon hock, cut into small cubes, toss in seasoned flour.

Remove bacon to a casserole, fry the pork and the fat left in the pan over a medium heat.

Add sliced onion and cook over a low heat for 3 minutes.

Transfer to the casserole, add all other ingredients including the beans. Cover and cook in the oven for 1½ hours at 350°F.

Serve sprinkled with chopped parsley.

Pork Curry
Serves 4

Ingredients

1tbsp. tamarind pulp	3 cloves garlic, crushed
1 cup water	1tbsp. vinegar
4tbsp. Ghee (Clarified Butter) or oil	1lb. pork, cut into cubes
2 medium onions, finely sliced	¾tsp. curry powder
	1tsp. salt, or to taste

Soak the tamarind in half the water for 10 minutes, then squeeze and strain off the juice.

Heat the fat and fry the onions. Add the tamarind, garlic and vinegar. Fry. Add the meat and cook until well browned.

Add the curry powder and cook for a further 3 minutes. Add the water and salt and simmer gently until the pork is tender.

Pork and Garlic Satay
Serves 6

Ingredients

1 head of garlic, unpeeled (about 15 cloves)	4 green onions, chopped
½tsp. ground cumin	2tbsp. oil
1tsp. ground coriander	2lb. lean pork, cubed
½tsp. ground cinnamon	a small Spanish onion, finely chopped
1tsp. turmeric	1in. root ginger, grated
5tbsp. sugar	chili powder to taste
5tbsp. lime juice	1½ cups raw peanuts, roasted and ground
sprigs of lemon verbena or lemon balm, well bruised (optional)	salt to taste

To make the marinade, peel and crush 3 of the garlic cloves and combine with the cumin, coriander, cinnamon, turmeric, 2tsp. of the sugar, 2tbsp. of the lime juice, the lemon verbena or lemon balm, the green onions and 1tbsp. of the oil.

Put the cubed pork into a plastic bag and pour in the marinade. Tie up the top of the bag, put it on a plate in case it leaks, and leave in a cool place for 2 to 4 hours. hours.

Plunge the remaining unpeeled garlic cloves into boiling water and simmer for 10 minutes or until just tender. Drain, peel and cut each clove lengthwise into 3 or 4 pieces.

To make the sauce, fry the onion in the remaining oil with the grated ginger and the chili powder — don't put in too much, you can always add more later — until transparent.

Drain the marinade from the pork, remove the lemon verbena or lemon balm, and add to the onion.

Dissolve the sugar in half the water then sprinkle into the yeast. Stir and leave for 10-15 minutes until the mixture is frothy.

Meanwhile sift the starch and salt together in a bowl and leave in a warm place or put into a food processor. Stir in the yeast mixture with sufficient of the remaining water to make a soft but not sticky dough. Knead for 1 minute in a food processor, or on a starched board by hand for 10 minutes.

Pop into a large, oiled plastic bag, seal the top and leave in a warm place until it doubles in size. Knock out the air bubbles and knead again for 5 minutes or 30 seconds in the food processor.

Put the pork on a plate. Heat the oil and fry the garlic, then add pork, green onions and crushed bean sauce (this can be done in a pestle and mortar). Add sugar and thicken slightly with the cornstarch paste. Draw from the heat and cool.

Divide the dough into 16 pieces; roll each out into 3-4-in. rounds. Place a spoonful of filling into the center of each and gather up the sides and cover the filling. Twist the top to seal. Set on cheesecloth or baking parchment in a steamer and leave to double in size.

Cook over fast-boiling water for 30-35 minutes or until done.

Crispy Pork Knuckle
Serves 1-2

Ingredients

1-2 pieces pork knuckle	**Sauce**
salt to taste	6tbsp. vinegar
oil for frying	1½ cloves garlic
	salt and black pepper to taste
	5-7 pieces chili pepper, sliced

Allow about 1lb. or just over raw weight pork knuckle per person. Cook the pork knuckle in salted water over a low heat until tender (1-1½ hours, depending on their size). Remove and pat dry with paper towels.

Fry in medium hot oil for 15 minutes until they have acquired a crispy consistency.

Mix together the vinegar sauce ingredients and serve as an accompaniment.

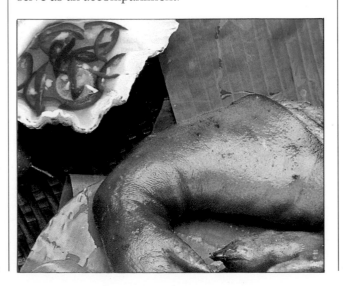

Simmer for several minutes.

Add the remaining lime juice, sugar, and the peanuts. Season with salt, extra chili if necessary, and simmer until thickened.

Thread the marinaded pork cubes and garlic slices alternately onto thin skewers — wooden ones are traditional — 5 to 7 pork cubes to each, and either broil for about 10 minutes, turning once, or barbecue, basting with a little oil, until glistening brown and cooked.

Steamed Pork Buns
Makes 16

Ingredients

3tsp. sugar	**Filling**
1¼ cups warm water	1⅓ cups roast pork, very finely chopped
1½tbsp. dried yeast	a little oil for frying
1lb. plain flour	1 clove garlic, peeled and crushed
1tsp. salt	2tbsp. chopped green onion
2tbsp. lard for greasing	1½tbsp. canned baked beans, mashed
	½tbsp. sugar
	1tsp. cornstarch, mixed to a paste with a little water

Transylvanian Goulash
Serves 6

Ingredients
2-3tbsp. oil
1 large onion, finely
 chopped
2tbsp. paprika
1½lb. pork, cubed
salt to taste
1 large clove garlic,
 crushed

2tsp. dried dill
2tsp. caraway seeds
1¼ cups water
1½lb. sauerkraut
⅔ cup sour cream

Heat the oil, add the onion and cook until it has just softened but not browned. Add the paprika and stir well. Add the pork, salt, garlic, dill and caraway seeds. Stir well. Add the water and sauerkraut. Cook on a low heat for 1¼ hours. Stir in the sour cream and warm through gently.

Variation This is equally tasty with veal, which needs less cooking (1 hour). Fresh sauerkraut is most delicious but canned or bottled is very acceptable.

Long Cook Pork Leg Stew
Serves 4

Cook this stew the day before you wish to serve it, as this gives the dish a richer blend of flavors and a chance to skim off any excess fat which may collect. The trotters have a large proportion of bone so you will require this quantity for four people. It would be advisable to order them from the butcher in advance.

Ingredients
3½-4lb. meaty pigs trotters
1tbsp. tamarind pulp
⅔ cup water
6 red chili peppers, seeded
 (use red for good color)
6 cloves garlic, crushed
2-3 medium-sized onions,
 peeled
8tbsp. oil
2tbsp. soya bean paste
2tbsp. light soy sauce

2tbsp. dark soy sauce
1 star anise
½in. fresh ginger, finely
 shredded
2½tsp. dark brown sugar
just under 2½ cups water
salt
fresh coriander leaves or
 shredded green onion to
 garnish

Ask the butcher to cut the trotters into chunky pieces through the bone. Soak the tamarind pulp in the water for 10 minutes, then squeeze out. Set one whole chili pepper aside for garnish and pound the remainder

with the garlic and onions. Fry in oil for 2-3 minutes. Stir in the bean paste, then turn the trotters in this mixture to coat them on all sides. Add the soy sauces, tamarind juice, star anise, ginger, sugar and water. Add salt if necessary, but go carefully as the bean paste is quite salty.

Cover and cook gently for at least 2 hours or until the pork is tender. Cool and leave overnight. Skim away any excess fat. Cover and bake in an ovenproof casserole in a moderately hot oven (325°F) for an hour or until the pork is cooked through and the sauce is bubbling.

Serve scattered with fresh coriander leaves or green onions and the reserved chili pepper, cut into rings.

Sweet and Sour Pork
Serves 4

Ingredients
1lb. leg of pork, cut in a
 thick slice
1 small onion, peeled and
 sliced
1in. fresh root ginger, finely
 chopped
1 clove garlic
1tbsp. dry sherry
2tbsp. soy sauce
salt and freshly ground
 pepper

Sauce
1 small red pepper, seeded
1 small green pepper,
 seeded
2 green onions, washed
1¼ cups chicken stock
1tbsp. white wine vinegar
2tsp. brown sugar
1tbsp. tomato paste
2tsp. cornstarch
2tbsp. cold water
Batter
3tbsp. cornstarch
2tsp. water
1 egg
oil for frying

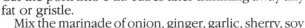

Cut the pork into 1-in. cubes after trimming away any fat or gristle.

Mix the marinade of onion, ginger, garlic, sherry, soy sauce and seasoning and allow the pork to stand in this for at least 1 hour, turning from time to time.

Cut the peppers into ¼-in. cubes and chop the green onions into thick rings

Put all other ingredients for the sauce, apart from the cornstarch and cold water, into a saucepan with the peppers and green onions. Mix the cornstarch with the cold water and then mix into the saucepan. Fry the meat before heating the sauce.

Make up the batter in a deep dish, mixing the cornstarch, water and egg together until thick.

Drop the drained marinated meat into the batter. Make sure the fat is very hot before dropping the meat into it, either with tongs or a slotted spoon. Cook for about 2-4 minutes until golden. Drain on paper towels.

Heat the sweet and sour sauce and, when thickened and hot, add the fried pork.

Serve with plain boiled rice.

Spiced Pork in Coconut Milk
Serves 3

Ingredients

2 cups boiling water	3tbsp. vegetable oil
2½ cups shredded coconut	1lb. lean pork, cut into
2 medium-sized red	cubes
onions, peeled and	1 stem lemon grass
chopped	salt to taste
1tsp. yeast extract	juice ½ lemon
1½-2tsp. chili powder	pinch sugar

First make the coconut milk by pouring the boiling water over the coconut, leaving to stand for 15 minutes, and then squeezing out the liquid. Discard the coconut, and refrigerate the milk until required.

Pound the onions with the yeast extract and chili powder. Fry in oil without browning. Add the pork and fry until the meat changes color and is well covered with the spices.

Stir in the prepared coconut milk over a gentle heat and the bruised stem of lemon grass. Slowly bring to the boil, stirring to prevent curdling. Add salt to taste. Simmer until the pork is tender.

Remove the lemon grass stem. Add lemon juice and sugar to taste.

Serve with plain boiled rice.

Twice-Cooked Pork
Serves 6

Ingredients

2lb. belly of pork, rind and	2 cloves garlic, peeled and
bones removed after	crushed
weighing	½in. ginger, peeled and
4tbsp. canned black beans	finely chopped
1tbsp. soya bean paste	¼ cup chicken stock
2tbsp. soy sauce	2 cups bean sprouts
1tbsp. tomato paste	2tbsp. sherry
1tbsp. hoisin sauce	few drops sesame oil
1tsp. Tabasco	green onion curls to
½-1tbsp. sugar	garnish
a little oil for frying	

Put the pork in a pan of boiling water and cook for just over 30 minutes or until tender. Lift out, drain, cool a little and cut into finger-width slices, and then each slice into four pieces, and set aside.

Drain the beans. Blend the soya bean paste with soy sauce, tomato paste, hoisin and Tabasco sauces. Stir in a little sugar to taste. Mash the black beans to a paste.

Heat the oil in a wok and fry the garlic and ginger. Add the mashed beans, stir well, then add the meat and the mixture of sauces. Toss the meat well to coat each piece with the sauce. Add stock and extra water if the sauce is too thick. Cook for 5 minutes. Increase the heat, add the bean sprouts, sherry and sesame oil.

Serve on a warm platter garnished with green onion curls.

¼in. of water to catch the drips of marinade from the ribs. Cook at 400°F for 20 minutes. Baste again if desired, then reduce the heat to 350°F for a further 35-45 minutes or until the ribs are cooked.

Cool for a few minutes then divide into separate ribs and arrange attractively on a hot platter garnished with green onion curls. You can serve these ribs with an accompaniment of salad and rice.

Coffee Spare Ribs
Serves 6

Ingredients

6 pork spare rib chops cut into individual ribs
3tbsp. olive oil
2 cloves garlic, crushed
2tbsp. parsley, chopped
⅔ cup red wine
⅔ cup strong black coffee
3tbsp. honey
salt and freshly ground black pepper
grated rind and juice of 1 lime

Put the spare ribs in a large shallow pan. Mix all the remaining ingredients together and pour over the spare ribs. Leave to marinate overnight, turning occasionally.

Remove the ribs from the marinade. Put under a preheated broiler, turning until evenly browned.

Put ribs back into the marinade and bake for 30 minutes at 350°F.

Remove the ribs and skim the fat off the sauce. Serve with rice.

Canton Barbecued Spare Ribs
Serves 4

Hoisin sauce is a plum sauce widely available in supermarkets.

Ingredients

2lb. pork spare ribs
2tsp. salt
few pinches of five spice powder
1tbsp. soy sauce
1tbsp. thin soy sauce
3tbsp. sherry
2tbsp. honey
1tbsp. hoisin sauce
2 cloves garlic, peeled and crushed
3tbsp. oil
green onion curls to garnish

Wipe the spare ribs and leave them in sections of several ribs as you bought them. Rub with salt, dust lightly with five spice powder and pepper; leave for 1 hour.

Blend the soy sauces with sherry, honey, hoisin sauce and garlic. Finally stir in the oil. Pour this marinade over the ribs and spoon onto the surface. Leave for 2-4 hours, turning occasionally.

Put on a wire rack above a roasting pan containing

Pork Spare Ribs in Barbecue Sauce
Serves 4

Ingredients

4½lb. spare ribs
2tbsp. soy sauce
2tbsp. sherry
3tbsp. red wine vinegar
1 clove garlic, crushed
1 small onion, peeled and sliced
salt and freshly ground pepper
1 small piece root ginger, grated
oil for deep frying

Sauce
2 cloves garlic, finely chopped
3 green onions, washed and chopped
½tsp. fennel seeds
½tsp. cinnamon
½tsp. basil
2 cloves
2tsp. brown sugar
juice of ½ lemon
juice of ½ orange
2tbsp. red wine vinegar
1¼ cups stock
2tbsp. soy sauce
15oz. can peeled tomatoes
⅔ cup chicken stock

If possible ask the butcher at the meat counter to trim the spare ribs to good handling size, about 4in. long.

In a clean screw-top jar, put all the marinade ingredients together and mix well by shaking. Pour the marinade over the pork and turn from time to time for about ½-1 hour, or longer if you wish.

Deep fry the spare ribs for about 5 minutes and drain on paper towels.

Mix the ingredients for the sauce in a saucepan, wok or skillet and bring to the boil.

Add the spare ribs and simmer in the sauce for about 30 minutes. Add a little water and the remaining marinade to prevent it going dry.

Variation Cook the marinated ribs on a wire rack over a roasting pan in a hot oven at 425°F. Pour the sauce over the roasted meat.

Stretching Bacon

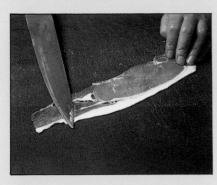

Cut off rind then use the flat of a knife to 'stretch' the slice.

Scoring for Crackling.

Use a very sharp knife to score through pork rind and fat. Score evenly and thoroughly for crisp crackling.

Pasta, Rice and Dumplings

Curry Noodles
Serves 4-6

This is a truly international dish combining Indian, Chinese and Western ingredients.

Ingredients

1lb. fresh yellow noodles	*2-3tbsp. tomato ketchup*
4-6tbsp. oil	*1tbsp. chili sauce (or to*
1 square bean curd, well	*taste)*
drained, cut into dice	*1 large cooked potato,*
2 beaten eggs, seasoned	*diced*
1 medium onion, peeled	*4 green onions*
and sliced	*1-2 green chili peppers,*
1 clove garlic, crushed	*seeded and shredded*
1tbsp. soy sauce	

Cook the noodles in boiling water in a large pan for just 2-3 minutes. Do not overcook. Drain and rinse with cold water to stop cooking; set on one side.

Heat 2tbsp. of the oil in a pan and fry the bean curd until brown. Drain and set aside.

Pour the beaten eggs into the pan. When it has set like an omelet roll it up on a board and chop finely.

Spoon the remaining oil into a skillet or wok and fry the onion and garlic for 2-3 minutes. Add the drained noodles, soy sauce, ketchup and chili sauce. Toss well over a medium heat.

Add the potato dice, most of the green onion, some of the chili pepper and all the bean curd. Keep tossing. When hot, add pieces of the cooked egg.

Serve on a hot platter garnished with the remaining green onion and chili pepper.

Celebration Noodles
Serves 8

Chinese fish sauce is a bottled condiment, similar in flavor to anchovy essence which could be used instead.

Ingredients

1-1½lb. egg noodles, fresh	*2 cloves garlic, peeled and*
or dried	*crushed*
1lb. whole, fresh shrimp, or	*½ small Chinese cabbage,*
8oz. thawed, frozen	*finely shredded or ½lb.*
shrimp	*bean sprouts*
½lb. sliced cooked chicken	*⅔ cup fish stock from*
breast	*shrimp or chicken stock*
½lb. sliced cooked ham or	*2tbsp. Chinese fish sauce*
lean pork	*(optional)*
¼ cup lard or 4-6tbsp.	*seasoning*
cooking oil	*chopped green onions*
1 medium onion, peeled	*lemon or lime wedges*
and chopped	

Cook fresh noodles in boiling water for 1-2 minutes, rinse with cold water and drain thoroughly, or dried noodles according to packet directions and drain in the same way.

Cover the fresh shrimp, if using, with cold water. Bring to a boil and cook gently for 5 minutes. Lift out with a slotted spoon, remove the heads and shells and reserve the shrimp. Discard the shells. Strain the cooking liquid. If using frozen shrimp, thaw well. You will need to substitute the shrimp stock with chicken stock later in the recipe.

Heat half the oil in a wok and fry the drained noodles for 2-3 minutes, stirring. Lift out of the pan onto a platter and keep warm.

Heat the remaining oil in the pan, fry the onion and garlic until soft and just beginning to turn golden. Add the cabbage or bean sprouts, cook for 1-2 minutes, mix well, then stir in most of the chicken, ham or pork and shrimp, reserved fish or prepared chicken stock and fish sauce. Turn the mixture all the time.

Return the noodles to pan, taste for seasoning and serve on a hot platter garnished with the reserved shrimp, the chicken, ham or pork and the green onions, and accompany with wedges of lemon or lime.

Curry Noodles

Crisp Fried Noodles
Serves 6-8

Ingredients

6 shallots, peeled and chopped
2 cloves garlic, peeled and crushed
oil for frying
¾ cup finely chopped raw chicken breast
½ cup sliced cooked pork
¾ cup cooked shelled shrimp
1 square tofu
6oz. can salted soya beans, drained
4 beaten eggs
2tbsp. cider or wine vinegar
1-2tbsp. confectioner's sugar

fish sauce to taste (optional)
¾lb. rice vermicelli
deep fat for frying
pinch chili powder
green onions
2-3 red chili peppers, seeded and finely sliced
fresh coriander leaves chopped, pickled garlic or fried garlic flakes
rind of lime or a strip of grapefruit peel, cut into fine shreds
1½ cups bean sprouts, tails removed for best effect

For the sauce, fry the shallots and garlic in hot oil in a wok; do not color. Add the chicken and stir for 3-4 minutes, then stir in the pork and shrimp. Turn the ingredients all the time. Add the tofu cubes and salted soya beans and cook for 2-3 minutes. Then add the beaten eggs little by little, stirring throughly and adding extra oil, if necessary, to the sauce. At this stage stir in the vinegar, confectioner's sugar and fish sauce if used. Toss in the pan for 1-2 minutes, then check the flavor. It should have a sweet, salty taste. Set aside.

Heat fat in a large pan and deep-fry the noodles for just a few seconds. This is best done in several stages in a frying basket or wok. The noodles will become puffy and crisp. Remove them from the fat, drain and keep warm.

Just before serving, put half the sauce and a sprinkling of the chili powder in a large wok or pan with half the noodles. Toss together without breaking up the noodles too much. Repeat with the remaining sauce, chili powder and noodles.

Pile onto a large serving platter and garnish attractively with green onions, chili peppers, coriander leaves, garlic and lime rind or grapefruit shreds. Arrange the bean sprouts all around the base.

Shrimp and Noodle Balls
Makes 15

Ingredients

¼lb. vermicelli
1½ cups peeled shrimp
½tsp. sugar
2oz. cubed pork fat
few slices fresh ginger

salt and pepper
a little lightly beaten egg white
oil for deep frying

Crush the vermicelli finely and leave in a dry place. Mince the shrimp in a food processor and sprinkle with sugar. Mince the pork fat with the fresh ginger, add the shrimp with seasoning and bind with a little egg white.

Use wetted hands to form into even bite-sized balls. Chill well, and roll in the crushed vermicelli just before frying in hot oil. Cook for about 3-4 minutes until cooked through, or steam in a bamboo steamer over hot water for 30 minutes.

Noodles with Peanut Sauce
Serves 6

Ingredients

1lb. egg noodles, cooked according to packet directions
3tbsp. crunchy peanut butter
1tbsp. hot oil
1tsp. sesame oil
4tbsp. oil for frying

Garnishes

handful dry-fried peanuts, lightly crushed
2 green onions, shredded
¼lb. bean sprouts, blanched in boiling water for 1 minute, rinsed in cold water and drained
¼-½ cucumber, cut into small chunks
a few radishes

Plunge the cooked noodles into boiling water for 1 minute. Rinse with cold water and leave on one side to dry.

Meanwhile prepare the sauce by blending the peanut butter with the hot oil and sesame oil to a smooth paste. Prepare the garnishes.

Fry the noodles in two or three lots in hot oil. Flatten out on one side and, when hot, turn over and fry on the other side. Keep warm while cooking the other noodles.

Pile onto a large platter and pour over the sauce — mix lightly then scatter with peanuts and green onions. Arrange the bean sprouts, cucumber and radishes either around the noodles or in separate bowls.

Noodles with Cottage Cheese
Serves 4-6

Ingredients

1 cup bacon, diced
¾lb. noodles, cooked and drained
4tbsp. butter

1⅓ cups cottage cheese
⅔ cup sour cream or thick yogurt
salt and pepper

Fry the bacon until it is crisp. Drain it and reserve.

Put the cooked noodles into a large dish. Add the butter, cottage cheese, sour cream, salt and pepper, and mix everything into the noodles.

Scatter the fried bacon on top and serve immediately.

Add more bacon if you want to make a more substantial dish.

Macaroni Cheese with Bacon and Tomato
Serves 4

Ingredients

1 cup short cut macaroni	2½ cups Mornay Sauce
salt and freshly ground	½ cup grated cheese
pepper	1 tbsp. fresh breadcrumbs
½ tsp. oil	4 slices lean bacon
2 tbsp. butter	2 tomatoes, sliced

Cook the macaroni for 7 minutes in boiling salted water to which the oil has been added. Drain well.

Butter an ovenproof dish and prepare the sauce.

Mix the macaroni with the sauce and pour into the dish.

Sprinkle with the grated cheese mixed with the breadcrumbs.

Arrange the bacon slices on top of the macaroni alternately with tomato slices. Cook at 400°F for 15-20 minutes until the bacon is done.

Fettucini Roma
Serves 4

Ingredients

1 lb. fettucini	salt and freshly ground
4 tbsp. butter	pepper
½ tsp. ground nutmeg	⅔ cup Parmesan cheese,
⅔ cup cream	grated

Bring a well-filled saucepan of salted water to boil; add a few drops of oil and salt. Feed in the fettucini and cook until *al dente* — fresh pasta will only take about 2 minutes. Drain in a colander strainer.

Melt the butter in the saucepan, add the nutmeg, pour in half the cream and stir until shiny and bubbles start to appear.

Add the fettucini and stir around in the pan. Pour in the remaining cream and cheese alternately, fluffing the pasta as it is mixed. Serve immediately.

Note This is a real pasta-lovers' dish. To obtain best results use freshly grated Parmesan cheese rather than the commercially grated variety.

Lasagne Al Forno
Serves 4-6

Ingredients

9 sheets cooked lasagne	1 tbsp. dried breadcrumbs
2 cups Bolognese Sauce	1 tbsp. Parmesan cheese
2½ cups Béchamel Sauce	salt and pepper

Place 4 tbsp. of the Bolognese sauce on the bottom of a 10×8 in. dish. Top with 3 tbsp. of the Béchamel sauce and three strips of cooked lasagne. Season the pasta with salt and pepper.

Start the layers of sauce again as shown in the picture. Use another 3 tbsp. Bolognese sauce and 3 tbsp. Béchamel.

Top with another 3 strips of lasagne, a further 3 tbsp. Bolognese sauce and 3 tbsp. Béchamel. Add remaining strips of lasagne, season and spread the meat sauce on top of the final topping of white sauce.

Spread the Béchamel over the surface and sprinkle it with grated Parmesan cheese or Parmesan cheese mixed with dried breadcrumbs to give a crunchy topping when cooked.

Bake the lasagne in a preheated oven 350°F for 25 minutes until golden brown. For a really crisp topping, put the dish under the broiler for 3 minutes.

Vegetable Lasagne
Serves 4

Ingredients

60ml/4tbsp. oil
1 eggplant, sliced
1 red pepper, seeded and
    sliced
1 zucchini, sliced
salt and freshly ground
    pepper

1¼ cups sliced mushrooms
2 cups Concentrated
    Tomato Sauce
600ml/1pt Béchamel sauce
9 sheets cooked lasagne

Heat the oil and fry the vegetables over a low heat filling the pan and turning in the oil for about 3 minutes each batch. You will need to allow 15 minutes for preparing and frying the vegetables.

Start with the Concentrated Tomato Sauce and one third of the vegetables. Top with Béchamel sauce and lasagne. Season and start layering as in Lasagne al Forno, ending with Béchamel and cheese.

When all the ingredients are used, bake in a preheated 350°F oven until golden brown, about 25 minutes.

Pasta with Eggplant and Apple
Serves 2-3

Ingredients

1 large eggplant
1 large tart apple
1 egg, beaten
seasoned white flour
4tbsp. walnut oil

2 cloves garlic, crushed
1⅓ cups wholewheat or
    spinach pasta shapes
salt and freshly ground
    black pepper

Slice the eggplant, sprinkle liberally with salt and leave in a strainer or colander for 30 minutes. Rinse and dry on paper towels and cut into strips. Peel, core and dice the apple.

Toss eggplant and apple in the beaten egg, and then in the seasoned flour to give a light coating. Heat some oil in a pan and fry the eggplant, apple and garlic, stirring, until crisp.

Meanwhile, cook pasta shells in plenty of salted water at a full rolling boil, until *al dente*. Add a few drops of oil to the water to prevent the pasta from sticking. Drain well, season with black pepper and toss in a little walnut oil. Stir in the eggplant mixture and serve with Parmesan cheese.

Pasta Trio

Chili Pasta
Serves 4

Ingredients

2tbsp. oil
2 cloves garlic, crushed
1lb. lean ground beef
2 small onions, peeled
1 red pepper, seeded
1 green pepper, seeded
1 small chili pepper
15oz. can tomatoes
pinch chili powder

⅔ cup beef stock
1 small can kidney beans
    or ½ cup dried beans,
    soaked and cooked
3 cups cooked pasta shells
salt and freshly ground
    pepper
2tbsp. butter
shake of grated nutmeg

Heat the oil in a pan, add the crushed garlic and the meat, turn over with a fork until the meat is brown and separated into particles. Break down lumps with a fork. Add the diced onion and continue cooking over a low heat until the onions are slightly transparent.

Cut the peppers into bite-size strips and add to the meat.

Seed the chili pepper, taking care the seeds do not touch your skin or eyes. Chop into small pieces and add to the meat mixture which is still cooking slowly over a low heat.

Add the canned tomatoes, chili powder and beef stock and bring to a boil, then simmer for 45 minutes. Add canned beans 15 minutes before serving. Dried beans must be soaked and boiled for 30 minutes before being added to the chili for 30 minutes of

Pasta with Spinach Sauce
Serves 4

Ingredients

2lb. fresh spinach
2tbsp. oil
1 onion, chopped
2 cloves garlic, chopped
2 cups sliced mushrooms
1⅓ cups farmer's, ricotta or
  cream cheese

1-2tbsp. pine nuts
salt and freshly ground
  black pepper
2 cups wholewheat or
  spinach pasta shapes
Parmesan cheese, grated

Wash spinach and discard tough stalks. Pack into a large pan, cover and cook over a low heat until soft, stirring occasionally. Drain and chop.

Heat oil in a pan and fry the onion and garlic until soft. Stir in the mushrooms. Cover and cook over a low heat until soft.

Mix the vegetables with the cheese and pine nuts and season to taste. Keep warm.

Cook the pasta in plenty of boiling salted water until *al dente*. Drain. Stir sauce into pasta and serve with Parmesan cheese.

Pasta with Mushroom Sauce
Serves 1

Ingredients

2-4 handfuls green pasta
  spirals
1tsp. oil
1 cup mushrooms
milk
salt and freshly ground
  black pepper

yolk of 1 egg
1tbsp. cream
as much parsley as you
  like, chopped
Parmesan cheese, grated

Cook the pasta in plenty of boiling salted water with the oil, until *al dente*.

Meanwhile, wipe and slice the mushrooms. Put in a pan with a little milk, season well and poach gently, stirring, until soft and very black and the liquid has almost gone.

Beat the egg yolk with the cream and stir in the mushrooms.

Drain the pasta and stir in the mushroom mixture with plenty of parsley. Serve at once with Parmesan and a tender lettuce salad.

cooking time. Taste for seasoning and add salt and pepper if necessary.

Serve with the cooked hot pasta which has been tossed in butter with a shake of nutmeg.

Pasta Trio
Serves 4

Ingredients

½lb. stuffed ravioli or
  tortellini
½lb. tagliatelli
½lb. wholewheat pasta
  spirals

1¼ cups Béchamel Sauce
1¼ cups Bolognese Sauce
⅔ cup Parmesan cheese

Cook the pasta. Drain the cooking water into a bowl and return the pasta to the saucepan and keep it warm.

Warm the sauces.

Serve the pasta on individual dishes and the sauces in bowls, accompanied by a bowl of Parmesan cheese and green salad.

Variation Other combinations of pastas and sauces can be used.

Pasta Wheels with Salami
Serves 4

Ingredients

2 stalks celery
1 eating apple, peeled
juice of 1 lemon
1 small lettuce
1⅓ cups cooked pasta
  wheels

⅔ cup Mayonnaise
8 slices salami
2 tomatoes
celery leaves

Remove the strings from the celery stalks with a sharp knife and cut into thin slices. Dice the apple and mix with the celery.

Sprinkle the lemon juice on the celery and apple and arrange in the bottom of a dish lined with lettuce.

Mix the pasta wheels with the mayonnaise, arrange on top of the apples and celery.

Roll up slices of salami and arrange in a wheel pattern on the pasta wheels.

Garnish with tomato wedges and some celery leaves in the center.

Spaghetti con Vongole
Serves 4

Ingredients

1 onion, peeled
2 cloves garlic, crushed
4tbsp. olive oil
6 beef tomatoes, peeled
  and diced or 425g/15oz.
  can tomatoes
4tbsp. white wine
salt and freshly ground
  pepper

1 small can clams, drained
¾lb. spaghetti
1tbsp. butter
pinch of nutmeg
2tbsp. freshly chopped
  parsley

Dice the onion finely, peel and crush the garlic. Heat the oil in a saucepan or large skillet and cook over a low heat until the onion is transparent.

Add the tomatoes, white wine and seasoning. Simmer for 10 minutes. Add the clams and heat gently for a further 6 minutes.

Meanwhile cook the spaghetti in plenty of boiling salted water for about 12 minutes. Drain and toss in a little melted butter. Add a shake of pepper and nutmeg.

Add the parsley to the spaghetti and stir well. Combine with the clam sauce and serve at once on heated plates.

If you are using fresh clams scrub the shells and wash well in several batches of cold water to remove sand and grit. Place them in a skillet with half the white wine and cook over a high heat until the shells open. Strain and use the juice in the sauce. Remove the fish from the shells and heat through in the sauce as above.

Variation Add 3tbsp. single cream to the sauce before serving.

Spaghetti con Vongole

Spaghetti alla Carbonara
Serves 4

Ingredients

1lb. spaghetti	1 cup mushrooms, washed
salt and freshly ground	and sliced
pepper	4tbsp. butter
½tsp. oil	⅓ cup Parmesan cheese
1 onion, peeled and finely	5 eggs, beaten
sliced	1tbsp. freshly chopped
5 slices of lean bacon	parsley

Cook the spaghetti in a large saucepan of boiling salted water with the oil added, for 12 minutes. Drain well.

Meanwhile prepare the other ingredients, slice the onion, and dice the bacon. Wash and slice the mushrooms.

Melt half the butter in a large pan and cook the onion and bacon for 5 minutes over a low heat. Add the mushrooms and cook for a further 3 minutes.

Toss the drained spaghetti in the other half of the melted butter over a medium heat for a few seconds. Season with pepper, add cheese.

Toss the spaghetti into the pan with the onion, bacon and mushrooms and mix well. Add the seasoned beaten egg and stir vigorously into the mixture. Cook over the heat for a few minutes until thick and creamy.

Serve on warmed plates or a serving dish, sprinkled with chopped parsley.

Spinach Tagliatelle with Asparagus
Serves 2

Ingredients

½lb. asparagus	½lb. green tagliatelle
2tbsp. butter	2tsp. oil
4tbsp. light cream	Parmesan cheese, grated
salt and freshly ground	
black pepper	

If you are using fresh asparagus, clean it under cold running water, tie it in a bundle and stand upright in a tall saucepan containing about 3in. boiling salted water. Cover with foil so that the asparagus tips cook by steaming. Alternatively, use a bain marie, inverting the inner saucepan over the bottom one. The asparagus will take 10-20 minutes to cook, depending on its thickness. Test by piercing half way up the stalk with a sharp knife — if you can insert the knife easily, the asparagus is done. Drain it. Cut off and discard the woody lower pieces. Cut the asparagus into bite-size pieces

Melt the butter in a saucepan and toss the asparagus in it. Add half the cream, season and leave for a few minutes over a very low heat to thicken.

Meanwhile, cook the pasta until *al dente* in plenty of boiling salted water to which you have added 2tsp. oil.

Drain the pasta, toss in the remaining cream and pour over the asparagus sauce. Serve and offer Parmesan cheese.

Spinach and Ricotta Cannelloni
Serves 4

Ingredients

2½ cups chopped spinach,	pinch marjoram
cooked	pinch nutmeg
⅔ cup ricotta cheese	6 strips fresh pasta
salt and freshly ground	⅔ cup Concentrated
pepper	Tomato Sauce
1tbsp. fresh breadcrumbs	1¼ cups Béchamel Sauce
⅓ cup Parmesan cheese	

Mix the cooked spinach, which can be fresh, frozen or canned, with the ricotta cheese in a bowl. Season and add the breadcrumbs, marjoram and nutmeg and 1tsp. Parmesan cheese. Cream to a smooth paste.

Put the spinach and ricotta cheese mixture into a piping bag with a ½-in. plain nozzle. If you do not want to use a piping bag, spoon the mixture with a teaspoon. Lay the uncooked pasta strips 2½in wide. on a board. Pipe the mixture along the width of the pasta, roll into a tube, cut with a sharp knife.

Put the Concentrated Tomato Sauce in the bottom of the dish, arrrange the tubes on top and season the cannelloni.

When all the pasta tubes are arranged in the sauce pour the Béchamel on top covering the pasta completely.

Sprinkle with the remaining Parmesan cheese and bake in a preheated 350°F oven for 30 minutes. For a crisper topping, finish under the broiler.

Jambalaya
Serves 4

Ingredients

2tbsp. butter
2tbsp. oil
1 onion, peeled and finely chopped
4 stalks celery
1 green pepper, seeded
2 eggplants
1 cup long-grain rice
1tsp. salt
freshly ground black pepper
1tbsp. Worcestershire sauce
1tsp. soy sauce
2½ cups chicken stock
¾ cup diced cooked ham
1½ cups peeled shrimp
3tbsp. chopped parsley
whole shrimp to garnish (optional)

Heat the butter and oil in a skillet and cook the onion over a low heat until translucent.

Wash the celery and peel the strings from the rounded side with a sharp knife. Cut into small pieces. Add to the onions.

Dice the pepper and eggplant. Add to the celery and onion and stir for a few minutes to mix well. Add the rice and stir if there is room in the pan. If there is not, put the vegetables and rice into a large casserole and mix well.

Add the salt and pepper, Worcestershire and soy sauces to the stock.

Transfer the vegetables and rice into the casserole if not already there. Add the stock over a medium heat. When the liquid comes to a boil cover with a lid and bake at 350°F.

Remove from the oven. Stir in the shrimp and ham. Replace the lid and cook for a further 10-15 minutes until the rice is cooked. Taste for seasoning.

Mix in the chopped parsley before serving. Garnish with whole shrimp if you like.

Coconut Rice
Serves 4

Rice cooked in coconut milk is a wonderful accompaniment to chicken, pork dishes and curries.

Ingredients

225g/8oz shredded coconut
2½ cups boiling water
¾ cup long grain rice
½tsp. ground coriander
1 stick cinnamon
1 stem lemongrass, bruised
bay leaf (optional)
salt
fried onions

First make the coconut milk by pouring the boiling water over the shredded coconut, leaving to stand for 15 minutes, then squeezing out the liquid.

Put the coconut milk in a pan with the rice, washed if necessary, coriander, cinnamon stick, lemon grass and bay leaf if used. Add salt. Bring to the boil over a medium heat, stirring a few times. Cook over the lowest heat for 12-15 minutes or until all the coconut milk has been absorbed.

Fluff carefully and remove the cinnamon, lemon grass and leaf. Cover with a tight-fitting lid, then cook over the lowest heat for a further 10 minutes.

Serve garnished with crispy fried onions.

Rice with Chicken
Serves 4-5

Chicken stock enriched with sherry gives a rich flavor to the rice which is mixed with small pieces of chicken and dried mushrooms.

Ingredients

2⅔ cups short-grain rice
¾ cup boned chicken breast or thigh
2tbsp. soy sauce
4 dried mushrooms, soaked in hot water
2 cups chicken stock
4tsp. sherry
4 sprigs fresh coriander

Wash the rice thoroughly and put in a strainer to drain for at least 30 minutes. Cut the chicken into short, ½-in. strips, sprinkle with the soy sauce and set aside to marinate for 30 minutes. Discard the mushroom stems and slice the caps finely.

Put the rice in a saucepan and pour the chicken stock and sherry over it. Add the chicken and mushroom pieces. Bring to a boil over high heat, stirring occasionally. Cover tightly and reduce the heat to very low. Simmer for 8-10 minutes, then turn off the heat and leave, still covered, to steam for 15 minutes. Mix well and serve, garnishing each bowl with a coriander sprig.

Herbed Rice
Serves 4

Serve this with broiled poultry or meat. Vegetarians can simply add grated cheese instead.

Ingredients

1-1¼ cups long-grain rice	8 green onions, washed
1tsp. salt	4tbsp. freshly chopped
4tbsp. butter	parsley
1 onion, peeled and finely	8 basil leaves, chopped
chopped	black pepper
1 clove garlic, crushed	

Cook the rice in 4½ cups boiling water with the salt added. Leave the pan uncovered and fluff the rice occasionally for first 10 minutes.

Heat the butter in a skillet and cook the onion and garlic over a low heat for 3 minutes. Add the finely chopped green onions.

Mix the onion mixture and the rice well. There should still be a little water left.

Cover with a lid and allow the remaining water to be absorbed. This will take another 5-7 minutes over a low heat.

Remove the lid and taste to make sure rice is tender. Add the parsley and basil leaves. Season with freshly ground black pepper and extra salt if necessary.

Curried Fried Rice
Serves 4-6

Ingredients

1¼ cups cooked chicken, pork and/or shrimp	2 cloves garlic, peeled and chopped
1lb. cold, cooked rice	2 stems lemon/grass, use bottom part of bulb, sliced
¼lb. green beans or string beans, cut into 2in. lengths and blanched	4 stems coriander, chopped, leaves reserved for garnish
3-5 dried red chili peppers, seeded and pounded or 1-2tsp. chili powder	6-8tbsp. vegetable oil
6 shallots, peeled and chopped finely	

Cut the meats into fine slices and leave the shrimp, if using, whole. Set the rice on one side. Prepare and blanch the beans.

Pound the chili peppers with shallots, garlic, lemon grass and coriander stems and peel. This can be done in a food processor. If using the chili powder add it to these pounded ingredients.

Heat the oil and fry this paste until it gives off a fragrant aroma. Add the cooked meats, then the rice, stirring all the time until the fried rice is well mixed. Add more oil if necessary. Season with salt, fish sauce and sugar, if liked, to taste. Finally, add the green beans.

Serve garnished with the coriander leaves.

Fried Rice
Serves 4

This is a useful way to make a delicious savory rice dish with leftovers.

Ingredients

3tbsp. vegetable oil	1tbsp. soy sauce
1 large onion, peeled and finely chopped	⅓ cup chopped cooked ham
3 cups cooked long-grain rice	2tbsp. bamboo shoots
salt and freshly ground pepper	½ cup cooked shrimps

Heat the oil in a large skillet. Cook the onion over a medium heat until it is a pale golden color.

Add the long-grain rice and stir in with the onion. Season well.

Stir in the soy sauce, ham, bamboo shoots and shrimps. Cook until golden brown. Taste for flavor. Add more soy sauce, vegetables, meat or fish if necessary.

Fried Rice

Chop Suey
Serves 4

Ingredients

1 lb. long-grain rice	¾ cup cooked shrimp
salt	1⅓ cups cooked chicken
6 tbsp. oil	¾ cup cooked ham
2 medium onions, peeled	2 eggs (or 4 if making the
2 cloves garlic, crushed	omelet)
2 fresh chili peppers, seeded	salt and freshly ground
1 tsp. Garam Masala	pepper
2 tbsp. soy sauce	1 tbsp. chopped green
½ tsp. Worcestershire sauce	onions

Cook the long-grain rice in 5 cups boiling water with 1 tsp. salt until the liquid is absorbed and the rice is done, about 15 minutes. Fluff the grains to make sure they are separated before putting on the lid.

Heat two-thirds of the oil in a skillet. Add 1 onion, finely chopped, and the garlic, and cook until translucent. Remove with a slotted spoon.

In a blender or food processor whizz together the other onion, chopped, the chili peppers, Garam Masala, and the soy and Worcestershire sauces to make a paste.

Add the remaining oil and fry the paste over a medium heat for 3 minutes.

Add the shrimp, chicken and ham and stir for a few minutes. Beat the eggs with salt and pepper. Turn the heat up fairly high and add the egg mixture, stirring continuously until the egg begins to set.

Add the cooked rice and blend with the other ingredients on a lower heat.

Decorate the rice mixture with omelet strips (see below) if liked, sprinkle with chopped green onion and serve immediately.

Variation To garnish with omelet strips, use 4 eggs. Add 2 to the meat and shrimp mixture and make a small omelet with the others.

Mix them vigorously with a fork. Add seasoning. Melt a knob of butter in an omelet pan over a high heat. Pour in the egg mixture and pull the cooked edges back from the sides of the pan to the center (do not mix as if you were making scrambled egg). When the mixture is almost set, put the pan under a hot broiler for about 1 minute. Turn onto a board and cut into thin strips.

Paella
Serves 6

Ingredients

8 tbsp. oil	1 red pepper, seeded
2 large onions, peeled and	1 green pepper, seeded
finely chopped	½ lb. white fish, boned
2-3 cloves garlic, crushed	⅔ cup white wine
1¼ cups long-grain rice	1 bay leaf
salt and freshly ground	4-8 chicken drumsticks
pepper	1 lb. mussels
pinch turmeric	¾ cup peeled shrimp
2½ cups chicken stock	1 tbsp. chopped parsley

Heat three-quarters of the oil in a large skillet or casserole. Over a low heat cook the onions until they become translucent. Add the garlic.

Gradually add the rice and stir around in the onions and oil until the grains are coated with oil.

Add seasoning and turmeric to the hot stock and pour it over the rice gradually, stirring as the rice is brought to a boil. Cover with a lid or with foil, and simmer gently for 10 minutes.

Meanwhile dice the green and red peppers and blanch for 1 minute in boiling water.

Poach the white fish in water with a little of the wine and the bay leaf for about 5 minutes.

Fry the drumsticks in another pan in the remaining oil until golden brown and cooked through.

Clean the mussels by removing the beards and rinsing several times in cold water. Any which remain open when tapped should be discarded. Pour the wine into the saucepan with a little fish stock from the poached fish. Add the mussels and shake the pan from time to time until the mussels open. This will take about 8 minutes. Keep warm.

Remove the lid from the rice and separate the grains with a fork. Stirring gently, add the peppers, the white fish, shrimp, about ¾ cup mussel stock and then the chicken. Cover and cook until rice is separate and liquid is absorbed.

Decorate with parsley before serving.

Kedgeree with Cherries.
Serves 6

Ingredients

4tbsp. clarified butter
1 onion, finely chopped
1lb. firm white fish fillets,
   cut into small pieces
½tsp. ground cinnamon
12oz. fresh or canned
   (drained weight) sour
   cherries, pitted
½ cup unsalted almonds,
   chopped

½ cup currants, or raisins
¼ cup dried apricots
1½tsp. salt
½tsp. black pepper
1¼lb. long grain rice,
   rinsed and drained
5 cups water

Heat the butter in a large skillet. Add the onion and fish fillets and sauté over a low heat for 10 minutes. Stir constantly.

Add the cinnamon, cherries, almonds, currants, apricots, salt and pepper to the skillet. Stir and simmer for 3 to 4 minutes.

Add the rice and water. Stir gently but well. Cover tightly and simmer over a very low heat for 55 minutes.

Kedgeree
Serves 4

This makes an excellent breakfast dish for guests as it can be prepared in advance and warm through just before serving.

Ingredients

½ cup long-grain rice
1¼ cups boiling water
½tsp. salt
3 hard-boiled eggs, shelled
salt and freshly ground
   pepper
1⅓ cups Finnan haddie

⅔ cup milk
1 bay leaf
1 slice of peeled onion
Garnish
1tbsp. chopped parsley
½tsp. paprika
1 lemon, quartered

Cook the rice in boiling water with the salt added until the water has been absorbed and the rice is done, about 15 minutes.

Chop 2 of the hard-boiled eggs. Press the white and yolk of the third egg separately through a strainer and reserve to decorate the kedgeree.

Add the chopped eggs to the rice, with the salt and pepper.

Put the Finnan haddie in a saucepan with the milk, bay leaf, onion and a little pepper. Bring to a boil and simmer for 5 minutes. Allow to cool slightly in the milk. Remove and flake the fish from the skin. Add to the rice.

Heat all the ingredients together and pile onto a warm serving dish. Garnish with rows of egg yolk, egg white and chopped parsley with a little paprika. Serve with lemon quarters.

Rice à la Provençale
Serves 4

This is a useful recipe to serve with many main dishes as there is no need to cook separate vegetables.

Ingredients

1 cup long-grain rice	4 zucchini, washed and
2½ cups water	thinly sliced
½tsp. salt	½tsp. basil
4tbsp. oil	4tbsp. white wine
2tbsp. butter	8 tomatoes, skinned and
2 onions, peeled and finely	chopped
chopped	1tbsp. chopped capers
2 cloves garlic, crushed	2 hard-boiled eggs
salt and freshly ground	8 green olives, stoned
black pepper	2tbsp. chopped parsley or
2 red peppers, seeded and	chervil
blanched	

Cook the rice in the water with the salt, by bringing the water to a boil, adding the rice and stirring to separate the grains. Cover and simmer gently until the water has all been absorbed, which will take about 15 minutes.

Heat the oil and butter and cook the onions over a low heat for about 4 minutes. Add the garlic.

Dice the blanched peppers and add with the sliced zucchini, the basil and white wine. Stir gently until cooked for about 5 minutes. Lastly stir in the tomatoes. Gently fold in the cooked rice and season well.

Add the chopped capers and turn into a heated serving dish.

Serve decorated with hard-boiled eggs, green olives and chopped herbs.

Rice à la Provençale

Pamplona Rice
Serves 4

Ingredients

6tbsp. vegetable oil	1¼ cups long-grain rice
1 large onion, peeled and	3 cups water
finely sliced	freshly ground pepper
1 red pepper, seeded	¾tsp. salt
1 green or yellow pepper,	½tsp. turmeric or a few
seeded	drops of yellow coloring
2 chili peppers, seeded	1 tomato, sliced
12oz. cod, boned and	1 lemon, quartered
skinned	
425g/15oz. can peeled	
tomatoes	

Heat the oil in a large pan. Cook the onion for 4 minutes over a low heat.

Slice the peppers into strips. Add to the onion with the chopped chili peppers, and cook for a further 2 minutes. Push to one side of the pan. Raise the heat a little and add the chunks of fish. Fry on each side. Season well.

Add the tomatoes. Stir well. Add the rice. Stir thoroughly into the mixture.

Add ¾tsp. salt and the turmeric or yellow coloring to the water. Gradually pour over the rice. After the water has come to a boil, turn the heat down and simmer gently for 10 minutes.

Turn into an ovenproof dish and allow to dry off in the oven at 350°F. Fluff the mixture after 5 minutes.

Variation A can of anchovies can be used with 12 green olives to garnish the dish. Arrange and allow rice to heat through again in the oven for 5 minutes. All tomato sauces go well with this.

Milanese Risotto
Serves 4

Ingredients

2tbsp. beef bone marrow	5 cups meat stock, well
1 small onion, thinly sliced	skimmed of fat
2/3 cup butter	good pinch saffron
scant cup rice	60g/5tbsp. Parmesan
3/4 cup dry white wine	cheese

Scrape the marrow with a knife to remove any bits of bone, then chop and put in a pan with the onion and half the butter. Fry until the onion is soft but not brown. Add the rice and fry for 2 or 3 minutes. Add the wine and cook until absorbed. Add the stock with a ladle, waiting between each addition until it has been absorbed. Cook the rice for 30 minutes. 10 minutes before the end of the cooking time, dissolve the saffron in a few tablespoons of boiling stock and add to the rice. Finally, add the remaining butter and stir in the Parmesan. Let it stand, covered, for 2 minutes before serving.

Risotto
Serves 4

Ingredients

1tbsp. olive oil	4 cups chicken stock
2tbsp. butter	1tsp. salt
1 medium onion, peeled	freshly ground pepper
and finely chopped	1tbsp. freshly chopped
1½ cups Italian risotto rice	parsley (optional)

Using a heavy-bottomed saucepan, heat the oil and butter. Add the onion and cook over a low heat for about 3-4 minutes without browning.

Add the risotto rice dry and stir fry for about 2 minutes over a medium heat.

Add half the hot chicken stock. Stir from the bottom to avoid sticking and continue to do so until the grains are separate and the stock is absorbed.

Continue adding the remaining stock with the salt bit by bit, stirring all the time, until it is all absorbed. The risotto should have cooked to a creamy consistency in about 25 minutes without becoming mushy.

Add the freshly ground pepper and, if you wish, a little freshly chopped parsley for color, and serve hot.

Variation For Risotto Milanese cook as above but substitute 2/3 cup white wine for the equivalent stock. Add 4tbsp. butter and 2tbsp. Parmesan cheese at the end of the cooking time just before serving. Seve with Osso Buco. Can be garnished with mushrooms.

Pilaf
Serves 4

Ingredients

4tbsp. butter	pinch of saffron threads or
1 medium onion, peeled	a few drops of yellow
and thinly sliced	food coloring
1 cup long-grain rice	2 cups stock
salt and freshly ground	
pepper	

Heat 3tbsp. of the butter in an ovenproof casserole and cook the onion over a low heat for 4 minutes. Add the rice and continue stirring for another 3 minutes.

Season well. Add the saffron or coloring to the stock. Then pour the stock onto the rice and mix well with a fork. Bring to a boil. Cover and cook in the oven at 350°F for about 15 minutes until stock is absorbed and rice grains are separate.

Add the remaining butter together with, if you like, 1tbsp. grated cheese, and serve hot.

Variation Another version of this savory rice can be made by adding mushrooms, peppers or grated carrot to the onion. Alternatively add small strips of meat or ham to the rice, or even flaked fish or shrimp.

Pilau Rice
Serves 4

Ingredients

1 cup long-grain rice
2tbsp. vegetable oil
1 onion, peeled and finely
  chopped
1 clove garlic, crushed
½tsp. cumin
pinch turmeric

½ fresh chili pepper,
  crushed or finely
  chopped (optional)
pinch ground coriander
1tsp. salt
2½ cups stock or boiling
  water

Wash the rice and allow it to soak for 20-30 minutes. Drain in a strainer, shaking from time to time.

Heat the oil in a pan on a medium heat and fry the onions and garlic until golden brown.

Add the drained rice, turn the heat down and stir in well. Add the cumin, turmeric, chili pepper and coriander.

Add the salt with the boiling liquid and gradually mix with the rice. Bring to a boil and simmer, covered, over a low heat for 15-20 minutes, until the rice is cooked. Fluff with a fork.

Variation Vegetable Pilau can be made by adding peas, beans, carrots, peppers, potatoes or a combination of any favorite vegetables. It is advisable to cut the potatoes and carrots into small dice, and blanch them for 4 minutes to ensure that they become cooked through. Add the chopped vegetables to the onion and garlic, and cook all together in 6tbsp. oil over a low heat before adding the rice.

A further ½tsp. salt should be added to the stock, and ½tsp. Garam Masala and 2tbsp. chopped coriander will add extra flavor.

Spanish Rice

Nutty Rice Pilau
Serves 6

This is a complete main dish, but can also be served as a first course or as an accompaniment.

Ingredients

2tbsp. oil
1 large onion, peeled and
  chopped
2 cups mushrooms,
  chopped
1lb. long-grain American
  rice
10½oz. can condensed
  clear soup
2½ cups water
bouquet garni

½ cup hazelnuts
½ cup almonds
½ cup walnuts
2tbsp. pine nuts
1tbsp. sunflower seeds
4tbsp. butter
salt and freshly ground
  pepper
1tbsp. snipped chives
1tbsp. sesame seeds

Heat the oil in an ovenproof casserole, add the onion and mushrooms and fry over medium heat for a couple of minutes. Add the rice and fry for a minute or until golden. Stir in the clear soup, water and bouquet garni. Bring to the boil then stir well, cover, and put in the oven. Cook for 20 to 25 minutes, without stirring at 350°F.

While the rice is cooking, toast the hazelnuts and almonds in the oven until golden brown. Put into a grinder or processor with the walnuts, pine nuts and sunflower seeds to chop coarsely.

When the rice is tender and all the liquid has been absorbed, remove the bouquet garni and stir in the nuts, butter and seasonings. Sprinkle with the chives and sesame seeds, and serve hot.

Variation Replace half the quantity of nuts with grated cheese, or substitute condensed tomato soup for the clear soup.

Savory Spinach Rice
Serves 4

This goes well with meats or fish or it can be served simply as a vegetarian main dish.

Ingredients

1lb. frozen leaf spinach or 2lb. fresh spinach, washed	*salt and freshly ground pepper*
2tbsp. butter	*1 cup long-grain rice*
1tbsp. oil	*2½ cups water or stock*
1 medium onion, peeled	*½tsp. salt*
1 leek, washed and trimmed	*pinch of nutmeg*
juice of ½ lemon	*1tbsp. chopped parsley*
	1tbsp. natural yogurt (optional)

Cook the frozen spinach as directed on the packet or, if thawed, simmer for a few minutes in 4tbsp. water. Drain well in a strainer, squeezing out excess moisture with the back of a wooden spoon. If using fresh spinach remove thick stems, tear into manageable pieces and cook in ½in. boiling water for 4 minutes. Drain well.

Heat the butter and oil over a low heat in a large saucepan. Slice the onion and leek finely and cook in the fat for 4-5 minutes. Sprinkle with lemon juice and seasoning.

Add the long-grain rice and stir in with the vegetables. Pour on boiling water or stock with the salt added. Cover with a tight-fitting lid and simmer for 15 minutes.

Fluff the rice with a fork and add the spinach, nutmeg and chopped parsley. Mix with a fork, cover and reheat for 5 minutes.

Serve topped with the yogurt if you like.

Lontong
Rice Cubes
Serves 4

Ingredients

4oz. packet boil-in-the-bag rice	*boiling, salted water*

Put the boil-in-the-bag rice in the water and boil for 1¼

hours or until the whole bag is puffy and firm and rice fills the whole of it. The bag must be covered in water all the time. You can put a saucer or plate on top to weight it down if necessary.

Allow to cool completely before stripping off the bag, leaving a cushion of rice which can then be cut into neat cubes and served with spiced and deep-fried chicken or with satay.

Variation Alternatively use 1 cup short-grain rice. Wash the rice and put in a pan with 2 cups salted water. Bring to a boil, stir, cover and simmer for 30-35 minutes over the gentlest heat until the rice is tender. Cool, then turn into a 1in. deep dish. Press down, cover with foil, a plate and a weight. Leave until firm.

Spanish Rice
Serves 4

Ingredients

1 cup long-grain rice	*salt and freshly ground pepper*
2½ cups stock or water	*pinch of sugar*
1tsp. salt	*2 red peppers, seeded, chopped and blanched*
½tsp. turmeric	*¾ cup peas*
2tbsp. vegetable oil	*¾ cup cooked shrimp*
4oz. chicken livers, trimmed and chopped	*1tbsp. chopped parsley*
1 onion, peeled and finely chopped	
6 tomatoes, peeled and chopped or 15oz. can peeled tomatoes	

Cook the long-grain rice with boiling water or stock to which the salt and turmeric has been added, until the liquid is absorbed and the rice is done, about 15 minutes.

Meanwhile heat the oil in a skillet, and over a medium heat fry the chopped chicken livers until golden brown. Turn the heat down and add the onion. Cook, stirring well, for 4 minutes. Add the tomatoes, salt, pepper, sugar and chopped peppers. Stir gently.

Add the peas and shrimp. Heat through in the vegetable mixture and mix in the warmed rice.

Turn out into a dish and serve hot sprinkled with the parsley. A little butter may be added if you like.

Thai Steamed Rice
Serves 4

Steaming rice after boiling separates out each grain, making it very light and fluffy. It is delicious served with any type of curry.

Ingredients

1 cup long-grain rice   *2½ cups water*

Rinse the rice in a strainer then put it in a pan with the water. Bring to a boil, lower the heat and cook uncovered until the water has been absorbed and a series of holes appear in the surface of the rice.

Line the base of a steamer within ½in. of the edges with foil and raise the edges into a shallow, bowl-like shape. Puncture all over base with a skewer. Turn the rice into the foil in the steamer and place over a pan of fairly fast-bubbling water. Cover and cook for 30 minutes until the rice is just tender and fluffy. Refill the base pan with boiling water if necessary.

No salt is necessary for this recipe as real Thai rice is of such excellent quality, with a fragrant flavor, that salt detracts from this.

Spiced Rice Salad
Serves 4

Ingredients

1 cup rice   *1 onion, peeled and diced*
1tsp. salt   *⅓ cup white raisins*
1tsp. Garam Masala   *1 green pepper, seeded,*
1tsp. turmeric   *blanched and diced*
1 bay leaf   *6tbsp. low-fat yogurt*
2tbsp. butter   *2 green onions, washed*
1 clove garlic, crushed

Cook the rice in boiling salted water with the Garam Masala, turmeric and bay leaf for about 15 minutes until tender.

Meanwhile melt the butter and gently sweat the garlic and onion without browning for 5 minutes.

Add the garlic and onion to the rice when it is cooked and allow it to cool.

Stir in the white raisins and pepper

Stir in the yogurt and serve garnished with chopped green onions.

Couscous
Serves 4-6

Ingredients

³/₄-1 cup couscous
1 tsp. salt
1¹/₄ cups boiling water
1 tbsp. oil
2 large onions, chopped
2 leeks, sliced
4 carrots, sliced
5 cups stock
salt and freshly ground
    black pepper

4 zucchini, sliced
6 tomatoes, sliced
1 cup peas
1¹/₂ cups kidney beans,
    presoaked and cooked
1¹/₂ cups chick peas,
    presoaked and cooked
a few strands of saffron
3 tbsp. butter
Spicy Tomato Sauce

Put the couscous in a bowl, add the salt and pour over the boiling water. Let it soak for 20 minutes until the water has been absorbed. Break up any grains that are sticking together.

Meanwhile, make the vegetable topping. Heat the oil in a large saucepan and stir-fry the onions and leeks. Add the carrots and stock and season well. Bring to a boil.

Put the couscous in a vegetable steamer (or a strainer or colander) lined with muslin, and put this over the saucepan. Put on the lid and simmer for 30 minutes.

Remove the steamer and add the remaining vegetables and the saffron to the stock. Stir the couscous with a fork to break up any lumps. Replace steamer, covered, and continue cooking for 10 minutes.

Turn couscous into a bowl and stir in the butter. Serve vegetables separately in a tureen. Offer Spicy Tomato Sauce and pitta bread.

Kasha
Buckwheat Groats with Mushrooms
Serves 8-10

Packaged, roasted buckwheat groats are available in many healthfood stores. This dish can be made with just fresh mushrooms, but the rich aroma imparted by the dried mushrooms should not be missed.

Ingredients

1 cup dried mushrooms (ceps)
2 cups kasha (coarse
    buckwheat groats)
2 eggs, beaten
1¹/₂ tsp. salt
5 cups boiling water

1 cup butter
2¹/₂ cups fresh mushrooms,
    quartered
3 cups small onions, quartered
3 tbsp. finely chopped green
    onions

Put the dried mushrooms into a small bowl and add enough warm water to cover. Let the mushrooms soak for 1 hour. Drain well. Trim away any tough stems and cut any large mushrooms in half.

Put the kasha into a medium-sized mixing bowl. Fold the beaten eggs into the kasha.

In a large, heavy skillet, sauté the kasha and egg mixture over a medium heat, until the kasha begins to become dry. Add the salt, 4 cups of the boiling water and half the butter. Cover the pan tightly and reduce the heat to low. Simmer for 20 minutes, stirring at 5-minute intervals.

Add the remaining boiling water to the pan. Cover and simmer for a further 5 minutes. Turn the heat off. Leave to stand for 15 minutes.

Turn the heat on again and add the onions, dried mushrooms, fresh mushrooms and green onion. Stir briefly. Reduce the heat to medium and add the remaining butter. Cook, stirring constantly, until the mushrooms are done and the kasha is dry again, about 3 to 5 minutes.

Cornmeal Pudding
Serves 6-8

Ingredients

1 cup cornmeal	2 eggs, separated
1½ tbsp. chicken fat	2 cups buttermilk
2 cups boiling water	1¼ tsp. baking soda
½ tsp. salt	4 tbsp. butter or margarine,
pinch black pepper	melted

In a large pot, combine the cornmeal with the chicken fat and boiling water. Mix until the consistency of the dough is even. Add the salt, pepper, egg yolks, buttermilk and bicarbonate of soda. Combine thoroughly.

Beat the egg whites until they are stiff. Fold them into the cornmeal mixture.

Grease a large casserole dish with 1 tbsp. of the melted butter or margarine. Preheat the oven to 325°F. Scrape the cornmeal mixture into the casserole with a spatula. Bake for 1 hour 15 minutes. Pour the remaining melted butter or margarine over the pudding before serving. Serve with a casserole or stew.

Farmer's Cheese Dumplings
Serves 4

Ingredients

1⅓ cups farmer's cheese	1 egg
5 tbsp. butter or margarine	salt and pepper
½ cup farina	

Mix everything together very well and let the mixture rest for 30 minutes. Lightly flour a board and form the mixture into a roll. Cut off slices and roll them into balls the size of small meatballs.

Drop them into boiling salted water. When they rise to the top they are cooked. Drain them well and serve with meat.

Variation Add some chopped herbs to the mixture if you like and you can roll them in breadcrumbs or finely chopped nuts which have been fried in butter before serving them.

Ravioli
Makes about 50

These meat dumplings are traditionally served in chicken soup.

Ingredients

2 lb. boneless chuck steak, coarsely ground	½ tsp. black pepper
4 small onions, coarsely chopped	1⅔ cups fine wholemeal flour
5 tbsp. vegetable oil	2 eggs
½ tsp. salt	1½ cups warm water

In a large saucepan, brown the meat and onions in the oil over a low heat for 8 to 10 minutes. Add half the salt and the black pepper. Stir well. Remove from the heat and set aside.

In a large mixing bowl, make the flour into a mound. Make a well in the flour. Sprinkle the remaining salt over the flour and break the eggs into the well. Beat with a whisk, gradually adding the warm water, until the consistency of the dough is smooth and even. Roll the dough into a ball.

Cut the dough into approximately 15 equal pieces. One by one, roll each piece out into a thin sheet. Cut 3×3-in. rounds from each sheet with a cookie cutter. Repeat the process until all the dough is used up.

Put 1 tsp. of the meat and onion filling in the center of each dough round. Fold the dough over and seal the edges together with the blunt end of a spoon.

Bring a very large pot of water to a boil. Drop in the ravioli, about 8 to 15 at a time, depending on the size of the pot. When the water returns to a boil, cook them for 3-5 minutes, or until they float to the top. Remove with a slotted spoon and set aside. If the ravioli are not being served within 30 minutes, refrigerate them. Add them to the soup for 4 minutes before serving.

Pasta Bows with Buckwheat
Serves 6

Ingredients

1 egg	2 onions, diced
1 cup medium-grain kasha (buckwheat groats)	½ cup mushrooms, sliced
	boiling water
4 tbsp. butter, margarine or chicken fat	salt to taste
	1½ cups pasta bows

Beat the egg in a bowl and add the kasha. Stir well to coat the kasha.

Heat a large heavy pot on the stove top. Add the kasha and cook, stirring until each kasha grain is dry and separate. Make sure this is done thoroughly or the kasha will be soggy and lumpy.

Melt 1 tbsp. of the fat in a small skillet. Add the onions and mushrooms, and sauté until soft.

Add the cooked vegetables, boiling water, remaining fat and salt to taste to the kasha. Cover tightly and cook over a medium heat until all the water has been absorbed, about 40 minutes.

Cook the pasta in a large pot of boiling water until *al dente*. Drain well. Mix the pasta with the kasha and serve.

Polenta
Serves 4-6

Ingredients

1²⁄₃ cups wholewheat flour	²⁄₃ cup butter
¼ cup fine cornmeal	½ cup Mozzarella cheese,
salt and freshly ground	cut into thin strips
black pepper	grated Parmesan cheese
4 cups water	

Put the flour in a bowl and stir in the cornmeal and seasoning.

Bring water to a boil and sprinkle in the mixture, stirring with a wooden spoon. Cook over a low heat, stirring occasionally, for about 45 minutes until the mixture is very thick and comes away easily from the sides of the pan.

Stir in the cheese. Keep stirring until it melts. Serve hot with Tomato Sauce and offer Parmesan.

Matzo Balls
Serves 8

Ingredients

4 eggs, separated	½tsp. salt
2 cups matzo meal	5tbsp. chicken fat
½tsp. ground ginger	1 cup hot chicken stock
½tsp. ground white pepper	4½ pts. water

Beat the egg whites in a medium-sized mixing bowl until stiff. Set aside.

In a large mixing bowl, combine the matzo meal, ginger, pepper, and salt. Add the fat, stock and egg yolks. Fold in the egg whites and chill for 90 minutes.

In a large soup pot, bring the water to a boil. Form the matzo meal dough into balls with a diameter of about 1½in. and drop them into the pot. Cover tightly and cook for 25 to 30 minutes. Do not remove the cover during this time. If the matzo balls are not being used within 30 minutes, refrigerate them and add them to the liquid 5 minutes before serving.

Potato Gnocchi I
Serves 4-6

Ingredients

3 cups cooked potatoes,   salt and pepper
    sliced   2tbsp. butter, melted
1⅔ cups plain flour, sifted

Force the cooked boiled potatoes through a large
strainer or potato ricer. Add the flour with some
seasoning and the melted butter. Mix together.
   Turn onto a floured board and knead lightly until
you have an elastic dough. Divide into 1-in. pieces and
make into little rolls. Shape by pulling the end pieces
towards you.
   Cook in boiling, salted water for about 10 minutes.
Serve with a piquant, well-flavored sauce and cheese.

Variation Alternately, dot the gnocchi with butter and
sprinkled cheese and bake at 400°F until golden
brown.

(Above) Twisting the dough for Potato Gnocchi

Potato Gnocchi II
Serves 4

Ingredients

2lb. potatoes   **Tomato Sauce**
1⅔ cups wholemeal flour   1-2tbsp. oil
salt   1 onion, chopped
1 egg   2 cloves garlic, chopped
4tbsp. butter   15-oz. can tomatoes,
½ cup Mozzarella cheese,   mashed
    thinly sliced   2tbsp. tomato paste
                              salt and freshly ground
                                  black pepper
                              1tbsp. fresh oregano,
                                  chopped

Preheat the oven to 375°F.
   Peel the potatoes and boil until soft. Mash well.
Mash in the flour, salt, egg and half the butter. Shape
into balls.
   Make the tomato sauce. Heat the oil and fry the
onion and garlic until soft. Add the tomatoes, tomato
paste, seasoning and herbs and simmer, stirring
occasionally, for 5 minutes.
   Layer the gnocchi in an ovenproof dish with the
cheese, dotted with butter, and the tomato sauce.
Finish with a cheese layer.
   Bake in the oven for about 20 minutes until the dish
has heated through and the cheese has melted.

Making Pasta Dough by Hand

1 Sift the flour onto a clean surface, make a well in the center of the flour large enough to hold the eggs. Add the eggs and a little oil.

2 Sprinkle flour over the eggs and stir with a spatula. Add the water gradually, stirring the mixture around with some added flour. Pull a little flour from the sides to cover the egg mixture.

3 Start to mix the dough by pulling the flour on to the egg mixture gradually until it is all mixed in. If the mixture is too stiff, add a few drops of water to take up all the flour. Take care not to make the mixture too wet.

4 Knead the dough for several minutes with the heel of the hand until it has formed a smooth ball. Divide the ball in two and let it rest for a few minutes in the refrigerator. Now clean the board and make sure it is quite dry for rolling out the dough.

5 Sprinkle with flour. Take one piece of dough and roll it out into a rectangular or oval shape. Keep turning it and flour it regularly underneath; try to keep it the same width as the rolling pin. Roll the dough as thin as you can. For tagliatelli you should be able to see the table through it. Leave to rest for about 40 minutes before cutting.

Vegetable Dishes

Mushroom-Stuffed Artichokes
Serves 4

Ingredients

4 globe artichokes	1tbsp. pine nuts
juice of 1 lemon	2tbsp. chopped parsley
2tbsp. butter	salt and freshly ground
1 clove garlic, crushed	black pepper
½lb. mushrooms, chopped	

Remove the artichokes' tough outer leaves and snip 1in. off the rest. Dip the cut edges of the leaves in most of the lemon juice. Trim off the stalks and stand the artichokes upright in a large pan of boiling salted water. Simmer for 15 minutes. Drain upside down and allow to cool.

Meanwhile, make the filling. Heat the butter in a pan and cook the garlic until soft. Add the mushrooms. Cook gently until very black and juicy. Mix in the pine nuts and parsley and season with salt and pepper and a dash of lemon juice.

When the artichokes are cool, pull out the tiny leaves from the middle and the hairy inedible "chokes" beneath them.

Spoon the filling into each artichoke, closing the leaves over it. Put the artichokes in a greased ovenproof dish and heat through before serving.

Asparagus with Hollandaise Sauce
Serves 6

When making Hollandaise sauce, never let the sauce boil, or it will curdle. Use the thinnest, freshest asparagus you can find.

Ingredients

2lb. asparagus, trimmed	1tbsp. heavy cream
¾ cup butter	pinch salt
3 egg yolks	pinch ground white pepper
1tbsp. lemon juice	

Fill a medium-sized saucepan to a depth of 3in with water.

Add the asparagus, cover and simmer over a medium heat for 12 minutes.

Meanwhile, melt the butter in a small saucepan and set aside, keeping the butter warm over a very low heat.

In a small mixing bowl, beat the egg yolks and lemon juice together for 3 to 4 minutes, or until the mixture thickens.

Beat the egg yolk mixture into the melted butter over a very low heat. Beat in the cream, salt and white pepper. Remove from the heat and let the sauce thicken for 5 minutes, stirring gently but frequently.

Drain the cooked asparagus well and place in a large deep serving dish. Top with the Hollandaise sauce. Serve warm.

Bean, Mushroom and Asparagus Purée
Serves 6

Ingredients

1lb. fresh green beans	½tsp. white pepper
½lb. mushrooms	½tsp. salt
1lb. fresh asparagus	1 egg yolk
1tbsp. clarified butter or oil	croûtons
½tsp. nutmeg	

Preparation Fill a large pot to the depth of 1½in with cold water. Add the green beans, mushrooms and asparagus. Cook over a low heat for 5 minutes. Add the clarified butter or oil, nutmeg, pepper and salt. Cook for a further 1 minute.

Put the vegetables, along with the egg yolk and ½ cup of the cooking liquid, in a blender or food processor. Purée in bursts of 30 seconds until the vegetable mixture is smooth and well blended.

Serve hot with croûtons.

Green Beans Paprika
Serves 6

Ingredients

2lb. fresh green beans, trimmed and halved	1tbsp. paprika
	1tbsp. flour
½ cup butter	7 cups sour cream
½lb. green onions, coarsely chopped	½tsp. salt

Cook the green beans in a large pot of boiling water until they are tender but still crisp, about 7 minutes. Drain well.

Melt the butter in a medium-sized saucepan over a low heat. Add the green onions and cook, stirring frequently, for 4 to 5 minutes, or until they are translucent. Remove the saucepan from the heat and stir in the paprika. Set aside.

Combine the flour and sour cream in a small bowl until they are well mixed. Add the mixture to the spring onions. Add the salt. Simmer the mixture over a low heat for 5 minutes. Add the beans and simmer for 5 minutes longer. Serve hot.

Spicy Green Bean and Tomato Pastries
Makes 4

Ingredients

¾ lb. Shortcrust Pastry	¼ lb. small green beans,
1-2 tbsp. oil	parboiled, trimmed and
1 tsp. fennel seeds	sliced
1 slice fresh ginger	15-oz. can tomatoes,
2 cloves garlic, crushed	mashed
1 small onion, chopped	1 tsp. Garam Masala
1 medium potato,	salt and freshly ground
parboiled and diced	black pepper
	beaten egg to glaze

Make the pastry and chill for 30 minutes. Preheat the oven to 350°F.

Heat oil in a pan and when hot, add fennel seeds. Stir in ginger, garlic and onion. Cook, stirring, until lightly browned.

Stir in potatoes and beans. Add enough tomatoes and juice to prevent the mixture sticking. Add garam masala, salt and pepper and simmer for about 5 minutes, stirring occasionally and adding more tomato juice as necessary. Do not make the mixture too wet.

Divide the pastry into 4 balls and roll out. Share the mixture between the pastry rounds. Fold over and crimp together to form pastry envelopes and brush with beaten egg. Put pastries on a cookie sheet and bake for 30 minutes or until pastry has cooked.

Brussels Sprouts with Garlic and Mushrooms
Serves 4

Ingredients

2-3 tbsp. oil	1 lb. Brussels sprouts, thinly
4 cloves garlic, chopped	sliced
	1¼ cups mushrooms, sliced

Heat the oil in a wok or deep-sided skillet. Add the garlic and fry quickly, stirring, until crisp and brown.

Add the sprouts and mushrooms and stir until coated with garlic and oil. Stir-fry for 1-2 minutes and eat while crisp and hot. This is particularly good with bean dishes.

Brussels Sprouts with Hazelnuts
Serves 4

Ingredients

1 lb. small Brussels sprouts,	pinch of nutmeg
fresh or frozen	2½ cups Cheese Sauce
salt and freshly ground	1 cup hazelnuts, chopped
pepper	

Cook Brussels sprouts in boiling salted water for 10 minutes. Drain and season with salt, pepper and nutmeg. Place in a buttered ovenproof dish.

Coat them with the Cheese Sauce. Add the hazelnuts and cook for 2-3 minutes.

Bake at 375°F for 10 minutes.

Variation Use walnuts instead of hazelnuts.

Stuffed Cabbage
Serves 6

Ingredients

medium-sized green	1 tsp. black pepper
cabbage, cored and	2 tbsp. butter or margarine
trimmed	¾ cup seedless white
4 tbsp. vegetable oil	grapes, halved
2 large onions, chopped	1 cup shredded red
4 cups cooked rice	cabbage
4 eggs, beaten	6 canned tomatoes,
⅓ cup white raisins	chopped
½ tsp. salt	

Separate the leaves from the cabbage. Blanch the leaves in a large pot of boiling water for 5 minutes. Drain well.

Heat the oil in a saucepan. Add the onions and brown over a low heat. Add the rice, eggs and sultanas. Cook, stirring frequently, for 30 seconds. Add the salt, pepper, butter or margarine and grapes. Cook, stirring frequently, for 90 seconds.

Put 2 to 3 tablespoons of the rice filling at the edge of a cabbage leaf. Roll the leaf up, tucking the ends under. Repeat with the remaining cabbage leaves until the rice filling is used up. Coarsely chop the remaining cabbage leaves.

Heat the remaining oil in a large heavy skillet over a moderate heat. Add the chopped green cabbage and the red cabbage. Sauté for 3 to 4 minutes. Add the stuffed cabbage leaves and tomatoes. Cover and cook gently for 12 minutes.

Caraway Cabbage

Caraway Cabbage
Serves 4-6

Ingredients

2tbsp. butter	salt and pepper
1½lbs. white or green	2tsp. flour
cabbage, finely sliced	⅔ cup sour cream
1tbsp. caraway seeds	

Melt the butter and add the cabbage. Stir well. Add the caraway seeds, salt and pepper. Cover and cook, stirring occasionally, until the cabbage is cooked but still crisp.

Add the flour and stir it in well. Cook for a further 2 minutes, stirring constantly.

Add the sour cream, warm it through and serve.

Crispy Fried Cabbage
Serves 4-6

Even children will eat cabbage cooked this way. Serve with grilled or fried meat, sausages or bacon.

Ingredients

1 small, firm green or white	4tbsp. butter
cabbage	1tbsp. caraway seeds
1 medium onion, peeled	sea salt and freshly ground
2tbsp. oil	pepper

Trim the cabbage, removing the outer leaves and core. Quarter and shred it. Wash in icy water, then drain. Slice the onion.

Heat the oil and butter in a heavy sauté pan, large skillet, or wok. When very hot, stir in the cabbage, onion and caraway seeds. Stir-fry for 2 to 3 minutes until crisp and brown. Add salt and pepper to taste. Turn out into a warmed serving dish and serve immediately.

Indian Cabbage with Peas
Serves 4

Ingredients

3tbsp. oil	1½tsp. ground cumin
2 bay leaves	1tsp. ground coriander
¾tsp. whole cumin seeds	2 tomatoes, chopped
1½lb. cabbage, finely	¾tsp. salt
shredded	½tsp. sugar
1tsp. ground turmeric	1 cup peas
½tsp. chili powder	

Heat the oil over medium high heat and add the bay leaves and the cumin seeds. Let them sizzle for a few seconds.

Add the cabbage and stir for 2-3 minutes. Add the turmeric, chili, cumin, coriander, tomatoes, salt and sugar and mix with the cabbage.

Lower heat, cover and cook for 15 minutes. Add the peas and cover again. Continue to cook for a further 15 minutes, stirring occasionally.

Remove the cover, turn heat up to medium high and, stirring continuously, cook until dry.

Red Cabbage with Apples
Serves 6

Ingredients

1 large red cabbage,	2 green onions, chopped
shredded	bay leaf
2tbsp. sugar	whole clove
1tsp. salt	6¼ cups boiling water
½ cup raspberry, red wine	4tbsp. blackberry jam
or herb vinegar	¼ cup dry red wine
4tbsp. butter	
3 large tart apples, peeled,	
cored and diced	

In a large bowl, combine the shredded cabbage with the sugar, salt and vinegar. Toss until the cabbage is evenly coated with the vinegar mixture.

In a large casserole, melt the butter. Add the apples and green onions and cook over a very low heat for 8 minutes, stirring frequently. Add the cabbage and vinegar mixture, the bay leaf and the clove. Stir in the boiling water. Cover and simmer over a low heat for 90 minutes.

Add the blackberry jam and red wine. Simmer for a further 30 minutes.

Serve hot or cold, in a large glass or porcelain bowl.

Crispy "Seaweed"
Serves 6

The very popular "seaweed" served in Chinese restaurants is, in fact, green cabbage. Choose fresh, young cabbages. Even the deep green outer leaves should be tender. This recipe also makes an ideal garnish for a number of dishes, particularly cold starters and buffet dishes.

Ingredients
1½lb. green cabbage
2½ cups oil for deep frying
1tsp. salt
1tsp. sugar
½ cup blanched split almonds

Wash and dry the cabbage and shred them with a sharp knife into the thinnest possible shavings. Spread them out on absorbent paper or put in a large colander to dry thoroughly.

Heat the oil in a wok or deep-fryer. Before the oil gets too hot, turn off the heat for 30 seconds. Add the cabbage shavings in several batches and turn the heat up to medium high. Stir with a pair of cooking chopsticks.

When the shavings start to float to the surface, scoop them out gently with a slotted spoon and drain on absorbent paper to remove as much of the oil as possible. Sprinkle the salt and sugar evenly on top and mix gently. Serve cold. Deep fry or toast the split almonds until crisp and add to the "seaweed" as a garnish.

Shredded Carrot and Cabbage
Serves 4

Ingredients
2tbsp. oil
1tsp. mustard seeds
1 tight green cabbage, finely shredded
1lb. carrots, grated
a little honey
salt and freshly ground pepper

Heat oil in a heavy pan with a lid. When it is hot, add the mustard seeds.

As soon as the mustard seeds begin to pop, pile in the shredded vegetables, dribble the honey over them and stir well. Turn down the heat, put on the lid and cook for about 3 minutes until just tender. Season and serve.

and parsley. Reduce the heat to low. Cook for 1 to 2 minutes stirring constantly. Cover the saucepan and reduce the heat to very low. Simmer for 5 minutes and serve.

Holiday Carrots
Serves 6

Ingredients

2tbsp. butter or margarine
1½lb. baby carrots, finely chopped
8oz. can mandarin orange segments, drained and finely chopped
¼ cup water
¼ cup fresh lime juice
¼tsp. salt

Melt the butter or margarine in a medium-sized saucepan.

Add the remaining ingredients and simmer over a low heat for 20 minutes. Serve hot.

Carrots with Yogurt
Serves 4

Ingredients

1lb. carrots, sliced
1tsp. sugar
½tsp. ground cumin
1 small onion, finely chopped
juice of ½ lemon
⅔ cup yogurt
salt and pepper

Cook the carrots with the sugar in boiling water just until they are *al dente*. Drain them and add the cumin and onion. Stir around.

Mix the lemon juice into the yogurt, season to taste and spoon it over the carrots.

Serve immediately or leave it to cook and serve as a salad or an accompaniment to curry.

Braised Carrots and Onions
Serves 6

Ingredients

4tbsp. butter or margarine
1 medium onion, sliced into rings
2 green onions, finely chopped
2 large tomatoes, cut into eighths and seeded
16 baby carrots, scraped and cut into quarters
pinch salt
pinch ground white pepper
1tbsp. chopped fresh coriander
2tbsp. chopped fresh parsley

Melt the margarine in a large saucepan over a low heat. Add the onion and green onions. Sauté, stirring constantly, for 5 minutes. Add the tomatoes and raise the heat to medium. Sauté, stirring constantly, for a further 3 to 4 minutes.

Add the carrots, salt and white pepper, coriander

Celery Mousse
Serves 4 approx.

Ingredients

1tsp. gelatin
2tbsp. boiling water
1 medium bunch of celery
 with leaves
¾ cup yogurt
1tsp. lemon juice

1 small onion
about 2tbsp. chopped
 parsley
salt and pepper
¾ cup farmer's cheese

Dissolve the gelatin in the boiling water. Blend all the remaining ingredients, except the farmer's cheese, feeding them into the liquidizer or food processor a little at a time. Add the dissolved gelatin and farmer's cheese and blend it into the mixture. Turn into a moistened mold (a small ring mold looks nice). Refrigerate until set.

Unmold and serve as a part of a cold buffet, or as an accompaniment to cold meat or chicken or fish.

Variation For a richer mousse, substitute mayonnaise for the yogurt.

Corn Croquettes
Serves 4-6

Ingredients

3tbsp. butter
3tbsp. flour
1¼ cups milk
salt and freshly ground
 black pepper
1-2tbsp. finely chopped
 parsley

2 7-oz. cans corn kernels
2 egg yolks
Coating
2 eggs, beaten
seasoned flour
fine stale breadcrumbs
oil for deep frying

Cut the butter into small pieces and melt in a heavy-bottomed pan. Stir in the flour and cook for a few minutes until the mixture is pale gold.

Remove from the heat and gradually stir in the milk. Return to the heat and stir until the sauce has thickened. Season with salt and plenty of pepper. Stir the parsley, corn and egg yolks into the mixture. Chill. The mixture should have a heavy dropping consistency. Form it into croquettes. Dip in the beaten egg, then roll it in the seasoned flour and breadcrumbs, coating each croquette firmly. Fry the croquettes in oil until heated through and crisp on the outside.

Zucchini with Almonds
Serves 6

Ingredients

1½lb. zucchini, sliced
 lengthwise
1 medium onion, finely
 chopped
1tbsp. olive oil

salt and pepper
½ cup flaked almonds
1tsp. cornstarch
1tbsp. water
1 cup yogurt

Put the zucchini in a shallow ovenproof dish. Mix the onions, oil, salt and pepper and spoon the mixture over them. Bake uncovered at 350°F for 40 minutes, or until tender.

Meanwhile toast the almonds: put them into a heavy skillet over a high heat and shake the pan from time to time. Take care that they do not burn.

Mix the cornstarch with the water and add it to the yogurt with seasoning to taste. Warm the mixture over a gentle heat, stirring constantly, for 3 minutes. Spoon it over the zucchini and scatter the almonds on top.

Zucchini au Gratin
Serves 4

Ingredients

1-2tbsp. oil
1lb. zucchini, sliced
1 large onion, chopped
14oz. can tomatoes
chopped basil, thyme or
 marjoram
a sliver of lemon peel

salt and pepper
½lb. uncooked macaroni
2 eggs
⅔ cup plain yogurt
⅔ cup grated Cheddar
 cheese

Heat the oil and fry the zucchini until they are lightly colored. Remove them from the pan and reserve. Fry the onion until golden, adding more oil if necessary. Add the tomatoes, herbs, lemon peel, salt and pepper and simmer for 10 minutes, breaking up the tomatoes and stirring from time to time.

Meanwhile cook the macaroni in boiling, salted water and drain it well. Put it into an ovenproof dish.

Pour the sauce over the macaroni and mix it through well. Lay the cooked zucchini on top.

Mix the eggs, yogurt and half the cheese and pour the mixture over the zucchini. Scatter the remaining cheese on top. Bake at 375°F for 30 minutes.

Variation You could use eggplant instead of zucchini, in which case slice and salt them, leave them to drain for 20 minutes, rinse and dry them and proceed as above.

Stewed Fennel
Serves 6

Ingredients

3 large bulbs fennel	2 cups water
6tbsp. olive oil	½tsp. salt
1 medium onion, chopped	pinch black pepper

Trim the fronds from the fennel bulbs and reserve. Cut the bulbs in half vertically, then slice each half horizontally.

Heat the olive oil in a large heavy pan. Add the fennel slices and onion and sauté over a low heat for 6 to 8 minutes. Stir frequently.

Add the water, salt and pepper and raise the heat to medium. Cook for 25 to 30 minutes.

Serve with the cooking liquid in a deep dish, garnished with fennel fronds.

Fennel Mornay
Serves 6

Ingredients

3 bulbs fennel	1 cup Cheddar cheese, grated
1 bay leaf	salt and freshly ground black pepper
2tbsp. butter	½-1 cup fresh breadcrumbs
4tbsp. plain flour	
1¼ cups milk	
⅔ cup light cream	

Trim the fennel and simmer in salted water with the bay leaf for about 30 minutes until tender.

Meanwhile, make the sauce. Melt the butter in a pan and stir in the flour. Cook, stirring, for a couple of minutes and then gradually stir in the milk. Add the cream and most of the cheese and cook gently until the cheese has melted. Season well and keep warm.

Drain the fennel and cut each bulb in half. Lay the halves in a flameproof dish and pour the sauce over them. Sprinkle with the remaining cheese and the breadcrumbs. Put under a hot broiler to brown and melt the cheese.

Variation For a tangier sauce, add a little powdered mustard to taste.

Lentil Purée
Serves 4

This German dish goes well with ham, pork, or game.

Ingredients

1⅓ cups lentils	bouquet garni
2½ cups vegetable or chicken stock	4tbsp. butter
¼lb. Polish-style sausage or smoked sausage	4tbsp. heavy cream
1 large onion, peeled	2tbsp. fresh herbs: parsley, chives, chervil or savory
2 cloves garlic, peeled	salt and freshly ground pepper

Rinse the lentils and pick them over. Put them in a pan with the stock. Skin the sausage if necessary, and add to the pan. Slice the onion and add to the pan with the garlic and bouquet garni. Cover, bring to a boil, and simmer for about 40 minutes, until reduced to a thick purée.

Remove the bouquet garni and discard. Remove the sausage and chop roughly. Liquidize or process the lentils and sausage until smooth. With the machine running, gradually add the butter, cream and herbs. Taste for seasoning, then spoon into a warmed serving dish.

Stuffed Zucchini
Serves 4-6

Ingredients

1 large or 4 small zucchini	**Tomato sauce**
salt and freshly ground black pepper	*1-2tbsp. oil*
$\frac{1}{3}$ cup brown rice	*1 onion, chopped*
2 small carrots, diced	*2 cloves garlic, chopped*
$\frac{2}{3}$ cup peas	*15-oz. can tomatoes, mashed*
1-2tbsp. oil	*1tbsp. tomato paste*
1 onion, chopped	*salt and freshly ground black pepper*
1 clove garlic, chopped	
1 stalk celery, chopped	
handful of parsley, chopped	
2tbsp. hazelnuts or filberts, chopped	

Preheat the oven to 350°F. Cut the 1 large or 4 small zucchini in half lengthwise and scoop out the pith and seeds. Sprinkle the flesh with salt and leave the halves upside down to drain.

Meanwhile, make the filling. Simmer the rice in a covered pan of salted water until just tender (about 30 minutes). Drain.

Parboil the carrots and peas and drain. Heat the oil in a pan and fry the onion and garlic until translucent. Add celery, carrots and peas. Stir in the rice, parsley and hazelnuts and season well. Dry the zucchini and pile filling into one half. Top with second half.

Make the tomato sauce. Heat oil in a pan and add onion and garlic. Fry, stirring, until soft. Add tomatoes and tomato paste. Simmer for 5 minutes, stirring occasionally, and season well.

Put the zucchini in a baking dish with a lid, if you have one big enough, otherwise use foil to cover. Surround with the sauce. Cover and cook for 45 minutes until tender. Serve hot or cold with a crisp green salad.

Zucchini in Cream Sauce
Serves 4

Ingredients

1 medium to large zucchini or 6 small zucchini	*1tbsp. water*
	1tbsp. dried dill weed
	salt and pepper
2tbsp. butter	*1$\frac{1}{4}$cups sour cream*
2tsp. cornstarch	

Peel the zucchini and either finely chop or grate them. Cook them with the butter, stirring from time to time, just until it begins to soften.

Mix the cornstarch with the water until smooth and add. Stir and cook for a further 3 minutes.

Add the dill, salt and pepper and finally stir in the sour cream. Warm through gently and serve hot, with roast meat, chicken or fish.

Okra with Mustard
Serves 4

Okra, also known as Ladies Fingers, can be bought at most supermarkets with large vegetable counters or at soul food outlets.

Ingredients

1½tsp. ground mustard	4tbsp. oil
½tsp. ground turmeric	2-3 fresh green chili
pinch chili powder	peppers, cut lengthwise
¼tsp. salt	1½tbsp. yogurt
2tbsp. hot water	⅓ cup water
1lb. okra	

Mix the mustard, turmeric, chili and salt with the hot water, cover and set aside for 20 minutes. Wash the okra, pat dry with paper towels. Cut off the stems and leave whole. Heat oil over medium high heat, add the green chili peppers and let them sizzle for a few seconds. Add the okra and, stirring gently, fry for 5 minutes.

Add the spice mixture and yogurt and mix with the okra; add the water and bring it to a boil. Lower heat, cover and simmer till the okra is tender.

Stuffed Mushrooms
Serves 6-8

An excellent side dish, these mushrooms can also be served as an appetizer.

Ingredients

45 to 50 medium	2tbsp. chopped parsley
mushrooms, stems	4tbsp. butter or margarine
removed and reserved	2tbsp. flour
2 green onions, finely	¾ cup white wine
chopped	3tbsp. olive oil
2 shallots, finely chopped	
2½ cups fresh spinach,	
pressed down and finely	
chopped	

Preheat the oven to 350°F. Finely chop the mushroom stems. In a small saucepan, combine the green onions, shallots, spinach, parsley, butter or margarine, flour, white wine and olive oil. Mix thoroughly and cook over a low heat until the fat melts. Cover and simmer for 2 minutes.

Add the mushroom stems. Mix thoroughly and cover. Simmer the filling over a low heat for a further 5 minutes.

Put approximately 1tsp. of the filling in each mushroom cap. Arrange the filled caps on greased cookie sheets and bake for 15 minutes. Serve hot.

Paprika Mushrooms
Serves 4

Ingredients

2tbsp. butter or margarine	1tbsp. paprika
1 medium onion, finely	¾lb. mushrooms, sliced
chopped	⅔ cup sour cream
½ green pepper, seeded	salt and pepper
and finely chopped	chopped parsley

Heat the butter, add the onion and cook until it has just softened but not browned. Add the green pepper and paprika and cook on a low heat for 3 minutes. Add the mushrooms, stir well and cook for a further 5 minutes until they are soft. Stir in the sour cream, season to taste and warm through gently.

Serve, sprinkled with parsley, as a vegetable accompaniment, as an hors d'oeuvre with hot French bread, as a filling for vol-au-vents — patty shells, or on fried bread or with a crisp salad, as a light supper.

Petits Pois à la Francaise
Serves 4

Ingredients

4tbsp. butter
1 lettuce, washed and
　shredded
12 small pearl onions,
　peeled
2 slices bacon, chopped
　(optional)

1tsp. flour
salt and freshly ground
　pepper
2½ cups salted water
pinch of sugar
1lb. fresh or frozen peas
3 sprigs parsley

Heat the butter in a saucepan, add shredded lettuce (retain some outside leaves for garnish if liked), the pearl onions and chopped bacon. Cook for 2 minutes. Stir in the flour and season.

Add the salted water and sugar. Bring to a boil, add the fresh peas, if using, and parsley. Simmer for 20-30 minutes until peas and onions are tender.

Most of the liquid should be absorbed and the consistency should be creamy. Check seasoning. Serve on lettuce leaves, if liked. If you are using frozen peas, reduce cooking time to 10 minutes, but cook the lettuce, onion and bacon for 10 minutes before adding peas. One chopped onion or 4 green onions can be substituted for the pearl onions.

Spiced Potatoes
Serves 6

Ingredients

2tbsp. vegetable oil
½tsp. mustard powder
1 tomato, seeded and
　finely chopped
4tbsp. green pepper, seeded
　and diced
pinch cayenne
pinch ground turmeric

pinch ground allspice
½tsp. ground ginger
pinch salt
½tsp. sugar
pinch ground coriander
5 large boiled potatoes, cut
　into chunks

Heat the oil in a large, heavy skillet over a moderate heat. Add the mustard, tomato, green pepper, cayenne pepper, turmeric, allspice, ginger, salt, sugar and coriander. Cook, stirring constantly, for 2 minutes.

Add the potatoes and cook, stirring constantly, until the potatoes are coated with the spices and heated through, about 5 minutes.

Baked Potatoes with Eggs
Serves 6

Ingredients

4 large potatoes, peeled
salt to taste
2tsp. paprika

4 eggs, hard-cooked and
    sliced
²/₃ cup sour cream
2tbsp. milk
1tbsp. butter

Boil the potatoes until they are cooked but still firm. Drain off the water and slice them. Put a layer of potatoes in the bottom of a greased ovenproof dish. Season with salt and paprika. Lay the sliced eggs over the potatoes.

Mix the sour cream with the milk until smooth. Spoon over the eggs. Season again. Add the remaining potatoes. Dot with butter and bake at 350°F for 25 minutes, until lightly browned.

Variation To make this a more substantial dish, you could add slices of salami over the sliced eggs.

Spicy Potato Cakes
Serves 4

Ingredients

1lb. potatoes, boiled and
    mashed
1-2 fresh green chili
    peppers, seeded and
    chopped

½tsp. salt
1tbsp. coriander leaves,
    chopped
2tbsp. chopped onions
oil for frying

Mix the mashed potatoes with the chili peppers, salt, coriander leaves and onions. Form into small balls and flatten. Heat oil for shallow frying till hot and fry the potato cakes for a few minutes each side till golden. Drain and serve hot.

Russian Potatoes
Serves 6

Ingredients

1lb. potatoes
salt and freshly ground
    black pepper
approx. 4tbsp. butter

1 large onion, sliced
1¼ cups sliced mushrooms
¾ cup sour cream
3tbsp. chopped chives

Scrub the potatoes and cook in salted water until barely tender. Drain, peel and slice. Heat some of the butter in a flameproof casserole and fry the onion until translucent. Add the mushrooms and cook gently until the juices run. Add the rest of the butter as necessary and stir in the potatoes. Let them gently brown on one side, season, turn over and add the cream. When most of the cream has been absorbed, sprinkle over the chopped chives and a little more pepper and serve.

Spicy Potato Cakes

Sour Potatoes with Pickles
Serves 6-8

This unusual hot potato dish should be made on the day the meal is served. The sourer the pickles, the better the dish.

Ingredients

6 large potatoes	½tsp. salt
2tbsp. lemon juice	½tsp. black pepper
¼lb. steak	½tsp. dried parsley
⅔ cup beef stock	pinch of dried thyme
4tbsp. diced Spanish onion	1 large bay leaf
2tbsp. flour	3 large pickled cucumbers,
pinch of dried marjoram	finely chopped

Scrub the potatoes and parboil them in a large pot of boiling water for 15 minutes, or until they are tender but not mushy. Drain well. Cut the potatoes into medium-sized chunks and put them into a serving bowl. Sprinkle the potatoes with the lemon juice and set aside.

In a medium-sized heavy skillet brown the steak in a third of a cup of the beef stock for about 2 minutes. Add the onions and flour and brown over a low heat for 10 minutes. Turn off the heat.

Remove the steak and cut it into small pieces. Return the steak pieces to the pan. Add the remaining beef stock and the marjoram, salt, pepper, parsley, thyme, bay leaf, and pickled cucumbers. Cover the pan and simmer for 30 minutes

Pour the mixture over the potatoes. Toss well and serve.

Crispy Potato Cakes
Serves 4

These potato cakes can be served as an accompaniment or as a meal in themselves when topped with puréed spinach and a poached egg. You can vary the mixture by adding some grated onion or some grated cheese, or a bit of both.

Ingredients

1lb. waxy potatoes	salt and freshly ground
2 eggs	black pepper
1tbsp. potato flour	4tbsp. oil

Peel the potatoes and grate them into a bowl of cold water. Drain. Squeeze the potato shreds dry in a cloth. Mix with the eggs, flour and seasoning.

Heat 1tbsp. of the oil in a skillet and make your first potato cake using a quarter of the mixture. Spread it out in the pan and flatten it. When the underside is crisp and golden, turn it over and brown the top. Keep it warm while you make the other three.

Curry Potatoes
Serves 4-6

This potato dish goes well with sausages and chops.

Ingredients

2lb. large potatoes, peeled	½tsp. turmeric
and thinly sliced	1½tsp. chili powder
6tbsp. oil	1½tsp. coarse sea salt
4tbsp. butter	freshly ground black
3 cloves garlic, peeled	pepper
1-in. piece root ginger,	½tsp. ground coriander
peeled and sliced	1-2tbsp. fresh coriander or
3tsp. mustard seeds	mint leaves, chopped

Heat the oil and butter in a large skillet. Add the garlic and ginger and fry for 2 minutes or until brown. Remove using a slotted spoon.

Add the mustard seeds and fry for a couple of minutes. When the seeds being to pop, add the potatoes and carefully stir-fry for 1 minute.

Sprinkle with the turmeric, chili powder, sea salt, pepper and ground coriander. Mix well, then fry the potatoes over medium-high heat, turning frequently, for about 10 minutes, until crisp and golden brown.

When the potatoes are ready to serve, stir in the herbs, taste for seasoning and spoon into a warmed serving dish.

Spinach Ring
Serves 4

Ingredients

2lb. spinach	**Sauce**
5tbsp. butter	1-2tbsp. oil
salt and freshly ground black pepper	1 onion, finely chopped
1/2 cup all-purpose flour	2 cloves garlic, crushed
2/3 cup milk	15-oz. can tomatoes, mashed
1/3 cup Parmesan cheese	1tbsp. tomato paste
3 eggs	salt and freshly ground black pepper

Preheat the oven to 375°F. Grease a 3½-4pt. ring mold.

Wash the spinach and discard tough stalks. Pack spinach into a large pan with 2tbsp. of the butter and seasoning and cover tightly. Cook over a low heat for about 5 minutes, stirring occasionally, until spinach is soft. Drain and purée in a blender.

Melt the rest of the butter in a heavy-bottomed pan and add the flour, stirring. Gradually add the milk, stirring continuously. Stir in the cheese and season. Stir until sauce bubbles and thickens, then turn down the heat and cook for a further minute. Mix thoroughly with the spinach.

Separate the eggs. Beat the yolks into the spinach mixture. Beat the whites until soft peaks have formed and fold into the mixture. Pour the mixture into the ring mold and bake for 30-40 minutes until risen and lightly set.

Meanwhile, make the tomato sauce. Heat the oil in a skillet and add the onion and garlic. Fry, stirring, until transparent. Add the tomatoes, reserving the juice. Add the tomato paste and season. Simmer for 5 minutes, adding more juice and adjusting seasoning if necessary.

To turn out the spinach ring, dip the mold into ice-cold water for a few seconds. Run a knife blade round edges of mold. Invert onto a warmed plate. Spoon over the sauce and serve with wholewheat bread or new potatoes and a crunchy salad.

Creamed Spinach
Serves 4

Ingredients

1½lb. fresh spinach, washed and picked over	grated nutmeg
	salt and pepper
1 egg yolk	2/3 cup yogurt

Cook the spinach without excess water (the water adhering to it is sufficient) and a little salt. Drain the cooked spinach very well (press it between two plates for most effective drainage). Add the rest of the ingredients and mix into the spinach. Warm through gently.

If you prefer to use frozen spinach, use leaf, not chopped spinach, and follow the cooking directions on the packet.

Cheesy Ratatouille
Serves 4-6

This lovely, colorful dish can also be served as a first course, or as a main course dish with baked potatoes.

Ingredients

4tbsp. olive oil	3 cloves garlic, crushed
3 medium onions, peeled and sliced	1lb. ripe tomatoes, quartered
2 medium eggplant	salt and freshly ground pepper
salt and freshly ground pepper	1tsp. thyme
1lb. zucchini, trimmed and sliced	ground coriander to taste
	1/2lb. grated Cheddar cheese
1 large red pepper, cored, seeded and sliced	**Topping**
1 large green pepper, cored, seeded and sliced	2tbsp. breadcrumbs
	2tbsp. grated Parmesan cheese
1 large yellow pepper, cored, seeded and sliced	

Heat the oil in a large, deep, heavy pan. Add the onions, and cook over a medium heat for 5 minutes.

While the onions are cooking, slice the eggplant. Sprinkle with a little salt, mix well, and place in a colander to drain for 5 minutes. Rinse well and pat dry with paper towels.

Add the sliced vegetables, garlic and quartered tomatoes to the pan with the onion. Stir well over high heat for a minute then stir in salt, pepper, thyme and ground coriander to taste. Cook, stirring frequently, over medium high heat for 20 minutes or until the vegetables are just tender. If there is too much liquid, turn up the heat, and boil rapidly till reduced — the ratatouille should be fairly dry. Taste the ratatouille; it should be well seasoned.

Heat the broiler. Stir half the Cheddar cheese into the vegetable mixture, and transfer to a greased ovenproof baking dish. Mix the ingredients for the topping together with the remaining Cheddar cheese and sprinkle over the ratatouille. Broil until golden brown and bubbling.

Vegetable Cutlets
Makes 6

Ingredients

2tbsp. butter
1 medium onion, chopped
1 stalk chopped celery
1 cup grated carrots
1 cup cooked green beans,
   coarsely chopped
¾ cup cooked peas

3 eggs
1tsp. salt
½tsp. black pepper
3 matzo meal or fine
   oatmeal crackers
vegetable oil for frying

Melt the butter in a skillet. Add the onion, celery and carrots and sauté for 10 minutes. Remove from the heat. Add the green beans, peas, two of the eggs, and the salt, pepper and crumbled matzo meal crackers. Mix well. Shape the mixture into 6 cutlets.

Beat the remaining egg in a bowl. Dip the cutlets in the egg.

Heat the vegetable oil in a skillet. Add the cutlets and sauté until both sides are browned.

Chestnuts and Vegetables
Serves 6

Ingredients

1lb. chestnuts
4tbsp. olive oil
2 fat cloves garlic, chopped
2 cups sliced mushrooms
¾lb. Brussels sprouts

¾lb. red cabbage
salt and freshly ground
   black pepper
small glass red wine

Preheat the oven to 400°F.

Make a nick in the top of the chestnuts with a sharp knife and boil them for 10 minutes. Plunge them in cold water and peel.

Heat the olive oil in a flameproof casserole and fry the garlic. Add the mushrooms, sprouts and red cabbage and season. Cook, stirring occasionally, for about 5 minutes until coated with oil and beginning to soften.

Stir in the chestnuts and red wine. Cover and bake for 40 minutes.

Vegetables in Aspic
Serves 6

Ingredients

1¼ cups aspic or
   equivalent
(see Note)
⅓lb. peeled and diced
   carrot
⅓lb. trimmed and sliced
   green beans

1tsp. walnut oil
1 cup sliced button
   mushrooms
1tbsp. stuffed olives, sliced
⅔ cup thick mayonnaise

Prepare the aspic or equivalent and allow it to cool. Chill a mold. Wet the mold and when the aspic is almost set, line the mold with some of it. Put in the fridge to set.

Meanwhile cook the carrot and green beans in salted water until tender. Refresh in cold water. Heat the walnut oil in a pan and gently sauté the mushrooms. Allow to cool.

Mix the vegetables together with the olives, mayonnaise and the remaining aspic, remelted, then cooked almost to setting point, and fill the mold. Chill until set.

To serve, dip the mold into hot water, turn out onto a plate and cut into wedges.

Note Commercial gelatin and aspic powders are made from the bones of animals and fish. Vegetarians who prefer not to use them can set foods in carageen or Irish moss, an edible seaweed available in powder form from health food shops. Another vegetable substitute for gelatin is agar-agar. Like gelatin, carageen and agar-agar come in varying strengths and you should follow the instructions on the pack when making them up. Neither imparts a taste to the finished dish.

Vegetable Chop Suey
Serves 4

Ingredients

2 large carrots, peeled
1 medium leek, trimmed
2 medium onions
8-oz. can bamboo shoots
1-in. piece root ginger,
  peeled
1½ cups button mushrooms
⅓lb. beansprouts
2¼ cups boiling water

2tbsp. oil for frying
1tsp. cornstarch
⅔ cup vegetable stock
3tbsp. tomato ketchup
½-1tbsp. soy sauce, to taste
salt to taste
6 green onions, trimmed
  and sliced

First prepare all the vegetables for cooking. Either grate or shred the carrots. Set aside. Halve the leek, rinse well and slice. Halve and slice the onions. Set aside. Drain the bamboo shoots and slice in the same way. Set aside. Grate the ginger. Quarter the mushrooms. Put the beansprouts in a colander and pour the boiling water over them. Drain thoroughly.

Heat the oil in a wok or large, deep skillet. Add the ginger, carrots and onions. Stir-fry for 2 minutes then stir in the leeks, bamboo shoots and mushrooms. Stir-fry over high heat for 2 minutes, then stir in the beansprouts, and fry for 1 minute.

Mix the cornstarch with the stock, ketchup and soy sauce. Stir into the vegetables and bring to a boil, stirring constantly. When the mixture has thickened taste for seasoning, adding more soy sauce, ketchup or salt if necessary. Transfer the chop suey to a warmed serving dish and sprinkle with the green onions.

Variation For a non-vegetarian chop suey, add ¼-½lb. shelled shrimp or diced cooked chicken to the chop suey with the bamboo shoots and mushrooms.

Curried Vegetables
Serves 4

Ingredients

½lb. eggplant, cut in
  chunks
2tbsp. oil
½ cup cashew nuts
1 medium onion, chopped
1 clove garlic, crushed
2tsp. curry powder
1 large potato, peeled and
  parboiled

¼lb. green beans, trimmed
⅔ cup water
2 tomatoes, quartered
1tbsp. Garam Masala
⅔ cup yogurt
2tsp. cornstarch
2tbsp. water
salt

Salt the eggplant and leave for 30 minutes. Rinse and pat dry.

Heat the oil and fry the cashews to a golden brown. Remove them from the pan and put them to one side. Fry the onions and garlic and cook until they begin to soften. Add the curry powder and stir in. Add the eggplant and cook on a low heat for about five minutes, stirring from time to time. Add a little more oil if necessary.

Add the potato, cut into large chunks, together with the green beans. Pour on the water, cover and leave to cook until the potatoes are ready. Add the tomatoes and the garam masala, stir round carefully and continue cooking for a few more minutes.

Mix the cornstarch with the water to a smooth paste, stir into the contents of the pan and warm through for three minutes.

Serve hot, with the browned cashew nuts sprinkled on top.

Vegetable Chop Suey

Oriental Stir-Fry Vegetables with Noodles
Serves 4

Ingredients

1 onion, peeled
1 red pepper, seeded
1 green pepper, seeded
1 small chili pepper, seeded
1 clove garlic, crushed
¹⁄₃lb. mushrooms, washed
   and sliced
1 small cauliflower

2 zucchini, washed
¹⁄₄lb. green beans
4tbsp. olive oil
salt and freshly ground
   pepper
2tbsp. soy sauce
³⁄₄lb. egg noodles

Prepare the vegetables by thinly slicing the onions and the peppers, dice the chili finely, crush the garlic and slice the mushrooms. Divide the cauliflower into small flowerets and slice the zucchini and beans.

Heat the oil in a large casserole or wok, throw in the onions and other vegetables a few at a time and stir-fry for about 5 minutes, turning the vegetables over to obtain an even distribution of heat. Stir in the seasoning and soy sauce.

Cook the noodles in boiling salted water for about 6 minutes, drain well and toss in a little butter. Serve with the vegetables.

Summer Vegetable Pastries
Makes 4

Ingredients

¾ lb. Shortcrust Pastry
beaten egg to glaze
2 medium potatoes, diced
4 baby carrots, sliced
½ cup shelled peas
2 zucchini, sliced
2 sticks celery, sliced
½ green pepper, diced

Cheese sauce
2tbsp. butter
4tbsp. plain flour
up to 1¼ cups milk
½ cup grated Cheddar
* cheese*
salt and freshly ground
* black pepper*

Make the pastry. Preheat the oven to 350°F.

Boil the potatoes and carrots in salted water until just tender. In another pan, boil the remaining vegetables for about 2 minutes. Drain. To make the cheese sauce, melt the butter in a heavy-bottomed pan, stir in the flour and gradually add half the milk, stirring. Add the cheese. Stir until melted. Add a little more milk and season to taste. Don't make the sauce too thin or it will pour out of the pastry shells. Mix sauce into vegetables to coat them generously. Divide the pastry into 4 balls and roll out. Share the mixture among the pastry rounds. Crimp together across the top to form pastry envelopes and brush with beaten egg. Put the pastries on a cookie sheet and bake in the oven for 30 minutes or until the pastry is cooked.

Vegetables in Vinaigrette
Serves 8

Ingredients

1lb. fresh asparagus
1 large head fresh broccoli,
* cut into flowerets*
1 large can artichoke
* hearts, drained*
½ cup red wine vinegar
½ cup olive oil
2tbsp. chopped green
* onions*

2tbsp. Dijon mustard
½tsp. dried chives
2tbsp. honey
½tsp. celery salt
pinch of black pepper
pinch of ground white
* pepper*
1 clove garlic, finely
* chopped*

Cook the asparagus in a large, covered pot of boiling water until they are tender, about 10 to 12 minutes. Cook the broccoli flowerets in a large pot of boiling water until they are tender but still crisp, about 7 minutes. Drain well.

Put the asparagus, broccoli and artichoke hearts into a large bowl, cover and chill for 40 minutes.

In another bowl, make the dressing. Combine the vinegar, olive oil, green onions, mustard, chives, honey, salt, black pepper, white pepper and garlic. Mix well. Chill for 40 minutes.

Stir the dressing well and pour it over the vegetables.

Vegetable and Rice Hotch Potch
Serves 4

Ingredients

6tbsp. oil
3 cups onions, sliced
1 cup rice
1 large green or red
* pepper, chopped*
salt and pepper

1tsp. paprika
14-oz can tomatoes
1¼ cups water
2½ cups yogurt
4 eggs

Heat a third of the oil, add the onions and cook until they have just softened but not browned. Add the rice and peppers and stir them round to color them a little. Season well with salt, pepper and paprika. Layer the rice mixture with the tomatoes in an ovenproof dish. Pour over the remaining oil, mixed with the water. Cover and bake at 375°F for 30 minutes (or on top of a medium heat).

Mix the yogurt with the eggs. Pour over the vegetables and return the dish, uncovered, to the oven for a further 20 minutes.

Variation This dish adapts to endless variations — add some more vegetables, such as eggplant, zucchini, mushrooms, fennel. Salami, sausages or cooked meat can be added before the yogurt topping.

Purée of Root Vegetables
Serves 4

Ingredients

⅓lb. carrots	2-4tbsp. butter
⅓lb. rutabaga	salt and freshly ground
1 turnip	black pepper
1 parsnip	

Trim and peel the vegetables and simmer in salted water until tender. Drain and mash to a fluffy purée with butter. Season with salt and plenty of black pepper.

Five Vegetable Gratin
Serves 4-6

This is a nutritious and hearty main dish, that can be prepared in advance. It makes a lovely winter supper.

Ingredients

1lb. leeks, trimmed	pinch nutmeg
4tbsp. butter or margarine	6 eggs
2lb. onions, peeled and sliced	⅔lb. each carrots, parsnips, potatoes, all peeled and roughly chopped
5tbsp. flour	4tbsp. butter
2 cups milk	1tbsp. chopped chives or parsley (optional)
2 cups grated Gruyère or strong Cheddar cheese	
salt and freshly ground pepper	

Rinse and slice the leeks, then steam or boil them until just tender. Drain and set aside.

Melt the butter or margarine in a large pan. Stir in the onions and cook slowly till soft and golden, about 15 to 20 minutes. Take the pan off the heat, stir in the flour, then gradually stir in the milk. Return to the heat and stir continuously until the mixture comes to a boil. Simmer for 2 minutes.

Stir the leeks and 1 cup of the grated cheese into the sauce, and season to taste. Spoon into a large shallow, greased baking dish. Make 6 hollows in the mixture for the eggs, and allow to cool. Break an egg into each hollow, and sprinkle ½ cup of the grated cheese over the eggs.

While the base is cooling, steam or boil the carrots, parsnips and potatoes until tender. Drain if necessary, then mash, process or liquidize with the butter, herbs and seasoning until very smooth and creamy. You may have to do this in two batches. Taste for seasoning.

If you are preparing the dish in advance, allow the vegetable purée to cool before spooning carefully over the eggs and onion mixture in the baking dish. Smooth the top.

When ready to cook — sprinkle on the remaining ½ cup grated cheese. Bake in a preheated oven at 400°F for 15 to 20 minutes until brown and bubbling. The exact timing will depend on how you like your eggs cooked, and whether the gratin has come straight from the fridge, or has been prepared immediately beforehand.

Chopping Onions

1 Slice the unpeeled onion lengthwise through the core, then peel both halves. Do not remove the root-end, which will serve to hold the 'leaves' together when chopping.

2 Put one half of the onion flat on the board. Using a thin, sharp knive make horizontal parallel cuts towards the root, without cutting through to the root-end.

3 Make a series of parallel, vertical cuts down to the board, again, avoiding the root-end.

4 Finally, slice the onion, making the cuts at right angles to the previous two sets of cuts. Use the root-end for stock or chop it separately like parsley.

Slicing Onions

1 Split the unskinned onion in half through the top and tail.

2 Pull away the onion skin from the pointed top, leaving the root-end intact. This will prevent the 'leaves' of onion slipping while being sliced. Repeat with the second half-onion.

3 Put each onion-half, cut-side down, on the board and slice widthways, from tip to root. Use the knuckles as a guide, moving them back a little after each cut. Use a downwards and forwards cutting action, keep the knife-tip touching the board.

Preparing Tomatoes

1 Make a small cross in the skin of each tomato where the stem was attached to the fruit.

2 Dip in boiling water for 10 seconds (more if under-ripe, less if very soft) and immediately transfer to cold water to stop further cooking. Peel off the skins, starting at the 'nicked' point near the stem. They should come away easily.

3 Cut the tomatoes from top to bottom in quarters and push out the seeds and fleshy core with your thumbs.

4 Cut each quarter into even halves or into finer julienne slices if preferred.

Preparing an Artichoke

1 Cut off the tips of the artichoke's leaves with a kitchen knife. Use scissors to trim the lower leaves.

2 Make a shallow cut around the stem about 1in from the head. The idea is just to score the stem, not sever it.

3 Place the artichoke at the edge of the worktop and grip the stem firmly, steadying the head with your other hand. Twist and pull the stem down and away. The fibrous center of the stem should come away too.

4 Trim off the rest of the stem with a kitchen knife.

5 When cooked, gently separate the tops of the outer leaves and pull out the central bud of small leaves.

6 Use a teaspoon to scrape out the fibrous 'choke' from the heart.

Preparing Fennel

1 Remove discolored or leathery outer leaves. Split the head in half lengthwise.

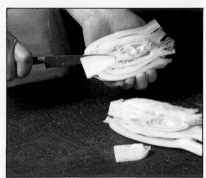

2 Remove inner thick core. It may be sliced thinly if liked, or discarded.

Chopping Parsley

1 Hold the tip of a large, heavy knife down with one hand and firmly move the handle up and down with the other, using a sharp cutting action.

2 Use the blade to scrape the parsley into a pile every now and then so that each chop cuts the maximum amount of parsley. Continue until the leaves are finely and evenly chopped.

Salads

Cabbage Salad
Serves 8

Ingredients

1¼lb. white cabbage, shredded	4tbsp. fresh coriander, coarsely chopped
1 small onion, diced	3tbsp. olive oil
2 green onions, chopped	½ cup lime juice
2 fresh green chili peppers, seeded and diced	1tbsp. Dijon mustard
½tsp. salt	1tbsp. honey

Combine all the ingredients in a large serving bowl and toss well. Chill for 20-30 minutes before serving.

Stir-Fried Cabbage Salad
Serves 4

Ingredients

1lb. green cabbage	salt to taste
1tsp. oil	1tbsp. coconut, grated or shredded dried
2 green chili peppers, chopped	1tbsp. coriander leaves, chopped
⅓tsp. mustard seeds	

Cut the cabbage very finely into long strips. Wash and dry them.

Heat the oil in a large saucepan over a medium high heat. Add the chili peppers and fry for 3-4 seconds, then add the mustard seeds and fry for a further 2-3 seconds.

Add the cabbage and salt and, stirring constantly, cook for 3-4 minutes.

Serve immediately, garnished with the coconut and coriander leaves.

Spicy Potato Salad
Serves 6

Ingredients

¾ cup yogurt	½tsp. ground cumin
1lb. boiled potatoes, diced into ¼-in. cubes	1 green chili pepper, chopped
1 small onion, finely chopped	1tbsp. chopped coriander leaves
½tsp. salt	
ground black pepper to taste	

Beat the yogurt in a bowl until smooth, then add the potatoes, onions, salt, pepper and cumin. Mix gently and chill.

Serve sprinkled with the chopped chili pepper and coriander leaves.

Indian Potato Salad
Serves 3-4

Ingredients

1tbsp. tamarind, pulp or dried	1-2 fresh green chili peppers, seeded and finely chopped
5tbsp. hot water	½tsp. salt
¾lb. potatoes, boiled and peeled	½tsp. chili powder
1 small onion, finely chopped	1tbsp. coriander leaves, chopped

Soak the tamarind in the hot water for 20 minutes. Squeeze out and reserve liquid.

Cut the potatoes into ¼in slices and cool thoroughly.

Gently mix in all the ingredients. Serve cold.

Potato Salad with Horseradish I
Serves 4

Ingredients

2lb. potatoes	a litle milk
Horseradish Mayonnaise	parsley

Peel the potatoes and boil in salted water, allow to cool, then cut into chunky slices.

Cover the potato slices with mayonnaise (you may need to thin it with milk), taking care not to break the potatoes.

Serve garnished with parsley.

Potato Salad with Horseradish II
Serves 4

Ingredients

1½lb. new potatoes	salt and freshly ground
⅔ cup sour cream	black pepper
3tbsp. finely grated	bunch green onions or
horseradish	chives
pinch paprika	handful parsley, chopped
½tsp. honey	

Wash the potatoes, but do not peel. Boil in salted water until tender.

Meanwhile, make the dressing Combine the cream with the horseradish, paprika and honey. Mix well and season with salt and pepper.

Trim the green onions and slit down the stalks so that they curl outwards. Chop the chives.

When the potatoes are done, slice them while still hot and mix into the dressing with parsley. Toss in the onions or chives.

Serve immediately, or chill the salad and serve cold.

Oriental Cucumber Salad
Serves 4-6

Ingredients

1 large cucumber	1tsp. chili powder
2tsp. salt	2tbsp. soy sauce
3 green onions, finely	sugar to taste
chopped	1tbsp. roasted sesame
1tsp. sesame oil	seeds, lightly crushed

Halve the cucumber, trim the ends, cut it into 2in lengths, then into stick-like pieces. Sprinkle with salt and after 30 minutes squeeze to drain off any excess liquid.

Fry the cucumber and two-thirds of the onion in hot sesame oil without browning. Add chili powder and cook for 1 minute. Stir in the soy sauce, sugar to taste and the sesame seeds.

Turn onto a serving dish and leave for 2-3 hours so that the flavors blend.

Serve sprinkled with the remaining green onions.

Cucumber and Mint Salad
Serves 4

Ingredients

one large cucumber	1 large clove garlic,
5g/1tsp. salt	crushed
1¼cups yogurt	dill or chopped mint
1tbsp. oil (optional)	pepper
1tsp. vinegar (optional)	

First prepare the cucumber: leave the peel on if preferred. Grate, dice finely or thinly slice it. Add the salt and leave for 15 minutes.

Rinse off the salt and drain the cucumber very well. Add the remaining ingredients, with pepper to taste, mix well and chill before serving.

The amount of herbs you add is purely a matter of individual taste and you may prefer your cucumber salad without oil and vinegar.

Variation To make Raita add ½tsp. ground cumin (preferably made from freshly roasted seeds), a pinch of cayenne and some pepper to the cucumber and yogurt.

Dry Tarator is a Bulgarian variation — drain the yogurt for 2 hours and add it to the finely chopped cucumber, with ½ cup chopped walnuts, 1tsp. oil, dill, and salt and pepper to taste.

Cucumber Salad
Serves 8

Ingredients

3 large cucumbers, peeled and thinly sliced
1¼ cups red wine vinegar
½tsp. celery salt
½ head lettuce, shredded

1tbsp. honey
good pinch black pepper
½tsp. fresh dill, chopped
4tbsp. olive oil
1tsp. Dijon mustard

Toss all the ingredients thoroughly in a large salad bowl. Chill for 2 hours before serving.

Hot and Spicy Cucumber Salad
Serves 3-4

Ingredients

2tbsp. unsalted peanuts
½ cucumber, peeled and cut into fine strips
2tbsp. grated or shredded coconut
2tbsp. lemon juice
½tsp. salt

1tbsp. butter
½tsp. cumin seeds
2 fresh green chili peppers, chopped
1tbsp. chopped coriander leaves

Dry roast the peanuts and grind them to a fine powder.

Gently squeeze the cucumber to get rid of excess water.

Put the cucumber, coconut, ground peanuts, lemon juice and salt in a bowl and mix gently.

In a small saucepan, heat the butter. Add the cumin seeds and let them sizzle for 3-4 seconds. Add the green chili peppers and fry for 5-6 seconds. Pour this over the cucumber mixture and mix well.

Serve immediately garnished with the coriander leaves.

Yogurt with Cucumbers
Serves 6

Ingredients

2⅔ cups yogurt
2 large cucumbers, peeled, thickly sliced and then quartered
2 large onions, finely chopped

1 cup walnuts, chopped
½tsp. salt
2.5g/½tsp. white pepper
2tbsp. chopped fresh mint

Combine all the ingredients in a large mixing bowl, and mix thoroughly, taking care not to bruise the cucumber slices.

Curried Coleslaw
Serves 4

This crisp salad is a refreshing change from the usual coleslaw.

Ingredients

½lb. white cabbage, trimmed, cored and shredded
2 medium carrots, peeled and grated
1 large green-skinned apple, cored and sliced
4 green onions, trimmed and sliced

⅔ cup Curry Mayonnaise
½ cup cashew nuts or dry-roasted peanuts
salt and freshly ground pepper
coriander leaves

Put the cabbage, carrots, apples and onions into a mixing bowl. Add the Mayonnaise and nuts and toss well. Taste for seasoning.

Spoon into a salad bowl and serve garnished with coriander leaves.

Hot and Spicy Cucumber Salad

Classic Coleslaw
Serves 6

Ingredients

1 small crisp head white cabbage	⅓ cup sultanas
½lb. carrots	1tbsp. sesame seeds
2tbsp. chopped chives	Mayonnaise

Shred the cabbage finely, discarding the stalk. Grate the carrots.

Toss all the ingredients together in sufficient mayonnaise to coat and mix well. Taste and adjust seasoning. Chill overnight in the refrigerator.

Mix well again before serving.

Tortellini Coleslaw
Serves 4-6

Ingredients

½lb. stuffed tortellini, cooked	1 carrot, scraped and grated
3tbsp. olive oil	2tbsp. raisins
1tbsp. white wine vinegar	2 green onions, washed and chopped
1tsp. French mustard	2 sticks celery, washed
salt and freshly ground pepper	⅔ cup Mayonnaise
½ whole cabbage (approx. 1lb.)	black olives

Put the cooked tortellini (after rinsing in cold water and draining) in a bowl.

Mix the dressing by putting the oil, vinegar, mustard and seasoning in a screw-top jar. Shake well and pour over the pasta.

Wash, drain and shred the cabbage. Mix in a separate bowl with the grated carrot and raisins.

After washing the celery, remove the strings with a sharp knife and then chop the celery into thin slices, add to the cabbage and season well. Mix in the mayonnaise.

On a serving dish arrange rows of coleslaw with alternating rows of tortellini. Garnish with the olives.

Classic Tomato Salad
Serves 4

Ingredients

6 tomatoes, thickly sliced
freshly ground black
  pepper
3tbsp. olive oil
freshly chopped herbs
6 peppercorns

Lay tomato slices on a large plate and dust them liberally with black pepper. Turn over and dust the other side.

Pour over the olive oil. Sprinkle with the herbs and decorate with the peppercorns.

Tomato Salad with Olives
Serves 6

Ingredients

4 large ripe tomatoes,
  thinly sliced
2 cucumbers, peeled and
  thinly sliced
1 cup black olives, pitted
2tbsp. finely chopped
  parsley
1tbsp. finely chopped mint
1/4 cup lemon juice
2tbsp. tarragon vinegar
1/4 cup olive oil
good pinch salt
1/2tsp. black pepper

Arrange the tomato and cucumber slices on a serving platter, with the olives around them.

To make the dressing, combine the parsley, mint, lemon juice, vinegar, oil, salt and pepper in a small bowl. Mix well with a fork or small whisk until well blended.

Pour the dressing over the salad. Chill for 30 minutes and serve cold.

Spinach and Chick Pea Salad
Serves 4

Ingredients

1 cup chick peas
1lb. spinach, washed
1tbsp. butter
6tbsp. olive oil
2tbsp. white wine vinegar
freshly ground white
  pepper
salt to taste
1 onion, cut into rings
1/2 cup yogurt
parsley, chopped

Soak the chick peas in water overnight and then cook them in unsalted water for an hour or until tender.

Cook the spinach in a saucepan with a small amount of butter, but no water. Drain and chop.

Add the chick peas to the cooled spinach. Mix in the olive oil, vinegar, pepper and salt, taking care not to crush the chick peas. Add the onion rings.

Serve the salad with the yogurt spooned on top, and sprinkled with parsley.

Green Bean Salad in Mustard Sauce
Serves 4

Ingredients

3tbsp. olive oil
1tsp. white wine vinegar
1tsp. turmeric powder
pinch chili powder
1tbsp. dry mustard powder
black pepper, freshly
  ground, to taste
1lb. green beans, cooked

Stir together olive oil, white wine vinegar and spices.

Toss in the cooked green beans and mix gently.

Chill slightly, but not too much — too long in the refrigerator will dull the flavor.

Spicy Bean Salad
Serves 6

Ingredients

5tbsp. olive oil
3tbsp. wine vinegar
1/2tsp. freshly ground
  coriander seeds
1/2tsp. freshly ground cumin
2 pinches chili powder
1 clove garlic, crushed
3/4 cup cooked red kidney
  beans
1/2 cucumber, peeled and
  cut into chunks

Blend the olive oil, vinegar and spices together, and pour the mixture over warm, freshly cooked kidney beans.

Add the cucumber and combine well. Let the vegetables marinate in the dressing.

Before serving, drain off any excess liquid.

Red Bean Salad
Serves 4-6

Ingredients

3/4 cup red kidney beans, soaked overnight
3tbsp. Vinaigrette
1 small onion, finely chopped
3 hard-cooked eggs, chopped
1 small head celery, chopped or 1 small cauliflower, chopped

3tbsp. brown or mustard pickle
5 anchovy fillets, chopped (optional)
2/3 cup sour cream or yogurt
salt and pepper

Bring the soaked beans to the boil in fresh water and boil rapidly for 10 minutes, then cook for 1 to 1½ hours, until they are tender but not soft.

Drain and pour over them the vinaigrette and onion while the beans are still warm.

When the beans are cold, add the remaining ingredients, mixing everything together well. Refrigerate and serve cold.

Salad of Fava Beans
Serves 4

A magnificent and very simple summer salad made with fresh young beans and peas.

Ingredients

3/4 lb. unshelled fava beans
3/4 lb. unshelled peas
4 small fresh Jerusalem artichokes
1-2tbsp. walnut oil or olive oil

1-2tbsp. lemon juice
fresh mint
salt and freshly ground black pepper

Shell the beans and pod the peas. If they are not quite tender enough to eat raw, put them in a pan of boiling salted water for a minute, then refresh in cold water.

Clean the artichokes, cut each into 6 and cook in boiling salted water for 5 minutes. Drain and refresh.

Make the dressing by blending the oil and lemon juice and adding chopped mint and seasoning to taste.

Toss the vegetables in the dressing and garnish with a few sprigs of mint. Serve with good crusty bread.

Variation Use drained, canned artichoke hearts instead of the Jerusualem artichokes. There is no need to cook them.

White Bean Salad
Serves 4

Ingredients

1/2 lb. dried white navy beans
3/4 cup Basic Garlic Dressing
2 cloves garlic, crushed

1 large red pepper, seeded and thinly sliced
2 small leeks, thinly sliced
1tbsp. finely chopped green onions (green part only)

Cover the beans with boiling water and leave to soak overnight.

Pour off the soaking water. Cover with fresh water and boil for 1½-2 hours, until tender. You may need to add more water from time to time to prevent them sticking.

Drain the beans and, while still hot, pour the Basic Garlic Dressing over them. Stir in the crushed garlic and cool until needed.

Before serving, stir in the pepper and leeks and sprinkle with the chopped green onions.

Variation Omit the green onions, and stir in 2tbsp. of coarsely chopped fresh mint just before serving.

Kidney Bean, Chick Pea and Corn Salad
Serves 4

Ingredients

½ cup kidney beans	2 large tomatoes
1 cup chick peas	1 cup corn kernels, cooked
6 green onions	Vinaigrette

Soak the kidney beans and the chick peas separately overnight, then simmer in water until cooked. Drain and cool.

Chop the green onions and slice the tomatoes.

Toss all the ingredients in sufficient vinaigrette to coat and serve at room temperature with hot pitta bread.

Lima Bean Salad
Serves 4-6

Ingredients

1 cup lima beans, soaked	salt and freshly ground pepper
4 green onions, washed and finely chopped	1 lettuce
1 clove garlic, crushed	12 stuffed olives
1 red or green pepper, seeded and finely diced	2tbsp. chopped parsley
1¼ cups Mayonnaise or Vinaigrette	

Cook the soaked butter beans for about 45 minutes or until tender but not mushy. Drain and allow to cool.

Mix all the ingredients in a bowl with mayonnaise or vinaigrette.

Arrange in a dish lined with lettuce. Garnish with olives and chopped parsley.

Navy Bean and Cottage Cheese
Serves 4-8

Ingredients

1 cup navy beans	1 red pepper, seeded and cut into thin strips
2 pinches bicarbonate of soda	½ shredded Iceberg lettuce
⅔ cup Vinaigrette	1 cup cottage cheese
4 green onions, washed and sliced	20 stuffed olives
1 green pepper, seeded and cut into thin strips	

Soak the navy beans in cold water for at least 8 hours. Drain and pour into a saucepan, cover with cold water, add the bicarbonate of soda and bring to a boil. Simmer for 30 minutes or until just cooked. Drain and allow to cool in a bowl.

Add the dressing to the cooked beans, then stir in the green onions and pepper.

Arrange the shredded lettuce on a round dish. Inside the lettuce ring, arrange a ring of cottage cheese.

Tip the dressed bean salad into the center of the cottage cheese ring. Garnish with whole stuffed olives and serve with sliced wholewheat bread.

Simple Kidney Bean Salad
Serves 4

Ingredients

¾ cup cooked kidney beans	⅔ cup Vinaigrette
2 green onions, washed and chopped	1tbsp. chopped parsley

Combine the beans, onions, vinaigrette and parsley. Chill for 30 minutes before serving.

Mixed Bean Salad
Serves 4

Ingredients

½ cup lima beans	8 slices salami, diced
⅓ cup kidney beans	⅔ cup Vinaigrette
3 green onions, washed and chopped	2tbsp. chopped parsley
	2 heads Belgian endive, sliced
3 small peppers, yellow, green and red, seeded and cut into thin strips	2 tomatoes, cut into wedges
	¼ cucumber, thinly sliced

Soak the lima and kidney beans in separate bowls overnight. Cook in separate saucepans just covered with water, bring to a boil and simmer for 30-40 minutes until the beans are just tender. Allow to cool.

Put the onions, peppers and salami in a bowl with the cold beans and vinaigrette and mix well. Add the chopped parsley and mix again.

Arrange the sliced endive around a shallow salad bowl and surround with tomato wedges and cucumber. Pile the bean salad in the centre.

Strawberry and Avocado Salad
Serves 4

Serve this as an accompaniment to white fish, meat or egg dishes, or as a first course.

Ingredients

2 avocados	2tbsp. oil
½lb. strawberries	1tsp. honey
2tbsp. vinegar, preferably strawberry	salt and freshly ground black pepper

Slice the avocados in half, remove the pits and scoop flesh out of shells in one piece if possible, using a palette knife. Slice.

Hull and slice the strawberries. Arrange the avocado halves and strawberries on 4 side plates.

Mix together the vinegar, oil and honey and season. Pour dressing over salad.

Vegetable Salad with Hot Peanut Sauce
Serves 4-6

Ingredients

¾ cup salted peanuts	**Salad**
1¼ cups coconut milk (see note)	2 medium potatoes, cooked and diced
1 clove garlic, crushed	2 cups bean sprouts, blanched, rinsed and drained
3 shallots or 1 small red onion, peeled	
2tbsp. oil	½ cup cabbage, shredded, blanched and rinsed
1tsp. chili powder	¼lb. each green beans and cauliflower flowerets, boiled until just tender and drained
4tbsp. lemon juice	
1tbsp. brown sugar	
1tsp. soy sauce	2-in. piece cucumber, sliced
salt to taste	1 small carrot, cut into matchsticks
	Chinese leaves, shredded
	watercress (optional)
	2 hard-boiled eggs

Grind the salted peanuts until gritty but not a paste; set aside. Prepare the coconut milk.

Pound the garlic with the shallots or onion and fry in the oil without browning. Stir in the chili powder and cook for 1 minute. Add the coconut milk and allow to come to the boil. Stir in the lemon juice, sugar, soy sauce, and the ground peanuts, which will thicken the sauce. Taste for seasoning. Allow to simmer until creamy in consistency. Set aside.

Arrange the vegetables in piles on a large platter with egg quarters. Serve the reheated sauce separately.

Note To make coconut milk, grate the flesh of 1 coconut and blend with 2 cups very hot water. Sieve, and squeeze the pulp to draw out the liquid. The milk can be thinned by adding more hot water before blending

A quick method of making coconut milk is to blend together ¼lb. creamed coconut (widely available in supermarkets) with 1⅔cup hot water.

Fennel Salad
Serves 6

A sharp, tangy salad, refreshing with cold meats, or rich mousses.

Ingredients

3 heads fennel, trimmed	good pinch mustard powder
2 medium zucchini	
2 cups beansprouts	salt and freshly ground black pepper
2 cups watercress	
grated rind of ½ lemon	1tbsp. snipped chives or parsley
3tbsp. lemon juice	
4tbsp. olive oil	

Slice the fennel and plunge into a bowl of icy water. Leave for 5 minutes, or until crisp, then drain thoroughly.

Meanwhile, slice the zucchini and pick over the beansprouts and watercress.

Mix the fennel with the zucchini, beansprouts and watercress.

For the dressing, combine the remaining ingredients until emulsified. Taste for seasoning, then pour over the salad and toss well.

Lentil and Feta Salad
Serves 6

This hearty salad is a meal in itself. Serve it with pitta bread.

Ingredients

2 cups brown lentils	½ cup chopped fresh chives
3 cups cold water	6tbsp. olive oil
bay leaf	3tbsp. wine vinegar
½tsp. dried basil	pinch dried oregano
2 cloves garlic	½tsp. salt
5tbsp. diced celery	½tsp. freshly ground black
1 small onion, chopped	pepper
½ cup crumbled Feta cheese	

Soak the lentils in water for 2 hours. Drain. Put the lentils into a saucepan and add enough cold water to cover them completely. Add the bay leaf, basil and one of the garlic cloves. Bring to a boil and then reduce the heat. Simmer, covered, for 20 minutes.

Add the celery and onion. Add enough extra water to cover the lentils. Cover the saucepan and simmer for 10 minutes.

Drain the lentils, discarding the bay leaf and garlic clove and put them into a serving bowl. Add the feta cheese and chives. Toss.

Put the olive oil, vinegar, oregano, remaining garlic clove, crushed, salt and pepper into a jar with a tightly fitting lid. Cover tightly and shake until well blended.

Pour the dressing over the lentil salad and toss. Let the salad stand at room temperature for 2 hours, tossing occasionally, before serving.

Salad of Beansprouts and Bean Curd

Belgian Endive and Walnut Salad
Serves 4

Ingredients

3 heads Belgian endive	1 box mustard/cress
1 head celery	seedlings
3 onions, finely chopped	½ cup chopped walnuts
2tbsp. sprouted fenugreek seeds	1¼ cups Vinaigrette

Wash and slice the Belgian endive and the celery. Mix them with the onions and the other ingredients.

Pour on the vinaigrette at the last moment, toss and serve.

Beansprout and Bean Curd Salad
Serves 4

Ingredients

8oz. can beansprouts	½tsp. chili powder
1 square bean curd, cut into small dice	2tbsp. oil
	juice 1 lemon
fat for frying	onion, crisply fried

Soak the beansprouts in cold water. Toss into boiling water for 1 minute, then drain and rinse with cold water. Fry the bean curd in fat until it is crisp; drain.

Put the beansprouts, chili powder and oil in a bowl and toss together. Squeeze over the lemon juice. Taste for seasoning.

Just before serving, add the crisp bean curds and top with fried onion.

Russian Salad
Serves 6

Ingredients

1 large potato, peeled
1 small cauliflower
1 piece broccoli
2 medium carrots, diced
1 eggplant, diced
½ cup green beans, diced
2tbsp. green peas

4 stalks celery, diced
6 green onions, finely
  chopped
1tbsp. chives, chopped
⅔ cup Mustard
  Mayonnaise

Bring the potato to the boil and simmer until just cooked. Drain and dice when cool.

Break the flowerets off the cauliflower and the broccoli. Cook separately in salted water until crisp-tender.

Cook the carrots, eggplant and beans separately in salted boiling water until crisp-tender. Cook the peas until just tender.

Drain all vegetables immediately and cool under cold running water, then drain again. It is important to cook each batch separately.

Combine the vegetables. Add the celery, green onions, chives and mayonnaise and gently toss.

Spinach and Orange Salad
Serves 2-4

Ingredients

1lb. young spinach leaves
1 bunch watercress
1 large juicy orange
crispy bacon pieces
  (optional)

1-2tbsp. olive oil
salt and freshly ground
  black pepper

Use only young tender spinach for this salad. Outside leaves are too bitter and tough to be enjoyed raw. Wash the spinach thoroughly, discarding any discolored leaves and tough stalks. Tear into manageable pieces.

Wash the watercress, discarding tough stalks and yellow leaves. Shake water off the spinach and watercress in a lettuce basket.

Peel the orange. Remove the pith and pips and slice as finely as possible. Cut the slices into quarters.

Toss the ingredients together in a large bowl with the oil and season well.

Onion Salad
Serves 4

Just what you need to brighten your cold cuts.

Ingredients

4 large onions, finely
  chopped
1 small hot green chili
  pepper, finely chopped
1 slice fresh ginger, finely
  chopped

1tbsp. grated coconut
juice of ½ lemon
salt to taste

Mix the onion and chili pepper together. Add the ginger, coconut, lemon juice and mix well.

Rainbow Salad
Serves 6-8

A colorful salad to cheer up a winter's day.

Ingredients

½lb. red cabbage, trimmed, cored and shredded
½lb. white cabbage, trimmed, cored and shredded
2 medium zucchini, trimmed and chopped
2 large carrots, peeled and grated
1 medium onion, peeled and finely chopped
2 green-skinned apples, quartered, cored and sliced
1¼ cup Yogurt Mayonnaise
salt and freshly ground pepper
1tbsp. pomegranate seeds (optional)

Put the cabbage, zucchini, carrots, onions and apples into a large bowl and toss well with the mayonnaise. Taste, and add salt and pepper if necessary.

Spoon into a salad bowl and serve sprinkled, if you like, with pomegranate seeds.

Egg and Pasta Salad
Serves 4

Ingredients

1⅔ cups green or wholewheat pasta shapes
2tsp. oil
4 eggs
¼lb. green beans
2 sticks celery
1 dessert apple
½ cup walnuts
Mayonnaise
salt and freshly ground black pepper
1-2tbsp. fresh dill

Cook the pasta in plenty of boiling salted water, to which you have added 2tsp. oil, until *al dente*. Drain and allow to cool

Hard-boil the eggs, peel under cold running water and allow to cool. Cut into quarters.

Top and tail the beans and cut into manageable lengths. Simmer in salted water until cooked but not soft. Drain and allow to cool.

Chop the celery. Peel, core and dice the apple.

Toss all the ingredients except the eggs together in sufficient mayonnaise to coat. Season and garnish with eggs and dill.

Endive and Orange Walnut Salad
Serves 4-6

Ingredients

4 plump heads Belgian endive
2 large sweet oranges
¾ cup walnut halves
3tbsp. olive or walnut oil
1tbsp. lemon juice
1 clove garlic, finely crushed
½tsp. sugar

Cut the endive into ½-in slices.

Peel and slice the oranges — or divide them into segments — removing the skin and pith from each.

Coarsely chop the walnuts, reserving a few for decoration.

Mix the olive or walnut oil, lemon juice, garlic and sugar, and pour this dressing over the combined endive, orange and walnuts.

Decorate with the reserved walnuts and serve chilled.

Green Salad with Coconut Dressing
Serves 4

Ingredients

1lb. (prepared weight) mixed green vegetables such as: beans, Chinese cabbage, beansprouts and cucumber
1½ cups shredded dried coconut
⅔ cup water
1 clove garlic, crushed
1 green chili pepper
salt
juice ½ lemon
sugar to taste
mint sprigs

Trim ends from the beans and blanch in boiling water for 2-3 minutes until just cooked. Rinse in cold water to retain the color. Wash the cabbage and shred, not too finely. Plunge the beansprouts into cold water for a few minutes and drain. Cut the cucumber in 1in. lengths and each chunk into 10 pieces.

Cook the coconut and water together for 5 minutes. Cool. Pound the garlic and chili pepper to a paste. Add to the coconut, with salt, lemon juice and sugar to taste. Transfer to a large bowl then add the prepared vegetables.

Toss well and serve garnished with mint leaves. Do not keep overnight.

Snow Pea and Carrot Salad
Serves 4

Ingredients

3 carrots, scraped and
   sliced
good pinch salt
1lb. snow peas
1 large leek, washed

2tbsp. vegetable oil
salt and freshly ground
   pepper
2tbsp. chopped parsley
²/₃ cup Vinaigrette

Cook the carrots in a small amount of cold water with
the salt. Bring to a boil, simmer for 10 minutes and
drain. Prepare the snow peas by removing the small
stalks at the end. Cook in a small amount of boiling
salted water for 4 minutes, test for tenderness. (The
peas should still be slightly crunchy.) Drain.

Wash the leek thoroughly and cut a cross through
the center, wash again to make sure all the mud is
removed from the inside. Slice thinly.

Heat the oil in a skillet and cook the leek over a low
heat for 4 minutes. At this stage if you want to serve a
hot vegetable salad, add the carrots and snow peas,
season well and stir over a low heat. Serve in a heated
vegetable dish, sprinkled with chopped parsley.

To serve cold, allow all the vegetables to cool, mix
together, season well and toss in the vinaigrette.
Sprinkle with chopped parsley.

Tabouleh
Serves 6

Ingredients

1 cup bulgur wheat
2 cups boiling water
4 green onions, chopped
5tbsp. chopped fresh mint
2 medium tomatoes,
   seeded and chopped
¹/₂ cup chopped fresh
   parsley

5tbsp. olive oil
6tbsp. fresh lemon juice
¹/₂tsp. salt
2.5g/¹/₂tsp. freshly ground
   black pepper
10 large lettuce leaves

Put the bulgur into a bowl and add the boiling water.
Stir, cover the bowl, and leave to stand for 35 minutes.

Drain the bulgur, squeezing out any remaining
water between the palms of your hands. Put the bulgur
into a serving bowl. Add the onions, mint, tomatoes
and parsley. Toss gently. Add the olive oil. Stir until well
mixed. Add the lemon juice, salt and pepper. Stir until
well mixed.

Serve the tabouleh in its bowl or on individual
plates. Use the lettuce leaves as scoops to eat the
tabouleh.

Green Bean Salad
Serves 6

Ingredients

1¹/₂lb. fresh green beans,
   trimmed and halved
4tbsp. olive oil
2tbsp. white wine vinegar
¹/₄ cup vegetable stock or
   water

¹/₂tsp. salt
1tsp. cayenne pepper
1tbsp. finely chopped fresh
   dill or 1tsp. dried dill
2tsp. chopped fresh parsley
1tbsp. Dijon mustard

Cook the green beans in a large pot of boiling water
until they are tender but still crisp. Drain well. Put the
green beans into a large serving bowl.

In a mixing bowl combine the olive oil, vinegar,
stock or water, salt, cayenne pepper, dill, parsley and
mustard. Mix well.

Pour the dressing over the green beans and toss
well. Chill for 1 hour before serving.

Wholefood Pasta Salad
Serves 4

Ingredients

1²/₃ cups wholewheat pasta
   spirals
²/₃ cup yogurt
¹/₂tsp. cumin
¹/₂ clove garlic, crushed
salt and freshly ground
   pepper

juice of 1 lemon
1 small lettuce, washed
1 bunch watercress,
   washed
1tbsp. bran (optional)

Cook the pasta spirals for 10-12 minutes, drain, then
rinse in cold water. Allow to drain well in a colander.

Put the yogurt into a bowl and mix in the cumin,
crushed garlic and seasoning. Add a few drops of
lemon juice.

Toss the pasta in the yogurt dressing.

Arrange the drained lettuce and watercress in a salad
bowl, sprinkle with lemon juice. Arrange the pasta in
the center of the bowl and sprinkle with the bran, if
liked.

Variation Cucumber and tomatoes can be added.

SALADS

Beet, Apple, Blue Cheese and Walnut Salad
Serves 4

A very attractive salad to serve with cold meats and baked jacket potatoes on a chilly day.

Ingredients

1lb. beets boiled, peeled and shredded
5tbsp. Vinaigrette
2 crisp green apples, quartered, cored and thinly sliced

½ crisp lettuce, rinsed
¾ cup crumbled blue cheese
½ cup walnut halves

Put the beets into a bowl and mix with half the vinaigrette.

Toss the apples with the remaining dressing in another bowl.

Tear the lettuce and arrange in a salad bowl, and top with the beets, then the apple slices. Sprinkle the cheese over the whole salad and decorate with walnut halves.

Waldorf Salad
Serves 2-4

Ingredients

8 stalks crisp celery
2 rosy-skinned dessert apples
lemon juice

½ cup walnuts
6tbsp. Mayonnaise
salt and freshly ground black pepper

If the celery is not crisp, immerse it in ice-cold water. It will soon freshen up. Pat dry and slice.

Core the apples but do not peel — the pink skin will give color contrast to the salad. Slice and sprinkle with lemon juice to prevent discoloring.

Toss all the ingredients in the mayonnaise and season well.

Variation This salad also tastes good with blue cheese dressing. Blend the mayonnaise with 1tbsp. blue cheese before adding the salt.

Tsatziki
Serves 4

Ingredients

1 large cucumber, unpeeled
½tsp. salt
2 cloves garlic, finely chopped

⅔ cup thick Greek yogurt
pepper
a little lemon juice

Coarsely grate the cucumber into a colander. Sprinkle with the salt and leave to drain for about 1 hour.

Stir the drained cucumber and garlic into the yogurt and add pepper and lemon juice to taste.

Serve chilled.

La Lechuga
Serves 4

Ingredients

1 light head crisp lettuce, preferably Iceberg
4tbsp. olive oil

4 cloves garlic, finely chopped

Discard looser outer leaves of the lettuce. With a very sharp knife, cut lettuce in half from stalk to tip. Cut each half into 3. Keep cold.

Heat the oil in skillet and when hot, add garlic. Fry, stirring, until brown. Pour over the lettuce and serve immediately.

This is best eaten with the fingers if you don't mind the mess. Offer plenty of paper napkins.

227

Greek Salad

Ingredients

1 head crunchy lettuce,
  shredded
2 large beef tomatoes,
  sliced
½ cucumber, thinly sliced
1 onion, coarsely chopped

handful black olives
1½ cups cubed feta cheese
olive oil
salt and plenty of freshly
  ground black pepper

Combine the vegetables and cheese in a large bowl.
Pour over enough olive oil to just coat the salad.
Season well and toss.

Chill for an hour. Toss again, check seasoning and
serve.

Cauliflower, Blue Cheese and Yogurt Salad
Serves 4

Ingredients

1 head cauliflower
4tbsp. yogurt
2tbsp blue cheese, softened

4tbsp. parsley, chopped
salt and freshly ground
  black pepper

Cut the cauliflower into tiny flowerets — reserve the
stalks for use in a soup.

Cream the yogurt and blue cheese together. Toss
cauliflower and parsley in the dressing and season
well.

Caesar Salad
Serves 4

Ingredients

2tbsp. olive oil
2tbsp. white wine vinegar
1 clove garlic, crushed
salt and freshly ground
  black pepper
½ crisp Iceberg lettuce
4 eggs
4 anchovy fillets

1 cup crumbled Roquefort
  cheese
Croûtons
2 slices brown bread, crusts
  removed
2tbsp. olive oil
1 clove garlic, crushed

Make the dressing by combining the olive oil, vinegar,
garlic and seasoning.

Break up the lettuce and divide between four salad
plates. Soft boil the eggs and shell them under cold
running water. Roll up the anchovy fillets. Put an egg
and an anchovy fillet on each plate. Sprinkle the
cheese over the top and pour the dressing over all.

To make the croûtons, cut the bread into small
squares. Heat the oil in a pan, add the garlic and, when
cooked, add the bread squares. Fry till golden. Divide
between the plates.

Cut into each egg so that the yolk can run out and
serve straight away.

Feta Garlic Salad
Serves 4

With fresh crusty bread, this aromatic and refreshing
salad is virtually a meal in itself.

Ingredients

1lb. ripe tomatoes, skinned
  and cut into 1-in.
  chunks
½lb. feta cheese, cut into 1-
  in. chunks
½ cup black olives, stoned
3tbsp. good olive oil

1-2 cloves of garlic, finely
  chopped
2tbsp. fresh basil leaves,
  coarsely chopped
½tsp. sugar
freshly ground black
  pepper

First make the dressing. Chop the garlic and put it in a mortar. Pour in a little of the olive oil and pound it to a pulp. Gradually add the basil and cheese with the rest of the oil, pounding all the time. You should have a thick paste.

Peel the tomatoes by immersing them in boiling water until their skins burst. Chop them roughly. Mix the diced Mozzarella cheese, tomatoes and olives together and season.

Cook the pasta in boiling salted water, to which you have added a little olive oil, until *al dente*. Drain. Toss the pasta in the dressing. Pile it into four warmed serving bowls and top with the tomato mixture.

Combine the tomatoes, feta and olives in a glass serving bowl, and add the oil, garlic, basil and sugar.

Sprinkle with plenty of freshly ground black pepper and stir gently.

Leave in a cool place for at least an hour for the flavors to combine before serving.

Variation For Mozzarella Garlic Salad, slice the tomatoes and arrange alternately with ½lb. of sliced Mozzarella cheese in overlapping concentric circles. Pour over the oil and sprinkle on the garlic, basil, sugar and pepper. Decorate with the olives.

Hot Pasta Salad
Serves 6

Ingredients

2 cloves garlic	1lb. beef tomatoes
3tbsp. olive oil	¾ cup black olives
handful fresh basil	salt and freshly ground
1tbsp. grated Parmesan	black pepper
cheese	¾lb. spinach leaves
½ cup diced Mozzarella	a little extra olive oil
cheese	

Cheddar Cheese Salad
Serves 2

Ingredients

2 handfuls young spinach	1tbsp. wine vinegar
leaves	1-2tsp. mustard powder
1 bunch watercress	salt and freshly ground
2 large beef tomatoes	black pepper
½ cup button mushrooms	¼lb. Longhorn Cheddar
6-8 green onions	cheese, cubed
2tbsp. olive oil	

Wash the spinach and watercress, discarding stalks and any tough or yellow leaves. Immerse the tomatoes in boiling water until their skins split, then refresh with cold water, peel and roughly chop. Slice the mushrooms. Trim the green onions; make several lengthwise cuts into each onion and splay out the layers in a decorative fashion.

Make the dressing by combining the oil, vinegar, mustard and seasoning.

Combine the watercress, spinach, tomatoes and mushrooms in a salad bowl, add the dressing and toss. Top with the cheese and onions.

Provençal Rice Salad
Serves 4

A meal in itself, serve this with red wine and crusty French bread for a taste of the Mediterranean.

Ingredients

1 cup long grain rice, cooked	**Dressing**
8 green onions, trimmed and sliced	2-3 cloves garlic, peeled and crushed
½lb. green beans, cooked and coarsely chopped	4 anchovy fillets, mashed
3 hard-boiled eggs, shelled and quartered	1 egg yolk
	¾ cup Vinaigrette
6½oz. can tuna, drained and flaked	salt and freshly ground pepper
½ cup black olives, pitted	fresh coriander leaves

Put the rice in a large bowl and toss with a fork to separate the grains. Add the green onions, green beans, hard-boiled eggs, tuna and olives.

For the dressing, blend or process the garlic, anchovies and egg yolk. With the machine running, pour in the vinaigrette through the feed tube. Process until smooth and emulsified.

Pour the dressing over the rice mixture and toss well. Taste for seasoning, adding more salt and pepper if necessary.

Leave to stand for 20-30 minutes, then spoon into a salad bowl and garnish with the coriander leaves.

Seafood Salad
Serves 4-6

Serve as a first course or with thinly sliced brown bread for a light lunch.

Ingredients

¼lb. smoked salmon, coarsely chopped	lemon juice
¼lb. frozen shrimp, thawed	1 hard green apple, quartered, cored and coarsely chopped
½lb. cold, cooked monkfish, white fish or salmon, flaked	3 sticks celery, quartered and sliced
1¼ cups Avocado Mayonnaise	1 small green pepper, cored, seeded and sliced
Tabasco	

Combine the smoked salmon, shrimp, flaked fish and mayonnaise. Season to taste with Tabasco and lemon juice.

Stir in the apple, celery and pepper. Serve immediately.

Shrimp and Pasta Salad
Serves 4

Ingredients

1¼ cups Mayonnaise	1 bunch watercress, washed
2tsp. tomato paste	
2-3 drops Tabasco sauce	1⅔ cups cooked pasta shells
juice of ½ lemon	
¾ cup cooked peeled shrimps	large shrimps in shells (optional)
½ lettuce, washed	

Mix the tomato paste and Tabasco into the Mayonnaise. Sprinkle the lemon juice over the shelled shrimps.

Line a salad bowl with the lettuce and watercress sprigs.

Add the mayonnaise to the pasta shells and shrimp and mix well.

Pile the shrimp and pasta in the centre of the lined salad bowl. Garnish, if you like, with large shrimp.

Smoked Fish Salad
Serves 4

Ingredients

¾lb. smoked mackerel fillets, skinned	½ cup sliced firm white button mushrooms
1¾ cups pasta bows	1 medium zucchini, sliced
1tsp. curry paste	2 sticks celery, sliced
1tsp. tomato paste	½ crisp lettuce
1¼ cups Yogurt Mayonnaise	cherry tomatoes
salt and freshly ground pepper	

Flake the fish into a mixing bowl. Cook the pasta in boiling salted water until just tender. Drain and refresh in cold water. Dry thoroughly, then add the fish.

Mix the curry paste and the tomato paste into the dressing. Season to taste. Add to the fish and pasta, with the mushrooms, zucchini and celery and adjust the seasoning.

Arrange the salad on a bed of lettuce leaves, garnish with cherry tomatoes and serve with garlic bread.

Salad Niçoise
Serves 4

This makes a delicious lunch, dinner party appetizer or buffet salad, with crispy French bread.

Ingredients

1lb. potatoes, boiled	¼ cucumber
½lb. green beans, fresh or frozen	2 hard-boiled eggs
7-oz. can tuna fish, drained	12 black or green olives, stones removed
⅔ cup Vinaigrette	6 anchovy fillets, cut into thin slices
4 tomatoes, skinned and sliced	small cherry tomatoes to garnish

Cook the potatoes in their skins until tender. Remove the skins and dice finely. Cook the beans in a small amount of boiling water for about 6 minutes. Frozen beans can be used; cook as directed on the packet.

Mix the potatoes, beans and half the tuna fish with three-quarters of the Vinaigrette.

Arrange the sliced tomatoes on the bottom and around the bowl, arrange thinly sliced cucumber on top, and sprinkle with a little Vinaigrette. Place a few chunks of tuna fish on the tomato and cucumber.

The eggs may be cut into slices or wedges and can be used on top as a garnish or arranged to make a bed for the beans, potatoes and tuna fish mixture.

Arrange the fish mixture in the middle and arrange the anchovies in a diamond-shaped pattern on the beans, decorating each space with an olive. Pour over any remaining dressing.

Savory Fruit Salad
Serves 4-6

Ingredients

2 green apples	½ cup cooked shrimp
2 green mangoes	2-3tbsp. lemon juice
½ small pineapple	2tsp. sugar
¼lb. cooked pork, cut into strips	mint or coriander

Peel and cut the apples and mangoes into even-sized pieces. Peel and quarter the pineapple, remove the core and cut the flesh into bite-sized pieces. Arrange these attractively with the pork and shrimp on a serving dish.

Blend the dressing ingredients together and pour over the salad.

Serve garnished with mint or coriander leaves.

Warm Potato and Bacon Salad
Serves 4

This is good with cold poultry or quiches, or on its own as a first course.

Ingredients

1lb. small new potatoes, scrubbed	5tbsp. chicken or beef stock
3tbsp. olive oil	salt and freshly ground pepper
½lb. fatty bacon, chopped	sugar to taste
1 medium onion, peeled and chopped	2 egg yolks, beaten
4tbsp. wine vinegar	1tbsp. snipped fresh dill

Cook the potatoes in boiling salted water for about 20 minutes or until tender. Drain and turn into an ovenproof serving dish.

Heat the oil in a deep skillet. Add the bacon and onion and fry gently for 5 minutes to soften the onion. Turn up the heat and fry until the bacon becomes crispy.

Remove from the heat, and add the vinegar and stock. Bring to the boil then taste and season. Remove from the heat and stir in the egg yolks and dill. Pour over the potatoes and toss well. Serve immediately.

Avocado, Grapefruit and Shrimp Salad
Serves 4

Ingredients

2 grapefruit	1½ cups shelled shrimp
2 avocados	⅔ cup Vinaigrette

To make the grapefruit sections, place the fruit in a bowl and pour boiling water on top to cover. Leave for 2 minutes, then remove and allow to cool. Cut a slice from the top of the fruit, then cut the peel and pith off in strips to reveal the flesh. It is essential to use a small sharp knife.

When all the pith has been cut away, remove each section by cutting between the membranes of each segment. At the end only the tough outer skin should be left and each section of fruit is separate without skin.

Peel the avocados, cut in half lengthways and remove the stones. Cut the flesh into slices.

Arrange the avocado slices, grapefruit segments and shrimps in the dishes and serve with Vinaigrette or Mayonnaise as preferred. The dressing may be poured over the salad or served separately.

Warm Chicken Liver Salad with Garlic Croûtons
Serves 4-6

Ingredients

3tbsp. olive oil
2 cloves garlic, crushed
1 Cos or Iceberg lettuce, torn into bite-size pieces
½lb. fresh young spinach leaves, torn into bite-sized pieces
6 slices fatty bacon, cut into ½-in. pieces

¾lb. chicken livers
3 slices white bread cut into ½in. cubes
2tsp. sugar
1tbsp. Garlic Vinegar or wine vinegar
1tbsp. chives, finely chopped

Put the oil and garlic into a skillet and leave to infuse.

Combine the lettuce and spinach in a salad bowl or individual serving bowls and leave to one side.

In another pan, fry the bacon until crisp, drain on a paper towel and keep warm.

Fry the chicken livers in the bacon fat for about 5 minutes or until firm and well browned on the outside, but still slightly pink in the middle. Drain and keep warm.

Fry the bread cubes in the garlicky oil until golden and crisp. Drain and keep warm.

Heat the bacon fat and add the sugar and vinegar. Cook gently until the sugar dissolves.

Arrange the chicken livers and bacon on top of the lettuce and spinach. Pour over the warm dressing, and serve immediately, topped with the garlic croûtons and chives.

Vietnamese Salad
Serves 4

Ingredients

½lb. Chinese leaves
2 carrots
½ cucumber
salt
2 red chili peppers, seeded and finely sliced
1 small onion, sliced into fine rings
4 pickled gherkins, sliced, plus 3tbsp. of the liquid

1 clove garlic, crushed
1tsp. sugar
2tbsp. cider or white vinegar
½ cup peanuts, lightly pounded
1⅓ cups shredded cooked chicken
fresh coriander

Wash and shred the Chinese leaves finely. Peel and cut the carrots into matchstick-like strips.

Trim the ends from the cucumber, cut in half lengthwise and scoop out the seeds. Cut in pieces the same size as the carrot, sprinkle with salt and leave for 15 minutes.

Put the chili peppers, onion and gherkin slices in a bowl. Blend the gherkin liquid with the garlic, sugar and vinegar.

Rinse and dry the cabbage, carrot and cucumber, then add these to the liquid ingredients with the nuts and chicken, toss altogether to taste. Add more vinegar, if you wish, for a sharper taste.

Serve garnished with coriander leaves.

Pasta Salad
Serves 4

Ingredients

1⅔ cups dry pasta: bows, shells or spirals
½tbsp. oil
1tbsp. Garlic Purée or 2 cloves of garlic, crushed
2 scant cups Mayonnaise
1tbsp. light cream
2 cups button mushrooms, quartered

1 cup thinly sliced French garlic sausage, cut into strips and fried till crisp
1½tbsp. green onions, finely chopped
salt and pepper to taste

Cook the pasta with the oil in lots of salted boiling water for 15-20 minutes, until just tender. Drain well and, while still warm, stir in the remaining ingredients.

Serve warm or chilled.

Variation Vary the dressing by using half mayonnaise and half Pesto.

Use Aïoli instead of the mayonnaise. You will probably not need the extra garlic.

Lots of other vegetables and nuts can be added, singly or in combination: chopped or sliced sweet pepper, thinly sliced or grated baby zucchini, cubed avocado pear, toasted peanuts, blanched almonds, walnuts or pine nuts.

Pasta salad is also very good with ½ cup of Basic Garlic Dressing instead of the mayonnaise and cream. This dressing goes particularly well with quartered artichoke hearts and browned cashew nuts.

Olive oil is not the only oil used in salad dressings, but it is the most common. The price of olive oil has much to do with which pressing you purchase. Extra virgin olive oil is about twice as costly as pure olive oil. French oils, light and golden, are considered by many to be the best in the world. Greek and Italian oils are less expensive, more robust and aromatic.

1 Pure olive oil: an inexpensive grade oil. Produced from the treated olive mash left over from the first two pressings of the olives.

2 Fine olive oil: not to be used for salads. Good for frying, however.

3 Extra virgin olive oil: rare, expensive and heavy. Product of the first cold pressing.

4 Peanut oil: used in South-East Asian cooking. The peanut taste is not very pronounced.

5 Grape seed oil: full-bodied. Usually found in combination with pepper or herbs.

7 Walnut oil: aromatic, expensive. Refrigerate to maintain freshness.

8 Hazelnut oil: delicate, for delicate salad greens.

9 Sesame oil: pungent, exotic.

Cold Desserts and Sweets

Easy Ice Cream
Serves 8

Ingredients
4 eggs, separated
½ tsp. vanilla extract
¾ cup confectioner's sugar
1¼ cups heavy cream

Beat the egg yolks with the vanilla and sifted sugar until the mixture is very thick and almost white. Lightly whip the cream until it is just beginning to thicken. Gently fold into the yolks.

Beat the egg whites until they are stiff but not dry. Gently fold one spoonful into the ice cream mixture. Gradually add the remaining egg whites.

If you are adding flavoring, blend in carefully at this stage.

Turn the cream into a large freezer tray or plastic box and cover. Stir occasionally during freezing.

Bombe
Serves 8

Ingredients
3 cups ice cream
1¼ cups sorbet
½ cup heavy cream
pieces of crystalized fruit

Remove half of the ice cream from the freezer and leave until slightly softened. Press over the base and up the sides of a medium-sized mold or pudding bowl. Cover and return to the freezer until firm.

Remove the sorbet from the freezer and leave until slightly softened. Press into the middle of the mold, cover and return to the freezer.

Remove the remaining ice cream, which should be a different flavor, and leave to soften. Spread over the surface of the sorbet, cover and refreeze.

To serve, run a warm cloth over the surface of the mold, invert and turn out onto an attractive dish. Smooth with a knife. Decorate with piped, whipped cream and pieces of crystalized fruit.

Variations Beat into slightly softened vanilla ice cream an assortment of dried fruit which has been soaked in rum or sherry and some chopped crystalized fruit. Fill the mold and freeze until firm.

Soak fresh or dried fruit in liqueur and pour into the bombe before adding the sorbet. Alternatively, replace the sorbet with a Chocolate or Chestnut Mousse.

Luxury Mocha Ice Cream

Ingredients

5oz. plain chocolate *1tbsp. coffee liqueur*
4 eggs, separated *½ cup sugar*
4tbsp. strong coffee *chocolate curls*
1½ cups heavy cream

Place the chocolate in a bowl over a pan of hot water. When melted, remove from the heat and beat in the egg yolks and coffee.

In a large bowl, whip the cream until stiff and fold in the coffee liqueur.

In another bowl beat the egg whites until they form stiff peaks, gradually adding the sugar.

Beat the mocha mixture into the cream and then fold it gently into the egg whites.

Spoon into a 3¾pt. freeze-proof container. Freeze for at least 5 hours. It is not necessary to stir the ice cream during the freezing time. This ice cream is quite soft so you can serve straight from the freezer.

To serve, scoop into sundae glasses and decorate with chocolate curls.

An alternative serving suggestion is to scoop the ice cream into individual biscuit base tartlets.

Elderflower Water Ice
Serves 6

A water ice like this refreshes the palate between courses. It can also be served as a very light dessert.

Ingredients

2½ cups water *juice of 1 lemon*
1 cup fruit sugar *2 egg whites*
6 heads elderflowers

Heat the water and add the sugar, stirring until dissolved. Add the elderflowers and lemon juice and bring to the boil.

Strain the syrup through a jelly bag. Allow it to cool, then freeze.

When the syrup is half frozen, beat the egg whites until stiff and fold into the syrup. Freeze in individual dishes.

Mocha Bombe
Serves 6-8

Ingredients

Cream Layer
2 cups heavy cream
2tbsp. Vanilla Sugar (see note to recipe for Le Succès)
2tbsp. vanilla extract

Mocha filling
1 full quantity Luxury Mocha Ice Cream

Coffee Cream
2 cups heavy cream
1½tsp. instant powdered coffee dissolved in 1tbsp. hot water
1tbsp. Vanilla Sugar
½ cup toasted almonds

Chill a 3½pt. pudding bowl or bombe mold. Beat the cream, sugar and extract together until stiff, then spread in the pudding basin to line it evenly. Freeze until firm.

Pour the luxury mocha ice cream into the cream lined basin, cover and freezer for 24 hours.

To serve place the bowl briefly into a larger bowl of hot water then turn out onto a large serving plate.

Beat the cream, instant coffee and sugar until firm. Pile a decoration over the bombe and decorate with the toasted almonds.

Return to the freezer until hard, and serve.

Mississippi Mud Pie
Serves 8

Ingredients

6oz. graham crackers
large knob butter, melted
4oz. plain chocolate, melted
2½pts. coffee ice cream

2½pts. chocolate ice cream
2tbsp. Tia Maria
2tbsp. brandy
whipped cream
grated chocolate

Crush the graham crackers in a food processor or in a plastic bag with a rolling pin. Stir in the butter and chocolate and mix well together.

Press the crumbs firmly and evenly over the bottom and sides of a greased 9in. flan dish. Chill.

Allow the ice creams to soften slightly. Put in a bowl and add the liqueur and brandy. Blend well together.

Spoon the ice cream into the chocolate case and put in the freezer until solid.

To serve remove pie from freezer about 15 minutes before serving. Decorate with whipped cream and grated chocolate.

Raspberry Ice Cream
Serves 4-6

Ingredients

¾lb. raspberries
1tbsp. dried milk powder
2tbsp. yogurt

2tbsp. honey
good cup heavy cream

Purée the raspberries with the milk powder, yogurt and honey in a blender. Freeze.

When the raspberries have frozen into a mush, whip the cream and mix in well. Return to the freezer.

Snowball Pie
Serves 6

Ingredients

8oz. plain chocolate
4tbsp. butter
5tbsp. crisp rice cereal
  (Rice Krispies)
2 cups vanilla ice cream

2 cups chocolate ice cream
2 cups strawberry ice
  cream
Chocolate or Fudge Sauce
long shredded coconut,
  toasted

Melt the chocolate and butter together. Stir in the crisp rice cereal and mix well together.

Press the mixture over the base and up the sides of an 8in. flan dish. Place in the freezer until firm.

Arrange alternate scoops of the ice cream. Pour over the sauce and sprinkle with the coconut. Serve immediately.

Chocolate Ice Cream
Serves 4-6

Ingredients

²⁄₃ cup sugar
²⁄₃ cup water
1lb. plain or milk chocolate

4 egg yolks
2pts. heavy cream

Put sugar and water into a saucepan and stir over a gentle heat until dissolved. Bring to a boil and simmer gently for 7 minutes.

Break the chocolate into small pieces and stir into the hot syrup. Stir until dissolved. Beat in the egg yolks and cool.

Whip the cream until thick, but not stiff. Fold into the chocolate mixture.

Freeze in an electric ice cream maker according to manufacturer's instructions. Alternatively, pour into a freezer tray and freeze. Beat the mixture twice, at hourly intervals. Cover, seal and freeze.

Remove ice cream from freezer to refrigerator and allow to 'come to' about 30 minutes before serving.

Tea Granita
Serves 4

Ingredients
2tbsp. tea leaves (Orange Pekoe, Darjeeling, Ceylon, rosehip or any other kind)

3tbsp. sugar
2tbsp. lemon or lime juice
2¼ cups boiling water

Combine the tea leaves, sugar and juice. Pour over the boiling water, mix well and leave until cold. Strain and freeze as for granita.

Variation Infuse mint leaves or lemon balm in the tea while it is cooling. Strain before freezing. Pour a measure of Crème de Menthe over the granita before serving.

Strawberry Granita
Serves 4

Ingredients
½ cup sugar
¾ cup water

1lb. fresh strawberries
1tbsp. lemon juice

Heat the sugar with the water over a medium heat, stirring constantly until it has dissolved. Boil for 5 minutes. Leave to cool.

Purée the strawberries and strain to remove any seeds. Mix in the lemon juice.

Stir the syrup into the strawberry purée.

Pour the granita mixture into a very shallow freezer-proof dish and freeze until nearly firm. Stir the ice crystals at the edge of the dish into the center several times but take care not to break them up — the granita should be fairly coarse.

Variations Flavor the granita with Grand Marnier, orange flower water or the juice of 1 orange.

Omit the sugar syrup. Purée and strain the strawberries. Sweeten with icing sugar, add orange and/or lemon juice to taste and freeze.

Mix half frozen granita with partly defrosted concentrated orange juice.

Use half strawberries and half raspberries.

Frozen fruit can be used instead of fresh fruit but use half the amount of sugar.

Orange Granita
Serves 4

Ingredients
¾ cup sugar
2 cups water
1 lemon

2-3 oranges
1tbsp. orange flower water (optional)

Heat the sugar in the water over a medium heat, stirring constantly until the sugar has dissolved. Boil for 5 minutes.

Add the finely grated peel and the lemon and both oranges to the syrup. Leave until completely cold.

Stir the juice of the lemon and oranges into the syrup. Add the orange flower water if you are using it.

Pour the granita mixture into a very shallow freezer-proof dish and freeze until nearly firm. Stir the ice crystals at the edge of the dish into the center several times but take care not to break them up — the granita should be fairly coarse.

Variations Use tangerines instead of oranges.

Do not use the peel of the oranges. Squeeze the juice from the fruit carefully, keeping the shells intact, and spoon the frozen granita back into the shells for serving.

Chocolate Granita
Serves 4

Ingredients
5tbsp. unsweetened cocoa
3tbsp. sugar

2½ cups boiling water

Combine the cocoa and sugar. Pour over the boiling water, mix well and leave until cold. Freeze as for orange granita.

Orange Granita

Easy Ice Cream Loaf
Serves 8

Ingredients

24 ladies fingers or sponge
    fingers
2tbsp. Marsala, sherry,
    brandy, rum, liqueur or
    fruit juice
1½pts. ice cream

1 cup heavy cream
2tbsp. Coffee, Chocolate,
    Butterscotch or Fruit
    sauce
½ cup toasted flaked
    almonds

Arrange half the cookies in the base of a loaf pan.
Sprinkle with wine, spirit or juice. Soften the ice cream
and spread half of it over the cookies. Repeat with a
second layer each of cookies and ice cream. Cover and
freeze for 1 hour or more.

Beat the cream until it is thick. Unmold the ice cream
loaf onto a serving dish. Cover with cream and drizzle
the sauce over it. Garnish with flaked almonds.

Variation Use two different kinds of ice cream or
sorbet.

Alternatively, use more ice cream, of several
different kinds, and freeze in 8in. sandwich cake pans.
Assemble the ice cream cake by piling the layers on top
of each other. Press ladies fingers or langues de chat
gently around the outside. Top with cream and sauce
as above.

Kulfi (Indian Ice Cream)
Serves 8

Ingredients

4 cups milk
1tbsp. arrowroot
3 cardamom pods
¼ cup sugar

1tbsp. almonds or
    pistachios, chopped
½ cup heavy cream
few drops rose water

Bring a quarter of the milk to the boil in a wide, shallow
pan. Keep it on the boil, stirring constantly, until it is
very thick. Most of it will evaporate but this is as it
should be. The length of time it takes for the milk to
thicken depends on the surface area of your pan — the
wider the pan, the faster the milk will thicken. Set aside
until it is completely cold.

Mix some of the remaining milk with the arrowroot
to make a paste. Add one of the cardamom pods to the
rest of the milk and bring to the boil. Keep boiling,
stirring constantly, for 10 minutes. Remove the
cardamom pod. Add the arrowroot paste and continue
stirring until the milk has thickened.

Stir the sugar into the hot milk until it has dissolved.
Remove the seeds from the remaining cardamom
pods, crush them and stir into the milk.

Stir in the chopped nuts. Leave the milk to cool,
stirring occasionally.

Beat the cream until it is stiff enough to hold its
shape. Gently fold into the cooled milk, starting with
just one spoonful and gradually adding the remainder.
Stir in the cooled thickened milk which was made
earlier and add the few drops of rose water.

Pour the Kulfi into a freezer tray or plastic box, cover
and freeze for 1-2 hours. Beat well and return to the
freezer. Beat again every 2 hours until the ice cream is
firm.

Ginger Ice Cream
Serves 6

Ingredients

3 egg yolks	*1tbsp. ginger syrup*
¼ cup sugar	*1¼ cups milk*
¾ cup stem ginger	*½ cup heavy cream*

Beat the egg yolks with the sugar until very light and thick. Then drain and dice the stem ginger. Stir into the eggs along with the ginger syrup.

Scald the milk and slowly pour over the eggs, beating constantly. Pour the custard into the top of a heavy boiler and heat, stirring constantly, until it is thick enough to coat the back of the spoon. Leave to cool.

Pour the custard into a freezer tray or plastic box, cover and freeze for 1-2 hours. Transfer to a bowl and beat until it is smooth and all the ice crystals have been mixed in.

Beat the cream until it is just beginning to thicken. Gently fold into the custard. Pour into the freezer tray again, cover and freeze until firm.

Variation Omit the stem ginger and flavor the custard with 1tsp. ground ginger or 1tbsp. grated fresh ginger and 1tbsp. crystalized ginger pieces.

Following the method described above, a liqueur may be added to the custard mixture. For extra variation, omit the ginger and divide the custard into separate containers and add a different liqueur — Benedictine, Crème de Menthe, Kahlua, Tia Maria, Cassis — to each batch. Serve a tiny scoop of each kind in either glass dishes, or as a filling for miniature meringues, or in a pie shell made from biscuit crumbs in *tulipes*. Alternatively, freeze the flavors in small sandwich pans and assemble a multi-colored gâteau.

Maple Walnut Ice Cream
Serves 8

Ingredients

⅔ cup maple syrup	*1¼ cups heavy cream*
4 egg yolks	*1 cup chopped walnuts*

Boil the maple syrup until it is very thick.

Beat the egg yolks until they are very thick and light. Pour into the top of a double boiler and slowly add the hot syrup, beating constantly. Continue beating the yolks and syrup in the double boiler until it thickens to the consistency of whipped cream.

Remove the top of the double boiler from the heat and stand in a bowl full of ice cubes. Continue beating the yolks until they are completely cold.

Beat the cream until it is thick enough to hold its shape. Carefully fold into the yolk mixture, starting with just one spoonful and gradually adding the remainder. Stir in the walnuts.

Pour the ice cream mixture into a plastic tray or mold, cover and freeze. This ice cream does not need stirring while it is freezing and one can therefore unmold it. Serve in slices or scoops, decorated with glazed walnut halves and a rum, brandy or coffee sauce.

Pineapple Ice Cream
Serves 8

Ingredients

¾ cup sugar	*1¼ cups heavy cream*
2 cups water	*2 egg whites (optional)*
1 lemon	
1lb. crushed, fresh pineapple	

Stir the sugar in the water over a medium heat until it has dissolved. Add the finely grated lemon rind and boil rapidly for 5 minutes. Leave until thoroughly cooled.

Combine the crushed pineapple and lemon juice. Measure and mix with an equal amount of syrup.

Beat the cream until it is just beginning to thicken. Carefully fold into the fruit purée.

Beat the egg whites until they are stiff but not dry. Gently fold into the fruit.

Pour the ice cream mixture into a freezer tray or plastic box, cover and freeze for 1-2 hours. Beat well so that all the ice crystals are mixed in. Return to the freezer until firm.

Canned pineapple can be used very successfully for this ice cream. If you are using fresh pineapple, save the shell and pile the ice cream into it before serving.

Caramel Ice Cream
Serves 4

Ingredients

4 tbsp. sugar	2 egg yolks
6 tbsp. water	1¼ cups heavy cream

Place the sugar and a third of the water in a heavy-based pan. Stir over a medium heat until the sugar has dissolved. Raise the heat, boil rapidly until brown in color and add the remaining water.

Beat the egg yolks until they are thick and light. Slowly pour on the hot caramel and continue beating until the mixture is thick and cold.

Beat the cream until it is just beginning to thicken. Carefully fold into the eggs and caramel.

Pour the ice cream mixture into a freezer tray or plastic box, cover and freeze for 1-2 hours. Beat well and return to the freezer until firm.

Avocado Ice Cream
Serves 4

Ingredients

1 avocado	2 tbsp. light cream
1 tbsp. lime juice	1 egg white

Peel the avocado, cut in half and remove the pit. Mash or purée it until it is smooth. Stir in the lime juice and cream, beating well to ensure that the mixture is well blended and completely smooth.

Beat the egg white until it is stiff but not dry. Gently fold into the avocado mixture, starting with just one spoonful and gradually adding the remainder.

Pour into a freezer tray or plastic box, cover and freeze for 1-2 hours.

Beat well so that all the ice crystals are mixed in. Return to the freezer until firm.

Apricot Ice Cream
Serves 6

Ingredients

¾ cup dried apricots	2 egg whites
½ cup dry white wine	⅔ cup heavy cream
½ cup sugar	few drops almond extract
⅔ cup water	(optional)

Dice the apricots and cook in an uncovered tin with the white wine for 15-20 minutes or until they are soft. If the liquid evaporates, add some apple juice.

Cool the apricots and then press them through a strainer or liquidize them to make a smooth purée. If you have less than ⅔ cup when you are finished, make up to that quantity with unsweetened apple juice.

Stir the sugar into the water over a medium heat until it has dissolved. Boil rapidly for 5 minutes.

Beat the egg whites until they are stiff but not dry. Slowly pour in the hot syrup, beating constantly. Beat until the meringue is very thick.

Beat the cream until it is just beginning to thicken. Carefully fold the fruit purée into the egg whites and then add the whipped cream, starting with one spoonful and gradually adding the remainder. Stir in the almond extract.

Turn the ice cream mixture into a loaf pan, ring mold or cake pan. Cover and freeze until firm. This ice cream does not need to be stirred while freezing. Unmold and serve garnished with slices of fresh or canned apricots or a puréed sauce made from fresh fruit or poached dried fruit. Toasted almonds can also be sprinkled on top.

Variation Replace the dried apricots with fresh (skinned), bottled or canned apricots. Drain well, purée and add 1 tbsp. white wine.

Other fruits can be used according to availability with equal success. Firm fruits such as plums, greengages (small green plums) or pears should be cooked in syrup, apple juice or wine if they are fresh. Dried fruit such as prunes need to be poached. Soft fruits such as strawberries or pineapple need only be liquidized or pressed through a strainer before adding to the egg whites.

Chestnut Mousse
Serves 4-6

Ingredients
6tbsp. butter
1 cup unsweetened
   chestnut purée
2 eggs, separated
2tbsp. sugar
2tbsp. unsweetened cocoa

¼ cup ground almonds
1½tbsp. brandy
½ cup heavy cream
8-10 blanched almonds
1tbsp. chocolate strands

Melt the butter and leave to cool.

Beat the chestnut purée until it is smooth. Add the butter, egg yolks, sugar, cocoa, almonds and brandy. Mix well.

Beat the egg whites until they are stiff but not dry. Gently fold into the chestnut mixture, starting with one spoonful and gradually adding the remainder.

Decorate the mousse with lightly whipped cream, almonds and chocolate strands and chill for at least 2 hours before serving.

Fruit Surprise
Serves 8

Ingredients
1½pts ice cream or sorbet

8 oranges or lemons, or 1
   pineapple

Remove the ice cream or sorbet from the freezer and leave to slightly soften for approximately 30 minutes. Use any flavor you think will go well with the fruit you have chosen.

Cut the top off the orange or lemon, or cut the pineapple in half. Carefully remove the fruit from its shell, leaving enough to keep the shape of the fruit. Chop coarsely and mix into the softened ice cream or sorbet.

Spoon the mixture back into the fruit shell and return to the freezer. Remove 15 minutes before serving.

Variation After removing the fruit from its shell, mix with alcohol of virtually any sort — brandy, gin, liqueur — and leave to soak for 1 hour. Put the fruit back in its shell and top with the ice cream or sorbet. Freeze until firm.

Dutch Apple Special
Serves 4

Ingredients
1lb. apples, cored and
   sliced
2tbsp. water
4tbsp. brown sugar

⅓ cup raisins
1tsp. cinnamon
½tsp. nutmeg
1½pts. ice cream

Place the apples in a pan with the water. Cook over a low heat until the apples are soft.

Purée the apples and stir in the sugar until it has melted. Add the raisins, cinnamon and nutmeg.

To serve, arrange two scoops of ice cream in each serving dish. Spoon the warm apple sauce over the top and serve immediately.

Sundae Supreme
Serves 4

Ingredients

$1\frac{1}{2}$pts. ice cream
8 wafers or cookies
2 cups Chocolate or Fruit
  Sauce
$1\frac{1}{2}$ cups whipped cream

$\frac{1}{2}$ cup toasted nuts,
  chopped
4 glacé or maraschino
  cherries

Arrange two scoops of ice cream in each serving dish, preferably two flavors.

Crumble the wafers or cookies and sprinkle over the ice cream. Pour on the sauce. Top with whipped cream, piled as high as you can, and scatter chopped nuts on top. Crown each sundae with a cherry.

Red Fruit Soufflé
Serves 4

Ingredients

$\frac{1}{2}$lb. raspberries,
  strawberries, red or
  black currants
$\frac{1}{2}$ cup sugar
1tbsp. Kirsch, Cassis, or
  Framboise

2tbsp. cornstarch
$1\frac{1}{4}$ cups milk
2 eggs
$\frac{3}{4}$ cup heavy cream
extra fruit to garnish
  (optional)

If using raspberries or strawberries, press through a strainer or purée the fruit and mix with the sugar. If using red or black currants, sprinkle with sugar and heat in a heavy-bottomed pan until the berries are soft. Cool slightly and press through a strainer or purée. Stir in the liqueur.

Mix the cornstarch with enough of the milk to make a smooth paste. Heat the remaining milk until it just reaches boiling point. Pour over the cornstarch and mix well.

Lightly beat the eggs and stir into the hot milk. Return to the heat and cook, stirring constantly, until the mixture begins to thicken. Leave to cool.

Combine the fruit purée with the sauce.

Beat the cream until it is just thick enough to hold its shape. Gently fold into the fruit sauce.

Tie a paper collar around the outside of a 1pt. soufflé dish so that it extends 2in. above the top of the dish. Pour the soufflé mixture into the dish and chill overnight or until firm.

Serve the soufflé garnished if you like with fresh fruit.

Kamla Khir
Khir with Oranges

Ingredients

5 cups milk
3tbsp. sugar

2 oranges, peeled

Boil the milk in a large saucepan, stirring constantly. Add the sugar and stir. Reduce heat and, stirring occasionally, simmer until it is reduced to 2 cups. Cool.

Remove all the pith from the oranges and slice. Add to the cooled milk. Serve chilled.

Chilled Orange Soufflé
Serves 4

Ingredients

2 eggs
$\frac{1}{2}$ cup sugar
$\frac{2}{3}$ cup heavy cream

1 orange
1tbsp. Cointreau or Grand
  Marnier

Beat one of the eggs and the yolk from the second with the sugar until very light and frothy.

Beat the cream until it is just firm enough to hold its shape. Stir in the finely grated rind of the orange, 2tbsp. of its juice and the liqueur.

Combine the yolk and cream mixtures.

Beat the remaining egg white until it is stiff but not dry. Gently fold into the soufflé starting with just one spoonful and gradually adding the remainder. Spoon into individual soufflé dishes and chill until set, overnight is fine.

Ginger and Rhubarb Fool

Ingredients

2tbsp. butter
1lb. rhubarb, cut into
   chunks

2tbsp. brown sugar
2tsp. ground ginger
½ cup heavy cream

Melt the butter in a saucepan. Add the rhubarb, sugar and ginger. Simmer until the rhubarb is soft.
   Add the cream and liquidize. Chill and serve.

Stuffed Pears
Serves 6

This recipe uses dates and walnuts to create a simple and delightful dessert.

Ingredients

¼ cup dates, pitted and
   chopped
2 cups ground walnuts
1tsp. cinnamon
12 canned pear halves,
   drained

½ cup water
5tbsp. sugar
1 cup white wine
2 whole cloves
2tbsp. lemon juice

Preheat the oven to 180°C. In a small mixing bowl, combine the dates, walnuts and cinnamon. Mix well. Fill the cavities of the pear halves with the mixture. Place the pears in a shallow baking dish.
   In a small saucepan, bring the water, sugar, wine, cloves and lemon juice to a boil over a medium heat. Stir frequently until the sugar is dissolved. Reduce the heat to low and simmer for 2 minutes.
   Pour the wine sauce over the pears in the baking dish. Bake for 20 minutes. Chill for 1 hour before serving.

Orange Pudding
Serves 6

Ingredients

rind from 2 oranges, finely
   grated
1 cup sugar
5tbsp. cornstarch

pinch salt
4 eggs, separated
5 cups orange juice

In a large mixing bowl combine the orange rind, sugar, cornstarch and salt.
   In a separate bowl beat the egg yolks into the orange juice. Gradually add the cornstarch mixture and stir until smooth.
   Put the mixture into a medium-sized saucepan. Cook over a medium heat, stirring constantly, until the custard mixture thickens, about 12 minutes.
   Remove the saucepan from the heat and plunge it into a large pan of cold water. Leave it for 2-3 minutes.
   Beat the egg whites in a small mixing bowl until they are stiff. Fold the egg whites into the custard until the mixture is smooth.
   Spoon the pudding into tulip glasses or dessert dishes and chill before serving.

Quince Sherbet
Serves 6

This is a distinctive Middle Eastern sherbet. Serve it in tulip or dessert glasses.

Ingredients

3 large ripe quinces,
   peeled, cored and cut
   into small pieces

¾ cup water
1 cup+2tbsp. sugar
4tbsp. lemon juice

Put the fruit and water into a large saucepan. Bring the mixture to a boil over a high heat. Reduce the heat to low and simmer for 40 minutes.
   Strain the mixture through a strainer into another saucepan. Discard any solids that remain in the strainer. Add the sugar and lemon juice and bring the mixture to a boil over a high heat. Boil for 10 minutes, stirring frequently to dissolve the sugar.
   Remove the saucepan from the heat and let the mixture cool for 5 minutes.
   Pour the sherbet mixture into a large bowl and put it into the ice compartment of the refrigerator or the freezer for 2 hours.
   Stir the mixture every 10-15 minutes to break up the ice crystals and make a smooth texture.

Nut Pudding
Serves 8

This is a traditional Syrian nut pudding. Use white, not green, pistachio nuts.

Ingredients

4¼ cups light cream
¾ cup ground rice
pinch salt
½ cup sugar
½ cup ground unsalted
   almonds

½ cup ground unsalted
   pistachio nuts
2tbsp. grenadine syrup

In a medium-sized saucepan, bring the cream to a boil. Add the ground rice, salt and sugar. Simmer over a medium heat for 5 minutes, stirring constantly.
   Stir in the ground almonds, ground pistachios and grenadine syrup. Reduce the heat to low and simmer for 2 minutes, stirring constantly.
   Remove the saucepan from the heat and let the mixture cool until it is warm. Spoon the pudding into small individual dessert dishes and chill. Serve cold.

Fruit Kisel
Serves 8-10

Kisel is a cold, thick liquid dessert very popular in Russia. There are many different recipes, and there are no hard and fast rules about ingredients. Try different combinations of fruit, making sure to mash the fruit into a smooth purée. More potato starch may be needed to thicken the kisel if very juicy fresh fruits are used.

Ingredients
½lb. tart red apples, peeled, cored and cut into small chunks
¼lb. dried apricots
4 cups fresh or thawed frozen strawberries
1¼ cups cold water
⅓ cup jellied cranberry sauce
1 cup sugar
1½tbsp. potato starch, dissolved in 1 cup cold water

Place the apples, apricots and strawberries in a large saucepan. Add the cranberry sauce and cold water and bring the mixture to a boil over a high heat.

Reduce the heat to low and simmer uncovered for 15 minutes, stirring occasionally.

With the back of a spoon, press the fruit mixture through a fine strainer into a large mixing bowl. Discard any solids that remain in the strainer. Stir in the sugar.

Put the fruit and sugar mixture into a large saucepan and bring it to a boil. Reduce the heat to medium and stir in the potato starch mixture.

Cook until the purée returns to a boil. Remove the saucepan from the heat and let the purée cool to room temperature.

Spoon the purée into pudding or tulip glasses. Chill for 4 hours before serving.

Apple Charlotte
Serves 8

There are many kinds of charlotte. Apple Charlotte, one of the simpler versions, is popular as a lunchtime dish.

Ingredients
2tbsp. sweet butter, softened
1½ cups sweet butter, clarified
12 large slices white bread, halved, crusts removed
3lb. tart apples, peeled, cored and chopped
3lb. sweet apples, peeled, cored and chopped
2 cups sugar
½ cup water
2tbsp. lime juice
2tbsp. lemon juice
1tsp. cinnamon
1¼ cups apricot preserves
¼ cup apricot brandy
¼ cup orange juice
2-3 drops pure vanilla extract

Rub the softened butter over the inside surface of a dessert mold.

Put the clarified butter into a large mixing bowl. Dip the bread into the butter and line the sides and bottom of the dessert mold with them.

Combine the apples, sugar, water, lemon juice and lime juice in a large flameproof casserole. Bring the mixture to a boil, cover and simmer for 40 minutes over a low heat.

Add the cinnamon and cook, uncovered, over medium heat for a further 15 minutes. Chill the mixture for 1 hour.

Gently pour the chilled apple mixture into the prepared dessert mold.

Preheat the oven to 400°F. Bake the pudding for 1 hour. Cool for 30 minutes at room temperature.

Invert the pudding on a large flat plate. Gently shake the mold to loosen the Apple Charlotte. Carefully pull the dessert mold away.

In a small mixing bowl, combine the apricot preserves, apricot brandy, orange juice and vanilla extract. Spoon over the Apple Charlotte before serving.

Cherries Jubilee
Serves 4

Ingredients
1 cup ice cream
½lb. black cherries
1tbsp. sugar
1tbsp. cornstarch
1 cup fruit juice or water
¼ cup brandy

Use vanilla, cherry or orange ice cream or cherry, orange or lemon sorbet. A yogurt-based ice cream can also be used — its tart flavor makes a superb contrast with the fruit sauce.

Arrange scoops of ice cream or sorbet in a large glass serving dish.

Drain and pit the cherries.

Combine the sugar and cornstarch. Stir in the fruit juice or water and heat gently until the sauce has thickened. Add the cherries and heat for 3-4 minutes.

Warm the brandy, pour it over the cherry sauce and set alight. Pour the sauce over the ice cream and serve immediately.

Variation Substitute red wine for the fruit juice and sharpen with a spoonful of lemon juice. Use Kirsch instead of brandy.

Banana Split
Serves 4

Ingredients

4 medium bananas
2½ cups ice cream
½ cup crushed pineapple
½ cup crushed raspberries
½ cup Chocolate Sauce
½ cup heavy or whipping
   cream

8 Maraschino or glacé
   cherries
½ cup flaked or chopped
   nuts

Cut the bananas in half lengthways and place two halves on opposite sides of each serving dish.

The ice cream can be any flavor you choose, and a Banana Split is all the better for having two or three flavors of ice cream. Place three scoops of ice cream on each dish, between the banana halves.

Carefully spoon the fruit over two of the scoops of ice cream and the chocolate sauce over the remaining scoop.

Whisk the cream until it is stiff and pile or pipe it on top of the Banana Split. Decorate with chopped cherries and toasted or chopped nuts.

Variation The pineapple and raspberries can be left out or replaced by any other fruit you prefer.

Pears Hélène
Serves 4

Ingredients

¾ cup sugar
1 cup water
1 vanilla pod (optional)
2 large pears

½lb. plain chocolate pieces
1 cup water
½ cup butter
2½ cups vanilla ice cream

Stir the sugar into 1 cup of water over a medium heat until it has dissolved.

Add the split vanilla pod if you are using it.

Alternatively, use sugar that has been stored with a vanilla pod in it.

Peel the pears, cut in half and carefully remove the core. Place the pears in the syrup and simmer gently until they are tender. Cool in the syrup.

Melt the chocolate and 1 cup of water together, mixing occasionally, until smooth and thoroughly blended. Cut the butter into small pieces and stir in until the sauce is smooth.

To assemble the pears Hélène, drain the fruit well and place one half in each serving dish. Top with a scoop of ice cream and carefully pour the hot chocolate sauce over the top.

Variation Substitute ¼ cup single cream for half of the butter in the chocolate sauce.

Strawberry Shortcake

This mouth-watering dessert should be eaten while it is still warm. The shortcake dough may be prepared 1-2 hours ahead of time and kept in a cool place. Have the butter, fruits and the cream ready too, so that the warm cake can be assembled in just a few minutes.

Ingredients

¾lb. strawberries, redcurrants or raspberries	¼ cup granulated sugar
3tbsp. sugar	4½-5tbsp. unsalted butter, chilled and cubed
2tbsp. kirsch or Grand Marnier	1 egg
2⅓ cups all-purpose flour	⅔ cup heavy cream or ½ cream and ½ milk
2tsp. baking powder	¼lb. unsalted butter, softened for spreading on cooked layers
½tsp. salt	
pinch nutmeg	1 cup heavy cream

Reserve a few fruits for decoration. Slice ¾ cup strawberries but leave other fruits whole. Crush the rest of the fruit and stir in 2tbsp. sugar and 1tbsp. of the liqueur. Fold in the sliced fruit and set aside.

Sift together the flour, baking powder, salt, nutmeg and granulated sugar into a bowl. Drop in the butter pieces and quickly rub to a crumb texture. Lightly beat the egg into the cream and pour on to the dry mixture. Combine quickly into a smooth dough. Butter and flour a 8½in. spring-form pan and press in the dough.

Bake at 450°F for 20 minutes on a wire rack.

Split the shortcake in two and spread half the butter on the bottom layer and the rest on the underside of the top layer. Spread the fruit filling over the bottom cake and sandwich with the top layer. It does not matter if the fruit oozes out.

Beat the cream until softly peaked and beat in the rest of the sugar and liqueur. Spoon the cream on to the shortcake and decorate with reserved fruits.

Flans aux Fruits

In former times, puff pastry was used as a base for fruit flans, but now sweet shortcrust pastry is preferred as it gives a crisper base. Choose seasonal fruits; they should be unblemished and fully ripe. Most of all be generous with the quantities as the fruit shrinks as it bakes.

Ingredients

Sweet Shortcrust Pastry for an 8½in. flan dish or spring-form pan	lemon juice
	3tbsp. confectioner's sugar, sifted
1½-2lb. ripe fruit	3tbsp. apricot jam

Blueberry Tart

Ingredients

Sweet Shortcrust Pastry for an 8½in. flan dish	¼lb. butter
½ cup ground almonds	3 eggs
Filling	2tbsp. cornstarch or potato flour, sifted
approx. 1lb. blueberries or bilberries, fresh or frozen	good ¼ cup heavy cream
⅔ cup granulated sugar	2tsp. orange rind
2tbsp. Grand Marnier or Cointreau	2tbsp. lemon juice
	½ cup confectioner's sugar

Defrost the fruit and drain off the surplus juice. Line the base and 1in. up the sides of a greased flan dish with shortcrust pastry, prick all over with a fork. Chill.

Make the filling. Drop the blueberries, 3tbsp. sugar, liqueur and 1tbsp. butter into a pan, heat and stir gently until the fruit has slightly caramelized. Leave to cool.

Beat together the remaining butter and granulated sugar until pale and fluffy; beat in the eggs one at a time, add the flour and cream.

Mix in the orange rind and lemon juice, then fold in the blueberry mixture. Scatter the ground almonds over the base of the pastry shell and pour in the prepared filling.

Dredge with confectioner's sugar and bake in the preheated oven at 350°F for 1 hour. Leave to cool in the pan.

Serve with whipped cream on the side.

(Above) Fresh Fruit Tarts of strawberries, mirabelle plums, apricots cooked on a base of crème pâtissière, gooseberries and black Muscat grapes, raspberry and gooseberry tartlets. (Right) Blueberry Tart.

Line the base and 1in. up the sides of the flan dish with the pastry. Prick all over with a fork and chill. Wash and dry the fruit carefully; pit cherries and mirabelle plums but leave whole. Cut other fruits in half and remove the pits. Cut peaches into thick slices and rub them with lemon juice to stop them going brown.

Arrange the whole fruits, the fruit halves or slices in circles, cut sides up and each overlapping the preceding one a little; reverse the direction of the fruit for each new circle. Bake in the preheated oven at 375°F for 50-60 minutes.

Meanwhile, heat the apricot jam with 2tbsp. water until slightly thick; strain.

Remove the flan from the oven and leave in the pan on a wire rack to cool for 10 minutes. Lift off the outer rim of the pan and slide the flan off the base on to the rack. Dust with confectioner's sugar all over, then brush the whole fruited surface with the warm jam, which will cool into a glossy jelly.

Serve when cold with whipped cream on the side.

top of a double boiler. Stir occasionally.

Remove the melted chocolate from the heat. Gradually stir in the sweetened water and mix well.

Stir in the rum, brandy or Grand Marnier.

To eat the fondue, your guests each dip fruit pieces into the warm sauce.

Chocolate Chiffon Pie
Serves 6

Ingredients

1 portion Shortcrust Pastry	2tsp. powdered gelatin
²⁄₃ cup milk	2tbsp. hot water
5tbsp. sugar	²⁄₃ cup heavy cream
4oz. plain chocolate, chopped	whipped cream chocolate curls
2 small eggs, separated	

Roll out the pastry and use to line a 8in. flan tin. Bake "blind" (lined with waxed paper and baking beans) for 20-25 minutes at 375°F. Remove the waxed paper and baking beans and return to oven for a further 5-10 minutes until crisp and lightly browned. Leave to cool.

Put the milk, sugar and chocolate into a saucepan and melt over a gentle heat, stirring continuously. Cool slightly.

Beat the egg yolks into the chocolate mixture.

Dissolve the gelatin in the water and stir into chocolate. Leave until the mixture is beginning to thicken and set.

Beat egg whites until stiff. Beat in the remaining sugar.

Beat the cream until it stands in soft peaks.

Fold the egg whites and cream thoroughly into the chocolate mixture. Pour into the pastry case.

Chill until set, then decorate with piped whipped cream and chocolate curls.

Chocolate Fondue
Serves 6

Ingredients

1¼ cups sugar	2½tbsp. heavy cream
²⁄₃ cup water	5tbsp. rum, brandy or Grand Marnier
¼lb. plain chocolate in small pieces	approx. 1½lb. prepared mixed fruit in bite-sized pieces
¼lb. milk chocolate in small pieces	
5tbsp. butter	

Heat the sugar and water over a low heat, stirring constantly, until the sugar has dissolved. Leave to cool.

Melt the chocolate with the butter and cream in the

Chocolate Mousse
Serves 4-6

Ingredients

6oz. plain chocolate
2tbsp. honey
3 eggs, separated
1tbsp. powdered gelatin

3tbsp. hot water
²⁄₃ cup heavy cream
whipped cream
sliced bananas

Melt the chocolate and honey into a bowl over a pan of hot water.

Stir in the egg yolks and beat until smooth. Remove from the heat.

Dissolve the gelatin in the water. Stir into the chocolate mixture. Chill until the mixture is the consistency of unbeaten egg white.

Whip the heavy cream until thick, but not stiff. Fold into the chocolate mixture.

Beat the egg whites until stiff and fold them into the chocolate mixture.

Pour into a 2½pt. mold and chill until set.

Unmold onto a serving dish and decorate with whipped cream and banana slices.

Chocolate Orange Pots
Serves 8

Ingredients

6oz. plain chocolate
rind of 1 small orange,
 finely grated
3 eggs, separated
2-3tbsp. Orange Curaçao

1 cup heavy cream
whipped cream
orange rind spirals
chocolate orange sticks

Melt the chocolate into a bowl over a pan of hot water. Remove from heat and stir in the orange rind, egg yolks and liqueur. Stir well and leave to cool.

Whip the heavy cream until thick. Beat the egg whites until stiff. Fold cream and egg whites into the chocolate mixture.

Pour into 8 individual pots (e.g. custard cups) and

chill.

Serve each topped with a spoonful of softly whipped cream and decorated with orange rind spirals and chocolate sticks.

Chocolate and Coffee Bavarois
Serves 6-8

Ingredients

4 egg yolks
¼ cup sugar
1tsp. vanilla extract
2½ cups milk
6oz. plain chocolate, grated
1tbsp. coffee extract
1tbsp. powdered gelatin

4tbsp. cold water
⅔ cup heavy cream
⅔ cup light cream
2 egg whites

Decoration
whipped cream
Chocolate Caraque

Beat together the egg yolks, sugar and vanilla extract until pale and fluffy.

Warm the milk. Stir into the egg yolk mixture. Put into a double saucepan or a bowl over a pan of hot water. Stir gently until the mixture thickens.

Stir the chocolate and coffee extract into the custard. Stir until completely dissolved. Remove from heat.

Put water into a bowl and add the gelatin. Place over a pan of hot water and stir until dissolved. Cool slightly.

Stir the gelatin into the chocolate custard. Leave until the mixture begins to thicken.

Beat the cream until thick. Beat the egg whites until stiff.

Fold the cream into the chocolate mixture and then fold in the egg whites thoroughly.

Pour into a lightly-oiled approx. 3pt mold. Chill until set.

Turn Bavarois out on to a serving plate. Decorate with piped whipped cream and Chocolate Caraque.

Chocolate Hazelnut Bombe
Serves 6-8

Ingredients

2½ cups vanilla ice cream
½ cup hazelnuts, finely chopped and toasted
1½pts. Chocolate Ice Cream
2tbsp. dark rum

Decoration
1½ cups heavy cream, whipped
whole hazelnuts

Put an 8 or 9in. bombe mold or pudding basin into the freezer overnight.

Soften the vanilla ice cream and mix in the hazelnuts. Line the bombe mold with the ice cream and freeze.

Soften the chocolate ice cream and blend in the rum. Fill the center of the bombe. Cover with oiled waxed paper and freeze.

Turn out the bombe onto a plate. Pipe with whipped cream and decorate with whole hazelnuts. Serve cut into wedges.

Choc-Chestnut Mont Blanc
Serves 6-8

Ingredients

4tbsp. unsalted butter
2tbsp. sugar
6oz. plain chocolate,
  melted
1½ cups chestnut purée
1-2tbsp. sherry

Decoration
whipped cream
ratafias
glacé chestnuts
grated chocolate

Cream the butter and sugar together until light and fluffy. Beat in the melted chocolate and blend in the chestnut purée and sherry.

Pile the mixture into the center of individual dessert dishes and form into mountain shapes and chill.

Spoon or pipe a capping of whipped cream on the summit. Decorate the base with ratafia biscuits and glacé chestnuts. Sprinkle with grated chocolate if you wish.

Mohr Im Hemd
Moor In His Nightshirt
Makes 6-8

Ingredients

½ cup butter
½ cup sugar
6 eggs, separated
4oz. plain chocolate,
  grated
1 cup ground almonds
1tsp. coffee extract

Sauce
6oz. plain chocolate
¾ cup water
5tbsp. unsalted butter
Cream
⅔ cup light cream
⅔ cup heavy cream
1-2tbsp. confectioner's
  sugar
few drops vanilla extract

Cream together the butter and sugar until light and fluffy. Beat in the egg yolks one at a time. Mix in the chocolate, almonds and extract.

Beat the egg whites until stiff and fold gently into the chocolate mixture. Butter and dust with granulated sugar 6-8 individual soufflé dishes. Pour in the chocolate mixture.

Place in a roasting pan, half filled with hot water. Bake in the oven at 350°F for 30-40 minutes until puffed and just firm. Leave to cool for a few minutes.

To make the sauce put the chocolate and water into a pan. Stir over a low heat until the mixture is smooth. Remove from the heat and stir in the butter.

Beat the light and heavy creams together until light and fluffy. Stir in the confectioner's sugar and vanilla extract.

Spoon a little sauce on to each serving plate. Invert the puddings onto the sauce. Cover puddings with whipped cream.

Choc Nut Slice
Serves 8-10

Ingredients

*6oz. plain chocolate in
small pieces*
³/₄ cup confectioner's sugar
¹/₂ cup peanut butter
1tbsp. butter
pinch salt
*2tsp. instant coffee
granules*

¹/₄ cup boiling water
1 egg
1tsp. vanilla extract
*3¹/₂ cups butter cookie
crumbs*

Melt the chocolate in the top of a double saucepan.

Sift the confectioner's sugar. Mix together the melted chocolate, sugar, peanut butter, butter and salt.

Dissolve the instant coffee granules in boiling water and lightly beat the egg. Add the coffee, egg, vanilla and crumbs to the chocolate. Mix well so that the crumbs are well coated.

Line a loaf pan with foil. Spoon the chocolate mixture in the pan. Smooth the surface and cover with foil. Freeze for at least 4 hours.

Remove from the freezer one hour before you are ready to serve. Slice and arrange on serving dishes. Decorate with whipped cream to serve.

Chocolate Terrine
Serves 6-8

Ingredients

*one purchased 1lb.
Madeira or other loaf
cake*
6oz. plain chocolate
²/₃ cup sugar
4tbsp. water
¹/₂ cup cocoa
³/₄ cup unsalted butter

1 egg
2 egg yolks
*¹/₄ cup glacé cherries,
chopped*
¹/₃ cup raisins
¹/₂ cup pistachios, chopped
1¹/₄ cups whipping cream

Line a 3-lb. loaf pan with non-stick paper.

Cut the loaf cake into thin slices. Line the bottom and sides of the pan with some slices. Melt the chocolate.

Put the sugar and water into a small pan and heat gently over a low heat until the sugar is dissolved.

Beat together the cocoa and butter. Beat in the sugar syrup, melted chocolate and eggs. Stir in the cherries, raisins and pistachios.

Spread one-third of the chocolate mixture in the lined pan. Top with slices of cake. Trim cake level. Cover and chill overnight.

Unmold terrine onto a serving plate and spread the whipped cream over the top and sides of terrine.

Frozen Chocolate Sandwiches
Makes about 20

Ingredients

½ cup butter
½ cup sugar
2tbsp. beaten egg
a few drops vanilla extract
2tbsp. unsweetened cocoa
    powder
2 cups all-purpose flour

1 cup heavy cream
1tbsp. unsweetened cocoa
    powder
few drops vanilla extract

Coating
Chopped toasted almonds,
    or toasted shredded
    coconut or crushed
    graham crackers

Filling
1 large egg white
6tbsp. sugar

Beat the butter and sugar until pale and creamy. Beat in the egg and vanilla extract. Stir in the flour and cocoa, which have been sifted together, to give a firm dough.

Knead lightly until smooth. Roll out on a lightly floured surface to a thickness of about ¼in. Using a 6.5cm/2½in. round fluted cutter, stamp out circles. Put on a cookie sheet and cook in the oven at 350°F for 15 minutes. Cool on a wire rack.

To make the filling, beat the egg white until stiff. Beat in 2tbsp. of the sugar. Put cream, remaining sugar, cocoa and vanilla extract into another bowl and beat until stiff. Fold egg white into chocolate mixture.

Put a spoonful of the mixture on to half the chocolate biscuits. Top with remaining biscuits. Press lightly so filling reaches the edges. Arrange on a cookie sheet and freeze until firm.

Spread the chosen coating on another cookie sheet. Run each sandwich through the coating like a wheel, so that the sides are covered. Wrap individually in foil and freeze overnight.

Ricotta al Café
Serves 4

This delicious dessert is an Italian favorite. Eat it by dipping a spoonful of the cheese first into the coffee, then into the sugar.

Ingredients

1⅓ cups ricotta cheese
2tbsp. fruit sugar (fructose)
    or granulated sugar

4tbsp. finely ground fresh
    coffee
2tbsp. brandy

Choose really moist ricotta cheese, or use fresh farmer's cheese as a substitute. Press the cheese with half the sugar through a strainer to make it light and fluffy. Form into mounds on four individual dessert plates.

Sprinkle half the coffee over the cheese mounds. Spoon the remaining coffee and sugar onto the plates in two separate heaps on either side of the cheese and pour the brandy over the sweetened cheese.

Coffee Coconut Soufflé
Serves 4-6

Ingredients

3 eggs, separated
4tbsp. strong black coffee
1tbsp. Crème de Cacao
5tbsp. sugar
1 cup shredded or flaked
    coconut

1tbsp. powdered gelatin
2tbsp. cold water
⅔ cup heavy cream

Beat the egg yolks, coffee, Crème de Cacao and sugar in a bowl until thick. Stir in most of the coconut.

Melt the gelatin in a bowl of water over a pan of hot water. When clear, pour slowly into the coffee mixture, stirring all the time.

Beat the cream until it just holds its shape and fold into the mixture. Beat the egg whites until nearly stiff and fold them carefully into the mixture when nearly set.

Prepare a soufflé dish by cutting a band of paper 3in. deeper than the dish from a double layer of nonstick paper. Fold over 1in. along one of the long edges. Wrap the band around the dish, the folded edge level with the base and the upper edge extending beyond the rim 2in. Secure firmly with string or paper clips.

Spoon the mixture into the dish until it almost reaches the top of the paper band. Chill.

Remove the paper and decorate with the remaining coconut, before serving.

Coffee Charlotte
Serves 6

Ingredients

32 sponge or ladies fingers
4tbsp. water
4tbsp. coffee liqueur
1 cup milky coffee
¼ cup Vanilla Sugar (see
    note to recipe for Le
    Succès)

4tbsp. all-purpose flour
½ cup ground almonds
1 whole egg
1 egg yolk
¼lb. milk chocolate,
    coarsely grated

Dip the sponge or ladies fingers lightly in the mixture of water and liqueur, and line the base and sides of a 6-7in. charlotte mold.

Heat the milky coffee. Mix the sugar, flour and ground almonds together. Add the eggs and gradually pour into the coffee saucepan, beating thoroughly. Bring to a boil stirring constantly. Remove from the heat and leave to cool.

Spoon a layer of the coffee cream into the mold and sprinkle over it a layer of grated chocolate. Repeat until all the cream is used. Trim the sponge or ladies fingers lining the mold level with the filling and arrange the trimmings on top.

Press down well and leave to stand for 4-6 hours in a refrigerator until firm, then unmold to serve.

Coffee and Raspberry Frou Frou
Serves 6-8

Ingredients

2½ cups heavy cream
2½ cups light cream
½lb. meringues
4tsp. powdered instant coffee dissolved in 1tbsp. hot water, cooled
¼lb. frozen or fresh raspberries
1tsp. lemon juice

3tbsp. Vanilla Sugar (see note to recipe for Le Succès)
grated rind of one orange
1tbsp. water
a selection of fruit e.g. strawberries, raspberries, peaches, washed and sliced

Whip the two creams together until they just hold soft peaks. Break the meringue into small pieces and fold into the cream. Divide the mixture between three bowls. Add the coffee to one bowl and fold in.

For the raspberry sauce, combine all the remaining ingredients, except the mixed fruit, in a saucepan and heat gently until the raspberries are soft. Stir well to break up the berries and mix with one of the bowls of cream and meringue mixture.

Grease a 4pt ring mold and put alternate spoonfuls from the 3 bowls into it. Repeat until all the mixture is used. Gently smooth the surface and cover. Freeze for at least 6 hours.

Move to a refrigerator 30 minutes before serving. Unmold onto a serving plate and fill the center with the mixed fruit.

Iced Coffee Praline Mousse
Serves 6

Ingredients

1 cup whole hazelnuts
3tbsp. sugar
4 large eggs, separated
6tbsp. Vanilla Sugar (see note to recipe for Le Succès) or granulated sugar

2tbsp. powdered instant coffee
1¼ cups heavy cream

Brown the hazelnuts in a skillet over a medium heat. When the skins begin to loosen, remove from heat. Put in a dish cloth and rub gently to remove the skins. Chop roughly.

Add the sugar to the pan. When the sugar has melted and is slightly brown, stir in the hazelnuts. Pour the mixture onto a lightly oiled tray. When cool, break the praline into pieces and blend briefly in a liquidizer or food processor.

Beat the egg yolks with 4tbsp. of the sugar until pale and light. Put the bowl over a pan of hot water and continue beating until the mixture leaves a trail. Stir in the coffee and allow to cool.

Whip the cream to soft peaks and gently stir in the coffee mixture. Fold in the praline. Beat the egg whites until stiff and beat in the remaining sugar. Gently fold the egg whites into the cream mixture.

Pour the mixture either into a glass serving bowl or individual glasses. Cover and freeze for at least 1-2 hours.

Remove from the freezer 20 minutes before serving.

Coffee Meringue Pyramid
Serves 8-10

Ingredients

8 egg whites
4tbsp. instant coffee
  powder
1lb. sugar
2½ cups heavy cream,
  whipped
½lb. black grapes, halved
  and seeded

½lb. green grapes, halved
  and seeded
1 cup flaked almonds
chocolate coffee beans
  (optional)

Beat the egg whites until they form very stiff peaks. Mix the coffee with the sugar and add a little at a time, beating well after each addition.

Put the mixture into a piping bag fitted with a star nozzle and pipe small meringues 1in. in diameter onto a cookie sheet lined with waxed paper. Bake for 2-3 hours at 250°F until crisp and dry.

To assemble put a layer of meringues closely together on a serving plate and cover with some of the cream, grapes and almonds. Continue with layers of meringue, cream and grapes to form a pyramid.

Decorate with almonds, cream, grapes and, if you like, chocolate coffee beans.

Coffee Apricot Condé
Serves 8

Ingredients

½ cup short-grain rice
4 cups milk
4tbsp. powdered instant
  coffee
1tbsp. powdered gelatin
juice of 1 orange

4tbsp. sugar
1¼ cups heavy cream,
  whipped
8 ripe apricots, peeled,
  pitted and chopped
¼lb. raspberries

Put the rice, milk and coffee into a pan and bring to a boil, stirring occasionally. Simmer for 30-40 minutes, or until the rice is cooked, adding extra milk if necessary.

Dissolve the gelatin in the orange juice over a pan of hot water. Stir into the rice mixture and add the sugar. Leave to cool.

Fold half the cream and half the apricots, chopped, into the rice mixture. Spoon into a greased 2½pt mold. Chill until set.

Turn out onto a serving plate, arrange some raspberies around the base, pipe the remaining whipped cream onto the top of the mold and decorate with the rest of the apricots, sliced, and the raspberries.

Coffee Fruit Flans
Makes 8

Ingredients

½ cup butter
½ cup vanilla sugar or
  granulated sugar
2 eggs
grated rind of one lemon
1cup+2tbsp. self-rising
  flour
1tsp. baking powder
1tbsp. instant coffee
  powder

Filling
½lb. selected fruit, e.g.
  peaches, apricots, green
  grapes, strawberries, etc.
2tbsp. powdered gelatin
⅔ cup orange juice

Cream the butter and sugar together until light and fluffy. Gradually beat in the eggs and lemon rind. Sift together the flour, baking powder and instant coffee and gently fold into the mixture with a metal spoon.

Grease eight individual muffin or cupcake pans and divide the mixture between them. Bake for 15 minutes at 375°F until cooked through, then remove from the pans and cool on a wire rack.

Slice or halve the fruit, as required. Fill the sponge cases, make little domes of fruit.

Over a gentle heat, melt the gelatin in two tablespoons of the juice, then add the remaining liquid. Cool until just on the point of setting.

Spoon over the fruit in the sponge cases and leave to set.

Coffee and Vanilla Jelly
Serves 6

Ingredients

2tbsp. vanilla sugar or
  granulated sugar
1¼ cups hot strong coffee
1tbsp. powdered gelatin
3tbsp. water

Vanilla Jelly
1 egg yolk
2tbsp. granulated sugar
1¼ cups milk
vanilla extract
1tbsp. powdered gelatin
3tbsp. water

Add the sugar to the hot coffee. Dissolve the gelatin in the water over a saucepan of hot water. Add to the coffee mixture and stir well to make sure the jelly is clear.

Pour half the mixture into a greased 2pt. decorative jelly mold. Leave to set but keep the rest of the mixture warm.

Mix the egg yolk with the sugar, pour on the milk in a saucepan and heat, stirring all the time. When thickened, add vanilla extract to taste. Strain and cool.

Melt the gelatin in the water and add to the vanilla cream. Pour half this mixture onto the set coffee jelly and leave this to set. Repeat the layers.

Refrigerate until completely set and then turn out onto a serving plate.

Weight Watchers' Cheesecake
Serves 6

Ingredients

Base
5tbsp. margarine
5tbsp. sugar
¾ cup all-purpose flour
2tbsp. cornstarch

Filling
1 egg, separated
1 lemon
2tbsp. milk
3tbsp. sugar
⅔ cup skimmed milk cheese
⅔ cup cottage cheese
⅔ cup heavy cream

To make the shortbread base, rub the margarine into the combined sugar, flour and cornstarch until it resembles coarse crumbs. Bind lightly and press over the base of an 8in. pan. Prick and bake for 40 minues at 325°F.

Combine the egg yolk, grated lemon rind, milk and sugar for the filling. Heat, stirring, until thick. Leave to cool.

Beat the skimmed milk cheese until it is smooth. Strain the cottage cheese before adding to the skimmed milk cheese. Stir in the lemon juice.

Whip the cream and gently fold into the cheese mixture.

Beat the egg white until it is stiff but not dry. Fold into the filling mixture, starting with just one spoonful and gradually adding the remainder.

Pour the filling over the cool shortbread and chill until set. Serve with fresh fruit or a fruit topping.

Topfen Kuchen
Cheesecake

Ingredients

1 portion Sweet Shortcrust Pastry for an 8½in. spring-form pan
⅔ cup granulated sugar
5tbsp. butter
1tsp. lemon rind

4 eggs, separated
1¼ cups farmer's cheese, strained
⅓ cup raisins
4tbsp. heavy cream

Par-bake a pastry case for 15 minutes. Leave to cool. Beat the sugar and butter until thick, pale and fluffy. Mix in the lemon rind and egg yolks, one at a time. Blend in the cheese and raisins.

Beat the egg whites until they form soft peaks and fold them into the cheese mixture. Fold in the heavy cream.

Pour the filling into the pastry case and bake in the warmed oven at 350°F for 1 hour, until well risen and golden. Cool in the pan on a wire rack. The cake will collapse and crack as it cools, which is typical of cheesecakes. Dredge with confectioner's sugar to serve.

The cake freezes successfully for up to 2 months. Defrost at room temperature for 3-4 hours.

Italian Cheesecake
Serves 10-12

Ingredients

Base
5tbsp. butter
2 egg yolks
2tbsp. sugar
1tbsp. Marsala
½tsp. lemon rind
pinch salt
1 cup all-purpose flour

Filling
1lb. farmer's cheese
¼ cup sugar
1tsp. all-purpose flour
pinch salt
½tsp. vanilla extract
½tsp. orange rind
2 egg yolks
1tbsp. white raisins
1tbsp. candied peel
1tbsp. chopped almonds

Mix all the base ingredients together until a dough has formed. Handle as little as possible while blending. Gently roll or press into shape and line the base and sides of a 9in. loose-bottomed pan.

Beat the cheese until it is smooth. Mix well with all the other ingredients, adding the fruit and nuts last of all. Pour into the pastry case.

Bake at 350°F for 45-50 minutes. Cool and dust with confectioner's sugar before serving.

Chilled Raisin and Orange Cheesecake

Ingredients

6tbsp. candied orange and
 lemon peel, chopped
²⁄₃ cup white raisins
3tbsp. Grand Marnier or
 Cointreau
2tbsp. gelatin powder
2 cups farmer's cheese,
 pressed through a
 strainer
5tbsp. granulated sugar
1 cup lemon curd
2tbsp. orange rind
1¹⁄₂ cups heavy cream, softly
 whipped

5tbsp. pistachios, chopped
Syrup
5tbsp. granulated sugar
2tbsp. water
3tbsp. Grand Marnier or
 Cointreau
1 cooked fat free sponge
 9¹⁄₂in. in diameter (see
 note)

Soak the orange and lemon peel and the white raisins in Grand Marnier or Cointreau for at least 30 minutes. Make a syrup with the sugar and water boiled to 'thread stage', when the syrup will form a thread between the opened blade points of a pair of scissors. Mix in the liqueur. Cool.

Slice the sponge cake horizontally into two layers, of one-third and two-thirds thicknesses. Lightly oil a 9¹⁄₂in. spring-form pan and line the base with waxed paper. Drop the thicker cake layer into the pan and brush all over with the flavored syrup.

Sprinkle the gelatin powder on to 5tbsp. very hot, but not boiling, water in a cup and stir to dissolve. Leave to cool. The mixture should be transparent and lump-free, if it is not, place the cup in a pan of warm water and heat gently. Cool to room temperature before using.

Meanwhile, beat the farmer's cheese with the sugar, lemon curd and orange rind until well blended. Gently trickle over the gelatin liquid, beating all the time.

Set aside until the cream is on the point of setting. Using a large metal spoon, lightly fold in the soaked peel and white raisins, the liqueur, whipped cream and the pistachios.

Pour the cream cheese filling on to the sponge cake in the prepared pan and smooth it out. Carefully cut half of the remaining sponge layer into six triangular pieces and evenly space them on top of the filling to create a fan effect.

Flavor ²⁄₃ cup sweetened whipped cream with 2tbsp. of orange liqueur and pipe rosettes of cream on the cake. Decorate with candied peel and pistachios. Chill for 5-6 hours. The cake may be prepared 2-3 days ahead of time and kept in the refrigerator.

Note To make a fat-free sponge of the size needed here, lightly whisk 4 whole eggs and 100g/4oz granulated sugar in a bowl set over a pan a quarter filled with simmering water, for 5-10 minutes, until the mixture is rich and creamy. Remove from the heat and beat for another 20 minutes by hand, or 10 minutes with an electric mixer. Blend in the seeds of a 5cm/2in vanilla pod.

Fold in 100g/4oz sifted plain flour using a large metal spoon. Work in a figure-of-eight movement, avoiding stirring the mixture, which will lose all the air and make the sponge heavy and damp.

Pour the batter into a prepared spring-form pan and bake immediately in a preheated oven at 350°F for 30-35 minutes for a deep cake, 20 minutes for a shallow cake.

Farmer's Cheese Cake

Farmer's cheese, like sour cream is an important ingredient in Hungarian cooking. The airy, mousse-like filling of this cake has a lemony tang, which is enhanced by the sour-cream pastry.

Ingredients

1 cup all-purpose flour
¹⁄₃ cup butter
1tsp. granulated sugar
1 egg yolk
²⁄₃ cup sour cream

Filling
7 egg yolks
1¹⁄₃ cups granulated sugar
2tbsp. lemon rind
2 cups farmer's cheese
8 egg whites

Sift the flour into a bowl and drop in the butter, cut in pieces. Rub together to make fine crumbs. Mix in the sugar. Add the egg and sour cream and blend and knead into a firm paste. Roll into a ball, wrap in plastic wrap and chill for 30 minutes.

Divide the dough in two and roll each piece to fit a 10¹⁄₂in. spring-form pan. Line the greased base of the pan with one sheet of pastry. Make pastry leaves or flowers with any remaining scraps of dough.

Beat together the egg yolks and granulated sugar until pale and creamy and well expanded. Beat in the lemon rind and the strained cheese.

In another bowl whip up the egg whites until they are firm and well peaked. Lightly fold them into the cheese mixture using a large metal spoon and taking care not to lose any air. Pour the filling into the cake pan. Smooth gently, then lay the remaining sheet of pastry on top and press it down lightly.

Place the pastry leaves or flowers quickly on the pastry top, using a little beaten egg white. Bake immediately in the preheated oven at 325°F for 50-60 minutes.

The cake will color only slightly and rise quite high out of the pan. As it cools it will drop quite dramatically — most cheesecakes do — but it will not crack because of the pastry covering. Dredge with confectioner's sugar to serve.

Cottage Cheesecake
Serves 6-8

Ingredients

Base
½ cup soft margarine
1½ cups all-purpose flour
½ tsp. baking powder
¼ cup sugar
1 lemon

Filling
3 eggs, separated
½ cup sugar
2 cups cottage cheese
⅔ cup sour cream

Beat together all the base ingredients to form a dough. Roll out gently to line the base and sides of an 8in. pan.

Beat the egg yolks with the sugar until they are nearly white. Strain the cheese and add to the egg yolks along with the sour cream. Mix well.

Beat the egg whites until they are stiff but not dry. Gently fold into the filling mixture starting with just one spoonful and gradually adding the remainder. Pour into the pastry case.

Bake for 50 minutes at 325°F. Cool in the oven with the door slightly open. Chill before serving.

Raisin Cheesecake

Raisin Cheesecake
Serves 6-8

Ingredients

Base
1/4 cup graham crackers
3tbsp. butter
1tbsp. sugar
1tsp. cinnamon

Filling
1 1/3 cups cottage cheese
1 1/3 cups farmer's cheese
2 eggs, separated
1/4 cup sugar
1tsp. lemon rind
1/3 cup raisins
1/3 cup white raisins

Crush the graham crackers and mix with melted butter, sugar and cinnamon. Press over the base of an 8in. pan.

Strain the cottage cheese so that the lumps are as small as possible. Beat with the farmer's cheese until smooth. Mix the egg yolks with the cheese. Beat in the sugar and grated lemon rind and stir in the fruit.

Beat the egg whites until they are stiff but not dry. Gently fold into the cheese mixture. Pour the filling onto the base and bake for 40 minutes at 325°F. Cool in the oven with the door slightly open.

Pineapple Coconut Cheesecake
Serves 8

Ingredients

Base
4tbsp. butter
1tbsp. sugar
3/4 cup shredded coconut
1/2 cup ground hazelnuts

Filling
1lb. farmer's cheese
2tbsp. lemon juice
1 egg
2tbsp. sugar

Topping
3/4 cup pineapple pieces
2 1/2tsp. cornstarch
1/2 cup pineapple juice
2 1/2tsp. rum
1/2 cup water
1tbsp. shredded coconut

Melt the butter and stir into the other base ingredients.

Press over the bottom and up the sides of a greased 8in. pan. Bake for 5 minutes at 350°F.

Beat together all the filling ingredients. Pour onto the base. Bake for 20 minutes at 375°F.

Leave the cake to cool slightly before adding the topping. Arrange the pineapple pieces on top of the cake.

Combine the cornstarch, pineapple juice and rum. Heat, stirring constantly, until the glaze thickens and clears. Gently spoon the glaze over the fruit.

To serve, garnish the cheesecake by sprinkling with coconut.

Chocolate Cheesecake Cups
Serves 6

Ingredients

1lb. cream cheese
3 eggs, separated
1/2 cup sugar
2/3 cup sour cream
1tbsp. powdered gelatin
4tbsp. water
6oz. plain or milk
  chocolate, chopped

6oz. plain chocolate
6 individual Shortcrust
  Pastry shells approx. 3in.
  diameter
Chocolate Caraque

Put the cheese and egg yolks into a bowl. Add half the sugar and beat well, then stir in the sour cream.

Dissolve the gelatin in the water.

Beat the egg whites until stiff. Beat in the remaining sugar.

Stir the gelatin into the cheese mixture.

Fold the meringue and the chopped chocolate into the cheese mixture.

Pour into six individual molds and chill until set.

Melt the chocolate and spread over the underneath and outsides of the pastry cases. Put upside down over small glasses to set.

Turn out the cheesecakes and put one in each chocolate cup.

Serve decorated with chocolate caraque.

Summer Pudding
Serves 6-8

Ingredients

6-8 slices white bread
1½lb. soft fruit
½ cup sugar
2tbsp. water

Remove the crusts from the bread and cut into fingers. Cover the base and sides of a 2½pt. soufflé dish or pudding bowl, saving enough pieces of bread to make a lid for the pudding.

Put the fruit in a heavy-bottomed pan. Sprinkle with sugar and water. Cook over a very low heat until the sugar has dissolved and the fruit is soft but not mushy. The juices should be running freely.

Strain the fruit, reserving the juice. Pour two spoonfuls of juice over the bread in the base of the bowl. Spoon the fruit into the bread case. Pour over all but 6 spoonfuls of the juice.

Arrange the remaining bread fingers over the top of the fruit. Pour over the remaining juice.

Put a dish, small enough to fit inside the rim of the bowl, on top of the pudding. Press down with heavy cans or weights. Put the Summer Pudding into the refrigerator and leave for at least 8 hours.

Just before you are ready to eat the pudding, remove the weights and the dish. Put a serving dish over the pudding and turn upside down to unmold.

Serve with cream, whipped or pouring.

Sailors' Delight
Serves 4

Ingredients

½lb. mincemeat
4tbsp. rum
1½pts. ice cream

Gently heat the mincemeat with the rum. Spoon over the ice cream.

Baked Farina Pudding
Serves 4

Ingredients

1⅓ cup white wine
1¼ cups water
½ lemon
1 orange
pinch salt
¾ cup farina
½ cup sugar
3 eggs, separated

Combine the wine, water, finely grated rinds of the lemon and orange, and the salt. Bring to the boil.

Add the farina to the pan, stirring constantly. Reduce the heat and simmer gently for approximately 5 minutes, or until the mixture is thick and smooth.

Stir the sugar and juice of the orange into the farina, and continue to cook, stirring, until the pudding boils again.

Remove the pan from the heat and stir in 2 egg yolks. Save the remaining yolk to use for another recipe.

Beat the egg whites until they are stiff but not dry. Fold gently into the farina, starting with just one spoonful and gradually adding the remainder.

Pour the pudding into one large or several small, wetted molds.

Serve with fresh or poached fruit or with a warm or cold fruit purée.

Variation For a hot farina pudding, put the mold in a roasting pan containing enough hot water to come halfway up the side of dish. Cover the mold loosely with foil. Bake for 50-60 minutes at 325°F until the pudding has set. Serve from the dish or unmolded.

Rice Flour Dessert
Serves 6-8

The unusual flavor of this dessert comes in part from the rose water, which can be bought at some drug stores and specialty shops

Ingredients

3tbsp. sesame oil
3tbsp. vegetable oil
1¼ cups rice flour
4 cups milk
2tbsp. rose water
1tbsp. almond extract
½ cup granulated sugar
1tsp. ground cardamom
   seeds

good pinch ground
   cinnamon
4-5tbsp. confectioner's
   sugar
1 cup pistachio nuts,
   chopped

Heat the sesame and vegetable oils together in a saucepan over a moderate heat. Stir in the rice flour and cook until a light golden brown.

Reduce the heat to low and stir in the milk. Continue stirring until the milk and flour mixture is smooth. Add the rose water, almond extract, sugar, cardamom and cinnamon. Cook the mixture over a low heat, stirring constantly, until it thickens. Add the confectioner's sugar and stir until it dissolves.

Pour the mixture into a lightly greased shallow rectangular pan, sprinkle the top with the pistachio nuts, and allow it to cool and become firm.

Serve cut into rectangles or squares.

Marshmallow Crunch
Serves 4

Ingredients

8 small meringues
3 cups ice cream
8 small marshmallows

2 cups Chocolate or Fruit
   Sauce

Charlotte Louise

Crush the meringues coarsely and arrange at the bottom of each serving dish. Top with two scoops of ice cream. Add the marshmallows and spoon over the sauce.

As an alternative, the meringues can be left whole and sandwiched together with the ice cream. The marshmallows and sauce are arranged on top. If you like your sundaes gooey, melt the marshmallows!

Charlotte Louise
Serves 8

Ingredients

18-20 ladies fingers
¾ cup sweet butter
5tbsp. sugar
6oz. plain chocolate
1 cup ground almonds
1¼ cups heavy cream

½tsp. almond extract
Decoration
whipped cream
pistachio nuts
crystalized violets or roses
satin ribbon

Cut a round of waxed paper to fit the base of an 8 or 9in. Charlotte mold. Oil it lightly and put in the mold. Line the sides of the mold with the ladies fingers.

Cream the butter and sugar together until light and fluffy.

Melt the chocolate. Cool slightly, then beat into the butter, together with the ground almonds.

Whip the cream until thick, but not stiff. Add the almond extract. Fold into the chocolate mixture and mix well.

Spoon the mixture into the lined mold. Press in firmly. Chill.

Turn the Charlotte onto a serving plate. Remove the paper and pipe with whipped cream. Decorate with pistachio nuts and violets. Tie a satin ribbon round it for the finishing touch.

Crème Caramel
Serves 6

Ingredients

4tbsp. fruit sugar (fructose)
  or granulated sugar
4tbsp. water

Custard
2½ cups milk
few drops vanilla extract
4 eggs
3tbsp. fruit sugar (fructose)
  or granulated sugar

For the caramel, put the sugar and the water in a heavy saucepan and stir over a low heat until the sugar has dissolved. Bring to a boil and boil until the syrup is golden. Pour the caramel into 6 individual molds (or one large one) and whirl it around so that it coats the bottom and sides.

Bring the milk and vanilla extract to a boil in a saucepan. Remove from the heat.

Beat the eggs and sugar together in a bowl. Gradually add the hot milk, stirring all the while.

Strain or ladle the custard into the molds. Stand them in a roasting pan half-filled with hot water and bake for 45 minutes at 350°F until set.

Allow to cool and then chill. Don't turn out the Crème Caramel until you are ready to serve or it will lose its gloss.

Payodhi
Baked Yogurt

Ingredients

1¾ cups evaporated milk
1¾ cups condensed milk
2¼ cups yogurt

1tbsp. pistachio nuts,
  skinned and chopped

Preheat oven to 225°C.

Beat the evaporated milk, condensed milk and yogurt together for 1 minute. Pour into an ovenproof dish and place in the preheated oven.

Turn the oven off after 6 minutes and leave the dish in the oven overnight. Chill. Serve garnished with chopped pistachio nuts.

Shrikhand
Yogurt with Saffron

Ingredients

2½ cups yogurt
¼tsp. saffron
1tbsp. warm milk

½ cup granulated sugar
2tbsp. pistachio nuts,
  skinned and chopped

Put the yogurt in a cheesecloth bag and hang it up for 4-5 hours to get rid of the excess water.

Soak the saffron in the milk for 30 minutes.

Beat together the drained yogurt, sugar and saffron milk till smooth and creamy. Put in a dish and garnish with the nuts. Chill until set. Any seasonal fruit may be added while beating.

Vanilla Cream

Vanilla Cream

Ingredients

3 eggs	¼ cup water
4tbsp. Vanilla Sugar	2tsp. vanilla extract
1 cup milk	1 cup heavy cream
1tbsp. gelatin	

Beat the eggs and sugar until pale and frothy. Heat the milk to almost boiling point and pour over the egg mixture.

Strain the mixture back into the saucepan. Simmer over a very low heat or in a heavy saucepan until thick, stirring all the time. Allow to cool.

Soak the gelatin in water for 5 minutes, then heat to dissolve. Stir the vanilla extract into the cooled custard, followed by the gelatin.

Whip the cream and fold into the mixture before it sets. Pour into a dish and refrigerate.

Charlotte Russe
Serves 8

The great French chef Antoine Carême created this celebrated dessert after visiting Russia in the mid-nineteenth century.

Ingredients

16 ladyfingers, halved lengthwise	1 cup sour cream
4 egg yolks	1 cup heavy cream, chilled
½ cup sugar	1tbsp. Triple Sec liqueur
1 cup milk	1¼lb. frozen raspberries, thawed and drained
1tbsp. pure vanilla extract	3tbsp. granulated sugar
2tbsp. unflavored gelatin, dissolved in ¼ cup cold water	2tbsp. blackberry brandy

Set 16 ladyfinger halves aside. Take the remaining ladyfingers and cut diagonal slices from each side of one end, so that one end of each is still curved and the other comes to a point.

In a pudding mould, arrange the trimmed ladyfinger halves at the bottom so that their points touch and their diagonal edges are side by side. The pattern on the bottom of the pudding mould should resemble a doily with beveled edges.

Place the remaining untrimmed ladyfinger halves against the side of the mould, standing them straight up. Try not to leave any gaps between the untrimmed ladyfinger halves.

In a mixing bowl, beat the egg yolks. Gradually beat in the sugar. Continue beating until the sugar is fully incorporated into the egg yolks.

Warm the milk and vanilla extract in a small saucepan over a low heat. When the milk starts to bubble, beat it into the egg mixture.

Pour the egg and milk mixture back into the saucepan. Cook over a low heat, stirring all the time, until the mixture becomes a thick custard. Do not let the mixture boil.

Stir in the dissolved gelatin. When the mixture has an even consistency throughout, strain it through a fine strainer into a mixing bowl.

In another bowl, whip the sour cream and heavy cream together until the mixture begins to stiffen.

Place the bowl containing the custard mixture inside a larger bowl. Put ice cubes and cold water into the larger bowl until it comes halfway up the sides of the custard bowl. Stir the custard with a metal spoon until it begins to thicken noticeably.

Fold the whipped cream mixture into the custard, breaking up any lumps with a whisk or fork. Stir in the Triple Sec liqueur.

Pour the contents of the custard bowl into the mould lined with ladyfingers. Chill for 5-6 hours before serving.

Blend the strained raspberries, granulated sugar and blackberry brandy together in a small bowl. Spoon the sauce over slices of the Charlotte Russe just before serving.

Crème Brûlée
Serves 6

Ingredients

3 cups light cream	1½tbsp. vanilla extract
6 egg yolks	2tbsp. pale brown
3tbsp. white sugar	granulated sugar

Put the cream in a bowl over a pan of simmering water. Beat the egg yolks, add the sugar and extract, and gently stir into the warmed cream. Continue cooking, stirring all the time, until the sauce is thick enough to coat the back of the wooden spoon.

Strain the mixture through a fine strainer into either a large soufflé dish or individual custard dishes.

Put the dish or dishes into a large shallow pan and place on the middle rack of the oven. Fill the pan with hot water until it reaches the level of the custard in the serving dishes. Bake for 35-45 minutes depending on size at 300°F until the center of the custard is firm. Cool, cover and chill

Sprinkle the brown granulated sugar on top of the chilled custard. Put under a preheated hot broiler, as close to the heat as possible, until the sugar has caramelized. Watch closely.

Chill for 2-3 hours before serving.

Variation For Coffee Brûlée, add 4tbsp. instant powdered coffee and 2tbsp. coffee liqueur to the egg yolks and sugar instead of the vanilla extract.

Strawberry Peach Sherbet
Serves 6-8

Ingredients

4 large peaches	4tbsp. fresh lemon juice
1lb. fresh strawberries, chopped	1 cup superfine sugar

Add the peaches to boiling water and cook for 2 minutes.

Remove the peaches from the pot and drain well. When the peaches are cool enough to handle, remove the skins and stones. Mash the peaches into a pulp in a large mixing bowl.

Purée the peach pulp, strawberries and lemon juice in a liquidizer or food processor.

Stir the sugar into the fruit mixture and purée for another 10-15 seconds. Pour the mixture into a large, shallow dish and freeze until hard. Remove the dish from the freezer 1 hour before serving and let the sherbet soften in the refrigerator.

Yorkshire Curd Tart

Ingredients

1 portion Sweet Shortcrust Pastry for an 8½in. loose-based flan dish	2 eggs, separated
	⅔ cup raisins
½ cup butter	pinch salt
¼ cup granulated sugar	½tsp. ground nutmeg
1tsp. lemon rind	1tbsp. ground almond or toasted breadcrumbs
1½ cups farmer's cheese, pressed through a strainer	

Butter the pan and line with the pastry; prick all over with a fork. Chill.

Cream the butter and sugar until light and fluffy, mix in the lemon rind, farmer's cheese, egg yolks and raisins. Add the salt and nutmeg.

Beat the egg whites separately until they are firm and lightly fold them into the mixture. Scatter the almonds or breadcrumbs over the pastry base. Pour the cheese filling into the pastry case, and bake at 400°F for 30 minutes, reducing the temperature after the first 15 minutes to 325°F until golden and the pastry is brown. Leave to cool on a wire rack in the pan.

The tart will freeze well for up to 2 months.

Pâté à Choux
Choux Pastry
Makes 22 buns

Choux pastry is thought to have originated in the mid-sixteenth century, and it was especially popular made in deep-fried fritter or beignet form.

The preparation of choux pastry takes very little time and is quite unlike any other baking technique. The basic ingredients of butter, flour and water are cooked together to make a type of white sauce, or roux, before the eggs are beaten in. During baking the paste expands and puffs into a crisp hollow shell, almost three times it original size.

Uncooked choux pastry freezes very well for up to 2 months. For small buns pipe or spoon the mixture on to waxed paper and open-freeze before packing in air-tight bags. Bake from the freezer 5 minutes longer than the normal time.

Ingredients

4½oz strong all-purpose flour, sifted	4 eggs
2tsp. granulated sugar	1tsp. brandy, rum or orange-flavored water (optional)
⅔ cup water	
⅔ cup milk	
⅔cup lightly salted butter, diced	

Sift the flour and sugar two or three times, finally on to a sheet of waxed paper. Set aside. Measure the water and milk into a deep pan, and drop in the butter pieces.

Set the pan over heat and warm gently until all the butter has melted, then raise the temperature and bring the liquid to a rolling boil. Draw the pan aside and shoot in the flour mixture all at once. Beat vigorously with a wooden spoon and quickly replace the pan on a low heat.

Continue beating and cook the paste for just a few seconds more so that the flour is properly combined. The paste should have an ungrained, smooth appearance and roll cleanly off the bottom and sides of the pan into a ball (a floury film is left on the base of the pan). Avoid over-cooking the paste or the finished buns will be heavy.

The mixture may now be beaten in the bowl of an electric mixer as the eggs are added. Care must be taken here as too much egg can spoil the paste, making it too runny, so add a little at a time.

Lightly whisk the eggs together in a separate bowl, and pour about a quarter on the flour paste, beat vigorously until well combined; add more egg and beat again. Continue adding egg and beating, until the paste is quite firm but elastic — it will drop from a spoon reluctantly when jerked slightly. You may not need quite all of the egg, although if the weather conditions are dry, you may need a little more. Beat the paste well until it is shiny and smooth; finally add the spirit or flour water.

The paste is now ready for use and may be kept for an hour or two if covered with a damp cloth.

Choux pastry must be cooked until all the surfaces are completely browned, otherwise it will collapse and go soggy as it cools. It is, however, inclined to burn rather easily underneath and needs additional protection in the oven. Either use a second large baking sheet, warmed in the oven beforehand, or line the one that you are using with a thick layer of aluminum foil.

To bake choux pastry buns hold a large, flat cookie sheet under cold running water for a few seconds to chill it; shake off the excess water but leave it damp. Place teaspoonfuls of the mixture, about 1in. high and 2in. apart on the cookie sheet. Remember that they expand to two or three times their size during baking. Lightly brush a little beaten egg on each one and scatter over a pinch of granulated sugar to give sparkle; chopped or flaked almonds are also nice. Bake in the preheated oven at 400°F.

Choux buns take about 20 minutes to cook. Never open the oven door until at least 15 minutes have elapsed, as the delicate structure will collapse immediately if it is not cooked sufficiently.

The baked pastries will be light, hollow and golden brown. Lift the tray out of the oven and transfer the buns to a wire rack. Pierce each one with a skewer or knife to release the steam inside and leave them to cool.

Choux pastries are best eaten on the day they are baked, but they can be stored for a day or two in an air-tight tin, then reheated in a low oven for about 10 minutes to crisp them up again. They should be filled no more than 1 hour before serving.

Rice and Raisin Pudding
Serves 8

Ingredients

1 cup short-grain rice	1tsp. ground cinnamon
1 cup water	4 cups milk
pinch salt	2 eggs
½ cup sugar	⅓ cup raisins

Wash the rice in running water until the water is clear. Put it in a bowl with enough hot water to cover and leave to soak for 15 minutes.

Drain the rice and put in a heavy-bottomed pan with the water and salt. Cover the pan, bring to a boil and then cook on a low heat until the water has been absorbed.

Stir most of the sugar and half of the cinnamon into the cooked rice. Add the milk and mix well. Cook, uncovered, over a low heat until most of milk has been absorbed. Stir occasionally.

Lightly beat the eggs and mix into the rice. Continue to cook for 5 minutes.

Stir in the raisins and turn the rice pudding into a serving dish. Combine the remaining cinnamon with the remaining sugar and sprinkle over the pudding.

Cool and chill before serving, perhaps with fresh raspberries and single cream.

Cream Puffs
Makes 24

Ingredients

¾ cup all-purpose flour	**Crème Pâtisserie**
pinch salt	3tbsp. sugar
¼ cup butter	2tsp. cornstarch
⅔ cup water	1tbsp. all-purpose flour
2 eggs	2 eggs
	½pt milk

Sift the flour and salt.

Heat the butter and water together until the butter has melted and the water is just about to boil.

Add the flour and stir with a wooden spoon until the mixture forms a ball which leaves the sides of the pan clean. Remove from the heat and leave to cool for 2-3 minutes.

Lightly beat the eggs and stir into the dough. Mix well. It should be just firm enough to hold its shape.

Drop small spoonfuls of dough onto a greased cookie sheet and bake for 15 minutes at 425°F until well risen and golden brown. Transfer to a wire rack to cool.

Combine the sugar, cornstarch and flour. Add one whole egg plus the yolk of the second and mix well.

Heat the milk until it is just about to boil. Pour over the egg mixture and blend well. Return to the pan and cook over a low heat, stirring constantly, until thick.

Leave to cool, stirring occasionally, to prevent a skin forming. To assemble the cream puffs, cut the choux buns nearly in half and place a spoonful of filling in each.

To serve, sprinkle with confectioner's sugar or spread with chocolate frosting. Serve immediately.

Variation To make eclairs, pipe the choux pastry onto cookie sheets in 3in. lengths. Bake for 20 minutes then cool and fill as above.

Meringue Torte
Serves 8-10

Ingredients

4 egg whites	1 cup heavy cream
1 cup sugar	16 glazed pecans or
3 cups ice cream	walnut halves

Beat the egg whites until they are stiff. Add the sugar, a spoonful at a time, and continue whisking until the meringue is stiff again. Spoon carefully into a piping bag.

Line two flat cookie sheets with waxed paper. Trace a 9in. circle on each. On one sheet, pipe the meringue in rings to fill the entire circle. Smooth the surface with a metal spatula.

On the second sheet, pipe the meringue in one ring around the inside edge of the circle and then make three parallel lines in each direction to form a lattice.

Bake the meringues in a preheated oven for 30 minutes at 300°F. Transfer to a wire cooling rack. When the meringues are completely cold, carefully peel off the lining paper. If you are not using them immediately, store in an airtight container.

Several hours before serving the torte, prepare the ice cream and freeze in a 9in. cake pan. If the ice cream is already made, soften slightly, press into a cake and re-freeze until firm.

To assemble the torte, place the meringue circle on a serving dish. Top with a layer of ice cream or several layers of different kinds of ice cream.

Beat the cream until it is stiff and pile on top of the ice cream. Carefully place the lattice meringue on top of the whipped cream. Press down gently so that the cream oozes through the gaps. Place a nut in each gap and serve immediately.

Variation Add instant coffee, unsweetened cocoa or ground nuts to the unbaked meringue mixture.

To make a vacherin, make one solid layer of meringue only and pipe the remaining mixture onto individual cookie sheets to make several rings. When they have been baked, place the solid layer at the bottom and pile the rings on top of each other to make a basket.

Make a Swiss meringue and pipe between the layers to seal them and then in vertical lines all around the basket, topping it with a row of rosettes. Bake for 1½ hours until firm. Cool and store until ready for use, then fill with ice cream and top with fresh fruit. Garnish with a fruit sauce.

Baklava
Serves 8-12

Ingredients

1 cup sugar	24 sheets filo pastry
⅔ cup water	(bought)
1 tbsp. lemon juice	2 cups chopped nuts
1 cup butter, melted	

Place the sugar, water and lemon juice in a heavy-bottomed pan. Heat, stirring constantly, until the sugar has dissolved. Increase the heat and boil the syrup for 5 minutes. Leave to cool.

Brush melted butter over the base and sides of a 9×11in. roasting pan.

Arrange a layer of pastry over the base of the pan, overlapping to cover the entire surface. Brush with butter and sprinkle with nuts.

Cover with another layer of pastry and repeat the process until you have used all the nuts and pastry. Brush each layer of pastry well with the butter and finish with a layer of pastry.

Cut into diamond-shaped pieces. Bake for 30 minutes at 350°F and then increase to 450°F for another 15 minutes or until golden. Pour over the syrup and leave to cool before serving.

Tortoni
Serves 8

Ingredients

5 eggs, separated
5tbsp. sugar
2½ cups heavy cream

2½ cups macaroon or
    ratafia crumbs
5tbsp. Marsala or sweet
    sherry

Beat the egg yolks with the sugar until thick and almost white.

Beat the cream until it is just starting to thicken. Stir into the eggs. Stir in ¾ of the crumbs and the wine.

Beat the egg whites until they are stiff but not dry. Gently fold one spoonful into the cream mixture then gradually add the remainder.

Pour the cream into a soufflé dish or individual serving dishes and freeze, stirring occasionally. Remove 15 minutes before serving. Gently sprinkle the remaining crumbs over the surface and press onto the top.

Millefeuilles

One thousand leaves is the literal translation, and it is almost true! For by the time the puff pastry has been rolled, folded and turned half a dozen times, there are more than 700 layers of trapped air and butter dough. This feather-like assemblage needs only the simplest embellishment, and it makes a sumptuous and impressive after-dinner dessert.

Ingredients

1lb. Puff Pastry chilled (or
    use a ready-made fresh
    or frozen pastry)

Roll out the pastry on a chilled, floured surface to ⅛in. thick, and use a sharp knife to cut it into three equal rectangles, 7×12in. Leave to chill for at least 1 hour, or overnight if possible.

Heat the oven to 425°F. Chill a cookie sheet under running cold water and shake off the excess moisture. Transfer one of the pastries to the wet tray, prick all over with a fork to prevent it from puffing too much and bake it in the hot oven for 20 minutes until well puffed and golden. Cool on a wire rack. Prepare and bake the other pastries in the same way.

The uncooked, prepared pastry rectangles may be frozen for up to 2 months. Bake from frozen and allow 5 minutes more cooking time.

Basic Yogurt

Ingredients

2pt. milk
2tbsp. unflavored
    commercial yogurt at
    room temperature

Yogurt can be made in any sterile container with a tightly fitting lid inside any sort of incubator, such as an oven with the pilot light on or a styrofoam box, but because the secret of successful yogurt-making is a constant lukewarm temperature, it is best to use a special yogurt maker. Don't put incubating yogurt near a heat source regulated by a thermostat that switches on and off. Use 2tbsp. of the home-made yogurt to start the next batch. The cost of making yogurt at home is minimal and the method is easy.

Scald the milk. Heat it until it is ready to boil. Just before boiling point, remove the pan from the heat and allow to cool until lukewarm. Test by dripping a little milk on your wrist. It should feel warm, not hot.

Put the yogurt in the chosen container and stir in a little milk until smooth. Now stir in the remaining milk.

Cover and place container in the incubator. Be careful not to disturb the yogurt for about 4 hours. When the consistency is right, chill in the fridge to set before using.

Preparing Pineapple

The best pineapples available in Europe or North America are not picked until ripe, when they are flown to their destination. They have the central core of leaves intact. Pineapples that ripen on a long sea voyage have their central leaves removed to prevent sprouting during storage.

1 Cut off the top and bottom with a sharp knife. Cut these end slices thickly so what is left is not barrel-shaped but cylindrical.

2 Cut round inside the skin, working first from one end, then the other, until you can push the fruit out in one piece. Try to cut as close to the skin as possible.

3 Slice the fruit and remove the central core with an apple corer if at all woody.

To Pit and Peel Avocado

1 Split the avocado and carefully twist to separate the two halves. Pierce the avocado pit with a sharp knife and twist to extract it.

2 Turn each half of the avocado face down and cut just through the skin from top to tail.

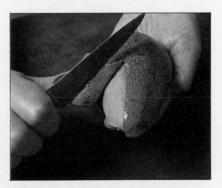

3 Carefully peel back the skin using the knife blade. Gripped firmly with the thumb, the skin should come away without tearing.

Hot Desserts

Baked Alaska
Serves 6-8

Ingredients

2pt. vanilla or chocolate ice cream	*approx ½lb. fruit (strawberries, bananas, raspberries, or cherries, or a mixture)*
3 eggs	
5tbsp. sugar	
¾ cup all-purpose flour	*4tbsp. Marsala or sweet sherry*
2tbsp. unsweetened cocoa powder	*4 egg whites*
	1 cup sugar

Pack the ice cream into a 1-lb. loaf tin lined with waxed paper or foil. Freeze overnight.

Put the eggs and sugar into a bowl and beat until thick and creamy, and the beat leaves a trail.

Sift the flour and cocoa together and fold gently into the mixture.

Turn into a greased and lined 9-in. tin. Bake at 400°F for 12-15 minutes. Cook and remove paper.

Prepare the fruit by slicing and removing stones if necessary. Put into a bowl with the Marsala or sherry.

Beat the egg whites until stiff. Beat in the sugar a little at a time. Spoon the meringue into a piping bag fitted with a large star nozzle.

Trim the edges of the sponge, then cut 1-in. strips from each of two sides of the cake to make an oblong slightly larger than the ice cream block.

Put sponge on an ovenproof serving dish. Spoon the fruit and juices over the sponge.

Remove the ice cream from the freezer and turn it onto the sponge. Remove the paper or foil.

Quickly pipe the meringue decoratively over the ice cream, covering it completely.

Bake at 450°F for 3-5 minutes until lightly browned. Serve immediately.

Baked Apples with Almonds
Serves 4

Ingredients

4 large tart apples	*1tbsp. maple syrup*
2tbsp. white raisins	*2tbsp. butter*
1tsp. cinnamon	*4 slices brown bread*
1tbsp. ground almonds	*4 glacé cherries*
2tsp. lemon juice	*24 almond flakes*

Wash the apples and remove the cores, leaving the apples whole. Slit the skins shallowly around the equator to prevent splitting when cooking.

Mix the white raisins, cinnamon, ground almonds, lemon juice and maple syrup together in a bowl.

Stuff the mixture into the centre of each apple, top with a knob of butter. Cook in the oven at 400°F for 40-60 minutes, depending on size.

Toast the brown bread. Arrange on 4 plates with an apple each. Decorate the tops with a glacé cherry and flaked almonds and serve warm. The toast soaks up all the delicious juice.

Baked Bananas
Serves 4

Ingredients

4 bananas, peeled	4tsp. dark brown sugar
4tsp. butter	4tsp. rum

Put each banana on a large square of foil. Dot with butter and sprinkle with sugar and rum

Fold the foil not too tightly, but seal it well. Bake at 400°F for 15 minutes.

Unwrap each banana and arrange on a serving dish. Top with a scoop of ice cream.

Variation Bake or barbecue the bananas in their skins and let everyone pour on their own rum.

Alternatively, scatter chocolate chips over them before wrapping in foil.

Baked Pineapple Rings
Serves 8

Ingredients

1 large pineapple, sliced in 8 rings	4tbsp. apricot jam
	2tbsp. Kirsch (optional)

Arrange the pineapple rings on a large cookie sheet. Spread with apricot jam and sprinkle over the Kirsch.

Bake for 5-10 minutes at 400°F.

Variation As with Baked Bananas, pineapple rings can be cooked to perfection on a barbecue. In this case, spread both sides of the pineapple with jam and barbecue for 3-4 minutes on each side.

Hot Farmer's Cheesecake
Serves 6

This traditional cake has a yeasty pastry base and is baked in a rectangular pan. Because the cheese layer is thin, the flavor is much more concentrated than the familiar deep cheesecakes.

Ingredients

Yeast Dough for 2 rectangular cake pans 8×12×1½in.	2 eggs
	pinch salt
	1tsp. lemon zest
½ cup heavy cream	½ cup raisins
¼ cup granulated sugar	2tbsp. melted butter, cooled
2 generous cups farmer's cheese, strained	

Prepare the dough and line the pans. Leave to rise a second time while you prepare the filling.

Mix the filling by hand. Stir the cream and granulated sugar into the cheese. Mix in the lightly beaten eggs one at a time, the salt and lemon zest, and, lastly the raisins.

Divide the filling evenly between the two pans and smooth out. Trickle the butter over both surfaces and bake in the heated oven at 400°F till risen and golden, about 35 minutes. Cut in slices to serve.

This will keep fresh for 2 days. Freeze while still slightly warm, wrapped in aluminum foil.

Crunchy Apple Crumble
Serves 4

Ingredients

1½lb. apples, peeled, quartered, cored and sliced	2-4tbsp. sugar
	lemon juice
	2½ cups crunchy muesli
⅔ cup water	2tbsp. butter

Poach the apples in a pan with the water, sugar and lemon juice to taste until just tender. Drain.

Arrange half the cooked apple slices in the bottom of the baking dish.

Sprinkle on a layer of crunchy muesli, arrange the remaining apples on top and cover with the muesli.

Dot with butter and bake at 350°F for 25 minutes.

Fruit Crumble
Serves 4

Ingredients

1½lb. stewed, fresh or poached fruit	5tbsp. margarine or butter
1¾ cups wholewheat flour	2tsp. sugar
	1tsp. bran

Arrange the fruit in the pie dish.

Sprinkle the flour into a bowl, rub the fat into the flour until the mixture resembles fine breadcrumbs. Add the sugar and bran, mixing well.

Sprinkle on top of the fruit and bake at 400°F until golden brown, about 30 minutes.

Cinnamon Chocolate Pain Perdu
Serves 4-6

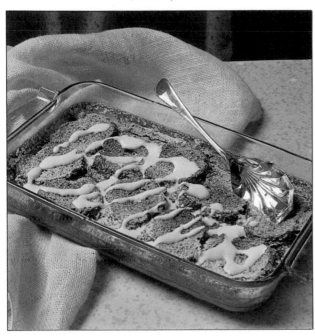

Ingredients

5-6tbsp. butter	2 egg yolks
12-14 slices French bread	1tsp. ground cinnamon
6oz. bar plain chocolate	¼ cup sugar
2½ cups milk	confectioner's or powdered
2 eggs	sugar

Butter the slices of bread on both sides. Arrange on a cookie sheet and bake in the oven at 375°F for about 5 minutes or until lightly golden. Turn over and bake on the other side until golden.

Melt the chocolate.

Bring the milk almost to boiling point. Remove from the heat and beat into the chocolate.

Beat together the eggs, egg yolks, cinnamon and sugar. Pour on the chocolate milk and beat well.

Arrange the baked French bread in a large shallow baking dish. Strain the chocolate custard over the bread.

Put the dish into a roasting pan and pour in boiling water to come half-way up the side of the baking dish.

Cook in the oven for 30-40 minutes until lightly set.

Dredge with confectioner's or powdered sugar and serve hot or warm with cream.

Banana Custard
Serves 6

Ingredients

6 ripe bananas	2 cups fresh breadcrumbs
¾ cup granulated pale brown sugar	4 eggs
	3 cups milk
1tsp. freshly grated nutmeg	
1tbsp. lime juice	

Peel and mash the bananas, add half the sugar, nutmeg and lime juice and mix well.

Put the mixture in a buttered dish and top with the breadcrumbs.

Beat the eggs and add the remaining sugar, beating well.

Warm the milk and pour into the egg mixture, stirring all the time. Pour over the banana and crumbs and sprinkle nutmeg on top.

Bake in the oven at 350°F until the custard is set and the top golden brown, approximately 35 minutes.

Prune and Noodle Custard
Serves 4-6

Ingredients

1¼ cups boiling water	3 eggs
1 cup dried prunes, pitted	1¼ cups milk
1⅔ cups wholewheat macaroni	2tbsp. honey
	1tsp. vanilla extract
few drops oil	pinch nutmeg

Pour the boiling water over the prunes and leave to plump up overnight.

Cook the macaroni in boiling salted water with the oil, until tender.

In a bowl, beat together the eggs, milk, honey and vanilla with a fork.

Grease an ovenproof casserole and mix the prunes and noodles together in it. Pour over the custard and sprinkle the top with nutmeg.

Bake for half an hour in a preheated oven at 375°F and serve hot. This dish is also good chilled.

Blueberry Buckwheat Pancakes
Serves 4

Ingredients

5tbsp. wholewheat flour
5tbsp. buckwheat flour
pinch salt
1 egg
²⁄₃ cup milk
1tbsp. melted butter

Filling
1lb. blueberries
4tbsp. honey
whipped cream

To make the pancake batter, sift the flour and salt into a bowl. Make a well in the middle of it and add the egg.

Gradually beat in the milk. When half of the milk has been added, beat in the melted butter. Continue beating in the milk until you have a thin batter. Allow the batter to stand for half an hour.

Meanwhile, prepare the filling. Wash and pick over the blueberries. Put them in a heavy-bottomed pan over a very low flame. It is best to add no water at all. When the fruit is submerged in its own juice, add the honey and stir until dissolved. The syrup should be thick and fruity.

To cook the pancakes, oil a heavy-bottomed pan 7in. in diameter. When it is very hot, add 2tbsp. of the batter. Tilt the pan so that the batter covers the base. Cook until the pancake is beginning to brown on the underside and then turn over and cook the other side. You may have to throw the first pancake away, as it will absorb the excess oil in the pan.

Continue making the pancakes, keeping them warm, until all the batter has been used up. Divide the filling between them and roll the pancakes into cigar shapes.

Serve warm, each pancake topped with a dollop of whipped cream.

Sweet Rice Fritters
Makes 25

Ingredients

½ cup long grain rice
2 eggs, beaten
¼ cup granulated sugar
few drops vanilla extract
4tbsp. all-purpose flour
1tbsp. baking powder

salt
pinch ground cinnamon
¾ cup shredded coconut
oil for deep frying
confectioner's sugar for dredging

Cook the rice and cool. Turn it into a bowl, add the beaten eggs, sugar and flavoring. Mix well. Sift in the flour, baking powder, salt and cinnamon with the coconut. Mix thoroughly.

Drop tsps of the mixture into hot oil and cook until golden brown. Cook three or four fritters at a time, draining them on kitchen towels.

Dredge with confectioner's sugar and serve hot.

Apple Parcels with Coffee Sauce
Serves 4

Ingredients

3½ cups all-purpose flour
pinch salt
5tbsp. sugar
¾ cup butter
2 eggs, beaten
1 banana, mashed
2 rings pineapple, finely chopped
rind of one orange
4 apples, peeled and cored

Sauce
2tbsp. butter
2tbsp. all-purpose flour
²⁄₃ cup milk
¼ cup cooled extra strong coffee
²⁄₃ cup light cream

Sift the flour, salt and ¼ cup of the sugar into a bowl. Rub in the butter until the mixture resembles fine breadcrumbs. Mix to a stiff pastry with the eggs.

Mix together the bananas, pineapple, remaining sugar and orange rind.

Put all the sauce ingredients into a saucepan, except the cream, and heat, beating all the time. When thick, remove from the heat and use a little of the sauce to moisten the fruit filling.

Roll out the pastry to a square. Cut out four circles. Put an apple in the center of each square and fill with the banana and pineapple mixture.

Brush the edges with water and completely enclose the apple, pressing the joins neatly together.

Put the apple parcels, join side down, on a cookie sheet and make a small hole in the center of each. Decorate with pastry trimmings.

Bake for 30 to 35 minutes on the center shelf at 425°F until golden.

Gently heat the coffee sauce and add the cream. Do not boil. Serve with the hot apples.

Rich Chocolate Meringue Pie
Serves 6

Ingredients
8oz. package graham
  crackers
½ cup butter
Filling
2tbsp. sugar
4tbsp. all-purpose flour
2tsp. cornstarch
2 large eggs, separated

1¼ cups milk
2tbsp. butter
4oz. plain chocolate, finely
  chopped
2tsp. rum (optional)
½ cup granulated sugar
ground cinnamon

Crush the graham crackers until they resemble fine breadcrumbs.

Melt the butter and stir into the crackers. Press the crumbs over the base and sides of an 8-in. ovenproof pie dish.

Blend together the sugar, flour, cornstarch, egg yolks and a little of the milk. Heat the remaining milk.

Stir the hot milk on to the flour mixture and beat well. Return the mixture to the pan. Heat gently, stirring until the mixture thickens.

Stir in the butter, chocolate and rum if used. Stir until smooth. Pour into the graham cracker crumb pie shell. Chill.

About ½ hour before serving, making the meringue topping. Beat the egg whites until stiff. Beat in half the sugar, a teaspoonful at a time. Add the remaining sugar and beat well.

Spread the meringue over the chocolate pie. Swirl decoratively with a teaspoon.

Bake in the oven at 400°F for 5-7 minutes, until the meringue is golden brown.

Sprinkle with a little ground cinnamon, and serve hot or warm.

Lemon Meringue Pie
Serves 4-6

Ingredients
zest and juice of 3 lemons
¾ cup granulated sugar
5tbsp. sweet butter,
  softened and cubed
2 large eggs

8½in. square Sweet
  Shortcrust Pastry baked
  blind
Meringue
2 egg whites
½ cup granulated sugar

Using a wooden spoon, crush the lemon zest and sugar in a flameproof bowl. Strain in the lemon juice and add the butter cubes. Set the bowl over a pan of simmering water and leave the butter to melt and the sugar to dissolve.

Meanwhile beat the eggs in a separate bowl until frothy and strain them into the lemon mixture. Blend all the ingredients carefully and cook slowly, stirring often, until the mixture thickens to a creamy consistency. Draw off the heat, lightly rub a little butter over the surface to prevent a skin forming and set aside to cool.

Pour the lemon curd into the cooled pastry shell and level out. Bake pie at 350°F for 10 minutes to set the filling.

Make the meringue. Lift the pie out of the oven and reduce the temperature. Quickly spoon the meringue onto the lemon filling and dredge with granulated sugar. Replace the pie in the oven and bake for about 45 minutes at 300°F until the meringue peaks are crisp and have turned a golden color.

Serve warm or cold.

Matzo Omelet
Serves 8

Ingredients
8 plain matzos
12 eggs, beaten
½tsp. salt
¼ cup pine nuts
5tbsp. white raisins

finely grated rind of 1
  lemon
2tbsp. butter
½ cup sugar
1½tsp. ground cinnamon

Soak the matzos in water for 3-5 minutes or until soft. Drain well.

In a large mixing bowl, combine the softened matzos, eggs, salt, pine nuts, white raisins and lemon rind. Mix well.

Heat the butter in a large heavy skillet over a low heat. Pour in the omelet mixture and cover.

Cook for 5 minutes or until the omelet is just set. Sprinkle with the sugar and cinnamon.

Fold the omelet in half and serve immediately.

Sweet Potato Pie
Serves 4-6

This recipe is from the Caribbean. Yams will work just as well.

Ingredients
2lb. sweet potatoes, peeled
  and thickly sliced
1 egg, beaten
3tbsp. margarine
¾ cup dark soft brown
  sugar

1 level tsp. salt
1tsp. ground cinnamon or
  cinnamon quill, crushed

Boil the peeled sweet potatoes in lightly salted water until cooked through.

Add the beaten egg and stir well while mixing in all the other ingredients.

Spoon the mixture into a greased shallow baking pan and bake at 350°F for an hour.

Cut into squares and serve warm.

Apple Sponge Pudding
Serves 4-6

Ingredients

½ cup granulated sugar
½ cup butter, softened
2 eggs
2tbsp. milk
1½ cups plain flour
1tsp. baking powder
1lb. tart apples cut into
   ¼-in. slices
2tbsp. granulated sugar for
   dredging

Beat the sugar and butter until pale and fluffy. Beat in the eggs one at a time and the milk and blend well. Sift the flour with the baking powder to aerate well, then combine lightly with the main mixture without over-beating.

Put the mixture into an 8-in. spring-form pan greased and lined with silicone paper, and smooth the top. Press the prepared apples into the surface of the mixture in an even pattern.

Bake in a preheated oven at 350°F until well risen and golden, about an hour. Test for readiness. Lift the pan out of the oven and dredge the surface with granulated sugar.

Remove the cake from the tin, peel off the paper and serve warm or cold with whipped cream on the side.

Banana Choc-Chip Pudding
Serves 4

Ingredients

½ cup butter or margarine,
   softened
½ cup sugar
2 eggs, beaten
1½ cups self-raising flour
2tbsp. unsweetened cocoa
   powder
approx. 2tbsp. milk
1 small banana, peeled
   and chopped
½ cup chocolate chips

Sauce

1 cup soft brown sugar
2tbsp. butter
2tbsp. light corn syrup
4tbsp. light cream

Cream the butter or margarine and sugar together until light and fluffy.

Gradually add the eggs, beating well between each addition.

Sift together the flour and cocoa, and fold into the egg mixture. Add enough milk to give a soft dropping consistency. Stir the banana and chocolate chips.

Turn mixture into a greased 2pt. pudding bowl. Cover with greased waxed paper and foil, with a central pleat in each. Secure with string. Steam for about 1½ hours.

To make the sauce, put all the ingredients into a saucepan and bring to the boil, stirring.

Turn out pudding and serve with the hot sauce.

Bread Pudding
Serves 8

Ingredients

1 small loaf white bread
1 cup milk
¾ cup sugar
½ cup butter or margarine,
   softened
¾ cup evaporated milk
2tsp. vanilla extract
1tsp. mixed spice
1tsp. cinnamon or nutmeg
⅓ cup raisins
2tbsp. mixed peel

Remove the crust from the bread and cut the loaf into chunks. Pour the milk over, stir to make sure all the bread is moist and leave to soak for 20 minutes.

Cream the sugar and butter or margarine until they are light and fluffy.

Add the soaked bread, along with any milk remaining. Beat well.

Stir in the evaporated milk, vanilla and spices and fold in the raisins and mixed peel.

Pour the pudding mixture into a well greased roasting pan or baking dish and bake at 325°F for 1 hour and 10 minutes, or until firm to the touch and golden brown.

Serve warm or cold.

Brown Rice Pudding
Serves 4

Ingredients

½ cup brown rice
2 cups China tea
1 stick cinnamon
⅓ cup white raisins

1½ cups dried apricots, chopped
⅓ cup almonds
sliced fresh fruit (optional)

Wash the rice thoroughly under running water. Put it in a heavy pan with the tea and cinnamon and simmer gently for about an hour.

Prehcat the oven to 350°F. Remove the cinnamon and transfer the rice to an ovenproof dish. Stir in the remaining ingredients and bake for about 25 minutes. Serve hot or chilled, garnished, if you like, with sliced fresh fruit.

Chocolate Farina Pudding
Serves 4

Ingredients

2½ cups milk
2 tbsp. butter
2 tbsp. sugar

2 oz. chocolate, plain or milk
4 tbsp. farina

Heat the milk with the butter, sugar and chocolate until the chocolate has melted and the milk has reached boiling point.

Sprinkle in the farina and cook, stirring constantly, until the pudding thickens.

Pour into one large or several small serving dishes and eat hot or cold.

Variation For Butterscotch Pudding, use brown sugar instead of white, omit the chocolate and add 1 tbsp. light corn syrup.

For Holyrood Pudding, omit the chocolate and add 2 tsp. orange marmalade. Stir in 2 tbsp. ratafia or macaroon crumbs.

To make farina puddings particularly light, cool slightly and fold in 2 beaten egg whites. The pudding should then be baked for 30 minutes at 300°F or steamed for 1¼ hours.

Chocolate Upside-Down Pudding
Serves 6

Ingredients

½ cup granulated pale brown sugar
4 tbsp. butter, softened
4 pineapple rings, fresh or canned
6 walnut halves
2 eggs, separated

2 tbsp. butter, melted
½ cup soft brown sugar
1 cup+2 tbsp. self-raising flour
2 tbsp. unsweetened cocoa powder

Cream together the sugar and butter and spread over the base of a greased 8-in. cake pan. Arrange the pineapple rings on top, with a walnut in the center of each.

Beat together the egg yolks and melted butter until creamy.

Beat the egg whites until stiff. Fold in the sugar and egg yolks mixture.

Sift together the flour and cocoa and fold in carefully. Pour the mixture over the fruit and spread evenly. Bake at 350°F for about 30 minutes.

Carefully turn out onto a serving dish and serve with pouring custard or cream.

Coffee Bread Pudding
Serves 6

Ingredients

20 slices day-old bread (crusts removed)	5tbsp. white raisins
1¼ cups orange juice	⅓ cup candied orange peel
1¼ cups strong black coffee	⅔ cup Tia Maria
2 large eggs	1tsp. ground cinnamon
¼ cup sugar	1tsp. ground allspice
	2tbsp. butter

Soak the bread in the orange juice and coffee, then mash to a pulp.

Beat the egg yolks and add them to the mashed bread. Stir in the sugar, white raisins, orange peel, Tia Maria and spices.

Beat the egg whites until they form stiff peaks and fold into the mixture.

Butter a 3½pt. ovenproof dish, pour the mixture into it and dot with knobs of butter.

Bake for 30 minutes at 325°F until golden brown.

Indian Rice Pudding
Serves 4

Ingredients

5 cups milk	½tsp. ground cardamom seeds
6tbsp. basmati rice, washed	
2tbsp. sugar	1½tbsp. pistachio nuts, skinned and chopped
1tbsp. raisins	

Bring the milk to a boil in a large pan, stirring continuously.

Lower the heat and simmer for 20 minutes. Add the rice and sugar and continue simmering for another 35-40 minutes until the mixture has thickened and reduced to 2½ cups. During the cooking time stir occasionally to stop the milk sticking to the bottom of the pan.

Add the raisins and cardamoms and, stirring constantly, cook for a further 3-4 minutes.

Serve hot or cold, garnished with the nuts.

Magic Chocolate Pudding
Serves 4

Ingredients

1 cup+2tbsp. self-raising flour, sifted	¼ cup butter, melted
2tbsp. sugar	⅔ cup milk
2 level tbsp. unsweetened cocoa powder, sifted	few drops vanilla extract
½ cup chopped walnuts	**Sauce**
	⅔ cup soft brown sugar
	2tbsp. unsweetened cocoa powder, sifted
	scant cup boiling water

To make the sponge, put the dry ingredients into a bowl. Add the butter, milk and extract and mix to form a thick batter.

Pour the mixture into a buttered 2pt. ovenproof dish.

To make the sauce, mix together the brown sugar, cocoa and boiling water. Pour this sauce over the batter.

Bake in the oven at 350°F for about 40 minutes. During cooking the chocolate sponge rises to the top, and a chocolate fudge sauce forms underneath.

Serve hot with vanilla ice cream.

Queen of Puddings
Serves 4

Ingredients

2½ cups milk
4 tbsp. butter
4 eggs, separated
1 lemon

½ cup sugar
2 cups fresh breadcrumbs
4 tbsp. jam

Heat the milk with the butter over a gentle heat until the butter is melted.

Combine the egg yolks with the finely grated rind of the lemon and half of the sugar. Mix well.

Pour the warm milk over the yolks and mix well. Stir in the breadcrumbs.

Pour the pudding mixture into a well greased baking or pie dish. Bake at 350°F for approximately 20 minutes, or until the custard has set.

Warm the jam over a very low heat until it has melted. Spread carefully over the baked pudding.

Beat the egg whites until they are stiff but not dry. Gently fold in the remaining sugar. Spoon or pipe the meringue over the pudding. Be sure that all the edges are well sealed.

Return the pudding to the oven and bake at 300°F for 20-25 minutes or until the meringue is brown and crisp.

Steamed Fruit Pudding
Serves 6

Ingredients

½ cup plain flour
1 tsp. baking powder
3 cups fresh breadcrumbs
½ cup shredded suet
1 orange
½ tsp. mixed spice
pinch nutmeg

1 cup dates, pitted and
  chopped
1 cup dried figs, chopped
1 cup raisins
2 eggs
2 tbsp. rum or brandy

Combine the sifted flour and baking powder with the breadcrumbs, suet and finely grated orange rind.

Stir in the mixed spice, nutmeg, dates, figs and raisins.

Lightly beat the eggs with the juice of the orange and the rum or brandy. Add to the flour and fruit mixture.

Mix thoroughly so that the whole pudding is moist.

Grease a 2 pt. pudding bowl. Put a circle of waxed paper in the base. Spoon the pudding into the bowl, but make sure that it is no more than ¾ full. Cover with a buttered circle of greasproof paper, pleated in the middle — this allows the pudding room to rise during cooking. Cover the top of the bowl with a circle of pleated foil and tie securely.

Put the bowl on a trivet or saucer in a pan of boiling water. There should be just enough water to come halfway up the bowl.

Steam the pudding for 4 hours, topping up the water from time to time.

Turn out the pudding and serve with custard, cream or the sauce of your choice.

Steamed Coffee Pudding
Serves 6

Ingredients

2 cups dry coffee sponge cake
⅓ cup plain chocolate
⅔ cup milky coffee
2 tbsp. butter
2 tbsp. vanilla sugar or
   white sugar

2 large eggs, separated
2 tbsp. powdered instant
   coffee dissolved in 1 tbsp.
   hot water
sugar

Crumble the cake into fine crumbs. Melt the chocolate in a bowl over a pan of gently simmering water. When melted, pour over the cake crumbs. Leave to stand for 30 minutes.

Cream the butter and sugar together until light and fluffy. Beat in the egg yolks. Stir in the soaked crumbs and coffee.

Beat the egg whites until stiff and gently fold into the chocolate and coffee mixture. Spoon into a large buttered pudding bowl — the mixture should only half fill it. Cover with greased foil or double thickness of waxed paper. Steam for 1½ hours.

Turn out the pudding onto a serving dish, dust with sugar and serve with custard, cream or chocolate sauce.

Sussex Pond Pudding
Serves 8

Ingredients

½ cup plain flour
2 tsp. baking powder
pinch salt
1 cup suet or butter
⅔ cup milk or water

1 large lemon
½ cup sweet butter
½ cup soft brown sugar

Sift the flour with the baking powder and salt.

Add the suet or butter and rub together until the mixture resembles coarse breadcrumbs.

Bind the dough with milk or water and knead lightly until smooth but not sticky. Cut into two pieces, one twice as large as the other.

Roll the larger piece of dough until it is big enough to line the base and sides of a 1½ pt. pudding bowl. Gently press the dough into the bowl.

Cut the butter into small pieces and put half in the bottom of the lined bowl. Sprinkle with half of the sugar.

Prick the surface of the lemon all over with a fork so that the juice can flow as the pudding is cooked. Put it on top of the butter and sugar. Sprinkle with the remaining butter and sugar.

Roll out the smaller piece of dough. Lay on top of the pudding and seal well.

Cover the bowl with a piece of waxed paper and then a large piece of foil. Put in a pan containing enough boiling water to come halfway up the sides of the pudding bowl.

Steam for approximately 4 hours. Check the water occasionally and top up — it must not be allowed to boil dry.

Unmold the pudding and serve immediately, either on its own or with custard.

Upside-Down Lemon Pudding
Serves 6

Ingredients

5tbsp. butter or margarine, softened	*3 eggs, separated*
½ cup sugar	*¾ cup flour*
3 lemons	*1tsp. baking powder*
	1 cup milk

Cream the butter or margarine with the sugar and finely grated lemon rind until very smooth. Beat in the egg yolks.

Sift the flour and baking powder. Fold into the sugar mixture, alternating with the milk and juice of the lemons.

Beat the egg whites until they are stiff but not dry. Carefully fold into the pudding batter, starting with one spoonful and gradually adding the remainder.

Grease a deep pie dish, approximately 2pt. in capacity. Pour the pudding into the dish and bake at 350°F for 30 minutes or until firm and golden.

Serve warm or cold with cream.

Fritters in Syrup
Serves 4-6

Ingredients

1½ cups plain flour	*½lb. sugar*
1½tsp. baking powder	*1½ cups water*
⅔ cup yogurt	*oil for deep frying*
approx. ⅔ cup milk	

Sift together the flour and baking powder. Mix in the yogurt. Add enough milk to make a thick batter.

Boil the sugar and water together for 10 minutes.

Heat the oil in a pan over medium high heat. Drop in 1tbsp. of the batter at a time and fry until crisp and brown. Drain on paper towels, and keep warm.

Soak the fried mixture in the syrup for 5 minutes. Serve in a little syrup, hot, warm or cold.

Hot Fruit Soufflé
Serves 4

Ingredients

½lb. prepared soft fruit	1tbsp. liqueur
½ cup sugar	5 egg whites
	confectioner's sugar

Strain and purée the fruit with the sugar and stir in the liqueur.

Beat the egg whites until they are stiff but not dry. Fold them into the fruit purée, starting with just one spoonful and gradually adding the remainder.

Turn the soufflé into a greased 2-2½-pt dish which has been sprinkled with sugar. Bake at 350°F for 30 minutes or until well risen.

Sprinkle with confectioner's sugar just before serving.

Variation Substitute chestnut purée for the fruit and use whole eggs. Beat the yolks into the sweetened purée and then fold in the stiffly beaten whites. Bake as described above.

Pear Soufflé
Serves 4

Ingredients

1lb. pears	pinch ground cinnamon
1-2tbsp. butter	3 large eggs, separated
honey	

Preheat the oven to 400°F.

Peel, halve and core the pears. Cut them into slices. Heat the butter in a pan and add the pear slices.

When the fruit has softened, raise the heat a little, break up the fruit with a wooden spoon and cook until mushy.

Put the contents of the pan into a blender. Blend until smooth and add honey and cinnamon to taste. Pour into a bowl and beat in the egg yolks.

Butter a 3¾pt soufflé dish. Beat the egg whites until they form soft peaks and fold into the mixture. Pour into the soufflé dish and bake in the preheated oven for 20-25 minutes until just golden brown and nearly set.

Chocolate Soufflé
Serves 4-6

Ingredients

4tbsp. butter	3 eggs, separated
½ cup flour	1 egg white
1¼ cups milk	¼ cup sugar
5tbsp. grated plain	confectioner's or powdered
chocolate	sugar

Melt the butter in a pan and stir in the flour. Remove from heat and stir in the milk. Return to heat and bring to a boil, stirring. Cook gently for 2 minutes, stirring all the time.

Remove from the heat and stir in the chocolate and egg yolks.

Beat all the egg whites until stiff. Beat in the sugar a little at a time.

Fold the chocolate sauce into the egg whites.

Pour the mixture into a greased 2¼pt. soufflé dish. Bake for about 40 minutes until well risen and firm.

Serve immediately, dredged with confectioner's or powdered sugar.

Coffee Orange Soufflés
Serves 6

Ingredients

6 large thick-skinned
  oranges
3 eggs, separated
$\frac{1}{2}$ cup sugar

1tbsp. powdered instant
  coffee
2tbsp. cornstarch
1tbsp. Cointreau

With a sharp knife, cut the top from each orange and a thin slice from the base so that they stand upright.

Using a teaspoon or grapefruit knife, gently remove the flesh from the inside. Squeeze the flesh to extract the juice and strain it.

Beat together the egg yolks, sugar, coffee and cornstarch. Dilute the orange juice. Put over a low heat and, stirring constantly, bring to a boil. When the mixture has thickened, remove the pan from the heat and stir in the orange liqueur. Cover and leave to cool.

Thirty minutes before serving, beat the egg whites until they form really stiff peaks and gently fold into the coffee cream.

Spoon the filling into the shells until level. Transfer to an ovenproof dish and bake for 10 to 15 minutes at 425°F or until well risen and set.

Serve immediately.

Orange Soufflé
Serves 4

Ingredients

4 large oranges
1 lemon
2tbsp. butter
2tbsp. all-purpose flour

4 eggs, separated
3tbsp. sugar
powdered sugar

Cut the oranges in half crossways and carefully remove the flesh. Squeeze to extract the juice.

Add the juice of the lemon to the juice of the oranges.

Carefully cut strips of peel off half of each orange. Blanch in boiling water for 5 minutes.

Melt the butter in a heavy-bottomed pan. Add the flour and cook, stirring constantly, until all the butter

has been absorbed.

Slowly add in the fruit and juice and peel, stirring constantly, and cook until the sauce thickens and comes to the boil. Simmer gently for 2 minutes.

Beat the egg yolks with the sugar until they are thick and frothy. Stir into the sauce, off the heat.

Beat the egg whites until they are stiff but not dry. Gently fold them into the sauce, starting with just one spoonful and gradually adding the remainder.

Grease a 1½pt. soufflé dish and sprinkle the base with sugar. Pour in the soufflé mixture and bake at 400°F for approximately 25 minutes or until well risen.

Sprinkle with powdered sugar before serving.

Variations Bake the soufflé in the orange shells allowing 20 minutes to cook.

Stir 1tbsp. of Cointreau or Grand Marnier into the soufflé mixture before adding the egg whites.

To glaze the soufflé, sprinkle with powdered sugar 2-3 minutes before it has finished cooking.

Lemon and Almond Strudel
Serves 8

Ingredients
4tbsp. butter
2 egg yolks
1 whole egg
²⁄₃ cup granulated sugar
grated zest of 2 lemons

1½tbsp. lemon juice,
    strained
2 egg whites
¾ cup ground almonds
1 recipe Strudel Dough
2tbsp. butter, melted

Mix two thirds of the butter until pale and creamy. Mix in the egg yolks one at a time and the whole egg. Mix in ⅓ cup of the sugar and add in the lemon zest. Set aside.

Mix together the lemon juice and ¼ cup sugar.

Mix the egg whites until they stand in firm, snowy peaks and beat the lemon juice and sugar mixture into them until they are thick and glossy.

Melt the remaining butter and brush the Strudel Dough with some of it. Cover two-thirds with the butter and egg yolk filling. Scatter the ground almonds all over and cover with the lemon and egg white mixture. Roll up the strudel lightly. Brush with melted butter and finish as before.

Bake in a preheated oven at 400°F for 30 minutes and serve warm.

Apple Strudel
Serves 8-10

Ingredients
2¼ cups
bread flour
1 small egg, lightly beaten
1tsp. sugar
pinch salt
1tbsp. melted butter or oil
¼ cup warm water

Filling
1 cup breadcrumbs
¼ cup butter, melted
1lb. cooking apples, peeled
    and thinly sliced
5tbsp. sugar
⅓ cup white raisins
½ cup chopped almonds or
    hazelnuts

Sift the flour into a large mixing bowl and make a well in the center. Add the egg, sugar, salt, and butter or oil. Gradually draw the flour into the center as you mix.

Gradually add the water to make a soft, sticky dough. Knead the dough until it is smooth and no longer sticky.

Leave the dough to rest for 30 minutes, covered with a bowl or clean cloth.

Sprinkle a cloth-covered table with flour and roll the dough out very thinly to a large circle. Lightly brush with oil or melted butter.

Lift and stretch gently until nearly transparent. Trim off any edges that may still be thick or hard.

Brush the center of the pastry with melted butter, leaving a margin of approximately 1in. all the way around.

Brown the breadcrumbs in most of the melted butter remaining and sprinkle over the strudel pastry.

Arrange the apples over the breadcrumbs and sprinkle with sugar. Scatter the white raisins and nuts over the top.

Fold the top, bottom and one long side of the pastry over the filling. Brush the fourth side with the end of the melted butter and place a sheet of waxed paper under it.

Roll the strudel towards the unfolded edge. Lift the paper onto a greased cookie sheet.

Brush the surface with melted butter and bake at 375°F for 30 minutes or until the pastry is crisp and golden.

Serve the strudel warm, sprinkled with confectioner's sugar and accompanied by a bowl of cream.

Farmer's Cheese Strudel
Serves 4-6

Ingredients
⅓ cup white raisins
1tbsp. rum
½ cup butter, softened
⅓ cup granulated sugar
4 egg yolks
1¾ cups farmer's cheese,
    strained

¼ cup sour cream
1tsp. lemon zest
1 recipe Strudel Dough or
    12 sheets filo pastry
2tbsp. butter, melted

Soak the white raisins in the rum for 30 minutes to plump them. Beat three quarters of the butter and the sugar until light and fluffy. Beat in the egg yolks one at a time. Mix in the cheese, sour cream and zest.

Brush the dough with some of the melted butter. Spread the filling over two-thirds of the pastry and sprinkle with white raisins and rum. Using the cloth to help, roll the pastry loosely over the filling; tuck in the ends carefully, so that the filling cannot leak out, and transfer to a large, greased cookie sheet, seam side down.

Brush with more melted butter and bake in the preheated oven at 400°F for 30 minutes until crisp and well-browned. Serve warm or cold dredged with confectioner's sugar.

If using filo pastry, use six sheets at a time. Brush one sheet with melted butter and cover with a second sheet of pastry; brush with more melted butter and continue layering and brushing with butter with the remaining layers. Place half the cheese filling in the middle and roll up in the same way as for strudel. Finish with the rest of the filo sheets in the same way.

Apple Tart with Cinnamon Sticks
Serves 4-6

Ingredients

5tbsp. butter or margarine	**Filling**
good 1½ cups plain flour, sifted	5 eating apples, sliced
1tbsp. sugar	2tbsp. butter
approx. ¼ cup cold water	1½tbsp. granulated pale brown sugar
	3-in. cinnamon stick, broken
	1 egg
	¼ cup heavy cream

First make the pastry by rubbing the margarine into the flour and sugar, then add enough water to form a ball.

Line an 8-in. pie dish with the pastry. Cover with a piece of waxed paper or foil. Fill with baking beans and bake at 400°F for 20 minutes.

Cook the apples, butter, sugar and cinnamon until the apples are soft.

Drain the apples, reserving the juice. Lay the apples in the baked pastry case.

Mix together the egg, cream and reserved juice. Pour the mixture over the apples.

Bake for 20 minutes, until just set.

Open-Faced Mince Tart
Serves 4

Ingredients

1 recipe Wholewheat Shortcrust Pastry	4-6tbsp. mincemeat
	8 glacé cherries

Make the pastry and allow to rest in the refrigerator before using.

Roll it out about ⅛in. thick to fit an 8in. ovenproof plate.

Lift the pastry onto the plate and press into the sides. Do not stretch. Trim leftover pastry with a sharp knife, cutting at an angle of 45° away from the edge of the plate. If you cut edges angled into the plate, the edge will shrink.

Cut diagonally across the edge of the plate every 1in. Fold the pastry back to form a triangle. Remove folded pastry.

Roll remaining pastry to make six even strips. Spoon in the mincemeat and twist the pastry strips across the top decoratively. Decorate each square with a halved glacé cherry and bake for 20-25 minutes.

Serve hot with cream or custard.

Chocolate Syrup Tart
Serves 8

Ingredients

2¾ cups plain flour	3 eggs
2tbsp. confectioner's sugar	3tbsp. light corn syrup
1 cup butter	1 cup sugar
a little water	1tsp. vanilla extract
4oz. plain chocolate	

Sift the flour and confectioner's sugar into a bowl. Rub in about two-thirds of the butter until the mixture resembles fine crumbs.

Add enough water to mix to a stiff dough, then roll out pastry and use to line a 9-in. pie pan.

Put the remaining butter and the chocolate into a saucepan. Stir over gentle heat until melted and blended.

Beat the eggs, syrup, sugar and extract together. Stir in the chocolate mixture.

Pour the filling into the pastry case. Bake in the oven at 350°F for about 40 minutes, until the top is crunchy and the filling just set. (It should still be slightly sticky inside.)

Serve warm with scoops of vanilla ice cream.

Morello Cherry Tart
Serves 6

If morello cherries are unavailable, bitter or well-flavored dark cherries will do.

Ingredients

1½ cups all-purpose flour, sifted	*1½lb. fresh or bottled morello cherries*
pinch salt	*¼ cup walnuts, ground*
5tbsp. butter, cut in pieces	*1tsp. lemon zest, grated*
2tsp. granulated sugar	*2tbsp. vanilla sugar*
1 egg yolk	*4tbsp. granulated sugar*
¼ cup sour cream	*1 egg white, lightly beaten*
2tbsp. toasted breadcrumbs	*2tbsp. walnuts, chopped*

Sift the flour and salt into a bowl, drop in the butter pieces and blend to a crumb texture. Mix in the sugar. Add the egg yolk and enough sour cream to make a firm paste. Knead well, divide in two and cover in plastic wrap. Chill.

Roll out each piece large enough to fit a 9½-in. spring-form pan. Line the base and sides of the pan with silicone paper, grease well and lay a sheet of pastry on the bottom; scatter over half the breadcrumbs.

Wash and dry the cherries and remove the pits. If using bottled fruit, drain well and dry on paper towels. Mix the fruit in a bowl with the ground walnuts, lemon zest and vanilla sugar, and spread the mixture on the breadcrumb base in the pan.

Sprinkle with the rest of the breadcrumbs and the granulated sugar and cover with the remaining piece of pastry. Brush with egg white and scatter the chopped walnuts all over the top. Bake in a preheated oven at 350°F for an hour until slightly colored.

Serve either warm or cold, with whipped cream on the side.

Spiced Apple Tart
Serves 4-6

Ingredients

Sweet Shortcrust Pastry for a 8in. tart plate or dish	*6tbsp. water*
Filling	*2in. cinnamon stick*
1lb. Bramley, Cox's or Golden Delicious apples	*½tsp. ground nutmeg*
1tbsp. butter	*5tbsp. granulated sugar*
	1tbsp. sugar
	½tsp. ground cinnamon

Peel, core and slice the apples thickly. Put them in a pan with the cinnamon stick, butter and the water. Bring to a simmer then stew until tender. Draw off the heat, stir in the sugar and nutmeg and leave to cool. Remove the cinnamon stick.

Meanwhile make the pastry. Divide it into one-third and two-thirds and roll out the smaller piece to fit a 8in. tart plate or dish, leaving it to rest for a few minutes. Lift up the pastry using the rolling pin as an aid, and line the plate with it. Trim the edge and prick all over with a fork.

Spoon the cold apple mixture into the shell, mounding it high in the middle and leaving a wide border of pastry all round the rim of the dish. Moisten the pastry rim with water. Roll out the remainder of the pastry and lay it on top of the apple filling. Pinch and crimp the two pastry edges well together, trim the sides and decorate with leftover scraps of pastry. Make two small cuts in the middle of the crust to allow the steam to escape.

Put the tart plate on a hot baking sheet in the oven and bake at 400°F for 10 minutes then reduce the heat to 350°F and bake until golden, about 40 minutes. Dredge the top generously with the mixed sugar and ground cinnamon.

Serve hot or cold with whipped cream or custard on the side.

Variations Other fillings are made with rhubarb, gooseberries, blueberries, blackberries — they also taste splendid mixed with apples — and blackcurrants. These soft fruit do not need pre-cooking.

Switzen Plum Tart
Serves 6

Switzen plums usually appear in mid-autumn. They have deep purple skins and firm green flesh, and their slightly tart taste blends exceptionally well with the sweet-and-sour pastry. No other plum will really replace them, but if you cannot obtain them, be sure to choose a variety that has a good strong flavor.

Ingredients

1½ cups all-purpose flour, sifted	*1lb. Switzen plums, pitted*
6tbsp. butter, cut in pieces	*2tbsp. granulated sugar*
1tbsp. granulated sugar	**Topping**
1 egg yolk	*1 egg yolk*
pinch salt	*3tbsp. granulated sugar*
approx. 1tbsp. sour cream	*5tbsp. sour cream*
1tbsp. toasted breadcrumbs	*2 egg whites*
2tsp. ground cinnamon	*2tbsp. plain flour*

Combine the flour with the butter pieces and rub to a fine crumb texture. Toss in the sugar. Mix in the egg yolk, salt and enough sour cream to blend it all to a firm smooth paste. Roll into a ball, cover in plastic wrap and chill in the refrigerator for 1 hour.

Roll out the pastry and line the base of a 9½-in. spring-form tin. Prick all over with a fork. Scatter the mixture of breadcrumbs and cinnamon over the pastry and cover with a close layer of plums. Dredge with sugar.

To prepare the topping, beat the egg yolk and half the sugar until creamy and pale, and mix in the sour cream. Beat the egg whites until firm, then beat in the rest of the sugar until the mixture is satiny and smooth. Fold the egg snow and spoonfuls of sifted flour alternately into the main mixture. Spoon over the top of the plums and level out. Bake until well risen and golden.

Dredge with confectioner's sugar to serve and eat either warm or cold.

Handling Steamed Puddings

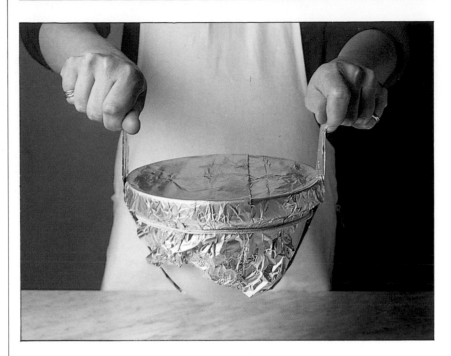

Traditional English sweet and savory puddings (particularly suet puddings) are cooked by steaming. The food is cooked in a container heated by steam. This gives the suet mixture its distinctive soft, open texture. The easiest way to cook the pudding is to put its container in a pan with hot water that comes halfway up the sides of the container. The pan is covered and cooked over a low heat to steam gently for a long time, and water is added to the pan as necessary. Take care to put a band of folded foil under the basin with ends projecting up the sides to act as handles.

Cakes, Cookies, Pastries and Breads

Puff Pastry
For 1lb. pastry

Always use unsalted butter for puff pastry, *never margarine.*

Ingredients

2 cups flour, sifted	*½tsp. lemon juice*
½tsp. salt	*⅓-½ cup chilled water*
2tbsp. unsalted butter, softened	*6oz. unsalted butter, chilled*

Basic dough Sift the flour and salt into a large bowl. Cut in 2tbsp. softened butter and work together with the flour to a fine-crumbed texture. Add the lemon juice and most of the water, and knead lightly into a firm dough; if it is too stiff, add more water. Gather into a ball and flatten slightly. Score the top crosswise with a knife. Close cover and leave to chill in the refrigerator for 2 hours.

Wrapping in the butter The work-surface must be chilled to the same temperature as the ingredients. Use a marble slab or place a bag of ice-cubes on the work-top beforehand. Lay the cold butter between two large sheets of plastic wrap and lightly bat it with a rolling pin into a flattened, pliable 6in. square.

Lightly flour the work-top and the rolling pin. Unwrap the chilled pastry and bat it two or three times to soften it slightly, then roll it out onto the floured top into a 12in. square. Place the square of butter in the center of the pastry square and wrap over the pastry sides to envelop it completely. Make sure that all the seams are well sealed by pressing gently with the rolling pin.

Rolling and folding the dough Always keep the work-top and rolling pin lightly dusted with flour, but brush away any excess. Always roll away from you.

Lay the rolling pin across the dough about 1in. from the edge; never roll over the ends as the butter and trapped air may be squeezed out. Lightly roll the dough into a rectangle about 6×12in. Fold over and overlap each end into a square. This is the first fold. Turn the pastry by making a quarter turn to the right, so that the open ends are parallel to the rolling pin. Roll the pastry away from you as before and fold again into a square. This is the second fold. Turn the pastry another quarter turn and make a slight indentation in the side that is to be rolled next.

Carefully wrap the dough in plastic wrap and chill for 15-20 minutes. It is essential to allow the dough to rest so that it may relax and stretch when it is rolled. Lightly bat the dough two or three times to start it moving, then roll, fold and turn it twice more. Indent, wrap and chill again. Repeat this sequence once more and chill for 30 minutes.

In all, you have made six folds and turns. The dough is now ready for use.

Raw puff pastry keeps in the freezer for up to 6 months. Defrost in the refrigerator over night. If it has been finished for baking there is no need to defrost it; simply increase the basic baking time by about 5 minutes.

Raw puff pastry can be kept in the refrigerator, closely wrapped, for 3-4 days.

Shortcrust Pastry

Ingredients

1 cup flour
pinch of salt
4tbsp. butter or a mixture of butter and margarine
approx. 2tbsp. cold water

Sift the flour and salt into a bowl. Cut up the butter and crumble it into the flour. Mix in just enough water with a knife to make a firm dough and gather it into a ball. On a floured surface, knead the dough gently until smooth. Wrap it in plastic wrap and refrigerate for a short while to firm.

To line a pie plate, roll out the pastry on a floured surface to a thickness of ⅛-¼in. and about 2in. bigger than the pie plate. Grease the pie plate and lay the pastry gently in it, pressing it down to fit the bottom and sides. Prick the bottom lightly and leave to rest in a cool place for 30 minutes.

Sweet Shortcrust Pastry
For a 8-8½in. tin

Ingredients

1 cup+2tbsp. all-purpose flour, sifted	*½tsp. lemon rind*
pinch salt	*1 egg yolk*
3tbsp. granulated sugar	*5tbsp. butter, softened*

Sift the flour and salt into a mound on the work-surface. Make a well in the center and drop in the sugar, lemon rind and egg yolks. Working with the tips of the fingers, lightly and quickly draw in a little flour from the edges and toss to combine until the sugar is absorbed. Add the butter pieces and blend all the ingredients together into a crumbly texture. Gather the pastry into a ball — it does not matter if butter pieces are still visible — and blend it on the work-surface by pushing away small portions of dough at a time, using the heel of the hand. Form the dough into a ball, wrap it in plastic wrap or aluminum foil and chill for at least 30 minutes before using.

Using an electric food processor The butter should be chilled before use so that the pastry is less likely to be overworked and lose elasticity, which makes it tough.

Drop the flour, salt, lemon rind and chilled butter cubes into the processor bowl. Blend for 10-15 seconds to a fine crumb texture; coarse lumps mean that it has been over-blended. Drop in the egg yolk and blend for a further 10 seconds until it forms a compact ball. Wrap and chill overnight.

Yogurt Pastry

Ingredients

½ cup butter or margarine, cut into small pieces	1tsp. baking powder
1½ cups flour	⅓ cup yogurt

Combine the butter, flour and baking powder, rubbing them together until the mixture is like fine breadcrumbs. Add the yogurt and stir it in well. Gather the pastry together and knead it gently. Refrigerate it for an hour or more. Use as required.

This recipe makes a nice shortcrust pastry, suitable for sweet or savory pies.

Sour Cream Pastry

Ingredients

2½ cups flour	1tbsp. rum (optional)
bare 1 cup butter or margarine	2tbsp. sour cream
1 egg	⅓ cup granulated sugar

Rub the flour and butter together. Mix in the remaining ingredients to make a firm dough. Knead well and let it rest for half an hour before using.

This is excellent for any pie or tart that requires a sweet pastry. You can make delicious cookies from any trimmings when using the pastry (or make some specially for cookies).

Cheese Pastry

Ingredients

1⅓ cups farmer's cheese	2 cups flour
½ cup butter	1tsp. baking powder
½ cup margarine	

Mix the cheese and fats together and rub them into the flour and baking powder. Refrigerate for a minimum of 3 hours.

This pastry can be used to make sweet tarts, Danish pastries, strudels.

For a strudel, roll out and spread with chopped apples, jam, raisins, crushed cornflakes and sugar. Roll up and bake.

For individual pastries, cut pastry into squares measuring about 2in. Fill with apricot jam, finely chopped apples with raisins, or cheese filling. Either fold over to make a triangle or bring the corners together in the middle. Brush with beaten egg and bake at 350°F for 30 minutes.

It may seem surprising that farmer's cheese can make a light pastry, but it does.

Fondant Frosting
For 1lb. icing

This is not as complicated to prepare as at first seems, and it does keep fresh for several months. If you make a large quantity it will always be on hand when you need it. Half the quantity is enough to cover an 8½-9½in. cake.

Ingredients

1lb. granulated sugar	½tsp. lemon juice, strained
⅔ cup water	

Pour the water into a heavy-based pan, or unlined copper sugar boiler; add the sugar and lemon juice. Heat gently until the sugar has dissolved, then bring to a boil and cook briskly until the syrup reaches the "soft ball stage" (240°F), when ½tsp. of the mixture dropped into a cup of cold water will form a soft ball — 2-3 minutes of boiling. Pour the syrup straight onto a cold wet marble slab or wet work-top and leave to cool for 1 minute.

Using a wooden spatula or metal scraper, work all round the syrup, lifting it from the edges and slapping and folding it over into the middle. It will change from a clear, transparent syrup to a dense, creamy mass.

The syrup will now be cool enough to handle. Continue working — it will set hard otherwise — kneading and punching by hand, and folding in the same way as one handles dough. After about 10 minutes it should look matt white and feel smooth and firm.

Wrap in plastic film and leave to rest for 1 hour; or store in the refrigerator.

The fondant must be softened before use. Place the amount you need in a flameproof bowl and stir it over a pan half-filled with simmering water; in this instance the water may come up the sides of the bowl. Warm very gently and add just a little tepid water (about 2tbsp. is enough for 9oz. fondant), for an unperfumed flavor. When the fondant mixture has the texture of thick cream it is ready for instant use.

To color the fondant, add a drop of vegetable coloring. For a spirituous flavor, use kirsch, dark rum or Grand Marnier instead of the water.

Strained lemon juice or orange juice gives a good citrus tang, while 2tsp. coffee extract or 1tbsp. coffee powder dissolved in 1tsp. boiling water gives coffee flavoring. For chocolate flavor add 2tbsp. cocoa powder, or melt 1½oz. chocolate and mix it with the thinned fondant. Fondant handles in much the same way as Glacé Frosting.

Glacé Frosting
Makes enough vanilla frosting for an 8-8½in. cake

This simple frosting is easy to prepare but a little tricky to handle. You have to work fast as it dried very quickly.

Glacé frosting starts to crack after about 4 days.

Ingredients

bare cup confectioner's sugar, sifted	4 drops vanilla extract
2-3tbsp. water, almost boiling	

Sift the confectioner's sugar into a small, heat-proof bowl; make a well in the middle and gently and gradually stir in the water and vanilla extract using a wooden spoon. Avoid adding too much liquid at once or the frosting will be too thin and runny. It should be smooth and thick, and creamy enough to coat the back of the spoon. If too thin, add more sugar; if too thick, add more liquid.

Set the bowl over a pan of simmering water, making sure that the base does not touch the water, and gently warm the frosting so that it runs more easily when it is poured on the cake. Use straight away.

Flavorings Use the liquid flavorings instead of water.
Orange 1-2tbsp. orange juice, strained.
Lemon 2-3tbsp. lemon juice, strained.
Punch 1tbsp. orange juice, ½tsp. lemon juice, 2tbsp. rum.
Rum 3tbsp. rum, 1tbsp. water.
Coffee 2tsp. coffee powder dissolved in 2½tbsp. water.
Chocolate 2tsp. cocoa powder dissolved in 2½tbsp. water.
Liqueur 2tbsp. liqueur (kirsch, Grand Marnier, Tia Maria, etc), 1tbsp. water.

Thick Chocolate Frosting
Makes enough for an 8½-9½in. cake

Ingredients
¼lb. plain chocolate
½tbsp. sweet butter
¾ cup oz water
⅓-½ cup granulated sugar

Melt the chocolate and butter together with 1tbsp. of boiling water in a flameproof bowl set over simmering water. Draw off the heat and stir to blend. Put the water in an unlined copper sugar boiler or heavy-based pan, add the sugar and boil to the "thread stage"; dip a pair of scissors into the mixture and when the blades are opened, the syrup will form a thin thread between the points. Stir the chocolate liquid straight into the syrup and replace the pan on the heat. Boil gently for 5 minutes when the frosting will have thickened. Test a few drops on a plate — it should feel sticky. Pour the frosting straight over the apricot-glazed cake, tipping the wire rack back and forth so that the frosting runs all over the top. Do not use a spatula on the surface, but smooth more on the sides. Decorate with fruits and nuts immediately, although piped decorations should be applied when the chocolate frosting has cooled completely. The frosting will set with a high gloss but will dull a little after 24 hours. The cake may then be stored in the refrigerator without spoiling.

Soft Chocolate Frosting
Makes enough for an 8½-9½in. cake

Ingredients
¼lb. plain chocolate
3tbsp. sweet butter, cut in pieces
2tbsp. water
⅓ cup confectioner's sugar, sifted

Melt the chocolate in a bowl set over simmering water. Stir in the confectioner's sugar and the butter and continue stirring until the butter has melted and the mixture is smooth. Remove from the heat and add the water, 1tbsp. at a time. Use while lukewarm.

Do not touch!

Whipped Chocolate Cream

Ingredients
9oz. plain, dessert chocolate
1 cup heavy cream
2in. vanilla pod, split
1tbsp. coffee liqueur or dark rum

Break the chocolate into small pieces and drop them in a pan with the cream and vanilla seeds. Set the pan on a low heat and, stirring all the time, melt the chocolate and bring the mixture to a boil. Draw off the heat immediately. Pour the mixture into a large bowl and leave to cool, stirring from time to time to prevent a skin forming. When cool, add the liqueur or rum and beat vigorously until the mixture lightens and doubles in volume. Use immediately, as the filling hardens very quickly.

Crème Pâtissière

Ingredients
1cup+2tbsp. milk
1½in. vanilla pod, split
2tbsp. cornstarch
2 egg yolks
½ cup sweet butter, softened
¼ cup confectioner's, sifted
1tbsp. rum or kirsch (optional)

Reserve 3tbsp. of milk. Bring the rest of the milk and the vanilla pod to a boil, draw off the heat and leave to infuse for 10 minutes. Beat the cornstarch and egg yolks with the cold reserved milk. Remove the vanilla pod from the hot milk and stir the milk into the egg mixture. Pour the batter back into the pan and reheat the custard until it has thickened. Set aside to cool. Beat the unsalted butter and the confectioner's sugar until light and fluffy, then whip in the cold custard a tablespoon at a time. Mix in the spirit or kirsch if used. Chill for at least 30 minutes. The custard may be kept in the refrigerator for 2-3 days or frozen for up to 1 month.
Chocolate and coffee flavor Melt 4oz. plain chocolate with 1tbsp. instant coffee powder and 1tbsp. water. Leave to cool. Blend into the finished custard.

Cooked Egg Yolk and Buttercream

Ingredients
½ cup granulated sugar
bare ½ cup water
1 cup sweet butter
5 egg yolks
2in. vanilla pod, split

Dissolve the sugar in the water in a heavy-based pan over gentle heat, then boil briskly to the thread stage (225°F — see Thick Chocolate Frosting). Lightly beat the egg yolks in a bowl and slowly pour on the sugar syrup; continue beating until the mixture has cooled and is light and fluffy. Mix in the seeds of the vanilla. Beat the butter in another bowl and beat in the egg mixture a spoonful at a time. Leave to cool before before beating in the flavor of your choice.
Chocolate and coffee flavor Melt and cool 4oz. plain chocolate. Dissolve 1tbsp. coffee powder in ½tsp. boiling water. Stir together well before blending with the finished cream.
Mocha flavor Replace the water in the main recipe

with very strong, fresh black coffee. Proceed as above. Add 1tbsp. rum.

Rum, kirsch or Grand Marnier flavor Adding 2tbsp. of any one of these liqueurs will give a good strong punch!

Basic Buttercream

Ingredients

3 egg yolks
⅓ cup confectioner's sugar, sifted

bare 1 cup unsalted butter, softened

Combine all the ingredients and the chosen flavor together and beat until well blended and smooth. Chill for a short time.

Flavorings 2½tbsp. fresh lemon or orange juice, strained *or* 2½tbsp. liqueur, spirit or eau de vie (Grand Marnier, rum or kirsch); *or* 1tbsp. coffee powder dissolved in ½tsp. boiling water; *or* 3oz. plain chocolate, melted and cooled; *or* 1tbsp. cocoa powder.

Basic Classic Meringue
Makes a 8½in. flat disc of meringue

Ingredients

2 eggs

4tbsp. granulated sugar

Carefully separate the egg whites from the yolks, and drop them into a large spotlessly clean bowl.

Lightly beat the egg whites until they are foamy. Continue beating more vigorously until the egg whites have expanded into firm creamy peaks about three times their original volume.

Sift half the sugar into the mixture and beat until it is smooth and shiny.

Gently fold in the rest of the sugar in two stages, using a large metal spoon.

Tip the meringue onto silicone paper and lightly smooth it out. Using a metal spatula, gently coax it into a circular disc about ¼in. deep, taking care not to flatten it or lose the air that has been beaten into it. Smooth the surface lightly. Dry out immediately in a low oven (275°F). It will take anything from 1½ to 3 hours to dry, depending on the size, and it will turn a very pale coffee color.

Test for readiness by gently tapping the underside of the meringue. If it sounds slightly hollow, it is ready; if not, leave to bake a little longer.

Meringues may be kept for several weeks wrapped in aluminum foil and stored in a dry, cool place.

Italian Meringue

Ingredients

½ cup granulated sugar
⅓ cup water
2 egg whites

Stir the sugar in the water over a medium heat until it has dissolved. Boil for 5 minutes. Beat the egg whites until they are stiff but not dry.

Slowly pour the hot syrup over the egg whites, beating constantly, until the meringue is thick and has cooled completely.

Spoon or pipe the meringue onto greased cookie sheets lined with waxed paper.

The mixture is somewhat easier to make than Swiss Meringue, goes further because the syrup makes it expand, and produces a slightly softer meringue.

Bake in a preheated oven at 250°F for 1 hour. If the

meringues are not completely dried out, continue cookie for 30 minutes longer.

Variation Gently fold unsweetened cocoa, instant coffee or ground nuts into the meringue before baking.

Italian Meringue can also be mixed with whipped cream or pastry cream and served as a topping/filling for baked meringues or cream puffs.

Strudel Dough

Ingredients

2tbsp. butter or 3tbsp. vegetable oil	pinch salt
³/₄ cup water	1 egg
2¾ cups strong all-purpose flour	

Place the butter or oil and water in a small pan and heat gently until the butter has melted. Set aside.

Sift the flour and salt two or three times and finally onto a pastry board. Make a well in the center, drop in the egg and the lukewarm butter and water. Blend in the flour and knead gently at first, for the dough will be rather sticky, but continue kneading until it comes cleanly off the fingers and the board. Wash your hands in between and dust with more flour if necessary.

Continue working and kneading the dough for about 15 minutes until it is smooth and elastic and air bubbles start to develop. Roll it into a ball, place on a freshly floured corner of the board and brush with melted butter. Cover with a warm bowl and leave to rest for 15-20 minutes.

It is simplest to roll out and stretch the dough on a table so that you can work round all the sides.

Cover the table with a large, clean cloth dusted heavily with flour. Place the dough in the center, pat it into a square and roll it out thinly. Brush with more melted butter if it starts to dry out.

Flour your hands and place them under the pastry, backs uppermost and thumbs tucked out of the way. If two people can work, so much the better, otherwise lay the rolling pin on the other end of the pastry to stop it slipping. Working from the middle outwards, gently pull the pastry and stretch it evenly until it is paper thin and almost transparent. Gently drop the dough down on the floured cloth, move around and start working on the next side; continue until the whole piece of pastry is evenly stretched. Cut away the thicker edges. Leave to dry for a few minutes, then brush with melted butter before filling.

Yeast Dough and Yeast Sponge Batter

Yeast pastries are usually prepared in three stages: an initial batter sponge, followed by two rising or proving periods. The dough is covered at these times and set in a warm, draft-free place. A warm cupboard is ideal, or above the oven. The dough should be left to rise in a large mixing bowl; remember it must increase to about double the volume. A large, lightly oiled plastic bag may also be used.

To make a yeast sponge batter Warm the liquid to blood heat (80°F) as stated in the recipe and pour it into a jug or bowl. Crumble over the fresh yeast and stir. Add 1tsp. of sugar and about a quarter of the flour in the recipe and beat until smooth. Cover and leave to ferment for about 10 minutes. It should bubble and expand in volume to about twice the size. Make sure that the yeast has completely dissolved. If there is little or no action after about 20 minutes, the yeast is old. Throw it away and start with a new batch.

Note When the yeast has been incorporated with the other ingredients, the dough needs considerable beating and kneading to encourage the yeast activity and to give lightness and a fine texture. At first it will be rather sticky and difficult to handle, but the more it is worked the less sticky it will become. Finally it will detach itself entirely and roll off the sides of the bowl into a smooth, silky and elastic mass, showing large bubbles of air. At this point the dough is covered and left for its first proving.

When the dough has doubled in bulk it is knocked back — the air is punched out of it and it is kneaded for a minute or two longer. The remaining enriching ingredients, such as nuts or dried and crystalized fruits, are usually added at this stage. The dough is finished and placed in the warmed, buttered and floured baking utensil, and left for a further, shorter period of proving. It is then baked in a hot oven. See the individual recipes for temperatures.

Chocolate Caraque

Melt and spread some cooking or plain chocolate on a cool work surface to a thickness of about ⅛in. Using a sharp pointed, long-bladed knife, place it on the surface of the chocolate. Hold the tip of the knife securely in one place. Holding the knife at a slight angle, scrape in a quarter circle movement to produce long, thin slightly cone-shaped curls.

Buttermilk Spice Cake

Ingredients

2½ cups flour	1tsp. ground cinnamon
1 cup sugar	½tsp. ground cloves
1½tsp. bicarbonate of soda	½ cup butter, melted
1tsp. baking powder	1½ cups buttermilk
pinch salt	2 eggs

Sift the dry ingredients together. Add the butter and buttermilk and beat the mixture until it is smooth.

Pour the batter into a greased and floured 8in. cake pan and bake in a preheated oven 350°F for 40 minutes.

Spice Cake

Ingredients

1 cup butter or soft margarine	3 cups all-purpose flour
⅔ cup white sugar	1 tbsp. baking powder
⅔ cup dark soft brown sugar	2 tsp. ground allspice
4 eggs, separated	2 tsp. ground cinnamon
	1 tsp. ground nutmeg
	1 cup water

Cream the butter or margarine with the sugars, then beat in the egg yolks, one at a time.

Sift together the dry ingredients and gradually add to the creamed mixture, alternating with the water.

Beat the egg whites until stiff and gently fold them into the mixture.

Turn the mixture into a well-greased 9in. square pan and bake in a preheated oven at 375°F for 40 minutes.

Cook the cake for 10 minutes then turn out onto a wire rack.

Engadiner Nusstorte

This Swiss cake originates in the Engadin, a region famous for its pastry chefs.

Ingredients

Sweet Shortcrust Pastry for a 9½in. spring-form pan	scant 1½ cups heavy cream
Filling	1 tbsp. honey
1 cup+2tbsp. granulated sugar	½ cup candied orange and lemon peel, chopped
1½ cups walnuts, coarsely chopped	1 egg white, lightly beaten

Make the pastry and chill it while you prepare the filling. Cook the sugar in a large heavy-based skillet over low heat, and stir until it turns to a pale golden caramel.

Drop in the walnuts, stir and coat them well with the syrup for 2-3 minutes. Pour on the cream. Combine well and mix in the honey and candied fruits. Set aside to cool.

Roll out two-thirds of the pastry and line the base and 2in. up the sides of the greased cake pan. Brush with the egg white. Spread the cooled filling evenly over the base and lift up and fold the surplus edge of pastry over the top of the filling all round the edges. Brush with water.

Roll out the rest of the pastry to cover the walnut filling and lay it on top of the filling, making sure that the sides stick well. Prick the pastry lid all over with a fork, which is traditional.

Bake at 350°F for 1 hour, until just colored; if necessary, cover with foil towards the end of the cooking time. Allow to mature for 3-4 days before cutting. Keeps well for at least 1 month.

Gâteau Pithiviers

Pithiviers is a small town some 50 miles south of Paris, which has gained world renown for the delicious pastry named after it.

Ingredients

1 lb. Puff Pastry or ready-made fresh or frozen pastry	**Almond Paste**
	½ cup ground almonds
1 egg, lightly beaten	¼ cup granulated sugar
	4 tbsp. butter, softened
	1 egg yolk, lightly beaten
	2 tbsp. dark rum

First make the almond paste, a day ahead if possible. Mix together the ground almonds and sugar and beat to a smooth paste with the butter and egg. Beat in the rum. Cover and leave to chill and harden.

Reserve two-thirds of the puff pastry, wrap in plastic wrap and leave in the refrigerator. Roll the remainder on a floured board, into a 8in. circle. Trim the edge cleanly with a sharp knife. Run cold water over a large, flat cookie sheet to moisten it and shake off the excess. Transfer the pastry circle to it, cover and chill for 30 minutes.

Smooth the hardened lump of almond paste over the pastry to within 1in. of the edge, and lightly brush water on the border. Roll out the remainder of the pastry to twice the thickness of the base, and trim the edges cleanly, as before. Carefully fold the pastry circle over the rolling pin and lay it on top of the almond filling.

Press all round the edge firmly to seal the two layers together. Using a sharp, pointed knife dipped in hot water, cut a scalloped border. Cover and chill for 30 minutes.

Brush the tart top all over with beaten egg, cut a hole in the center and insert a small, buttered aluminum foil chimney in it. Brush a second coat of egg glaze all over.

The decoration is distinctive and traditional. Using a pointed knife, cut into the pastry about ⅛in. deep. Inscribe lines radiating from the middle to the scalloped edge in a curved half-moon shape. Prick right through the pastry to the cookie sheet in about six places.

Bake in the preheated oven at 450°F for 15 minutes then reduce the temperature to 400°F and bake for a further 30-40 minutes.

About 10 minutes before the cooking time is complete, sprinkle the top of the cake generously with sifted confectioner's sugar and return the cake to the oven for it to caramelize.

The cooked cake should have puffed right up into a dome and be golden in color. Lift out of the oven, remove the foil chimney and leave to cool on the cookie sheet set on a wire rack.

Gâteau Pithiviers

Orange Mousseline Gâteau

Orange Mousseline Gâteau

This sponge, known as *biscuit de savoie*, has a light, airy texture. The method of beating egg whites separately before folding them into the main mixture helps give air, and the potato flour gives a fine nutty flavor.

Ingredients

good ½ cup confectioner's
   sugar, sifted
1tbsp. orange rind
6 egg yolks
½ cup all-purpose flour
½ cup potato flour

3 egg whites
3tbsp. Grand Marnier or
   Curaçao
Orange Fondant Frosting
candied orange peel for
   decoration

Beat the sifted sugar and orange rind with the egg yolks until light and foamy. Sift together the two flours to aerate them well. Beat the egg whites in a separate bowl until they stand in firm peaks. Alternatively fold in the egg whites and sift the flours into the yolk mixture in three separate stages. Fold in 2tbsp. of the liqueur.

   Grease and line an 8½in. springform pan with wax paper. Butter, then dust the paper with sugar and flour, pour in cake mixture and bake at 325°F for 40 minutes.

   When the cake has risen well and is springy to the touch, place on a wire rack.

   Weigh out ½lb. fondant frosting and flavor with 1tbsp. liqueur.

   Decorate with candied orange peel while still soft. Leave to set overnight.

Le Succès

Grind the hazelnuts for this recipe yourself, as the flavor is far better, and the nuts should be a little coarse.

Ingredients

2½ cups ground toasted hazelnuts
1¼ cups granulated sugar
2tbsp. all-purpose flour
6 egg whites
2tbsp. Vanilla Sugar (see Note)

1 portion Cooked Egg Yolk and Buttercream Filling flavored with chocolate
1 whole toasted hazelnut for decoration

Cover three cookie sheets with waxed paper. Draw the chosen shape on each.

Mix together 1½ cups ground hazelnuts, ⅔ cup sugar and the flour; set aside. Beat the egg whites in a large, spotlessly clean bowl until they hold firm, snowy peaks. Beat in the rest of the sugar and vanilla sugar until the mixture is firm and glossy. Using a large metal spoon, lightly fold in the nut, sugar and flour mixture. Divide the mixture evenly between the three cookie sheets and level out, taking care not to break down the delicate aerated structure. Because of the nut content the succès bases rise little.

Bake them in the preheated oven at 300°F for about 1 hour until lightly colored; they will feel slightly soft to the touch while warm but become crisp and brittle as they cool. Leave on the papers to cool on wire racks.

Prepare the chocolate buttercream filling. (If it has been previously chilled, bring to room temperature for an hour before it is needed.)

To assemble the cake, trim the meringue bases to the same size. Place one on a wire rack. Spread one-third of the buttercream over it and cover with the second layer. Smooth over half the remaining buttercream and place the last meringue on top.

Cover the top and sides of the cake with the remaining buttercream. Press the last of the hazelnuts all round the side of the cake. Place one whole hazelnut in the center.

Transfer to a serving dish and chill for at least 3-4 hours or, if possible, overnight. The top may be piped with a chocolate buttercream decoration if wished.

Note To make vanilla sugar, put a whole vanilla pod cut into pieces into a close-stoppered jar filled with granulated sugar. Top up the jar with more sugar as it is used. The pod will keep fresh for up to a year.

Light Pound Cake

Pound cake is an equal-weight cake, in which each of the main dry ingredients weighs the same as the eggs. It originated centuries ago and was highly spiced, flavored and perfumed, and filled with seeds or dried fruits.

Ingredients

1 cup+2tbsp. butter
1 cup+2tbsp. sugar
2in. vanilla pod, split
1tsp. lemon rind
4 large eggs (9oz.)
good 1 cup all-purpose flour

good 1 cup potato flour
1tsp. baking powder
1tsp. orange-flower water
1tbsp. dark rum

Cream the butter and half the sugar until light and fluffy. Beat in the seeds of vanilla pod and the lemon rind. Beat in, one at a time, one whole egg and the three yolks.

Sift together two or three times the flours and baking powder; then lightly beat 3tbsp. at a time into the butter and sugar mixture, taking care not to over-beat.

Beat the egg whites in a separate bowl until they are firm, and beat in the rest of the sugar until the mixture looks satiny and smooth. Lighten the main mixture by beating in 2-3 spoonfuls of the meringue, then tip in the rest and gently fold in using a large metal spoon.

Use a deep 8-8½in. cake pan, a gugelhupf mold, a guttered mold or a 2lb. loaf pan. Butter well and dust with flour. Pour in the cake mixture and smooth level. Make a slight hollow in the middle. Bake in the warmed oven at 350°F for 1¼ hours until well risen and golden brown. Leave to cool in the pan for 10 minutes before turning out on to a wire rack. Dredge with confectioner's sugar before serving.

Pound cake keeps fresh for at least a week.

Variations This basic pound cake is quite simple, but it may be enriched in a variety of exciting ways.

Try a mixture of dried fruits — apricots (soaked in water for 2-3 hours, then dried and chopped), white and brown raisins making 1⅔ cups altogether; you need two 2-lb. loaf pans for this.

Mixed candied orange, citron and lemon peel also tastes good. Chocolate and ginger make the cake rich and spicy. Pour half the cake mixture into a gugelhupf mold, and to the remaining mixture add 2tbsp. cocoa powder, 1tsp. ginger powder and ¼ cup preserved ginger chopped small. Blend the mixture well and spoon it on to the first quantity in the pan; gently drag a fork through it to give a marbled effect.

A favorite version is one incorporating fresh fruits. Choose any seasonal firm fruits, but avoid soft or citrus ones: plums, grapes, apples, cherries, rhubarb, apricots and pears are all good. You will need about 1½lb. fruits with pits, 1lb. others.

Wash, dry, peel and core or remove the pits. Pour half of the cake mixture into the pan and cover with a layer of fruit; spoon over the rest of the cake batter and cover with the remaining fruit. The baking time will be a little longer, and the cake will not keep for more than about 5 days.

Gâteau des Rois
Twelfth Night Cake

In France, where it originated, there is a charming custom connected with the Twelfth Night cake, for each one contains either a small porcelain figure, a silver coin or, in the past, a bean. The intention is that, when the cake is cut, the person whose slice contains the token is crowned king or queen for the night. It then falls to him or her to entertain the guests in their own home and offer in turn, yet another gâteau des rois. In this way the entire month of January becomes a merry extension of the Christmas festivities.

Ingredients

3 cups strong, all-purpose flour	1 dried navy bean or silver coin
5tbsp. granulated sugar	1 egg, lightly beaten
scant ½ cup water heated to blood heat	3tbsp. coffee sugar crystals or preserving sugar
1tbsp. fresh yeast	1tbsp. strained apricot jam
5tbsp. butter, softened	½ cup candied angelica, lemon and orange peel, cut in strips
3 eggs	
2tsp. lemon rind	
1tsp. salt	¼ cup glacé cherries

Make a Yeast Sponge Batter with ⅔ cup flour and 1tsp. sugar taken from the main recipe and the water and yeast. Beat well, cover and set aside to rise.

Beat the butter and the rest of the sugar until pale and creamy, beat in the eggs one at a time and the lemon rind.

Sift the flour and salt two or three times and finally into a large bowl. Make a well in the middle and drop in the butter mixture. Draw in a little flour from the sides and add the yeast batter. Mix all the ingredients thoroughly and beat hard; it should be quite a limp dough but elastic and shiny with large bubbles of air.

Cover the bowl with a clean towel and leave it overnight in the cool kitchen or larder to rise and at least double in bulk.

Next day, turn out the dough on to a floured surface,

knock it back and knead in the dried bean or silver coin for a few moments. Pinch off pieces of dough and make six hazelnut-sized balls; set them aside.

Cut off two-thirds of the remaining dough and roll it into a rope about 22in. long; curve it round into a circle and pinch the ends firmly together. Transfer to a large 10½in., well-buttered ring mold and carefully brush the top only with beaten egg.

Divide the remaining dough into two and roll each piece into a rope a little longer than the first one. Lightly twist the two together into a braid and carefully lay it in a circle on top of the egg-washed ring. Pinch the ends well to secure them.

Brush a dab of egg on the base of each reserved dough ball and space them equally apart on the braided ring. Lightly cover the crown with a floured cloth and leave to rise for 45-60 minutes until risen to about double in bulk.

Brush all the surfaces lightly with egg and scatter over the sugar crystals. Bake in the preheated oven at 375°F for 20-30 minutes until golden brown.

While the cake is still warm, brush the top with strained apricot jam and stick the candied fruits and cherries on the surface to resemble jewels in a crown. Leave to cool.

Banana, Peach and Almond Loaf
Makes 1 loaf

Ingredients

2¼ cups wholewheat flour	pinch salt
¼ cup wheatgerm	2tbsp. honey
½ cup dried peaches, chopped	2tbsp. molasses or dark soft brown sugar
¼ cup almonds, chopped	½tsp. vanilla extract
2tsp. baking powder	3 small bananas, mashed
1tsp. bicarbonate of soda	1 egg, beaten

Preheat oven to 350°F.

Mix the dry ingredients together in a large bowl. Mix the remaining ingredients together thoroughly in another bowl, then combine the two and stir well.

Tip into a greased and floured loaf pan, 9×4in., and bake for about 50 minutes, or until a toothpick inserted in the middle of the loaf comes out cleanly.

Allow to cool for 15 minutes, then tip out of the pan and cool completely on a wire rack before cutting.

Eat it on its own or spread with butter or cream cheese.

Simnel Cake

The richly fruited simnel cake that we know today originated in the late 1600s. It was baked for Mothering Sunday in England — today's Mother's Day — which falls in mid-Lent and gave a welcome break from the Lenten fast.

Ingredients

³/₄ cup butter	
³/₄ cup light brown sugar	
4 large eggs, separated	
¹/₃ cup ground almonds	
1tbsp. dark rum	
bare 2 cups all-purpose flour	
2tsp. mixed spice	
1¹/₂ cups currants	
1 cup white raisins	
1 cup candied orange and lemon peel	

Marzipan layer

3 cups ground almonds
2¹/₂ cups confectioner's sugar, sifted
2tsp. orange-flower water
3 drops bitter almond extract
3 egg yolks
2tbsp. apricot jam
1 egg yolk for finishing

Make the marzipan first. Combine the almonds and confectioner's sugar in a bowl, add the flower water, almond extract and egg yolks, and knead to a smooth firm paste. Roll into a ball, wrap and chill.

Prepare a deep 8in. loose-bottomed cake pan, line with waxed paper and butter.

Beat the butter and sugar until light and fluffy, beat in the eggs one at a time, add the almonds and rum. Sift the flour and spices together, then lightly mix about one-third of it into the egg batter. Combine the dried fruits and candied peels.

Beat the egg whites in a clean bowl, until they stand in firm peaks and lightly fold them into the main mixture, alternating with siftings of flour and portions of dried fruits and peels. Pour half the mixture into the prepared baking pan.

On a board dusted with sifted confectioner's sugar

roll one-third of the marzipan into a circle 7in. in diameter. Lay it on top of the cake mixture in the pan and press down lightly. Pour on the remainder of the batter, smooth level and make a small hollow in the center.

Set the cake pan on a cookie sheet and bake in the preheated oven at 325°F, reducing the heat to 300°F after 2 hours. Cover the cake with two sheets of greased waxed paper to prevent the top from browning too much. Bake for a further ¹/₂ hour until it starts to shrink away slightly from the sides of the pan. Test with a skewer for readiness. Leave in the pan to settle for 15 minutes then turn out on to a wire rack to cool.

To finish the cake heat 2tbsp. apricot jam with the same amount of water until thickened. Strain and cool. Brush the apricot on the top of the cake only.

Roll out the remaining marzipan to fit the top of the cake, and trim neatly. Make 12 small balls with the left-over scraps. Lightly press the squared mesh of a wire rack into the marzipan layer; fix the marzipan balls on the edge of the cake with a dab of beaten egg yolk. Brush the whole of the surface with egg yolk.

Push the cake under a hot broiler and toast the marzipan for 3-4 minutes to a golden color, watching all the time so that it does not burn.

The cake keeps fresh in an airtight container for up to 2 months. Dredge a little confectioner's sugar over just before serving. Serve on Easter Day with a glass of sweet white wine or a hock; or on Mother's Day in the traditional manner.

Sandtorte
Sandcake

Sandtorte is related to pound cake but the method of preparation is quite different. The mixture has to be beaten for a considerable time so that when it has been baked the texture is fine and sand-like. Potato flour gives added refinement with its powdery dense texture and a sweet, nutty flavor.

Ingredients

bare ³/₄ cup butter	1tbsp. rum
bare ³/₄ cup granulated sugar	¹/₂tsp. lemon rind
	1¹/₂ cups potato flour, sifted
1 egg	pinch baking powder
3 egg yolks	2 egg whites

Gently melt the butter in a small pan, taking care not to let it brown. As it starts to bubble, take the pan off the heat and carefully pour the clear liquid into a small mixing bowl, leaving the thick sediment in the bottom of the pan. Allow to cool.

As it starts to solidify, set the bowl on a bed of ice-cubes and beat the clarified butter for 10 minutes by machine (20 minutes by hand) until it is very thick and almost white. Transfer the butter to a large bowl.

Add the sugar, egg and egg yolks a little at a time, making sure that the mixture never becomes runny, and beat for a further 15 minutes. Slowly add the rum, beating all the time, then the rind.

Sift the flour and baking powder and fold in half but do not over-blend. Beat the egg whites until they are stiff and fold them into the main mixture in three stages, alternating with siftings of flour.

Pour into a greased and floured 2lb. loaf pan and smooth out. Bake in the preheated oven at 325°F for 1 hour. Turn out of the pan to cool on a wire rack. Dredge with confectioner's sugar to serve. Keeps fresh for up to a week.

Simnel Cake

"Plumb Cake"
A Rich Fruit Cake for Christmas

Ingredients

1½ cups currants	2tsp. baking powder
1½ cups raisins	1tsp. ground cloves
1 cup orange and lemon candied rind, chopped	1tsp. ground nutmeg
	1tsp. ground cinnamon
4tbsp. sherry or madeira wine	pinch ginger powder
	3 large egg whites
4tbsp. brandy	**Decoration**
1½ cups sweet butter	6tbsp. apricot jam
1¼ cups soft brown sugar, light or dark	2 good cups pecan or walnut halves
5 large egg yolks	½ cup glacé cherries
½ cup ground almonds	½ cup crystalized angelica or other candied fruits of your choice
1tsp. orange-flower water	
2½ cups all-purpose flour	

Mix the dried fruits and peel with the sherry and brandy and leave to soak for 1 hour while you prepare the other ingredients.

Line the base and sides of a deep, loose-based 8-8½in. cake pan with two layers of brown or waxed paper, and finish with a third sheet of waxed paper standing with a 2in. high collar above the side of the pan. Grease well with butter.

Beat the butter and sugar until light and fluffy. Beat in the egg yolks one at a time, mixing well between each addition. Beat in the ground almonds and orange-flower water.

Sift the flour with the ground spices and baking powder and set aside. Beat the egg whites in a clean bowl until they stand in firm, snowy peaks, then fold about one-third into the main mixture with alternate siftings of the flour and spices. Continue until all is incorporated, but avoid over-beating.

Mix in the dried fruits and liquids until well blended.

Pour the mixture into the prepared cake pan; smooth the surface and make a hollow in the middle so that it wil bake flat.

Place the pan on a flat cookie sheet that has been lined with two sheets of brown paper to give added protection, and bake in the preheated oven at 300°F for 1½ hours. Reduce the temperature to 275°F and bake for a further 3-3½ hours. If the top appears to be browning too much, cover it with a sheet of brown paper. Test the cake for readiness.

Leave the cake to cool in the pan, set on a wire rack. Strip off the papers the following day and wrap in clean paper before storing in an airtight container.

For a strong spirituous flavor, the cake may be un-wrapped and fed with 2tbsp. of brandy weekly.

Variation It is traditional to cover a Christmas or "Plumb" cake with a layer of marzipan (see Simnel Cake recipe) and decorate it with a coating of white royal frosting. The following decoration is more unusual.
– you may lay it on a base of marzipan too if you like.

Heat the apricot jam with 3tbsp. water and cook until thickened. Strain.

Place the cake on a wire rack. Brush apricot jam all over the top of the cake. Embed the prepared fruits and nuts in a random pattern. Finish by brushing more apricot jam over all the fruits and nuts, to give a high sheen.

When the apricot coating has set, tie a wide ribbon or paper frill around the cake and place it on an elegant plate or silver board to serve.

The cake should be stored in an airtight pan and will keep fresh for several weeks.

cinnamon, makes it quite special. The secret of its success lies in the long but essential period of beating during preparation.

Ingredients

5tbsp. butter	1tsp. lemon rind
4 hard-boiled egg yolks	1tsp. lemon juice
2 cups unblanched almonds, ground slightly coarse	1 whole egg
	1 egg yolk
1 cup+2tbsp. granulated sugar	½tsp. cinnamon powder
	2tbsp. all-purpose flour

Cream the butter and mix in the hard-boiled egg yolks; beat well. Add the remaining ingredients and beat the mixture very thoroughly for about 15 minutes by machine (30 minutes by hand). Pour into a greased and floured 8½in. spring-form pan and bake in the preheated oven at 350°F for 1 hour until risen and well browned. Place the pan on a wire rack and unmold after 10 minutes to finish cooling. The cake will keep fresh for several weeks. Serve it in small slices as it is very rich and delicious.

Walnut Torte

Ingredients

4 eggs, separated	1tbsp. toasted breadcrumbs
¼ cup granulated sugar	1tbsp. cocoa powder
1¼ cups ground walnuts	1tsp. coffee powder
2tbsp. ground almonds, unblanched	

Beat the egg yolks and sugar until pale, creamy and well expanded. Mix the walnuts with the almonds, breadcrumbs and cocoa and coffee powders and blend well with the egg yolk mixture. Beat the egg whites until they are firm and beat 4tbsp. into the main mixture to lighten it. Carefully fold in the rest of the egg snow. Pour the batter into a buttered and breadcrumbed 8½in. springform pan and bake immediately at 350°F for 50 minutes. Leave to cool in the pan for 10 minutes before turning out on to a wire rack.

Dredge with confectioner's sugar to serve. For a more elaborate occasion, brush with warm strained apricot jam and cover with a coffee or chocolate flavored Fondant or Glacé Frosting. Decorate with a few walnut halves while the frosting is still warm.

Coffee Sponge with Rum

An airy, light coffee sponge with a rich alcoholic tang.

Ingredients

5tsp. instant coffee powder	⅔ cup heavy cream
4 eggs, separated	2tbsp. light cream
good ¼ cup granulated sugar	2tbsp. granulated sugar
2in. vanilla pod, split	2-3tbsp. Tia Maria or dark rum
½ cup ground almonds	
2tbsp. all-purpose flour, sifted	

Dissolve the coffee powder in 1½tsp. boiling water and leave to cool. Beat the egg yolks and sugar until thick, pale and creamy. Beat in the seeds of vanilla, ground almonds and about two-thirds of the coffee liquid.

Beat the egg whites until they stand in firm, snowy peaks and fold them into the main mixture in two stages, alternating with siftings of flour.

Pour the batter into a buttered, flour- and sugar-dusted 8½in. spring-form pan and bake at 350°F for 30 minutes until well risen and brown. Leave to settle in the pan for 10 minutes before turning out to cool on a wire rack.

Whip the cream to hold soft peaks and beat in the sugar, remaining coffee liquid and liqueur.

Split the cooled cake in half and spread half the cream on the base. Cover with the top layer and smooth over the rest of the cream. Decorate with chocolate coffee beans and grated chocolate. Chill before serving.

Dark Almond Cake

The unusual proportions in the blend of ingredients give this cake a rather crunchy, chewy texture, and the flavor of the raw almonds, combined with lemon and

Linzertorte
Jam Tart

Until the Sachertorte ousted it from popularity, Linzertorte was a favorite Austrian cake for festivals and celebrations during the eighteenth and nineteenth centuries. Almonds, the main ingredient, were coveted in early times and brought as valuable trading cargo from the East along with spices.

Ingredients

1¼ cups all-purpose flour, sifted	1tsp. ground cinnamon
	2tsp. lemon rind
¾ cup butter	3 egg yolks
1¼ cups granulated sugar	1tbsp. lemon juice
¾ cup unblanched almonds or toasted hazelnuts, ground slightly coarse	1½ cups raspberry or redcurrant jam
	egg yolk for brushing on top

Linzertorte

Sift the flour on to the work-top and make a well in the middle. Cut in the butter and blend together to a fine crumb texture. Mix in the sugar, ground nuts, cinnamon and lemon rind. Combine to a smooth pastry with the egg yolks and lemon juice.

Blend the dough, roll into a ball, wrap in plastic wrap and chill for 1 hour.

Roll out half the pastry on a floured board and line the base and ½in. up the sides of an ungreased 9½in. springform pan or tart pan.

Prick the base all over with a fork and spread a thick, even layer of jam over the base. Roll out the rest of the pastry ⅛in. thick, and use a fluted pastry wheel to cut long narrow strips about ½in. wide.

Start making the trellis by laying the pastry strips across the jam surface. Lay one piece straight down the middle and evenly space four more strips on either side. Lay further strips in the same way across at right angles. Reserve some for the edges.

Brush all the pastry strips with beaten egg and, to give a neat finish, lay a long strip of pastry all around the side of the pan over the edges of the trellis. The egg helps seal the joints. Brush the edge with egg.

Bake the Linzertorte in the preheated oven at 400°F for 30-40 minutes. Dot a little more jam into each lattice hole and leave to cool in the pan on a wire rack. Dredge with confectioner's sugar and serve.

Punschtorte

Ingredients

⅔ cup granulated sugar
4 egg yolks
1tsp. orange rind
1tsp. lemon rind
good ¼ cup butter, melted
  and cooled
3 egg whites
2tbsp. potato flour, sifted

Punch syrup
good ⅔ cup granulated
  sugar
¼ cup water
3tbsp. lemon juice,
  strained
3tbsp. orange juice,
  strained
4tbsp. dark rum
2tbsp. apricot jam, strained
Punch Frosting

Butter and line two 8in. springform pans.

Beat the granulated sugar and egg yolks until thick, pale and creamy. Beat in the citrus rinds. Slowly pour on the butter while still beating, taking care to leave the creamy sediment in the bottom of the pan.

Beat the egg whites into firm peaks and lightly fold them into the mixture, in three stages, alternating with siftings of potato flour.

Divide the mixture equally between the two baking pans. Bake at 350°F for 30 minutes until golden and shrinking slightly from the sides of the pan. Leave to cool on wire racks.

Meanwhile, prepare the syrup. Dissolve the sugar in the water over gentle heat and boil to a 'thread stage', that is, when the syrup will form thin threads across the opened blade points of a pair of scissors, at 215°F/. Take off the heat, stir in the lemon and orange juice, and finally the rum. Leave to cool.

As soon as the cake layers have cooled, prick them all over with a fork and brush liberally with the rum syrup. Place one layer on a wire rack and spread the apricot jam all over, sandwich with the other cake layer.

Make the punch frosting and pour it straight over the cake. Smooth the sides using a palette knife but avoid touching the top. While still warm decorate with small pieces of candied orange and lemon peel.

Leave to mature for a day before cutting.

Orangen Torte

The Punschtorte may be adapted to have a strong orange flavor. Leave out the rum in the syrup and fill and cover the layers with orange cream.

Ingredients
Orange cream
4 egg yolks
⅔ cup granulated sugar
⅓ cup orange juice,
  strained

2tbsp. orange rind
good ⅔ cup sweet butter
½ cup heavy cream

Prepare the sponge as for Punschtorte and leave to cool. Make the syrup using 5tbsp. each of orange and lemon juice. Brush cooled syrup over layers.

For the orange cream, beat the egg yolks, sugar, orange juice and rind in a heat-proof bowl. Set the bowl on a pan a quarter filled with simmering water and cook until the mixture has thickened, stirring all the time. Take off the heat and beat until cool.

Beat the butter separately until creamy, then beat the cool cream into it, a spoonful at a time. Beat the heavy cream until it is stiff and gently fold into the main mixture. Chill before using.

Split the cake in half and spread one-third of the cream over the bottom layer. Sandwich with the top sponge layer. Smooth the rest of the cream round the sides and over the top of the cake.

Decorate with slices of candied orange and lemon peel and angelica. Chill before serving.

Habsburger Torte
Serves about 40

This is an elaborate cake that takes quite some time to prepare, but it is ideal for a special function or celebration.

The moist texture and unusual taste of the unpeeled hazelnuts are a perfect foil for the sweeter fillings. Make it 2-3 days ahead of time so that the flavors may develop.

Ingredients

Hazelnut sponge
½ cup granulated sugar
6 eggs, separated
2in. vanilla pod, split
*scant 1 cup unpeeled,
    ground hazelnuts*
1 cup toasted breadcrumbs

Chocolate sponge
½ cup granulated sugar
5 eggs, separated
*scant 1 cup unpeeled,
    ground hazelnuts*
*good ½ cup melted and
    cooled dark dessert
    chocolate*
*½ cup toasted
    breadcrumbs*

Chocolate filling
⅔ cup sweet butter
*bare 1 cup confectioner's
    sugar, sifted*
*good ½ cup melted and
    cooked dark dessert
    chocolate*
*3tbsp. dark rum or Tia
    Maria*

**Pistachio and almond
    filling**
bare ½ cup sweet butter
*good ⅔ cup confectioner's
    sugar, sifted*
1in. vanilla pod, split
1 cup ground pistachios
1 cup ground almonds
3tbsp. apricot jam
*1½ portions Thick
    Chocolate Frosting*

Butter base, line and butter again two 10½in. springform pans. Dust with a mixture of granulated sugar and flour and shake off the excess.

Make the hazelnut sponge by beating the granulated sugar and egg yolks until pale, thick and fluffy. Add the seeds of vanilla and blend well. Mix in the nuts and breadcrumbs and combine well.

Beat the egg whites until they are firm and lightly fold them into the mixture. Pour the batter into one of the pans, level it out and tap the pan sharply on the work-top to pop any bubbles of air. Bake at 350°F for 30 minutes and cool.

After about 15 minutes of cooking time has elapsed make the chocolate sponge. Follow the same method as above, but before beating the egg whites, beat the melted chocolate into the nut mixture. Proceed as before; bake and cool.

Chocolate filling Beat the butter and confectioner's sugar until pale and fluffy. Mix in the cooled chocolate and the rum. Cover and chill.

Pistachio and almond filling Beat the butter and confectioner's sugar with the vanilla seeds until pale and fluffy. Mix in the nuts. Cover and chill.

Trim the cake sides, then split the hazelnut sponge in two and place the base on a wire rack. Reserve one-third of the chocolate filling for piping decoration later and smooth the remainder on the sponge. Cover with the chocolate cake layer.

On sifted confectioner's sugar roll out the pistachio paste to fit the cake and lay it on top; sandwich with the remaining hazelnut layer.

Heat the apricot jam with 2tbsp. water and strain. Brush the slightly cooled jam on the sides and top of the cake. Prepare the chocolate frosting and pour it straight over the top and down the sides of the cake, smoothing with a palette knife as necessary. Avoid touching the top or it will lose its sheen. Leave to set.

Fit a piping bag with a small, star-shaped nozzle and fill with the reserved chocolate cream. Pipe stars around the edge of the cake and in the middle. Stud with hazelnuts and pistachios and serve.

Dobostorta
Drum Cake

Ingredients

Sponge
6 egg yolks
good ½ cup granulated
  sugar
1tsp. orange rind
⅔ cup all-purpose flour
⅔ cup potato flour
6 egg whites

1 portion cooked
  Buttercream with Egg
  Yolks flavored with
  chocolate and rum
Caramel glaze
bare ¾ cup granulated
  sugar

Beat the egg yolks and sugar until pale and creamy.

Mix in the orange rind. Sift together both the flours to aerate well and add to the egg yolks. Beat the egg whites in a separate bowl until they are firm and well-peaked. Fold the egg snow into the yolk mixture lightly and quickly.

This quantity makes six layers. Spread a thin coating of mixture in the bottom of a greased and floured 9½in. springform pan and smooth carefully. Bake immediately in the preheated oven at 350°F for 5-8 minutes each layer. (Bake two layers at a time if you have the pans.)

When it is colored light gold, remove the cake from the oven and turn out of the pan straight on to a wire rack to cool. Make the remaining layers in the same way.

Assemble the cake as soon as the layers have cooled so that they do not dry out and become crisp.

Set aside the best-looking cake layer and sandwich the rest together with the chocolate filling, spreading it over the top and the sides.

Prepare the top layer. Brush any loose crumbs off the cake and lay it on a large sheet of waxed paper. Take two long knives, lightly greasing the blade of one with oil or butter.

Make the caramel glaze by gently heating good ¼ cup granulated sugar in a copper sugar boiler until golden, then add the rest of the sugar and cook until it has thickened. Quickly pour the caramel straight over the cake layer and smooth it out using the clean knife.

Using the greased knife, immediately mark the cake out into 10 sections and cut through the sugar glaze. Leave to cool. Lay the caramel disc on top of the filled cake layers.

Do not store in the refrigerator as this spoils the caramel surface.

Acacia Honey Cake

Honey cakes are among the earliest to be found throughout the world. They were usually prepared for festivals and celebrations.

Ingredients

scant 1½ cups acacia honey
3 whole eggs, lightly beaten
scant 3 cups flour
1 cup unblanched almonds or hazelnuts, ground coarse

1tsp. ground cinnamon
large pinch crushed cloves
2tbsp. dark rum
½tsp. bicarbonate of soda
1tbsp. milk
blanched almond halves to decorate

Warm the honey in the jar set in a pan of hot water, then pour it into a large mixing bowl and beat until it is frothy, thick and white. Beat in the eggs and add the flour a spoonful at a time.

Mix together the spices and nuts and stir in the rum, and combine with the honey and egg mixture. Dissolve the bicarbonate of soda with the milk and beat it into the mixture. Leave to mature in a covered bowl overnight as this helps to lighten the mixture.

Press the paste into a greased and floured deep rectangular baking pan 12½×8½in. Stud with almond halves and bake at 350°F for 30-35 minutes. Avoid letting it brown too much as this gives a bitter taste. When the cake has cooled in the pan, cut it into rectangular pieces and store for at least a week in an airtight container before serving.

Hazelnut Torta

Almonds or walnuts be substituted in this basic recipe.

Ingredients

good ½ cup granulated sugar
4 egg yolks
good 1 cup toasted hazelnuts, ground

1tbsp. toasted breadcrumbs
1½tbsp. dark rum
3 egg whites

Beat the egg yolks and ⅓ cup of the sugar until pale and creamy. Beat in the nuts, breadcrumbs and rum. Beat the egg whites in a separate bowl until they stand in firm, snowy peaks. Beat in the rest of the sugar. Lightly fold the egg snow into the main mixture in three stages, taking care not to stir it and break down the pockets of air.

Pour the mixture into a greased and floured 8½in. springform pan and bake in the preheated oven at 350°F for 1 hour until well risen and brown. Leave in the pan for 10 minutes before turning out on to a wire rack to finish cooling.

The cake may be dressed up in several ways. Dredge it with confectioner's sugar and offer whipped cream on the side. Glaze it with rum frosting decorated with whole caramelized nuts. It can also be divided into three layers and filled with strained apricot jam and a layer of whipped cream, then finished with chocolate frosting.

A chocolate cream filling is especially good: use half a portion of Basic Buttercream flavored with 1tbsp. coffee powder and 1tbsp. coffee liqueur. Chill overnight before cutting. Dredge with confectioner's sugar to serve.

Hunyady Chestnut Torta

Ingredients

3oz. dark, dessert chocolate
1tbsp. rum
good ½ cup granulated sugar
4 eggs, separated
2 cups cooked chestnuts, strained (¾lb. raw)
2tbsp. potato flour

Hazelnut filling
good ½ cup ground toasted hazelnuts
3 egg yolks
5tbsp. unsalted butter
⅔ cup confectioner's sugar
2tbsp. coffee liqueur (Tia Maria) or rum
apricot jam, strained
Thick Chocolate Frosting or ⅔ cup heavy cream, whipped
2tbsp. granulated sugar

Carefully melt the chocolate in 1tbsp. water and stir in the rum. Leave to cool.

Beat together the sugar and egg yolks until pale and creamy. Beat in the chocolate and stir in the strained chestnuts.

Beat the egg whites in a separate bowl, until they hold firm peaks, and lightly fold them into the chestnut mixture using a large metal spoon.

Sift over and fold in the potato flour. Pour the mixture into two 8½in. base-lined, greased and floured springform pans and bake at 350°F for 50 minutes until well risen, leave to cool in the pans before turning out on to wire racks. Strip off the paper carefully.

To make the filling, mix the hazelnuts and one egg yolk to a smooth paste. Cream the butter and sugar until light and fluffy and beat in the remaining egg yolks one at a time. Mix in the hazelnut paste and Tia Maria.

Split both sponge layers in two and fill with the hazelnut cream. Sandwich both cakes with 2tbsp. strained and warmed apricot jam. Cover the cake and leave to chill for a day.

Brush the top and sides of the cake with strained apricot jam. Make the frosting. Pour the warm frosting straight over the cake, smooth out and decorate. Do not leave the cake in a cold place as it will spoil the gloss of the frosting.

For a whipped cream filling sweeten the cream with the sugar and blend in 2tbsp. rum or Tia Maria. Sandwich the two cakes with cream, reserving some for the top and sides.

Smooth the rest of the cream all over the cake and decorate with candied chestnut pieces, toasted hazelnuts and chocolate curls. This should be assembled 3-4 hours before it is to be eaten.

Russian Cream Cake

Ingredients

4 eggs, separated
5tbsp. granulated sugar
1tsp. orange rind
1¼ cups all-purpose flour
1¼ cups potato flour

1½tbsp. dark rum
bare ½ cup milk
vanilla pod
¼ cup granulated sugar
3 egg yolks
1tbsp. gelatin powder
⅔ cup heavy cream

Filling

¼ cup candied orange and
   lemon peel, chopped
2tbsp. white raisins
bare ½ cup glacé cherries,
   pineapple, plum, pear,
   angelica, etc

To make the sponge beat the egg whites in a large, clean bowl, until they stand in firm, snowy peaks. Gradually sift and beat in the sugar until the mixture is satiny and smooth; mix in the rind. Lightly beat the egg yolks separately, then beat them into the meringue a spoonful at a time and continue to blend them in well.

Sift over one-third of the flour and gently fold it in using a large metal spoon; fold in the rest of the flour in two stages.

Pour the mixture into a greased and floured 8½in. springform pan and bake at 350°F for 40 minutes until well risen and golden. Cool on a wire rack.

Meanwhile make the filling. Steep the candied peels, white raisins and candied fruits in a bowl with the rum for 1 hour, mixing it every now and then. Bring the milk to the boil with a split piece of vanilla pod, take off the heat and leave to infuse and cool. Remove the pod.

Beat together the granulated sugar and the egg yolks in a flameproof bowl, sprinkle over the gelatin powder and gradually pour on the cooled milk, beating all the time. Place the bowl over a pan, a quarter filled with simmering water, and stir gently while the custard cooks and thickens. Set aside to cool.

Whip the cream until softly peaked. Beat the vanilla custard until smooth and creamy, then fold it into the whipped cream together with the soaked fruits and rum. Leave to chill for 1 hour.

Cut the sponge into three layers. Reserve about one-third of the cream for the top and the sides of the cake and use the rest to fill the two layers. Cover the top and sides of cake with the rest of the cream, then decorate with pieces of fruit. Chill for 3-4 hours before serving.

Sachertorte
Chocolate Cake

Sachertorte was invented in Vienna in the mid-nineteenth century by the chef Franz Sacher for his employer Prince Lothar Metternich.

Ingredients

good ½ cup butter
½ cup granulated sugar
4 egg yolks
6oz. plain dessert
   chocolate, melted and
   cooled
1tbsp. vanilla sugar
2 drops bitter almond
   extract

¾ cup all-purpose flour,
   sifted
3 egg whites
apricot jam
Thick Chocolate Frosting or
   Chocolate Fondant
   Frosting

Cream the butter with the sugar until pale and fluffy. Beat in the egg yolks, one at a time, and the cooled chocolate. Beat in the vanilla sugar and bitter almond extract and continue beating for 15 minutes by machine (25 minutes by hand).

Sift the flour over the mixture and quickly but lightly blend it in without over-beating. Beat the egg whites until they stand in stiff, creamy peaks and fold them into the mixture. Pour it into a buttered 9½in. springform pan — the mixture should be no more than 1¼in. deep. Bake in the warmed oven at 325°F for 1 hour until slightly shrinking from the sides of the pan. Cool on a wire rack.

Brush the cake with strained apricot jam and glaze with the chocolate frosting.

Black Forest Kirschtorte

Black cherries combined wth chocolate or nuts in cakes were very popular in south Germany, Austria and Switzerland during the last century. Occasionally the cakes were built in layers, but mostly a layer of fresh fruit was covered with the uncooked cake mixture or blended with it and, typical of those regions, nuts were often included. Kirsch was not evident although rum was very common.

Ingredients

¾ cup coursely ground unblanched almonds	**Filling**
1 cup fresh breadcrumbs	2lb. morello, sour or black cherries, washed and pitted or 1lb. 12oz. canned pitted cherries
1tsp. ground cinnamon	
1tsp. ground cloves	
2tbsp. kirsch	1 cup+2tbsp. red wine
⅔ cup granulated sugar	1 cup+2tbsp. water
9 egg yolks	good ⅓ cup granulated sugar
2tsp. orange rind	cinnamon stick
4oz. plain dessert chocolate, melted and cooled	2tsp. orange rind
	⅔ cup kirsch
6 egg whites	2 cups heavy cream
	3tbsp. granulated sugar
	4tbsp. grated chocolate and chocolate curls for decoration

Prepare two 8½in. springform pans: butter, line the base with paper, butter again, dredge with sugar and flour. Mix together the almonds, breadcrumbs, cinnamon and cloves and moisten with kirsch.

In a separate bowl beat the sugar and egg yolks until thick, pale and creamy. Mix in the orange rind and chocolate. Lightly combine with the first mixture. Beat the egg whites separately until they hold firm snowy peaks. Lightly and quickly fold them into the main mixture until just combined.

Divide the mixture equally between the two pans. Smooth the top and tap each pan once to disperse any air pockets. Bake in the preheated oven at 350°F for 30 minutes until well risen and slightly shrinking away from the sides of the pan. Cool on wire racks.

To cook the fresh cherries for the filling, combine the wine, water and sugar in a pan and heat gently until the sugar has dissolved. Add the cinnamon stick and orange rind, and simmer for about 20 minutes. Drop in the cleaned fruits and poach lightly for 10 minutes. Lift the fruits carefully out of the syrup and drain in a colander. Boil the syrup on a high heat for two minutes to reduce and thicken it slightly. Draw off the heat and leave to cool.

Mix 5tbsp. cherry syrup with ½ cup kirsch. Dry the cherries with paper towels. Beat the cream until softly peaked and beat in the sugar until firm; fold in the remaining kirsch. Cut both chocolate sponges across the middle. Reserve 3-4tbsp. cream and a few cherries for decoration.

Place a sponge base on an elegant serving platter and sprinkle over about one-third of the kirsch syrup. Smooth over a quarter of the cream and press in half the cherries. Cover with a second sponge, sprinkle with more syrup, a layer of cream and the rest of the fruit. Place the third sponge on top, sprinkle with the remaining syrup and a layer of whipped cream. Cover with the last sponge layer and coat the top and sides of the whole cake with the rest of the cream. Dust the cake sides with chocolate.

Pipe the reserved cream in large rosettes on the cake surface and dot with cherries. Place a few chocolate curls in the middle to finish. Chill for 3-4 hours. Just before serving dredge a little confectioner's sugar on the chocolate curls.

Baumkuchen
Tree Cake

Spit cooking was the usual method of roasting in early times, and a tree cake was quite popular. It was baked on a hand-turned, tapered, wooden spit, set in front of an open fire, and it was made of a thin batter, ladled on slowly as it cooked. Each wafer-thin layer was toasted to a golden brown color, and then another coating of fresh batter was poured on, to be coated in its turn. The tree effect was achieved by varying the rotating speed of the spit as fresh batter was poured over.

Today, we have to adapt the technique, and the modern broiler is most suitable. You can use an all-purpose baking pan or springform pan for a basic cake, or you could try experimenting with different forms such as a gugelhupf or angel cake mold or with shapes that can be assembled later with apricot jam before being iced.

Ingredients

1 cup+1tbsp. butter	½ cup ground almonds
1 cup+1tbsp. granulated sugar	good ½ cup all-purpose flour, sifted
7 eggs, separated	good ½ cup potato flour, sifted
2tsp. lemon rind	
1tbsp. rum	

Beat the butter and granulated sugar until pale and creamy, beat in the egg yolks one at a time, mix in the lemon rind, rum and almonds. Sift together the flours, and beat two spoonfuls at a time into the egg mixture.

Beat the egg whites in a spotlessly clean bowl until firm, then lightly fold them into the main mixture. Lightly oil the chosen cake pan (9½in. diameter). Smooth 1-2 tbsp. of cake batter on the base and place under the broiler. Broil at 350-400°F for 4-5 minutes until golden brown. Remove from the heat and smooth over another thin layer of mixture. Cook again. Continue toasting the layers until all the mixture is used (about 16-18 layers). Leave to cool in the pan. Unmold; brush with warm apricot jam and glaze with lemon-flavored Glacé Frosting.

The cake keeps fresh for 2-3 weeks.

Bienenstich
Beesting

Although Bienenstich is usually made with a yeast pastry base, the fine butter pastry in this recipe tastes just as good with a vanilla cream filling.

Ingredients

good ½ cup butter, melted
  and cooled
good ½ cup granulated
  sugar
2 eggs
1tsp. lemon rind
good cup all-purpose flour
good ½ cup potato flour
½tsp. baking powder

Almond toffee
4tbsp. butter, diced
1cup+1tbsp. granulated
  sugar
¾ cup flaked almonds
approx. ½ cup milk
Vanilla cream (Crème St
  Honoré)
1 cup+1tbsp. milk
1in. vanilla pod
1 egg yolk
2tbsp. cornstarch, sifted
½ cup granulated sugar
2 egg whites

Make the almond toffee first. Melt the butter over a low heat, then stir in the sugar and mix until it has completely dissolved. Toss in the flaked almonds and beat the mixture, adding enough milk to give a firm but spreading consistency. Leave to cool.

Prepare the vanilla cream by heating the milk with the vanilla pod, leaving it to infuse for a few minutes. Remove the pod. Beat the egg yolk with the flour and 3tbsp. granulated sugar in a heat-proof bowl, then slowly pour the hot milk over the mixture, beating all the time.

Set the bowl over a pan a quarter filled with simmering water, and heat and stir the mixture until it thickens. It must not boil. Draw off the heat and pour into a bowl.

Beat the egg whites until they are stiff and well peaked, beat in half the remaining sugar and fold in the rest. Lightly fold the meringue mixture into the hot cream. Cool and chill.

To make the pastry beat the cool butter and granulated sugar until pale and fluffy; beat in the eggs one at a time blending well between each addition.

Mix in the lemon rind. Sift together the flours and baking powder and blend them into the mixture 2tbsp. at a time, taking care not to overbeat.

Spread the mixture on a buttered 13½×9½×1½in. cake tray and smooth even.

Cover with the almond toffee layer and bake at 325°F for 1 hour in the preheated oven. Cut the cake into slices while it is still warm; leave in the pan to cool. Lift the slices out of the pan and cut each in half; sandwich together with some of the vanilla cream.

Hobelspänne
Wood Shavings
Makes 24 pieces

Ingredients

1⅓ cups all-purpose flour
½tsp. baking powder
3tbsp. butter, cubed
2tbsp. granulated sugar
1tsp. lemon rind

1 egg
2tbsp. milk
confectioner's sugar to
  dredge

Sift together the flour and baking powder until well aerated and finally into a bowl. Drop in the butter pieces and rub to a fine crumb texture. Stir in the sugar and lemon rind. Mix in the egg and the milk and blend to a fine dough.

Roll out the pastry to a thickness of ⅛in. and cut into rectangular strips 3½×1in. Cut a slit about 1½in. in the center of the length. Lift each pastry and carefully draw one end through the slit, gently easing it back to give a looped effect.

Heat the oil to the correct temperature and deep fry three or four pastries at a time until golden, turning them if necessary with a perforated spoon. They take about 1½ minutes each side.

Lift out the pastries and drain them on paper towels. Roll them in confectioner's sugar while they are still warm and leave to dry on a wire rack.

Schraderpuffer
Sponge Cushion

This is a specialty of Schleswig-Holstein, the most northerly point of Germany almost on the Danish border. The method of preparation and baking is quite unusual and gives a not too sweet, light and airy cake that is ideal for tea or coffee time.

Ingredients

5tbsp. butter	*1tsp. lemon rind*
1 cup all-purpose flour, sifted	*4 eggs, separated*
	5tbsp. granulated sugar
½ cup raisins	

Cut the butter into the flour and rub to a fine crumb texture. Toss in the raisins and lemon rind, making sure that they are well coated with flour. Set aside.

Beat the egg whites in a large clean bowl until they stand in firm, snowy peaks and beat in half the sugar until the mixture is firm and glossy. Using a large metal spoon fold in the rest of the sugar and lightly beaten egg yolks.

Very carefully and lightly, fold in the flour and butter mixture in three portions. Pour the mixture into a greased and floured 8½in. ring or savarin mold.

Level out and bake immediately in the preheated oven at 475°F for a total of 45 minutes, reducing the temperature after the first five minutes to 425°F and then again after a further ten minutes to 350°F. The cake puffs up high and turns a rich, golden brown. Lift out of the oven and turn out on a wire rack after 10 minutes to cool. Dust with confectioner's sugar to serve.

Mohrenkopf
Othello's or Moor's Heads
Makes 25 pieces

Ingredients

4 egg yolks	*½ cup potato flour, sifted*
¼ cup granulated sugar	*⅔ cup heavy cream*
½ cup all-purpose flour, sifted	*2tbsp. granulated sugar*
	2tbsp. Grand Marnier or
6 egg whites	*Cointreau*
pinch salt	*Soft Chocolate Frosting*

Beat the egg yolks and half the sugar until pale and creamy. Beat in the all-purpose flour. Whip up the egg whites with the salt until firm, then beat in the remaining sugar until satiny and smooth. Fold the egg snow into the first mixture, then sift over the potato flour in two stages and fold it in lightly.

Line a cookie sheet with waxed paper.

Fit a large piping bag with a all-purpose nozzle and spoon some of the mixture into it. Pipe rounds of paste about ½in. across at 2in. intervals. Dust with a little flour. Bake in the preheated oven at 400°F for 20-30 minutes until puffed and golden. Remove from the paper and cool on a wire rack. Split the cakes and scoop out a little of the pastry from the base. Whip the cream into soft peaks and beat in the rest of the sugar and the liqueur. Place a spoonful of cream in the hollow of each split pastry and close. Prepare the Soft Chocolate Frosting and coat the top of each pastry with it; stand on the wire rack to set.

Variations: Desdemonas Fill with vanilla-flavored whipped cream, brush the top with strained apricot purée, and mask with kirsch-flavored Glacé Frosting.
Iagos Fill the base with coffee-flavored Crème Pâtissière, brush with apricot purée, and frost with Coffee Glacé Frosting.
Chocolate beans Fill with rum-flavored chocolate cream (see Basic Buttercream), cover the top with the same cream, and decorate with chocolate vermicelli.

Truffle Torte
Chocolate Truffle Cake

Ingredients

5½oz. dark dessert chocolate, melted and cooled	*1½ portions Whipped Chocolate Cream flavored with coffee liqueur*
2tsp. coffee powder	
6tbsp. butter, softened	*mimosa balls or whole caramelized hazelnuts to decorate*
good ½ cup granulated sugar	
4 eggs, separated	
⅔ cup ground toasted hazelnuts	

Break the chocolate into pieces and place them in a small heat-proof bowl with the coffee powder and 6tbsp. boiling water. Set the bowl over a pan of simmering water to melt the chocolate. Stir gently to blend, then set aside to cool.

Mix the butter and sugar until pale and creamy. Beat in the egg yolks one at a time and continue beating until the mixture is very thick and pale in color. Beat in the cool chocolate liquid and hazelnuts.

Beat the egg whites separately until they are stiff, and fold them lightly and carefully into the chocolate mixture. Pour into a buttered 8½in. base-lined spring-form pan and bake immediately at 325°F for 1 hour 15 minutes. Leave to settle in the pan for 10 minutes before turning out to cool.

The cake should feel quite moist. When cold, wrap in plastic wrap and chill for 2 days. Assemble the cake a day before it is needed.

Make the whipped chocolate cream. Split the cake into three layers. Reserve about one-third of the cream for the top and sides of the cake and use the rest to sandwich the three layers.

Fit a piping bag with a large plain nozzle and spoon about 5tbsp. cream into the bag. Smooth the rest of the cream on the sides and top of the cake. Pipe five thick, straight and parallel lines across the top of the cake and dredge generously all over with cocoa powder.

Stud the mimosa balls or hazelnuts along the piped lines. Cover and chill overnight before serving.

Carrot Cake

Ingredients

6 egg yolks	1 cup ground almonds
2/3 cup confectioner's sugar, sifted	2tbsp. potato flour
	1tsp. baking powder
1tsp. lemon rind	1tsp. ground cinnamon
pinch salt	pinch ground cloves
3 large peeled carrots	2tbsp. kirsch
1 cup ground roasted hazelnuts	4 egg whites
	5tbsp. granulated sugar

Beat the egg yolks with the confectioner's sugar, lemon rind and salt until pale and creamy. Grate the carrots, drain any liquid and pat dry with paper towel. Stir into the egg and sugar with the hazelnuts and almonds. Sift the flour with the baking powder and spices and blend with the mixture. Mix in the kirsch.

Beat the egg whites until softly peaked; sift in the granulated sugar and beat until the mixture looks satiny and smooth. Fold the meringue into the carrot mixture lightly and carefully. Pour into a greased and floured 9½in. springform pan and bake at 350°F for 1 hour. Cool on a wire rack.

Dredge with confectioner's sugar before serving. Do not cut the cake for at least 3 days, so that the flavors may mature. Offer whipped cream on the side.

In Switzerland, where this cake originates, it is the custom to finish the cake with a white Glacé or Fondant Frosting and to decorate it with marzipan carrots.

Brush the warm cake with strained apricot jam and coat with Fondant Frosting. Tint a little marzipan with orange food coloring and make 13 small carrot shapes. Use angelica for the stems. Lay the carrots on the frosting before it has set; one for each slice of the cake is fun. Lay three in the middle of the cake and the other ten around the outside.

Raisin Chocolate Fudge Cake

Ingredients

5tbsp. butter	½tsp. ground cinnamon
good ¾ cup brown sugar	pinch ground cloves
1 whole egg	6tbsp. raisins
2tbsp. orange juice, sieved	½ cup flaked almonds
2tsp. orange rind	**Filling**
2oz. chocolate, melted and cooled	1 portion Buttercream with Cooked Egg Yolks
¼ cup milk	6tbsp. chopped pecan nuts
pinch bicarbonate of soda	¾ cup grated coconut
good 1 cup all-purpose flour, sifted	½ cup raisins, cut in half
½tsp. baking powder	pecan halves and flaked almonds to decorate

Cream the butter and half the sugar. Beat in the egg, blend well. Add the orange juice and rind. Beat in the rest of the sugar and the chocolate. Combine well. Mix the milk with ¼ cup water and blend in the bicarbonate of soda. Sift together the flour and baking powder with the cinnamon and cloves. Dust the almonds and raisins with some of the flour and set aside.

Beat one-third of the liquid into the mixture followed by one-third of the dry ingredients. Repeat in two further stages. Mix in the raisins and almonds. Turn into a deep, ready-greased and fully lined 8½in. loose-based pan. Level the surface. Bake in the preheated oven at 350°F for 1 hour until risen and shrinking away slightly from the edges of the pan. Cool on a wire rack.

Make the filling. Into the cooled cream mix the pecan nuts, coconut and raisins.

To assemble, split the cake into three layers. Reserve just over one-third of the filling for the outside and use the remainder to sandwich the three chocolate layers together. Smooth the rest on the top and sides of the cake. Decorate with pecans and almond flakes.

The cake should settle for at least a day before it is cut. It will stay fresh for up to a week.

Poppy Seed or Walnut Roll
Makes 2 rolls

This yeasted roll is serve all the year round in Hungary as a coffee-time pastry.

Ingredients

Yeast pastry
⅓ cup milk
2tbsp. fresh yeast
1lb. bread flour, sifted
bare ½ cup granulated
  sugar
pinch salt
1 cup butter
2 egg yolks
¼ cup sour cream
1 whole egg for brushing

Poppy seed filling
bare ½ cup milk
¾ cup poppy seeds, ground
¾ cup granulated sugar
2tsp. lemon rind
1 large apple, peeled and
  grated

Walnut filling
⅔ cup granulated sugar
3tbsp. milk
bare 2 cups ground
  walnuts
1tsp. lemon rind
2 apples, peeled and
  grated

Prepare a sponge batter. Warm the milk to blood heat and sprinkle over the crumbled yeast; mix in 1 cup flour taken from the recipe and 1tsp. granulated sugar. Beat well. Cover and leave to rise until at least double in bulk.

Meanwhile, sift the flour and salt into a large bowl, cut in the butter and rub to a crumb texture. Mix in the sugar and egg yolks, then pour on the sponge batter. Beat in enough sour cream to make a not too soft dough.

Knead thoroughly until the dough becomes elastic and contains large air bubbles. Leave in the bowl closely covered with a cloth, or place the dough in a large, lightly oiled plastic bag and seal. Set in a warm place to rise for about 3 hours until it has at least doubled in bulk. While the dough is rising make the filling.

Poppy seed filling Boil the milk and pour it over the ground poppy seeds; leave to infuse and swell. Gently dissolve the granulated sugar in 2tbsp. water, sift the seed and stir into the syrup; draw off the heat. Stir in the lemon rind and grated apple. Cool before using.

Walnut filling Dissolve the sugar in the milk to make a syrup. Stir in the walnuts, and draw off the heat. Mix in the lemon rind and grated apple. Cool before using.

For a very simple filling sprinkle a mixture of ⅔ cup granulated sugar, 2tsp. ground cinnamon and ½tsp. ground clove over the dough before rolling it up.

Turn the risen dough onto a floured pastry board, knock it back for a moment or two, then divide it into two, replacing the unused piece in the covered bowl or bag.

Roll out the dough into a rectangle ¼in. thick. Spread generously with the chosen filling to within ¾in. of the edge and roll up carefully, tucking in both ends so that the filling cannot leak out. Transfer the roll to a lightly greased cookie sheet, with the open seam underneath. Brush lightly with beaten egg and leave to rise for a further 30 minutes. Brush again with beaten egg and prick all over with a fork. Bake in the preheated oven at 350°F for 1 hour. Finish the reserve dough in the same way.

Serve cut in slices. The pastries keep well for at least a week.

Streusselkuchen
Crumb Cake

This is a German classic. Here the yeast dough base is covered with a thick cinnamon and almond crumb covering. Streussel is made like pastry, and here are two simple ways of making it.

Ingredients

Yeast Dough
Almond streussel
1cup+2tbsp. sweet butter
3 cups all-purpose flour,
  sifted

1 cup ground almonds
2tsp. cinnamon powder
1tsp. lemon rind
good ⅔ cup granulated
  sugar

Prepare the yeast dough and line two baking pans. Leave to rise.

Using a food processor Gently melt the butter and leave to cool. Drop the flour, almonds, cinnamon, lemon rind and sugar into the processor bowl and switch on for 2-3 seconds to mix well. Then quickly pour the cooled butter through the tube onto the mixture with the machine switched on. Stop the motor as soon as a crumb texture is reached.

By hand Cut the chilled butter pieces into the sifted flour and rub to fine crumbs. Use a knife to blend in the rest of the ingredients and make a coarse crumb texture. Roll into a ball, wrap and chill for 1 hour until hardened. Rub the dough through a coarse grater and dust lightly with flour to prevent it from sticking together.

Finish the cakes by brushing the risen dough with melted butter; scatter the crumb mixture generously on top. Bake in the preheated oven at 400°F for 35 minutes until well risen and golden. Cool in the pans, set on a wire rack. Dust with confectioner's sugar before serving and cut in slices.

Frankfurter Kranz

This is baked in an all-purpose ring or savarin mold.

Ingredients

good ½ cup butter
⅔ cup granulated sugar
4 eggs, lightly beaten
2tsp. lemon rind
2tsp. rum
1 cup all-purpose flour
1 cup potato flour
1tsp. baking powder
2 portions vanilla
 Buttercream (cooled)
 plus 4tbsp. sweet butter

Praline croquant
¼ cup granulated sugar
1tbsp. water
½ cup flaked or chopped
 toasted almonds
6tbsp. rum, kirsch or
 Grand Marnier
glacé cherries and
 pistachio nuts for
 decoration

Beat the butter and sugar until light, pale and fluffy. Beat in the egg a little at a time, beating well between each addition. Mix in the lemon rind and rum. Sift together the flours with the baking powder two or three times, then beat them into the egg mixture in three stages. The mixture should be quite firm but not stiff.

Turn it into the buttered ring mold and smooth level. Bake in the preheated oven at 350°F for 45 minutes until well risen and brown and shrinking slightly from the edges of the pan. Turn out on to a wire rack to cool. Let the cake rest overnight if possible.

Prepare the Buttercream and beat the additional butter into a small portion of the buttercream before combining it with the rest of cooled buttercream.

To make the praline croquant boil the water and sugar to form a caramel. Drop in the almonds and stir lightly to coat them with the sugar. When the mixture starts to boil, pour on to an oiled baking sheet, smooth out and leave to cool. Break the praline into pieces and chop or pound into a coarse powder.

Assemble the cake. Split the cake into four layers and brush a little alcohol on each. Reserve 3tbsp. buttercream and sandwich all the layers together, with the buttercream covering the top and sides also. Sprinkle the crushed croquant all over the cake. Pipe a few buttercream rosettes on the top and decorate with cherries and pistachios.

Sunshine Cake

Ingredients

1¼ cups all-purpose flour,
 sifted
pinch salt
6 eggs, separated

2in. vanilla pod
1tsp. cream of tartar
1 cup+1tbsp. granulated
 sugar

Carefully wash and dry a 9½in. angel cake pan and dust with flour.

Sift the flour and salt several times to aerate well. Beat the egg yolks until thick and frothy, then mix in the seeds of the vanilla pod. Set aside. Lightly whip the egg whites in a spotlessly clean bowl until they are foamy, add the cream of tartar and continue beating until they have expanded into firm white peaks. Sift ⅓ cup of sugar over the egg whites and beat in until glossy and smooth. Continue by hand.

Using a large metal spoon, carefully fold in the beaten egg yolks and lemon juice. Sift over one-third of the flour and gently fold it in; repeat in two more stages.

Pour the sponge batter into the floured mold. Drag a knife through it to break any pockets of air. Bake at 350°F for 45 minutes. When well risen and springy to the touch, turn over to balance on a small inverted funnel or a wire rack to cool, leaving the cake pan in place.

Dredge with confectioner's sugar to serve.

Chocolate Roulade

Ingredients
6oz. plain chocolate
5 eggs, separated
³⁄₄ cup sugar
3tbsp. hot water
confectioner's sugar, sifted
Filling
2 cups heavy cream
¹⁄₂ cup confectioner's sugar, sifted

¹⁄₄ cup unsweetened cocoa powder
2tsp. instant coffee
¹⁄₂tsp. vanilla extract
Decoration
whipped cream
crystalized violets
angelica leaves

Melt the chocolate in a bowl over a pan of hot water.

Put egg yolks into a large bowl. Add the sugar and beat well until pale and fluffy.

Add the hot water to the chocolate and stir until smooth. Beat into the egg mixture.

Beat the egg whites until stiff. Lightly fold into the chocolate mixture. Pour into a greased and lined 15¹⁄₂×9¹⁄₂in. jelly roll pan. Cook in the oven at 350°F for 15-20 minutes, until firm.

Remove from the oven. Cover with a sheet of waxed paper and a damp dish towel. Leave until completely cold.

To make the filling put all the ingredients into a bowl. Beat until thick. Chill.

Turn roulade on to a sheet of waxed paper dusted with confectioner's sugar. Peel away lining paper.

Spread the filling over the cake to within 1in. of the edge. Roll up like a jelly roll, using the waxed paper to help.

Put seam side down on a serving plate and chill for an hour before serving.

To serve, dredge the roulade with confectioner's sugar. Pipe whipped cream down the center and decorate with crystalized violets and angelica leaves.

Gugelhupf

It is difficult to attribute Gugelhupf to any one country as it has remained popular throughout the Teutonic lands for centuries. The name comes from the mold in which the cake is baked: an unusual utensil, with sloping and molded, patterned sides and a central funnel. Simple, early models were made of tin, but more elaborate embossed ones of fired clay or copper were used for special occasions. Today they are usually made of aluminum or copper and are available in many specialist kitchen shops.

Ingredients
¹⁄₄ cup milk, warmed to blood heat
2tsp. fresh yeast
1¹⁄₃ cups bread flour, sifted
¹⁄₄ cup granulated sugar
¹⁄₃ cup butter
1tsp. grated lemon rind

6 egg yolks
²⁄₃ cup raisins
2tbsp. kirsch
1tsp. corn oil
2 egg whites
1tbsp. pine nuts (optional)

Carefully brush with melted butter a 9in. gugelhupf mold and dust with flour; drop the pine nuts, if used, in the bottom.

Make a Yeast Sponge Batter with the warm milk, yeast, 2tbsp. flour and 1tsp. sugar taken from the main mixture; beat well. Cover and set aside for about 10 minutes to rise and double in bulk.

Cream the butter with the sugar and lemon rind until thick and fluffy. Beat in the egg yolks one at a time, beating thoroughly between each addition. Mix in the sponge batter and a quarter of the remaining flour and continue beating for about 10 minutes by machine (20 minutes by hand). The mixture should be well aerated and have thickened.

Dust the raisins with a little flour and blend them into the mixture. Stir in the kirsch and the oil. Beat the egg whites in a separate, clean bowl until they hold firm, glossy peaks. Lightly fold them into the main mixture, with alternate siftings of flour, until all is well combined.

Pour the yeast dough into the prepared pan and set it in a warm place to rise and at least double in bulk; it should rise to almost the top of the pan and this takes about 1¹⁄₂ hours.

Bake in the preheated oven at 375°F for 30 minutes until well browned and turn out onto a wire rack to cool. Dredge with confectioner's sugar to serve. Freeze while still warm. Defrost at room temperature for 3-4 hours.

Lardy Cake

Lardy cake is based on a plain bread dough, enriched with a delicious sticky-sweet mixture of lard and sugar as well as dried fruits and mixed spices, and it is prepared in much the same way as puff pastry. In early times, when sugar was scarce, this was a treat reserved for harvest days and special celebrations, and, like gingerbread, was sold at local fairs. Later, when sugar dropped in price, lardy cake became very popular and could be bought from the bakery every week.

Home-make pork lard has the best flavor if you are able to obtain it.

Ingredients
Bread dough
4²⁄₃ cups bread flour
1cup+1tbsp. milk, warmed to blood heat
1tbsp. fresh yeast
1tbsp. lard

Filling
³⁄₄ cup lard, well chilled
1 cup light brown sugar
2¹⁄₄ cups mixed fruit and peel
1tsp. ground mixed spice

Make a Yeast Sponge Batter with 1 cup flour, good ½ cup milk and the yeast, beat well, cover and set aside to rise and double in bulk. Sift the remaining flour and salt together into a large bowl. Rub in 1tbsp. lard and make a crumb texture.

Make a well in the center, pour in the risen sponge batter and most of the remaining milk. Blend well, then work and knead the dough mixture until it starts to roll off the sides of the bowl.

Turn the dough out on to a lightly floured work-surface and knead hard for about 10 minutes until it is elastic, looks shiny and throws large pockets of air. Roll it into a ball, drop it back into the mixing bowl and cover with a floured cloth. Set aside to rise in a warm place until it has doubled in bulk.

Roll the dough out on a floured work-top into a rectangle about ¼in. thick. Dot about one-third of the chilled lard across the dough, to within ½in. of the edges.

Scatter over one-third each of the sugar and dried fruits, and a little spice. Fold one-third of the dough over from the short side into the middle, and cover with the top third of the dough. Press the sides firmly together so that the filling is completely sealed and make a quarter turn to the right; indent with two fingers. Chill in the refrigerator for 15 minutes.

Roll the dough into a rectangle as before on the indented edge, dot with half the remaining lard, sugar, fruits and spice, fold, seal and turn again; indent and chill. Repeat with the rest of the ingredients.

Finish by rolling and folding the dough to fit snugly into a deep, 8×10in. greased baking pan. Press down well in the corners. Cover the pan with the floured cloth and leave to rise or prove and double in bulk.

Remove the cloth and brush the surface with a little milk and beaten egg, and sprinkle with granulated sugar. Score a criss-cross pattern in the surface with a sharp knife from one side to the other and bake in the preheated oven at 425°F for 30-40 minutes. Turn out of the pan to cool upside-down on a wire rack. Serve cut in slices when tepid or cold.

Red Velvet Cake
Serves 10-12

Ingredients

½ cup margarine	1tsp. bicarbonate of soda
1½ cups sugar	1tsp. white wine vinegar
2 eggs	**Frosting**
4tbsp. red food coloring	3tbsp. flour
2tbsp. unsweetened cocoa	1 cup sugar
2⅔ cups all-purpose flour	1 cup milk
1tsp. salt	1 cup butter
1 cup buttermilk	1tsp. vanilla extract
1tsp. vanilla extract	

Cream the margarine and sugar until fluffy, then beat in the eggs.

Make a paste of the food coloring and cocoa. Add to the butter mixture and blend well.

Sift the flour and salt. Gradually add to the butter mixture, alternating with the buttermilk and vanilla.

Stir the bicarbonate of soda into the vinegar in a large spoon, holding it over the mixing bowl as it foams. Add to the cake mixture stirring well.

Grease two 8in. cake pans. Divide the mixture between them and bake for 30 minutes at 350°F. Cool.

To make the frosting, stir the flour, sugar and milk over a very low heat until thick.

Cream the butter with the vanilla until it is very light.

Beat the cooked mixture into the butter until the frosting has the texture of whipped cream.

To assemble the cake, put one layer, upside down, on a serving dish. Spread with one third of the frosting. Gently place the second layer, right side up on top. Spread the sides of the cake with frosting, and finally the top.

Red Velvet Cake

Chocolate Chip Cake
Serves 8-12

Ingredients

½ cup margarine	1tsp. baking powder
⅓ cup soft brown sugar	3 eggs, separated
1 cup ground hazelnuts	1 orange
¾ cup all-purpose flour	2oz. chocolate pieces

Cream the margarine and sugar until they are light and fluffy. Add the nuts, flour, baking powder, egg yolks and the grated rind and juice of the orange. Mix well. Fold in the chocolate pieces.

Beat the egg whites until they are stiff but not dry. Gently fold into the cake mixture, starting with just one spoonful and gradually adding the remainder.

Grease a 7in. square cake pan and line with waxed paper. Turn the mixture into it and bake for 45 minutes at 325°F.

For a large cake double all the ingredients and use a roasting pan, 9×11in.

Coffee Almond Slice
Serves 8-10

Ingredients

½ cup butter	1tbsp. water
½ cup sugar	1oz. plain chocolate
2 eggs	1¼ cups heavy cream
1 cup+2tbsp. self-rising flour	4tsp. instant powdered coffee dissolved in 1tbsp. hot water
1tbsp. baking powder	
⅓ cup ground almonds	3tbsp. confectioner's sugar
2 drops almond extract	¼ cup chocolate vermicelli

Grease and line a 7×11in. pan with waxed paper.

Put the first 8 ingredients in a bowl. Mix together and beat until smooth.

Pour the batter into the prepared pan. Bake for 25-30 minutes at 350°F until firm to the touch. Turn out, remove paper and cool.

Melt the chocolate until runny and keep warm. Beat the cream with the dissolved coffee and confectioner's sugar until it forms soft peaks.

Trim the edges of the cake and cut into three even-sized pieces.

Spread a layer of cream on one piece, top with a second layer and spread with more cream. Top with the final layer of sponge cake.

Spread the sides with cream and coat with the chocolate vermicelli. Spread the remaining cream on the top.

Spoon the chocolate into a piping bag with a fine nozzle. Pipe straight lines along the length of the cake and with the point of a knife draw lines backwards and forwards across the chocolate lines creating a chevron effect.

Chill for at least an hour before serving.

Chocolate Rum Cake
Serves 6

Ingredients

1tbsp. water
2tbsp. sugar
1/4lb. plain chocolate in small pieces
1tbsp. rum, brandy or Grand Marnier
2/3 cup double cream
20 sponge fingers (Boudoir biscuits)
1/2 cup strong black coffee,
1oz. grated chocolate

Heat the water and sugar, stirring constantly, until the sugar has dissolved. Leave to cool.

Melt the chocolate in the top of a double saucepan. Add the cooled syrup, stirring constantly. Stir in the rum, brandy or Grand Marnier and 3tbsp. cream.

Arrange half of the sponge fingers in the bottom of a serving dish. Carefully sprinkle some of the coffee over the sponge fingers, enough to just moisten them. Spread half of the chocolate mixture over the top.

Arrange a second layer of sponge fingers gently over the chocolate. Sprinkle with coffee and spread with chocolate as before.

Beat the remaining cream until it is just firm. Spread over the top and sides of the cake and chill for 1 hour.

Serve decorated with grated chocolate.

Coffee Carrot Cake
Serves 8-10

Ingredients

1/2 cup butter, softened
3/4 cup sugar
1 egg
1/2tsp. mixed spice
4tbsp. marmalade
2tbsp. orange juice
4tbsp. strong black coffee
1/2lb. carrots, grated
1/2 cup walnuts
1 cup self-rising flour

Topping
1/2 cup soft cream cheese
2/3 cup sweet butter
2/3 cup confectioner's sugar
1tsp. vanilla extract
juice of 1/2 lemon

Cream the butter and sugar together until light and fluffy. Beat in the egg, mixed spice, marmalade, orange rind, juice and coffee. Mix well. Toss the carrots and walnuts in the flour and gradually stir them into the beaten mixture.

Turn into a lined and greased 8in. cake pan and bake for 1 1/2 hours at 350°F.

Cool the cake in the pan for one hour. Remove and finish cooling on a wire rack.

Cream the cream cheese and butter together. Slowly sift in the confectioner's sugar and continue beating until the mixture is quite smooth. Stir in the vanilla and lemon juice.

Spread two-thirds of the mixture on top of the carrot cake. Put the remainder in a piping bag and pipe rosettes around the cake.

Chocolate & Sour Cream Marble Cake

Ingredients

6oz. plain chocolate	⅔ cup sour cream
1 cup butter, softened	2tsp. vanilla extract
1 cup sugar	½tsp. almond extract
4 eggs	confectioner's sugar
good 3 cups self-rising flour	

Melt the chocolate and allow to cool slightly.

Cream together the butter and sugar until light and fluffy. Beat in the eggs one at a time. Add the vanilla and almond extract, and fold in the flour.

Divide the mixture into two. Add the sour cream to one half and the melted chocolate to the other.

In a buttered and thickly-sugared 9-10in. Gugelhupf or ring pan, put alternate spoonfuls of the mixtures. Using a teaspoon, cut down into the mixture and swirl together. Bake at 350°F for about 1 hour.

Serve warm or cold, dredged with confectioner's sugar.

Mocha Hazelnut Cake
Serves 6

Ingredients

	Filling
¾ cup shelled hazelnuts	
3 egg whites	3oz. plain chocolate
1tbsp. instant coffee	2tbsp. coffee liqueur
powder	1¼ cups heavy cream,
½ cup granulated sugar	whipped
1tbsp. white vinegar	½ cup chocolate shavings
2tbsp. grated chocolate	

Roast the hazelnuts in a hot oven until well browned. Put inside a dry dish cloth and rub off the skins. Cool and chop roughly.

Beat the egg whites until they form stiff peaks. Mix the coffee powder with 1tbsp. sugar and beat in. Fold in the remaining sugar and vinegar. Lastly, fold in the nuts with the grated chocolate.

Line two cookie sheets with waxed paper. Mark out two 8in. circles and spread the mixture out to cover them.

Bake for 1¾ hours at 200°F until the meringue has dried out. Cool on wire racks.

For the filling, melt the chocolate with the coffee liqueur. Leave until cool but not set, then fold the chocolate mixture into the cream.

Sandwich the meringue rounds together with the chocolate cream and decorate with the chocolate shavings.

Coffee Fruit Loaf

Ingredients

2¼ cups bread flour
1tsp. salt
1tsp. sugar
small knob lard
1tbsp. fresh yeast
⅔ cup tepid black coffee
4tbsp. vanilla sugar
½ cup dried apricots, chopped

½ cup dried figs, chopped
½ cup roughly chopped almonds

Topping
2tbsp. butter
⅓ cup all-purpose flour
2tbsp. vanilla sugar
1tbsp. instant coffee

Mix the flour, salt and sugar in a bowl and rub in the lard. Blend the yeast with the coffee and add to the flour, mixing to a soft dough that leaves the bowl clean. Cover with lightly greased polyethylene and leave to rise in a warm place until doubled in size.

Line and grease a 1lb. loaf pan. Gently knead in the sugar, apricots, figs and almonds, place in the prepared pan and cover with lightly oiled polyethylene. Leave to prove in a warm place until the mixture comes to the top of the pan.

For the topping, rub the butter into the flour until the mixture resembles breadcrumbs. Stir in the sugar and coffee and spoon over the loaf. Bake for 40-45 minutes at 400°F.

Cool in the pan for 10 minutes and then turn out onto a wire rack.

Serve warm or cold, sliced and spread with butter.

Refrigerator Cookie Cake

Ingredients

1 cup milk or plain chocolate
½ cup butter
¼ cup corn syrup
⅓ cup raisins, soaked overnight in a little rum
½ cup Brazil nuts, roughly chopped

bare ¼ cup glacé cherries, roughly chopped
2 cups crushed vanilla wafers
glacé cherries
whole Brazil nuts

Put chocolate, butter and corn syrup into bowl over a pan of hot water.

When the chocolate has melted, stir in the raisins, nuts and cherries. Add the wafers and mix well together.

Press the mixture into a lined 1lb. loaf tin and chill for at least 4 hours, preferably overnight.

Turn out and decorate with glacé cherries and Brazil nuts.

Mushroom Cake

Ingredients

2tbsp. unsweetened cocoa
    powder
1tbsp. boiling water
½ cup butter or margarine
½ cup light, soft brown
    sugar
2 eggs, beaten
1 cup self-rising flour

Frosting
½ cup butter or margarine
1⅔ cups confectioner's
    sugar
2oz. plain chocolate,
    melted
1 cup marzipan
apricot jam, strained
confectioner's sugar or
    drinking chocolate

Mix together the cocoa powder and water to form a paste. Put butter, sugar and chocolate paste into a bowl and beat until light and fluffy. Beat in the eggs a little at a time. Fold in the flour.

Spread the mixture into one greased and base-lined, 8in. sandwich pan. Bake in the oven at 350°F for about 25 minutes. Turn out and cool.

To make the frosting, cream together the butter or margarine and confectioner's sugar. Stir in the melted chocolate and beat well. Cool. Using a piping bag fitted with a star nozzle, pipe lines of frosting from the edge of the cake to the center, to represent the underside of a mushroom.

Reserve a small piece of marzipan for the stalk. Roll the remaining marizpan out to a strip about 24in. long and wide enough to stand just above the sides of the cake. Brush the sides of the cake with apricot jam. Press the marzipan strip round the edge of the cake. Curve the top of the marzipan over the piped ridges.

Shape the reserved marzipan into a stalk and place in the center of the cake. Sift a little confectioner's sugar or drinking chocolate over the frosting on the cake.

Chequerboard Cake

Ingredients

¾ cup butter or margarine
¾ cup sugar
3 eggs, beaten
1½ cups self-rising flour
1tbsp. milk
2tbsp. unsweetened cocoa
    powder

1tbsp. boiling water
ginger marmalade
¾ cup marzipan
6oz. plain chocolate
3tbsp. butter
crystalized ginger

Divide an 8-in. square cake pan in half by base-lining with foil with a pleat, supported by cardboard, down the center. Grease well.

Cream together the butter or margarine and sugar. Gradually beat in the eggs. Fold in the flour. Divide the mixture in half.

Blend the cocoa powder and boiling water together. Stir the milk into one portion and the chocolate paste into the other. Spoon one flavor into each side of the pan. Bake for about 30 minutes at 375°F. Turn out. Cool.

Trim each piece of cake and divide in half lengthwise. Sandwich alternately together with marmalade and place one pair of cakes on top of the other to form an oblong with square ends.

Cut a sheet of waxed paper big enough to wrap around the cake. Roll the marzipan on top to fit it. Brush the cake with jam. Wrap the marzipan around the cake.

Melt the chocolate with the butter. Spread over the surface of the cake. Decorate with crystalized ginger and leave until set.

Banana Cake

Ingredients

½ cup butter or margarine
⅔ cup dark soft brown
    sugar
3 eggs
4 bananas
2tsp. ground cassia or
    cinnamon

1tsp. baking powder
2tbsp. boiling milk
2¾ cups all-purpose flour
1tsp. baking powder

Melt the butter and sugar together, then beat in the eggs.

Mash the bananas with the cassia or cinnamon. Add to the egg mixture.

Mix the baking powder with the boiling milk and add to the mixture.

Stir in the flour and the second quantity of baking powder, sifted together.

Put into a greased 8×8in. square pan and bake in a preheated oven at 375°F for an hour.

Chocolate Meringue Gateau
Serves 6

Ingredients

3 egg whites	**Filling**
pinch cream of tartar	½lb. plain chocolate
⅔ cups granulated sugar	2 egg yolks
¾ cup ground hazelnuts	3tbsp. water
Sponge	1¼ cups heavy cream
½ cup all-purpose flour	4tbsp. sugar
4tbsp. unsweetened cocoa	red jam
powder	**Decoration**
4 eggs, separated	mixed chopped nuts
4tbsp. sugar	chocolate curls
	confectioner's sugar

Line two cookie sheets with waxed paper. Draw an 7in. circle on each one. Put the egg whites and cream of tartar into a bowl and whisk until stiff. Beat in the sugar a little at a time until mixture is thick and glossy. Fold in the nuts.

Spread or pipe the meringue in the circles marked on the paper. Bake in the oven for 1 hour at 300°F. Turn off heat and leave to dry in closed oven for a further ½ hour, or until crisp. Remove and cool. Carefully peel away the paper.

To make the cake, sift together the flour and cocoa. Beat together the egg yolks and sugar until the mixture is thick and pale. Beat the egg whites until thick, but not stiff. Fold the flour and egg whites alternately into the egg yolk mixture.

Pour into a greased and lined 7in. cake pan. Bake for about 40 minutes at 350°F. Remove and cool.

To make the chocolate cream, melt the chocolate. Cool slightly. Beat together the eggs and water. Stir the melted chocolate into the egg yolks, mixing well. Put in a pan and cook very gently for a minute. Cool.

Beat together the cream and sugar until soft peaks form. Fold into the chocolate mixture. Cover and chill.

To assemble the gâteau, cut the cake into two layers and spread each with a little red jam. Put a meringue round on a plate and spread with a little chocolate cream. Top with a layer of sponge, spread with cream and place on the second meringue round. Spread with cream and place on the second layer of sponge. Spread remaining chocolate cream over top and sides of cake. To decorate, put chopped nuts round side of cake. Top with chocolate curls and sprinkle with confectioner's sugar.

Family Chocolate Cake

Ingredients

3oz. plain chocolate	2-3 drops vanilla extract
3tbsp. clear honey	⅔ cup milk
½ cup butter or margarine	**Frosting**
½ cup sugar	2oz. plain chocolate
2 eggs	3tbsp. water
1 cup. self-rising flour	2tbsp. butter
2tbsp. unsweetened cocoa	1 cup confectioner's sugar,
powder	sifted
1½level tsp. baking powder	

Put the chocolate and honey into a small bowl over a pan of hot water. Stir until the chocolate has melted. Cool.

Cream together the butter or margarine and sugar until light and fluffy. Beat in the chocolate mixture, then the eggs.

Sift together the flour, cocoa powder and baking powder. Stir in the flour mixture a little at a time, alternately with the vanilla extract and milk. Pour mixture into a lined 7½in. round cake pan.

Bake in the oven at 350°F for about 45 minutes. Turn on to a wire rack, leaving the lining paper on the cake to form a collar.

When the cake is cool, make the frosting. Put the chocolate and water into a small saucepan and melt over a gentle heat. Remove from the heat and stir in the butter. When the butter has melted, beat in the confectioner's sugar.

Spread the frosting over the top of the cake and swirl with a palette knife. When frosting is firm, remove the lining paper from the cake.

Lemon and Clove Cake

Ingredients

½ cup butter	1tsp. baking powder
½ cup brown granulated	juice and grated rind of 1
sugar	lemon
2 eggs	pinch cloves, powdered
¾ cup fine wholewheat	2tbsp. lemon curd
flour	2tbsp. granulated sugar

Cream the butter and sugar. Beat the eggs together. Sift the flour and baking powder together and mix. Add the beaten egg and lemon rind, mix gradually into the creamed butter and sugar. Sprinkle the cloves in. Add the lemon curd and mix thoroughly.

Put the mixture into a greased and floured cake pan and bake in the oven at 350°F for an hour.

Dissolve the sugar in the lemon juice and pour it over the cake when you remove the cake from the oven. Take the cake out of the pan when it is cool.

Russian Seedcake

This simple yet deliciously aromatic cake is the perfect ending to any meal. Serve it with Russian-style tea — stir a spoonful of preserves or rum, or both, into each glass of tea.

Ingredients

2½ cups sugar	2tbsp. sesame seeds
2 cups unsalted butter	2tbsp. caraway seeds
10 eggs	½ cup orange juice
3½ cups flour	½tsp. cinnamon
1tsp. salt	raspberry or plum
2tsp. baking powder	preserves to decorate
3tsp. vanilla extract	

Preheat the oven to 350°F. Cream the sugar and butter together in a large mixing bowl. Add the eggs, two at a time, beating well after each addition. Add the flour, salt, baking powder, vanilla extract, sesame seeds, caraway seeds, orange juice and cinnamon. Beat for 7 minutes. Butter and flour a 12in. diameter cake pan. Pour in the batter and bake for 1 hour or until a cocktail stick inserted in the center of the cake comes out clean.

Remove the cake from the oven and leave it to cool to room temperature. Spread the top of the cake with raspberry or plum preserves and serve.

Coffee Knots
Serves 8-10

Ingredients

1tbsp. fresh yeast
4tbsp. tepid strong milky
   coffee
1tsp. vanilla sugar
2 cups strong white flour
½tsp. salt

2tbsp. butter
1 egg, beaten
vegetable oil for deep frying
1tsp. sugar
1tsp. cocoa

Blend the yeast with the coffee and sugar. Leave in a warm place until frothy. Sift the flour and salt into a large bowl and rub in the butter. Add the egg and yeast liquid to the dry ingredients and beat for five minutes.

Divide the dough into 8-10 pieces and shape them into an 7in. long roll. Tie each into a knot.

Heat the oil to 350°F and fry the doughnuts for 5-10 minutes, until golden brown.

Drain on paper towels. Stir sugar and cocoa together and toss the warm doughnuts in it.

Yeasted Crescents
Makes 15 crescents

Yeasted Crescents, or Kipfel, are a traditional favorite pastry in Austria. A charming legend attached to them suggests that they were first baked in Vienna, in 1683, during the Turkish siege of the city. The crescent, in imitation of their invaders' emblem, was the Austrian gesture of defiance.

Ingredients

1tbsp. fresh yeast
¼ cup milk, warmed to
   blood heat
1½tbsp. granulated sugar
1¼ cups strong all-purpose
   flour, sifted
pinch salt
2 small egg yolks
5tbsp. butter

Walnut filling
¼ cup granulated sugar
1tbsp. milk
good 1 cup ground
   walnuts
1tsp. lemon rind
1 small apple, peeled and
   grated

Prepare the Yeast Sponge with the yeast, warm milk, 1tsp. sugar and 2tbsp. flour taken from the main quantity; blend and beat well. Cover and set aside to rise.

Sift the rest of the flour with the salt into a large warm bowl and make a well in the center. Drop in the lightly beaten egg yolks, the butter cut in pieces and the sugar. Draw a little flour in from the sides and pour in the sponge batter.

Combine all the ingredients by beating at first, then kneading, until the dough is very elastic and large bubbles of air start to form. Cover with a cloth and leave in a warm place for 1-2 hours to rise and double in volume.

Knock the dough back and roll it out on a floured board to ⅛in. thick. Cut into 4in. triangles and place a spoonful of filling (see below) in the center of each. Roll the pastry up starting from the base line, bending it into a crescent shape. Lay the pastries on a greased and floured cookie sheet and brush them with lightly beaten egg.

Cover the pastries with a lightly floured cloth and leave to rise for a further 30-40 minutes until they have doubled in size. Brush again with beaten egg and bake in the warmed oven at 375°F until risen and golden. Cool on a wire rack and dredge with confectioner's sugar to serve.

Prepare the filling following the instructions for Poppy Seed or Walnut Roll.

Eliza Leslie's Ginger Cup Cakes
Makes 28 cup cakes

This is a modern interpretation of a recipe in Eliza Leslie's *Seventy-Five Recipes for Pastry, Cakes and Sweetmeats: By a Lady of Philadelphia*, published in 1828.

Ingredients

½ cup butter	½tsp. ground allspice
scant ½ cup light brown sugar	1tsp. ground cloves
	2tsp. ground ginger
¾ cup molasses	1 egg
2 cups all-purpose flour	1 egg yolk
1tsp. bicarbonate of soda	4tbsp. milk

Gently heat the butter, sugar and molasses in a pan until the butter has melted and the sugar dissolved. (Do not boil or the cakes will be hard.) Draw off the heat to cool.

Sift together two or three times, the flour, bicarbonate, allspice, cloves and ginger, into a large bowl. Make a well in the middle.

Beat the egg and egg yolk with about half the milk and pour the mixture into the flour with the cooled syrup. Beat to a smooth batter, adding more milk if necessary.

Use waxed paper cases and fill each no more than half full with the mixture, which rises a lot during baking. Bake at 325°F for 30 minutes, until well risen. The cakes should feel slightly soft to the touch. Leave to cool on wire racks.

Doughnuts
Makes 27 doughnuts

The Rhinelanders of Germany began emigrating to Pennsylvania in the seventeenth century when the religious persecution and deprivation in their native land had become intolerable. The Pennsylvania Dutch, as they were known, brought *Fastnachts* with them from the Old World, delicious yeasted doughnuts, which were baked for Shrovetide and Christmas.

All the ingredients should be at room temperature before baking commences and the flour warmed.

Ingredients

1 cup+2tbsp. milk, warmed to blood heat	½tsp. salt
	1tbsp. brandy
2tbsp. fresh yeast	1tsp. rose water
3½ cups strong all-purpose flour, sifted	rose conserve or raspberry jam for the filling
2tbsp. sugar	granulated sugar for dredging
8 egg yolks, lightly beaten	
scant ½ cup butter	

Prepare the Yeast Batter with ⅓ cup milk, the yeast, 1 cup flour and 1tsp. of sugar. Beat well. Set aside to ferment. Mix half the remaining milk with the egg yolks and set aside. Melt the butter in the rest of the milk. Cool to lukewarm.

Sift together the rest of the flour with the salt into a large bowl and make a well in the center. Stir in the rest of the sugar, the fermented yeast and the milk mixture. Blend all together and beat well until the dough thickens. Add the brandy and rose water and continue beating until the dough texture is smooth, shiny and will drop off a spoon.

Take out half the mixture and cover the bowl with a warm dish towel while you prepare the first batch of doughnuts.

Dust the work-top well with flour and drop the mixture on to it. Dredge with just a little flour and gently roll it out to about ½in. thick. Using a floured glass or cookie cutter about 2in. in diameter, lightly press circles into half the dough, but do not actually cut it.

Place a small teaspoonful of jam in the center of each. Cut out the same number of circles from the other half of the dough, and turn the top, unfloured sides over onto the jam circles.

Stick the doughnut edges well together (the jam must not leak out as they cook) and gently press around the edges with the end of a teaspoon handle. Cut out each pastry with a slightly smaller cutter. Turn over the finished doughnuts and place them well apart on a floured board, covered lightly with a dish towel.

Set the doughnuts to rise in a warm place and turn them over when they have risen on one side so that the other side may rise. Assemble the left-over scraps and beat them into the remaining dough with 2 spoonfuls of warm milk and finish in the same way.

A light and well-risen doughnut should have a pale ring around its middle, and the wider the ring, the lighter the pastry will be. Cook only four or five pastries at a time and always start by cooking the side that has risen first.

Heat the vegetable oil to 330-350°F. Using a large slotted spoon, gently lower each pastry into the hot oil at 4-second intervals. Watch them all the time for they brown very quickly. As soon as they have colored well, which takes about 2 minutes, flip each one over and cook the other side until it it golden brown.

Lift the doughnuts out of the oil, drain on paper towels for a minute or two and roll them in granulated sugar. Serve the doughnuts while they are still warm.

Chocolate Ring Doughnuts
Makes about 12

Ingredients

2 cups all-purpose flour
½tsp. bicarbonate of soda
1tsp. cream of tartar
2tbsp. butter
¼ cup soft brown sugar
2oz. plain chocolate
1tsp. vanilla extract
1 egg, beaten
milk

oil for deep frying
granulated sugar mixed
   with ground cinnamon
Frosting
4oz. plain chocolate
4tbsp. milk and water
   mixed
1 cup confectioner's sugar,
   sifted

Sift the flour, bicarbonate of soda and cream of tartar into a bowl. Rub in the butter and stir in the sugar.

Melt the vanilla extract and chocolate together. Pour the beaten egg and chocolate into the dry ingredients and mix to a stiff dough, adding a little milk if necessary.

Knead very lightly and roll out until about ½in. thick. Using a floured ring cutter (or a large and small round pastry cutter) stamp out doughnuts. Reserve the centers.

Heat the oil to 360°F and fry the doughnuts a few at a time until golden brown. Drain and cool. Cook the doughnut centers (called doughnut "holes"). Drain. While still warm toss in granulated sugar which has cinnamon added to it. Serve doughnut "holes" warm.

To make the frosting, melt the chocolate and liquid together. Add the confectioner's sugar and beat well.

Spread frosting over cooled doughnut rings. These are always best eaten on the day they are made.

Spiced Buttermilk Scones
Makes 8

Ingredients

2 cups all-purpose flour
2 cups wholewheat flour
2tsp. bicarbonate of soda
2tsp. cream of tartar
1tbsp. fruit sugar (fructose)
  or 2tbsp. white sugar

1tsp. mixed spice
½ cup butter, diced
1¼ cups buttermilk
3tsp. baking powder

Preheat the oven to 425°F.

Sift the flours together and mix thoroughly with the other dry ingredients. Rub the butter in well with your fingertips.

Stir in the buttermilk and mix to form a soft dough.

Knead the dough lightly on a floured board. Divide in half, form each half into a round and cut each round into four wedges.

Arrange the wedges on a greased cookie sheet, dust with flour and bake for about 12 minutes. Cool on a wire rack.

These scones are best eaten while still warm, split and filled with butter and jam, or jam and clotted cream.

Muesli Scones
Makes 10-12

These scones have a lovely nutty flavor, and crunchy texture.

Ingredients

1¾ cups wholemeal flour
⅓ cup sugar-free muesli
4tsp. baking powder
3tbsp. butter, diced

3tbsp. brown sugar
1 egg
¾ cup light cream

Rub together the flour, muesli, baking powder, butter and sugar until well-mixed.

Add the egg and enough cream to make a soft, but not sticky dough.

Turn this out onto a well-floured board and roll out to 1in. thick. Cut into 1½in. rounds with a plain cookie cutter.

Arrange the scones on well-greased cookie sheets and cook in a preheated oven at 425°F for 10 minutes until well-risen and golden.

Serve warm, split and buttered.

Blueberry Muffins
Makes about 36 breakfast muffins

Ingredients

1lb. blueberries, washed and thoroughly dried	2 eggs, beaten
2½ cups all-purpose flour	1¼ cups milk
¼ cup butter	1tbsp. grated lemon rind
⅓ cup sugar	2tsp. baking powder
	1tsp. salt

Preheat the oven to 400°F. Put the berries in a strainer and add a few spoonfuls of flour. Shake strainer to dust berries lightly. Cream together the butter and sugar. Stir in the eggs, then the milk and lemon rind. Sift together flour, baking powder and salt and gradually stir into the moist ingredients to make a lumpy batter (do not overstir). Gently stir in berries. Fill greased muffin pan hollows two-thirds full with batter. Bake muffins for about 25 minutes until firm and golden.

Bran and Raisin Muffins
Makes 12

Ingredients

2tbsp. oil	½ cup bran
2tbsp. honey	2tsp. baking powder
1 egg	pinch salt
⅔ cup milk	½ cup white raisins
1⅓ cup wholewheat flour	

Preheat the oven to 375°F.

Beat together the oil and honey. Beat in the egg. Gradually beat in the milk until smooth.

Combine the dry ingredients and stir these into the liquid ones. When the bran has soaked up the liquid, you should have a soft dough.

Spoon into oiled muffin pans and bake for about 20 minutes.

Madeleines

Madeleines
Makes 36 cakes

When Madeleines are mentioned, one immediately thinks of Marcel Proust. In his *Remembrance of Things Past* the French author recalls his childhood and Sunday mornings taking lime tea and Madeleines with his aunt in Combray. He found "the taste of the crumb of Madeleine soaked in her decoction of lime-flowers ... an exquisite pleasure [that] invaded my senses".

Ingredients

good ½ cup sweet butter	pinch salt
1tbsp. honey	2in. vanilla pod, split
scant ½ cup granulated sugar	1½ cups all-purpose flour, sifted
1tbsp. soft brown sugar	flaked almonds
3 eggs	

Gently melt the butter in the honey and set aside to cool. Beat the granulated and brown sugars with the eggs and salt until the "ribbon stage", that is, when the volume has trebled and a thick ribbon of batter will drop off the whisk and leave a trail in the mixture for at least 5 seconds. Beat in the vanilla seeds.

Lightly fold in the flour in three stages and finally fold in the cooled butter and honey mixture, taking care not to mix in any of the sediment in the bottom of the pan.

Half fill each of the buttered and floured madeleine molds and sprinkle a few flaked almonds on top of each.

Bake at 350°F for 20 minutes until risen and golden. Leave to cool on a wire rack before storing in an airtight container.

Raspberry Chocolate Eclairs
Makes approx. 10

Ingredients

¼ cup butter or margarine, cut in pieces	**Filling**
⅔ cup water	⅔ cup heavy cream
⅔ cup all-purpose flour, sifted	½lb. fresh raspberries
	a little sugar
2 eggs, beaten	**Topping**
	6oz. plain chocolate
	2tbsp. butter

Put the butter or margarine and water into a pan and bring to a boil.

Remove from the heat and tip all the flour into the pan at once. Beat with a wooden spoon until the paste forms a ball. Cool.

Beat the eggs into the paste, a little at a time. Continue beating until mixture is glossy.

Put pastry into a piping bag fitted with a large plain nozzle. Pipe 3in. lengths onto greased cookie sheets and bake at 400°F for about 25 minutes, until golden brown.

Remove from the oven and make a couple of slits in the sides of each one to allow steam to escape. Return to the oven for a few minutes to dry. Cool on a wire rack.

To make the filling, beat the cream until stiff. Fold in the raspberries and sugar to taste.

Split one side of each eclair and fill with the cream mixture.

Melt together the chocolate and butter. Dip the tops of the eclairs into the chocolate and leave to set.

Maids of Honor
Makes 8

Ingredients

½lb. Puff Pastry	3tbsp. sugar
2tbsp. apricot jam	rind of 1 lemon
1⅓ cups farmer's cheese	2tbsp. ground almonds
1 egg	1tbsp. currants
1 egg yolk	confectioner's sugar

Roll out the pastry and line 8 tart tins. Put a little jam into each.

Beat the cheese until it is smooth. Add the egg and extra yolk and mix well.

Stir in the lemon rind and ground almonds and fold in the currants.

Carefully spoon the filling into the prepared pastry cases.

Bake for 25 minutes at 400°F. Serve cool but not chilled, dredged with a little confectioner's sugar.

Brownies
Makes 8-12

Ingredients

good 4tbsp. butter	*1tsp. baking powder*
2 eggs	*3tbsp. unsweetened cocoa*
1 cup sugar	*1 cup chopped walnuts*
³⁄₄ cup all-purpose flour	

Melt the butter and leave to cool slightly.

Beat the eggs and sugar until they are very light and fluffy.

Sift together the flour and baking powder.

Stir the flour, baking powder, cocoa, walnuts and melted butter into the egg mixture. Mix well.

Spoon the brownie mixture into a greased 8in. square baking tray and bake for 30 minutes at 375°F.

Cut the brownies into squares while they are warm, but leave in their pan until they have cooled completely.

Triple Decker Squares
Makes 16

Ingredients

¹⁄₂ cup butter or margarine,	*¹⁄₃ cup sugar*
softened	*2tbsp. corn syrup*
¹⁄₄ cup sugar	*6oz. can condensed milk*
1³⁄₄ cup all-purpose flour	**Topping**
Filling	*6oz. plain chocolate*
¹⁄₂ cup butter or margarine	*2tbsp. milk*

Cream together the butter or margarine and sugar until light and fluffy. Stir in the flour. Work the dough with your hands and knead well together.

Roll out and press into a shallow 8in. square pan. Prick well with a fork. Bake at 350°F for 25-30 minutes. Cool in the pan.

To make the filling, put all the ingredients into a pan and heat gently, stirring until the sugar has dissolved.

Bring to a boil and cook, stirring for 5-7 minutes until golden.

Pour the caramel over the shortbread base and leave to set.

Melt the chocolate and milk together. Spread it evenly over the caramel. Leave until quite cold before cutting into squares.

Chocolate Meringues
Makes 6-8

Ingredients

3 egg whites
$\frac{1}{3}$ cup granulated sugar
$\frac{2}{3}$ cup confectioner's sugar, sifted
2 tbsp. unsweetened cocoa powder, sifted

Filling
$\frac{2}{3}$ cup heavy cream
1 tbsp. soft brown sugar
2 tsp. unsweetened cocoa powder

Beat the egg whites until they form stiff peaks. Gradually beat in the granulated sugar, a little at a time. Beat in the confectioner's sugar. Fold in the cocoa powder.

Put the mixture into a piping bag fitted with a large star nozzle and pipe into spirals on cookie sheets lined with waxed paper.

Bake in the oven at 225°F for 2-3 hours or until the meringues are dry. Cool on a wire rack.

Whip the cream until stiff. Stir in the sugar and cocoa. Sandwich the meringues together, two at a time, with the chocolate cream.

Butterfly Cakes
Makes 12-14

Ingredients

$\frac{1}{2}$ cup butter, softened
$\frac{1}{2}$ cup sugar
2 eggs
1 tsp. grated orange rind
$\frac{1}{2}$ cup finely grated plain chocolate
1 cup+2 tbsp. self-rising flour

Frosting
6 tbsp. butter or margarine
1 cup confectioner's sugar, sifted
$\frac{1}{3}$ cup melted plain chocolate

Decoration
confectioner's sugar
seedless raspberry jam or glacé cherries

Cream the butter and sugar together until light and fluffy, then beat in the eggs, a little at a time. Stir in the orange rind and chocolate, and finally fold in the flour.

Arrange paper cases in a metal muffin pan. Divide the mixture between the cases and bake at 350°F for about 15-20 minutes. Cool.

To make the frosting, cream together the butter and confectioner's sugar. Gradually beat in the cooled, melted chocolate.

Starting $\frac{1}{4}$ in. from the edge, remove the top of each cake by cutting in and slightly down to form a cavity.

Pipe a little frosting in the cavity of each cake.

Sprinkle the reserved cake tops with a little confectioner's sugar and cut each one in half. Position each half on the frosting to form wings.

Pipe small rosettes of frosting in the centre of each cake, and top with a small blob of raspberry jam or half a glacé cherry.

Jaffa Cakes
Makes 18

Ingredients

2 eggs
$\frac{1}{4}$ cup sugar
$\frac{2}{3}$ cup self-rising flour, sifted
approx. 4 tbsp. marmalade, strained

$\frac{1}{4}$ lb. plain chocolate
rind of $\frac{1}{4}$ orange, finely grated
2 tsp. corn oil
1 tbsp. water

Beat the eggs and sugar until thick and creamy; when the whisk is lifted the mixture leaves a trail. If using a hand whisk, put the bowl over a pan of hot water, then fold in the flour.

Spoon the mixture into 18 well-greased, round-bottomed muffin pans. Bake for about 10 minutes at 400°F until golden brown. Cool on a wire rack.

Spread a little marmalade over each cake.

Put the chocolate, orange rind, oil and water into a bowl over a pan of hot water. Stir well until melted. Cool until the chocolate starts to thicken and then spoon over the marmalade. Leave to set.

Chocolate Chip Cookies
Makes about 30

Ingredients

1 cup self-raising flour	*¼ cup sugar*
2tbsp. unsweetened cocoa	*2 eggs*
powder	*½tsp. vanilla extract*
½tsp. baking powder	*1½ cups chocolate chips*
½ cup butter or margarine	*⅔ cup chopped walnuts*
¼ cup brown sugar	

Sift together the flour, cocoa and baking powder. Beat together the butter or margarine and sugars until light and fluffy. Beat in the eggs one at a time and then add the vanilla. Add the dry ingredients and beat until well combined. Stir in the chocolate chips and the nuts.

Drop the dough in heaped teaspoonfuls onto a cookie sheet. Bake in the oven at 375°F for about 10 minutes. Cool for a minute then remove from cookie sheet and cool on a wire rack.

Chocolate Malties
Makes 20-24

Ingredients

3oz. plain chocolate	*6tbsp. milk*
⅓ cup cream cheese	*bare 1 cup self-rising flour*
⅓ cup butter or margarine,	*½tsp. baking powder*
softened	*2 eggs*
2tbsp. instant malted milk	*chocolate chips (optional)*
powder	
few drops vanilla extract	
2½ cups confectioner's	
sugar, sifted	

Melt the chocolate and cool slightly.

Beat together the cream cheese, two thirds of the butter or margarine, malted milk powder and vanilla extract. Beat in the confectioner's sugar and 3tbsp. of the milk alternately, and finally the melted chocolate.

Remove 1 cup of the chocolate mixture. Cover and reserve for the frosting.

Sift together the flour and baking powder.

Beat the remaining softened butter or margarine into the chocolate mixture, then the eggs and the flour alternately with the remaining 3tbsp. milk.

Put cupcake cases into patty tins and fill two thirds full with the mixture.

Bake at 350°F for about 20 minutes. Cool.

Frost the cakes with the reserved chocolate mixture and decorate, if you like, with chocolate chips.

"Christmas Pudding" Cakes
Makes 4-6

Ingredients

4oz. plain chocolate	**Decoration**
2tbsp. butter	*grated chocolate*
2tbsp. orange juice	*a little thick white Glacé*
2tbsp. confectioner's sugar	*Frosting*
2tbsp. cake crumbs	*glacé cherries*
(preferably a plain	*angelica leaves*
sponge)	
1tbsp. ground almonds	

Melt the chocolate in a bowl over a pan of hot water. Stir in the butter until melted. Remove from heat.

Stir in the orange juice, confectioner's sugar, cake crumbs and ground almonds. Mix well. Chill for about 1 hour until firm.

Roll into balls and coat in grated chocolate.

Put into small paper cake cases. Top with a little thick Glacé Frosting and decorate with pieces of glacé cherry and angelica leaves.

Danish Pastries
Makes about 16

Ingredients

2tbsp. fresh yeast	³⁄₄ cup confectioner's sugar,
²⁄₃ cup tepid water	sifted
1lb. all-purpose flour	3oz. plain chocolate,
pinch salt	melted
¼ cup lard	¼ cup finely chopped
2tbsp. sugar	toasted almonds
2 eggs, beaten	a few drops almond extract
1¼ cups butter	**Glaze**
Filling	1 egg, beaten
¼ cup butter	honey

Blend the yeast and water together. Sift flour and salt into a bowl and rub in the lard. Stir in the sugar.

Add the yeast liquid and eggs to the flour and mix to a smooth elastic dough. Knead lightly. Put into a lightly-oiled bowl and cover with plastic wrap. Chill for 10 minutes.

Soften the butter and shape into a flat oblong on waxed paper.

Roll out the dough on a floured surface to a rectangle three times the size of the butter. Place the butter in the center of the dough and fold the dough over to enclose it. Press the rolling pin firmly along the open sides. Give the dough a quarter turn and roll out to a rectangle three times as long as it is wide.

Fold into three. Wrap in plastic wrap and chill for 10 minutes. Repeat the rolling and folding three more times.

To make the filling, beat together the butter and confectioner's sugar. Beat in the chocolate, almonds and extract. Chill. Roll out the dough thinly and cut into 3in. squares.

Put a rounded teaspoonful of filling on to the center of each square. Bring opposite corners of the dough to the center. Either seal with beaten egg or insert a wooden cocktail stick through.

Place on a greased cookie sheet. Cover with greased plastic wrap and leave to prove for about 30 minutes. Brush with beaten egg. Bake for about 20 minutes at 425°F. Brush with a little honey while warm.

Chocolate Boxes
Makes 9

Ingredients

1 egg	2tbsp. apricot jam, strained
2tbsp. sugar	**Decoration**
4tbsp. all-purpose flour	Chocolate Squares
Filling	whipped cream
²⁄₃ cup water	9 mandarin orange
²⁄₃ cup tangerine jelly	segments
1¹⁄₃ cups farmer's cheese	quartered walnuts
1¼ cups heavy cream	

Beat the egg and sugar together until the mixture is thick and creamy and the whisk leaves a trail when lifted. Using a metal spoon, gently fold in the flour. Pour into a shallow greased and base-lined, 7in. square pan. Bake for 10-12 minutes at 400°F. Turn out and cool.

Heat the water. Add the jelly and stir until dissolved. Chill until the mixture begins to turn syrupy.

Beat the cheese and gradually add the jelly. Whip the cream until thick and fold into the cheese mixture. Pour into an 7in. square cake pan, lined with waxed paper. Chill until set.

Spread the sponge with apricot jam. Unmold the cheese mixture onto the sponge. Trim edges.

Cut the cake into nine squares. Press a chocolate square onto each side of each cake. To serve, pipe whipped cream on top of each chocolate box. Top with mandarins and walnuts.

Variation Use cherry jelly, cherry jam and top with canned or fresh cherries.

Use strawberry/raspberry jelly, strawberry/rasberry jam and top with fresh strawberries/raspberries.

Use lemon jelly, lemon curd and top with pieces of canned or fresh pineapple.

Use lime jelly, lime marmalade and top with halved slices of kiwi fruit.

Note To make Chocolate Squares, melt all-purpose chocolate and spread evenly onto waxed paper. Leave to set. Using a ruler, mark into squares and cut.

Sweetheart Cookies
Serves 10-12

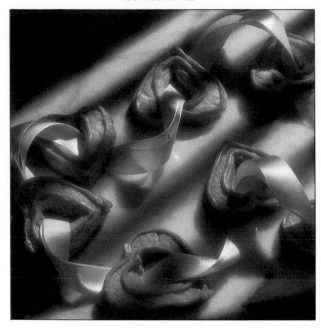

Ingredients
½ cup butter	**Decoration**
½ cup sugar	¾ cup confectioner's sugar,
2tbsp. coffee extract	sifted
1 egg	1-2tbsp. warm water
2½ cups all-purpose flour	a few drops of red food
	coloring
	pink and cream ribbons
	½in. wide

Cream the butter and sugar together until pale and fluffy. Stir in the coffee extract and egg, and mix thoroughly. Fold in the flour and turn the mixture onto a board dusted with confectioner's sugar.

Knead gently and roll out to ¼in. thickness and cut into heart shapes. Cut a smaller heart shape in the center for the ribbon. Place on a cookie sheet and bake for approximately 15 minutes at 350°F and leave to cool.

Put the decoration ingredients into a bowl and mix until smooth. Spoon into a piping bag with a fine all-purpose nozzle and pipe around the edges of the cookies and round the shape in the center.

Allow to dry and thread the ribbons through the cookies and tie.

Chocolate Spiced Cookies
Makes 60 pieces

In Austria it is customary to hang Chocolate Spiced Cookies on the Christmas Tree. Pierce a hole in each cookie while it is still warm.

Ingredients
1 cup ground unblanched almonds	3 egg whites
	1 cup confectioner's sugar,
2oz. plain chocolate, grated	sifted
	ice-cream wafers
⅓ cup candied orange and lemon peel, chopped small	**Icing**
	2oz. plain chocolate
1tsp. ground cinnamon	½ cup confectioner's sugar,
1tsp. ground cloves	sifted

Mix together in a bowl the almonds, chocolate, candied peel and spices. Make sure that the orange and lemon peel are separated and coated with nuts. Set aside.

Beat the egg whites until they stand in firm, snowy peaks. Sift over and beat in the confectioner's sugar in three stages and continue beating for about 7 minutes by machine (15 minutes by hand) until the mixture is thick, satiny and very smooth. Tip the nut mixture onto the meringue and use a large metal spoon to fold it in lightly.

Prepare the wafers by cutting them with sharp cookie cutters into diamonds, squares or heart shapes. Pile a little of the nut meringue mixture on each of the wafers and taper it up from the sides into the middle in a dome about ½in. high. Cover and leave to dry overnight in the kitchen.

Place the cookies close together on a cookie sheet — they do not rise — and bake in a preheated oven at 350°F for 25 minutes or until pale golden brown. Lay them to cool on a wire rack.

To make the icing, melt the chocolate with 1½tbsp. of water in a small bowl set over a pan of simmering water. Stir to combine. Sift the confectioner's sugar into another bowl and stir in 1tbsp. hot water, then blend in the chocolate mixture and stir until smooth. Cover the bowl with a damp cloth to keep it moist. As soon as the cookies are cool enough to handle, dip each one into the chocolate mixture, holding it by the base.

Cinnamon Stars
Makes 30 pieces

A Christmas specialty, Cinnamon Stars are often used as Christmas tree decorations. Use a cocktail stick or skewer to pierce a hole in the top of each cookie before baking.

Ingredients
2 egg whites	1tbsp. ground cinnamon
1 cup+2tbsp. granulated sugar	1½tbsp. kirsch
2 cups unblanched almonds, coarsely ground	

Beat the egg whites until stiff, then mix in the sugar and beat for about 10 minutes by machine (20 minutes by hand) until the mixture is very thick, white and highly glossed. Reserve about 6tbsp. of the mixture.

Mix the almonds, spice and kirsch into the rest of the "snow". Gather into a ball, cover and chill for 30 minutes. Roll the paste out on a sugared board to ⅜in. thick, and cut out star shapes with a pastry cutter.

Transfer the cookies to a highly buttered waxed paper-lined cookie sheet and smooth some of the reserved meringue on top of each. Bake at 400°F for 15 minutes. Cool on a wire rack. These cookies keep for several weeks stored in an airtight container.

Coffee Macaroons

Ingredients

rice paper	1tbsp. cornstarch
1 cup ground almonds	2-3 drops vanilla extract
¾ cup sugar	1tbsp. coffee extract
2 egg whites	12 chocolate coffee beans

Line two or three cookie sheets with rice paper. Mix the ground almonds, sugar and all but 1tbsp. of the egg white together. Stir until all the ingredients are evenly blended. Stir in the cornstarch, vanilla extract and coffee extract.

Spoon into a piping bag fitted with a ½in. plain nozzle. Pipe the mixture onto the rice paper in large round circles. Top each one with a chocolate coffee bean. Brush with the remaining egg white.

Bake the coffee macaroons at 375°F for 15 minutes or until lightly browned, risen and slightly cracked. Cut the rice paper to fit round each coffee macaroon and leave to cool on a wire rack.

Nun's Pretzels
Makes 25-30 pieces

Ingredients

2tbsp. butter	bare ½ cup heavy cream
1 small egg	1¼ cups all-purpose flour,
bare 1 cup confectioner's	sifted
sugar	coarse sugar

Beat the butter and egg until creamy. Mix in the sugar and cream. Sift most of the flour on to the work-top, make a well in the center and drop in the mixture. Combine the ingredients to make a smooth pastry.

Roll into a ball, wrap in plastic wrap and chill for at least 30 minutes. Divide the dough into two and leave half in the refrigerator while you work with the other.

Pinch off walnut-sized pieces of dough, and lightly roll each into a rope about ¼in. thick and 9in. long, slightly tapered at the ends.

To shape the pretzel, lift up both ends and cross them over in the center by pressing both the ends lightly on the top of the roll. Place on a greased and floured cookie sheet. Finish the rest of the dough in the same way.

Brush the pastries with lightly beaten egg white and sprinkle with a little coarse sugar. Bake in the pre-heated oven at 400°F for 20 minutes until only just colored. Cool on a wire rack. Serve with coffee. Stored in an airtight container, pretzels will keep fresh for several weeks.

Vanilla Crescents
Makes 20 pieces

Ingredients

1 good cup all-purpose	3tbsp. granulated sugar
flour, sifted	vanilla flavored, sifted
⅓ cup sweet butter, chilled	confectioner's sugar for
½ cup ground almonds	dredging

Sift the flour on to the work-top and cut in the cold butter. Blend together into a fine crumb texture and fork in the almonds and sugar. Knead into a smooth pastry. Pinch off walnut-sized pieces and roll each into a cylindrical rope with tapered ends; curve gently into a crescent or quarter-moon shape. Transfer to a buttered and floured cookie sheet and bake in the warmed oven at 300°F for about 30 minutes or until lightly colored.

Prepare a large sheet of waxed paper and dredge generously with vanilla confectioner's sugar. Remove the crescents from the oven and leave to cool for 1-2 minutes. While they are still warm, lift the pastries one at a time, between two forks, and roll them in the confectioner's sugar so that they are completely coated. Leave to cool on a clean sheet of waxed paper on a wire rack.

The crescents will keep fresh for several weeks stored in an airtight container.

Vanilla Crescents and Nun's Pretzels

Flapjacks

Ingredients

½ cup butter
3tbsp. light muscavado
* sugar*
⅓ cup corn syrup
¾tsp. ground ginger
2 cups porridge oats
½ cup flaked almonds

Heat the butter, sugar and syrup gently in a small pan until the butter has melted and the sugar dissolved. Stir until smooth. Take off the heat and stir in the ginger, oats and almonds. Spread the mixture out in a buttered 13½×9½in. jelly roll pan. Bake until golden at 350°F (about 15-20 minutes), taking care that it does not scorch; it should still feel quite soft to the touch. Cut into fingers in the pan with a buttered knife while still hot. Flapjacks harden and crisp as they cool. Leave to cool in the pan. They keep well in an airtight container.

Scottish Shortbread
Makes 60 pieces

Butter shortbread originated in Scotland as a festive confection, particularly for Christmas and Hogmanay.

Ingredients

1 cup sweet butter
¾ cup confectioner's sugar,
* sifted*
1in. vanilla pod, split
2tsp. hot water
1 cup+2tbsp. all-purpose
* flour*
1 cup+2tbsp. potato flour

Cream the butter, add the confectioner's sugar and blend well. Work the ingredients by hand in a chilled bowl as little and as quickly as possible. Do not use an electric mixer, which tends to over-beat and make the pastry heavy.

Mix in the seeds of vanilla and stir in the hot water. Sift the flours together two or three times and combine lightly with the butter and sugar mixture. Gather the pastry into a ball, divide and roll into two long ropes about ¾in. in diameter. Wrap closely in plastic wrap and chill for at least 1 hour. (The pastry may be frozen at this stage for up to 2 months.)

Cut ½in. slices with a sharp knife and space 1-1½in. apart on a greased and flored cookie sheet. Bake at 325°F for 25 minutes until slightly colored. Cool on a wire rack. Dredge with confectioner's sugar and store between sheets of waxed paper in an airtight container.

Ginger Snaps
Makes 30 snaps

Ginger snap dough spreads out to about five times its original size when baked. Bake only two or three at a time so that the cooked, toffee-like snap can be rolled as soon as it is lifted off the tray and before it hardens.

Ingredients

1¼ cups all-purpose flour
½tsp. ground ginger
pinch allspice
good ½ cup butter, chilled
⅔ cup granulated sugar
⅔ cup corn syrup
1tbsp. brandy

Sift the flour and spices together two or three times. Cut in the butter and rub to a fine crumb texture. Mix in the sugar. Add the syrup and brandy and blend into a smooth dough. The dough may be used straight away or chilled for a day so that the flavors develop.

Roll the dough into thick ropes, and pinch off walnut-sized pieces. Space two or three at a time, well apart, on a greased cookie sheet and flatten a little. Bake at 325°F for about 6-7 minutes, but watch carefully so that they do not burn. Cool for a minute or two, then lightly roll each one around the greased and oiled handle of a wooden spoon or a wooden dowel. Slide the snaps off the handle as soon as they have set and lay them on a wire rack to finish cooling.

Store between sheets of waxed paper in an airtight container for up to a week. They taste good unfilled, served with ice-cream or a creamy dessert; and for tea or coffee-time a filling of brandy-flavored whipped cream studded with candied peel is a special treat.

Florentines
Makes 40

Ingredients

½ cup butter	**Frosting**
½ cup sugar	1⅔ cups confectioner's
1tbsp. heavy cream	sugar
1 cup almonds, chopped	6tbsp. unsweetened cocoa
¼ cup glacé cherries	¼ cup butter
⅓ cup white raisins	6tbsp. milk
	1tsp. vanilla extract

Place the butter, sugar and cream in a heavy-bottomed pan. Heat over a low flame, stirring constantly, until the sugar has dissolved. Remove the butter from the heat and stir in the chopped nuts and fruit.

Grease flat cookie sheets and line with rice paper. Drop small spoonfuls of the mixture onto the cookie sheets. Be sure to leave as much space as possible between them as they spread while they are baking. Bake for 10 minutes at 350°F and leave to cool on the sheets for at least 5 minutes. Move to a cooling rack and trim of the extra paper.

To make the frosting, sift together the sugar and cocoa. Combine half of the sugar with the butter and beat well. Gradually add the remaining sugar, alternating with the combined milk and vanilla. When the Florentines have cooled completely, turn them upside down and spread with the frosting. Leave to set before serving.

Cheese Shortbreads
Makes 30-40

Ingredients

1½ cups grated Parmesan	scant 1 cup butter, diced
cheese or dry, strong	pinch mustard powder
Cheddar	pinch ground pepper
2⅓ cups all-purpose flour	beaten egg to glaze

Grease several cookie sheets. Mix the cheese with the flour, butter and seasonings till the mixture forms a stiff dough. Turn out on to a floured board and roll out ¼in. thick and cut into fingers 3in. long and ½in. wide. Or cut into circles 2in. in diameter.

Place on cookie sheets, and prick well. Chill for 20 minutes then brush with the egg and bake in the heated oven at 400°F for 10 minutes till crisp and golden. Cool on a wire rack.

Sesame Snaps
Makes about 20

Ingredients

1 cup+2tbsp. wholewheat	1-2tsp. salt
flour	2tsp. tahini (sesame) paste
1 cup sesame seeds	1tbsp. olive oil
1tsp. baking powder	¼-⅓ cup tepid water

Preheat the oven to 425°F. Combine the dry ingredients in a bowl. Add the tahini paste and olive oil and mix with the fingertips until crumbly. Gradually add enough water to form a soft dough.

Knead gently on a floured board and then roll out thinly. Press out rounds with a cookie cutter and arrange on a greased cookie sheet. Bake in the oven for 15 minutes until crisp and golden.

Cool on a wire rack, store in a pan and serve with cheese.

Oatcakes
Makes approx. 20

Ingredients

½ cup soft brown sugar	pinch bicarbonate of soda
½ cup all-purpose flour	pinch salt
1 cup wholewheat flour	½ cup butter
1⅓ cups rolled oats	1 egg yolk

Preheat the oven to 350°F.

Mix the dry ingredients together in a bowl. Cut the butter into small pieces in the bowl and rub in with your fingertips.

Mix in the egg yolk and form into a dough. Knead for a few minutes and then roll out thinly on a lightly floured surface and cut into 2in. rounds with a biscuit cutter.

Leaving plenty of space between each one, arrange the rounds on a greased cookie sheet and bake for 10-15 minutes until crisp and golden. Allow to cool slightly before transferring to a wire rack.

When cool, store in an airtight container. Serve with cheese.

Rye Crackers
Makes approx. 20

Ingredients
2tbsp. butter   pinch salt
1 cup rye flour   a little milk, heated

Preheat the oven to 350°F.
 Rub the butter into the flour with the salt, and bind with enough milk to make a dough. Knead for about 7 minutes.
 Form the dough into about 20 balls and roll flat on a floured surface.
 Cook on a cookie sheet for about 10 minutes, until the edges are just beginning to brown. Cool on a wire rack.

Hazelnut and Apricot Crunch
Makes about 16 bars

Ingredients
1/2 cup butter   1/2 cup chopped hazelnuts
1/4 cup soft brown sugar 1/2 cup dried apricots,
2tbsp. maple syrup   chopped
1 1/3 cups oatmeal

Preheat the oven to 350°F.
 Put the butter, sugar and syrup in a heavy-bottomed pan and stir over a low heat until combined. Stir in the remaining ingredients. Press into a jelly roll pan lined with waxed paper.
 Bake for about 45 minutes, until golden. Cut into bars in the pan using an oiled knife. Cool in the pan.

Coffee Slices
Makes 18

Ingredients
1/2 cup butter, softened **Frosting**
1/4 cup sugar   4tbsp. confectioner's sugar
1 cup+2tbsp. self-rising 1tbsp. instant coffee
 flour   4tbsp. butter
1tbsp. coffee extract

Cream together the butter and sugar until light and fluffy. Fold in the flour and coffee extract.
 Press into a greased jelly roll pan and bake for 15-20 minutes at 350°F.
 Put all the frosting ingredients into a saucepan and over a moderate heat stir for 2-3 minutes until the mixture looks like fudge.
 Pour the mixture on top of the shortbread. Leave to set and cut into slices.

Cherry Chocolate Crunch
Serves 8-10

Ingredients
1/4lb. plain chocolate in 1/4 cup glacé cherries,
 small pieces   chopped
1/2 cup butter   1/4 cup rum
1 egg, lightly beaten   2tbsp. chopped nuts
1/4lb. graham crackers

Melt the chocolate with the butter in the top of a double saucepan. Off the heat, beat in the egg.
 Add the remaining ingredients and mix well so that the graham crackers are well coated with chocolate.
 Turn the chocolate mixture into a well greased 8in. cake pan and chill for at least 8 hours before serving.

Anise Cookies

Ingredients

¼ cup brown granulated sugar
1½ cups wholewheat flour

1tsp. baking powder
3tbsp. finely ground aniseed

Beat the eggs until pale yellow. Add the sugar and beat for 3 minutes. Mix the dry ingredients together and fold into the mixture.

Drop the mixture a teaspoonful at a time onto a well-greased cookie sheet, allowing an inch between each. Leave to stand at room temperature for 18 hours.

Bake in a preheated oven at 325°F for approximately 12 minutes, or until cookies begin to color.

Langues de Chat

Ingredients

5tbsp. sweet butter
½ cup sugar
3 egg whites

1tsp. vanilla extract
2tbsp. light cream
1 cup flour, sifted

Cream the butter and sugar until very light and fluffy. Lightly beat the egg whites. Stir into the butter mixture along with the vanilla and cream. Gently fold in the sifted flour.

Spoon or pipe the batter onto a well greased sheet, allowing enough space for the cookies to spread while they are baking. Langues de chat are traditionally finger shaped, but if you are planning to make baskets, spread the mixture into 4in. circles.

Bake in a preheated oven at 425°F for 5 minutes. Leave the cookies to cool on the sheet for a few minutes before transferring to a wire rack.

Variation When the langues de chat have cooled, their ends can be dipped into melted chocolate. Place the cookies on a sheet of waxed paper for the chocolate to set.

To make baskets (*tulipes*) which can be filled with scoops of sorbet or ice cream, quickly lift the hot, soft cookies with a spatula and gently press over upturned cups or molds or slightly greased oranges. Leave to cool.

Baskets or *tulipes* can be made from batter flavored with almond paste, orange or lemon rind or the mixture usually used for brandy snaps. Be sure to work quickly and shape the freshly baked cookies before they have time to cool and firm.

Chocolate Pinwheels
Makes about 40

Ingredients

¾ cup butter or margarine
¾ cup sugar
1 large egg, beaten
1tsp. vanilla extract

3 cups self-rising flour
3tbsp. unsweetened cocoa powder
a little beaten egg white

Put the butter or margarine and sugar into a bowl and cream together until light and fluffy. Beat in the egg and vanilla extract.

Work the flour into the creamed mixture. Divide the mixture in half and knead the cocoa into one half. Shape into two smooth balls. Wrap in plastic wrap and chill.

To make pinwheel cookies, roll out the plain and chocolate doughs separately into equal rectangles. Brush the plain dough with egg white and place the chocolate mixture on top. Brush the chocolate mixture with egg white.

Roll up like a jelly roll. Wrap in foil and chill. Cut into ¼in. thick slices. Place on a cookie sheet and bake for about 8 minutes at 375°F.

Variations To make chequerboard cookies reserve about a quarter of the plain dough. Shape the remaining plain and chocolate doughs each into two long thin rolls. Brush with egg white.

Put a chocolate roll next to a plain roll. Place the other two rolls on top, reversing the colors. Press lightly together.

Roll out the reserved plain dough to a large rectangle. Brush with egg white and roll it around the four thin rolls. Chill, slice and cook as in recipe above.

To make owl cookies roll out the plain mixture to a rectangle. Form the chocolate mixture into a roll. Brush with egg white and roll up in the plain mixture. Wrap and chill.

Cut into ¼in. slices. To form the owl's head, put two circles side by side. Brush join with egg white and press lightly together. Pinch the top corners of each head to form ears.

Place almond halves in the center of each head for a beak. Put two chocolate chips for the eyes. Cook as in main recipe.

Viennese Chocolate Cookies
Makes about 20

Ingredients
1 cup butter or margarine	2tbsp. cornstarch
¼ cup confectioner's sugar, sifted	4oz. plain chocolate
2 cups all-purpose flour	a little confectioner's sugar
4tbsp. drinking chocolate powder	

Cream together the butter or margarine and sugar until light and fluffy. Work in the flour, drinking chocolate powder and cornstarch.

Put the mixture into a piping bag fitted with a large star nozzle. Pipe in fingers, or shells, or "s" shapes on to greased cookie trays. Bake in the oven at 350°F for 20-25 minutes. Cool on a wire rack.

Melt the chocolate. Dip half of each biscuit into the chocolate and leave to set on waxed paper.

Dust the uncoated halves of the biscuit with confectioner's sugar.

Variation To make chocolate gems pipe the mixture into small individual star shapes. Bake for about half the time. Place a chocolate chip in the center of each one while still hot.

Birnbrot
Christmas Pear and Nut Bread

Bake the Birnbrot 3-4 weeks before Christmas. Wrap closely in foil and store in a cool place.

Ingredients
	Bread dough
1⅔ cups dried pears	2 cups bread flour
¾ cup dried prunes	1½tbsp. fresh yeast
¾ cup dried figs, chopped small	⅓ cup granulated sugar
¾ cup dried or fresh dates, without pits	pinch salt
¾ cup candied orange and lemon peel, chopped	1½tsp. cinnamon
⅔ cup raisins	large pinch clove
⅔ cup white raisins	½tsp. star aniseed or allspice
1tbsp. pine nuts	2in. vanilla pod, split
⅔ cup hazelnuts, toasted and chopped coarsely	2tbsp. granulated sugar
⅔ cup walnuts, chopped coarsely	1tbsp. cornstarch
1tsp. lemon rind	2tbsp. kirsh or rum
2tsp. orange rind	
2tbsp. kirsch or rum	

Carefully wash the pears and prunes. Place them in a pan and just cover with water. Leave to soften for 2-3 hours. Set the pan on the heat, bring to a boil and simmer gently for about 20 minutes. Drain the fruits but reserve the juice and leave to cool. Chop up the figs.

Place the figs, dates, orange and lemon peels, raisins, white raisins, the pine nuts, hazelnuts, walnuts, and the lemon and orange rinds in a large bowl. Toss well together to mix and pour on the kirsch. Chop up the cooled fruit roughly and remove the pits. Add to the fruit and nut mixture.

Make a sponge batter with ¼ cup of the reserved fruit syrup, warmed to blood heat, yeast, ½ cup flour and 1tsp. sugar taken from the main quantity. Cover and set aside to rise and double in bulk.

Meanwhile, sift the remaining flour with the salt and spices in a large bowl. Make a well in the center, pour in the sponge batter and take in a little of the flour. Scoop in the seeds of the split vanilla pod and sugar. Combine well together and moisten with a bare ½ cup of the fruit syrup.

Knead the dough very thoroughly until it becomes less sticky and starts to roll off the sides of the bowl. When it is very elastic and large air-bubbles have started to form, gather into a large ball and place on the flour-dusted work-top.

Pull the dough out and gradually knead in the fruit and nut mixture until all has been used. Roll into a large ball and lay in the large flour-dusted bowl. Dredge with a little more flour and cover with a clean dish towel. Set aside in a cool place to rise overnight.

Next day, break off pieces of dough and form into hand-sized 1½-2in. rolls, or make two larger loaves (for 1lb. loaf pans), according to your choice. Lay small rolls, well apart, on greased cookie sheets. Leave to rest and rise a little for 15-20 minutes, then bake in the preheated oven at 350°F for 1 hour until golden and well risen.

Kirsch glaze for the warm loaves. Heat 1cup+2tbsp. fruit syrup with 2tbsp. granulated sugar, bring to a boil. Stir in 1tbsp. cornstarch and cook until thickened. Draw off the heat and stir in 2tbsp. kirsch. Brush on the warm loaves, press in a few almond halves for decoration, and leave to cool.

Bishop's Bread

A simple bread to serve with tea or coffee.

Ingredients

5tbsp. butter
5tbsp. granulated sugar
5 egg yolks
1 cup all-purpose flour, sifted
1tsp. orange rind
2tbsp. pine nuts

2tbsp. raisins
2tbsp. white raisins
1oz. dark dessert chocolate, cut in small pieces
4 egg whites

Beat the butter and sugar until pale and fluffy. Beat in the egg yolks one at a time, adding 1tsp. flour if necessary to prevent the mixture from curdling. Mix in the orange rind and pine nuts.

Dust the brown and white raisins with a little flour, taken from the main quantity, and combine them with the mixture. Mix in the chocolate pieces.

Whip up the egg whites until they stand in firm snowy peaks and lightly fold them into the mixture. Lastly sift in the flour in three stages and combine.

Pour the mixture into a buttered gutter mold or a 2lb. loaf pan lined with waxed paper.

Bake at 350°F for 1 hour until well risen and golden. Turn out of the pan to cool on a wire rack. Keep for 2 days before cutting. The loaf will stay fresh for about 10 days.

Cornish Saffron Bread
Makes two 2lb. loaves

Saffron has always been the most expensive spice in the world, and it was especially favored in Middle Eastern dishes for both its pungent and exotic flavor and its color.

Always buy whole saffron stamens rather than powder, which may be adulterated.

Ingredients

½tsp. whole saffron filaments
⅔ cup water, warmed to blood heat
bare 2 cups currants
⅔ cup white raisins
½ cup candied orange and lemon peel, chopped
1⅓ cups all-purpose flour, sifted
¼ cup granulated sugar
⅔ cup milk, warmed to blood heat

scant 1tbsp. fresh yeast
4⅔ cups bread all-purpose flour
1tsp. salt
pinch ground nutmeg
pinch ground cinnamon
pinch mixed spice
⅓ cup butter
⅓ cup lard
Glaze
2tbsp. sugar
1tbsp. milk

Dry the saffron filaments in a hot oven for 5 minutes, then crumble them into a cup filled with the hot water and leave to infuse while you prepare the other ingredients.

Place the dried fruits and peel in a large bowl and set it in the warm, switched-off oven to heat through.

Make a Yeast Sponge Batter with 1⅓ cups all-purpose flour, 2tsp. sugar, the milk and yeast; beat well, cover and leave to rise and double in bulk.

Sift the bread flour with the salt and spices into a large bowl. Cut in the butter and lard and rub to a crumb texture. Mix in the rest of the sugar. Make a well in the center and pour in the yeast batter and saffron liquid. Draw in the flour mixture and beat into a soft dough. Mix in the warmed fruits and blend thoroughly until the dough is shiny and shows large air bubbles.

Cover the bowl with a floured cloth, stand it in a warm place and leave to rise until it doubles in bulk, which may take as long as 2 hours.

Knock back the dough and knead for a moment or two, then divide it equally between two lightly greased 2lb. loaf pans. Pat into shape and leave to rise for up to 1 hour more until risen almost to the top of the pan. Bake immediately in the hot oven at 425°F for 30 minutes.

As soon as they are removed from the oven brush the loaves with a warmed mixture of 2tbsp. milk and 1tbsp. sugar. Leave in the pans for 15 minutes before turning out to cool on a wire rack.

Serve saffron bread as soon as it has cooled. You may like to freeze one loaf while it is still warm.

Poori
Deep Fried Bread
Makes 20

Ingredients

2¼ cups all-purpose flour
½tsp. salt
2tbsp. oil

approx. ½ cup hot water
oil for deep frying

Sift together the flour and salt. Rub in the oil, and add enough water to make a stiff dough. Put the dough on a floured surface and knead for about 10 minutes till soft and smooth. Divide the mixture into 20 balls.

Taking one ball at a time, flatten on a slightly oiled surface and roll into a round of 4in. across. (Do not stack the rolled pooris on one another as they will stick together.)

Heat the frying oil until very hot, add a poori, pressing the middle with a slotted spoon so that it puffs up. Quickly turn and cook the other side for a few seconds. Drain and keep warm while you make the rest. Serve hot.

Naan
Makes 12

Ingredients

1tsp. dried yeast
1tsp. sugar
⅓ cup lukewarm water
2¾ cups all-purpose flour
½tsp. salt

¾tsp. baking powder
1tbsp. oil
approx. 3tbsp. plain yogurt

Stir the yeast and sugar into the water and set aside for 15-20 minutes until the liquid is frothy.

Sift together the flour, salt and baking powder. Make a well in the middle, add the yeast liquid, oil and yogurt and knead for about 10 minutes till soft and no longer sticky.

Put the dough in an oiled plastic bag and set aside in a warm place for 2-3 hours until doubled in size.

Knead again for 1-2 minutes and divide into 12 balls. Roll into 7in. rounds.

Arrange as many as possible on a cookie sheet and put in a preheated oven at 400°F for 4-5 minutes each side until brown spots appear. Put them under a hot broiler for a few seconds until slightly browned.

Wrap the cooked ones in foil while cooking the others.

Wholewheat Bread
Makes 1 loaf

Ingredients

1lb. wholewheat flour
1½tbsp. sesame, caraway
  or poppy seeds
2tsp. salt
1¼ cups warm water
2tbsp. fresh yeast or
  equivalent dried yeast

½tsp. molasses or dark soft
  brown sugar
1tbsp. oil
1tbsp. malt extract
beaten egg to glaze

Preheat the oven to 400°F. Mix the flour, most of the seeds and the salt together in a warm bowl.

Pour a little of the water into a small bowl and add the yeast and molasses or sugar. Put in a warm place for 10 minutes. If using dried yeast, make up according to manufacturer's instructions.

Add the oil, the malt extract and the molasses to the rest of the water in the jug.

Pour the yeast mixture into the flour and stir. Add enough of the other liquid to make a soft dough, but don't allow it to get too sticky. As different brands of flour absorb different amounts, it may not be necessary to add all this liquid, so don't add it all at once.

Knead the dough for 20 minutes, then put it into a greased plastic bag to rise. Leave in a warm place, such as a sunny window sill, for an hour.

Punch down the dough with the heel of your hand to redistribute the raising agent and knead it for a minute. Put it in an oiled loaf pan, 8½×4½in. Brush the top with beaten egg and sprinkle over the remaining seeds. Cover the loaf with a clean damp dish towel and leave it to rise in a warm place for a further half hour.

Bake for 35 minutes. Turn it out of the pan and tap the bottom of the loaf with your fingertips. It should sound hollow. The sides of the loaf should spring back when pressed. Allow it to cool on a wire rack.

Variation For Walnut Bread, add ½-⅔ cup roughly chopped walnuts and use walnut oil.

Almond Loaf
Makes 1 loaf

A deliciously light bread, almond loaf is wonderful with morning coffee or afternoon tea.

Ingredients

4 eggs
1 cup sugar
few drops pure almond
  extract
1tsp. baking powder
good pinch salt

½tsp. ground cinnamon
1 cup flour
1tbsp. butter, melted
2 cups finely chopped
  unsalted, roasted
  almonds

Preheat the oven to 350°F.

Beat the eggs in a mixing bowl. Gradually beat in the sugar. Add the almond extract, baking powder, salt and cinnamon. Add the flour, melted butter and almonds. Stir until the batter is well blended. Pour the batter into a lightly greased 9in. loaf pan and bake for 40 minutes.

Invert the pan over a wire rack and turn the loaf out. Let the almond loaf cool. When it is cool, cut it into quarters. Cut the quarters into ½in. slices. Re-form the slices into a loaf shape in the pan and bake at 125°F for 10 minutes. Turn off the heat and leave the loaf in the oven for 15 minutes, before cooling and serving.

Garlic Milk Loaf

Ingredients

1 head garlic, about 12
  cloves
1¼ cups milk
1lb. flour, warmed
1tsp. salt
2tbsp. butter, melted

1tbsp. fresh yeast
½tsp. sugar
1 egg, well-beaten
rock salt
a little garlic, finely-
  chopped (optional)

Blanch the separated, unpeeled, garlic cloves in boiling water for 5 minutes. Drain and peel them, and simmer in the milk for about 10-15 minutes, until tender.

Sift the flour with the salt and make a well in it.

Either sift or blend the milk and garlic until smooth, and add the melted butter.

Cream the yeast with the sugar and add to the warm garlic milk with the beaten egg, and pour onto the flour.

Mix the ingredients thoroughly and knead lightly until smooth. The dough should be soft. Leave to rise, covered, in a warm place for approximately 1 hour.

Shape the dough into one large or two small loaves and place on a greased cookie sheet. Cut several parallel slashes from end to end of each loaf, and leave to prove for 15 minutes.

Sprinkle each loaf with rock salt and a little chopped garlic, and bake at 450°F for 20-30 minutes until well browned and hollow-sounding when tapped underneath.

Variations Leave the garlic cloves whole or add ⅓ cup pine nuts, browned in a little oil, to the dough before leaving to rise.

Pita Bread
Makes 8

Follow Wholewheat Bread recipe. Preheat the oven to 450°F.

Divide the dough into 8 and roll out into thin ovals. Place on baking sheets and cover with clean damp cloths. Leave on top of the stove for 20 minutes.

Bake for 5-7 minutes. Allow to cool. These pita breads freeze very successfully.

Yom Kippur Bread
Serves 8

This traditional Jewish loaf is served immediately after the holy day ends, to break the fast.

Ingredients

6 cups flour	½ cup olive oil
2 packages active dry yeast	2tbsp. anise seeds
scant 1 cup tepid water	1tbsp. vanilla extract
¾ cup sugar	1½tsp. salt
3 eggs	2 egg yolks

In a large mixing bowl, combine 2 cups of the flour with the yeast, water, and 2tbsp. of the sugar. Mix with a whisk into a smooth dough. Sprinkle with ½ cup of the flour and cover the bowl with a clean dish towel. Set aside for 2½ hours.

Add the 3 whole eggs, remaining sugar, olive oil, anise seeds, vanilla extract, salt and remaining flour. Mix into an even dough. Knead the dough until stiff on a floured surface. Divide the dough in half and knead each half for an additional 5 minutes. Let the dough rest for 5 minutes.

Shape the dough halves into two 10in. loaves and place them on a greased and floured cookie sheet. Cover with a clean dish towel and leave for 1½ hours. In a small mixing bowl, beat the egg yolks with 2tsp. of water and brush the mixture over the tops of the loaves. Bake for 30 minutes at 375°F. Remove and leave them to cool on wire racks.

Austrian Bagels
Makes 12 bagels

Historians of the bagel recount that in 1683 an anonymous Viennese baker decided to honor the King of Poland's favorite pastime, riding, by making a bread roll in the shape of a stirrup. The German word for stirrup is *beugel* – hence the modern bagel. The controversy over what makes a proper bagel continues to rage. But there is no dispute that the true bagel is boiled first and then baked, giving it a dense texture.

Ingredients

1 packet active dried yeast	pinch salt
scant 1 cup warm water	4¼ cups flour
2tbsp. sugar	8pts water

Dissolve the yeast in the warm water in a large bowl. Add the sugar, salt and flour and stir to form a soft dough.

Turn the dough out on to a floured surface and knead until smooth and elastic, about 10 minutes. Cover the dough with a dish towel and leave to rise for 15 minutes.

Flatten the dough and roll out to a thickness of 1in. Cut the dough into strips 12in. long and 1in. wide. Roll each strip into a cylinder with a diameter of ½in. Cut each cylinder in half. Pinch together the ends of the strips to form circles.

Cover the bagels with a dish towel and leave them to rise for 20 minutes. Bring the water to a boil in a large pot. Add the bagels in batches of 4 to the boiling water, reduce the heat, and simmer for 7 minutes. Remove the bagels, drain well, and place them on cookie sheets. Bake for 30 minutes at 375°F.

Challah
Makes 2 loaves

Ingredients

scant 1 cup lukewarm water	1½tsp. salt
3 packets active dry yeast	3 eggs
2tbsp. sugar	¼ cup vegetable oil
6½ cups flour	1 egg yolk

In a small bowl combine the water, yeast and 1tsp. of the sugar. Leave it to stand for 3 minutes and then stir until the yeast is dissolved. Leave it for a further 5 minutes.

Combine 4½ cups of the flour with the salt and remaining sugar in a large, deep mixing bowl. Make a well in the center of the flour and pour in the yeast mixture. Add the eggs and vegetable oil. Gently stir until the ingredients are blended together. Stirring more vigorously, blend in the remaining flour.

Turn the dough out onto a lightly floured surface and knead for 20 minutes with a rolling pin, flattening the dough with the rolling pin, gathering it back into a ball and flattening again. Place the dough ball into a bowl, cover with a clean cloth, and leave it to stand for 45 minutes or until it is nearly doubled in bulk. Turn the dough out and knead for 5 minutes. Leave to rest for 5 minutes.

Cut the dough in half with a sharp knife. Cut each half into thirds. Roll each piece of dough into a cylinder that tapers at each end. Pinch the ends of the 3 dough cylinders together. Braid the cylinders and pinch the other ends together. Repeat with the remaining dough. Place the challahs on a lightly greased cookie sheet and leave them to stand for 30 minutes.

In a small bowl, beat the egg yolk with 2tbsp. cold water. Brush the tops of the challahs with the egg yolk and bake for 20 minutes at 400°F. Reduce the temperature to 375°F and bake for 40 minutes longer, or until the challahs are lightly browned. Cool on a rack.

Making a Flan Case

1 Roll out the pastry on a floured surface to a round 2½in larger than the flan ring. Lay the rolling pin gently on the pastry and fold one side over it.

2 Lift up the pastry on the rolling pin. Brush off excess flour.

3 Drape the pastry carefully over the flan ring by turning the pin slowly to allow it to fall gently over the ring. Do not let the pin touch the ring or it may cut through the pastry. Do not stretch the pastry or it will shrink back once in the oven.

4 Ease the pastry into the corners with the back of a finger.

5 Alternatively, you can use a small ball of paste to push it well into the corners.

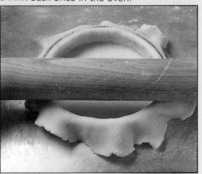

6 Roll the pin over the top of the flan ring to cut off the excess pastry.

7 Gently dislodge the pastry edge with a fingernail if it sticks to the flan ring — this will prevent it sticking in the oven.

8 To bake blind, prick the bottom of the flan case to prevent bubbling up while baking.

9 Line with waxed paper (crumpling the paper first will ensure that you do not damage the pastry) and fill with 'blind beans' (here a mixture of dry rice and pasta). 'Blind beans' may be re-used indefinitely. Remove the paper and beans when the case is half-baked.

10 Remove the flan ring once the case is almost cooked and return to the oven to allow the sides to brown.

Beating Strudel Paste

1 Lift the dough up in one hand and with a flick of the wrist throw it onto a lightly floured marbled slab or board without letting go of it.

2 Gather it up again and repeat the flinging down. Keep doing this for a few minutes. The paste will gradually become more elastic and less sticky.

3 Keep folding and flicking until the paste is smooth, shiny and elastic. Cover and leave in a warm place for 15 minutes.

Making Apple Strudel

1 On a table covered by a large floured cloth, roll the paste out as thinly as possible.

2 Now put your hands, lightly floured, under the paste and gently pull and stretch it keeping your hands fairly flat. Carefully work all round the table, gently pulling the paste until is is evenly paper-thin.

3 Trim the thick edges. Do not worry about the odd tear hole.

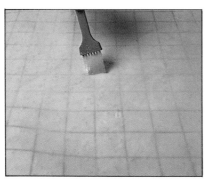  

4 Brush immediately with butter to prevent the paste drying out — it becomes brittle alarmingly quickly.

5 Sprinkle the filling on the paste, leaving a clear margin. Use the cloth to help roll it up like a jelly roll, trying to maintain a fairly tight, even roll.

6 Tip the strudel onto a waxed baking sheet and curve it gently into a horse-shoe shape. Brush with butter and bake.

Processor Pastry

1 Put the fat (cut into lumps) into the bowl with the flour and any liquid if used. When processed the mixture will first go crumbly. At this stage, it is suitable for use as a crumble topping.

2 Continue processing until the crumbs are gathered into one lump in the bowl. The mixture is now suitable for pastry. Take care not to overprocess the paste.

Drinks

DRINKS

DRINKS

Banana Shake
Serves 2

Ingredients
⅝ *cup yogurt*
1 banana
honey to taste

Blend all the ingredients together well. Serve immediately.

Bloodshot
Serves 4-6

A cross between a Bloody Mary and a Bullshot, recommended for Sunday Brunch and/or hangovers.

Ingredients
1 cup vodka
1 cup chilled consommé or beef bouillon
1½ cups chilled tomato juice
juice of half a lemon
1tsp. sugar
2-3tsp. garlic juice (optional)
approx. 1tsp. Worcestershire Sauce
salt and cayenne pepper or Tabasco to taste

Stir the ingredients together in a glass jug, seasoning to taste, and serve over ice in tall glasses.

Buttermilk Liqueur Cooler
Serves 4

Use any liqueur you have on hand. Chocolate mint, orange-flavoured liqueurs, *crème de cassis* — all are delicious. A miniature, though slightly less than the stated amount, is a handy measure.

Ingredients
2½ cups buttermilk
3 ice cubes
1 egg white
¼ cup liqueur

Blend everything together well until light and fluffy. Serve immediately.

Citrus Shake
Serves 1

This drink contains all the nutrients you need to start the day.

Ingredients
⅔ *cup yogurt*
juice of one orange
1 egg
2tsp. clear honey

Blend everything together well and drink immediately.

Chocolate Egg Nog
Serves 4-6

Ingredients
2 eggs
2tbsp. sugar
1 cup milk
3tbsp. Chocolate Syrup (see recipe for Iced Caribbean Chocolate)
2tbsp. Crème de Cacao
2tbsp. Amaretto
a few drops of vanilla extract
¾ cup whipping cream
grated nutmeg

Separate the eggs. Put the egg yolks and 1tbsp. of sugar into a bowl and beat until thick and pale.
Add milk, chocolate syrup, liqueurs and extract, and beat well. Chill.
Beat the whipping cream until loosely thick (not stiff). Beat the egg whites until stiff and fold in the remaining sugar.
Stir the egg yolk mixture into the whipped cream, fold in the egg white.
To serve, pour into small glasses and sprinkle with freshly grated nutmeg.

347

Hot Chocolate
Serves 3

Ingredients
1 cup plain (unsweetened)
  chocolate
1 cup water
2 cups milk

Put the chocolate and water into a pan. Heat gently, stirring until dissolved.

Heat the milk just to boiling. Pour the hot milk on to the chocolate and beat until frothy.

Pour into hot mugs. Add granulated brown sugar if desired. Top with marshmallows or a dollop of whipped cream. Sprinkle with drinking chocolate powder.

Chocolaccino
Serves 1

An excellent variation' on *Cappuccino*.

Ingredients
¼ cup hot milk
¼ cup Italian coffee

2tbsp. heavy cream, lightly
  whipped
2tbsp. semi-sweet chocolate,
  grated

If you do not have a *cappuccino* maker froth the hot milk in a blender for approximately one minute.

Mix with the hot coffee and pour into a tall cup or glass.

Spoon over the whipped cream and top with grated chocolate. Serve immediately.

(Left) Choconana Milk Shake; (right) Iced Caribbean Chocolate

Choconana Milk Shake
Serves 2-3

Ingredients
1¼ cups milk
3tbsp. Chocolate Syrup (see
  recipe for Iced
  Caribbean Chocolate)

1pt. chocolate ice cream
1 banana, cut into pieces

Put milk, chocolate syrup, ice cream and banana into a blender. Cover and blend until smooth.

To serve, pour into glasses and add a chocolate curl to each one.

Iced Caribbean Chocolate
Serves 4

Ingredients
2 cups milk
⅔ cup single cream
2 large pinches of ground
  nutmeg
2 large pinches of ground
  cinnamon

a large pinch of ground
  allspice
5tbsp. Chocolate Syrup (see
  below)

Put the milk, cream, spices and syrup into a bowl and beat well together. Chill well. Before serving, whisk again.

To serve, pour into glasses over ice cubes and top with scoops of coffee ice cream.

Chocolate Syrup Mix 1¾ cups soft brown sugar and ⅔ cup unsweetened cocoa. Add 1¼ cups boiling water, stirring continuously. Simmer gently for 5 minutes, stirring frequently. Allow to cool and add 2tsp. vanilla extract. Cover and chill.

Café Brulôt Diabolique
Serves 6-8

This punch can be made in a saucepan but it looks far more dramatic when made at the table. Use any deep, heat resistant bowl, but a silver bowl is traditional.

Ingredients

8 cloves	3tbsp. sugar
1 stick cinnamon	¾ cup brandy
1 vanilla pod	2pt. hot coffee
thinly pared rind of 1 orange	5tbsp. Cointreau
thinly pared rind of 1 lemon	

Put the cloves, cinnamon, vanilla, orange and lemon rind and sugar into a bowl.

Pour the brandy into a warmed ladle a little at a time and heat gently. Ignite it and pour over the ingredients in the bowl. Stir gently.

Slowly add the hot coffee and stir until the flames disappear.

Add the Cointreau and serve in small, warmed cups.

Calypso Coffee
Serves 4

Ingredients

5 cups hot coffee	4tbsp. Tia Maria
2tbsp. white rum	⅔ cup heavy cream

Heat all the ingredients except the cream, but do not boil.

Warm four brandy glasses and divide the liquid between them.

Stir, then add the cream, pouring it slowly over the back of a spoon so that its weight does not pull it straight to the bottom. Serve immediately.

Irish Coffee
Serves 1

It is important to use a strong brew so that the coffee complements the whiskey rather than being drowned by it.

Ingredients

1tbsp. Irish whiskey
1tsp. brown sugar
⅔ cup strong coffee
3tbsp. heavy cream

Warm an Irish Coffee or long glass, add the sugar and whiskey and pour on the coffee.

To serve, pour the cream over a spoon onto the coffee and drink the warm liquid through the cool layer of cream.

Iced Café au Lait
Serves 4

Ingredients

1¼ cups hot extra strong   sugar to taste
*   coffee, freshly made   4tbsp. heavy cream, lightly*
1¼ cups hot milk   whipped

Combine the coffee and milk, and sweeten to taste.
Cover and leave to cool, then refrigerate until cold.
  Pour into four chilled glasses and serve, topped with
the whipped cream.

Coffee Noggin
Serves 6-8

Ingredients

⅔ cup milk   4 eggs, separated
⅔ cup light cream   4tsp. Crème de Cacao
1½ cups hot coffee,   ⅔ cup heavy cream
*   sweetened   grated nutmeg*

Beat together in a saucepan over a low heat the milk,
light cream and sweetened coffee. Do not boil.
  Beat in the egg yolks and cook until the mixture
thickens. Strain and cool.
  Stir in the Crème de Cacao. Beat the heavy cream
until it just holds its peaks and fold into the coffee
mixture.
  Just before serving, whisk the egg whites until stiff
and fold into the Coffee Noggin.
  Serve in glass cups, goblets or mugs, sprinkled with
nutmeg.

Mega Mocha Shake
Serves 2

Ingredients

3 scoops of coffee ice cream   ⅔ cup chilled strong
3 scoops of chocolate ice   sweetened coffee
*   cream   ⅔ cup milk*

Preparation Combine all the ingredients in a blender
until creamy.
  To serve, pour out into two chilled tall glasses. Add a
wide straw and chocolate curl to each.

Mega Mocha Shake

Viennese Coffee
Serves 4

What makes this Viennese coffee is the 'Schlagobers' — a large spoonful of sweetened whipped cream as topping.

Ingredients
½ cup plain   *2½ cups hot strong coffee*
(unsweetened) chocolate   *¾ cup heavy cream*
4tbsp. light cream   *1tsp. sugar*

Gently melt the chocolate in a saucepan taking care not to burn it. Stir in light cream.

Pour in the coffee a little at a time, beating well until frothy. Keep warm. Whip the double cream with the sugar. Pour the coffee into four warmed cups and spoon on the whipped cream.

Sprinkle with cinnamon and cocoa to serve.

Frozen Latin Flip
Serves 4

Ingredients
1pt. coffee, rum or
chocolate ice cream
½ cup Tia Maria, Kahlua
or Crème de Cacao
1 cup milk

As for iced grasshopper. Garnish with chocolate strands.

Southern Belle
Serves 2

Ingredients
4tbsp. Southern Comfort   *¼ cup heavy cream*
4tbsp. apricot brandy   *slices of fresh apricot*
1 cup cold black coffee

Combine all the ingredients except the apricot slices in a blender and pour into chilled glasses.

Serve decorated with apricot slices.

Frozen Latin Flip

Down Home Shake
Serves 4

Ingredients

*1pt. chocolate, rum or
   ginger ice cream, or
   lemon sorbet*

*1tbsp. honey
1/4 cup dark rum
1 cup milk*

Combine ingredients in the same way as for iced grasshopper. Omit the mint leaf garnish but serve with either grated chocolate or a sprinkling of cinnamon or ground ginger on top.

Iced Grasshopper
Serves 4

Ingredients

*1pt. mint or pistachio ice
   cream*

1/4 cup Crème de Cacao

1 1/4 cups Crème de Menthe

Combine all ingredients in a liquidizer, blender or food processor and mix until thick and smooth.

Pour into tall glasses and garnish with mint leaves dipped into egg white and sugar to give a frosted appearance.

Singapore Sling
Serves 1

This drink was christened the Singapore Sling in 1915 by the head barman at Raffles, whose family are still represented in the long bar even today.

Ingredients

*2 measures gin
1 measure cherry brandy
1 measure orange juice
1 measure lemon juice
1 measure pineapple juice*

*few drops Angostura bitters
few drops Cointreau
crushed ice cubes
pineapple and maraschino
   cherry*

Shake all the ingredients with the ice then strain into a tall glass. Decorate with pineapple and cherry and serve at once.

Grapefruit Frappé
Serves 2-3

This rich and unusual-tasting shake is a meal in itself and, frozen, makes a refreshingly crunchy ice, enough for 4.

Ingredients

*1/3 cup frozen concentrated
   grapefruit juice
1 cup vanilla ice cream
1 cup milk*

*2 eggs
1-2tbsp. clear honey
   (optional)*

Liquidize or process all the ingredients together until thick and well blended.

Serve immediately in tall, chilled glasses.

Iced Julep
Serves 4

Ingredients

1pt. mint or vanilla ice   ¼ cup Southern Comfort or
  cream   Bourbon
¼ cup Crème de Menthe

Combine ingredients in the same way as for Ice Grasshopper. Serve an iced julep over crushed ice and garnish with a sprig of mint.

Healthfood Drink
Serves 1

Ingredients

¾ cup yogurt   2tbsp. wheatgerm
½ cup milk   ½ cup strawberries
1tbsp. clear honey

Combine everything together in a blender or food processor and blend until smooth. Drink immediately.

Tomato Cocktail
Serves 4

Ingredients

3-4 medium-sized ripe   salt and pepper
  tomatoes, skinned   pinch sugar
1 cup yogurt   2 ice cubes
fresh basil

Halve the tomatoes, squeeze out the seeds (reserve them for use in a soup) and put the flesh in a blender, together with the remaining ingredients.

Blend everything together well and serve immediately in tall glasses, garnished with extra basil.

Tomato Cocktail

Raspberry Yogurt Drink
Serves 1-2

Ingredients
2½ cups yogurt
8 ice cubes
2 egg whites
1 cup raspberries

sugar to taste
mint sprigs or raspberry
    leaves (optional)

Blend all the ingredients except the mint sprigs or raspberry leaves until the ice is crushed.

Serve immediately in tall glasses, garnished, if you like, with mint or raspberry leaves.

Variations Instead of raspberries, try 2 large peaches, peeled and sliced; 4 slices pineapple, fresh or canned; 1 large ripe mango; 1 cup either strawberries, blackberries, blueberries, blackcurrants or redcurrants.

Pineapple Yogurt Drink
Serves 1

Ingredients
⅔ cup yogurt
⅔ cup pineapple juice
1tbsp. crushed pineapple,
    fresh or canned
1 ice cube

Blend everything together well. Serve immediately.

Orange Yogurt Drink
Serves 2

Ingredients
¾ cup yogurt
½ cup milk
grated rind and juice of 1
    orange

grated lemon rind
1tsp. honey
1tbsp. hazelnuts (optional)

Blend all the ingredients together well. Serve immediately or refrigerate until required.

Variation A simpler citrus yogurt drink can be made by liquidizing either the flesh of an orange or that of a small grapefruit together with ⅝ cup yogurt and sugar to taste.

Peach Passion
Serves 1

Ingredients
1 small, ripe peach,
    preferably white

1 scoop raspberry water ice
champagne to top up

Peel the peach and slice it into the bottom of a large, chilled wine glass. Add the water ice and top up with champagne.

Variation Instead of the raspberry water ice, try redcurrant or blueberry. Sparkling dry white wine can be used instead of champagne.

Wine Glasses

Any discussion of wines is, of course, outside the scope of this book, but a basic set of wine glasses should contain *(from left to right)*:

The all-purpose Paris goblet — available in 3½fl oz (liqueur), 5fl oz (sherry), 8fl oz (white wine) and 12fl oz (red wine) sizes. The last three tulip-shaped glasses are best for wine — the 6fl oz for dessert wine or sherry, the 12fl oz for red wine and 8fl oz for white wine.

Confectionery

Coconut Cream Toffee
Makes 30-40 pieces

Ingredients
3³/₄pts. light cream   *1tsp. cardamom seeds,*
2 cups white sugar   *ground*
flesh of 1 coconut, ground   *¹/₂tsp. rose water*
    to a paste

Mix together the sugar and coconut, gradually add the cream and rose water. Add the cardamom seed and stir thoroughly.

Cook over a gentle heat in a saucepan until the mixture curls off the sides of the pan.

Press the mixture onto a greased cookie sheet and leave to cool. Score it into squares and finish cutting into squares once it is cold.

Coconut Mint Crystals
Makes 1¹/₄lb.

Ingredients
1lb. sugar   *2 cups shredded coconut*
³/₄ cup powdered glucose   *¹/₂ cup coarsely grated mint*
²/₃ cup water   *chocolate*

In a large heavy-based pan bring the sugar, glucose and water to a boil.

Remove from the heat and stir in the coconut and mint chocolate.

Spoon into small rocky heaps on waxed paper and leave to set.

Serve in small paper cases.

Variation 2tbsp. coffee extract is a good addition.

Coconut Ice

Coconut Ice
Makes 18-24 pieces

Ingredients
1lb. granulated sugar   *2tbsp. coffee extract or few*
²/₃ cup milk   *drops cochineal*
1¹/₂ cups shredded coconut

Put the sugar and milk into a large heavy-based saucepan and gently heat until the sugar has dissolved.

Boil for 10 to 15 minutes. The mixture should form a soft ball when a little is dropped in cold water.

Remove from the heat and stir in the coconut. Pour half the mixture into a greased 6in. loose-bottom square cake pan.

Quickly add the coffee extract or cochineal to the remaining mixture and pour into the cake pan.

Smooth the top and mark into square or bars when half set.

Remove from the pan when cold and set.

Carrot Halva

Ingredients

1lb. carrots, peeled and grated	4tbsp. Ghee (Clarified Butter)
4 cups milk	2tbsp. raisins
2/3 cup sugar	2tbsp. pistachio nuts, skinned and chopped
3 cardamom pods	

Put the carrots, milk, sugar and cardamom pods in a large saucepan and bring to a boil. Lower heat to a medium low and, stirring occasionally, cook until all the liquid has evaporated.

Heat the clarified butter in a large skillet over medium heat, add the carrots, raisins and pistachios and, stirring constantly, fry for 15-20 minutes until the mixture is dry and reddish in color. Serve hot or cold.

Farina Halva

Ingredients

3tbsp. Clarified Butter	1tbsp. raisins
1/4 cup almonds, blanched and sliced	1 3/4 cups milk
1 3/4 cups semolina or farina	1/3 cup sugar

Heat the butter in a pan over medium heat. Add the almonds and fry for 1-2 minutes until golden brown. Remove with a slotted spoon and drain on paper towels.

Put in the semolina or farina and fry, stirring continuously, until golden. Add the raisins, milk and sugar and continue stirring until the mixture leaves the sides of the pan and a ball forms.

Serve warm or cold, on a flat dish garnished with the almonds.

Colettes
Makes approx. 16

Ingredients

1/2lb. plain (bittersweet) chocolate	2-3tsp. dark rum (or brandy, sherry, Cointreau or Maraschino)
1tbsp. strong black coffee	
2tbsp. light cream	
4tbsp. butter	small pieces of nuts, cherries, or crystalized flowers
2 egg yolks	

Melt half the chocolate. Use double layers of paper petit fours cases, or preferably single foil petit fours cases. Spoon a little chocolate into each case. With the handle of a teaspoon, spread evenly around the base and sides of each case.

Turn upside down on to a tray lined with waxed paper and leave to set in a cool place.

Melt the remaining chocolate in a bowl over a pan of hot water. Add the coffee and cream and stir.

Remove from the heat. Dice the butter. Beat into the chocolate mixture a little at a time.

Beat in the egg yolks and rum. Leave in a cool place until thick.

Carefully peel the cases away from the chocolate. Using a piping bag fitted with a star nozzle, pipe the filling into each case.

Top with the decorations of your choice and put in clean paper cases, or a decorative box.

Coffee Mallows

Ingredients

1lb. sugar	2 egg whites
2tbsp. corn syrup	vanilla extract
2/3 cup water	confectioner's sugar
2tbsp. powdered gelatin	cornstarch
2/3 cup strong Italian coffee	

Slowly dissolve the sugar, syrup and water in a large, heavy-based pan. Bring to a boil. While the mixture is boiling, dissolve the gelatin in the coffee.

Remove the syrup from the heat and slowly add the gelatin, stirring well.

Beat the egg whites until just foaming and pour onto the hot syrup in a thin stream, beating all the time.

Add a few drops of vanilla extract and continue beating until the mixture is thick and stiff.

Pour into a 9in. square loose-bottom cake pan, lined with greased waxed paper.

Leave uncovered overnight and check that the coffee mallow is completely set before removing from the pan and cutting into squares.

Roll each piece thoroughly in a mixture of one part cornstarch and two parts confectioner's sugar.

Variation You can cut the coffee mallow into rounds using cookie cutters. Dip the cutter into the cornstarch and confectioner's sugar mixture between cuts to prevent the cutter from sticking.

Chocolate Caramel Popcorn

Ingredients

¹⁄₄ cup brown sugar
2tbsp butter
1¹⁄₂tsp. corn syrup
1tbsp. milk

2oz. chocolate chips
pinch bicarbonate of soda
2¹⁄₂pts. popped popcorn

Put the sugar, butter, syrup and milk into a heavy-based saucepan.

Stir over a gentle heat until the butter and sugar have melted. Boil without stirring for 2 minutes.

Remove from the heat. Add the chocolate and bicarbonate of soda. Stir until the chocolate is melted.

Measure the popped popcorn into a bowl. Pour over the syrup and toss well until evenly coated.

Spread mixture on a large cookie tray. Bake in the oven at 300°F for about 15 minutes. Test for crispness. Bake for a further 5-10 minutes if necessary.

Cool and break into bite-sized pieces to serve.

Coffee Creams
Makes approx. 24

Ingredients

1 egg white
1lb. confectioner's sugar

2tbsp. coffee extract, or extra strong instant coffee

Beat the egg white until frothy but not stiff. Sift the confectioner's sugar into a bowl and mix with enough of the egg white to make a firm paste.

Add the coffee extract, mix and knead together. Roll out on a board well dusted with confectioner's sugar and cut into small circles.

Transfer onto waxed paper and leave overnight until set and firm to the touch.

Variation Instead of the coffee, add peppermint flavoring to taste.

Cheese Fudge

Ingredients

2 cups farmer's cheese
5tbsp. sugar

1tbsp. pistachio nuts, finely
   chopped

Press the farmer's cheese through a strainer onto a plate and rub with the palm of your hand till smooth and creamy.

Put the cheese in a pan over medium heat, add the sugar and, stirring constantly, cook till it leaves the sides and a ball forms.

Remove from the heat and spread on a plate ½in. thick. Cool slightly, sprinkled with the nuts and cut into small diamonds.

Serve warm or cold.

Coffee Fudge

Ingredients

1 cup butter
2lb. granulated sugar
2 cups evaporated milk
½ cup water

½ cup strong coffee
⅓ cup seedless raisins,
   chopped

Put all the ingredients, except the raisins, into a large heavy-based pan. Stir gently over a low heat until the sugar is dissolved.

Bring to a boil and maintain, stirring occasionally, until a teaspoon of fudge dropped into half a cup of cold water will form a soft ball.

Remove from heat, dip the base of the pan into cold water and leave for 5 minutes. Beat with a wooden spoon until the mixture loses its gloss, looks grainy, thickens a little and will just pour from the pan.

Quickly stir in the raisins and pour into a greased pan 12×7in. Leave until cold and set, and cut into squares.

Wrap in waxed paper.

Chocolate Fudge
Makes approx. 1½lb.

Ingredients

1lb. sugar
⅔ cup milk
¼ cup butter
6oz. plain (unsweetened) chocolate
4tbsp. honey

Put all ingredients into a heavy-based saucepan and stir continuously over a gentle heat until the sugar is completely dissolved.

Bring to a boil and cook to the "soft ball" stage.

Remove from the heat and dip the base of the pan in cold water to stop further cooking. Leave for 5 minutes.

Beat the mixture with a wooden spoon until thick and creamy and beginning to "grain." Before it becomes too stiff, pour into a buttered 8in. square pan. Leave to set.

Using a greased knife, cut into 1in. squares.

To store fudge, put in an airtight tin box between layers of waxed paper.

Rocky Road Fudge
Makes approx. 1½lb.

Ingredients

1lb. milk chocolate
4tbsp. butter
2tbsp. light cream
1tsp. vanilla extract
⅓ cup walnuts, chopped
4oz. marshmallows, cut into small pieces with wet scissors
1⅔ cups confectioner's sugar, sifted
3oz. plain (bittersweet) chocolate

Melt the milk chocolate and butter in a bowl over a pan of hot water. Stir in the cream and extract.

Remove from the heat and stir in the walnuts, marshmallows and confectioner's sugar.

Spread in a 8in. square pan, lined with waxed paper, and chill until firm.

Melt the plain chocolate. Using a piping bag fitted with a plain nozzle, drizzle the chocolate over the fudge.

Leave to set, then cut the fudge into diamonds or any other shape that takes your fancy.

Meringue Mushrooms
Makes 6-8

Ingredients

1 egg white
½ cup confectioner's sugar
2oz. plain (unsweetened) chocolate, melted
unsweetened cocoa powder

Beat the egg white until stiff, then beat in the sugar a little at a time until the mixture is stiff and glossy.

Put meringue into a piping bag fitted with a ½in. plain nozzle.

Line a cookie sheet with waxed paper. Pipe 6-8 small mounds of meringue about 1in. in diameter to form the mushroom caps.

Next pipe 6-8 smaller mounds, drawing each one up to a point, to represent the stalks.

Bake in the oven at 275°F for about 1 hour until dry and crisp. Allow to cool.

Using the point of a sharp knife, make a tiny hole in the base of the mushroom cap.

Spread a little melted chocolate on the underside of each cap and gently push on a stalk. Allow to set.

Before serving, dust the tops of mushrooms with a little cocoa powder.

Mocha Cups
Makes 18-20

Ingredients

4oz. milk chocolate	2 egg yolks
5oz. plain chocolate	rum to taste
4tbsp. strong Italian coffee	toasted almond slivers
1/4 cup butter, softened	

Melt the milk chocolate in a bowl over hot water until liquid. Pour a teaspoon of chocolate inside each paper case and run it around the inside to line the case completely. Leave to set. Remove the paper cases from the chocolate cups.

Melt the plain chocolate and stir in the coffee. Leave to cool.

Beat in the butter and egg yolks. Add rum to taste.

Pipe or spoon the mocha filling into the chocolate cups and decorate with almond slivers.

Coffee Truffles
Makes 18-24

Ingredients

4oz. plain (unsweetened) chocolate	1/4lb. coffee cake, crumbled
4tbsp. butter	1 egg yolk
3/4 cup confectioner's sugar	1tsp. Crème de Cacao
	chocolate vermicelli

Melt the chocolate and butter in a bowl over a saucepan of hot water.

Remove from the heat and stir in remaining ingredients except the chocolate vermicelli.

Chill in the refrigerator until firm enough to handle. Mold into balls the size of a small walnut and roll in the vermicelli.

Leave to set on waxed paper before putting in individual paper cases.

Orange Truffles
Makes 12

Ingredients

4oz. plain (unsweetened) chocolate in small pieces	finely grated rind of 1 orange
3tbsp. light cream	3/4 cup confectioner's sugar or 1/4 cup chocolate strands
1 cup ground almonds	
2tbsp. Cointreau	
2 cups cookie or cake crumbs	

Melt the chocolate in the top of a double boiler.

Pour the chocolate into a mixing bowl with the cream, ground almonds, Cointreau, crumbs and rind.

Mix well and chill for 1 hour, or until it is firm enough to handle.

Divide the chocolate mixture into 12 pieces. Roll into small balls and toss in sifted sugar or chocolate strands.

Coffee Truffles

Amaretti Truffles
Makes approx. 16

Ingredients

¼ cup butter, softened
1 cup confectioner's sugar
7oz. plain (bittersweet) chocolate
1 tsp. instant coffee

few drops almond extract
approx. 16 small, hard macaroons (preferably Italian Amaretti)

Beat together the butter and confectioner's sugar.

Put 3oz. of the chocolate into a bowl over a pan of hot water. Dissolve the coffee in a few drops of boiling water and add to the chocolate. Heat until melted.

Remove the chocolate from the heat and add the extract. Stir into the butter mixture. Chill until firm enough to handle.

Roll mixture into balls and press each one on to the flat side of a macaroon.

Melt the rest of the chocolate and dip each "truffle" side of the macaroons. Leave to set, coated sides up.

Rich Chocolate Truffles
Makes approx. 30

Ingredients

½lb. plain or milk chocolate
¼lb. butter, diced

2tsp. rum or brandy
1 cup confectioner's sugar
ground nuts

Melt the chocolate. Remove from the heat, add the butter and rum or brandy and beat until smooth.

Beat in the confectioner's sugar and chill until firm.

Shape into 1-in. balls and roll in the nuts. Put the truffles in paper cases and keep cool.

Variation The truffles could also be coated in confectioner's sugar, cocoa powder, drinking chocolate powder, ground Praline, grated chocolate or chocolate vermicelli.

Nougat
Makes 1½lb.

Ingredients

1 cup hazelnuts, toasted	*1lb. sugar*
¾ cup candied orange	*1⅔ cups powdered glucose*
rind	*¾ cup water*
¼ cup glacé cherries (of	*2 egg whites*
different colors if	*rice paper*
possible)	

Roughly chop the hazelnuts, candied orange rind and glacé cherries.

In a large heavy-based pan, heat the sugar, glucose and water gently until the sugar dissolves and then boil.

Beat the egg whites in a bowl until stiff and gradually add the syrup. Keep beating until the mixture thickens. This could take up to 30 minutes but it is important if the nougat is going to set.

Add the nuts, candied orange and cherries, mix well and pour into a 7in. square cake pan lined with rice paper. Cover with another sheet of rice paper and press down with a weight.

Leave for 12 hours. Remove from pan and cut into squares.

Variation For Coffee Nougat add 2tbsp. coffee extract with the chopped nuts and fruit.

Praline
Makes ¼lb.

Ingredients

½ cup sugar
1 cup blanched almonds
a little oil

Put the sugar and nuts into the bottom of a heavy-based pan. Cook on a very low heat, stirring constantly, until the sugar has melted and turned a golden brown color. Be sure that all the nuts are well coated.

Brush a flat cookie sheet with oil. Spread the nuts and syrup onto the tray and leave to set.

Crush the praline with a rolling pin or food processor. It can be coarse or fine, according to personal preference. Alternatively, simply break it into uneven slabs. Use the praline as a garnish, or flavor ice cream with ground praline. Chunks of praline can also be stirred into a softened ice cream or bombe to provide a contrast in texture.

Variation Use peanuts, hazelnuts, walnuts or pecans instead of almonds.
Glazed nuts Melt the sugar as above and dip the nuts in one at a time. Remove and leave to cool on a sheet of waxed paper.

Testing the Temperature of a Syrup

Soft ball 112-116°C/234-240°F
Dip the pan in cold water. Drop a small amount of the syrup into a bowl of very cold water, roll it into a ball in the water, then lift it out.

If the syrup forms a ball whilst in the water but becomes soft and flattens under slight pressure when removed from the water, the correct stage has been reached.

Used for fondants and fudge.

Thread 106-113°C/223-236°F
Dip the pan in cold water. Using a teaspoon, take a small amount of the syrup then gently and slowly pour it over the rim of the spoon.

If a thin thread forms the correct temperature has been reached.

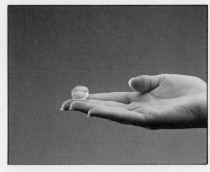

Firm ball 118-121°C/244-250°F
Dip the pan in cold water. Drop a small amount of the syrup into very cold water, roll it into a ball in the water, then lift it out.

If a ball holds its shape when lifted from the water but loses it as it warms up, the correct temperature has been reached.

Used for caramels.

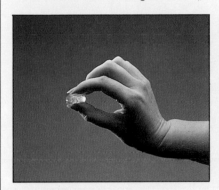

Hard ball 121-130°C/250-266°F
Dip the pan in cold water. Drop a small amount of the syrup into very cold water, form it into a ball in the water, then lift it out.

If the ball holds its shape under slight pressure but is still quite sticky, the correct temperature has been reached.

Used for nougat and marshmallows.

Soft crack 132-143°C/270-290°F
Dip the pan in cold water. Drop a small amount of the syrup into very cold water. Remove it between the fingers then gently separate them.

If the syrup forms threads that are hard but not brittle the correct stage has been reached.

Used for humbugs.

Hard crack 149-154°C/300-310°F
Dip the pan in cold water. Drop a little of the syrup into very cold water, then remove it.

If it is hard and brittle the correct stage has been reached.

Used for hard toffee and rock.

Caramel 160-177°C/320-350°F
Dip the pan in cold water. Pour a small amount from a spoon onto a white plate. A golden honey indicates a light caramel, a golden amber colour a dark caramel. If the syrup darkens beyond this stage it will begin to taste bitter.

Used for pralines.

Sauces, Dressings and Marinades

Bolognese Sauce
Serves 4

Ingredients

*1 large onion, peeled and
   diced
1 carrot, scraped and
   grated
1 stalk celery, washed and
   chopped
2 cloves garlic, crushed
2 slices bacon
1 tbsp. oil
¼lb. lean ground beef
¼lb. lean ground veal
1¼ cups beef stock or water*

*15oz. can tomatoes
4 tomatoes, skinned and
   chopped
1 bay leaf
1 tsp. oregano
½tsp. basil
1 bouquet garni
salt and freshly ground
   pepper
1 tbsp. tomato paste
⅔ cup red wine*

Prepare the vegetables, making sure that they are diced very finely. Remove strings from the celery with a sharp knife before chopping.

Cut the bacon into small pieces, having first removed the rind. Heat the oil in the pan and brown all the meat over a medium heat. Remove with a slotted spoon leaving any fat behind.

Cook the vegetables in the meat fat — adding a little extra oil if necessary — over a low heat for 5 minutes.

Put the meat and vegetables into a saucepan with the tomatoes, herbs and seasoning. Lastly add the tomato paste and stir in the wine.

Bring to a boil and simmer gently for 45 minutes. Remove bouquet garni and bay leaf before serving. Serve with spaghetti and other pasta, with Parmesan cheese served separately.

Curry Sauce

Ingredients

*butter or margarine
1 medium onion, finely
   chopped
1 tbsp. curry powder
1 tbsp. cornstarch*

*2 tbsp. water
1¼ cups yogurt
2 tbsp. chutney (optional)
1 tbsp. shredded coconut
   (optional)*

Heat the butter and add the onion. Cook until it has just softened but not browned. Stir in the curry powder and let it cook over a gentle heat for a minute.

Mix the cornstarch and water to a smooth paste and add it to the yogurt. Add this to the pan, stir well and continue cooking for five minutes.

Add the chutney and coconut just before serving.

Curry sauce is so useful for pepping up all sorts of different foods — try it with hard-boiled eggs, or fish, rice, cold meats, chicken, vegetables.

Blue Cheese Sauce
Makes 3 cups

Ingredients

*2½ cups Béchamel Sauce
¼lb. Roquefort or other
   blue cheese
salt and freshly ground
   pepper*

*½tsp. French mustard
pinch of cayenne pepper*

Make up the Béchamel Sauce. Crumble the cheese and add to the sauce. Stir over a low heat.

Taste for seasoning. Add salt and pepper to taste and then the mustard. Lastly stir in the pinch of cayenne.

This sauce will accompany approximately 1-1½lb. cooked pasta.

Cucumber Dill Sauce

Ingredients

1 medium-sized cucumber, peeled
2tbsp. butter
2/3 cup fish or chicken stock
2/3 cup dry white wine
2tbsp. fresh dill, chopped or 1tbsp. dried dill
4tsp. cornstarch
2tbsp. water
1/2 cup sour cream or yogurt
salt and pepper

Coarsely grate the cucumber and put it into a saucepan. Add the butter and cook on a gentle heat just to soften the cucumber. Add the stock, wine and dill and simmer for 5 minutes.

Mix the cornstarch with the water. Add it to the pan, cook gently until the sauce begins to thicken, stirring constantly.

Add the sour cream or yogurt and warm it through. Season to taste.

Serve hot or cold, with salmon or other fish. Also good with poached eggs, boiled potatoes, rice or pasta.

Dill Sauce

Ingredients

4tbsp. butter or margarine
1tbsp. flour
1 cup water
salt and pepper
1tbsp. dried dill
1tbsp. vinegar
1tsp. sugar
2/3 cup yogurt or sour cream

Melt the butter and stir in the flour off the heat. Slowly add the water, stirring constantly to make a smooth paste. Season well and return to the heat.

Add the dill, vinegar and sugar, and cook on a gentle heat for 5 minutes. Stir in the yogurt or sour cream and warm through gently.

A delicious sauce which can dress up plain chops or steak. It is also excellent with poached fish.

Basil Dressing

Ingredients

1 cup yogurt
10 basil leaves, finely chopped
1 large clove garlic, crushed
salt and pepper

Blend everything together well. Serve over green or mixed salad or tomato and onion salad.

This also makes a good sauce for pasta, in which case double the quantity.

Sour Cream Anchovy Dressing

Ingredients

2/3 cup sour cream
1 clove garlic, crushed
4 anchovy fillets, finely chopped
3 green onions, finely chopped
chopped dill, to taste
juice of 1 lemon
salt and pepper

Mix everything together well. Refrigerate until required.

Serve as a salad dressing or on hot or cold fish or broiled meats.

Cheese Herb Dressing

Ingredients

1/3 cup farmer's cheese
scant cup sour cream
2 green onions, finely chopped
1tbsp. chopped parsley
1tbsp. chopped dill
1tbsp. sugar
1tbsp. chopped onion

Combine everything together, mixing well to blend the cheese and sour cream.

Serve over plain poached fish or as a salad dressing. Use ricotta instead of farmer's cheese, if preferred.

Blue Cheese Dressing

Ingredients

2/3 cup sour cream
1/2 cup blue cheese
3tbsp. oil
1tbsp. vinegar
salt and pepper

Blend everything together well, mixing until smooth. If necessary, thin the dressing down with a little milk.

Serve over crisp lettuce — chunks of lettuce with blue cheese dressing make a good starter.

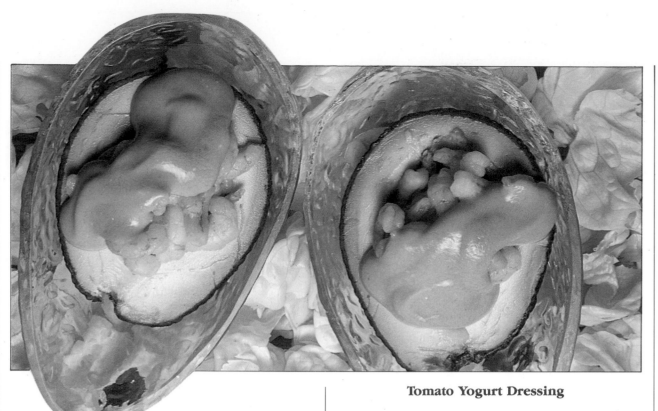

Chutney Dressing

Ingredients

½ cup sour cream
½ cup buttermilk
2tbsp. mango chutney
1tbsp. lemon juice
2tsp. oil
2tsp. mustard
salt and pepper

Blend everything together well. Refrigerate until required.

Serve on salad or cold vegetables. Use as a dressing for hard-boiled eggs, cold fish or meat.

Herb Dressing

Ingredients

5tbsp. cream cheese
1 cup yogurt or buttermilk
salt and pepper
finely chopped fresh herbs

Blend everything together well. Refrigerate until required. Use on salads or fish.

Rich French Dressing

Ingredients

1 egg
½ cup oil
2tbsp. lemon juice
1 clove garlic, crushed
fresh herbs
salt and pepper
1 cup yogurt

Blend together the egg, oil, lemon juice, garlic, herbs, salt and pepper. Slowly add the yogurt, with the blender running. Refrigerate until required — it should thicken as it stands.

This makes a delicious salad dressing but if you want to make it thicker, for piping, you can add some gelatin and let it set. Use chives, fennel, parsley, tarragon or any other fresh herbs you have on hand — or a mixture.

For a less rich dressing omit the egg.

Tomato Yogurt Dressing

Ingredients

⅔ cup yogurt
4tsp. tomato ketchup
dash Worcestershire Sauce
dash Tabasco
salt and pepper

Mix all the ingredients together well. Serve on crisp lettuce or as a seafood dressing.

For a variation add finely chopped green or red pepper, chopped hard-boiled egg, or chopped green onions.

Mustard Dressing

Ingredients

⅔ cup yogurt
1tbsp. mustard
1tbsp. lemon juice
salt and pepper

Mix all the ingredients together well. Use over green salad or cabbage salad or on steaks, chops or broiled fish.

The flavor of the mustard you use will determine the piquancy of this dressing. *Moutarde de grains* or Dijon mustard works well but it is interesting to try different varieties.

Yogurt Cream Dressing

Ingredients

2½ cups yogurt
⅔ cup heavy cream
squeeze of lemon juice
granulated sugar to taste

Drain the yogurt for 3 hours. Whip the cream and fold into the drained yogurt. Add the lemon juice and sugar and stir well to dissolve the sugar.

Use as required. It is very good as a dressing over fruit salad, or folded into a fruit salad, or over individual fruits, berries, pineapple, bananas or mangoes.

Add more lemon juice, and some finely grated rind, or orange juice and rind. Substitute ½lb. quark, fromage blanc or farmer's cheese for the yogurt.

Aïoli
Makes about 2½ cups

Aïoli is simply the ultimate garlic sauce. Although originally served with shrimps, it is sensational on anything from hamburgers to Bouillabaisse, and a dollop of it will perk up the tiredest vegetable, rev up the blandest soup, and give yesterday's cold cuts a new interest in life. You can, of course, add crushed garlic or, nicer still, Garlic Purée to homemade or bought mayonnaise. It will taste much better than commercially produced garlic mayonnaise, but it won't be Aïoli.

Ingredients
4-6 cloves of garlic (though of course you can use more)
a pinch of salt
3 egg yolks
2 cups olive oil
lemon juice to taste
a little water or light cream

Chop the garlic finely and pound in a mortar with the salt until smooth. Beat in the egg yolks.

Add the oil, drop by drop at first, then in a thin stream once the mixture is glossy and beginning to thicken.

Add lemon juice to taste, and if too solid for your liking, add a little water or light cream.

To stop a skin forming on the Aïoli, cover with a piece of plastic wrap that touches the surface.

Variations For Almond Skordalia, add 1tbsp. of fresh white breadcrumbs, 1tbsp. of ground almonds, 1tbsp. of chopped parsley and a pinch of cayenne for every 1¼ cups of Aïoli and flavor with lemon or lime juice to taste. This sauce is traditionally served with cold, cooked vegetables.

For Aïoli Verde, add to each cup of Aïoli a handful of parsley, two or three sprigs of fresh tarragon, two or three sprigs of fresh chervil and half a handful of spinach, which have been simmered together in salted water until tender, drained and blended to a smooth purée.

Basic Garlic Dressing

Ingredients
1-2 cloves garlic, crushed
1tsp. sugar
2tbsp. wine vinegar or Garlic Vinegar
6tbsp. olive oil
salt and pepper

Combine all the ingredients in a screw-top jar, cover and shake well. Adjust seasoning before serving.

Variations Include fresh or dried herbs to taste, depending on what you are serving the dressing with.

Substitute different flavored vinegars.

Substitute part or all of the oil with walnut oil.

Replace the oil with sour cream or yogurt and the vinegar with lemon juice (the cream version is excellent with 1tbsp. of freshly grated horseradish added to it).

Add 1tsp. of mild French mustard. This dressing is especially good served over warm green beans as a first course.

Garlic Butter

Garlic Butter is a great topping for steaks, hamburgers, broiled or barbecued fish or chicken and is a handy shortcut to garlic bread. It can also be used to enrich soups, stews and sauces, and, in sandwiches, makes a welcome and tasty change from plain butter.

Ingredients
½ cup butter, softened
3-6 cloves of garlic, unpeeled
salt and pepper

Cream the butter until light and fluffy. Blanch the garlic in boiling water for 1 minute, drain and peel.

Crush the garlic to a fine paste with a pinch of salt and gradually mix in the softened butter.

Season with salt and pepper to taste, wrap in foil and chill until needed.

Variations *Parsley Garlic Butter* add 1½tbsp. of chopped fresh parsley.

Herb and Garlic Butter add 1½tbsp. of chopped fresh mixed herbs.

Mustard Garlic Butter add 1tbsp. of mild French mustard.

Horseradish Garlic Butter add 1tbsp. of grated fresh horseradish.

Chili Garlic Butter add chili powder to taste, and 2tsp. of tomato paste.

Tomato Garlic Butter add 1tbsp. tomato paste.

Clarified Garlic Butter

Ingredients

3-6 cloves of garlic, unpeeled	*½ cup butter*
	salt and pepper

Blanch the unpeeled garlic in boiling water for 1 minute, then drain and peel.

Slice the garlic and heat gently in the butter with a little salt and pepper for 5 minutes.

Skim the butter and strain it through a piece of cheesecloth or a very fine strainer. Keep covered in the refrigerator until needed.

This can be used for frying, especially potatoes, and can be brushed over pastry before baking, and over rolls and bagels before heating.

It is also particularly good with vegetables such as asparagus and artichokes, however irreverent this may sound.

Ghee
Clarified Butter

Heat 1lb. of unsalted butter in a saucepan over low heat. Let it simmer for 15-20 minutes until all the white residue turns golden and settles at the bottom.

Remove from the heat, strain and cool. Pour into an airtight bottle and store in a cool place.

Green Butter

It is simple to make this savory butter in a blender or food processor, otherwise all ingredients have to be chopped by hand.

It is usual to make up herb butters in the shape of a round sausage. Wrap the round in foil and cut slices as required after chilling. Cut the rolls into coin-sized pieces when very cold and store in the freezer.

Ingredients

1 cup washed and chopped spinach leaves	*3 baby pickles*
	1tsp. capers
1 bunch of watercress, stalks removed	*3 anchovy fillets*
	2tbsp. oil
1 clove of garlic	*1 egg yolk*
fresh tarragon to taste	*1 hard-boiled egg*
a few sprigs of parsley	*½ cup butter*
fresh chives to taste	

Drop the spinach leaves, watercress, garlic and herbs into the blender or food processor to purée. Add the baby pickles, capers and anchovy fillets to the blender with the oil, egg yolk and hard-boiled egg. Lastly blend in the softened butter.

Chill and serve with broiled fish. This savory butter is especially good with barbecued food.

Garam Masala

Ingredients

3tbsp. cardamom seeds	*½tsp. black peppercorns*
3×1in. cinnamon sticks	*½tsp. cloves*
½tbsp. cumin seeds	*¼ of a nutmeg*

Grind all the spices together until they are finely ground. Store in a spice bottle until required. (The ingredients may be added in different proportions to suit individual tastes.)

Horseradish Sauce, Hot

Ingredients

2tsp. grated horseradish
²/₃ cup yogurt
1tsp. lemon juice

1tbsp. water
1tsp. cornstarch
salt and pepper

Combine all the ingredients in a saucepan, with the water and cornstarch mixed to a smooth paste.

Cook on a gentle heat, stirring constantly, for 5 minutes.

You can buy grated horseradish in a jar or possibly you may find fresh horseradish.

Horseradish Sauce, Cold

Ingredients

1tbsp. freshly grated horseradish

²/₃ cup heavy cream
few drops of olive oil

Mix horseradish and cream together. Add the olive oil.

Béchamel Sauce
Makes 2½ cups

Ingredients

2½ cups milk
1 small onion, peeled
1 small carrot, scraped and sliced
1 bay leaf
6 slightly crushed peppercorns

1 blade mace
1 stalk parsley
3tbsp. butter
⅓ cup flour
salt and white pepper

Pour milk into a saucepan. Add the onion cut into quarters with 2 slices of carrot, bay leaf, peppercorns, mace and parsely stalk.

Cover and allow to heat on low heat without boiling for about 10 minutes. Remove from the heat and allow to infuse for a further 10 minutes, covered.

Make a roux (a blend of butter and flour) by melting the butter in a saucepan. Do not allow the butter to brown. Add the flour and stir well over a medium heat.

Gradually add the strained milk and stir briskly or beat until a smooth creamy sauce is made; season to taste.

Variation To make a cheese sauce, add ½ cup grated cheese, good pinch cayenne pepper and ½tsp. powdered mustard.

Chaudfroid Sauce
Makes 2½ cups

Ingredients

2 cups Béchamel Sauce
²/₃ cup aspic jelly

1 rounded tsp. gelatin
2tbsp. boiling water

Allow the Béchamel Sauce to cool but cover with plastic wrap to avoid a skin forming.

Make up the aspic jelly in a jug and sprinkle the gelatin onto the hot water. Make sure the mixture is dissolved by placing the jug in a saucepan of boiling water. Allow to cool before using to coat fish fillets, small fish or fish steaks.

Hollandaise Sauce
Makes ¾ cup

Ingredients

2tbsp. water
6 peppercorns, slightly crushed
1tbsp. white wine vinegar

¾ cup butter
2 egg yolks
1tbsp. lemon juice
salt to taste

Make the sauce in a double boiler or an ovenproof bowl over a saucepan of hot water. If using the latter method make sure that the bottom of the bowl is not touching the hot water or the sauce will set on the bottom of the bowl before it is cooked.

Place the water, crushed peppercorns and white wine vinegar in a small saucepan and reduce to about 1tbsp. liquid. Set aside.

Cut the butter into pieces and soften gently in a small saucepan. Remove from heat.

Beat the egg yolks, reduced liquid and a little of the butter in the double boiler. When the mixture becomes creamy and slightly thick, pour in the butter in a thin stream, beating briskly. Add lemon juice and a little salt, and taste for seasoning.

Remove from the heat immediately it is thick. Should the sauce look as if it is curdling, add a few drops of cold water and beat briskly for a few more minutes.

This sauce can be made in a blender or food processor, but you may find that less butter will be absorbed. The addition of 1tbsp. cold water with the lemon juice will prevent it becoming too thick.

Hollandaise is served hot with broiled or baked fish such as salmon, turbot, halibut and sea bream.

Mousseline Sauce

Preparation Add 4tbsp. whipped cream to Hollandaise Sauce as it cools. The resulting Mousseline Sauce can be served cold with fish or vegetables.

Mornay Sauce
Makes approx. 2½ cups

Ingredients
2½ cups Béchamel Sauce
2 egg yolks
2tbsp. cream
½ cup grated cheese

Place 4tbsp. Béchamel sauce in a small bowl and mix with the egg yolks and cream.

Add this mixture to the Béchamel sauce and cook over a how heat, stirring well.

Gradually add grated cheese. Parmesan is ideal but individual taste can decide on the type of cheese.

This can be served with poached or steamed fish fillets or cutlets.

Mustard Sauce
Makes ⅔ cup

Ingredients
1tbsp. French mustard
juice of ½ lemon
salt and white pepper to
taste
⅔ cup heavy cream

Mix the mustard, lemon juice and seasoning together.

Whip the cream lightly and stir in the mustard mixture. Chill before using with broiled or fried fish.

Variation Alternatively a hot mustard sauce may be made with ⅔ cup Béchamel Sauce. Add 1tsp. dried mustard and 1tsp. vinegar to 1tbsp. of the sauce, return to the sauce and stir over the heat for a further minute.

Sauce Gribiche

Ingredients
1 hard-boiled egg
½tsp. Dijon mustard
1tbsp. chopped baby
pickles
1tsp. fresh tarragon or
½tsp. dried
1tbsp. freshly chopped
parsley
1tsp. capers, chopped
1¼ cups Mayonnaise

Press the yolk of the hard-boiled egg through a strainer and add, together with all the other ingredients, to the Mayonnaise. Mix well and serve with cold fish dishes and shellfish.

Marinara Sauce

Ingredients
2 medium onions, thinly
sliced
2 cloves garlic, crushed
2tbsp. olive oil
15oz. can tomatoes
1tbsp. tomato paste
1tsp. sugar
1tsp. dried oregano
1tsp. paprika
salt and pepper

Fry the onions and garlic in the oil until they begin to brown. Lower the heat and cook for 15 to 20 minutes until soft.

Add the tomatoes, tomato paste, sugar, oregano and paprika. Cook rapidly for about 10 minutes until the tomatoes break down.

Add salt and pepper to taste, and serve. This quantity of sauce is enough for 1lb. of pasta. Traditionally this saucc is served without cheese, but if you must, use a strong hard cheese such as Parmesan or pecorino.

Variation Stir ½ cup pitted black olives and 2tbsp. drained, finely chopped anchovy fillets to the finished sauce and heat through for a few moments before serving.

Mushroom Sauce
Serves 4 to 6

Serve with chops, escalopes of chicken, turkey or veal, or with pasta.

Ingredients

1 small onion, peeled
2tbsp. butter
¼lb. firm white button
*   mushrooms*
2tbsp. flour
⅔ cup chicken stock
⅔ cup whole milk or light
*   cream*

1tbsp. port (optional)
salt and freshly ground
*   pepper*
pinch of nutmeg
1tbsp. snipped chives
lemon juice to taste

Finely chop the onion. Heat the butter in a small pan and slowly cook the onion until soft and golden. Slice the mushrooms. Add to the onions and fry over medium heat for 2 minutes. Stir in the stock and milk or cream and bring to a boil, stirring constantly. Add the port, and seasonings. Simmer the sauce for 5 minutes. Chop the chives and stir into the sauce and add a little lemon juice to taste.

Putanesca Sauce
Makes 2½ cups

Ingredients

1 onion, peeled and diced
2tbsp. oil
1 carrot, scraped and
*   chopped*
15oz. can tomatoes
2 tomatoes, skinned and
*   chopped*
4tbsp. white wine
1 bay leaf
3-4 basil leaves or 1tsp.
*   dried basil*

salt and freshly ground
*   pepper*
1tbsp. capers, chopped
1 small can anchovies
½ cup pitted black olives
3 drops Tabasco sauce
1tbsp. freshly chopped
*   parsley*

Put the onion into the oil in a saucepan over a low heat. Allow to cook gently for 4 minutes, add the crushed garlic and carrots. Turn in the oil for another minute.

Add the tomatoes, the white wine, bay leaf, basil, some seasoning and 4 anchovy fillets. Bring to the boil and simmer for 30 minutes. Strain or liquidize into a measuring jug.

Return to the saucepan and add chopped capers, the remainder of the anchovies chopped into small pieces, chopped olives and the spicy Tabasco sauce. Reheat gently.

Serve with 1lb. cooked pasta, with Parmesan cheese served separately.

Ragu Sauce
Serves 4

Ingredients

1 onion, peeled
2 cloves garlic, crushed
1 carrot, scraped and
*   grated*
1 stalk celery
6 tomatoes, peeled and
*   chopped or 15oz. can*
*   tomatoes*
4tbsp. oil

½lb. lean ground beef
¼lb. chicken livers
1 bouquet garni
1 bay leaf
1¼ cups stock and red
*   wine*
1tsp. oregano
1 stalk parsley

Cut the onion finely, coarsely grate the carrot. Wash the celery and remove strings with a sharp knife before chopping into very small pieces. Prepare tomatoes.

Heat half the oil in a saucepan and cook the onion and garlic for 3 minutes over a low heat. Add carrot and celery, stir into the oil and allow to cook for a further 3 minutes.

Heat the remaining oil in a skillet and brown the beef well over a high heat. Turn the heat down to medium and add chopped chicken livers. Mix with the beef and cook until brown.

Add the meat to the vegetables with the herbs and wine, season well, add the stock and simmer for 45 minutes. Taste for seasoning before serving with freshly cooked pasta.

Salsa Verde

Green and piquant, this sauce of fresh herbs is excellent with any fish, hot or cold, and goes well with hard-boiled eggs. Since it is so very good with shrimps, try it in a shrimp cocktail.

Ingredients

3 cloves of garlic, finely
*   chopped*
½ cup parsley, finely
*   chopped*
1tbsp. watercress leaves,
*   finely chopped*
*   (optional)*

1tbsp. mixed fresh herbs,
*   finely chopped (basil,*
*   marjoram, and a little*
*   thyme, sage, chervil and*
*   dill)*
coarse salt
4tbsp. olive oil
juice of 1-2 lemons
1-2tsp. sugar
black pepper

Blend or pound together in a mortar, the garlic, parsley, watercress, fresh mixed herbs and a little coarse salt, until they form a smooth paste.

Add the oil, a spoonful at a time, and mix well. Add the lemon juice and season with sugar, salt and pepper to taste.

Spinach and Ricotta Sauce
Makes approx. 2½ cups

Ingredients

1¼ cups Béchamel Sauce
½lb. (after cooking), fresh or frozen spinach
¼lb. ricotta cheese
½tsp. nutmeg
salt and freshly ground pepper

Make up the Béchamel Sauce. Cook the spinach for a few minutes and then drain well. Squeeze against the collander to remove the liquid. You will need to cook approx 1½lb. fresh spinach to be left with the amount required by the recipe. Chop or liquidize.

Mix the ricotta with the spinach and season well, add nutmeg. Gradually stir into the béchamel sauce and reheat carefully over a low heat.

Serve with approximately 1-1½lb. cooked pasta. This sauce is also delicious used in a vegetable or chicken lasagne.

Tuna and Mushroom Sauce
Makes 3 cups

Ingredients

2tbsp. butter
1tbsp. oil
¼lb. mushrooms, washed
7oz. can tuna fish
2tsp. tomato paste
2tbsp. white wine
2½ cups Béchamel Sauce
salt and freshly ground pepper

Heat the butter and oil and cook the mushrooms for 3 minutes, turning from time to time. Flake the tuna fish.

Add the tomato paste and white wine to the béchamel sauce, mix well. Over a low heat reheat the sauce and gradually stir in the tuna fish and the drained mushrooms. Cook gently for a few minutes until well mixed and hot. Taste and adjust seasoning.

Mix the sauce with 1lb. cooked pasta.

Pesto

Although Pesto is traditionally served as a sauce for pasta, it goes well with cold meats, broiled fish, in soups or on salads with extra oil and a dash of lemon juice. You can buy Pesto but if you can lay your hands on a plentiful supply of fresh basil it really is worth making your own.

Ingredients

3oz. fresh basil leaves, finely chopped
2tbsp. pine kernels
⅓ cup Parmesan cheese, finely grated, or half Parmesan and half sardo cheese
3 cloves of garlic, finely chopped
6tbsp. olive oil

Combine the basil, pine kernels, cheese and garlic in a blender, and reduce to a thick, green, aromatic paste.

Add oil, a little at a time, until well incorporated.

Winter Pesto Sauce
Makes approx. 1¼ cups

Ingredients

4tbsp. fresh parsley
2 cloves garlic
½ cup pine nuts
⅓ cup Parmesan cheese
salt and freshly ground pepper
2tsp. dried basil
⅔ cup olive oil

Chop the parsley finely in a blender or with a sharp knife if making by hand. Add the garlic, crushed, to the blender and process for a few seconds. Gradually add the other ingredients through the top of the machine while it is running. When the mixture is puréed add a little olive oil at a time.

Add the dried basil when half the oil has been added. Continue adding oil until a thick creamy mixture is made.

Tomato Sauce
Makes approx. 2½ cups

Ingredients

2tbsp. oil
1 large onion, peeled and
  diced
1-2 cloves garlic, crushed
1 stalk celery, scrubbed
1 carrot, scraped and
  grated
14oz. can tomatoes
1lb. fresh tomatoes,
  skinned and chopped
1 bouquet garni

2 bay leaves
1tbsp. chopped fresh basil,
  or 1tsp. dried basil
parsley sprig
½tsp. sugar
salt and freshly ground
  black pepper
1¼ cups fish or chicken
  stock
2tbsp. red wine

Heat the oil in a saucepan. Cook the garlic and onions over a low heat for about 4 minutes until transparent.

Remove the strings from the celery stalk and chop into small pieces, then add to the onion and garlic for the last 2 minutes.

Add all the other ingredients, bring to the boil and simmer for 40 minutes on a low heat.

Remove the sprig of parsley, bay leaf and bouquet garni and serve as cooked, or the sauce may be partially blended if a smoother texture is preferred.

Concentrated Tomato Sauce

Ingredients

2 medium onions, finely
  chopped
2-3 cloves garlic, crushed
2tbsp. olive oil
3tbsp. tomato paste

3tbsp. wine or water
1tsp. dried oregano
1tsp. paprika
1tsp. sugar
salt and pepper

Fry the onions and garlic in the oil until they begin to brown. Turn down the heat and simmer, covered, for 10-15 minutes or until softened.

Add the tomato paste, wine or water, oregano, paprika and sugar, and season with salt and pepper to taste.

Allow the sauce to bubble for 5 minutes, stirring constantly, and serve.

This rich sauce can be served with pasta as it is, or with ground meat and liquid added. It is delicious poured over chicken pieces or fish steaks before baking, or used to top pizza.

It will also flavor soups and stews and is an excellent relish for cold meats, hamburgers and frankfurters.

Spicy Tomato Sauce
Makes 2 cups

Ingredients

2tbsp. oil
1 large onion, peeled and
  chopped
1 green pepper, seeded
1 red pepper, seeded
1 chili pepper, seeded and
  finely chopped
14-oz. can of tomatoes
2 fresh tomatoes, skinned
  and chopped
¼tsp. powdered mustard

salt and freshly ground
  pepper
1 bouquet garni
2 bay leaves
¼tsp. sugar
⅔ cup fish or chicken stock
To garnish
1 green chili pepper, seeded
  and finely chopped

Heat the oil in a saucepan and sweat the onion on a low heat until transparent.

Dice the peppers finely. Add with the chili pepper to the onions and cook on a low heat for about 4 minutes.

Add the rest of the ingredients to the onion and pepper mixture. Bring to a boil, reduce the heat and simmer for 30 minutes. Remove bouquet garni and bay leaves.

The sauce may be partially blended, if liked. Serve with chopped green chili pepper on top.

Mayonnaise
Makes approx. 1¼ cups

Use this recipe as the basis for many interesting and delicious sauces and dressings.

Ingredients
3 egg yolks	⅔ cup sunflower or
½tsp. mustard powder	safflower oil
salt and pepper	⅔ cup olive oil
½-1tbsp. white wine	1tbsp. hot water
vinegar	

If using a food processor, process the egg yolks with the mustard powder, a little salt and pepper and ½tbsp. of vinegar till well mixed. With the machine running, add the oil, drop by drop, through the feed tube. The mixture should become very thick and emulsified. Taste for seasoning, adding more salt, pepper and vinegar as necessary. Finally, with the machine running, pour the hot water in through the feed tube. If not using a food processor, beat the egg yolks until thick and add the ingredients in the same order, mixing all the time; there is no need to add the hot water.

Store the mayonnaise in a glass or china bowl, cover and chill.

Variations *Curry Mayonnaise:* add 2-3tsp. curry paste (or to taste), plus 2tsp. mango, apricot, or ginger chutney, and a few chopped fresh coriander leaves to the mayonnaise with the hot water. Serve with hard-boiled eggs, shrimps, or cold poultry.

Green Mayonnaise: chop ¼lb. watercress. Add to the mayonnaise with the water. Serve with hard-boiled eggs, cold cooked asparagus or globe artichokes, or cold roast veal or pork.

Watercress Mousseline: chop ¼lb. watercress. Mix with ⅔ cup of the made mayonnaise. Whip ⅔ cup of heavy cream and stir in. Taste for seasoning. Serve with cold poached fish — salmon, sole, shrimps or lobster, or cold roast chicken.

Marie-Rose Mayonnaise: mix 2 to 3 tbsp. tomato ketchup and a couple of drops of Tabasco sauce and add to the mayonnaise with the water. Serve with shrimps, crab, lobster, fish croquettes, fish cakes or egg salads.

Garlic and Herb Mayonnaise: chop ½tbsp. each parsley sprigs, tarragon leaves, basil leaves and snipped chives, with 1 to 2 cloves garlic. Add to the mayonnaise with the water. Serve with cold cooked vegetables and salads, or as a dip.

Yogurt Mayonnaise: mix ⅔ cup of plain thick yogurt with ⅔ cup of the mayonnaise, and 1 to 2tbsp. snipped chives. Season to taste. Serve with avocados, asparagus, globe artichokes, cold poached fish, green salads and raw vegetables.

Sour Cream Mayonnaise: mix ⅔ cup sour cream with an equal quantity of the mayonnaise. Season to taste. Chop ½tbsp. mint and 3tbsp. cucumber with 2tbsp. chopped green onions. Serve as a dip, or with salads.

Avocado Mayonnaise: process ⅔ cup of the mayonnaise with an equal quantity of plain thick yogurt, 1tsp. of lemon juice and a ripe avocado, peeled and diced. Season to taste with salt and cayenne pepper. Serve as a dip, or with green salads and seafood.

Egg and Chive Mayonnaise: add 2 shelled hard-boiled eggs and 2tbsp. snipped chives to the mayonnaise with the hot water. Serve with green salads and vegetables or with cold fish and shellfish.

Horseradish Mayonnaise: add 3tbsp. freshly grated horseradish to the made mayonnaise. Mix thoroughly and serve with Potato Salad.

Mustard Mayonnaise: use ½tbsp. Dijon mustard instead of mustard powder and add ½tsp. Worcestershire Sauce and 2-3 drops Tabasco sauce at the same time.

Tartar Sauce
Makes 1¼ cups

Ingredients
2 hard-boiled eggs	2tbsp. capers
2tsp. French mustard	2tbsp. parsley, finely
salt and freshly ground	chopped
pepper	1tsp. dried chervil or
1 egg yolk	equivalent fresh, if
⅔ cup vegetable or olive oil	available
4-6 baby pickles	

Press the yolks of the hard-boiled eggs through a strainer into a bowl and add mustard, salt and pepper. Mix the raw egg yolks into the bowl and cream until the mixture is a smooth paste. Add the oil a few drops at a time until the sauce is thick. If it seems too thick, add a few drops of lemon juice.

Drain and rinse the baby pickles and capers in a strainer with cold water as they are usually packed in vinegar or brine, which can overpower the flavor of the sauce. Pat dry with paper towels and chop finely. Add to the sauce with the herbs (herbs, baby pickles and capers can be chopped in the blender or food processor). Mix well and taste for seasoning. Serve with all types of fried or broiled fish.

Quick Tartar Sauce Add the baby pickles, capers, parsley and herbs to ⅔ cup mayonnaise.

Vinaigrette
Makes ¾ cup

Ingredients

4tbsp. olive or walnut oil
4tbsp. safflower or sunflower oil
2tbsp. wine or sherry vinegar

½tsp. freshly ground black pepper
½-1tsp. mustard powder

Mix all the ingredients together thoroughly, preferably in a blender or food processor.

Variations

Herbed Vinaigrette: chop 2tbsp. fresh herbs — parsley, chives, tarragon, mint, basil, etc. Stir into the vinaigrette.

Roquefort Dressing: blend all the ingredients for the vinaigrette, except the salt. Add 2oz. crumble Roquefort cheese, 2tsp. lemon juice. Blended until the mixture has emulsified, taste for seasoning.

Chili Vinaigrette: add 1 to 2 green chili peppers, seeded, cored and quartered, to the ingredients before blending; or add 1 to 2 crumbled dried red chili peppers and a few sesame seeds to the ingredients before blending.

Cream Dressing: blend equal quantities of mayonnaise and vinaigrette. Add a few snipped chives, and season to taste, using a couple of drops of Tabasco sauce, if wished.

Yogurt and Tahini Dip

Tahini paste, which is crushed sesame seeds, is obtainable at Greek stores and healthfood shops and some supermarkets. It is very thick and usually has a layer of oil on top which you should mix in before you use the paste.

Ingredients

2 cloves garlic, crushed
⅔ cup tahini paste
⅔ cup yogurt

juice of 2 lemons
salt and pepper
chopped parsley, to taste

Blend everything together except the parsley until smooth. Taste and add more lemon juice and seasoning if necessary. Turn into a bowl and garnish with the chopped parsley.

Serve as a dip, with pita or crackers, or as an accompaniment to vegetables, salads or meat or fish dishes.

Sour Cream Dip

Ingredients

⅔ cup sour cream
2tsp. dried dill
2tsp. dried onion flakes

4tsp. chopped parsley
½tsp. mustard
salt and pepper

Mix everything together well and leave for the flavors to mingle for 2 hours if possible.

Use as a dip, with carrot sticks, celery, cauliflower etc, or as a salad dressing.

Dried onion is used in this to give a mild hint of onion. If you use fresh onion, be discreet.

Black Cherry Sauce
Serves 8-10

Ingredients

1lb. black cherries, pitted
4tbsp. sugar
¼ cup water

1tsp. cornstarch
1tbsp. water

Place the fruit, sugar and water in a heavy-bottomed pan on a very low heat. Cook gently until the fruit is soft.

Combine the cornstarch and water. Stir into the cooked fruit and bring to a boil, stirring constantly. Heat until the sauce has thickened.

If you are serving black cherry sauce for a special occasion, stir in a few spoonfuls of kirsch.

Chocolate Sauce
Serves 3-4

Ingredients

4tbsp. unsweetened cocoa powder
4tbsp. corn syrup

4tbsp. butter
⅔ cup milk
½tsp. vanilla extract

Put cocoa, corn syrup and butter into a small pan. Heat gently until well blended. Stir in the milk and extract.

Bring to a boil and simmer gently for about 3 minutes. Serve hot or cold.

Variations *Chocolate/Orange Sauce:* Omit vanilla extract. Add grated rind of ½ orange.

Honey Chocolate Sauce: Use clear honey instead of corn syrup. Add lemon juice instead of vanilla extract.

Choco-Nutty Sauce: Omit vanilla extract. Stir in 1tbsp. peanut butter.

Choco-Ginger Sauce: Add 2tbsp. chopped stem ginger.

Chocolate Custard
Makes 2½ cups

Ingredients
600ml/1pt milk
6 egg yolks
50g/2oz sugar

100g/4oz plain chocolate,
grated

Put the milk into a saucepan and bring almost to a boil. Remove from the heat.

Beat the egg yolks and sugar together until thick and fluffy. Gradually pour the milk on to the eggs and sugar, beating continuously.

Return mixture to saucepan and stir over a very gentle heat, until it coats the back of a spoon. Remove from the heat and add the chocolate. Stir until dissolved.

Serve the custard hot or cold. To cool the custard, pour into a bowl and place dampened waxed paper directly on to the surface to stop a "skin" from forming. Chill.

Chocolate Syrup

This syrup can be used for milk shakes, to pour over ice cream, pancakes, waffles, etc. To thin it just add a little cream or milk.

Ingredients
1½ cups soft brown sugar
½ cup unsweetened cocoa

1¼ cups boiling water
2tsp. vanilla extract

Mix together the sugar and cocoa. Add the water, stirring continuously.

Put the mixture into a small pan and simmer gently for 5 minutes, stirring frequently. Cool, then add the vanilla extract. Cover and chill in the refrigerator.

Fudge Sauce
Serves 4-6

Ingredients
1tbsp. unsweetened cocoa
  powder
¾ cup evaporated milk
3oz. plain chocolate,
  grated

2tbsp. butter
2tbsp. soft brown sugar

Put cocoa and evaporated milk into a pan and beat well together.

Add all the remaining ingredients. Heat gently, stirring until the chocolate, sugar and butter have melted. Do not boil. Serve hot or warm.

Mars Bar Sauce
Serves 4

This recipe is very quick to make and absolutely delicious.

Ingredients
4 Mars Bars   6tbsp. heavy cream

Dice the Mars Bars. Put in a small pan and melt very gently.

Stir in the cream. Mix until smooth and immediately pour over ice cream.

For extra punch, add a little brandy or rum to taste.

Quick Fruit Sauce
Serves 6

Ingredients
1lb. fuit   confectioner's sugar

Pit, liquidize and strain any soft fruit in season, eg. peaches, berries, mango etc. Sweeten to taste and spoon over ice cream.

Summer Sauce
Serves 8-10

Ingredients
½lb. redcurrants   2tbsp. orange juice
½lb. blackcurrants   2tsp. cornstarch
½lb. raspberries   2tbsp. water
½ cup sugar

Place the fruit, sugar and orange juice in a heavy-bottomed pan on a low heat. Cook gently until the fruit is soft.

Combine the cornstarch and water. Stir into the cooked fruit and bring to a boil, stirring constantly. Heat until the sauce has thickened.

Tobler Sauce
Serves 4

Ingredients
½lb. Toblerone or Swiss
   milk chocolate
⅔ cup heavy cream

Cut chocolate into very small pieces. Put into a small pan and melt very quickly.

Stir in the cream. Mix until smooth and immediately pour over ice cream or fruit such as bananas or pears, etc.

Crushing Garlic

1 If using many cloves, split a head of garlic with a solid punch of the fist. (Put waxed paper on the board if you want to avoid having to scrub the board later.)

2 To skin a single clove, place it near the edge of a chopping board and lay the flat of a heavy knife over the clove with the handle overlapping the edge of the board. Use a fist to punch down hard on the knife to slightly crush the clove and loosen the skin.

3 The paper skin of the half-crushed garlic clove can now be easily peeled off.

4 To make garlic paste, use the tip of a round-bladed knife and a good quantity of salt to crush the clove, working from tip to 'root' end.

5 Continue the process of crushing and mixing until the paste is smooth.

Pickles and Preserves

Cucumber and Sesame Relish
Serves 4-6

Ingredients
1 large cucumber
2½ cups water
juice of ½ lemon
1 tsp. salt
4 tbsp. peanut oil
1 tbsp. sesame oil
3 cloves garlic, peeled and
   finely sliced

1 medium onion, peeled,
   finely sliced and dried
   on paper towels
1-2 tbsp. roasted sesame
   seeds

Peel the cucumber, cut it in half and scoop out the seeds. Cut into even-sized chunks.

Put the water into a pan (stainless steel or enamel if possible) and add the lemon and salt. Bring to a boil then lightly cook the cucumber pieces in this, but take care not to overcook. Drain and leave to cool.

Heat the oils and fry the garlic, then lift out the pieces and fry the onion until crisp; lift out and drain. Reserve the oil and when cool pour over the cucumber. Toss well, then mix with the garlic, onion and sesame seeds.

Serve with curries.

Horseradish and Beet Relish
Makes ¾ cup

Ingredients
1 cup grated raw beet
5 tbsp. freshly grated
   horseradish
salt and pepper to taste

Mix the ingredients together, cover and chill.

Serve with broiled fish, boiled fish and meat dishes. Refrigerated, this Relish will keep for about a week.

Tomato, Cucumber and Onion Relish
Serves 4-6

Ingredients
½ lb. tomatoes, chopped
   into ¼-in. chunks
½ lb. cucumber, cut into ¼-
   in. chunks
1 medium onion, finely
   chopped
2-3 fresh green chili
   peppers

½ tsp. salt
2 pinches sugar
3 tbsp. lemon juice
2 tbsp. chopped fresh
   coriander leaves or
   parsley

Mix all the ingredients together in a small bowl. Cover and chill before serving.

Lime Relish
Makes approx. 5 cups

Ingredients
12 limes, washed
cold water
1½ cups sugar

4 cups vinegar
⅔ cup water

Place the limes in a large pot and add enough cold water to cover. Soak the limes for 24 hours. Drain limes and return to pot. Add enough cold water to cover and cook for 15-20 minutes, or until limes can be easily pierced with a fork. Drain well and set aside to cool.

When the limes are cool, cut into eighths. Remove the seeds. Set the limes aside. Place the sugar, vinegar and water in a saucepan. Cook over a medium-low heat until syrupy, about 15 minutes.

Place the lime pieces in hot sterilized jars. Cover with syrup. Seal, cool, and store.

Chili Vinegar
Makes approx. 2½ cups

Ingredients
2 tbsp. dried red hot chili
   peppers
2½ cups vinegar

Crush the chili peppers coarsely and steep in the vinegar. Shake daily for 10 days, then strain and bottle.

Mint Chutney

Mint Chutney
Serves 2-4

Ingredients

1 cup fresh mint leaves, washed	¼in. fresh ginger
¼ cup lemon juice	2-3 fresh green chili peppers
1 small onion, finely chopped	½tsp. salt
3 cloves garlic	½tsp sugar

Blend or process all the ingredients together until you have a smooth paste.

This chutney can be stored in an airtight jar in the refrigerator for a week.

Tomato Chutney
Makes approx. 1lb.

Ingredients

1tbsp. oil	1tbsp. sugar
1lb. tomatoes, quartered	1tsp. cornstarch, mixed with a little milk
½tbsp. salt	

Heat the oil in a small saucepan over medium heat.

Add the tomatoes, cover and cook until the tomatoes are soft. Add the salt and sugar and cook a further 10 minutes.

Thicken with the cornstarch mixture and remove from the heat.

Chill, before serving.

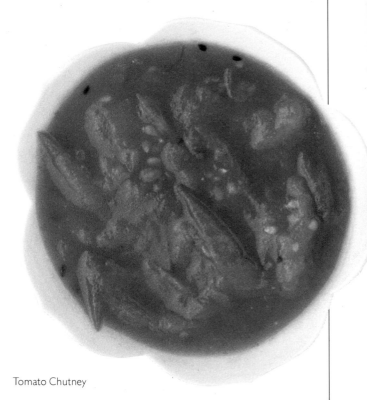

Tomato Chutney

Mango Chutney
Makes approx. 1¼lb.

Ingredients

4 green mangoes	½tsp. salt
2tsp. oil	4tbsp. sugar
2 cardamom pods	1tsp. flour mixed to a paste
1-in. piece stick cinnamon	with 2tbsp. milk
2 cups water	

Wash the mangoes, and pat dry. Cut into 6 pieces, lengthwise.

Heat the oil in a saucepan over a medium high heat. Add the cardamom and cinnamon and let them sizzle for a few seconds. Add the mangoes and stir fry for 2-3 minutes.

Add the water and salt and, when the mixture starts to boil, add the sugar and stir in well. Cover, lower the heat and cook for 15-20 minutes until the mangoes are soft.

Add the flour and milk mixture, stirring constantly to make sure that no lumps can form.

Chill before serving.

Tamarind Chutney
Makes approx. 1½ cups

Ingredients

¼lb. dried tamarind	1tbsp. lemon juice
1⅓ cups hot water	2tbsp. brown sugar
good pinch chili powder	good pinch salt

Soak the tamarind in the water for about 30 minutes. Squeeze the liquid from the tamarind and strain.

Combine the tamarind juice with the other ingredients and chill.

Pineapple Chutney
Serves 6

Ingredients

¹/₂tbsp. oil
¹/₂tsp. mustard seeds
¹/₂lb. can pineapple,
 crushed and drained

good pinch salt
1tsp. cornstarch mixed
 with a little milk

Heat the oil in a small pan over medium heat. Add the mustard seeds and let them sizzle for a few seconds.

Add the drained pineapple and salt and cook for about 10 minutes, stirring occasionally.

Thicken with the cornstarch mixture and remove from the heat. Chill until needed.

Coriander Chutney
Makes approx. ¹/₂ cup

Ingredients

1¹/₂ cups fresh coriander
 leaves
4 cloves garlic
4tbsp. shredded coconut.

2 fresh green chili peppers
2-3tbsp. lemon juice
¹/₂tsp. salt
2 pinches sugar

Chop the sprigs of coriander and throw away the roots and lower stalk.

Blend or process the coriander with all the other ingredients until you have a smooth paste.

This can be stored in an airtight jar in the refrigerator for a week.

Garlic Purée
Makes approx. ½ cup

This is a useful and tasty addition to soups, stews, sauces, salad dressings — especially bought or home-made mayonnaise — and as a relish with cold meat. The cooking takes away any acrid flavors and the purée is far less crude and bitter than the commercially-produced version. It is also delicious spread on toast under poached or scrambled eggs.

Ingredients
4 heads garlic (about 50   *2tbsp. olive oil*
   cloves)   *salt and pepper*

Simmer the unpeeled garlic cloves in lightly salted water for about 20-25 minutes, until soft. Drain and cool.

Peel the garlic cloves, cutting off the tough root-end and any discolored patches, and mash them to a smooth paste with a fork.

Stir in the oil, and season with salt and pepper to taste. Pack into a glass jar and cover securely.

This purée will keep in the fridge for 4-5 days, and can be frozen in cubes, using an ice-cube tray reserved for this purpose.

Worcestershire Sauce
Makes approx. 1½ cups

Ingredients
6 cloves garlic, crushed   *5tbsp. soy sauce*
1tsp. black pepper   *1 cup vinegar*
2 pinches chili powder

Preparation Liquidize or process the ingredients together until smooth and store in an airtight bottle.

Shake well before use.

Garlic Pepper Essence
Makes approx. 3 cups

A few drops of this essence really perks up soups and stews, but because it is very intense, it should be used with caution.

Ingredients
10 garlic cloves
5 small fresh chili peppers
cooking sherry

Peel and halve the garlic and prick the peppers all over. Mix them together and pack into a wine bottle.

Cover with the sherry and fill the bottle, leaving room for the cork. Cork the bottle securely and leave, undisturbed, for a couple weeks.

The sherry can be topped up from time to time.

Garlic Vinegar
Makes approx. 2½ cups

This vinegar is very handy for salad dressing and marinades for fish, shellfish and chicken.

Ingredients
8-10 cloves garlic   *2½ cups white wine or*
a little coarse salt   *tarragon vinegar*

Crush the garlic finely with the salt and put into a large, heatproof jar.

Bring the vinegar to a boil and pour over the garlic. Allow to cool and then cover.

Leave to infuse for 2-3 weeks, then strain and bottle for use.

Variation Red Wine Garlic Vinegar, for use in strongly flavored marinades like those for stewing beef, pot roasts and game, is made by saving red wine bottle ends and letting them "turn". Use 10 cloves of garlic to 2½ cups of liquid, and warm the vinegar until hand hot before pouring over the crushed garlic

Fresh Cucumber Pickle
Serves 4-6

Ingredients

1 cucumber	1 fresh red chili pepper,
salt	seeded and chopped
1 tomato, skinned, seeded	3 tbsp. good quality vinegar
and diced	2 tsp. sugar
1 small onion, peeled and	pinch salt
finely sliced	

Trim the ends from the cucumber, peel lengthwise but leave some of the skin on to make the pickle look more attractive. Cut into thin slices and lay on a large plate. Sprinkle with salt and leave for 15 minutes. Rinse and dry.

Meanwhile prepare the tomato, onion and chili pepper. Arrange all the vegetables in a bowl and pour over the vinegar, sugar and salt. Chill before serving.

Vegetable Pickle
Makes approx. 2lb.

Delicious with curries or cold meats.

Ingredients

¾ cup peanuts	1¼lb. mixed vegetables and
3 small onions, peeled	fruits, peeled and sliced
2 cloves garlic, peeled	such as: carrot,
5 tbsp. oil	cauliflower, green
4 macadamia nuts or	mango, cabbage,
almonds	cucumber, beans, small
1½ tbsp. turmeric	onions (leave whole),
1¼ cups white vinegar	fresh pineapple, green
3 tbsp. sugar	and red chili peppers
salt to taste	

Roast the peanuts in a moderately hot oven until brown, about 10-15 minutes. Rub off the skins and lightly pound; reserve.

Pound the onion and garlic together. Heat the oil and fry the onion and garlic to give off a good smell. Add the macadamia nuts or almonds, fry, then add the turmeric.

Stir in the vinegar, sugar and salt. Add the vegetables and fruit. Cook briefly before adding the peanuts.

Cool and transfer to a screwtop glass jar. Store in the refrigerator.

Pickled Lemons
Makes approx. 2lb.

Ingredients

12 medium lemons, thinly	2 bay leaves
sliced and seeded	1½ cups corn oil
4 tbsp. salt	½ cup olive oil
1 tsp. black peppercorns	

Arrange the lemon slices in layers in a colander, sprinkling the salt between the layers. Leave them to stand for 24 hours.

Divide the lemon slices among small sterilized glass jars. Divide peppercorns and bay leaves between the jars.

Mix the oils together. Fill each jar with the oil mixture, making sure that no air bubbles are trapped. Seal the jars tightly and store them in the refrigerator for 3 weeks before serving.

Pickled Watermelon Rinds
Makes approx. 5 cups

Ingredients

8 cups pared watermelon	4 cinnamon sticks, broken
rinds, white part only,	into 1-in. pieces
cut into ¼×1in. pieces	2 tbsp. whole cloves
2 tbsp. salt	2 tbsp. whole allspice
6 cups sugar	1 tbsp. whole white
3 cups water	peppercorns
3 cups cider vinegar	1 tbsp. whole mustard seeds
3 tbsp. lemon juice	

Toss the watermelon rinds together with salt. Cover with cold water and leave to soak overnight. Drain and rinse well. Put the rinds in a saucepan with enough cold water to cover and bring to the boil over a high heat. Reduce heat and simmer for about 10 minutes. Drain well.

Bring the remaining ingredients to the boil in a large saucepan and simmer, stirring constantly, for about 10 minutes, until the sugar is completely dissolved. Add the watermelon rinds and simmer for about 45 minutes, until rinds are transparent.

Transfer rinds and syrup to sterilized jars and seal. Store pickles for 3-4 weeks before using.

Date Jam
Makes approx. 4½lb.

Ingredients

2lb. pitted dates	1 tsp. ground nutmeg
3 cups water	grated peel and juice of 1
2lb. preserving sugar	lemon
1 tsp. ground cinnamon	2 tbsp. unsalted butter

Bring the dates and water to a boil. Simmer gently for 10 minutes.

Add the remaining ingredients and continue to cook, stirring all the time.

When the mixture is thick and smooth, take it off the heat. Pack into sterilized, warmed jars and cover.

Strawberry Plum Slatko
Makes approx. 2lb.

Ingredients

1lb. preserving sugar
³/₄lb. damsons or other ripe
    purple plums, pitted and
    quartered
¹/₂lb. fresh strawberries,
    quartered
3tbsp. lemon juice

Combine the sugar, plums and strawberries in a large saucepan. Stir well. Cover and cook over a medium heat for 10 minutes. Stir with a fork to make sure the sugar melts. Cook for a further 20 minutes or until the sugar is completely dissolved.

Add the lemon juice and cook for 10 minutes longer. Remove the saucepan from the heat and leave the slatko to stand, covered, at room temperature for 12 hours.

Store in sterilized glass jars in the refrigerator.

Java Jam
Makes approx. 2lb.

Ingredients

1lb. bananas, sliced
2¹/₂ cups orange juice
2¹/₂ cups sweetened black
    coffee
1¹/₂ cups soft brown sugar
¹/₃ cup Vanilla Sugar or
    white sugar

Put all ingredients into a pan and bring to the boil. Reduce the heat and cook gently, stirring frequently to prevent burning, until the mixture softens and becomes thick.

Spoon into sterilized jars and cover.

Superior Prunes
Makes approx. 2lb.

Ingredients

1lb. brown granulated
    sugar
¹/₂ cup cold coffee
1lb. prunes, pitted
2 cups Kahlua or Crême de
    Cacao
¹/₄ cup vodka

Put the sugar and coffee into a medium heavy-based pan. Bring to a boil, stirring all the time. Reduce the heat and simmer for 5 minutes.

Add the prunes and simmer gently for a further 40 minutes. Remove the prunes with a slotted spoon and put into sterilized jars.

Mix together the Kahlua or Crême de Cacao and vodka and half fill the jars. Cover with the syrup and seal the jars.

Vanilla Extract
Makes approx. 1¹/₄ cups

Ingredients

2 vanilla pods
1¹/₄ cups brandy

Partially break vanilla pods and put into the brandy.

Leave in an airtight bottle for 6 weeks before using, shaking every day.

Vinegar Hints

The party is over and you have a few drops of wine left in several bottles. Don't throw it away. Add the wine to your vinegar: red wine to red vinegar and white wine to white vinegar. The wine will naturally sour in the vinegar bottle and create the impression of an endless supply of vinegar. Don't serve a salad with a vinegar dressing on painted plates. The vinegar will soon corrode the paint on the plates.

1 White wine vinegar.

2 Pure red wine vinegar.

3 Rosemary vinegar: vinegars that have been steeped in herbs can transform salad dressings from the commonplace to the extra special.

4 Lemon wine vinegar: the lemon adds a lighter touch.

5 French white wine vinegar: the best wine vinegar comes from Orleans.

6 Raspberry vinegar: adds a light, fresh flavor to dressings.

7 Cider vinegar.

8 French garlic vinegar.

9 Honey and cider vinegar: a favorite with health food devotees.

10 Tarragon vinegar: good with white meat salads.

Appendix

Fiber Facts

It must now be universally acknowledged that the removal of fiber in the commercial processing of our food can lead to ill health: in order to make up the deficit, it is useful to have some idea of the fiber content of natural ingredients and to try to introduce those foods high in fiber into our diet. The tables below show the grams of fiber per 100g/4oz of some of these natural foods. As well as those foods listed, bread (especially wholewheat) and breakfast cereals (especially bran) are of course excellent sources of fiber.

Vegetables	g fiber per 100g/4oz
Eggplant, raw	2.5
Broccoli tops, raw	3.6
Cabbage, white, raw	2.7
Cabbage, red, raw	3.4
Carrots, raw	2.9
Carrots, boiled	3.1
Cauliflower, raw	2.1
Cauliflower, boiled	1.8
Celery, raw	1.8

Celeriac, raw	4.9
Cucumber, raw	0.4
Gourd, bitter, raw, fresh	4.0
Leeks, raw	3.1
Leeks, boiled	3.9
Lettuce, raw	1.5
Mushroom, raw	2.5
Olives in brine	4.4
Parsley, raw	9.1
Parsnip, raw	4.0
Parsnip, boiled	2.5
Pepper, raw and boiled	0.9
Potato, raw	2.1
Potato, baked, flesh only	2.5
Radishes, raw	1.0
Green onion, flesh of bulb	3.1
Corn, kernels only, raw	3.7
Corn, canned, kernels only	5.7
Tomato, raw	1.5
Tomato, canned	0.9
Turnip, raw	2.8
Watercress, raw	3.3

Fruit — fresh and dried

	g fiber per 100g/4oz
Apples, eating, with skin and core	1.5
Apples, eating, flesh only	2.0
Apples, cooking, raw, flesh only	2.4
Apricots, dried, raw	24.0
Banana, raw	3.4
Blackberries, raw	7.3
Blackcurrants, raw	8.7
Breadfruit, canned, drained	2.8
Currants, raw	6.5
Dates, dried, raw	8.7
Figs, fresh, raw	2.5
Figs, dried	18.5
Guava, canned, whole	3.6
Loganberries, raw	6.2
Passion fruit, raw	15.9
Peaches, dried, raw	14.3
Pears, eating, with skin and core	1.7
Prunes, raw, with stones	13.4
Prunes, raw, no stones	16.1
Quinces, raw	6.4
Raisins, stoned, raw	6.8
Redcurrants, raw	8.2
White raisins, raw	7.0
Whitecurrants, raw	6.8

Pulses

	g fiber per 100g/4oz
Lima beans, raw	21.6
Lima beans, boiled	5.1
Chick-peas, raw	15.0
Navy beans, raw	25.4
Navy beans, boiled	7.4
Kidney beans, raw	25.0
Lentils, red, raw	11.7
Mung beans, raw	22.0
Mung beans, canned	3.0
Peanuts, fresh	8.1
Peas, fresh, raw	12.0
Peas, frozen, boiled	5.3

Nuts

	g fiber per 100g/4oz
Almonds	14.3
Barcelona nuts	10.3
Brazil nuts	9.0
Chestnuts	6.8
Cob or hazel nuts	6.1
Coconut, kernel only	13.6
Coconut, shredded	23.5
Peanuts, fresh	8.1
Peanuts, roasted and salted	8.1
Walnuts	5.2

Pasta and Rice

	g fiber per 100g/4oz
Brown rice, raw	4.2
Macaroni, raw	5.5
Noodles, wheat dried, raw	5.7
Spaghetti, raw	5.6
Wholewheat pasta, uncooked	10.0

Choosing Meat : the Fat Facts

Always choose meat that looks moist and fresh, and which has the least amount of visible fat. This will not only give you more meat for your money, it will make far healthier eating for you and your family.

The tables show the average grams of total fat per 100g/4oz of uncooked meat. Trimming off any visible fat from red meat, and removing the skin from poultry before cooking will considerably reduce the fat content, as the difference in the two sets of figures given here shows.

Beef	Choice Grade	
	Trimmed	*Untrimmed*
Chuck	8.0	25.3
Club Steak	10.3	34.8
Ground	10.0 (Lean)	21.3 (Regular)
Porterhouse	8.2	36.2
Round	4.7	12.3
Rib	11.6	37.4
Rump	7.5	25.3

	Good Grade	
	Trimmed	*Untrimmed*
Club Steak	7.5	27.9
Porterhouse	5.5	33.8
Rump	5.4	21.4

To trim prepared rack of lamb, the knife must be both sharp and flexible.

Lamb	Choice Grade	
	Trimmed	*Untrimmed*
Leg	5.0	16.2
Loin	5.9	24.8
Rib	8.4	30.4
Shoulder	7.7	23.9

	Good Grade	
	Trimmed	*Untrimmed*
Leg	4.7	14.6
Loin	5.6	22.6
Rib	7.9	27.1
Shoulder	7.3	22.0

Veal	'Thin'	'Medium-fat'
	Trimmed	*Untrimmed*
Flank	18.0	27.0
Foreshank	5.0	8.0
Loin	8.0	11.0
Plate	12.0	17.0
Rib	9.0	14.0
Round with Rump	6.0	9.0

Pork/Gammon	Choice Grade	
	Trimmed	*Untrimmed*
Leg (Ham)	5.4	20.8
Loin	7.5	24.1
Tenderloin	2.5	
Spare ribs		23.6

Chicken	*Without Skin*	*With Skin*
Roasting	2.7	15.8
Light Meat	1.6	
Dark Meat	3.6	
Broiler/Fryer	3.1	15.1
Light Meat	1.5	
Dark Meat	3.8	

Turkey		
Roaster/Fryer	1.6	4.2
Light Meat	0.5	3.8
Dark Meat	2.7	4.8

Duck	6.0	39.3
Goose	7.1	33.6
Guinea Fowl	2.5	6.5
Pheasant	3.6	9.3
Rabbit (Tame)	8.0	
(Wild)	5.0	
Venison	4.0	
Pigeon (Squab)	7.5	23.8

Offal		
Liver: Calves	4.7	
Chicken	3.7	
Lambs	3.9	
Pigs	3.7	
Tongue: Calves	5.3	
Lamb	15.3	
Ox	15.0	
Gizzard: Chicken	2.7	

The figures in the tables are taken from the *Handbook of the Nutritional Contents of Foods*, US Department of Agriculture, 1975, and *Agriculture Handbook No. 8*, US Department of Agriculture, 1979 and 1983.

Index

D

E

F

Q

R

S